THE HISTORY OF ANTI-SEMITISM

LÉON POLIAKOV

THE HISTORY OF ANTI-SEMITISM

VOLUME THREE
From Voltaire to Wagner

Translated by Miriam Kochan

PENN

UNIVERSITY OF PENNSYLVANIA PRESS

Philadelphia

CONTENTS

FOREWORD

The author of this thesis could not be more aware of the numerous defects and gaps in his work. They were to a certain extent inevitable in view of the breadth of the subject which demanded very varied research covering two centuries of political, ideological and literary European history. This is responsible for a discursive style which in some places might seem more suited to an essay. It also explains why the data only meet the usual requirements of scholarship in some chapters. Finally, it is the reason why the focus of attention is almost solely on those countries which make up the modern world, at the expense of those (Austria-Hungary, Russia) which before 1850 still remained governed by the customs and attitudes of the past in the sphere with which I am concerned.

Another criticism which I would be the first to make of myself might perhaps seem even more serious. The present book was as far as possible intended to be a work of historical sociology, following the method I set out to use in the two volumes which preceded it. But this principle has only been carried out in the "Prologue" and, after a fashion, in Book II. For the most part, the work has against my will slipped into a study of the history of ideas—if this description can be applied to the series of sketches in which opinions on Jews and Judaism voiced by eminent people, both Christian and Jewish, alternate with biographical data and attempts at psychological interpretation, insofar as the documents make it possible. Thus a systematic study of the role Jews played in the development of industrial society will not be found in this book. The reader will find only one short chapter in which I explain why the idea of "economic anti-Semitism" seems to be devoid of real explanatory value, in a field where, in my opinion, the primordial role (that of a sub-structure if you like) belongs to theology. In my defense, let me point out that the moment French and German Jews became "assimi-lated," that is to say became, in theory and in accordance with their own and their emancipators' wishes, French or German citizens on the same basis as their non-Jewish compatriots, they seem to elude the methods of investigation in use in the human sciences at the present stage of their development.[1] A difficulty of a purely technical nature at first sight—the absence from the archives for the periods after emancipation, of dossiers devoted to what was formerly called the "Jewish nation"[2]—actually reflects a basic irresolution, the origin of which must be sought with the ideologists and thinkers. "Sect" in the eighteenth century, "race" in the nineteenth, the Jews, of whom it could in the twentieth be said that they existed by virtue of the anti-Semites' conception of them, thus seem to elude the categories recognized by sociology. In my attempt to render the phenomenon of modern anti-Semitism intelligible, perhaps I had no option but to forgo the original plan and adopt an eclectic method, dictated by the index cards accumulated as I went along?

In fact, taking the above difficulties into account, my first step consisted of collecting texts in which great Europeans of the past discussed Jews and Judaism. At first, the dossier built up in this way left me with the impression of a monumental collection of nonsense. These texts are generally little known. Historians and commentators tend to pass them over in silence. In almost every case, scruples as to method apart, sheer necessity obliged me to go back to the original sources. The reasons why twentieth-century scholarship prefers to keep quiet about the anti-Jewish diatribes of people like Voltaire or Kant, Proudhon or Marx can, I think, be guessed. (Karl Marx's ferocious *Judenfrage* in a sense lends itself to the description of "prophetic," since Soviet and Polish practice in fact bear witness to the fundamental incompatibility between a communist régime and the right to be a Jew.) Nonetheless these texts exist. We can regard them as comments of no great consequence, tributes negligently paid to the accepted ideas of the time; we can, on the other hand, ask ourselves if they do not express a basic trend in Western thought. I have quoted contexts, but it is not for me to be dogmatic about a question which concerns the historians of philosophy. Nonetheless, I thought it was worth posing.

Another related question is of more concern to the sociologist. Might not the precautions taken by so many men of good will have contributed, just as much as the inadequacy of traditional methods, towards hiding from scholars a semi-indestructible reality of a psychological nature, which is there to be noted? However, the choice of terms to use creates a problem (habits of thought? permanence of attitude? collective memory?) and this is perhaps not the least difficulty. I do not think the problem is new; remember the polemics around such varied concepts as Durkheim's "collective soul" or C.G. Jung's "original images." It seems as if specialists in the different disciplines each in his own way had attempted an appropriate conceptualization. In this context, the historian Alain Besançon recently asked "what exactly the fact of being Jewish, Catholic or Protestant meant in psychology," and he cited "the phenomenon already noted by the historian that a French schoolteacher coming from a secular tradition can behave like a jansenist, a bolshevik like the arch-priest Avvakum, and in his writings a positivist scholar like Freud can remember the Zohar which he had never read."[3]

However inadequate my work may seem to me, I think that its virtue will perhaps be to bring into the open the persistence of an archaic attitude on a particular point amongst the men of the enlightenment and much later. It is a fact that survivals of this type find their strangest illustration in the case of the Judeo-Christian relationship. My temerity lay in undertaking a historical study of it and thus setting out over unexplored territory, where my precursors were few and which the human sciences, from psychology in depth to human genetics, only imperfectly illuminated. Might this be a final reason for begging the reader's indulgence?

Such as it is, this work could not have been undertaken without the kind understanding and encouragement of M. Raymond Aron. Numerous friends have given me the benefits of their scholarship. François Furet took the trouble to read the chapters relating to the century of enlightenment, and Rita Thalmann did the same with those concerning German history; their comments have been valuable to me. With Jean-Pierre Peter, I discussed the strange case of Richard Wagner. I re-wrote the conclusion on the advice of Norman Cohn and Gavin Langmuir; but the whole work has been greatly stimulated by my exchanges of views and correspondence. Dr Béla Grunberger was kind enough to discuss the legitimacy of my psychological interpretations. Dealing with a subject which is inter-disciplinary par excellence, the discussions I had with Alexandre Kojeve, Emmanuel Levinas and Alexis Philonenko were no less valuable to me, notably where questions of the history of ideas were involved. Lucette Finas generously sacrificed numerous evenings to read the manuscript from cover to cover, pen in hand; the corrections she suggested often helped to qualify or clarify my ideas. To all of them, as well as to all the people who, at some time or other, helped with advice, criticism or bibliographical suggestions—the list would be too long—I hereby give my most sincere thanks.

PROLOGUE

one

The Jews of Europe in the Eighteenth Century

In eighteenth-century Europe, there were about two million Jews, almost half of whom lived in Poland. Although their status varied from country to country, the major distinction was between "Sephardi" (Spanish and Portuguese) Jews and "Ashkenazi" (German and Polish). The Sephardim numbered about a hundred thousand and were most frequently descendants of the Marranos, whom I discussed at length in my previous volume; they were able to settle in any European country except their native peninsula where the funeral pyres of the Inquisition continued to flare up from time to time. But, in actual fact, they were primarily settled in the large ports of Europe or overseas, where they engaged in international trade on a world scale. An English author, Joseph Addison, at the beginning of the eighteenth century compared them to the "pegs and nails in a great Building, which, though they are but little value in themselves, are absolutely necessary to keep the whole frame together."[1]

All governments regarded them as useful subjects; in addition to their commercial and financial activities a fair number of them cultivated arts and letters while others won distinction on the political scene, as negotiators and secret agents. In their principal centers—in London, Amsterdam, Hamburg, Bordeaux, Leghorn—they enjoyed a privileged status and generally adopted the elegant and polite manners of the period. Those of Holland, according to a German traveler in 1678 "have such a good appearance that one hardly thinks of them as Jews."[2] The following year, when the Duke of

Hanover fell ill passing through Amsterdam, his wife wrote to her brother:³

> Thank Heaven he is getting better through the care of Signor Robbio, a Jewish doctor, and our host, Signor de la Costa, the Portuguese minister and a member of the same tribe, who is accommodating us magnificently and makes broth for Ernest Augustus with his own hands. He and all those of his nation are so clean that they do not want to have any truck with the German Jews because of their filthiness and stench. . . .

These civilized and (*avant la lettre*) "assimilated" Jews therefore carefully kept away from their co-religionists. Nothing better sums up their typical opinion of themselves, a reflection of how cultured Christians saw them, than the terms in which they were defended by Pinto. Pinto, an eighteenth-century Jew from Bordeaux, made the following reply to Voltaire's anti-Semitic generalizations:⁴

> If M. de Voltaire had on this occasion referred to that soundness of argument which he professes, he would have begun by singling out from other Jews, the Spanish and Portugese Jews who have never intermingled with or been incorporated into the masses of the other children of Jacob. He should have pointed out this great difference. I am aware that it is little known in France generally speaking and that this has harmed the Portuguese nation of Bordeaux on more than one occasion. But M. de Voltaire cannot be unaware of the scrupulous fastidiousness of the Portuguese and Spanish Jews not to mix, by marriage, alliance or in any other way, with the Jews of other nations. He has been to Holland and knows that they have separate synagogues and that although their religion and articles of faith are the same, their ceremonies are frequently not alike. The customs of the Portuguese Jews are quite different from those of other Jews. The former do not wear beards and do not affect any peculiarity in their dress, the well-off amongst them carry refinement, elegance and display in this respect as far as the other nations of Europe, from whom they differ only in their form of worship. Their divorce from their brethren goes to such

lengths that if a Portuguese Jew in Holland or England were to marry a German Jewess, he would immediately lose his prerogatives; he would no longer be acknowledged as a member of their synagogues; he would be excluded from all ecclesiastical and civic offices; he would be completely cut off from the body of the nation; he would not even be buried amongst his Portuguese brethren. The idea they quite generally hold that they are descendants of the tribe of Judah, the main families of which were sent to Spain at the time of the Babylonian captivity, cannot but lead them to make these distinctions and contribute to that loftiness of feeling that one observes in them, and which even their brethren of other nations appear to recognize. . . .

People who know the Portuguese Jews of France, Holland and England are aware that, far from having an invincible hatred *of all the nations who tolerate them,* as M. de Voltaire says, they think themselves so identified with these same nations that they consider that they form part of them. Their Spanish and Portuguese origin has become a pure ecclesiastical discipline which the harshest criticism would accuse of pride and vanity, but in no way of greed and superstition. . . .

These distinctions and protestations by an eighteenth-century assimilated Jew recur with innumerable variations after the general emancipation of the Jews. It was on the basis of similar arguments that rich Jews later set themselves apart from poor Jews, native-born Jews from foreign Jews, and strangely, German Jews from Polish Jews. The complexity of emancipation always demands the existence of someone more of a Jew than oneself. It is only fair to add that M. de Pinto then took up the defense of his co-religionists, explaining their mistakes by the status they were given (this is another instance where he anticipates the future):

Is it surprising that, deprived of all the advantages of society, multiplying in accordance with the laws of nature and religion, despised and humiliated on all sides, often persecuted, always insulted, the degraded and debased nature in them no longer appeared to be concerned with anything but immediate need? . . . One can pity them, if they are wrong, but it would be unfair

not to admire the constancy, courage, good faith, disinterested-
ness with which they sacrifice so many temporal advantages. . . .

These traditional Jews were officially tolerated in
contemporary Europe only in the Germanic countries, Poland
and Italy; nonetheless, they succeeded in infiltrating
gradually and in growing numbers into France and England.

I have examined their position in Poland in my first book, to
which I refer the reader; until the Polish partitions at the
end of the eighteenth century, that position hardly changed.
More to the West, on the other hand, where the first
symptoms of the Industrial Revolution were beginning to
appear and where the ideas which were to shake the world
were taking shape, the new political and social climate of the
period was favorable to the Jews' commercial and financial
prowess. There were many different reasons for this but the
most important derived from their medieval status as money-
lenders, in other words "privileged pariahs." (The definition
of the Jew given in a famous fifteenth-century treatise, the
Summa Angelica by Ange de Chivasso, in its own way reflects
this ambiguous situation : "To be a Jew is an offense, though
one that is non-punishable by the Christian.") I studied this
medieval status in my book about Jewish *banchieri* in Italy,
which contains a more detailed account.[5] In the period of
absolutism, the Jews' special privilege disappeared as the
medieval prohibition on money-lending at interest fell into
disuse; but at the same time, the consolidation of the power of
the princes, their traditional allies, opened up for them the
possibilities of action in other fields. In fact *raison d'État* was
replacing medieval ethics with the men in power; at the same
time, the idea of the general good, as opposed to the
corporate privileges of former times, was taking shape. We
cannot discuss the structural development of the Jews'
economic status in detail—it would take a large book to study
it as it deserves[6] and some of its effects persist on both sides of
the Atlantic to this day. But in view of the tenacity of preconceived ideas about a congenital and quasi-biological

aptitude on the part of the Jews for business and for making money, the brief remarks which follow seem necessary. What does follow is therefore a sketch which will be partially illustrated later in the present "Prologue" (nor can there be any question of specifying the relative importance of the different factors enumerated below, some of which overlap, as will be seen, so that as far as the economic role of the Jews in modern times is concerned, it is possible to talk about positive over-determination).

1) The advantage that the Jews had over their Christian competitors was partly derived objectively (technically) from their old specialization in pawnbroking. In particular:

a) Handling the pawned goods posed problems of their safe-keeping, and of disposing of items left in the lenders' hands. This led to Jews specializing in such activities as renovation, utilizing waste products and trading in used articles (the widespread commercialization of these goods before the Industrial Revolution must not be forgotten). It will be noticed that Jews still play an important role in the textile industry, and the jewelery and second-hand goods trade in many countries today. All these specializations follow historically from the old pawnbroking.

b) For the same sort of reasons, that is to say the heteroclite nature of the transferable wealth pawnbrokers handle, the Jews to the extent to which they were henceforth authorized to go into business, had a tendency to trade in all types of merchandise (a prefiguration of the modern "big store"). Christian merchants, on the contrary, were traditionally confined by corporate statutes to one single type of business.

c) From the financial point of view, a pawnbroker is nothing but an owner of capital who gives credit to the public; consequently, the Jews were the pioneers of hire-purchase selling to individuals. In my book about the Jewish bankers, I established that such operations were already widespread amongst the Jews in Italy in the fifteenth century. They appear again in French and German documents of the eighteenth century, and it is easy to understand that they constituted one of the reasons why the customers preferred the Jews.

d) Another reason for the popularity of Jewish trade was its low prices, prices which defied all competition, according to innumerable concordant testimonies. This went so far that, in places where Jews were authorized to open shop, the Christian trade guilds felt ruin facing them. On this point, too, the professional practice of lending at interest had taught the Jews (starting from the idea of the importance of a rapid circulation of money) the elementary and now universally known fact that rapid turnover of a stock of merchandise sold at a low profit (in other words, mass production) normally works to the entrepreneur's or trader's advantage. Christian merchants, for their part, took time to draw the inferences from this important fact, because they were bound by the traditions and rules of the guilds. These were based on the medieval idea of the "just price" which in practice involved Malthusian sales offset by large profit margins, so that every member of the guild could be certain of security and a living wage.

> In matters of commerce, the fault of the Dutch
> Is giving too little, and asking too much

ran a seventeenth-century English couplet; it was certainly not applicable to the Dutch alone.

2) Other factors contributing to the superior position of the Jewish merchant or entrepreneur also derived from his medieval status, but via respective attitudes and customs, from the reciprocal relationship between the contempt in which the Jew was held and the treatment inflicted on him. From this point of view, a genuine complementary connection can, I think, be established between Christian macrocosm and Jewish microcosm. On the Jewish side, the main factors noted are:

a) As a general rule, a much more sober way of life than the Christian merchant, concerned with keeping up his prestige or corporate "standing"; for the Jew this meant considerably lower expenses for maintaining himself and his family.

b) A traditional vitality linked to the insecurity of the Jew's political status, in contrast to the pleasant unconcern of the Christian entrepreneur; a hunger for wealth due to the cruel secular experience, since in a Christian society, money is the Jew's sole protection. Moreover, since this society was becoming middle-class and the old framework was beginning to disintegrate, it became a means of escaping the contempt which surrounded him and of becoming, once a certain income level was reached, a person of quality, as I will show further on.

c) In matters more specifically requiring a spirit of enterprise or involving deliberate acceptance of risk, elements to which the Jew was accustomed from the very fact of his precarious status predisposed him to take purely commercial risks sanguinely and to forge boldly ahead.

d) Lastly, remember the international connections and solidarity of the Jews, as a result of persecution and expulsion. What has recently been said about the French Protestants could be applied to them, but on a very much vaster scale: "In every sphere, persecution and insecurity of status has made them a particularly restless minority, and forced on them a mobility which, though often cruel, has been of great advantage to them. . . ."[7]

On the Christian side, a tendency is apparent, particularly in the nobility and amongst officials, to reach an understanding with the Jews in order to negotiate, in partnership with them, profitable transactions hardly compatible with upper-class status or contemporary custom. In this way, the Christian honor of a high and mighty personality was not compromised or was less compromised (one did not blush before the most lowly of men), and the secret of the agreement and transaction seemed best guaranteed. Pure and simple corruption can be closely related to these practices since, for the same reasons, the Jew was well placed to play the part of tempter. There were innumerable variations on such combinations to enable a man to become rich without openly losing caste. We will mention two categories :

a) Lucrative capital investments, usurious or speculative transactions when all the opprobrium was thrown on the Jew whether partner or figurehead. The meteoric rise of the Rothschilds, to a large extent due to speculation undertaken with capital belonging to the ultra-wealthy Margrave of Cassel, provides the best historical example of this.

In fact, the capital with which the Jewish financiers and great merchants were operating was most frequently Christian in origin. It is interesting to note that the debts thus contracted contributed in another respect to maintaining the Jews' precarious freedom of the city: their creditors became, *ipso facto*, their protectors for their own ends since the debts were irrecoverable in the event of expulsion. At certain periods and in some countries, Jewish communities made systematic use of this method of insurance against expulsion. This was notably the case in Renaissance Italy,[8] as well as in Poland in the eighteenth century. As far as Poland was concerned, the Finance Minister to Emperor Paul I, Gabriel Derzhavin, stated:[9]

... and in order not to be exposed to the fate they met in Spain, they have devised or applied a means already known to them, to borrow money from the people amongst whom they are living, and in this way to become tolerated by them. They pledge as security for the sums they borrow the mobile property of all the community by the intermediary of their congregations, which thereby win from their creditors attachment and respect.

b) Tips and bribes accepted by officials who in return granted the Jews both the right of residence in a country or a town and the privilege of carrying on several types of trade. In Germany, these tips bore the suggestive name of "douceurs" (they were current in seventeenth- and eighteenth-century Europe in a general way; a great Roman theologian, Cardinal de Lugo, had declared that he found nothing to say against the practice provided that the bribed official or minister undertook nothing contrary to his prince's interests; there is no certainty that this clause was always honored).[10]

c) The accuracy of the above remarks and the importance that such psychological factors assumed in the economic rise of the Jews emerges from the example of the institution of "court Jews." It flourished particularly in Germany but the germ of its equivalent can be found in the entourages of some great French nobles. The reason why princes entrusted the management of their financial, personal and even sentimental affairs to factotums chosen from the Children of Israel cannot be understood if the psychological affinities between nobles and Jews, partly deriving from similar collusion, were not given due place. Needless to say the favor they enjoyed as a result put the Jews in an essentially strong position, very advantageous to Jewish economic activities as a whole.

3) Lastly, certain other factors in the Jews' success must be considered from the point of view of the commercial ethics, if not simply the ethics, of past centuries. The routine governing Christian trade was historically linked to a Christian or agrarian-Christian tradition which was hostile to money-making and trade, and which slowed down European economic development. "The guild spirit is in principle opposed to the spirit of innovation" (Charles Moraze). The Christian class of producers and merchants had prescribed very tight rules of conduct and opposed the slightest change in established customs and practices. The Jews, strictly excluded from the guilds, did not feel bound by these rules of conduct, and the spirit of innovation, developed by their chequered and dangerous existence in exile, might almost be said to have become second nature to them.

Some of the commercial stratagems the Jews employed, to the fury and despair of their Christian competitors, have long since come into modern usage. Some are still condemned. All brought them the favor of their *clientèle*, as well as a scarcely flattering renown; but in this respect they did not have very much to lose. Here are a few examples of the practices they followed:

a) Advertising and canvassing for custom, in other words "sales promotion." It was strictly forbidden by guild rules but a favorite economic weapon with the Jews, in the form of soliciting customers in market places, inn rooms and the streets of the ghetto, assiduously frequented by Christian buyers.

b) The manufacture and sale of inferior quality goods, not conforming to guild standards; displaying the merchandise attractively, particularly old clothes, renovated or patched up by skillful ghetto craftsmen.

c) The disposal of merchandise of dubious origin, war plunder, contraband, soldier's loot, or stolen or burgled goods. (Typical of this point, is the promise not to obtain supplies from receivers and soldiers which the Ashkenazim made to the Sephardim of Hamburg when they were admitted to the town.[11]) Volume I dealt with the phenomenon of Jewish brigandage in Germany in the seventeenth and eighteenth centuries.[12]

This can be linked up with the question of "Talmudic ethics," that is to say ethics which permit practices in respect of non-Jews forbidden in relations with co-religionists.

We know the fate which befell in this respect certain texts or precepts of the Jewish religion, some of which were authentic, others fabricated, as a result of anti-Semitic propaganda. But on this subject, in the first centuries AD the scholars of the daughter-religion were imitating those of the parent (cf. the "exception of Ambroise," authorizing loans at interest to heretics *ubi jus belli, ibi jus usurae*).[13] Later, both sides discriminated against the "Infidel" by the political methods within their scope, that is to say, violence and trickery respectively. Christians and Jews practiced the system of one law for one's friends and another for enemies, and found themselves caught up in an inextricable reciprocal relationship. Traditionalists on both sides seemed to think this a good thing, for example Bonald wrote: ". . . Christians can be cheated by Jews, but they must not be ruled by them, and this dependence offends their dignity even more than the greed of the Jews encroaches on their profits."[14] But just because the Jews were only a small minority, this sort of arrangement acted to their advantage (to the extent to which flexibility in commercial matters constitutes an advantage) since the Jew's economic activity most frequently concerned a Christian, while the converse was only true in an infinitesimal proportion of cases.

These are the major factors. In comparison, the causes most often cited—the high level of culture of the "people who have been reading for two thousand years," or a sort of natural selection—seem only to have played a subsidiary role, which ensured the economic advance of the Jews in countries where they were tolerated. It must be added that, despite their advance, Jewish businessmen did not acquire supremacy in any Western country, and did not play the role of "creators of capitalism" sometimes attributed to them.

We now come down to concrete facts, country by country.

Germany

In a general way, the Jews' economic progress at the dawn of the modern period goes hand in hand with the rise of centralizing absolutism and the consolidation of the power of the princes at the expense of medieval bourgeois rights and guild privileges. This development was particularly apparent in Germany, where these rights and privileges persisted longer than in the Western monarchies and where the Christian bourgeoisie fought the Jews, the tools of absolute power, with especial passion. Nothing is more typical of this than the episode of the settlement in Berlin of the Jews expelled from Vienna in 1671.

The expulsion of the old and wealthy Viennese community was decreed in the purest medieval style for motives consisting of an indistinguishable blend of commercial hypocrisy and pious superstition. The Emperor of Austria, Leopold I, a former Jesuit, was renowned for his piety. For the first ten years of his reign, his attitude to the Jews was benevolent, but in 1669 doubt was sown in his mind by a series of misfortunes which struck the Imperial family. There was a fire in the palace; the heir to the throne died; and the Empress miscarried. The Empress's confessor took it upon himself to suggest to the Emperor that these were signs or warnings from on high. His argument was supported by an offer from the Viennese bourgeoisie to compensate the Imperial Treasury for the financial consequences of the Jews' departure. The Emperor decreed their expulsion on February 28, 1670; all Jews had to leave the capital before Pentecost. (They were recalled some fifteen years later, and henceforth considered indispensable: "chiefly in Vienna by the influence and credit of the Jews, business of the greatest importance is often transacted," declared Leopold I's new minister, Chancellor Ludewig.)[15] As soon as he heard of the expulsion, the "Great Elector," Frederick-William, the first of the kings who made modern Prussia, decided to invite fifty rich Jewish families to come to his state. He was trying to develop Prussia's industry and trade by every means and had already welcomed numerous foreign colonists or entrepreneurs, in particular the French Huguenots. He therefore granted the Jews, on payment of a corresponding protection tax (*Schutzgeld*), a special and irrevocable charter which laid down the activities Jews were allowed to follow as well as their rights and duties, according to custom.[16] The competition which immediately broke out between Christian and Jewish merchants was all the keener because their respective culture and customs were as different as their commercial practices and legal status. Some forms and effects of this competition were to persist in the nineteenth century, well after the emancipation of the Jews. In addition, the Chancellery of the Prussian state was flooded, for generations, with representations and counter-representations. Reading them takes us straight to certain major factors in modern anti-Semitism.

The Christian merchants of Berlin and Cologne complained in 1673:[17]

Then these infidels run from village to village, from town to town, offer this and take that, whereby they do not only dispose of their discarded and wretched goods and deceive the people with old rags, but they spoil all commerce and particularly the retail trade, especially in silver, brass, tea and copper.

... That is the urgent reason, your illustrious Highness, why we are compelled in our humility to put our misfortunes before you, which are so great that we must be ruined and with us the whole town and its churches and schools in which the glory of God is to be taught. ...

From this, one sees how easily a connection was made between the glory of God and the profits of Christian trade, as early as the seventeenth century. The same type of resentment can be held responsible for a somewhat scatological libel in the same year, 1673, directed against the banker, Israel Aron, who had succeeded in securing the key position of purveyor to the Great Elector's court.

As well as the Jew, the libel also attacked the officials who favored him and whom he was said to have showered with gold and gifts.[18] Recriminations by Christian guilds against competition from Jews were repeated year after year and in one province after another. A copious selection can be found in two volumes of documents recently published by Selma Stern.[19]

We need only quote the powerful metaphors the merchants of the town of Stendal employed in 1734:[20]

For if the matter is looked at in its true light then the Jew amongst Christian merchants is like a pike in a fishpond, he ... snatches the bread from the mouth of the Christian merchant, sucks the blood of the poor, he lives sordidly and does not contribute his due taxes to the churches, schools and towns. ...

In 1673, the Great Elector supported the Jews, reckoning that "the Jews and their trade are not harmful to ourselves and our country, but they are useful." His successors most frequently adopted the same line of conduct, it being understood that this usefulness was measured by the contents of the purses of the Children of Israel. The Jews, for their part, behaved in a humble and lowly manner, and confined themselves to invoking the principles of healthy trade to justify their tolerance in a Christian state:[21]

We ask simply: who are those ruined by us or by our trade? . . .
Are the vaults of each one of these great merchants not filled
with a larger quantity and more precious goods than we poor
Jews can hardly assemble all together over a long period? And
besides they do not lack magnificent and finely furnished houses
and buildings. Who of us can, like them, maintain a coach and
horses and drive out of the gates to his own country seat and
pleasant gardens? Has any of us ever made enough profit from
his small trading to imitate them and buy country houses, and
eventually leave trading altogether and become a fine banker?
. . . If we were guilty of the ruin of a Christian merchant then
none of them should ever go bankrupt in places where no Jew
lives. . . . But what is more common than to see Christian
merchants enter on a transaction which they do not
understand? What good can result when the master relies on
the servant and does not conduct the affair himself but much
prefers his fine eating and drinking? . . . How can the Jew be
responsible for the ruin of such a merchant? . . . Third parties
do not trust the Jews, but they must themselves travel in search
of new goods, they do not trade beyond the capacity of their
purses and therefore they are not overburdened with goods
as credit. . . .

The intertwining of the interests of religion and trade
can again be illustrated by incidents which broke out in the
Prussian town of Halberstadt in 1669. Without official
permission, the Jews allowed to trade in the town had built a
synagogue. Without referring to the authorities, the Halberstadt bourgeoisie, accompanied by some fifty armed
musketeers, according to the Jewish petition,[22]

burst into our synagogue, seized the windows and doors and
partially broke them down and razed the whole building to the
ground, destroyed and smashed everything, cut it into pieces
and caused such violent tumult and confusion, fear and terror
that we could not but think that we were to be cut down and
chased away to the last man, and then when the mob came
running up from every corner we had to have soldiers on guard
day and night for our protection.

The Prussian government ordered an investigation. The Halberstadt bourgeoisie justified themselves as follows:[23]

> Because it is unfortunately drawn from experience what evil is caused to the Jews and their eternal damnation by the establishment of such seminaries in which superstition and a perverted understanding of all divine prophecy and revelation as well as contempt for Christ and his holy word is inculcated from childhood onwards and thus the way to their conversion is made more difficult and remote; also, this people nowhere grows more numerous than where they are permitted to exercise their damnable religion and we and the whole country are overburdened with this mob to the great ruin of many Christians. . . .

From which it can be seen how the demands of Christian trade maintained and stimulated the Church's millennial struggle against the synagogue.

If the Christian bourgeoisie's businesses really seemed to have suffered greatly from the Jews' presence, it was extremely advantageous to the princes and nobility, their natural protectors (so much so that the economist Werner Sombart would like to regard the Jew as the authentic co-founder of the modern state). But over and above the principles of political equilibrium which had to be respected in a state which remained Christian, religious feelings were present to limit the protection and favors accorded the sons of the deicidal people on the grounds of their economic and financial usefulness. The personal temperament and convictions of the autocrats played an unmistakable part at this juncture. The conduct to be adopted to reconcile *raison d'État* with the demands of Christian morality were ingenuously described by the "sergeant king," Frederick-William, advising his son, the future Frederick the Great, on good government:[24]

> So far as the Jews are concerned there are unfortunately many in our hands who have no letters of protection from me. These

you must chase out of the country for the Jews are locusts in a country and ruin the Christians. I ask you, issue no new letters of protection, even if they offer you much money ... if you need something for your pleasure, then put all the Jews down for 20-30,000 thalers every 3 or 4 years, in addition to the protection money they must give you. You must squeeze them for they betrayed Jesus Christ, and must not trust them for the most honest Jew is an arch-traitor and rogue. Be convinced of this.

A realist like his father, but as cynical as the latter was bigoted, Frederick the Great had none of these moral qualms and went back to the Great Elector's golden rule: a Jew is as useful as he is rich. He therefore hunted down and mercilessly expelled the penniless Children of Israel, the "little Jews," and continued to distribute privileges to those who were proving capable of creating industries, opening up commercial outlets, taking a lease on money and, particularly, of lending money.[25] Government action like this, observed, moreover, in several European states at that period, has contributed to the persistence even today of a certain connection between Judaism and money (both in the conception that the Christian world has formed of Judaism, and in the internal life of the Jews). This is proof, if proof is needed, that feelings outlive for generations the situations which give birth to them and, in so doing, cause the continuing existence of certain after-effects of these situations.

The German Jews played an increasing economic role in the great commercial centers in the seventeenth and eighteenth centuries. In Leipzig, twenty-five percent of those participating at fairs at the end of the eighteenth century were Jews.[26] In Hamburg, the senate of the free town which had expelled them in 1648, and only re-admitted a few families fifteen years later, recorded in 1733 that they had become a "necessary evil" for trade, because their interests were bound up with those of the Christians.[27] Above all, in Frankfurt, a ghetto fire in 1711 was said to have made the finances of the Empire quake. But the ghetto ramparts, which had become a promenade, were decorated with the inscription: "No Jew and no pig can enter here."[28] Jews were particularly numerous in Frankfurt, the main financial center of Germany: over 3,000, sixteen percent of the population of the town, in around 1711. Obviously, alongside a few rich financiers, the ghetto from which the Rothschilds emerged included a large plebeian class, crammed into a few narrow alleys and engaged in a hundred and one wretched dealings to make ends meet.

> Lending or trafficking, they know how to draw people
> into their net.
> He who lets himself be trapped will never escape.
> There is no longer anyone in the whole of your country
> Who is not tied to Israel in one way or another.

So Goethe, fascinated by this sight from his youth,[29] described the Jews' dealings in his *Jahrmarktfest zu Plundersweilern* (1788). A popular song gives a pithy description:[30]

> If you want to buy a suit,
> to the Jew run back.
> Silver dishes, linen, tin—
> anything the households lack,
> you will find the Jew has by him,
> taken as a pledge for loans.
> Stolen goods, abducted items
> with him, make their happy homes.
> Coats and trousers—what you will,
> he will sell it cheap.
> The craftsmen can sell nothing.
> To the Jew all creep.

The small folk in the German towns and countryside, unlike the merchants and craftsmen, certainly profited from the presence of Jews, but all types of evidence unanimously indicate that the "silent classes," those who had no say in the matter, also despised and detested them. "To diddle the Jew" was considered a supreme feat, as a variety of popular tales shows; "The Jew in the Thorns" (*Der Jude im Dorn*) for example, which the Grimm brothers included in their classic collection.

The traditional Christian identification: "Judaism" as equivalent to a lie, from which we get "a Jew" equivalent to a swindler, could not have been more in keeping with such a moral philosophy. In the seventeenth century, the belief in the Jews' congenital double-dealing seems to have been shared by all classes of society. Spener, the founder of Lutheran pietism and one of the first to rise to their defense, even offered a sort of natural explanation for it:[31]

> As for the poor amongst them, whose number, as it is amongst the Christians, is always the largest, it is quite impossible for them to live without cunning and ruses for they, having only a few thaler capital, must turn this over through trade so that they can meet the needs of their family as best they may; so the wretched people can day and night think and wrack their brains about nothing else than how to spend their miserable lives in cunning, intrigue, deception and theft.

In the following century, such views were beginning to be classed as prejudiced by the enlightened. According to Christian-Wilhelm Dohm, a Prussian official who was one of the forerunners of Jewish emancipation:[32]

> It is only the mob which considers itself allowed to deceive a Jew, accuses him of being allowed by his law to deceive members of another religion, and it is only intolerant priests who have collected myths of the prejudices of the Jews which serve simply to prove their own.

Popular anti-Semitism can be said to have rested on two bases which were its two necessary and sufficient preconditions: the priests of the two faiths taught both children and adults in the catechism and from the height of the pulpit that the Jews were a deicidal and perfidious race. In real life and at adult age, these views were only rarely belied, drawing daily justification from the tension *sui generis* inherent in business relations, in the masked or open conflict which every purchase and every sale, any haggling and any exchange involve—and the contact between Christians and Jews was limited for the most part to aggressive relationships of this sort.

Much more complex were the Jews' relationships with the men in power and the ruling classes. These relationships constituted their vital position of strength. At a period when the traditional order of things and ideas was being disturbed particularly from beneath, they sometimes reached a degree of real intimacy. It is to their credit that the figureheads of the ghetto were able to make these meteoric ascents and, once they had made their fortunes, experience the pleasures of power and even a certain glory, and still remain Jews.

There are some extraordinary stories of baroque Germany. Take the case of Alexander David of Halberstadt, a poor Jew, who in 1707, when he was twenty, went to seek his fortune in Brunswick, capital of the Duchy of the same name, where Jews were not tolerated. When he arrived, the gatekeeper of the town is said to have protested: "Am I to see with my own eyes a Jew living in Brunswick?"[33] In actual fact, Alexander David did succeed in obtaining the right to reside. But in the early days, he had to sleep on a bench in the open, because he could not find a resident prepared to house him.

From the documents, we then learn of recriminations by tradesmen in the town indignant at the Jew's unfair practices, such as delivering orders to clients' homes. But right from the beginning, he had been able to get the heir to the throne on his side, in all probability by lending him money. In return, the latter granted him a "secret charter" in advance, and openly showered him with favors when he succeeded his father in 1714. Alexander David was then authorized to build a house, set up a tobacco factory, import English and Dutch cloth, and he received the title of court purveyor, which protected him from ordinary law. When his counselors protested, the young duke is said to have replied: "Will one ever find his equal, blessed with such divine inventive genius?"

As the years went by, Alexander David, simultaneously trader, banker and official, like nearly all court Jews, expanded and diversified his activities, which included supplying the army, organizing a lottery, advancing money to the duke, and granting loans to other German princes (among them the future Frederick the Great, via his fiancée, Elisabeth Christina von Bevern). He prospered under five successive dukes, expanding his collection of titles and functions as his wealth increased: he was court *banker,* court *jeweler,* court *minter,* court *purveyor,* and carried out several political missions. He could hold his own with officials. One of his old coachmen was accused of theft, and condemned to death. The ducal minister, Schrader von Schliestedt, refused him pardon, with the words: "As true as my name's Schrader von Schliestedt, he will hang," to which the Jew replied: "I was called Alexander David before you were called von Schliestedt" and won his case. He spent his leisure studying the Talmud and built a sumptuous synagogue at Brunswick. He died in 1765, aged nearly eighty. The ducal hearse, followed by court servants, carried his body to its final resting place.

It can be assumed that the origins of his dazzling success lay in the services he was able to render the crown prince from the moment he arrived, with the addition of gifts. Expensive gifts the court Jews regarded as an investment for the future, provided that they were judiciously distributed. In her memoirs, Glückel of Hamelin[34] tells a very typical story on these lines. She describes the lavish marriage in 1670 of her eldest daughter to the son of a banker, Elias Cleve, which was honored by the presence of the second son of the Prussian "Great Elector":

... Among the guests there were also many distinguished Portuguese Jews, one of whom was a jeweler of the name of Mocatta. He had with him a beautiful little gold watch set in diamonds, worth 500 reichstaler. Reb Elias asked Mocatta for this little watch, as he desired to make a present of it to the young Prince. But a good friend standing close by said to him, "Why do this? To give such an expensive present to the young prince? If he were the Elector it would be worth while." But as I have already mentioned, the Elector died not long after and the young Prince succeeded him and is still Elector. Thereafter, whenever Reb Elias Cleve saw the friend who dissuaded him from giving the present, he would throw it up at him angrily. And in truth, if he had given the present, the Prince would never have forgotten it, for great people never forget such things.

This brings us back to the cordial relations between Jews and German princes, both of them characters outside the common run or outside the framework of contemporary German society. But whatever the true reasons for the affinity between the members of the two classes, each in its own way permeated with a sense of its own superiority, an eighteenth-century German princely court without its Jew had become inconceivable. During a struggle in 1741 between the knackers' guild and the Jews in the ecclesiastical principality of Hildesheim, Rabbi Herschel Oppenheimer appealed to the Prince-Bishop to put the craftsmen in their place:[35]

> ... But if the knackers had only had some experience of courts, they would not reason so stupidly since there is almost no prince or potentate in the German Reich without his Court Jew who can always see the ruler—not like the knacker; who daily favors the Jews with privileges, even monopolies, so that the principle falls to the ground: that the Jews do not have the favor of the ruler, as their subjects do.

The three hundred or so German principalities gave hundreds of Jews the chance of making a career and a fortune. The tinier the principality, the more intimate the relationship between the prince and his Jew, which sometimes ended with the sovereign under his factotum's thumb. Heinrich Schnee has published some letters which the Count of Lippe-Detmold wrote to his banker Joseph Isaac in about 1730. The following is an extract:[36]

> Joseph, we have no more butter for this evening, so I am hereby telling you that you should make arrangements to have a full tun here this very night. There is no time to lose for otherwise we cannot sit down at table, so I hope you will do your best.

In another letter, the count begs the Jew to obtain some candles for him urgently; otherwise he will have to sit up in the dark. In the same supplicatory tone he asks for money advances. This subservience is more like H. G. Wells's sinister Morlocks, or Joseph Losey's film *The Servant*, than the relationship between Mephistopheles and Faustus (Sombart's romantic comparison). But we cannot trust literature. Remember, that if ever there was a field where imagination and literary clichés have done all too much harm, it is truly that of anti-Semitic obsessions which have always involved a typical exaggeration of the power the Jews exercised.

Nevertheless, this exaggeration, however obsessional, has one of its roots in certain past financial practices. Within the nobility particularly, there were a number of Christians hungry to speculate or to lend at interest in secret without losing face. For this purpose, the obliging and discreet Jew, impervious to the shame of acting as a Jew, was the ideal figurehead. This façade is still misleading a number of contemporary historians! He was sometimes no more than a puppet with a Christian capitalist pulling the strings. More often, there was a partnership in which the Christian element, the invisible portion of the iceberg, played a dominant part. Thus, the career of Baruch Simon (grandfather of the writer, Ludwig Börne) at the court of the Prince-Archbishop of Cologne was due to the protection of the Minister, Count Belderbusch, the principal member of a partnership which eventually amassed a fortune of a million ducats. According to public rumor, the Court Chaplain, Father Paulin, also participated in their partnership: of him it was said, *sub vesperum cum ministro et Baruch spolia dividebat.*[37] In Saxony, under the Brühl Ministry (1733-63), Count Joseph Bolza had become the richest man in the kingdom. He used Jewish figureheads, notably the "court-factor," Samuel Ephraim Levy, for his speculations and usurious loans to the crown. "The gains he derived thereby were a little too Jewish, and the services of this nobleman cost us very dear," wrote Brühl in 1761. In the end, Count Bolza's rapacity aroused suspicions that he was a Jew in disguise, so that in the Nazi era his descendants had to make genealogical investigations to "obtain certificates of Aryanity."[38] Saxony again saw the last act of the tragi-comedy when Voltaire, who had instructed the son of the jeweler Herschel to buy Saxon bonds for him, succeeded in cheating the young man in masterly fashion. The father died of a broken heart. The poet Lessing, who was working as the philosopher's translator sums up these transactions in the following epigram:[39]

> To give in short
> The reason why
> The cunning of the Jew
> Was not so spry
> The clue must roughly be
> Mr V . . . was an even bigger
> Rogue than he.

The Rothschilds, as we have already said, laid the foundations of their own fortune by investing profitably the fortune built up by the Margraves of Cassel in accordance with instructions they received.

The Jews' aptitude for covering with their Jewish label all types of unscrupulous transactions or dealings which went against the code of honor, certainly facilitated a good many spectacular ascents. Once he had arrived, the court Jew escaped from the main disabilities of his class. He could choose his residence outside the ghetto, and carry weapons. The designation "Jew" was replaced by "Mister" in official correspondence; his name appeared in the official court almanac in that form. Alexander David's funeral in the Duke of Brunswick's hearse was no isolated fact: the great German nobles often honored with their presence Jewish funerals, circumcision, and especially weddings, sometimes celebrated in the residence of the local ruler. It really seems as if attentions or compliments of this sort irritated the Christian bourgeoisie more than the sight of the financial successes of the Children of Israel. This irritation emerges in the reasons the Frankfurt magistrates gave for refusing the Jews access to the town's famous "promenade," despite their complaints: "It is only pride and the desire to think themselves equal to the Christians which provoke these ambitious thoughts,"[40] they wrote in conclusion.

France

The picture in eighteenth-century France is the same as in Germany, though the colors are not as bright. The Jews were protected to their finger tips by the central power, actively opposed by the rising bourgeoisie, and Christianly hated by the population as a whole, with the relative exception of enlightened and privileged circles. As the ancient edict banishing them from France (reiterated by Louis XIII in 1615) had not been repealed, their gradual spread over the kingdom took place semi-clandestinely starting from Alsace and Metz, the pontifical enclave of the County of Avignon, and the harbor towns. In France, they did not enjoy the specific support they found in a Germany divided amongst individual princes, to the irritation of their subjects. But perhaps the human climate of a country wide open to the ancient Mediterranean played a part in making contrasts and hatreds less sharp.

All the same, the settlement of Jews in a town could be resented as a crime of divine *lèse-majesté,* as the minor clergy of Nancy insinuated in its request to Duke Leopold of Lorraine in 1708:[41]

Are we to lose within minutes what has always so happily distinguished us from the most flourishing kingdoms, and will we, like the nations surrounding us, be forced to mourn the deadly wounds that eternally contagious trade can inflict on a state and a religion? These are no vague alarms, Monseigneur. How many visions of ruined merchants, devastated fields, oppressed and penniless families rise up before our eyes! Will you grant to the Jews, the most mortal enemies of Jesus Christ, his church and the Christian name, what you have so firmly refused to heretics who have forgotten nothing in order to settle in your states? Will these people, so visibly cursed and damned by God, banished from almost every state, find asylum in yours, Monseigneur?

When the threatened merchants appealed direct to the authorities, without using the clergy as spokesmen, they expressed their concern without any theological digression.[42] "The Jews will soon monopolize France's trade ..." (Gien merchants, 1732). "This infidel and deceitful Jewish nation spreads in our cantons every day ..." (trade delegates from Montpellier, 1739). "This Jewish nation only seems to grovel the better to raise and enrich itself ..." (delegates from the Toulouse Chamber of Commerce, 1744). "We implore you to halt the advance of this nation, which would inevitably throw all trade into confusion ..." (Montpellier, 1744). The royal administration did not let these alarms deceive them:

The best course that they [the Toulouse merchants] could follow would be to stock their shops with the same quality as the Jews and be satisfied with lower profits than they are making. ...
... If the merchants [of Beziers] are complaining about the loss the Jews are causing them, it is their fault. They should not fleece the public and try to make large profits. ...

... The merchants of Montpellier ... offer their fabrics at such exorbitant prices that, although they talk about the poor quality of those the Jews carry at fairs, theirs are not worth less at the prices they sell them than the fabrics found on the merchants' stalls. The Jews have all qualities at all prices. I have heard no reports that they carry any not marked with the fabric stamp. Consequently, it is the difference between the small profits the Jews are prepared to accept and the excessively high prices the merchants place on their materials, which has decided the public to obtain its supplies at the fairs rather than place orders at Lyons. ...

But the Jews' modest profit margins alone were not enough to explain their success. Characteristically, the very fact that they were forced to operate semi-clandestinely worked in their favor, appealing to the customers' imagination:[43]

At present, there are men of this type outside the Stock-Exchange [at Nantes] who sell all sorts of haberdashery and hardware and whose cry to attract custom is "Giving it away! Giving it away!" ... Last year, these vagabonds offered all sorts of muslins, prints and handkerchiefs for sale outside the Stock-Exchange. Nonetheless they were sold surprisingly quickly.

Another method for these illicit or stealthy street sales consisted of disposing of the goods in an inn room or, better still, coming to an agreement with a hard-up noble who put his château at the Jew's disposal, as was done by the Marquis de La Grave at Montpellier, or M. de Saint-Simon at Saintes.[44] An administration which was already half converted to the ideas of the Century of Enlightenment and anxious for the general good, let these practices go on, or even approved of them, particularly when they also benefited the immediate interests of the state. This was certainly true of the horse-dealers' war in Languedoc, when a few enterprising Avignon Jews ended the shortage of cart—and saddle—horses, current in the south in about 1735, by importing animals from Poitou and Auvergne and in so doing ruined the guild of Christian horse-dealers. "The Jews sold their beasts at prices which were fair and fitted the means of the country folk . . . ," recorded Bernage, the administrator of Languedoc.[45]

The traditional trade in money had more difficulty in finding men to defend it. However, in 1768 a high magistrate gave the following verdict on such trade by Alsatian Jews:[46]

Jews can certainly be of some use in Alsace. In hard times and when there is war on the frontier, they supply the peasants with the means of supporting their expenses. If they have been pillaged, if they have lost their animals in corvées, the Jews make them advances which put them in a position to buy seeds and animals; these loans are not made cheaply; but in extreme need, it is better to pass through the usurer's hands than to perish completely. The Jews are also engaged in remounting the cavalry; they scheme to bring horses from foreign countries; and that they have rendered this kind of service during all past wars cannot be denied.

It is therefore no evil for there to be a few Jews in Alsace; but look at the evil too many could entail. . . . The Jews do not work at tilling the land, and they occupy a number of houses in the country which could be usefully occupied by agriculturalists. The peasants, finding the Jews have money they can borrow, either to pay their lord's or the King's taxes, become listless and lazy and soon fall into a state of poverty, while their property, ill-cultivated, is sold to pay their creditors. . . .

In the second half of the eighteenth century, the climate of opinion seemed favorable to the Jews' requests for official authorization to practice "commerce and the arts" in Paris. The guilds opposed it on grounds of tradition, but some of the arguments put forward on that occasion reflect the fact that the old order had been shaken, that irreligion was increasingly prevalent, that the "age of reason" had arrived. Very instructive on this count is the memorandum drafted in 1765 by a famous lawyer, Maître Goulleau, at the request of the merchants and traders of Paris (the six guilds). This memorandum is mainly a long historical account of the crimes and misdeeds of the Jews, studded with picturesque comparisons and metaphors in the style of the period.[47] Maître Goulleau lists all the traditional criticisms and revives them to serve his purpose, from unsociableness to usury, and from ritual murder to the propagation of the plague—with the exception of the original and major crime, i.e. the murder of Christ, which the memorandum does not even mention. Thus, though the framework was still intact, the cornerstone of the anti-Jewish argument had been removed by this writer. We have already reached the age of reason. Likewise, during another lawsuit, the lawyer and polemicist, Linguet, was choosing his words with this in mind when he said: "Habit, religion, policy, reason perhaps, or at least an instinct justified by many reasons, drives us to attach both scorn and aversion to the name of the Jews. . . ."[48] The new ideas, the deism in the air, had even reached the old-clothes-men of Montpellier, when they invoked the Supreme Being in 1789:[49]

> There is no one who does not carry in his heart the conviction of the evil that the Jewish people does throughout the world. The Supreme Being, when he created nature, expressly wished this race to be confined in a specific area, and forbade it to communicate in any way with other nations. . . .

But in the main, anti-Semitism in the eighteenth century in France, as elsewhere, continued to rest on the ancient union between the impulses of traditional religion and the interests of trade—as the Minister of State, Malesherbes, reminded Louis XVI on the eve of the Revolution:[50]

> There still exists in the hearts of most Christians a very strong hatred of the Jewish people, a hatred based on the memory of the crime of their ancestors and corroborated by the custom whereby Jews in every country engage in trade which the Christians regard as their downfall. . . .

Militant anti-Semitism was thus essentially a bourgeois-

Christian phenomenon: the vital commercial interest apart, Jews bent on practicing their Jewish professions without the slightest hypocrisy inevitably seemed scandalous to merchants professing to worship the God of the poor and lowly. (According to Savary's *Dictionary of Trade*, "a merchant is said to be as rich as a Jew when he is reputed to have accumulated great wealth.") We will see how even the attitudes of philosophers and encyclopedists towards the Children of Israel seemed colored by their social origin. Only the nobility, whose prestige rested on birth and whose prejudices indiscriminately enveloped everybody who was not one of themselves, evinced some sympathy for the Jews. Perhaps they even gave them preference over the Christian bourgeoisie, whose mounting jealousy and hatred they realized. To the extent to which there were distinctions and contrasts within the ranks of the nobility, this conclusion, not surprisingly, primarily applies to the old sword-bearing nobility. It is extraordinary to see the heroes and great captains, men with only the king and the heavens above them, surrounding themselves with Jews and protecting them. Such was the case with Prince Eugène of Savoy, Marshall Maurice of Saxony,[51] Prince Charles de Ligne. This latter wrote a *Mémoire sur les Juifs,* towards the end of his life, in which good will was barely veiled by the irony befitting a great lord. "The Jews have various types of virtue," he wrote in conclusion; "never drunk, always obedient, precise and attentive to ordinances, loyal subjects to the sovereign at times of revolt, and never angry; united amongst themselves, sometimes hospitable, and their rich helping their poor." There follows an appeal for the emancipation of the Jews, of a stronger brand of irony.[52]

And lastly the Israelites, while awaiting the impenetrable decrees of Providence on their obduracy in the matter of the wrongs of their ancestors, will at least be happy and useful in this world, and will cease to be the meanest people on earth. I well understand the origin of the horror the Jews inspire, but it is time this ended. Eighteen hundred years seems to me long enough for anger to persist!

The nobility's philo-Semitism under the *ancien régime* probably rested first on the manifold services the Jews were able to render it, in the form of monetary loans, indeed on the speculation they undertook together (the type, for example, that the Princess of Rohan indulged in, under cover of one Salomon Levy, in Law's time).[53] But the absence of bourgeois prejudice on their part facilitated such relationships, which were not necessarily selfish. It is quite understandable that only a high-born and self-confident priest could have set out to work for a Jew in trouble in the way the Abbé de La Varenne de Saint-Saulieu did in 1744 (the Abbé de La Varenne de Saint-Saulieu to the Lieutenant of the Paris Police, March 14, 1744):[54]

> I have not forgotten that you told me that I seemed like a rabbi when I spoke to you of this affair; but when you hear that the Jew on whose behalf I am speaking has done at least as much good in the prison where he is as all the charitable offices, when he has been in good health, and that few prisoners have left it without feeling the effects of his liberality, you will probably no longer accuse me of Judaism, and I am even convinced that you will become as much of one [a rabbi] as me, and that your sense of justice will commit you to imitate the Lord who rewards even in this world the good faith of these miserable victims of their blindness.

Let us conclude with a glimpse of the social status of the Jews in Paris at the end of the *ancien régime*. It is provided by a lawsuit brought in 1776 by a Bordeaux Jew, Mendès, against two negroes, Gabriel Pampy and Amynte Julienne (slaves whom Mendès had brought back from the West Indies, they had given their master the slip in Paris, and he had appealed to the law to obtain their return). In the course of the case, the Jew and the Negroes, via their lawyers, bandied the unflattering opinions that Europe nursed on their respective counts. One side described all the sons of Ham as "swindlers and liars"; the other retorted "that they could make the same criticism of the Jewish people, and that the parallel would not perhaps be favorable to it." They also accused Mendès of cruelty, bringing forward manifold examples to support the charge. But the most terrible pain they had suffered was that "their master prevented them from fulfilling the duties of the Catholic religion, in which they had the good fortune to have been brought up."

But why had Mendès come to live in Paris? The lawyer representing Pampy and Julienne disclosed that it was because[55]

> the capital seemed to him the most propitious spot. All ranks are almost merged together there, and if a wealthy Jew did not enjoy that pleasant consideration which was the first need of a well-born man, he could at least enjoy all the pleasures which could be bought with gold. . . . If residence in that town promised many pleasures to Monsieur Mendés. it was very pernicious for his Negro and Negress. For the Jew, far from making them feel the effects of the sweetness that characterizes the French, on the contrary made them mourn the hard work on which they had been employed in the colonies.

The tribunal decided in favor of Pampy and Julienne.[56]

Great Britain

The originality of English customs, which appeared in modern times in so many spheres, was evident in the status given to the Jews.

The chapter entitled "Anti-Semitism in the Pure State" in my first volume[57] recalled the terror which greeted Cromwell's intention to re-admit them to the British Isles in 1656 (whence they had been expelled in 1294). It tells how, faced with popular opposition, he had to back down while tacitly allowing a colony of rich ex-Marrano merchants to settle in London—the British art of compromise. Later, these valuable taxpayers were useful to the host country, both as financiers and political informants on Spanish affairs, and London became one of the main centers of the thriving "Marrano dispersion." We have also seen[58] how their eventful history had led Jews from the Iberian peninsula to comply with Christian customs, to "assimilate" *avant la lettre*. In the course of the eighteenth century, Jews born of the German and Polish ghetto and held at a distance, clustered around them and eventually outnumbered them. Great Britain counted a total of twenty to twenty-five thousand Jews in 1800.

On the continent, the dispersion of the Children of Israel was proof of their downfall. In the eyes of the English rulers it became the value symbol of a people who were in many respects displeasing. As early as 1712, the statesman and publicist Joseph Addison proclaimed their usefulness for the human race:[59]

> They are indeed so disseminated through all the trading parts of the world, that they are become the instrument by which the most distant nations converse with one another, and by which mankind are knit together in a general correspondence. . . . They are like pegs and nails in a great building, which, though they are but little value in themselves are absolutely necessary to keep the whole frame together.

There was nothing in such peaceful functions to shock the ruling classes and public opinion in an island which was already "a nation of shopkeepers," and where (if Max Weber is to be believed) early capitalist impulses had diverted the vitality of the Calvinist revolution to their own advantage. Because of the flexibility, or perhaps the "modernity," of English trade, it could face Jewish competition without excessive fear. Moreover, in the event, this competition came primarily from the so-called Portuguese Jews, who, as we have seen, troubled the Christian imagination much less than their

German and Polish brethren. On another score, some of the direct fundamentals of Calvinist Protestantism, such as the popularity of the Old Testament and the prestige of its heroes (reflected in the fashion for Biblical Christian names), as well as the multiplication of sects and the principles of religious freedom which derived from them, contributed to under- standing and sometimes sympathy. In this way, the two fundamental and perhaps indissoluble activators of anti- Semitism were extenuated. It is a fact that English merchants only indulged in exceptional circumstances in the agitation and anguished protests which characterized the attitude of French and German guilds.

Some English historians think that it is the country's com- mercial ability which saved it from anti-Semitic disturbances and upheavals in modern times: G. M. Trevelyan, for example:[60]

> . . . Between the time when the Jews were expelled by Edward
> I, and the time when they were re-admitted by Cromwell, the
> English had learnt to manage their own financial and business
> affairs. There was therefore no danger of Hebrew domination
> and of the answering reaction of anti-Semitism. By Hanoverian
> times, England was strong enough to digest a moderate influx of
> Jews.

This "digestion" was not always easy, and the very term the author uses could suggest that it is not completely finished at the present time. However that may be, if eighteenth-century England did not experience the phenomenon (classic on the continent) of anti-Jewish campaigns stirred up by commercial interests, Judaism had no shortage of disinterested enemies.

In the cradle of religious and political toleration, there is hardly an author, at least among names which have come down to posterity, who has not unleashed his shaft at the deicidal people, permanent enemy of the Christian name. For example Daniel Defoe cursed "the execrable Jews crucifying the Lord of Life"; or Alexander Pope raised the following prayer in one of his satires:

Keep us we beseech thee, from the hands of such barbarous and cruel Jews, who albeit they abhor the blood of black-puddings, yet thirst they vehemently after the blood of the white ones. And that we may avoid such like calamities, may all good and well-disposed Christians be warned by these unhappy wretches woeful example, to abominate the heinous sin of avarice.

As for Jonathan Swift, he put English public opinion on its guard against the indomitable dissenters, by waving the specter of the Jewish danger:

What if the Jews should multiply and become a formidable party among us? Would the dissenters join in alliance with them likewise, because they agree already in some general principles, and because the Jews are allowed to be a stiffnecked and rebellious people?

M. F. Modder's book, from which we are borrowing these quotations,[61] offers many more of the same type, extracts from the works of Samuel Richardson, Henry Fielding, and Laurence Sterne. Amongst the novelists, only Tobias Smollett was entirely favorably disposed towards the Jews (we will deal with political and religious thinkers in the following chapter). But these were minor pinpricks that can partly be attributed to a sort of literary convention. More significant was the furious and ephemeral anti-Jewish explosion of 1753, which echoed the events of 1656, and proved that medieval hatreds and terrors persisted in the hearts of the English population.

The pretext was trifling.[62] In 1753, the Duke of Newcastle's government, probably at the instigation of a group of rich Sephardim, submitted a Bill (the Naturalization Bill) for the approval of the House to simplify procedures for their naturalization and to authorize them to acquire land. Both the House of Lords and the Commons adopted the bill without any difficulty. But the ensuing popular agitation against this law was of a violence rarely equaled in the annals of English history. Petitions from all sections of the population multiplied, seditious inscriptions appeared in the streets of English towns. Pamphleteers outdid each other in their warnings against the influx of Jews and their accession to landed property, which would lead to their seizure of the nation's land, after the style of the division of the land of Canaan between the twelve Biblical tribes. One of the agitators even gave a detailed and not unamusing forecast of the sad state of England in 1853: St Paul's Cathedral transformed into a synagogue, trade ruined by the obligatory observance of the Sabbath, a ban on pork and a Christian Naturalization Bill rejected by the Great Sanhedrin. But the Archbishop of Canterbury who supported the Bill had serious fears at the time of a general massacre of the Jews.[63]

In the long run, the government had to give in to popular agitation and repeal the unpopular law six months after its publication. And yet nothing in it constituted a material threat to any economic interest whatsoever. What had come to the surface simply at the thought of seeing members of the deicidal race admitted to the full rights of man and of Christians were the haziest apprehensions, dark atavistic fears. Likewise, Jews in Anglo-Saxon countries even today are surrounded by subtle social barriers and tacit discriminations; an unavoidable ransom, perhaps, for the material security they enjoy.

It was not until the last years of the eighteenth century that in the British Isles a new image of the Jew began to be superimposed on the one which had disturbed and frightened all Christian states since the time of the Crusades. At the period when France and, in its train, the Continent, was entering the whirlpool of revolutionary wars, Great Britain was falling in love with a different type of conflict: boxing with naked fists. To public amazement, several children of the ghetto found their vocation as professional boxers, and the names of Abraham de Costa, Samuel and Israel Belasco, Isaac Bitton and particularly Daniel Mendoza filled the sporting columns. "Dan" Mendoza eventually became a national idol; even present-day connoisseurs agree that he was one of the

pioneers of the "noble sport."⁶⁴ Thus it was that the prototype of the young Jewish athlete came shyly into competition
with the archetypes of Judas and his thirty pieces of silver
and the hook-nosed Shylock, which brings us back to the
originality of British customs.

A glance at the other European countries

The case of the Jews in Britain brings out the connection
between the level of a country's economic development and
the status it gave the Jews. If we wanted to reduce anti-
Semitism to a phenomenon of commercial competition, leading to a revolt by the natives against Jewish supremacy, we
could find even better arguments in another exceptional case,
the Netherlands. Jews who had settled there at the beginning
of the seventeenth century, at the time when the Dutch
"waggoners of the seas" were lording it over the English,
eventually formed two or three percent of the population.
Amsterdam, their main place of residence, deserved the title
of "new Jerusalem." Neither density nor prosperity gave rise
to persecution or even recrimination in the flourishing United
Provinces.

However, the fact that the Jews were well-established did
not necessarily mean that the people, whose opinion was not
asked, cheerfully accepted their presence. Taken all in all,
anti-Semitism is a phenomenon with several concentric levels
or layers, and economic jealousy is only the most superficial or
the most recent of them. Likewise, the image of the Jew in the
other European countries at the same period presented a
whole gamut of tones, not related to his socio-economic
function.

In Italy, for example, all the conditions for intense Judeophobia seemed to be united. Jews there played a major
economic role in a country where trade was languishing and
the distant descendants of the merchants and financiers who
once dominated Europe spent their days in increasing idle-

ness. Side by side with the great Jewish entrepreneurs of Venice or Leghorn, enfranchised and sometimes over-bearing, nearly every town had a poor Jewish proletariat crowded into ghettoes—remember, both the word and the fact are Italian in origin. From the time of the Catholic reform, the Holy See had intended to illustrate in this way both the triumph of Christianity and the intransigent purity of its own principles ("one ghetto of Jews is better proof of the truth of the religion of Jesus Christ than a school of theologians," claimed the Catholic publicist G. B. Roberti at the end of the eighteenth century). But judging by the peaceful history of the Children of Israel, and the indifference men of letters evinced towards them, this un-Christian lesson had no great effect in Italy. Neither rich nor poor in this country of old and high culture created the prejudice and obsessions noted on the other side of the Alps. Furthermore, Italy was the only large country in Europe where the Jews after emancipation integrated easily and harmoniously into Christian society, and which in practice did not experience anti-Semitism in its modern forms.[65] To the Italian man-in-the-street, the Jew is an eccentric who is still waiting for the Messiah and who knows how to rub along in life while waiting; neither of these characteristics constitutes an ir-redeemable vice in his eyes.

If the Italian population enjoyed some sort of basic immunity to anti-Jewish agitation, in Spain on the other hand anti-Semitism was perpetuated in the absence of Jews. In this context, let me refer to my preceding volume, where I tried to establish the long genealogy of a phenomenon that in the last analysis goes back to the socio-religious conflicts in the Middle Ages and whose roots are therefore plunged in the distant past. At the opposite end of Europe, Russia experienced nothing resembling these conflicts except the ephemeral "heresy of the Judaizers" in the fifteenth century. However, Muscovite Judeophobia almost equalled in intensity the anti-Semitism raging in the Iberian peninsula and equally found concrete expression in a *cordon sanitaire* erected against those who followed the Law of Moses and maintained down the centuries by each successive tsar. In both cases, it is tempting to make a connection between economic and cultural backwardness and horror of the Jews. Horror was no less intense in Poland and Hungary but backwardness, from the point of view which interests us, led to quite different results, since Jews were numerous there and deeply embedded in the economy. It was Hungary in the last century which produced a definition of anti-Semitism which is perhaps as good as any other: "The anti-Semite is a man who detests Jews more than is reasonable." It can be seen that if almost every country in Old Europe satisfied this definition, variations on it, if not contradictions to it, were no less numerous.

The state of Judeo–Christian relations in the New World enables us to add some highly significant details to the quick sketch we have drawn.

two

The United States of America

The powerful American Jewish community usually dates its foundations from the year 1654, when some twenty Jews, fleeing the Brazilian inquisition, came and settled in New York. Towards the middle of the seventeenth century, Jews, mostly merchants, also appeared in other colonies (Massachusetts, Connecticut, Virginia, Maryland). The formation of American Jewry was slow and apprehensive at first; in the middle of the nineteenth century, the United States only counted a few thousand Jews, generally of Sephardi stock. At times, the representatives of colonial power or the local assemblies protested against their presence, as they did against the admission of other religious minorities, such as the Catholics or even Quakers.[1] In a virgin country where men were in short supply and each new colonist was valued in terms of his industry and not his genealogy, these tendencies did not prevail. They gained as little ground as the paradox of the opposite tendency, which seems to have appeared in the Puritan colonies (during a lawsuit in Connecticut, for example, the judges reduced the punishment imposed on a Jew, "cause, considering he is a Jew, to show him what favore they may . . .").

Puritanism, which was a determining factor in forming American attitudes, sought its first truth in Old Testament Judaism. The historian James Adams even wrote:[2]

in spirit they [the Puritans] may be considered as Jews and not Christians. Their God was the God of the Old Testament, their laws were the laws of the Old Testament, their guides to conduct were the characters of the Old Testament.

The spiritual leaders of these "spiritual Jews" certainly placed a high value on the testimony of flesh and blood Jews, and this was also true of the founders of some other sects. The Puritan Cotton Mather celebrated every Jewish conversion as an important event, and wrote a special treatise on the subject. The founder of Methodism, John Wesley, started learning Spanish when he was staying in America so that he could better convert the Jews, "some of whom seem nearer the mind that was in Christ than many of those who call Him Lord." The Quaker William Penn said that they should be regarded with "tender compassion," adding that they should only be converted by kindness. The Puritan Ezra Stiles seems more sceptical, noting in his journal:[3]

> I remark that Providence seems to make every Thing to work for Mortification to the Jews, and to prevent their incorporating into any Nation; that thus they may continue a distinct people. ... [It] forbodes that the Jews will never become incorporated with the people of America, any more than in Europe, Asia and Africa.

For theologians scrutinizing Christian tradition, the Jews remained marked with special significance; but nascent public opinion did not look so closely in a new country where everything was still to be done and "where the inhabitants had come to forget and not to remember."[4]

It was in this way that the specifically American tolerance came about, stimulated by solidarity in the face of the work of clearing the land and building, and leading to civil and religious egalitarianism. De Tocqueville was already pointing out that in the United States public opinion, rather than imposing the true religion, required that every man practice *his* religion. As a general rule, the Jews obtained equal civic and electoral rights as early as the end of the colonial era, the victory on the whole being easier in the northern states than in the south. A good many of them distinguished themselves in the War of Independence and some rose to become officers on the battlefield. The shared experience of war and bloodshed has always been a powerful agent in the integration of minorities. The political philosophy of the United States put the final touch to this integration, and when they drew up the birth certificate of the American nation, its founding fathers were opening up the "age of the rights of man," solemnly proclaimed by the Declaration of Independence.[5] In a message in 1790, George Washington expressly extended these rights to the Jews:

> May the children of the stock of Abraham who dwell in this land continue to merit and enjoy the good will of the other inhabitants; while every one shall sit in safety under his own vine and fig tree and there shall be none to make him afraid.

But the most generous declaration of intention requires a propitious climate of opinion to be put into practice. The declarations formulated in Europe at the same period by the enlightened despots or the French Constituent Assembly, crowned by the emancipation of the Jews there, did not prevent the ferocious explosions of anti-Semitism of the nineteenth and twentieth centuries. Perhaps they contributed to them, as we shall see further on. If Judaism found in the American Republic the security and peace that the founders promised it, it was for reasons that lay deeper than ideology.

It is a good idea to begin by recalling an adventitious factor which acted in the Jew's favor: the existence of a black community which polarized the aggressive instincts of the white community in the way we know too well. But above all, every generation of Americans was confronted with new immigration, with wretched individuals with different and therefore shocking habits. In the nineteenth century, the Irish first and then the Italians were no better treated or looked on than the Polish or Russian Jews who flowed in at the end of the century, or the Mexicans and Puerto Ricans today. All the human groups who successively populated the United States had to suffer the same transplantation and the same ordeal, and this led to much less "Jewish otherness." So it is possible to talk of a veritable historical predisposition towards the Jews, since the habits and customs which govern American community life in the last analysis also arise from a vast collective uprooting.

In the same way, the mobility and vitality which characterize the Children of Israel and make them objects of envy, scarcely offended a Christian majority which was evincing exactly the same qualities. In the nineteenth century, the American myth of the frontier seemed to be creating a new wandering people. De Tocqueville has given a perceptive description of them:[6]

> These men left their first country to improve their condition; they quit their resting place to ameliorate it still more; fortune awaits them everywhere, but happiness they cannot attain. The desire of prosperity is become an ardent and restless pattern in their minds which grows by what it gains. They early broke the ties which bound them to their natural earth, and they have contracted no fresh ones on their way. Emigration was at first necessary to them as a means of subsistence; and it soon becomes a game of chance, which they pursue for the emotions it excites as much as for the gain it procures.

Such characteristics, common to Jews and Americans in the past, also imply a desire or a need for innovation which as we know is the primary driving force behind capitalist expansion. In the same connection, half a century ago, the German economist Werner Sombart went so far as to write that "America in all its regions is a land of Jews."[7]

In these circumstances anti-Semitism was unknown in the United States until relatively recently, like many other "old opinions which guided the world for centuries [and which] have disappeared,"[8] to quote another of de Tocqueville's comments. In particular everything suggests that Christian tradition dropped its anti-Jewish component when it was transplanted into North America. It can be concluded from this that if the myth of the deicidal people and its various historico-theological extensions are necessary pre-conditions of anti-Semitism, they alone are not sufficient condition for its occurrence. At the beginning of the twentieth century, quali-fied observers, both Christians and Jews, were declaring that it was non-existent in the United States.[9] It is significant that its slow rise coincided with the completion of colonization, with a certain stabilization or a movement towards middle-class respectability in American society, and with the restric-tions on all immigration which this society brought in to pro-tect the positions gained. (Nevertheless the causes in such matters are rarely simple, and it can also be argued that the rapid multiplication of Jews in the United States—tenfold between 1880 and 1914[10]—and the hostility which all new immigration arouses, were determining factors.)

In these circumstances as well, the Jews living within a nation without a past carried the weight of their own millen-nial past more lightly. They enjoyed the same security as their Christian compatriots ("a vital security in insecurity"), and in the process their image altered completely to produce a remarkable and sometimes aggressive self-confidence, a high opinion of themselves and an unqualified, naïvely sponta-neous admiration for their new fatherland.[11] Another by-product, as the heartbreak of exile faded into the past, was the transformation of the dialectic of the Exile and the promised land into a purely theoretical exercise (as their historians point out).[12] This is the reason why today, despite anti-Semitic campaigns which were particularly virulent in the inter-war period, it is still, with some qualifications, as respectable to be a Jew in the United States as a Protestant or a Catholic. Priests and pastors can be seen holding up the Jews as examples to their flocks, and not only in the realm of philanthropy. "Where are *our* Einsteins, Oppenheimers and Salks?" the President of the great Catholic University of Notre-Dame recently reproached Catholic educationalists.

Likewise, a Protestant theologian bewailed the absence in authors of his faith, of the visionary faculties of Jewish writers.[18] Such semi-official expressions of esteem for the old Jewish name as well as certain specifically American types of co-operation between Christians and Jews (pastors preaching in synagogues and vice-versa) remain unimaginable in old Europe, where the past continues to weigh heavily on the present.

We return now to this past and to the strange fate of German Jewry.

three

The Men of the Ghetto

Strange indeed was the fate of the human group, barely larger than an Australian or North American Indian tribe, whose descendants were exterminated (like the Australians' or North American Indians'), after having borne supermen who turned the intellectual map of the West inside out. What made their fate even stranger was the fact that the generation of German Jews we are considering seemed stricken with cultural sterility, even from a strictly rabbinical point of view. As their most recent historiographer puts it:[1]

> In spite of everything, the German Jews of that period possessed neither literature nor a science in the true sense. They utterly lacked the mobility and empathetic power of Hellenized Jewry, the depth of philosophic speculation of Spanish Jewry, the general education and high cultural level of Dutch Jewry, the creative fantasy of Italian Jewry, the religious ecstasy of Polish Jewry. . . .

"My nation, alas, is kept so far distant from all culture that one might almost despair of the possibility of an improvement!" declared the philosopher, Moses Mendelssohn.[2] The only trace of their passage on this earth that these men might be said to have left, came from their clever financiers; and they were hardly in the habit of writing down what they thought about themselves or the world around them. In these circumstances, the portraits of the ancestors of Marx, Freud and Einstein can only be a sort of archaeological reconstruction for which we will be using a few contemporary sources together with what is known about medieval ghetto life in other contexts. We have several physical descriptions of these German Jews. The following, for example, was given by the Prince de Ligne :[3]

> Is a picture of them required? Always sweating from running about selling in public squares and taverns; almost all hunch-backed, such dirty red or black beards, livid complexions, gaps in their teeth, long, crooked noses, fearful, uncertain expressions, trembling heads, appalling frizzy hair; knees bare and pocked with red; long, pigeon-toed feet, hollow eyes, pointed chins. . . .

The word "run" appears frequently in eighteenth-century writings about them: "They are particles of quick silver which *run about,* wander . . ." said Maître Goulleau in his statement and the apologist Zalkind-Hourwitz uses the same verb describing their struggle for existence:[4]

> Here you have the state of the Jews . . . those who *run* about the provinces may breathe freer air, but are no less wretched for it. Apart from the expense, the difficulties and the dangers inseparable from a wandering life, they are continually harassed by trade, custom and inspection officials and very often arrested by the mounted constabulary on the slightest suspicion: they are obliged to carry their dishes and meat around with them, those of other nations being forbidden them; this annoys the greedy and intolerant inn-keepers who make them pay very dearly for the little they sell them. As oppression makes them suspicious, as people are likewise prejudiced against them, and as moreover they have no fixed domicile, they can barely buy or sell at all except for ready cash. . . .

This constant running, this behavior peculiar only to themselves, probably contributed to the persistence of legends of a specifically Jewish physical constitution and of their congenital deformities. Zalkind-Hourwitz tells us that such views were the subject of discussions in learned societies in his day,[5] and La Harpe in his famous *Histoire des Voyages,* to emphasize their ugliness, compared the cross-eyed pygmies to the Jews.

John Toland, an English author who traveled a great deal in Europe (we will have more to say about him later), reports :

> Yet so strong is the force of prejudice, that I know a person, no fool in other instances, who labor'd to perswade me, contrary to the evidence of his own and my eyes (to mine I am sure) that every *Jew* in the world had one eye remarkably less than the other, which silly notion he took from the Mob. Others will gravely tell you, that they may be distinguish'd by a peculiar sort of smell. . . .

This smell (the *foetor judaicus*),[6] the opposite of the Christian "odor of sanctity," was a mark of the Jews' depravity. The way in which contemporaries thought that their hideousness originated directly from the great crime their ancestors had committed, can be illustrated by another traveler's comment:[7]

> . . . I did not separate the idea of a Jew from that of a man with a swarthy head, dull eyes, flat nose, large mouth; in fact I saw that God had printed a stamp of reprobation on their foreheads.

To flee from danger, to obtain money, a pledge of security; these were the incentives behind the perpetual motion which struck observers (but in their descriptions, the latter placed the emphasis on the pursuit of money : *"Der Jude liebt das Geld, und fürchtet die Gefahr,"* as Goethe says).[8] The Jewish obsession with money led to a scale of values within Jewish communities which gave priority to wealth— and such a hierarchy was not, of course, limited to eighteenth-century German Jews. But inside the ghetto, the pursuit of money did not degenerate into worship of the golden calf, contrary to the tendency which henceforth developed in the Christian bourgeoisie. In fact, because of their status, money remained purely a means for the Jews, as long as the end (i.e. their toleration, the right to live) had to be acquired by means of this money. It was a means equally of marrying, of procreating[9] and in this way of perpetuating the People of the Covenant which the Holy One, Blessed be He, urgently required for his glory to be celebrated. An old Talmudic fable compares the Jew's position to that of the king's servant hated by the people:

> To whom can the peoples of the earth be compared? To a man who hates the king, would like to attack him but is powerless to do so. That is why he blames the man who serves the king, because him he can attack. The peoples of the earth would like to attack God; as they can not, they strike at Israel.

This Talmudic scholar also recognized how important the hatred of the nations was for the preservation of Judaism: "When King Ahasuerus gave Haman his ring to seal the persecution that the latter demanded, he did more for Israel than all the prophets."[10]

In this way we are looking more closely into the fascinating interweaving of external pressure and internal tradition in the fabric of Jewish history. The internal tradition glorified wealth but assigned it the role of the servant of a wisdom which taught that there was no better way of serving God than by stimulating the intellect of the sons of the Chosen People by study. In addition, the Jews' world to come, their "paradise," was traditionally depicted as a sort of eternal Talmudic academy. In daily life, the priority they accorded spiritual things was expressed in typical practices such as the plutocrats' pursuit of learned sons-in-law to buy with their daughters' dowries, as well as in the weight given to the rabbi's voice in communal affairs. A boy's transition to marriageable age consisted of a reading exercise (*bar mitzvah* – religious and social majority). From tender years, he was initiated in the rudiments of the art of dialectic. The theme of the Jewish child disputing with scholars, which appears in a scene of the Gospel according to St Luke, was an everyday feature of ghetto life.[11]

To Voltaire's contemporaries, even more than to preceding generations of Christians, Jewish wisdom was all Talmudic fables and chimeras. However, the plutocratic régime of the ghetto might be likened to a sort of approximation to Plato's Republic, where a city ruler had to be a dialectician, excelling in knowledge of the True and Good. In their internal relationships, particularly within the family, the pariahs of Europe sometimes evinced a delicacy of feeling, an exquisite pride[12] which it would be hard to find equaled in contemporary Europe. But the men of the ghetto completely disregarded the "point of honor," an unspoken code befitting a republic governed by sages. Zalkind-Hourwitz notes this characteristic of the Jews of his day in the following terms:[13]

> It is true that they are absolutely insensible to what is appropriately called the point of honor, but this is because they simply believe with Socrates that an honest man cannot be dishonored by being insulted by a ruffian; that it is the gentleman who pays his debts with blows who is vile, and not the Jew who receives them; lastly, they believe that skill in swordsmanship is not proof of bravery, nor bravery proof of honesty. It must be admitted that these prejudices of the Jews are very justifiable, if it is considered that the Barbary pirates are very bad fencers, very brave and very dishonest.

This is a typical argument. The relativity of ethics and customs had already become commonplace for the public of the time, and some philosophers had already drawn devastating conclusions from it. With the Jews, this type of critical sense (but where radicalism was still tempered by the system of references constituted by the Torah) had found plenty to work on in the course of their millennial Dispersion. It had been fed by peregrinations which were more instructive than reading travelers' tales, and stimulated still more by the persecution and abuse as well as the hypocrisy of surrounding society. Let us quote Zalkind-Hourwitz again:[14]

What must the Jews think of the people who oppress them solely because of their religion, and treat as friends all who abjure it, that is to say cease to be Jews, without worrying if they become Christians, or if they are decent people; what, I say, what must the Jews think of this behavior? Behavior which, in this enlightened century, they can no longer attribute either to fanaticism or bad policy. Are they not right in concluding from it that Christianity ordains it, or that Christians, even the most honest and enlightened, are less zealous about moral principles and their own religion, than hostile to Judaism, and consequently to God, its author. . . ?

The Jews' critical sense and intellectual faculties, their mistrust of absolute judgments and idols, were stimulated in very many ways. The trades they pursued assisted this, as did their position as a minority, and a whole set of beliefs which in practice involved a permanent defiance of the beliefs the "compact majority" professed. If the tendency to think and act in a different way from the rest, and, consequently, the talent to innovate in every sphere, partly originated in this, the peaceful means of resistance the Jews used cannot be detached from their religious respect for human life. Perhaps history had never known a human group to practice nonviolence so systematically, to follow, whether or not for want of the power to do otherwise, the Christian virtues of pardon and forgiveness of sins, of turning the other cheek. Here, we are at the source of a specifically Jewish attitude, of a behavior pattern, if not of a psycho-physiological condition. Its survival up to the present day sometimes causes reference to their "otherness." Moreover, do not various verses of the Old Testament explicitly state that God has *marked* the people of his Covenant for all time so that they shall not be mingled with other nations?[15]

The Jews' proverbial "restlessness" or "rootlessness" also partly originated in the mystical idea of the Exile, leading, through fascinating historical vicissitudes, to a very particular relationship between the scattered people and their "natural environment," heavy with psychological and social consequences.[16] But wherever such phenomena first originated, the link between the Jews' particular history and the vast gamut of their characteristic features cannot be seriously doubted. The Jews' non-violence is an example of this, a non-violence which was more or less balanced by so-called verbal aggressiveness, and which in its extreme form tended towards a characteristic "masochism."

It is true that Jewish masochism, with its numerous psychological extensions of all types, probably including a remarkable cultural creativity, was primarily to affect later generations of "emancipated" Jews. In the warm intimacy of the ghetto, it remained tempered by the mistrust in which the Christian world was held, by rejection of its values and indifference to its judgments. While they remained a globally oppressed community, and because they did so, the Jews faced their environment collectively and not individually. They looked at themselves in their own mirror and in the distorting mirror their detractors held up. Their faith in their moral superiority, culminating in the idea of the Chosen People, compensated for the feeling of insecurity that their physical weakness and vulnerability created. Let us repeat: a psychologically split *condition*, that is to say, the paradox of the debased–Chosen People, was intermingled with and balanced by a *tradition* whereby the Christians, significantly, were feared as wild animals much more than hated as men. This way, it is easier to understand how the Jews could endure the outrages, restrain their resentment and abstain fairly rigidly from any act of violence against their adversaries. Even more significant from this point of view seems their innate repugnance to the pleasures of hunting, abandoned by the wandering, hunted people, with their horror of blood, since the beginning of the Dispersion.

Another illustration of the intermingling of a historic condition with Jewish religious ethics and the behavior pattern of the men of the ghetto, is supplied by the cycle of annual festivals and their symbolic content. Whether solemn, like the Day of Atonement, or joyous, like Pentecost, they all emphasize the particular responsibility of the Children of Israel towards the Creator of the World, who never ceases to shower them with blessings and condescends to pardon their innumerable sins. They are all therefore devoted to the Covenant, to the thousand historic vicissitudes, between God and His People. There is one exception when the allegorical moral is pointed against the "nations" who persecute the Jews. This springtime festival, Purim, allows them to behave in a *non-Jewish* manner, that is to say to take symbolic vengeance on their oppressors, to ride rough-shod over them, to externalize themselves in extravagant gaiety. But the outlet this offers the repressed elemental instincts is only the annual carnival of the ghetto.

Christian people, on the other hand, could vent their feelings at any time. A hue and cry at the sight of a Jew was a daily spectacle. The philosopher Moses Mendelssohn wrote to a friend of his who was a Benedictine monk, that he preferred not to go out into the streets unless he had to:[17]

> everywhere in this so-called tolerant country I live so constricted, hemmed in on all sides by true intolerance that for the sake of my children I must shut myself up the whole day in a silk factory. At times, of an evening, I talk of it with my wife and children. "Father," an innocent child asks, "what does that fellow have against us? Why do people throw stones after us? What have we done to them?" "Yes, father dear," another says, "they chase after us in the streets and abuse us: Jews! Jews! Is it then such a reproach in people's eyes, to be a Jew? And how does that hamper other people?" Oh, I close my eyes and sigh to myself: Men! Men! How have you come to this?

Beside the sentimental effusion lurked a social reality, confirmed by evidence from a Christian source:[18]

> ... what more common than to see children in markets, fairs and inns, and one particular one who wants to exercise his temerity and malice, attack the Jews and torture them by mockery, insult, theft, even by blows and other pagan methods.

In an ode to the glory of the Emperor Joseph II, the poet Klopstock exclaimed: "who does not tremble with pity when he sees how our mob degrades [*entmenscht*] the people of Canaan."[19] But if the mere sight of a Jew whipped popular passions to white heat, it was because the horror and disgust existed before he was seen, and we come back to the phenomenon of "anti-Semitism in the pure state." We have an example of it in eighteenth-century Regency France.

Intending to establish *monti di pietà*, the Duc de Noailles sent an investigator to Italy to inform him on how they worked. This official was amazed to learn that the *monte di pietà* at Venice was run by Jews:[20]

> I am very much afraid that at first this report will fill you with a legitimate disgust because of the explanation of a peculiarity which cannot, however, be concealed. The Republic of Venice has realized, as have the other sovereign states of Italy, that it would be very useful for the poor to have a place where they can receive the wherewithal to relieve their immediate poverty, on the basis of their possessions; but it has made strange use of this idea, and I think it is only in Venice that the *monte di pietà* is run by Jews. . . .

The Christians' age-old disgust had communicated a sort of explosive charge to the very word "Jew." Even in enlightened circles, the name, with its emotive power, served as a standard of evil by virtue of custom, whether the language were Latin, Germanic or Slav. When he wanted to illustrate the vices of the Dutch, Montesquieu, the fairest of men, exclaimed: ". . . I do not think that . . . there had ever been Jews more Jewish than some of them."[21]

Thus although more and more voices were raised on behalf of the Jew as a *man* in this period, defenders and detractors alike abided by the same meaning of the *word*. The Jew was therefore only esteemed on condition that he was not a Jew: a semantic ambiguity which was to make its contribution to the everlasting quality of modern anti-Semitism. This cannot be emphasized sufficiently in relation to the chapters which

follow. In Germany, the Jews' first great advocate, the dramatist Lessing, made one of his characters exclaim: "There are
also Jews who are not Jews at all."[22]

In France, a member of the Constituent Assembly, M.
Rewbell, used similar arguments when he was opposing the
emancipation of the Jews of Bordeaux: "It is suggested that
you regard the Jews of Bordeaux as if they were not Jews."[23]

Some Jewish emancipators pleaded the cause of their co-
religionists in the same terms: "Look for the man in the Jew;
do not look for the Jew in the man."[24]

When Napoleon instructed his ministers to study the
future status of the Jews in 1805, one of the schemes
suggested that: ". . . The appellation 'Jew,' to which unfortunate prejudices are attached, should be omitted from official
acts."[25]

Champagny, the Minister of the Interior, sceptically
commented: "I am very much afraid that custom will prevail
over the decree forbidding this appellation."[26]

This pessimism was not entirely justified. In the long run,
operations of verbal magic like this, which various European
governments were using to try and "resolve the Jewish question" by influencing things through words, did not prove
totally ineffective. In France, for example, it can be said that
the Jews did to some extent become Israelites, both to themselves and to a part of the Christian population. The partial
substitution of the term *Evrei* (Hebrew) for the very derogatory *Jid* in Russian corresponded to this attenuation. But the
term *Mosaiste*, suggested for administrative purposes in
the German countries, remained a meaningless formula, since
a Jew there, even today, is still a *Jude*. Perhaps it is typical
that in German (contrary to French and English) the *wandering* Jew (that is to say someone whose running would one day
cease) is described as the *eternal* Jew (*ewiger Jude*).[27]

PART ONE

THE CENTURY OF
ENLIGHTENMENT

From the earliest Middle Ages, there were men to challenge traditional belief, to question secretly the dogmas of the Revelation and even the existence of God. At the borders of the Western world, where Christianity and Islam lived side by side, these blasphemous doubts sometimes found expression; one such pamphlet described Moses, Jesus and Mohammed as "three impostors." Elsewhere, they remained uncommunicable, and even the variety of opinions born of the Reformation at first only succeeded in substituting manifold inquisitions for one single Inquisition: Michel Servet died at the stake, as did Giordano Bruno. Two more centuries passed before, in the wake of the new scientific ideas, this eternal questioning could be freely discussed in public. The universal challenge of accepted ideas, characteristic of the Century of Enlightenment, could not fail to extend to the circumstances and precise *significance* of the Jews. The different answers given, propagated by Voltaire and the encyclopedists, were to travel the world with the French Revolution; they still carry weight in some countries today. The answers to the part which concerns us, were primarily formulated in England in the first half of the eighteenth century in a controversy which served as an inspiration to, and a model for, future generations, and which is still not completely closed. This discussion shows how the idea formed of the Jew, that is to say anti- (or philo-) Semitism, is linked at a theoretical level with the supreme questions of the first cause and the last ends of man. That is why it is appropriate to begin this part of our book with a chapter on the English deists.

four

The English Deists

We must carefully distinguish between what the Scripture itself says, and what is only said of the scriptures.

(Robert Boyle)

The English revolutions and the rise of a commercial middle class led to a remarkable economic and cultural expansion in the British Isles. The boldness and vigor of English thought astonished contemporaries. As La Fontaine wrote:[1]

The English think deeply,
Their mind in this follows their temperament.
Digging into subjects, and strengthened by experience,
They extend everywhere the empire of science.

More hesitant, at first almost imperceptible, was the development of moral and religious ideas. The greatest English thinkers were reluctant to question traditional religion. Newton thought the main value of his discoveries lay in providing a rational demonstration of the existence of a God (did not the inexplicable "force of gravity" imply the existence of a "Great Clockmaker"?). Robert Boyle bequeathed his fortune to an endowment intended to reward the best works of the "new apologetic school with an astronomical basis";[2] John Locke, the first great apostle of tolerance, which he extended to Moslems and Jews, argued that Christianity and reason were perfectly compatible and protested against questioning the Biblical miracles. Bolder, less highly rated intellects, like Herbert of Cherbury or Charles Blount were going further (because reason is an extracting god). Even they, however, did not dare to profess atheism which was incompatible both with the intellectual climate of the period and its legislation. After 1693, the law relating to the freedom of the press allowed their subversive ideas to gain ground, at the same time as Bayle's *Diction-naire* was translated and Spinoza's Biblical criticism became known in England. English intellectuals were attracted by the ideas of a religion consistent with the message of the Gospel and yet compatible with the new scientific spirit, a religion which would be rational and *natural*, like the awe-inspiring spectacle of the natural laws. Thus, the great "deist discussion" was born. It had to find out how, for millennia on end, the human race could have remained enslaved to clerical superstition and paid tribute to the obscurantism of the traditional churches, particularly the Church of Rome. Who, therefore, had a motive to abuse reason and corrupt the innate good in men and systematically to adulterate the "natural religion"?

Newton himself had suggested the beginnings of an answer to this when he ascribed some corruptions of the Biblical text to St Jerome, but he did not draw any definite conclusions from this.[3] On the other hand, what John Toland, the "first freethinker in western history," drew up was a formal indictment of the fathers of the Church, corrupters of true Christianity. During his adventurous life, living off meager prebends, he never stopped preaching a "reasonable" Christianity, freed from its superstructure of mysteries[4] and in accordance with the teaching of Jesus Christ, as he found it in the Gospels. For him, this was the Christianity of the Ebionites, whom he described as Naza-renes or more simply as Jews. In fact, according to him:[5]

... the true Christianity of the Jews was over-born and destroy'd by the more numerous Gentiles, who, not enduring the reasonableness and simplicity of the same, brought into it by degrees the peculiar expressions and mysteries of Heathenism, the abstruse doctrines and distinctions of their Philosophers, an insupportable pontifical Hierarchy, and even the altars, offrings, the sacred rites and ceremonies of their Priests, tho they wou'd not so much as tolerate those of the Jews, and yet owning them to be divinely instituted ... and so this very Tradition is alleg'd by others to warrant the invocation of Saints, prayers for the Dead, the worship of Images, with the whole train of Greek and Romish superstitions, whereof the least footstep appears not in the *Bible*.

Consequently, he urged his contemporaries to go back to the purity of the two Testaments, which instructed the Jews to remain good Jews, and the Gentiles to become good Christians:[6]

It follows indeed that the *Jews*, whether becoming Christians or not, are forever bound to the Law of Moses, as now limited; and he that thinks they were absolv'd from the observation of it by Jesus, or that tis a fault in them still to adhere to it, does err not knowing the Scriptures; as did most of the converts from the Gentiles, who gave their bare names to Christ, but reserv'd their idolatrous hearts for their native superstitions. These did almost wholly subvert the True Christianity. ... So inveterate was their hatred of the Jews (tho indebted to them for the Gospel) that their observing of any thing, however reasonable or necessary, was a sufficient motive for these Gentile converts to reject it. ...

We see how the philosopher slips imperceptibly from a defense of the Jews of the past to a vindication of contemporary Jewry (in fact any meditation on the Scriptures seems to transform the "Jewish question" into a timeless theme *par excellence*). Did Toland also come round to his philo-Semitism through his own classless position as a wandering outlaw, which would have caused him to sympathize with the banished people? Was he spurred on at some stage by a prebend, his customary mode of subsistence? Nothing is known. But the fact remains that in 1714 he published his *Reasons for Naturalizing the Jews in Great Britain and Ireland . . .* , advocating collective immigration into the British Isles of Jews from the Continent. The work was dedicated to the bishops of the United Kingdom. Toland began by reminding them of the historical merits of the "educators of the human race" who had been able to inculcate monotheism into the Roman Empire, and whose first names contemporary Englishmen were proud to bear, but whom they hated and despised "no less inhumanely, than inconsistently." He attributed the main responsibility for this to the clergy, "their most inveterate enemies," the "priests who devoutly offered up these human Sacrifices, not only to share their goods with the rapacious Prince, but also to acquire the reputation of zeal and sanctity among the credulous vulgar. . . ." He also took into account popular xenophobia, and summed up the motives for it in the following three points :

> The vulgar, I confess, are seldom pleased in any country with the coming in of foreigners among 'em: which proceeds, first, from their ignorance, that at the beginning they were such themselves; secondly, from their grudging at more persons sharing the same trades or business with them, which they call *taking the bread out of their mouths;* and thirdly, from their being deluded to this aversion by the artifice of those who design any change in the government. . . .

He then assured his readers that a good number of them must have Jewish blood in their veins, notably the Scots, "which is the reason so many of them in that part of the Island, have such a remarkable aversion to pork and black-puddings to this day, not to insist on some other resemblances easily observable. . . ."[7]

He praised the teachings of Judaism, which commanded the Jews "to magnify to all the world the divine goodness, wisdom and power with those duties of men, and other attributes of God, which constitute *Natural Religion.*" Lastly, he listed the various advantages which an increased number of Jews would offer Great Britain; even if they did have a few faults, these "proceed from their Accident and not from Nature." Moreover, "they visibly partake of the Nature of those nations among which they live." He also declared that when they were settled in the British Isles, the Children of Israel would once again become the gallant soldiers and bold sailors they were in ancient times: "And I fancy they could kill the enemies of our *British* Islands, when they become their own, with equal alacrity."[8]

It would not appear that this strange document of Toland's had great repercussions. Most of his biographers today do not even mention it. At the time, it provoked an anonymous "confutation," primarily warning the English against the dangers of Jewish proselytism: ". . . where the latter [Christian priests] Convert one *Jew* to be a Christian, the *Jews* Pervert ten Christians to *Judaism* . . ." ". . . shall we not therefore rather separate from those, than Naturalize them, lest that God may Reject and Leave us, as he has rejected them. . . ." This danger would be all the more pressing because the Jews claimed to be the possessors of the sole uncorrupted Scriptures; but ". . . Hundreds of them that were born in *Spain, Portugal, Holland* and *England,* understand not one Word of *Hebrew* themselves. . . ."[9]

This was also the position, implied to a greater or lesser degree, of the main phalanx of deists who were denouncing the incoherence of the revealed doctrine. For them, the errors which had besmirched Christian tradition for centuries on end were mainly, if not entirely, due to the Jews. Moreover, if the Roman Church regarded the debasement of the Chosen People as proof of the truth of Christianity, these deists often based their arguments against traditional belief equally on this debasement. But manifold lines of argument were used. It is essential to consider them, because not only are they evidence of an atmosphere of Judeophobia (and more specifically the current identification of the Jew with a twister), they also supply the first historic landmarks on the slippery path of modern anti-Semitism. Passing through a number of stages, which will be discussed further on, deist thought became an active force, a historical factor several generations later.

Let us begin with the mathematician William Whiston, who succeeded Newton in his Cambridge chair. Like his great rival, he engaged in interminable calculations to integrate Biblical chronology in astronomic time. When these calculations did not work out, he attributed the residual difference to disturbance of the delicate machinery of the universe by a comet at the time of the flood. Mathematical inconsistencies were therefore only the result of human wickedness. Other errors he ascribed to the malice of the Jewish scribes. He also tried to reconstruct the authentic texts in his *Essay towards Restoring the True Text of the Old Testament* (1722). The penultimate proposal in this essay states: *"The Jews, about the Beginning of the Second Century of the Gospel, greatly alter'd and corrupted their Hebrew and Greek Copies of the Old Testament; and that, in many Places, on purpose; out of Opposition to Christianity."* Despite this, Whiston must have had the reputation of being a friend of the Jews, because it was he who was entrusted by an anonymous gentleman with one hundred pounds sterling to be distributed among them after a fire ravaged the Jewish district of London in 1736.[10]

Matthew Tindal's virulence took a different form. His treatise *Christianity as Old as Creation: or The Gospel, a Republication of the Religion of Nature* (1730) provoked over 150 refutations in England and on the Continent, including one from the illustrious Berkeley.[11] As the title of the book suggests, Christianity was identified as the "natural religion" which Moses would have perverted. To show the maleficence of Judaism, Tindal drew examples from contemporary history. Could not all its blood baths and crimes be justified by Biblical precedents?[12]

And I question whether the Spaniards would have murdered so

many millions in the Indies, had they not thought they might have used them like Canaanites. How many precedents, besides that of Ehud, (who, on a message from the Lord, stabbed the king to whom his people sent him with a present) did the Popish priests plead from the Old Testament for the assassination of the two Henries of France? And had the Gun-Powder-Plot succeeded here, they would, no doubt, have made use of the same plea to justify it. . . .

Tindal also recalled how the Gnostics, "one of the greatest sects in the primitive times," compared the cruel Jehovah to the true God of the Enlightenment; "so great a difference is there between the representations, which are made of God in the books of the Jewish and Christian religion."

Going two steps further, his continuator, Thomas Morgan, proceeded to an open defense of Gnosticism, consistent, in his eyes, with the true teaching of Christ. He extended the attack against the God of Israel to His people :

To imagine, that a Company of poor, contemptible egyptianiz'd Slaves, who having been delivered from one Yoke of Priesthood, were now to be put under another; a People scarce known to the rest of Mankind, and were never to mix or converse with them, but to be mew'd up in a little bye Corner of the Earth; that such a People, under such Circumstances, were intended in the divine Counsel and Wisdom, as a Light to the *Gentiles*, and the Means of preserving and keeping up the true Knowledge and Worship of God in the World, and of the true Religion or Way to Salvation; this, surely, is supposing what we speak with Scorn, that God was as much disappointed of his End, and took as wrong Measures to obtain it, as *Moses* himself. . . .

In short, the God of the Old Testament was to Morgan the "God of Israel, Lord of Hosts, or God of War, a local and tutelary god living amongst his people. . . ."[18] It has been pointed out that certain passages in his principal work, *The Moral Philosopher*, where he emphasized the purely "national and temporal" character of the Mosaic law, seem to have been paraphrased from Spinoza's *Tractatus Theologico-Politicus.*[14]

Another precursor of high Biblical criticism, Anthony Collins, adopted a similar position in his *Discourse on the Grounds and Reasons of the Christian Religion* (1724). It was he that Baron d'Holbach quoted as his authority in his ferocious *Esprit de Judaïsme,* which he claimed was a translation of Collins.[15]

The deist intellectual revolution was thus rapidly becoming more radical, like all genuine revolutions, and the "natural religion" was merged into a form of pantheism which was nothing more than thinly veiled atheism. Certain arguments which might seem funny to us were advanced with the greatest seriousness by their authors. For example, Bishop William Warburton tried to demonstrate in *The Divine Legation of Moses . . .* (1738) that God's choice of the coarsest and vilest of all peoples was the best proof of the truth of the Revelation.[16] (A distant echo of this argument was heard in an anti-Semitic controversy in England in the twentieth century under the slogan of "How odd of God to choose the Jews."[17])

Even more venomous was the famous pastor Woolston who was sentenced for blasphemy and was said to have died in prison. Tens of thousands of copies of his burlesque publications, which influenced Voltaire, were in circulation. Woolston's practice was to ridicule traditional methods of Biblical exegesis, under cover of defending them,[18] and the "noisy, stinking" Jews were a choice target for his wit. The following is a sample:[19]

And the World, according to the Proverb, and common belief of Mankind, may be said to stink with them. Hence *Ammianus Marcellinus* very appositely to the purpose before us, speaking of the *Jews*, calls them Tumultuating and stinking Jews. How this mark of Infamy was first fixt upon the *Jews*, whether from any ill smell that proceeds from them, according to the common Opinion, or otherwise; It is all one to the Prophesie and Type of them; and if their Bodies neither do, or ever did stink living; Yet their blasphemies against Christ, their Maledictions of his Church, and false Glosses on the Scripture, are enough to make their very Name odious and abominable. . . . And lastly, I can't but take notice again here that *St John* seems to hint that Frogs are a Symbol and Figure of Persons of a lying and devilish Spirit, and he speaks of three particularly unclean Spirits like Frogs. He means three *Jews,* I am well assured, and whose Names and Lyes, I very well know, and how they came out of the Mouth of the Dragon; but it is not my business at present to open and unfold this Prophesie.

It can be seen how the mere fact of the Jews' existence could be used indiscriminately to prove the falsity or truth of Christianity. These were intellectual exercises motivated by dark elemental passions whereby primary anti-Semitism could bolster up both simple faith and an *"Écrasez l'Infâme"* campaign.

In about 1750, the deist discussion in England ended as suddenly as it had begun at the beginning of the century. One of its last prophets was Peter Annet, a craftsman and a brilliant autodidact who intended to rid Christianity of its "Jewish legs" in order to embed it firmly in the "rock" of "Nature." King David, whose life he wrote, was his *bête noire.*[20]

These, Christians, are the outlines of the life of a Jew, whom you are not ashamed to continue extolling as a man after God's own heart! This, Britons! is the king to whom your late excellent monarch has been compared! What an impiety to the Majesty of Heaven! What an affront to the memory of an honest prince!

Lord Henry Bolingbroke, the last of the great deists, also attempted to show the contrast between the customs of the Patriarchs and the ideal of the English gentleman. In accordance with the views of his time, he had a tendency to use the Jews as a sort of standard of evil. For example, on the subject of Noah's curse on Ham's descendants (Genesis IX, 25): "Certain it is that no writer but a Jew could impute to the economy of Divine Providence, the accomplishment of such a prediction!"[21] But if the Jews were bad, their religion had made them worse, since they "thought themselves authorized by their religion to commit such barbarities as even they perhaps, if they had had no religion, would not have committed. . . ."[22] However, Lord Bolingbroke tended to share out the responsibility for the fables and lies in Christian tradition fairly between the Jews and the Fathers of the Church. All in all and contrary to legend, he should not be described as an *avant la lettre* "anti-Semite."[23]

A few additional comments are needed to conclude this rapid survey of deist propaganda.

The publications we have quoted do not necessarily give a great deal of space to the Jews. They most frequently consist of controversies between their authors which gather strength as they proceed.

Equally, there is no justification for thinking that these authors were "obsessed" with Jews (past and present). But when they do deal with them they remain imprisoned in the traditional Christian world of ideas. Only John Toland was able to break away from it, as is shown both by his book advocating the emancipation of the Jews and his optimism about the perfectibility of man through education, which he formulated with remarkable clarity.[24]

Nothing is more delicate than the subtle history of ideas, nothing more hazardous than establishing their genealogical channels. Typically, our specific problem leads us to ask if these neo-Gnostics owed anything to their distant predecessors, Valentinus and Marcion, or if their views were simply formulated under the combined stimuli of anti-clerical rebellion and anti-Jewish feeling. Before, after, or at the same time, other authors in other countries were formulating similar ideas, and the germ of the English deists' anti-Jewish arguments can already be found in Spinoza.[25]

Their intentions seemed noble: the apostles of the

"natural religion" were trying to escape the narrowness of Judeo-Christian horizons when they criticized the exclusivism of the Old Testament, sought the origin of civilization in Egypt or the cradle of the human race in India, subordinated Moses to Zoroaster or even identified Abraham with Brahma.[26] Yet this current of universalist-inspired thought —enriched by theories with scientific pretensions in the nineteenth century or by some other admixture—reached the twentieth century under the cloak of so-called "Aryan" internationalism as the racist dogma of Hitlerism. And in the eighteenth century a distinct path[27] connects the English deists to Voltaire, the great prophet of modern, anti-clerical anti-Semitism.

five

France in the Enlightenment

The Protestant attitude

Mme de Sévigné exclaimed in surprise:[1]

> *This hatred felt for them [the Jews] is extraordinary. But from where does this stench which confounds all perfumes come? —It is probably that unbelief and ingratitude smell bad as virtue smells good.... I feel pity and horror for them, and I pray God with the Church that he remove from their eyes the veil which prevents them from seeing that Jesus Christ has come....*

This seems to have been the general opinion of French society in the century of Bossuet. It is true that rigid censorship prevented the expression of contrary views; we mentioned the disappointments of the scholar Richard Simon in Volume I. Until the Sun-King died, only one official viewpoint on the Jews existed in France. Its canons can be illustrated by the misfortune which befell a pastor, Jacques Basnage, in 1710.

This Calvinist historian had published an *Histoire des Juifs*, in Holland, which tried to apply the rules of historical criticism to this difficult subject for the first time in the West. His book caused a sensation throughout scholarly Europe, and a well-known theologian, Abbé Louis Dupin, thought that it could usefully be copied in France, suitably adapted to the demands of Catholic dogma. There was nothing poor Basnage could do but helplessly protest: "My *Histoire des Juifs* has been stolen; my name has been deleted and sentiments inserted that are not mine. . . ."[2] In fact, Dupin's forgery contained over a hundred alterations, relating to facts or opinions which were not suitable for dissemination in France. For example, Basnage had questioned whether the Emperor Constantine had really had the Jews' ears cut off. Dupin gave the fact as true on the authority of John Chrysostom. Basnage had described King Dagobert, who expelled them, as a profligate. Dupin's heart was set on reinstating this monarch as a virtuous character. And so on, from century to century. The last alteration was also the most important. Dealing with the expulsion of the Jews in Spain, a subject fraught with references to the repeal of the Edict of Nantes, Basnage had criticized Ferdinand and Isabella for "devastating a great and vast kingdom." Obviously, Dupin lost no time in changing this to the highest praise for this legitimate and wise measure.

From this it can be seen how the historical role of cosmopolitan leaven in the general movement of ideas—a role which the French Protestants had played since the dawn of the eighteenth century—was prompting them to think about the meaning of the Jews' tribulations and to reconsider traditional ideas on the subject. It was in the "sanctuaries" of Holland and Geneva that the new views were formulated under the aegis of Pierre Bayle, the great apostle of tolerance. Later, throughout the century of Enlightenment, when more and more voices were heard calling for the raising of the position of the Jews in the name of an ideal of abstract humanity, Protestant authors were almost alone in showing interest in what "Judaism has to say," as Jean-Jacques Rousseau later put it. We have pointed out on various occasions the relative favor the Children of Israel enjoyed in countries with a Calvinist tradition. In the case of the French Protestants, this sympathy was increased tenfold by a tragic history which multiplied affinities and resemblances in the most varied forms. This was *sympathy* in the fullest meaning of the word, on the part of a human group which, to put it briefly, had passed through the same ordeals. All in all,

Drumont was not entirely wrong when he described French Protestants as "half-Jews."

The life of Pierre Bayle, whose famous *Dictionnaire historique* has sharpened the critical faculties of several generations of Europeans and is still worth studying today, bears some resemblance to a Marrano's. At the age of twenty, for reasons which remain obscure, he thought it proper to revert to Catholicism. However, he soon left the bosom of the Church of Rome. After some years of wandering, he settled at Rotterdam and devoted his life to denouncing the fanaticism and obscurantism of all persuasions, with a passion sharpened by personal tragedy. (As a result of one of his publications, his brother, who had stayed in France, was thrown into prison and died there.) At heart, this ardent anti-clericalist remained fundamentally Christian and warned of the "corrosive dust of philosophy." But he was a marvelous dialectician, able to demonstrate better than any other philosopher before David Hume the sterility of trying to bolster faith by arguments of reason. His *Dictionnaire* "remains the most overwhelming indictment that has ever been drawn up for the shame and confusion of men."[3] In it, he distributed his blows with perfect impartiality, and the fact that the Jews received a fair share of them, was not due to him but to the choice position which Christian tradition allotted them. He may have attacked the "prejudices of this wretched people," but he attacked the prejudices of past and present Christians even more vigorously. He criticized the Catholic Church of Spain for "treating Christianity like an old palace which needs supports, and Judaism like a fortress which has to be battered and bombarded incessantly,"[4] and he claimed the right to freedom of thought and worship for the Jews, as well as for all other sects, opinions or schools, "Jew, Pagan, Mohammedan, Roman, Lutheran, Calvinist, Arminian, Socinian . . ." (*Traité de tolérance universelle*, 1686).[5] From his immense but fragmentary output, it is difficult to distinguish a systematic viewpoint on the Children of Israel. But it can reasonably be supposed that he shared the ideas that his friend and the executor of his will, Jacques Basnage, developed in his *Histoire,* even though Basnage had been a much more conformist Calvinist than he. And this viewpoint probably reflects the prevailing opinions of French Protestantism of the period.

Basnage intended to write a history of the Jews, starting where "Josephus stopped," i.e. at the destruction of the second Temple. "We are not stirred by any passion," he announced in his preface:[6]

> We are reporting accurately and faithfully everything we have been able to unearth which refers to the Jews. The Christian ought not to find it strange that we very often exonerate the Jews from various crimes they are not guilty of, since Justice demands it; and to accuse of injustice and violence those who have pursued Justice is only to show bias. . . .

Basnage had therefore decided to put an end to the bloody legends which had grown up around the initial theme of deicide over the centuries, but his theological upbringing prevented him from challenging the root of the evil. When it came to this subject, the pastor again sounded like a man composing a sermon:

> How then did the daughter of Zion fall? The validity of a definite event cannot be disputed. It is sufficient to turn one's eyes to the present wretchedness of the Jewish people to be convinced that God is angry with them, and that their sins deserve the blindness which has made them rejected. . . . Instead of repenting of as black a crime as the crucifying of the Messiah, a spirit of sedition and revolt grew up. The Jews, when aroused, carried out terrible cruelties. . . .

Nevertheless, Basnage felt that the punishment that the Almighty had imposed on the Children of Israel was excessive; a cautious note of censure can even be discerned breaking through in some places. It may perhaps be significant that he does not use the term "miracle" in this context but refers to "marvels":

If God had been satisfied with punishing the leaders of the nation, the scribes and the Pharisees who cried: "Crucify! crucify!" If the punishment had fastened on the heads of the guilty, it would not be surprising; but it has passed from generation to generation, from century to century. Seventeen hundred years of wretchedness and captivity have already flowed by, with no prospect of relief. The event is unprecedented. A second circumstance heightens this *marvel*: for this unfortunate nation can find almost nowhere on the whole earth where it can lay its head or set its feet. It passes through torrents of blood which it has shed, and does not perish. Those thousands of Jews whom we will see slaughtered by cruel and barbarous zeal, have weakened the nation without extinguishing or destroying it. It still continues to exist despite the persecutions of Christian and idolater united for its destruction. . . .

No less characteristic of the Calvinist attitude is Basnage's conclusion: "God alone knows the time when He will remember this chosen nation. . . ." But his attempt at criticism was metaphorically paralyzed when it came to explaining the resemblance between the parables of the Gospel and the Talmud. Rather than admit a Judaic relationship, he almost preferred to believe that Christ "copied Greek documents"![7]

The new attitude also emerges with Marie Huber, a theologian from Geneva who enjoyed a momentary fame. In *Le Monde fou préféré au monde sage* . . . (1731), she features two pure and righteous Jews who feel drawn by the message of Jesus but are discouraged by Christian society because "all Christians, of whatsoever sect they may be, are very consistent in one repect. This is in the love of wealth, the insatiable desire to accumulate it; in this they are more Jewish than the Jews themselves. . . ." The Jew who makes this comment is surprised "to see men who acknowledge as their king, Jesus of Nazareth, son of a poor and abject carpenter, striving with all their might to raise their position and make money, in short to be his antipode in the world . . . ."[8] One of Huber's characters, Philo, remarks: "I want to get to know them; and although they are Jews, I will not be at all ashamed to take lessons from them on what constitutes the spirit of Christianity." The author's main mouthpiece, Erastus, who introduces the two Jews, is a trader, which cannot fail to be significant: the affinities between Protestants and Jews even before the persecutions reappear on the plane of their primary occupation, which, as we have already pointed out, benefited on the whole from their respective tribulations.

At the theological level, personal study of the Scriptures induced some people to "judaize" in various ways, and at the extreme, to decide to become Jews. The historian, H. J. Schoeps, in his *Philosemitismus im Barock,* has unearthed several cases of this type of courage in the Germanic world. Examples amongst French Protestants include the pastor Nicolas Antoine, who was burned in Geneva in 1632, and the famous critic and philologist Claude Saumaise, who declared on his deathbed that the Jewish religion was the sole truth.[9] Both of them had left Catholicism and found the final answer to their spiritual quest in this way.

But it was a strict upholder of orthodox Calvinism, Pastor Jurieu, Bossuet's great adversary, who (in his *Accomplissement des prophéties* ...) promised the Jews that "Jerusalem must be rebuilt for them and that they will be regathered in their land." So Protestant theology in its way was foreshadowing the future Zionist dream as early as the end of the seventeenth century. To the Catholic theologian, Richard Simon, it seemed that Jurieu "was patently propping up the religion of the Jews and at the same time destroying the Christian religion."[10] The multiplicity of direct and indirect ways in which the Reformation led Western society to revise its opinions on Jews and Judaism as well as on religion in general can be seen. We have therefore come back to its crucial role in challenging established beliefs since it allowed the doubters in every camp to lend an ear to adverse propaganda. As David Hume said:[11]

All religious systems, it is confessed, are subject to great and insuperable difficulties. Each disputant triumphs in his turn; while he carries on an offensive war, and exposes the absurdities, barbarities and pernicious tenets of his antagonist. But all of them, on the whole, prepare a complete triumph for the Sceptic. . . .

It would perhaps be wrong to place the Marquis Jean-Baptiste d'Argens in this latter category. He was one of the apostles of the French version of deism, that is to say of the significant phase in the history of ideas when a large part of enlightened society was rejecting Christian dogmas and calling for a scientific vision of the world. But they still did not dare to rid the Heavens of a Supreme Being and they still added faith to a scientifically provable "natural" religion.

Of Catholic origin, the Marquis d'Argens passed an adventurous youth and then settled in Holland where, on the advice and with the help of two Protestant publicist pastors, Pierre Chaix and Armand de La Chapelle, he devoted himself to literature,[12] and made it his career. The writings in which this advocate of natural religion (nonetheless the most superstitious of men) attacked the established churches, are singularly lacking in originality; as can easily happen, they were all the more avidly read and more widely circulated because of this, so that he could not be more representative of his time.

The only original thing about d'Argens's "Letters" was in the title he gave the first two series: *Lettres juives,* and *Lettres cabalistiques.* Perhaps the idea was suggested to him by his two mentors who "filed down and polished his style." In any case, it was certainly stimulating. But, cabalists or not, his Jews were even less Jewish than Montesquieu's Persians were Persian, although one of them, "Aaron Monceca," can only be the Dr Fonseca who taught him Hebrew in Constantinople. Another, Rabbi Isaac Onis, seems to be d'Argens himself. Voltaire, who showered hyperbolic praise upon the Marquis, comparing him to Montaigne and

Bayle, referred to him as "my dear Isaac" up to his death and even after.[13] These Jews are *philosophes* who gossip by letter about the affairs, customs, institutions and beliefs of Christian countries. They act as convenient weapons to poke fun at the Church and bolster the author's deist propaganda.

In his first "Letters" (which he first published on "half-sheets" from 1736 to 1739 at a rate of two letters a week), d'Argens, like John Toland, praised Judaism for approximating to the true natural religion (*Lettre juive* 4):

> Everyone who is called a freethinker here [in Paris], fashionable people, society ladies, only practice the religion of Nazareth externally; very few of them are really convinced at the bottom of their hearts. They are satisfied to believe in God; several think that the soul is immortal; many others, like the Sadducees, claim that it is subject to death. I regard these latter as people laboring under a misapprehension; as for the former category, I do not know if we can deny them the title of Jews. They believe in God who created the Universe, who rewards the good, and punishes the bad. What more do we believe? Is not this the whole of our religion except for a few ceremonies which our scholars and priests have prescribed for us. . . .

But quite quickly the tone changed: the Jews admitted that "the religion of Nazareth has even greater splendor" than their own which was directed towards "wealth and worldly goods. Only the hearts of the Nazarenes are those of sons for a good father; they serve God for him and not for the prospect of reward." The supporters of the Church were quick to take the point: "In his 26th letter, by a contradiction, as lucky for him as it is strange, he again becomes a Christian just as the Parisians and Turks are Jews, without knowing it," gloated the Jesuit review.[14] As far as it involved Christianity, this change of mind was shortlived; but where Judaism was concerned, things were going to worsen henceforth. To judge by his letter "To the rabbis of the synagogue of Amsterdam," it would seem as though the impecunious Marquis had asked the synagogue for a prebend or a pension, had been refused, and was taking his revenge by denigrating Judaism.[15] But at the same time, this tone must have been more in keeping with his deep-rooted feelings as well as those of his readers. Around Letter 100, he finally broke with the synagogue by making Isaac Onis abjure it, become a Karaite and flee to Cairo. Subsequently, he made the ex-rabbi admit the ritual crimes of the Jews and endorse the other customary charges, in the most conformist manner (cf. Letter 122, for example). Even more interesting, he made him discourse on the Jews' mysterious guilt as follows (Letter 157):

> When I think of the ills our fathers suffered, I am tempted to believe that they were guilty of some great crimes, knowledge of which has not come down to us; and I must confess to you that, if I was not as confident as I am of the truth of my religion, when I examine the ills which have overwhelmed us since the birth of Nazareanism, I would find it easy to believe that the prophecies had been fulfilled and that the God of Israel had abandoned his people, and chosen another. Is it possible, my dear Monceca, that the Divinity should expose a people to such great ills if they did not deserve them because of crimes which required such severe punishment? I think I am justified in asserting that our authors have not told us the real causes which can have forced the Lord thus to abandon his people to the cruelty of its enemies. The Jews must doubtless have committed some offense against the Romans which justifiably angered the Divinity.

A passage like this already presages the theme of the Jews' "bad conscience" in classical German philosophy, notably in Hegel. It can be seen how d'Argens, after first following the line his title promised, then set off down the slope of European deism. Not surprisingly, Voltaire greeted the publication of *Lettres juives* with enthusiasm: "I believe, my dear Isaac, that you will produce thirty volumes of *Lettres juives*. Continue, it is a fascinating piece of work. . . . I think absolutely as you do on almost everything. . . ."[16] In short the

Marquis's Jewish philosophers were model characters for the same reasons as were the converted Jews of the medieval legends and morality plays, and his deist wine is poured out of good old leather-bottles.

It should be added that a few years later, in his *Lettres chinoises*[17] (about 1742), the fickle Marquis was back on the Jews' side. Through the mouth of the sage Sioeu-Tcheou, he set out to treat the traditional accusations, notably ritual murder, as they deserved:

> Because what use would it be to the Jews to sacrifice a child on the day of the death of the Christians' Lawgiver? In which of their books is there the slightest trace of a like custom? How is it that in countries where they enjoy great freedom ... nothing similar has ever been attributed to them? Moreover, what is the purpose of this ridiculous sacrifice?

He also described the Jewish ceremonies with amused condescension, and took the opportunity this offered to poke fun at Catholic theology:

> You would not believe, dear Yn-Che-Chan, that the European pontiffs build their religion upon the spits and dripping pans of the Jews. ... All the greatest mysteries of Christianity are entirely contained in them: there, one finds the vindication of the sinner, the Trinity, and the death of the Christians' Lawgiver.

The reasons and motives behind the new direction in d'Argens's attitude to the Jews are unknown.

Montesquieu: the physiocrats

Theocracy has no place in the systems of government which the author of *L'Esprit des lois* describes, and there are hardly any references to the Old Testament in his principal work.[18] He refrains from any criticism or ridicule of Mosaic Law, though champion of the natural law as he was, it could not have failed to shock him.[19] The intrinsic quality of Montesquieu's mind can be seen in the treatment of the Jews in all his writings. He does not assign them a disproportionate place. Only in exceptional circumstances does he draw on them to prove either the truth or error of established beliefs and institutions. He makes a clear distinction between past and present Jews and he does not succumb to the easy temptation of being funny at the expense of either.

However, the paradoxical position of Judaism was occupying Montesquieu's attention from the time he wrote the *Lettres persanes*, LVIII:

(Usbek to Ibben, at Smyrna): Thou askest me if there are any Jews in France?

Know that wherever there is money, there are Jews. Thou inquirest what they do here? Just what they do in Persia: nothing can be more like a Jew of Asia, than a Jew in Europe.

They shew among the Christians, as well as among us, an invincible obstinacy for their religion, even to madness.

The Jewish religion is an old trunk, which has produced two branches that have covered the whole earth, I mean, Mohammedanism and Christianity: or rather it is a mother that has brought forth two daughters who have stabbed her with a thousand wounds: for, in point of religion, the nearest relations are the greatest enemies. But even though she has received ill usage from them, she nevertheless values herself greatly upon having produced them: she makes use of them both to take in the whole world, while she with her venerable great age takes in all ages.

The Jews therefore look upon themselves as the fountain of all holiness, and the foundation of all religion: on the other hand, they take us to be heretics, that have altered the law, or rather to be rebellious Jews. ...

Montesquieu expanded these ideas in *L'Esprit des lois* and declared that, all things considered, the Jews were right. The two chapters he devotes to them deal successively with trade and religion. He regards the intolerance of Christians as the source of their ills and the primary cause of their peculiar customs and appearance. "One sees trade emerge from the bosom of vexation and despair." Denouncing the scholastic prejudices against merchants, Montesquieu elaborates this idea as follows (*Esprit des lois,* XXI, 16; "How Commerce Broke Through the Barbarism of Europe"):

> Commerce was transferred to a nation covered with infamy; and was soon ranked with the most shameful usury, with monopolies, with the levying of subsidies, and with all the dishonest means of acquiring wealth.
>
> The Jews, enriched by their exactions, were pillaged by the tyranny of princes; which pleased indeed, but did not ease the people.
>
> What passed in England may serve to give us an idea of what was done in other countries. King John having imprisoned the Jews, in order to obtain their wealth; there were few who had not at least one of their eyes plucked out. Thus did that King influence his court of justice. A certain Jew who had a tooth pulled out every day for seven days successively, gave ten thousand marks of silver for the eighth. . . .
>
> I cannot help remarking by the way how this nation has been sported with from one age to another: at one time, their effects were confiscated when they were willing to become Christians; and at another, if they refused to turn Christians they were ordered to be burnt. . . .

Montesquieu is still harking back to the flames of the funeral pyres when he denounces religious intolerance, in the famous "Remonstrance" which he puts into the mouth of a Jew (*Esprit des lois,* XXV, 13: "A Most Humble Remonstrance to the Inquisitors of Spain and Portugal"):

> We conjure you, not by the mighty God whom both you and we serve, but by that Christ who, you tell us, took upon him a human form, to propose himself for an example for you to follow; we conjure you to behave to us, as he himself would behave was he upon earth. You would have us be Christians, and you will not be so yourselves. . . .

You put us to death, who believe only what you believe, because we do not believe *all* that you believe. We follow a religion, which you yourselves know to have been formerly dear to God. We think that God loves it still, and you think that he loves it no more; and because you judge this, you make those suffer by sword and fire, who hold an error so pardonable as to believe that God still loves what he once loved. . . .

The Montesquieu who talks about the Jews' "pardonable error," again appears in his intimate *Pensées* when, under the typical title of "Doubts," he ponders the mysteries of the Christian religion and, quoting St Paul, concludes that Jews cannot be excluded from salvation.[20] Under the same heading could be placed another reflection where his exacting intellect can see no conclusion except Tertullian's *credo quia absurdum:*[21]

What an outrageous thing is the torture of a God! It is much more so than all the monstrous opinions of paganism. . . . But this idea of the Cross, which has become the object of our respect, is not, by a long way as damning for us as it was for the Romans. There is more: there was no people who were so base in the mind of the Romans as the Jews. All the works are full of the ignominy with which they were covered. Yet it was a man from that nation that it was suggested that they worship; it was the Jews who foretold it, and Jews who offered themselves as witnesses. . . .

Discussing the ancient Jews again, he is astonished by their courage but criticizes their fanaticism.[22] He admired the "sublime" in Judaism, which he could no longer find amongst his contemporaries :[23]

There is, in the Jews' system, a great aptitude for the sublime because they had the custom of attributing all their thoughts and all their actions to individual inspiration from the Divinity: which gave them a very good agent. . . . What puts an end to the loss of the sublime amongst us and prevents us from striking and being struck is this new philosophy which only tells us of general laws and removes from our mind all individual thoughts of the Divinity. Reducing everything to the communication of movements, it only speaks of pure understanding, clear ideas, reason, principle, consequences.

Again he put forward the case of the Jews as an example of the "moral causes which can affect minds and characters."[24]

On the subject of contemporary Jews he speaks like a realistic reformer:[25]

To make the kingdom flourish and restore finances ... all the taxes given to individuals on the Jews would be removed and more extensive privileges would be sold to them in return for a sum payable in royal bills over three years, to a total value of one million in revenue. ...

He also states:[26]

A Jewish town should be made on the Spanish frontier, in a place suited to commerce, such as Saint-Jean-de-Luz or Ciboure. They would move there *en masse* and would end up by taking all the wealth they have to the kingdom. Only give them the same privileges they have in Leghorn, or even more, if it is wished. ...

But it was as an enlightened champion of tolerance that he exclaimed: "The Jews are at present saved: superstition will return no more, and they will no longer be exterminated on conscientious principles."[27]

Montesquieu's benevolent attitude to the Children of Israel can first be seen as a reflection of the period he lived in and the new spirit which had been alive in France since the death of Louis XIV. The passage from *Lettres persanes* quoted above, continues as follows:

They never enjoyed such a calm in Europe as they now live in. The Christians begin to lay aside that intolerant spirit, which used to sway them: the Spaniards are sensible of how much they have lost by driving the Jews out, and the French of having vexed the Christians whose belief differed a little from that of the prince. They are now convinced that the zeal for the progress of a religion is very different from the devotion she requires; and that to love and observe her, there is no manner of necessity for hating and persecuting those who do not.

The Seigneur de La Brède also comes into the picture both as a member of a class which was more ready to be philo-Semitic than any other, and also in his role of squireen wine exporter. He probably had business dealings with important Bordeaux Jews and, who knows, the suggestion about the "Jewish town on the Spanish frontier" or even the inspiration for the famous "Remonstrance to the Inquisitors" may have come from one of them. But in addition to these factors, the precise part played by the balanced temperament and generous nature of a happy man ("my soul clings to everything") who only worked for "love of good, peace and happiness to all men" must also be taken into account.[28]

We find the same sort of attitude in a little-known author, Espiard de la Cour, who, like Montesquieu, belonged to a great old legal family. In a collection of *Pensées* this original thinker argued as follows:[29]

If the Jews detest the Christians, it is certainly only in retaliation. They have suffered enough in the Christians' States to harbor violent resentment towards them.

The various banishments and recalls of the Jewish nation, which have taken place in turn in France and Spain, would barely be excusable if they had been dictated by religious motives: but the wealth of these unfortunates, which the king wanted to take advantage of, and the instigations of fanatical monks, have always been their primary cause.

Jesus Christ has condemned them to wander the Universe, without a land of their own; all the countries in the world should therefore be open to them. Nowhere are they strangers, nowhere citizens. . . .

It is a curious argument whereby this Christian boldly concludes that it devolves upon man to soften the mysterious decrees of Providence—reflecting in this the reforming tendencies of the time.

Other authors were appealing for recall of the Jews on the grounds of the general prosperity of France. An example of this is provided by Ange Goudar, a physiocrat (or "pre-physiocrat"), who was concerned with population problems. His case ran as follows:

Need to Recall the Jews to France to Increase the Population.
   It is not easy to say why our government shut its own door on a branch of population to which an infinite number of other European states have opened theirs.
   The reasons which were given for driving the Jews out of France in the past no longer exist. . . .
   The arguments cited against the Protestants in the past could have no basis in respect of the Jews.
   If this sect were settled amongst us it could not stimulate the ambitions of a party. Intrigue and plot are entirely unknown to them. This is in the nature of things. Their safety demands that it be so. If the Jews ceased to be loyal for one moment, they would be lost for ever. Wandering, leaderless, without a land of their own, and consequently without means of resisting the smallest power which might want to destroy them, their first political maxim is not to have one. . . .

This is not such a bad interpretation: in a way Goudar is putting his finger on the traditional reason why such a well organized state as the Republic of Venice showered favors on the Jews.[30] He went on to show the value of the services they rendered to governments in times of war, and passed on to his favourite subject, population growth:[31]

But the primary reason why our government should protect the Jews is their large population.
   No people on this earth multiplies more than they.
   There are natural causes for this large propagation. . . . The real ones are their restraint of their desires, a certain national continence and a natural absence of debauchery. There are no men on earth who, with so many faults, have so few vices. . . .

The Jews' rights were also upheld very amusingly by Abbé Coyer, a professional writer whose ideas resembled the physiocrats' and who had been instructed (probably by Turgot) to write a pamphlet against the guild system. His *Chimki, histoire cochinchinoise* ... describes the sad condition of the "Banians," but there can be no doubt as to who was actually involved, as we will see : [32]

> ... what criticism can be made of the Banians? Scattered over all Asia, without leader and without constitution, we only try to subsist by work and industry, while conforming to the laws, customs and decrees of princes everywhere. Your kings, on the basis of our reputation for skill in banking, exchange and brokerage, have allowed us to settle in their States. But people have discovered the secret of rendering null the protection they grant us. We are excluded not only from all offices and employments, we are still barred from all types of arts and crafts. We are forbidden to act in trade. No one is unaware of the abusive proceedings which your merchant guilds have just taken against us. They blame us for usurious lending: we might well have to come to this if it is the only means left to us to live. *Cheating—* We ask that cheats be hanged. And always *the original crime of our religion:* it is a little odd that merchants, craftsmen want to be more religious than the kings who protect religion; even more religious than the supreme Bonze, who sees us to the number of fifteen thousand in the holy town of Faïfo, who has allowed us to practice our religion and all the arts there. . . .[33]

But other people, who had likewise espoused the cause of the Banians, used different arguments on the subject of the Jews.

Voltaire

> I have noticed that the people who are quick to suspect a certain type of crime are those who practice it themselves; it is very easy to conceive what one allows but not so easy to understand what revolts you.
>
> De Sade, *Aline et Valcour*, ed. 1835, Vol. IV, p. 149.

During Hitler's domination of Europe, a history teacher, Henri Labroue, had no difficulty in compiling a two-hundred-and-fifty-page book of Voltaire's anti-Jewish writings.[34] The monotonous nature of the texts collected for this purpose adds nothing to the great man's glory; what strikes one first is the licence they take. In his free adaptation of Chapter XXIII of Ezekiel for example:[35]

> The most vital passages in Ezekiel, the ones which are most consistent with morality and public honesty, the most capable of inspiring modesty in young boys and young girls, are those where the Lord speaks of Aholah and her sister Aholibah. These admirable texts cannot be repeated too often.
>
> The Lord said to Aholah: "You have grown big; your breasts have filled out, your hair has sprouted . . .; but having confidence in your beauty, you prostituted yourself to every passerby, you built a brothel . . .; you have fornicated at the crossroads. . . . One gives money to all prostitutes, and yet it is you who gave money to your lovers." Her sister Aholibah did still worse: "She abandoned herself with passion to those whose members are like the members of asses and whose seed is like the seed of horses. . . ." The word seed is much more expressive in Hebrew. . . .

In his deist *Profession de foi* . . . Voltaire also made himself the guardian of morality:[36]

> The morals of theists are of necessity pure; since they always have the God of justice and purity before them, the God who does not descend upon the earth to order people to rob the Egyptians, to command Hosea to take a concubine in exchange for money and to live with an adulterous woman. Also one does not see us selling our wives like Abraham. We do not get drunk like Noah, and our sons do not insult the respectable member which gave them birth. . . .

Generally speaking, Voltaire's imagination was mainly stirred by the male sexual organ in this context: in pages 32 to 35 alone of Labroue's collection, the words "foreskin," "circumcised," "glans" and "penis" are repeated over twenty times! But was not the brilliant pupil of the English deists pursuing a higher motive by *castrating* the Jews in this way: i.e. the desire to combat ecclesiastical obscurantism, to *écraser l'Infâme*?

Nothing is more revealing than an analysis of Voltaire's main work, the *Dictionnaire philosophique*. Of its 118 articles,[37] thirty or more attack the Jews, "our masters and our enemies, whom we believe and whom we detest" (art. "Abraham"), "the most abominable people in the world" (art. "Anthropophagi"), "whose laws do not say a word about spirituality and the immortality of the soul" (art. "Soul"), and so on from "Torture"[38] down to Z. "Job" who finds favor in Voltaire's eyes, is not a Jew at all, but an Arab.[39]

The article "Jew" is the longest in the *Dictionnaire* (thirty pages).[40] The first part of it (written around 1745) concludes as follows:

... you will find them an ignorant and barbarous people, who for a long time have combined the most sordid greed with the most detestable superstition and the most invincible hatred for all the peoples who tolerate them and enrich them.

The famous injunction which follows sounds like a formality in such a context: "however, they must not be burnt." The last part of this article ("Seventh Letter") written in 1770 is even more significant. Here, the old man of Ferney harangues imaginary Jews in the name of Christianity:

We have placed *you* between the devil and the deep blue sea for centuries; *we* have torn *your* teeth out to force you to give us your money; *we* have driven *you* out several times through greed, and *we* have recalled *you* through greed and stupidity. ...

But in the long run the Jews are as guilty as their Christian hangmen, if not more so: "The only difference is that *our* priests have had you burned by laymen, and that your priests have always sacrificed human victims with their sacred hands. . . ." (We will come back to Voltaire's obsession with ritual murder later.) He then gives the following advice:

Do you wish to live peaceably? Imitate the Banians and the Guebres; their origins are much older than yours, they are scattered like you. The Guebres in particular, who are the ancient Persians, are slaves like you after having for a long time been your masters. They do not say a word; follow their example.

And in conclusion: "You are calculating animals, try to be thinking animals." This comparison between the Christian who thinks and the Jew who calculates, anticipates the *a priori* argument of racist anti-Semitism, decreeing the superiority of the creative intelligence of the Christians (who by then had become "Aryans"), over the Jews' sterile intellect. The modern side of Voltaire again emerges in his statement that the Jews are "plagiarists in everything,"[41] or in *Essai sur les mœurs* when he writes: "The Jews were regarded with the same eye as we see Negroes, as an inferior species of man."[42]

Not surprisingly, the same tone is found in Voltaire's correspondence: when, as a young adventurer, he offered to work for Cardinal Dubois by spying on a Jewish spy,[43] or half a century later when he wrote to Chevalier de Lisle:[44]

... But whether these circumcised men of Israel, who sell old knickers to savages, call themselves the tribe of Naphtali or Issachar, has very little importance; it does not make them any the less the biggest tramps who have ever soiled the face of the earth.

Voltaire's Judeo-phobia was well known to his contemporaries and their immediate descendants, and his friends were quite as struck by it as his enemies. "When I say," wrote Louis de Bonald, "that the Jews are the object of the benevolence of the philosophers, one has to except the head of the eighteenth-century school of philosophy, Voltaire, who has shown a decided aversion for this unfortunate people all his life."[45] It was about this time (1807) that Grattenauer, a German anti-Jewish pamphleteer, was suggesting that the Berliners replace the bust of Moses Mendelssohn by one of Voltaire.[46] On the philosophical side, the Prince de Ligne expressed the following opinion after having to listen to gems from the mouth of the irrepressible patriarch during eight days spent at Ferney: "M. de Voltaire has only stormed at Jesus Christ so much because he was born into a nation he abhorred. He was the Fréron of it, and this is M. de Voltaire's only mistake."[47] The sally gives food for thought and could have far-reaching significance.

Was Voltaire anti-Jewish because he was anti-clerical or was his battle against the *Infâme* motivated by his hatred of the people of the Bible? In his last important publication, *La Bible enfin expliquée* ... (1776), he again became "Christian," in order to contend with "six Jews." He had used the same ironic method in 1762 in his reply to Isaac Pinto,[48] who criticized him for "crushing an already too unfortunate people." On that occasion his irony was combined with polemical dishonesty; he promised the Jew that he would amend the offending passages but did not keep his word. This reply was dictated by Voltaire at the height of the Calas affair, the starting point of his great campaigns against intolerance. He signed it: *"Voltaire, chrétien, gentilhomme ordinaire de la chambre du Roi Très Chrétien."*[49] And this was the man who, five days later, informed his faithful Damilaville: "I end all my letters by saying *Écrasez l'Infâme*, as Cato always said: 'This is my opinion, and Carthage must be destroyed.' "[50] This seems like another appearance of the young Voltaire, who in his ode, *Le Vrai Dieu* in 1715, exclaimed: "Man is happy being treacherous, and guilty of deicide, you make us become Gods!"[51] It would really appear that anti-Semites experience this sort of divine pleasure.

Was Voltaire an anti-Semite? Let us be sure about the

basic meaning of the word. For the apostles of universal reason, a critical attitude towards Judaism went without saying, and they logically described it as superstition. But in practice, the importance they attached to the battles on this front showed infinite variation. The extent to which, in attacking the Revelation of Moses, they were challenging not only the authority of Church and State, but also the "internalized" authority of the father figure is significant in this respect. The turn their polemic took at this precise point cannot help but be indicative of their fundamental personality structure. A rebel of genius like the Marquis de Sade does not discuss the Jews anywhere except for a sympathetic mention in *Aline et Valcour*.[52] It was as though his prodigious aggressiveness, which was mainly directed against himself, had no need to project itself on to these symbols *par excellence* of a cruel and vengeful God the Father. In this context, present-day sociology and psychology in depth have shown up correlations between anti-Semitism and personality structure which are no longer open to doubt (even if authors, depending on which school they belong to, differ on interpretations).[53] It should be possible to extend them to the great figures of the past, provided a sufficient quantity of either literary or biographical material is available. We have given a few examples of the first category; let us now see what we have of the second.

Voltaire's biographers, each in his own way, have long brought out the infantile trauma which weighed on the life of this precocious genius. It was the life of a man who did not found a family and who, as far as we know, did not experience passionate physical love for a woman; of a man subject to indefinable illnesses and fevers, and tortured by fear of death. He was, lastly, a man tormented by anxieties and blood-thirsty obsessions, which his prodigious vitality only conquered by integrating them adequately, that is to say by transforming their mental energy into frenetic aggressiveness. An *Infâme* with somewhat vague contours may have been its main target but he also managed to deride

the human race in its entirety, with a vehemence that someone like Céline would not have disowned. Man became for
him a "miserable being who is hardly an image of the Being,
an embryo born between urine and excrement, excrement
itself, formed to fatten the filth whence it emerges."[54]
Literary critics too have not failed to note the repetition of
the parricide theme in Voltaire's tragedies, which suggests a
latent homosexuality, hence the anxieties about castration.
This hypothesis is confirmed not only by his writings, but
also by what is known of his early childhood. Without
apparent reason, he himself claimed that he was the offspring
of an adulterous union.[55] He was certainly an unloved child,
losing his mother when he was very young. And he certainly
suffered from his father's harshness and Jansenist fanaticism
(he describes him as a "grumbler, like Grinchard") and his
elder brother's "ferocious habits";[56] he harbored a grudge
against him all his life. It is worth noting that when Voltaire
was a grown man, his unmitigated venom towards the Biblical patriarchs made an exception in the case of Joseph who
was sold by his brethren. In this instance, he gave way to
sentimentality and was moved to tears by his fate.[57] Still
later, in old age, the immortal hurt child seems to be
revealed when Voltaire writes in his *Première lettre aux
Juifs:* "I know that the *instrument* with or without a foreskin
has been the cause of very grave quarrels. . . ."[58]

There remain the social factors, which could have
prompted the frustrated child to choose to settle his score
with one parental substitute, rather than another, to *invest*
his irrational hatred. For the specific character of anti-
Semitism consists precisely of the fact that the so-called
people of God, who are moreover circumcised, constitute the
most rational target for the logic of the Christian unconscious. Let us sum up these factors in Voltaire's case.[59]
On his father's side, he came from a pious middle-class
family, but on his mother's the influences were quite different. A friend of his mother's, the Abbé de Châteauneuf,

made him recite the verses of *La Moïsade* from his earliest youth:[60]

> The subtle lie passing for truth
> Was the basis of the authority of this law-giver [Moses]
> *And gave birth to the public beliefs*
> *with which the world was infected.*

Was he thinking of these free-thinking couplets some twenty years later, when he wrote *La Henriade*? The similarity can be seen:[61]

> The priest of this temple is one of those Hebrews
> Who, outlawed on earth, and citizens of the world
> Bear their deep misery from sea to sea,
> *And with an ancient accumulation of superstitions*
> *Have filled for so long all of the nations.*

This priest is a Jewish magician, officiating amongst Leaguers who want to assassinate Henri III in effigy. The operation fails and "the Sixteen lost, the Hebrew, gripped with horror, goes to hide in the night their crime and their terror."[62] (Voltaire states in a note that Catherine de Medici brought her Jews, possessors of the "secrets of the Cabala," to France; but history knows nothing of this.)

The specter of the ritual crime rears its head in Voltaire's mind on other occasions. For example in his memoirs he quotes the words of "that beautiful song" he had heard in Brussels forty years before:[63]

> Rejoice! rejoice each Christian man!
> For now gives up the ghost,
> That cursed Jew 'clep'd Jonathan,
> Who slew the sacred host.

In this context, he pokes fun at the Jesuit, Claude Nonotte, who "did not know that there are more than threescore towns in Europe, where the people give out that the Jews stabbed the *host* with knives, and that blood immediately followed." There was nothing Voltaire himself did not know about the "miracle of the rue des Ours in Paris, where the inhabitants every year burn at the end of the street the figure of a Swiss, who assassinated the Holy Virgin and the infant Jesus—nor the miracle of the Carmelites called Billettes, and a hundred others of the same kind." He obviously derided these "miracles," "celebrated by the dregs of the people, and brought in evidence by the dregs of writers, who would have us give the same credit to these nonsensical tales, as to the miracle at the marriage in Cana. . . ." But his indignation is not unadulterated. His happy memory of the bloodthirsty song is a partial confession of the other influences mingled with it.

The adolescent years Voltaire spent with the Jesuits of Louis-le-Grand probably did nothing either to alleviate his terrors[64] or to moderate his animosity towards the Children of Israel. (From certain points of view, the Jesuit education of that time was remarkably liberal, but precisely because of this, that is to say because the Society of Jesus actively propagated the concept of a "natural religion" common to all the people of the world, Abraham's revelation and its guarantors were held in even lower esteem.[65])

Then came Voltaire's wild years, the humiliation of the Chevalier de Rohan's blows, and exile in England. When he arrived in London, he had, he writes, a bill of exchange for 20,000 francs, drawn on a Jewish banker who had just gone bankrupt. The superb Voltairean retort is well known.[66]

When M. Medina, your compatriot, made me bankrupt of twenty-thousand francs, forty-four years ago, he told me that it was not his fault, that he was unlucky, that he had never been a child of Belial, that he had always striven to live as a son of God, that is to say as an honest man, a good "Israelite." He moved me to pity, I embraced him, we praised God together, and I lost twenty-four per cent."

It is interesting to find that in this English period when

Voltaire "was embracing Medina," he was in fact displaying some good will towards the Children of Israel. He associated with the family of another Jewish banker, d'Acosta, who finally extricated him from his difficulties (but whom Voltaire then regarded as an anonymous "English gentleman" sent by his lucky stars to save him).[67] To the anti-Semite, money is not odorless, and the Jews' money gives off its most pleasant emanations; their ambivalence, their secret attraction for the objects of their fury emerge in this way. To please his banker, Voltaire inserted some verses on anti-Jewish fanaticism in the English edition of the *Henriade*:[68]

It comes : Fanaticism is its terrible name

. . . when Rome at last submitted to the Son of God
from the ashes of the Capitol it passed into the Church:

In Madrid, in Lisbon, it lit its fires,
Those solemn stakes where every year
The priests send wretched Jews in pomp
for failing to discard their fathers' faith.

The following notes found in Voltaire's notebooks are much more significant:[69]

In my presence, Madame d'Acosta says to an abbé who wanted to make her Christian: "Was your God born a Jew?" "Yes." "Did he live as a Jew?" "Yes." "All right then, be Jewish."
England is meeting of all religions, as the Royal Exchange is the rendez-vous of all foreigners. When I see Christians cursing Jews, methinks I see children beating their fathers. Jewish religion is the mother of Christianity, and grand mother of the mahometism.

Were these thoughts inspired by Jewish friends? The fact remains that on his return from England he decided to snap his fingers at French prejudice against stock exchange and financial business and began to make money in the way we know. A few months after his return, skimming the surface of the law, he brought off the most wily and profitable trans-

action of his life: if he is to be believed, the Pelletier-
Desforts lottery coup earned him nearly a million livres.[70]
This was the conduct of a Jew, according to the terminology
of the day, and it did not fail to bring gibes upon his head,
and even some more serious insults. For example, twenty
years later, the famous Hirschel affair was a "low-down dirty
business" in Frederick II's opinion, and it also earned him
Lessing's harsh epigram. How, asked the poet, did the brilliant dramatist avoid the trap set for him by the most crafty
Jews of Berlin? Remember his reply:[71]

> To give in short
> The reason why
> The cunning of the Jew
> Was not so spry
> The clue must roughly be
> Mr V . . . was an even bigger
> Rogue than he.

What were Voltaire's motives for launching out into
dubious transactions like the Hirschel affair, which were not
even on a particularly large scale? A biographer of "Voltaire
the financier" thinks that: "having gone into business with
the intention of getting rich, he got caught up in the game,
and business became an end in itself . . . perhaps genius as a
businessman conceals genius as a writer more times than one
thinks."[72] Later on, Voltaire was not afraid to take shares in
a Nantes company engaged in the slave trade, a remunerative investment of the first order:[73] he became "one of the
twenty wealthiest men in the kingdom."[74] Such conduct was
hardly worthy of a philosopher, and while it helped to make
his independence as a writer and thinker more secure, it did
nothing to diminish his inner dependence (son of a notary as
he was) on kings and princes, as so many details of his life
demonstrate. That he should then seek to get rid of the Jew
in himself by attacking public and well-known Jews, and by
transferring his censure of himself to these scapegoats,
would be only too natural.

But the great anti-Semitic fervor reflected in his writing dates from the last period of his life. These were the fifteen years of his old age when the Calas and La Barre affairs had endowed him with a prophetic grandeur and he undertook to remake contemporary society and became the undisputed Messiah of the Century of Enlightenment. After destroying a great deal, he then turned to reconstruction. He ruled as a good *paterfamilias* over the minds of Europe, as over his Kingdom of Ferney. The artist in him had finally found the great role of his life.

"I have done more in my time than Luther and Calvin." So said Voltaire in this period of eschatological expectation. He was the head of a new deist church, which was hoping for a messianic era on the morrow, established as a result of his words and his "little band" of apostles, and which dreamt of enrolling the enlightened despots[75] in its crusade. This was the Voltaire who exclaimed in letters and writing: "A small reform was made in the sixteenth century, a new one is loudly called for."[76] "A beautiful century is in preparation. ... A new revolution is beginning. ..."[77] "Two or three years would be enough to make an eternal epoch."[78] D'Alembert, his favorite disciple, was the man "of whom Israel expects the most."[79] Forced to drink his Jewish chalice to the last dregs, the old man of Ferney was also the Voltaire who shot the most cruel shaft at the rival and eternal model, at everlasting old Israel. Looking at the life-stories of other great founders of religions like Mohammed or Luther, it might be asked whether there is not some ineluctable psychological need at such heights?[80]

Was Voltaire a Jew? If, perchance, he had been (after all, the most popular philosopher in Germany in his lifetime was called Moses Mendelssohn), posterity would have excelled in discovering a restless Jewish temperament, or a denying and eternal Jewish soul in this great demolisher (as he once described himself)[81]—even more than in Heine or Karl Marx. As it was, probably no man in modern times has so skillfully stirred up the anti-Semitic potential which slumbers in so many hearts, not excluding those of the Jews themselves. On this moving frontier, the Church sought to close its ranks against the campaigns of this one man and already seemed to be working towards a reversal of alliances. Evidence of this appears in the vindicatory *Lettres de quelques Juifs*, by Abbé Guénée, or the conclusions super-added to Abbé Fleury's *Mœurs des Israélites*: [82]

XX. This people, amidst so many setbacks, so many calamities, always preserve a firm hope of one day seeing the promises made to them fulfilled. They yearn for the Messiah, retain a firm hope of being re-established one day in their early splendor, and always have their eyes turned towards Jerusalem, as the place destined for their glory. This certainly gives food for thought to those who disparage the Jewish people and who do not see them as the instrument of Providence, but only as a vile nation, given over to the most absurd superstition, and the most insatiable greed.

As for the rare "enlightened" French Jews of the day, they do not seem to have borne Voltaire any grudge. Even today, the great majority of their descendants would accept what the sage, Zalkind-Hourwitz, who considered him the patron saint of future anti-Semites, wrote about this "patron saint of the democrats" (Julien Benda): [83]

It could well be that Voltaire would have felt less ill-will towards modern Jews than towards the old, that is to say towards the main stem of Christianity which he ceaselessly attacked. However that may be, the Jews forgive him all the ill he has done them, in consideration of the good he has done them, although involuntarily, perhaps even unknowingly; because if they are enjoying a little peace for a few years, they owe it to the advance of the Enlightenment, to which Voltaire has certainly contributed more than any other writer, by his numerous works against fanaticism.

For generations on end, in fact, emancipated Jews thought they could recognize themselves in the distorted mask of the champion of tolerance, in the mystical pacifist who detested the funeral pyres, and also in the inspired opponent of the Christian mysteries. "I can certainly not make head or tail of them; nobody has ever made head or tail of them, and it is for this that people are massacred."[84] Always massacred, they only saw Voltaire as the flag-bearer of bourgeois, pacific and secular democracy, without suspecting that the crushing of the *Infâme* would lead (via as many intermediaries as one could wish) to far vaster massacre.

Rousseau

> Rousseau indulges in Calvinist introspection; he searches his conscience and finds himself evil. Voltaire does not search his conscience and he finds himself good.
> (René Pomeau, *Voltaire par lui-même*, Paris, 1955, p. 16)

On reflection, one wonders whether the correlation between personality structure and attitude to Jews should not appear more clearly in eighteenth-century authors than in our contemporaries. In fact at present, and until a new order, the pattern seems set: people who, for a complex assortment of reasons and motives, choose a "left-wing" party, automatically condemn anti-Semitism because of this. This implies, at least in principle, a kindly attitude to the Jews. Obviously nothing resembling these allegiances or thought-patterns existed in the Century of Enlightenment. As a result, in the period when our present intellectual world was being shaped, each individual could take up a stand, freely, according to his own temperament, guided by obscure psychological factors or attractions, without considerations or demands foreign to these emotional predispositions intervening to mask or even distort them.

Be that as it may, when the grid just used for Voltaire is applied to Jean-Jacques Rousseau, it immediately reveals numerous elements combined to dispose him to regard the Children of Israel favorably. He came from a Calvinist family and background; he possessed an uneasy conscience, a morbid sensibility, a thirst for justice, an intolerance of success, a hatred of the complaisant philosophy of the rich and happy.[85] The way in which the man made a mess of his life, running away from his peers, and teetering on the brink of a persecution mania is already known. But we will not dig any deeper into the old theme of the relationship between genius and madness. For our purpose it is enough to note that, unlike Voltaire, the persecutor who chose to decide his own innocence, Jean-Jacques all his life pleaded guilty (to the point where he confused remorse with free will, when he was trying to prove the existence of a Supreme Being: "I am a slave in my vices, a free man in my remorse").[86] He asked only that a kindly ear be lent "to the arguments of the Jews." He made this request in a curious passage in his *Profession de foi du Vicaire savoyard* where, on the pretext of comparing the merits of the three great monotheist religions, he was in fact content to compare the Church triumphant with the muffled Synagogue, and pleaded in favor of the latter with its "best established" revelation—but was this because it was tyrannized? The passage has to be read:

> We have three principal forms of religion in Europe. One accepts one revelation, another two, and another three. Each hates the others, showers curses on them, accuses them of blindness, obstinacy, hardness of heart, and falsehood. What fair-minded man will dare to decide between them without first carefully weighing their evidence, without listening attentively to their arguments? That which accepts only one revelation is the oldest and seems the best established; that which accepts three is the newest and seems the most consistent; that which accepts two revelations and rejects the third may perhaps be the best, but prejudice is certainly against it; its inconsistency is glaring. ...
>
> Our Catholics talk loudly of the authority of the Church; but what is the use of it all, if they need just as great an array of proofs to establish that authority as the others need to establish directly their doctrine? The Church decides that the Church has

a right to decide. What a well-founded authority! Go beyond it, and you are back again in our discussions.

Do you know many Christians who have taken the trouble to inquire what the Jews allege against them? If anyone knows anything at all about it, it is from the writings of Christians. What a way of ascertaining the argument of our adversaries! But what is to be done? If anyone dared to publish in our day books which were openly in favor of the Jewish religion, we should punish the author, publisher and bookseller. This regulation is a sure and certain plan for always being in the right. It is easy to refute those who dare not venture to speak.

Those among us who have the opportunity of talking with Jews are little better off. These unhappy people feel that they are in our power; the tyranny they have suffered makes them timid; they know that Christian charity thinks nothing of injustice and cruelty; will they dare to run the risk of an outcry against blasphemy? Our greed inspires us with zeal, and they are so rich that they must be in the wrong. The more learned, the more enlightened they are, the more cautious. You may convert some poor wretch whom you have paid, to slander his religion; you get some wretched old-clothes-man to speak, and he says what you want; you may triumph over their ignorance and cowardice, while all the time their men of learning are laughing at your stupidity. But do you think that you would get off so easily in any place where they knew that they were safe? At the Sorbonne, it is plain that the Messianic prophecies refer to Jesus Christ. Among the rabbis of Amsterdam it is just as clear that they have nothing to do with him. I do not think that I have ever heard the arguments of the Jews as to why they should not have a free state, schools and universities, where they can speak and argue without danger. Then alone can we know what they have to say.

Note the *avant la lettre* Zionist argument at the end. Moreover, the question occurs as to whether Rousseau himself had "the opportunity of talking with Jews" as he put it. His biographers have nothing to say about this, but it is plausible. He could have met the old-clothes-men he talks about, on the road during his peregrinations, perhaps passing through the College of the Catechumeni like himself, and shy soul that he was, he could have seen the "men of learning, laughing at your stupidity," during his stay in Venice. When he was taking refuge at Montmorency, and saying that he wished to read nothing more, he agreed to make an exception for Mendelssohn's *Phädon* "because it is the work of a Jew."

However, also in the *Profession de foi* . . . Rousseau proves himself a child of his time by solemnly declaring his horror of the cruel Jewish God of battle:

> If then it [the Divinity] teaches us what is absurd and unreasonable, if it inspires us with feelings of aversion for our fellows and terror for ourselves, if it paints us a God, angry, jealous, vengeful, partial, hating men, a God of war and battles, ever ready to strike and to destroy, ever speaking of punishment and torment, boasting even of the punishment of the innocent, my heart would not be drawn towards this terrible God, I would take good care not to quit the realm of natural religion to embrace such a religion as that; for you see plainly I must choose between them. Your God is not ours. He who begins by selecting a chosen people, and proscribing the rest of mankind, is not our common father. . . .

Jean-Jacques also talks about the Jews of ancient times in the conventional way, on several occasions: "the vilest of peoples," "the baseness of [this] people, incapable of any virtue," "the vilest people perhaps who existed then."[87] Finally, this apostle of the religion of the heart, like the majority of his contemporaries, was embarrassed by the revelation on Sinai; hence the famous exclamation: "How many men between God and me!"[88] "Is it so simple, so natural that God should have sought out Moses to speak to Jean-Jacques Rousseau?"[89]

The fact remains that the love for the God of Sinai prevailed over the hatred in his mind. Moreover, he declared to the Duc de Croy that, like him, "he found more truth in Moses and the received objects than in anything else."[90]

What he meant is clarified by his statement that it is "easy to reconcile the authority of the Scriptures with ancient monuments, and one is not reduced to treating as fables traditions which are as old as the people who have transmitted them."[91]

Rousseau justified his admiration for Moses as follows (in his *Considérations sur le gouvernement de Pologne . . .*):[92]

> [Moses] planned and carried out the astonishing undertaking of setting up into a national body a swarm of wretched fugitives, without arts, without weapons, without talents, without virtues, without courage and who, not having a single inch of ground in its own right, made a strange troop on the face of the earth. Moses dared to make this wandering and servile troop into a political body, a free people, and, while it wandered in the deserts without a stone on which to rest its head, he gave it that institutional form which has stood the test of time, of fortune and of conquerors, which five thousand years have not been able to destroy or even alter and which still continues to exist today in full force even when the national body no longer exists.
>
> To prevent his people fusing with foreign peoples, he gave it customs and practices which are incompatible with those of other nations; he over-loaded it with ritual, specific ceremonies; he encumbered it in thousands of ways to keep it incessantly in good shape and to render it always a foreigner amongst other men; and all the bonds of fraternity that he placed between the members of his republic were so many barriers that kept it separate from its neighbors and prevented it from mingling with them. It is in this way that this strange nation, so often subjugated, so often apparently dispersed and destroyed, but always passionately attached to its code, has still been preserved up to the present day scattered amongst the others without mixing with them, and that its customs, its laws, its ritual continue to exist and will last as long as the world, despite the hatred and persecution of the rest of the human race.

Here, it is the author of the *Contrat social* who is in ecstasies over the excellence of the legislation Moses gave his "strange nation." An unpublished page shows his admiration clad in more mystical tones, foreshadowing, amongst other intuitions, the idea that the Jews were something quite other than a "race."[93] He states:[94]

... No longer as in earlier times are people to be seen boasting of being autochthons, aborigines, children of the land or country they are settled in. The frequent upheavals of the human race have so transplanted or merged nations that except perhaps for Africa, not one remains on earth which could boast of being native of the country it possesses. In this confusion of mankind, so many varied races have successively inhabited the same places and have followed or mingled with each other there that these races are no longer distinctive, and the different names that the people bear are no longer anything but those of the places they inhabit. If traces of descent remain in a few names, as with the Parsees or the Guebres, either they are no longer to be found in their ancient territory or it is no longer possible to say if they form the body of a nation.

But an astonishing and truly unique spectacle is to see an expatriated people, who have had neither place nor land for nearly two thousand years, a people mingled with foreigners, no longer having perhaps a single descendant of the early races, a scattered people, dispersed over the world, enslaved, persecuted, scorned by all nations, nonetheless preserving its characteristics, its laws, its customs, its patriotic love of the early social union, when all ties with it seem broken. The Jews provide us with an astonishing spectacle: the laws of Numa, Lycurgus, Solon are dead; the very much older laws of Moses are still alive. Athens, Sparta, Rome have perished and no longer have children left on earth; Zion, destroyed, has not lost its children.

They mingle with all the nations and never merge with them; they no longer have leaders, and are still a nation; they no longer have a homeland, and are always citizens of it.

What must be the strength of legislation capable of working such wonders, capable of braving conquests, dispersions, revolutions, exiles, capable of surviving the customs, laws, empire of all the nations, and which finally promises them, by these trials, that it is going to continue to sustain them all, to conquer the vicissitudes of things human, and to last as long as the world? Of all the systems of legislation which are known to us, some are theoretical creations the feasibility of which is even disputed; others have only produced a few followers, others have never made a well-constituted State, except this one which has undergone all the trials and has always withstood them. Jew and Christian agree in recognizing in this the finger of god, who according to one, is maintaining his nation, and according to the other, punishing it, but any man whosoever he is, must acknowledge this as a unique marvel, the causes of which, divine or human, certainly deserve the study and admiration of the sages, in preference to all that Greece and Rome offer of what is admirable in the way of political institutions and human settlements.

In the course of their memorable conversation, Rousseau told the Duc de Croy that the Hebrews were "the best established."[95] But nowhere does the originality of his standpoint emerge more powerfully than when he is expressing his adoration of the "Hebrew sage," i.e. Jesus. In this context, quite naturally, he disparages the witnesses that were the Jews: "The voice of loftiest wisdom arose among the fiercest fanaticism, most heroic virtues did honor to the most degraded of nations."[96] However, Jesus' historic mission, as Rousseau saw it, was strangely similar to the one the apostles of Zionism undertook to carry out in the following century: "Jesus, whom this century has failed to recognize because it is unworthy to know him, Jesus who died after having wished to make an illustrious and virtuous people out of his vile compatriots. . . ."[97] ("Rousseau was a Christian rather as Jesus Christ was a Jew," said Grimm ironically.) Rousseau expanded this idea:[98]

His noble plan was to raise up his people, to make them once again a free people and worthy of so being; for it was in this way that a beginning had to be made. The deep study that he made of the law of Moses, his efforts to re-awaken enthusiasm and love for it in people's hearts, showed their purpose, as much as it was possible so as not to alarm the Romans; but his base and cowardly compatriots, insteady of listening to him, conceived a hatred of him, precisely because of his genius and virtue, which were a reproach to their unworthiness. . . .

On the whole, there is nothing surprising about these views coming as they did from the eternal nonconformist, the man who despised fashionable philosophers, describing them as "ardent missionaries of atheism and very imperious dogmatics."[99] Nor are they unexpected on the part of the sworn enemy of Voltaire: ". . . Monsieur, I hate you," he spat at him.[100] Beyond the natural sympathy of a persecuted thinker for a persecuted people, they reveal the seismographic sensibility of the man who had what was perhaps the first presentiment of the dangers of "a philosophical inquisition, more insidious and no less bloody than the other."[101] The fact remains that Rousseau did not have the offensive and his arguments do not always appear to come up to scratch in the face of Voltaire's inexhaustible propaganda, particularly as the battle was unequal. An arsenal of pseudo-arguments, as amusing as they are varied, convince more easily than the lessons of reason and virtue.

One of the most curious relics of the Century of Enlightenment is Voltaire's annotated copy of *Émile*. He makes thirty-one mainly contemptuous comments on the *Profession de foi* . . . (which formed Volume III of *Émile*). But they are not continuous and suggest that Voltaire, who declared that "this absurd novel is unreadable," skipped the passage in which Rousseau argued in favor of Judaism. One finds oneself regretting this negligence which has perhaps deprived posterity of a literary bombshell.[102] A century and a half later, Charles Maurras took it upon himself to stand in for a "Voltaire, enlightened by the anti-Semitic spirit of the West," in order to give a piece of his mind to the "adventurer fed on biblical marrow"—his description of the "wretched Rousseau":[103]

He entered [French civilization] like one of those energumens which are thrown up by the desert, and rigged out in old sacks, parade their melancholy howling through the streets of Zion; tearing out their hair, rending their rags and mixing their bread with filth, they soil every passer-by with their hatred and contempt. . . . Nothing could, nothing should contain this man. He came from one of the points of the world where all mixtures of Judeo-Christian anarchy have swarmed for two centuries. . . .

We might, in this connection, examine the influence which Voltaire's diatribes and Rousseau's arguments exerted in France and throughout the world over generations. In the nature of things, the former appear to possess far greater striking power than the latter. It must also be remembered that we have quoted *all* the texts of the solitary walker that glorify the name of Israel, but only a fraction of those in which the Lord of Ferney ridiculed it.

The influence of these latter, or rather their audience, can be assumed to have been all the greater because Voltaire did not enter history as an anti-Semitic agitator but as a champion of tolerance and herald of democracy, and his authority was based on this. Commentators, editors and teachers usually avoid mentioning the anti-Jewish outbursts and writings of the defender of Calas. Notwithstanding, these texts still exist and probably continue to find their target at the opportune moment, keeping alight the flame of the "anti-Semitic genius of the West"; a genius who might only have been a specific expression of the relationship of Western man with God.

Diderot and the Encyclopédie

> If I think that I love you freely, I am mistaken. It is nothing of the sort. What a fine system for the heartless! I rage at being prevented by a devil of philosophy which my mind cannot prevent itself from sanctioning and my heart from denying.
>
> (*Diderot to Sophie Volland*)

In the summer of 1773, Diderot was invited to Russia by the Empress Catherine, and on the way, made a lengthy halt in the Netherlands. A letter he wrote to Mme d'Épinay tells us that in the Hague, he associated with Isaac Pinto, the enlightened Jew who corresponded with Voltaire:[104]

> . . . I have found a man here called Pinto, a Jew. He was very dissolute in Paris and he is none too sensible in the Hague. He has a little house, where he was only anxious that I should make the acquaintance of the Idumaean sex,[105] but these games have never been to my taste and are no longer of my generation. . . .

This interlude was reflected in *Le neveu de Rameau*, which already contained a persecuted Jew amongst its characters. When Diderot adapted his masterpiece in 1774, he added a second Jew, "affluent and spendthrift, who knew his Law and observed it as rigidly as a bar." He made him the inglorious hero of a scandalous affair, which actually happened in real life to a Christian merchant (so Diderot himself tells us).[106] This is only a small detail and it is a well-known fact that any funny story has only to be christened "Jewish" to gain additional *vis comica*. Otherwise, mention of Jews and Judaism in the philosopher's vast output are fairly rare.

In view of his fight against revealed religion, they could not be absent. In a youthful work, *La Promenade du Sceptique* . . . (1747), Diderot set out to put paid to Judaism and Christianity. From this first attack, he is found dismissing both these hostile superstitions non-suited, as equally absurd and equally noxious. He depicts them as two "armies": the Jews and the priests. The first had been "strongly recommended" by their leader (Moses) "to show their enemies no mercy and to be large-scale usurers, two commandments which they fulfilled excellently." The second, led by a viceroy (the Pope) who thought that "everyone is his slave . . . are really the wickedest race I know." And Diderot poked fun at the fight which took place between the two "armies," each equipped with its own "military code":[107]

The first contains strange rules, with a lengthy series of marvels performed to corroborate them; the second dismisses the first privileged people, and installs new ones who are likewise supported by marvels: there follows altercation between the privileged peoples. Those attached to the new creation claim that they are favored to the exclusion of those of the old, while the latter curse them as intruders and usurpers. . . .

This parity is found on other occasions, for example when Diderot was describing the Jansenists to Catherine II ". . . weeping over the fate of the Church as, under Julian, those tramps of Jews and Galileans wept, the first over the ruins of Jerusalem, the others over the destruction of their fanatical schools."[108] When he was drawing up a series of questions to the Empress about the economic state of the Russian Empire, he first asked the size of the population, then the number of monks, and third, the number of Jews.[109] When he wrote his long article for the *Encyclopédie* on the philosophy of the Jews, he still held the same sort of balance between the Galilean and the Talmudists; but with the censor watching over him, he had to cheat him by transforming "this obscure and fanatical Jew" into the "son of God," and by describing the Talmudic maxims as "playful and puerile."[110] Certain omissions appear equally significant: a note on usury he wrote for Catherine II contained no reference to Jews.[111] On the other hand, he did not evade the classic "proof by the Jews" in his polemic *Examen du prosélyte répondant à lui-même* (1763). We reprint below his closely reasoned answer to it:[112]

Reason demonstrates that in the course of nature the Jewish nation should have been extinct. Reason also demonstrates, on the contrary, that the Jews, marrying amongst themselves and producing children, the Jewish nation must continue to exist. But, you will say, how does it come about that one no longer sees either Carthaginians or Macedonians? The reason is that they have been incorporated into other peoples, but the religion of the Jews and that of the peoples with whom they live, does not permit them to incorporate themselves into them; they have to form a nation apart. Moreover, the Jews are not the only people who continue to exist dispersed in this way; for a great number of years, the Guebres and Banians have been in the same position. . . .

It will be noted that here again, on the subject of the "Jewish miracle," Diderot cites both the religion of the Jews and the religion of the "people with whom they live."

Such positivist reasoning is characteristic of this great champion of irreligion. For him, even the deism of his own day only became the last head to be cut off the obscurantist hydra.[113] On the other hand, his moral philosophy was, as J. Proust has shrewdly observed,[114] "secular, profane but in no way profaning." In fact, it can be noted that he treats problems of the Sacred with placid disrespect, without the slightest veneration (even for the person of Christ) but equally without iconoclastic passion. Perhaps no man in his day was so tolerant; he even advocated leaving his adversaries "the liberties to speak and write which they want to take away from us."

It might even be added that a few enthusiastic overtones can be noted at the beginning of Diderot's *Encyclopédie* article on the philosophy of the Jews, which make one wonder whether they were inspired solely by a desire to conciliate the censor:

> Without putting faith in the daydreams which pagans and Jews have propagated on the subject of Shem and Ham, what history teaches is enough to make them worthy of respect in our eyes; but what men does it offer who can compare in authority, in dignity, in judgment, in piety, in innocence, with Abraham, Isaac and Jacob? Joseph gained admiration for his wisdom with the most educated people in the world and governed them for forty years.
>
> And now we reach the time of Moses; what a historian! What a legislator! What a philosopher! What a poet! What a man!
>
> The wisdom of Solomon has become proverbial. . . .

In the rest of the article, Diderot relies primarily on Basnage's *Histoire des Juifs depuis Jésus-Christ*. . . . Towards the end, he enlarges on *Le Sentiment des Juifs sur la Providence et la liberté* in a way that suggests an interest in Maimonides' arguments on the problem of free will.

Diderot is the *Encyclopédie,* but the *Encyclopédie* is not Diderot. This awe-inspiring manifesto of the rising bourgeoisie was the work of over two hundred collaborators, with disparate opinions. From the point of view which interests us, it rapidly becomes apparent that the Jews, who are discussed in many contexts, if not out of context, are most frequently mentioned to prove an argument, and that the requirements of the proof in the majority of cases, lead to disparagement.

An exception to this in the form of a kindly disposed article appears curiously enough where one should least expect to find it: in the long article on "Usury." Its author, the economist Faiguet, was trying to prove the absurdity of the prohibition on lending at interest. Rather than openly criticize the anti-usury commandments in the Bible, he chose to argue from the difference in times and customs, which led him to give an idyllic description of the ancient Jews:[115]

This simplicity of customs is in contrast to our ostentation. . . . Whereas we barely know friendship, we, infinitely far away from that precious equality which makes the duties of humanity so dear and so urgent, we, slaves of custom and opinion, subject consequently to a thousand arbitrary demands, we are constantly borrowing large sums, and normally more from motives of greed than from real need.

It follows from these differences that the practice of lending free of charge was a stricter obligation for the Hebrews than for us, and it can be added that, in view of the influence of legislation on customs, this practice was also more natural and easier for them in so much as their laws and their government maintained amongst them a certain spirit of concord and fraternity which have not been seen in other peoples. These laws, in fact, breathe the sweetness and equality which must

prevail in a large family rather than the atmosphere of domination and superiority which appear necessary in a great state. . . .

But in the last analysis the ironic peroration in the article on
"Hebraic (Language)" should also rightfully be attributed to
this same desire to reform the existing order:

> It is not for us, blind mortals, to question Providence; also let us
> not ask it why it pleased it only to speak to the Jews in
> parables: why it has given them eyes so that they do not see,
> and ears so that they do not hear, and why of all the nations of
> antiquity, it chose particularly the one whose head was hardest
> and coarsest? It is here that proud reason must keep silent; the
> one who permitted the deviation of the favorite nation is the
> same one who allowed the deviation of the first man and
> thereafter no one can know eternal wisdom. . . .

The same can be said of that literary "cadence" in the article
"Cabala" (Abbé Pastré): "After having read this article, and
several others, one can quote the line from the *Plaideurs*:
'what madmen! I was never at such a feast.' "

Let us move on to the two articles on "Judaism" and
"Jews," where the Jews no longer merely supply evidence
but form the actual basis of the discussion. These are brief
accounts which can be described as objective. The first has
been attributed, wrongly, to judge by all appearances, to
Diderot.[116] It concludes as follows (see "Jews"):

> Today the Jews are tolerated in France, Germany, Poland,
> Holland, England, Rome, Venice, in exchange for taxes which
> they pay to the princes. They are also very widespread in the
> East. But the Inquisition does not suffer them in Spain or
> Portugal.

This second article is signed by the Chevalier de Jaucourt,
Diderot's right-hand man, and is obviously influenced by
Montesquieu. It concludes as follows:

Since that time princes have opened their eyes to their own

interests and have treated *Jews* with more moderation. It was felt in certain places in the north and south of France that people could not do without their help. But without speaking of the grand duke of Tuscany, Holland and England, moved by more noble principles, have granted them all possible favors under the constant protection of their governments. Thus scattered in our time with more security than they have ever had, in all the countries of Europe where commerce reigns they have become the instruments by means of which the most distant nations can converse and correspond together. . . .

People found themselves very badly off in Spain for having chased them [out] as well as in France for having persecuted subjects whose faith differed on some points from that of the prince. Love in the Christian religion consists in its practice: and this practice breathes only kindness, humanity and charity.

When he is discussing *medicine,* however, Jaucourt rages against the Jews, in the name of nascent somatic medicine, contemptuous of spiritual healing:

The ancient Hebrews, stupid, superstitious, separated from other peoples, unversed in the study of physics, incapable of resorting to natural causes, attributed all their diseases to evil spirits . . . in a word, their ignorance of medicine caused them to turn to soothsayers, magicians, enchanters or finally to prophets. Even when our Lord came to Palestine, it seems that the Jews were not more enlightened than formerly. . . .

Jaucourt appears again in the article entitled "Menstrual" where he obviously enjoys comparing Jewish women, their obsession with defilement and the absurd observances, with the negresses of the Gold Coast and the Congo kingdom. In the article on "Fathers of the Church," this "Maître Jacques de *l'Encyclopédie*" does not fail to recall the immorality of the patriarch Abraham, which gives him a better chance to criticize St John Chrysostom and St Augustine. Other authors dealing with quite different subjects (*Geography* or *Astronomy* for example) deny Moses all credit—he did nothing but learn from the Egyptians. Generally speaking, the encyclopedists tended to glorify the history of Egypt the better to belittle the sacred history of the Jews. The author of the article on "Political Economy," Nicolas Boulanger, criticizes "Judaic superstition" more traditionally, if one can use the term:

> The monarch, with the obdurate Jews and with all the other nations, was regarded less as a father and a God of peace than as an exterminating angel. The motive behind theocracy would therefore have been fear: this was also true of despotism: the God of the Scythians was represented by a sword. The true God of the Hebrews was also obliged, because of their character, perpetually to threaten them. . . . The Judaic superstition which fancied that it could not pronounce the terrible name of Jehovah, which was the great name of its monarch, in this way transmitted to us one of the conventions of this primitive theocracy. . . .

But the disparagement of the Jews involved in these gibes or criticisms was most often only a screen for totally different attacks. It fades to insignificance when compared with the great article entitled "Messiah," by Pastor Polier de Bottens, a disciple of Voltaire's. This article had been commissioned by the master himself. He had supplied the plan for it and put the finishing touches himself.[117] His style is clearly recognizable in the lengthy discourse on the ignominy of the Jews, which in passing enables him to ridicule the established Church, on the pretext of defending it:

> The Jews who revolted against the divinity of Jesus Christ, have resorted to all manner of means to invalidate and destroy this great mystery, fundamental dogma of the Christian faith; they distort the meaning of their own oracles, or do not apply them to the Messiah. . . . All these sophisms, all these critical comments have not prevented the Church from believing the celestial and supernatural voice which offered mankind the *Messiah* Jesus Christ as the *Son of God, the particular object of the dilection of the Most High, and from believing that all the fullness of divinity was embodied in him.*

If the Jews disputed Jesus Christ's role of *Messiah* and divinity, they have also neglected nothing to make him appear contemptible, to cast on his birth, his life and his death, all the ridicule and all the opprobium that their cruel relentlessness against this divine Savior and his heavenly doctrine could imagine; but of all the works that the blindness of the Jews has produced, there is probably none more odious or extravagant than the book entitled *Sepher Toldos Jeschut*, drawn from the dust by M. Wagenseil in the second volume of his work entitled *Tela Ignea* [etc.].

(What follows is a long summary of the *Toldoth Iéchouth*, a blasphemous work which was circulating in the ghetto; it probably dated from the first centuries of the Christian era. In it, Jesus was described as the son of a loose woman and a Roman legionary and his life story was adorned with much obscene detail. Duly attributed to the Jews and accompanied by abuse of them, the pamphlet was able to pass the censor and delighted the enemies of the Church. Pastor Polier seems to have been the unconscious tool of Voltaire in this affair. The "Holbachic Synagogue"—which will be discussed later—used a similar method when it published the anti-Christian treatise *Israël vengé* ... by the Marrano, Orobio de Castro, in 1770.)

... However, it is by means of all these odious calumnies that the Jews hold together in their implacable hatred against the Christians and against the Gospels; they have neglected nothing in order to alter the chronology of the Old Testament and spread doubts and difficulties about the time of the coming of our Savior; everything proclaims their stubbornness and ill-faith.

That there is a great deal of discussion of the Jews in the *Encyclopédie*, and that it contains a fairly large variety of opinions on them, can be seen. But what cannot be found in its twenty thousand folio pages, is a declaration of favorable feeling such as the Guebres enjoy—though the description of them could easily have been applied to the Children of Israel by changing a few words or proper nouns. We quote the praise of the Guebres, their customs, cult and even their messiahs, voiced by Nicolas Boulanger:

A wandering people, spread out over several provinces of Persia and the Indies. It is the sad remnants of the old Persian monarchy, which the Arab caliphs, armed with religion, destroyed in the seventh century, in order to set the god of Mohammed in the place of the god of Zoroaster, the doctrine of the magi and the worship of fire. They remain as if to serve as a monument to one of the oldest religions of the world.

Although there is a great deal of superstition and still more of ignorance amongst the Guebres, travelers are sufficiently in agreement to give us an idea of them which interests us in their fate. Poor and simple in their dress, gentle and humble in their manners, tolerant, charitable and hard-working, they have no beggars amongst them, but are all craftsmen, workers and big agriculturalists.

Although they have particular grounds for hating the Mohammedans, they have always relied on Providence to take charge of punishing these cruel usurpers, and they console themselves by a very ancient tradition which they talk of to their children, that their religion will one day regain the upper hand and that it will be professed by all the peoples of the world: to this article of their faith, they also join that vague and indeterminate expectation that is found with so many other peoples, of illustrious and famous personages who must come at the end of time to bring happiness to men and prepare them for the great revival. . . .

Moreover, the Guebres have no idols and no images, and they are seemingly the only people of the world who have never had such. . . .

People who have so simple a cult and such pacific dogmas probably ought not to have been the object of the hatred and contempt of the Mohammedans; but not only do the latter detest them, they have even accused them at all times of idolatry, impiety, atheism and the most infamous crimes. All religions which are persecuted and obliged to keep their assemblies secret, have endured calumnies and insults of this sort on the part of other sects. . . .

The "Holbachic Synagogue"

From the beginning of the eighteenth century, a number of anti-religious manuscripts were circulating in France, turned out in numbers by copyists, some actually specializing in this activity. According to Wade, the scholar who has studied this clandestine literature most fully, it bears in the majority of cases the imprint of Baruch Spinoza's ideas (notably from his *Tractatus Theologico-Politicus*). It is known that this Jewish name did in fact become the symbol of all "Spinozist" atheist propaganda. (It was said that the *Tractatus* "had been produced in hell by a renegade Jew."[118])

One of the most remarkable works of this type is the *Lettre de Thrasybule à Leucippe*. In it, its author, the scholar Nicolas Fréret, Secretary of the Académie des Inscriptions et Belles Lettres, makes the philosopher Thrasybulus describe and compare the bizarre superstitions of the Jewish and Christian "sects." After telling his correspondent about Christian ideas on the Christ-Messiah, Thrasybulus compares them to the Jewish views:

> . . . The Jews, on the contrary, maintain that not everything that has been prophesied about the man who is to raise up their nation can be taken allegorically. They say that he will be a powerful king, who will gather them together, restore their authority and extend it over all the nations. And it must in fact be admitted that their books do not give us a different idea and they contain nothing to favor the Christians' explanation.

Fréret therefore uses Jewish books to show the Christians' error. These books, he continues, remain the basis of the Christian religion; destroy the Jewish sect and Christianity will collapse like a house of cards:[119]

The sect of these latter depends on the truth of the Jewish sect,
on which it is entirely based; thus the first would only have to
be destroyed to remove the need to mention the latter; but by
itself it is devoid of adequate proof, we have no book by this
Christ; and although his disciples have written several, some of
them are only speaking from hearsay. . . .

It has often been said that Judaism was a convenient
target for anti-religious polemicists in the past because it
could be abused without danger. Fréret's work would seem
to suggest that, tactical reasons apart, the anti-Jewish
campaigns by the "Spinozists" and other atheists were
determined by the requirement of the discussion. Also to be
borne in mind is the Pauline metaphor, ". . . remember that it
is not you who sustain the root: the root sustains you"
(Romans, 11: 18).

But that is a question for theologians.

The *Lettre de Thrasybule à Leucippe* is a work of very
great dialectic strength, a cold demonstration, seemingly
devoid of passion. The tone of *La Moïsade,* also by Fréret, is
quite different. It is a pamphlet which seems to draw the
logical conclusions from the *Lettre* since it ends with a curse
on Moses and his followers:[120]

Die, Moses, die, destructive tyrant! Let the Heavens crush you
with thunderbolts of vengeance! Let the earth, as angry as the
Heavens with your treachery and cruelty, open beneath your
guilty feet and swallow you, abominable monster. . . . And you,
raging, senseless people, vile, coarse men, worthy slaves of the
yoke you bear, go back to your books; and keep away from
me!

Fréret's emulator and contemporary, Jean-Baptiste de
Mirabaud, Permanent Secretary of the Académie Française,
also produced anti-religious works on the quiet. In this way,
he composed three "Opinions" that can be regarded as successive parts of a single treatise. His *Opinions des anciens sur*
la nature de l'âme . . . is not related to the present subject; his

Opinions des anciens sur le monde ... is, in that it contains an argument against the Biblical creation story; his *Opinions des anciens sur les Juifs* ... concerns us most closely since it attempts to prove "that the disrepute into which the Jewish nation has fallen preceded the curse of Jesus Christ": [121]

> You will therefore see from this that, a long time before they had brought down upon themselves this curse, which is now regarded as the cause of their wretchedness, they were generally hated and generally despised in every country which knew them: after which you will agree that there is no mention of them in the old books except in connection with this contempt, and in relation to the general aversion felt for them. ...

This is Mirabaud's thesis, proved by a wealth of scholarship, using the Greek and Latin texts known in his day. His leitmotif is that:[122]

> Not only did all the nations despise the Jews; they even hated them and believed that they were as justified in hating as in despising them. They were hated because they were known to hate other men; they were despised because they were seen observing customs which were thought ridiculous.

More precisely:[123]

> Although its circumcision, its sabbath, its fasts, its gloomy ceremonies made the Jewish nation despised, nothing brought the insult and contempt of men down upon it so much as that ridiculous credulity of which the pagans accused it.

Speaking as an enlightened philosopher, Mirabaud then notes that the persecutions of which they are the object only attach the Jews all the more firmly to their superstitions. He compares them, from this point of view, to the early Christian martyrs. Nonetheless, his proof contains the germ of the arguments the future "racists" were to use since it extrapolates the ignominy of the Children of Israel in time, thus making it appear permanent and irremediable.

It is useless to ask why men like Fréret or Mirabaud chose to use anti-Jewish arguments for the purposes of their anti-clerical propaganda when other freethinkers neglected these arguments. Likewise, it will probably never be known why the principal center for this propaganda in the second half of the century, in Paris, was nicknamed the *synagogue de la rue Royale*.[124]

It was at this address that a rich, cultured German baron, Paul Henri Thiry d'Holbach, kept open house and twice weekly gave "philosophical dinners." This Amphitryon must have had a singularly strong personality. Diderot, a regular guest, has left a curious picture of him: "He is original in his manner and in his ideas. Imagine a satyr, gay, stimulating, indecorous and excitable, in the midst of a group of chaste, soft, refined figures. Such was he amongst us. . . ."[125] However, the ostentatious host of the "synagogue" concealed a discreet and methodical apostle of atheist propaganda. He raised it from the scale of a craft to an industry, by having the manuscripts, which were circulating illicitly, printed in London or Amsterdam and augmenting them with writings of his own.

Baron d'Holbach had over fifty works[126] published in this way between 1760 and 1775, either under assumed names or anonymously. It is not always easy to know who the actual authors were, though one of the manuscripts, the ambitious *Système de la nature,* is undoubtedly his own. Herald of the rising bourgeoisie, he proclaims his main principles in this work, with the slogan *Liberty, Property, Security*[127] and a philosophy of radical materialism. This materialism was pragmatically proved by the awe-inspiring conquests of a science which only recognized tangible and measurable matter. But although it declared war on the spiritualism of the Church, this materialism was dialectically established in terms of the Church and was trying to replace it by another unchanging, absolute truth.

It is difficult (and some people will think, very debatable) to establish to what extent the new philosophy, in its imperialistic approach, was modeled on theology, while still taking the opposite point of view. The problem becomes simpler when this philosophy makes the same value judgments as its enemy, and is content merely to change the reasons. It is not easy to shed the old intellectual world, and this continuity is found in many spheres, notably moral science;[128] the Jews have had major cause to rue it. There is no better evidence of this than the works d'Holbach popularized: for this untiring propagandist left no stone unturned and proved very eclectic in his choice. In fact, it ranged from *Israël vengé ou Exposition naturelle des prophéties que les chrétiens appliquent à Jésus, leur prétendu Messie*, by the Talmudist Orobio de Castro,[129] to *L'Esprit du judaïsme ou examen raisonné de la loi de Moïse*. . . . He attributes this book to the deist, Anthony Collins, but its real author is unknown. In it, Fréret's arguments reappear:

> It is obvious that Christianity is only reformed Judaism. The revelation made to Moses serves as a foundation for the one which was later made by Jesus Christ: the latter constantly declared that he did not come to destroy but to fulfill the law of this law-giver of the Hebrews. The whole New Testament is therefore based on the Old. In a word, it is clear that the Judaic religion is the true basis of the Christian religion. . . .

As for the Jewish people:

> This people, uniquely cherished by an unchanging God, has become very weak and very wretched. Victim at all times of its fanaticism, of its unsociable religion, of its senseless law, it is now dispersed among all the nations, for whom it is a lasting monument to the terrible effects of superstitious blindness. . . .

We recognize the great deist idea of the people as living evidence of the error of revealed Christianity. In conclusion, the author urges his contemporaries to turn away their eyes from this wretched "monument," from those "cowardly and degraded Asiatics . . .":

Dare therefore at last, oh Europe, to shake off the intolerable yoke of the prejudices which afflict you! Leave to the stupid Hebrew, to the imbecilic fanatics, to the cowardly and degraded Asiatics, these superstitions which are as degrading as they are senseless; they are not made for the inhabitants of your clime . . . close your eyes for ever to these vain chimeras, which for so many centuries have done nothing but impede progress towards real science and divert you from the road to happiness!

Other sentiments are even more reminiscent of twentieth-century anti-Semitic propaganda and, specifically, lofty Nazi propaganda:

It must in fact be admitted that even while they perished the Jews were well avenged on the Romans, their conquerors. From the ruins of their country, a fanatic sect emerged which gradually polluted the whole Empire. . . .

Such was *L'Esprit du judaïsme* . . . .[130] Obviously the running fire was not always so sustained. Its violence varied from work to work in d'Holbach's publications. For example, *La contagion sacrée* . . . attributed to an Englishman, Trenchard, is restricted to the classic imprecations against

the terrible god of the Hebrews . . . A God of blood; it is with blood that he wishes to be appeased; it is with waves of blood that his fury must be disarmed; it is with cruelty that zeal for him must be evinced. . . .

Le christianisme dévoilé . . . by the encyclopedist, Nicolas Boulanger, discusses the people of this God, "the most ignorant, the stupidest, the most abject people, whose evidence carries no weight with me. . . . The Jews remain dispersed, because they are unsociable, intolerant, blindly attached to their superstitions. . . ." But almost all the books, whoever their real authors, fire broadsides of this sort. A notable example is in the famous *Tableau des saints* . . . probably by d'Holbach himself, which scrupulously imitates the great Christian treatises of anti-Talmudic polemic:[131]

As for real morals, modern Jews are as completely unaware of them as the ancients. They are neither more honest nor more just to foreigners than were their ancestors. They still think that everything is permissible against infidels or heretics. . . . Jewish scholars have frankly said that if a Jew sees an infidel on the point of dying or drowning, he should not save him or pull him out of the water, although he is not allowed to kill him if he is not fighting against the Israelites . . . he is not allowed to treat a sick infidel, not even for money, unless it is feared that he will do some harm to the Israelites if met with a refusal. . . .

In general, the conduct of modern Jews indicates that, like their ancestors, they feel no obligation towards those who are not members of their holy nation. They are famous for their fraudulence and their bad faith in trade, and there is reason to believe that if they were stronger, they would on many occasions have revived the tragedies for which their country was formerly the continual theater. . . .

However, the optimistic Baron has no doubt that *good* Jews do exist—Jews who ride roughshod over the Mosaic law:[132]

If, as cannot be doubted, honest and virtuous people can be found amongst them, it is because they do not conform to the principles of a law which is obviously calculated to make men unsociable and maleficent, an effect which the Bible and the saints it holds up as models must have produced. By regarding such a book as divinely inspired and as containing the rules of conduct, a man can only become unjust, without faith, without honor, without pity, in a word completely devoid of morals.

Consequently, although the atheists of the Holbachic school regarded the name "Jew" as damned for eternity, the bearers of the name still had the means of escaping their opprobrium by abandoning their faith. Christian converters did not deny this and, on this head, the crusaders of irreligion were hardly innovating.

It can be seen that the Baron was no "racist" in the current meaning of the word. But although the idea was not clearly formulated, it can also be seen that general suspicion was fed by the opinion of the time on the subject of the Jewish people, over-submissive victims of outdated superstitions. Here too, this attitude seems copied from Christian thought: if the individual Jew can be improved, it is by the action of a sort of philosophic act of grace (what Voltaire wished for Isaac Pinto).

At the same period, totally different men, the missionaries of science and progress, working in a totally different field, were laying the first foundations of future racist theories. We will be dealing with them in the next chapter.

Today, d'Holbach is emerging from anonymity and achieving posthumous fame primarily as a result of research by Marxist authors. His main publications have been reprinted regularly in the Soviet Union since 1924. His most recent French editor praises his "great effort of rationalist criticism [which] destroyed at its source the divine right of the feudal lords and their monarch, shook the very structure of his feudal society."[133] Most of his modern commentators pass over the "Synagogue's" anti-Jewish propaganda in silence. Others—like the aforementioned editor—point it out and say that "this attitude was progressive at the time. It would be a serious error to confuse it with the anti-Semitism and barbarous racism of twentieth-century fascists."[134] But surely there are grounds for thinking that there is some relationship, since the atheists' crusade took the Jews as its primary targets from the start?

The system builders

Lastly, I would wish that the distinctions that have been made amongst the different species, by a praiseworthy zeal for knowledge, had not gone beyond sensible limits. Some people, for example, have thought it appropriate to use the term race to designate four or five divisions suggested initially

by the color of the peoples, but I cannot see the reason for this nomenclature. . . .
(J.-G. Herder, *Ideen zur Philosophie der Geschichte der Menschheit*, VII, 1)

In the twentieth century, racism has become a political problem, one of the most serious world problems of our time. In the previous century, it was first and foremost a scientific doctrine, accepted throughout the West, professed in the universities and even reflected in primary education. It was becoming a historical factor to the extent to which dogmatically stated beliefs are historical factors. But where did it originate? *"Fecit cui prodest"*: today, it is most frequently regarded as an ideological weapon of the Western bourgeoisie, intended to justify the black slave trade and colonial depredation. And there is certainly a great deal of truth in this interpretation.

But in the same way as armament manufacturers did not create patriotism, racism a short time ago was also based on sincere conviction, giving birth to a doctrine which took shape at the same time as the human sciences, of which it was an integral part. If it was a system of belief, this belief was held first and foremost by scholars. Today, such sponsorship is scarcely acknowledged. Historians of science and ideas are abandoning this field where, more than in any other, the science of the Century of Enlightenment was the servant of philosophy, proceeding by volleys of assumptions, based on value judgments. A tangle like this is not easy to unravel, particularly when the object is to trace the boundary between the new sense of human dignity and the arrogance of Western white man. To succeed, a careful distinction must first be made between a conceptual system which was trying to become a science, and elemental feelings as old as man himself.

It seems that all historic societies and all human groups had an implicit tendency to think that they were "superior" to the others. The emotional roots of racism obviously lie in this tribal arrogance. Several primitive populations reserve the title of "men" solely for their own members and have a different word to designate their neighbors. To a world where there were as many gods as groups of men, the universal religions brought the concept of man's equality before a single God. In this sense, it can be said that dogmatic anti-racism came long before racism. This theoretical barrier never prevented the expression of pre-racist claims everywhere and in very varied ways. As far as Christian Europe is concerned we have dealt in another book[135] with the phenomenon of Iberian racism and the "purity of blood" statutes, which grew out of the claims of the nobility to distinctive "blood." The Spanish kings themselves were thought to be of Gothic or Visigothic blood, and this vague recollection of the barbarian invasions corresponds to a strange feature in European history: the over-valuation of Germanic blood, from the most distant times. On this subject, the first propounders of the glories of "Germanity" were fond of referring back to Tacitus[136] and it might even be asked if the flattering descriptions in *Germania* did not in their way express certain cultural features of the old tribes east of the Rhine. Whatever the answer to that perhaps insoluble question, from the eighteenth century, the Germans, called "Germanomanes," whose numbers were ever-increasing, tried to conform to the ethnographic model the great Roman historian had drawn.[137] Moreover, such claims to biological superiority could feed on European historical tradition as well as on the geographical nomenclature of the Continent, from Lombardy to the land of the Angles and from the Island of Gotland to France.[138] For example, the French nobility's desire to maintain its privileges drove some of its defenders to claim the noble blood of the Franks as opposed to the "Gallo-Roman commonalty."

Over a century before Gobineau, Comte Henry de Boulainvilliers can count as one of the real ancestors of racism.[139] This curious character turns up at many significant junctures: he introduced Spinoza into France and was also one of the founders of a "scientific astrology," which also

denied free will.[140] As far as race was concerned, the French
nation had, since the chronicle of Fredegarius, that is to say
since the eighth century, been thought to go back to the
Trojans through Aeneas and King "Francion" (remember
Ronsard's *La Franciade*). An innovator on this point too,
Boulainvilliers set out to show that it was descended from
the Franks, but restricted this pedigree to the nobility, excluding the third estate. He wrote: [141]

> In the beginning the French were completely free and perfectly
> equal and independent . . . their sole reason for fighting against
> the Romans and Barbarians for such a long time was to secure
> that precious liberty which they regarded as their dearest
> possession . . . after the conquest of the Gauls, they were the
> only people acknowledged as nobles, that is to say as lords and
> masters. . . .

The phraseology used here identifies its ancient origins.
More rational than the Trojan genealogy, Boulainvilliers's
thesis formed part and parcel of the quarrel between
ancients and moderns, as well as reflecting the nobles' insurrection against the Sun King's policy. But it was a commoner
whom we have already mentioned, Nicolas Fréret (a protégé
of Boulainvilliers), who took it up. He expanded these ideas
in a long dissertation which tried to establish a sort of legal
basis for the claims of the bearers of Frankish blood. He
stated notably that the Gauls accepted the Germanic yoke
pacifically and even voluntarily. "The Gauls," he wrote, "wanted Frankish rule. . . . the conquest of Gaul and the occupation by the Franks took place without violence and in a way
which was pleasing to the people. . . ."[142] He was saying, in
fact, that the Gauls themselves had acknowledged their own
inferiority.

Such a thesis did not fail to arouse opposition, and after a
while authors such as Mably and Sieyès formulated systems
with contrary indications, though on the same genealogical
base, glorifying the third estate. In his famous pamphlet,
Sieyès even proposed sending the aristocrats back "to their

forests of Franconia."[143] Whatever the value judgment, the idea of a Gallo-Roman commonalty as opposed to a Frankish nobility, which was the subject of fresh discussion after the Revolution, could be used impartially to support the case for a "class struggle" or a "race struggle," to supply the key to universal history according to Marx or to Gobineau—as did in fact come to pass.

Neither Boulainvilliers nor Fréret was yet employing the term *race*, although it had already been in current use for a long time. The men who introduced it in its present generic sense did not have political ambitions and are rightly numbered amongst the founders of the human sciences. However, the choice of term remains significant.

It is a well-known fact that biology recognizes *sub-species* or *varieties* within a species. These terms are only replaced by the word "race" in the case of man and the domestic animals which surround him and which are linked to him by an emotional bond. Many naturalists and anthropologists have commented on this semantic anomaly.[144] The origin of the word "race" is uncertain but it appeared in Europe as early as the sixteenth century, notably in colloquial French, meaning "generation" or "descent." Right from the start it implied a value judgment: "nobility of race" as opposed to "common race," good race as opposed to bad.

> Race of the gods of France, honor of the world,
> My prince, my Lord, the support of my verses.
> (P. Desportes, *Angélique*)

> It was Jews. It was an insolent race.
> Spread over the world, they cover its face.
> (Racine, *Esther*, II, 2)

"Bon chien, chasse de race" ("what's bred in the bone comes out in the flesh"). It would seem that the term, in its generic and scholarly sense, was applied to animals before men. In France, around 1765, the *Encyclopédie* limits its use in this sense to "particular species of a few animals, primarily

horses."[145] In Germany, in about 1785, the philosopher Herder was doubtful about applying "this ignoble word" (*unedel*) to the human species.[146] These examples suggest that the word "race" applied to a man tended to carry the same pejorative overtone as calling him a "beast" or an "animal." Dictionaries show that a remnant of this overtone still exists today.[147]

However, as early as the beginning of the eighteenth century, a strange precursor of transformism, Benoît de Maillet, was talking about the human *races,* which according to him, had emerged from the sea.[148]

Another follower of *avant la lettre* "polygenism," Voltaire, strongly emphasized the Europeans' racial superiority, "men who to me seem superior to Negroes, as Negroes to monkeys and monkeys to oysters. . . ."[149]

Later, thinkers with a more methodical turn of mind laid the foundations of future anthropology. But the rejection of the Biblical cosmogony left them with a clear field for their theories which very often do not flatter the "savages." The value judgments thus made show the influence of the youthful bourgeois arrogance, characteristic of enlightened society at the time. The materialist thought of the Enlightenment brought to bear on tearing the secrets of the soul from the body, was probably also partially responsible. The general direction of anthropological thought was to continue on these lines. For generations, scholars were to do their utmost to find material and tangible proofs, contained within the body, of the intellectual and moral superiority of the white man, not resigning themselves to the fact that his biological composition is the same as a Negro's and similar to a monkey's. The rapid spread of the word and idea of "race" is very illuminating in all these respects.

Their great popularizer was first and foremost Buffon, whose status as an international authority in the Century of Enlightenment was second only to Voltaire's.[150] For the author of the *Histoire naturelle,* the universe was a pyramid with man at the top. He wrote:[151]

Everything about man, even externally, marks his superiority over all other living things: he holds himself straight and erect, his attitude is one of command, his head looks to the sky and presents a majestic brow bearing the stamp of his dignity; the image of the soul is reflected in his expression; the excellence of his nature breaks through the material organs and lights the features of his visage with divine fire; his majestic bearing, his firm, bold step announce his nobility and rank. . . .

But Buffon only found this dignity and these prerogatives to be fully present in European white man. He alone incarnated pure human nature: all other races would have "degenerated" from it. In his treatise *De la dégénération des animaux*[152] Buffon expands this idea, first introduced, it seems, by the mathematician, Maupertuis, in his *Vénus physique*.[153] A proponent of the concept of the unity of the human species, he assumes that man has undergone "alterations" of a degenerating nature as he has spread over the world:

> . . . they have been slight in temperate regions, which we assume are next to his place of origin: but they have got larger as he has moved further away, and when . . . he began to populate the sands of the South and the ice of the North, the change has become so substantial that there would be grounds for believing that the *Negro*, the *Lapp* and the *White* form different species, if there had not been only one single Man created. . . .

Buffon even suggested an experiment *in vivo* to establish how many generations of Negroes transplanted into Europe would be required to restore man's nature:

> These Negroes would have to be cloistered together with their females, and their race scrupulously maintained without allowing them to interbreed; this is the only means that could be employed to find out how much time would be required to restore man's nature in this respect, and by the same process of

reasoning how much was needed to change from white to black. . . .

The Negroes' degeneration might have made them inferior men, but Buffon gave the prize for sub-humanity to the Lapps. His *Histoire naturelle de l'homme* gives an eloquent description of these "abortions":[154]

> Not only are these peoples alike in their ugliness, their small stature, the color of their hair and eyes, but almost all of them also have the same propensities and the same morals, they are all equally coarse, superstitious, stupid ... without courage, without self-respect, without modesty: this abject people only has enough morals to make them despised.

To support his opinion, Buffon informed his readers that the Lapps carried immodesty to the point of bathing completely nude, all together, boys and girls, mothers and sons, brothers and sisters. He then let it be understood that the Lapps' only sign of humanity was that they were aware of their own abjection. In fact, they had the bizarre custom of offering their women to strangers. "As can happen with people who are aware of their own deformity and the ugliness of their women, they apparently find the ones that foreigners have not scorned less ugly."[155] This relationship between the "savages'" sexual customs and their awareness of their inferiority can also be found in Diderot. Offering his daughters and his wife to the Europeans, the Tahitian comments:[156]

> We are more robust and healthier than you, but we saw that you surpassed us in intelligence and we immediately destined a few of our most beautiful wives and daughters to receive the seed of a better race than ours.

This idea can firstly be explained by the state of knowledge at the time, and Buffon's opinion of the Lapps corresponds to what Régnard and Maupertuis said about them in their travelogues.[157] Other travelers brought back even more horrible stories[158] about the Negroes, whom the Europeans, Herder tells us, tended to regard as symbols of evil.[159] But these descriptions also reflected, in their very principle, the fundamental error in the method of anthropology at its beginnings. This lay in the arbitrary coupling of physical description, aesthetic appreciation and of a moral judgment based on the certainty of the existence of moral "laws" which were just as universal as the laws of Reason. In fact, the new eschatology of progress was patterned on the eschatology of the Church. The nascent science did not extricate itself from the imperialist domination of theology, its predecessor, and was living on a capital of thought habits fed by Christian moral science. From this, there came the belief in a *natural law* governing all spheres of life, and the confusion between facts and law, between explanatory science and the normative disciplines (a confusion maintained by the ambiguity of the term *law,* applied indiscriminately to the phenomena of the physical world, the precepts of the Revelation, the commands of the ruler, and the ethical standards: "the moral laws are the same everywhere," wrote Diderot in the *Encyclopédie*).[160]

The fallacious coupling of men's tangible "physical natures" and their intangible "mental" and even moral natures also occurs in the classification by Linnaeus, Buffon's great rival, although this pious Christian was infinitely less of an extremist than the French naturalist, whose religious beliefs were questionable.[161] In his *Systema Naturae*, Linnaeus postulated the existence of four varieties of the species *Homo sapiens* ("Americanus," "Europaeus," "Asiaticus," and "Asser") within the order of *Primates*, which included monkeys. The four varieties differed from each other not only in color of epidermis and hair but in customs and temperament. But although he compared the "gaudy, greedy" Asiatic, and particularly the "sly, lazy, negligent" African, the servile *Homo Asser*, with the "inventive and ingenious" European, he headed his classification with the "opinionated, self-satisfied, freedom-loving" American – which it is tempting to regard as the result of a certain Christian humility. About his order of Primates, Linnaeus wrote: "I can discover no difference between man and troglodyte [the anthropoid ape] without taking in doubtful characteristics, although all my attention has been given to this point. . . ."[162] But the very fact of "not discovering the soul at the end of his scalpel" served him as proof to support his faith. He wrote:[163]

> when we submit the human body to the anatomist's scalpel in order to find something in the structure of its organs not found *in other animals,* we are obliged to acknowledge the vanity of our research. It is therefore necessary to trace our prerogative back to something absolutely immaterial, that the Creator has only given man and which is the soul. . . .

His French emulators, who did not possess this teleological resort, clamored indignantly: for them, the dignity of human nature had been challenged. Criticizing Linnaeus's system, where horse and ass belonged to the same order (or "family"), Buffon exclaimed:[164]

> . . . it will equally be possible to say that the monkey belongs to the family of man, that it is a degenerated man; that man and monkey have a common origin. . . . Naturalists who so lightly establish families in animals and vegetables do not appear to be aware of the full extent of these consequences.

These are quarrels about method, it is true, but a new conception of man, specifically of white man, is also involved. Buffon wrote a little further on: "Men differ from black to white in color, from single to double in height, bulk, agility, strength, etc. and from everything to nothing in mind." His collaborator, Daubenton, likewise criticized Linnaeus for abusing *human nature*:[165]

> I am always surprised to find man in the primary genus, immediately below the general heading of quadrupeds, which is the title the class is given: a strange place for man! What

inappropriate classification, what spurious method, ranks man with four-legged animals! ... It is certain that by his nature, man should not be confused with any species of animal, and consequently should not be included in a class of quadrupeds, nor comprised in the same order as monkeys and sloths. ...

A priori metaphysics are evident on both sides, and Linnaeus was not embarrassed to find no structural differences where he *knew* that God had placed distinctions of another order. A polemic which the anatomist Johann Meckel senior, surgeon to Frederick II, directed against his famous Dutch colleague Peter Camper illustrates the opposite approach of a freethinker. After dissecting Negroes in 1757, Meckel discovered that their brains were darker than Europeans' and their blood black, "so black, that instead of reddening the linen, as blood usually does, it blackened it." From this, he concluded that Negroes formed "almost another species of men, in respect of internal structure."[166] Camper commented:

> The fact that he was unaccustomed to seeing Negroes probably gave him a sort of repugnance for and a horror of their color. ... I therefore resolved, if it were possible, to use this interesting material to throw some light on the belief of the Christian religion, whereby at the beginning of the world God only created one single man, who was Adam, to whom we owe our origin, whatever the cast of features and color of skin that differentiates us. ...

To support this thesis, Camper invoked the case of the Jews; there were dark ones ("Portuguese"), and fair ones ("Teutonics"); but everyone knew that they went back to the same root. Having first propounded his conclusions, he ended his proof by urging Europeans to "stretch out a fraternal hand to the Negroes and acknowledge them as descendants of the first man, whom we all consider as our common father."[167] His efforts were in vain. Another pioneer of experimental medicine, the anatomist Soemmering, announced in 1784 that, whatever might be said, Negroes were more closely related to monkeys than were Europeans.[168]

It is hardly necessary to add that Christian "anti-racism" of the time, however humanitarian it was, was fundamentally based on the defense of the Biblical cosmogony and only incidentally and secondarily involved in protecting the human dignity of exotic peoples. Jacques Roger devotes a chapter in his recent book, *Les Sciences de la vie dans la pensée française du XVIIIe siècle,* to "Opposition to the new science," the science of Maupertuis and Buffon. From this, it would appear that no critic attacked the views on the Negroes and Lapps, and that although Buffon was censured by the Paris Faculté de Théologie, it was for challenging the account of the Creation.[169] In the following century, the roles were reversed when the Churches faced with Darwin's evolutionism tried to emphasize the distance between man and monkey, since it is into man alone that God had breathed a soul (Genesis, II, 7).

Thus the growing tendency for the new Promethean man of the Century of Enlightenment, the artisan of science and progress, to take the place of God at the summit of Creation corresponded to the widening gap which separated him from other creatures, quadrupeds, monkeys and savages. The emancipation of science from ecclesiastical tutelage, the abandonment of the Biblical cosmogony and the neglect of Christian values left the way clear for racist theories. With some well-known scholars of the time, they were already assuming a Manichean character. The German philosopher Christoph Meiners, for example, believed that he had discovered the existence of two human races: the "pale, beautiful" race and the "dark, ugly" race, in contrast with one another like virtue with vice. This theory, he promised, made it possible to fathom the secret of the "superior men" who only sprang from noble peoples:

Only the peoples of Tatar stock knew true bravery, love of freedom and the other passions and virtues of great souls. . . .

Most Mongolian nations unite to an irritability born of weakness and an incredible sensitivity to the slightest insult and a revolting apathy to the joys and sorrows of others, even their closest relations, an unyielding hardness, selfishness and an almost complete lack of all sympathetic impulses and feelings.

From Buffon, Meiners borrowed the idea of the inferior peoples' awareness of their inferiority:[170]

Admittedly certain savages of the Mongolian tribe imagined themselves superior to the Europeans but on the whole they acknowledged the greater gifts of the more noble peoples and this acknowledgment is found most clearly in the custom of offering their wives and daughters to the superior men.

Within the framework of the moralizing estheticism of German pre-Kantian philosophy, the white race thus seems to Meiners to stand out against the other races like light to darkness, or good to evil. A French scholar who was something of an authority at the beginning of the nineteenth century, Jean-Joseph Virey, returned to this classification in 1800 in his *Histoire naturelle du genre humain*:

We will here describe the general characteristics of each of the human races which can principally be divided into beautiful whites, and ugly browns or blacks. . . . Celtic and even Sarmatian or Slavonic descendants in fact present oval, pleasant and very symmetrical faces. . . . Finally, the proud and noble forms, generous souls, frank and industrious natures, the beauty, valor, intelligence, perfection and the social virtues raise this race of men above the servile flock of other mortals who crawl, sadly attached to the earth, in base uniformity. What would our world be without Europeans?

The European was also destined to govern the world:[171]

The European, called by his high destiny to dominion of the world, which he can enlighten with his intelligence and subdue by his valor, is the man *par excellence*, and the head of the human race; the others, vile rabble of barbarians, are only as it were, the embryo. . . .

This did not prevent Virey, as a good son of the Revolution, from deploring the sad fate of the black slaves (while still letting it be understood that it was their own fault).[172] This is all the more remarkable in that he believed that the Negro was closer to the orang-utang than to white man,[173] and consequently tended towards the theory of polygenism. Scholars at that period had insight into the question of human origins which we no longer possess. Another son of the revolutionary generation, Saumarez, had the idea in 1798 of measuring intelligence by comparing the cranial capacity of Blacks and Whites.[174] He contributed in this way to jamming anthropology into the metric groove where it remained stuck for over a century.

It will be noticed that although all these scholars considered the white man superior to the colored, they did not generally make this sort of distinction between the various European populations. In this sense, they remained good eighteenth-century cosmopolitans (which after all, worked to the Jews' advantage; even the systems of Virey and Meiners implicitly ranked them with the "fair race"). New distinctions were to appear with the help of the Napoleonic Wars and the explosion of Chauvinism, tying up the patriotic singers of Arminius and the Teuton forest with the theories of Boulainvilliers, Fréret and their German homologues. At that time too, the craniological or physiological superstition, a legacy of French materialist philosophy, received the addition of the philological superstition sired by German spiritualistic philosophy and giving birth in its turn to the great myth of the "Aryan race." This will be discussed later.

Meanwhile, other men, with more strictly scientific minds, were guiding nascent anthropology on to better paths. Kant, who conferred his authority on the use of the unhappy word "race" to designate the great sub-divisions of mankind, refrained from any value judgment in the classification he suggested (copied from Linnaeus). In particular, he embarked on an epistemological discussion of the concept which is still valuable.[175] It contains an interesting passage in which he criticized a proposal for "eugenic selection" for purposes of improving the human race, made by Maupertuis, the first president of the Prussian Academy of Science.[176]

His contemporary and correspondent, Blumenbach, generally regarded as the true founder of anthropology, proposed a new classification of the human races on authentic scientific lines. His five races, which he described remarkably precisely, were neither "good" nor "bad." Nonetheless his caution deserted him at the end of his treatise, where he eulogized the faces of the white (or "Caucasian") people, which

> . . . generally makes them thought the most beautiful and the most pleasant. . . . I have given this variety, the name of Mount Caucasus because the most beautiful race of men, the Georgian, is found in its vicinity and because, if the cradle of the human race can be fixed, all physiological reasons combine to place it at that spot. . . . Finally, the Georgians' skin is white, and this color still appears originally to belong to the human race, but it easily degenerates into a darkish color. . . .

The theory formulated by Maupertuis and Buffon can be recognized here; Blumenbach was strengthening it with arguments drawn from the realm of esthetic contemplation, in accordance with the contemporary German attitude. And his academic enthusiasm glides from Georgian faces to Georgian skulls, "those beautifully shaped skulls, from which the others seem to be derived, until they come to the furthermost points, the skulls of Malayans and Negroes."[177]

The same enthusiasm is responsible for another craniological observation which originated with Blumenbach. He wrote:[178]

> It is known that the Jewish people have been spread over the whole world for centuries on end, and have nevertheless kept a

pure and very characteristic type; this strange fact has long worried naturalists and physiologists. But what is even more remarkable and as yet little known, is the fact that this type is clearly evident even in the skulls. I have had several opportunities of verifying this, because even laymen have been able to recognize Jewish skulls amongst the many skulls in my cupboards.

Nonetheless, this scholar made no value judgment on the Jews, whom he classified as a people and not a race.[179]

But contemporary opinion unanimously accorded this people a common descent, and writers and polemicists were applying the term "race" to it before professional scholars were so doing. It is difficult to escape the impression that scholars allowed the discussion by the writers and polemicists to influence their thinking, and that an interchange imperceptibly took place between the prejudices of the populace and the specialists' laboratories. In any case, the use of the word *race* in its scientific sense, and its extension to the Jews, spread within one or two decades. It was almost as if it corresponded to a secret need of enlightened society, notably in Germany, where racial systems multiplied at the dawn of the nineteenth century (as will be seen later). A remarkable example is supplied by a pamphlet, *Wider die Juden* (1803), by the lawyer Grattenauer: it shows the hesitant abandonment of the religious motive to justify the disparagement of the Jews, in favor of the argument supported by the prestige of science:[180]

That the Jews are an altogether separate race of men cannot be challenged by any historian and anthropologist. But the assertion of the curious antiquary, formerly universally maintained and accompanied by explanatory copper engravings, that God had punished the Jews with a special odor, with many hereditary defects, secret maladies and repulsive crimes can be fully proven as little as it can be completely refuted from any conceivable teleological viewpoint. . . .

In France at the same period, Napoleon was found applying the term "race" to the Jews, using it indiscriminately in the old theological meaning ("race covered with censure") or in the new anthropological sense ("race with polluted blood").[181] In this respect, the Emperor's ideas were no clearer than Grattenauer's, but both were expressing the common belief. The substitution of the racial for the old religious motives for anti-Semitism was loaded with consequences for the Jews, clothing their image in even more sinister tones. Their abasement in the eyes of those who despised them tended to become irremediable, and the outlook of the scientific age supplied the necessary support for this opinion. In effect, if they were biologically bad, their badness was identical with their supposedly material Jewish essence. No good faith, no submission, no pardon or baptismal water could alter this. Moreover, this view was in accordance with the new scientific ideas about living things.

According to the Christian or Judeo-Christian vision of the world, the course of all things was in the final analysis governed by the mysterious will of a transcendental God. After having made the heavens and the stars spring from nothingness, the creator of the universe formed the animal as well as the human species, and ensured its *procreation* from generation to generation, each human being receiving its immortal soul (to the Jews, the breath of life) from Him. Thus the moving impulse or animation was given to living things and conspicuously to human beings *from without*. To the Jew, this meant amongst other things, that if he was evil, it was not solely his own fault but also the result of a certain arbitrariness or whim of God, who in His omnipotence always remained free to revise His judgment. This gave rise to both hope for the Jew and extenuating circumstances.

When modern science had dismantled the great wheels of the physical world and embarked on an exploration of the mystery of life, it came up against insurmountable difficulties. In effect, no physical or mechanical model accounted satisfactorily for organic growth and in particular for its infinite reproduction from generation to generation, through the chain of living beings. The theory of the "pre-existence" or "nesting" of germs, germ within germ, came up against a mathematical impasse. It was therefore necessary, in the absence of a principle of transcendental and external action (such as the obsolete Biblical cosmogony provided), to acknowledge a principle of internal vital or motive organization, immanent in nature ("natural"). E. Voegelin has suggestively defined this major trend in the thought of the Century of Enlightenment, as the "interiorization of corporeality" (*Verinnerlichung des Leibes*).[182]

Some people continued to envisage this internal moving force as an immaterial soul, common to man and animals, constituting the "intrinsic animal." But the greater number relegated it to inside matter itself, a matter which felt, thought and formed organs. There was no shortage of suggestions for formulae to designate the principle of all organic life, invented *ad hoc* or borrowed from medieval terminology: genetic power, plastic or vital, motive or pervasive, internal mold or generating impulse. But this logomachy did not hide the resort to an occult quality. Driven out through the door, scholasticism came in at the window, and the opium induced sleep because it had soporific powers.

The great Blumenbach was one of the men most alive to the difficulty:[183]

> I call this force generating impulse to differentiate it from other actions of the vital power, insignificant expressions of plastic force and the like, which the ancients used without attaching any precise meaning to them. I am not claiming to designate a cause by this but rather a perpetual abstract effect, always true to itself in the constancy and universality of its phenomena. It is in this way that the words *attraction* and *gravity* are employed to designate certain forces, the causes of which remain buried in the deepest darkness. . . .

But scientific posterity most frequently lost sight of this problem. It was the generative impulse which became the adequate explanation for the nineteenth-century European mental concept of the universe, in which Newtonian attraction had taken the place of the "prime mover" of the past. This impulse, given the name of instinct (vital, racial), made everything in the realm of the phenomena of life explicable. Gone were the days of the universal scholar-philosophers of the Century of Enlightenment who, headstrong as they were, found the leisure and had the inclination to question the metaphysical assumptions of their science. The increasing specialization of scientific work, even the accumulation of knowledge, did the rest. Specialists and the public at large succumbed to the magic of words and formulae. The time of the scientistic religion and M. Homais had arrived.

As for the Jew, the new turn of mind had the effect of depicting him as bad "in himself" because he was biologically what he was, and no transcendental agent, God or Devil, had the power to change whatever it was that he was. The progress made by biology and the discovery of the genetic laws only confirmed this view. The Jew's responsibility became total and inexorable; the harmfulness inherent in his race and blood was derived from a scientific "necessity." Thus the implacable sentence carried out by the German Third Reich was justified metaphysically long beforehand.

The regenerators

> The real question in this case is to know if the Jews are men.
> (*Pierre-Louis Lacretelle*)

Being neither intrinsically good nor intrinsically bad, science could be used to guarantee all types of political philosophy in the same way as it could be influenced by them in formulating its working hypotheses and laying down its assumptions. Needless to say, this interpenetration was particularly close in the Century of Enlightenment, so much so that it could be called a fusion. This optimistic century believed in the infinite perfectibility of men. It believed that rational reforms and laws would be sufficient to ensure the blossoming and happiness of a human nature which was assumed to be fundamentally good. Even if prevailing opinion did not think that this goodness was strictly uniform, since it tended to vary as we have seen with customs and skin color, all races and all human groups were considered perfectible or open to improvement. And this applied, however far removed they might be from the norm, that is to say in the final analysis, from the image of enlightened society as it liked to see itself; witness Buffon's hypothesis on degeneration and regeneration.

When discussing the image of the large aberrant groups as they actually were and especially in a Catholic country like France, a distinction has to be made between Protestants, Jews and Negroes.

Enlightened French society unquestionably regarded the Protestants as having all the characteristics of human nature. Agitation had been systematically carried on on their behalf since the middle of the eighteenth century. This agitation could not help but be stimulated by the persistence the Catholic Church devoted to maintaining their subjection to special laws. From the clergy's point of view, they did in fact remain dangerous heretics. An anti-Protestant polemicist even wrote about them as follows:[184]

> ... God loved the Jews passionately in the past and has only temporarily suspended his love for them, whereas he has nothing but abhorrence for heretics and promises them nothing but punishment. ... After the Catholics, the Jews are unquestionably the most illustrious and most respectable people of all, whereas the heretics are the shame of Christianity and the ruin of all nations. However, I do not wish to conclude from all this that tolerance be owing to the Jews on grounds of justice. ...

An echo of this particular attitude on the part of the clergy recurs in Abbé Grégoire's famous work in favor of the emancipation of the Jews. Proposing to grant them complete religious freedom, he himself raised an objection: "But we are going to be told that the Protestants will demand the same privileges ..." and brushes it aside in confusion and embarrassment.[185]

On the other hand, a high official sympathetic to liberal ideas drew a completely different parallel between the descendants of Calvin and Moses. He wrote:

It is not possible to rank Protestants and Jews in the same class; the former have only been cut off from our society to its great detriment. Joined to us by all the ties of blood, by a great similarity of morals and principles, by every advantageous relationship, they cannot but be usefully and rightfully reinstated in their citizenship.

The Jews, on the contrary:

... in all places and at all times, have had only one plan, one line of conduct, which is to look on all the peoples of the land as enemies. . . . They see, they will always see, their descendants as the rulers of the nations; and it is by robbing us of all metals (that is to say, gold and silver) that they hope to accelerate the conquest. . . .

In another connection, this author demonstrated his enlightenment by declaring that he was not prejudiced "against the individuals of that nation, nor against their belief." In conclusion, he asked his "enlightened government" to repair a "twofold error":[186]

The Protestants, our co-citizens and our brethren, have been outlawed by the same kings who granted the Jews the right of natives of the country. Under a government as enlightened as ours, the prolongation of this double error can no longer be feared.

As for the Negroes, all classes of society probably felt an

even greater aversion to them than to the Jews. Montesquieu's cutting irony recalls it:[187]

> These creatures are all over black, and with such a flat nose, that they can scarcely be pitied.
>
> It is hardly to be believed that God, who is a wise being, should place a soul, especially a good soul, in such a black ugly body.

But these blacks were slaves, and the spectacular and quasi-metaphysical antithesis of liberty–slavery secured them consequential advocates (Turgot, Abbé Raynal, Bernardin de Saint-Pierre) in the third quarter of the eighteenth century, as well as a ready-made audience. On the plane of polemical argument, their case was faultless, from the very fact of their servile state: no corrupting ambition or plan for universal domination could be ascribed to them, or even enter into anyone's mind.

Where the Jews were concerned, enlightened circles were beginning to take an interest in their condition in around 1775-80. This interest coincided with the spread of a humanitarian attitude which was moved by the fate of all outcasts of fortune. It was not that the new bourgeois public opinion had perceptibly revised its views of Judaism, or even the Jew; it remained on the whole ill-disposed. It was more a question of an assumption of responsibility, of serious reflection on the part of enlightened society on its conduct: if the persecuted nation presented a multitude of defects, would not the fault devolve on us who had first persecuted it? And did we not owe it reparation?

This viewpoint was strongly expressed by the lawyer Pierre-Louis Lacretelle the younger, as early as 1775, in a plea which was later published at his clients' expense. It did not flatter

> this people who seem born for degradation, adversity and cunning. They are, if you like, a nation apart, a degenerated nation, to whom neither fame, nor honor nor anything what-

soever which gladdens the heart of man can belong. ... But is
this the fault of the man? Is it only the fault of his position?

Lacretelle was asking the tribunal to revise the "senseless
laws" in his clients' favor, and to pronounce their "decree of
regeneration. Let this low greed for profit, this despicable
callousness, this cruel defiance, this dark habit of double
dealing and usury leave their hearts!" He did not doubt that
this prayer could be fulfilled, once society had rendered
justice to the Jews:[188]

> It is not necessary before peoples like yourselves, messieurs, to
> refute the barbarous and senseless view which leads a few
> spirits who thrive on the suspicion of evil, to believe that the
> vices we have just outlined are inherent in the very nature of
> the Jews; that they are inseparable from their customs, their
> ideas, their religion itself. ...

The new campaigns on the Jews' behalf were not entirely
spontaneous. Rich Jews were stimulating them in a variety of
ways by supplying their protagonists with arguments, by
having their works printed or translated, by besieging
powerful or influential personalities, first and foremost court
circles. (An army contractor, Hertz Cerfberr, made numerous
attempts of this type in 1780-90.)[189] On the other hand, this
was an eminently international campaign, with its main
center in the Germanic countries. The question had been
on the agenda for a long time there and, in Berlin, Moses
Mendelssohn was offering an astonished world the spectacle
of regeneration incarnate, a Jewish philosopher. The vital
share the German Jews took in their emancipation will be
discussed in the following chapter. It is interesting to note, as
far as France is concerned, that the main works offered the
public were translated from German, like Lessing's *Les Juifs*
(1781) or *De la réforme politique des Juifs* by Dohm (1782),
translated by the mathematician Jean Bernouilli, a member
of the Berlin Academy of Sciences, at Cerfberr's expense.
This was also the case with the *Traité de droit mosaïque* by

J.-D. Michaelis and *L'Instruction salutaire* ... by Hartwig Wessely.[190] In 1787, Mirabeau, who had visited Jewish salons in Berlin, published his book *Sur Moses Mendelssohn* or *De la réforme politique des Juifs.* It began in a manner which was very typical of the time: "A man hurled by nature into the bosom of a debased horde." On the eve of the Revolution, he was preparing a second book on "this subject which is infinitely worthy of interest."[191]

This agitation did not fail to arouse misgivings, and these are reflected in a few fashionable publications (*L'Évangile du jour, La Défense de mon oncle, La Philosophie de l'Histoire*) which drew their clearest arguments from Voltaire's arsenal. In 1770, a fairly well known author, Louis-Sébastien Mercier, had published a novel of the future, *L'An 2440, rêve s'il en fût jamais.* In 1786, he added a chapter in which his dream was enriched by a vision which foreshadowed both the Protocol of the Elders of Zion and the Hitler genocide. The narrator of 2440 notes:[192]

> The Jews increased almost supernaturally, under the contempt of the nations who became so tolerant of them that they finally thought the time had come to revive the Mosaic law and announce it to the world by all the means which great wealth gave them ... regarding themselves as an earlier people than the Christians and created in order to subjugate them, [they] joined together under a leader to whom they attributed everything that is marvelous, made to stir the imagination and to prepare them for the greatest and most extraordinary revolutions. ... The title of *King of the Jews* bestowed on an ambitious person had given rise to a political storm, the reverberations of which did not fail to disquiet us. We did not want great bloodshed and this people, for its part, were prepared to renew all the horrors that its history offers, and of which it has been the agent or the victim. You had allowed this ferment which was silently penetrating all the countries of Europe to lie dormant. Its furor terrified us for it seemed to want no one left alive on the globe except believers attached to the Mosaic

law. . . . Decisive action had to be taken to repress the ferocious superstition.

Mercier, the author of *Tableaux de Paris,* can be regarded as the mouthpiece of the guilds.

Elsewhere, the Jews' merits and demerits continued to be discussed by way of proceedings brought against God. The case that the German baron, Anacharsis Cloots, opened in Paris in 1783, was based on the denial of the miraculous character of the survival of Judaism and his reasoning was not unlike John Toland's in places. The spokesman for the Parisian Protestants, Court de Gébélin, defended traditional belief, and the dispute was carried on over the heads of the Jews.

Court de Gébélin exclaimed:

How could you say that if Constantine had Judaized, everyone would have become Jewish? Only considering this emperor as a politician, he was too skillful to antagonize every pagan and every Christian in favor of the circumcised, vile despicable, out-and-out usurers, who are crassly ignorant and whose local religion could in no way serve as a rallying cry for men. As for the substance of your treatise which overlooks the fact that any people which has no resources only continues to exist through ingenuity and speculation, for the Jew is more of a speculator than a merchant, more of a usurer than a trader. . . .

"Everything M. de Gébélin says about Constantine and the Jews arouses pity!" replied Cloots. "The Judaic religion made incredible progress in the Roman Empire. . . ." He then moved on to the Carolingians "who had such a high regard for the Jews," and enlarged "on their usefulness in the development of trade." "France would be doing England a very bad service by recalling them in all its ports. . . ." (This was at the time of the American War of Independence.)

"As for the crass ignorance with which M. de Gébélin taxes the Jews, I do see this ignorance in places but not amongst the 'circumcised.'" To support this, Cloots listed the rabbis of Amsterdam "whose very names make Christian theology tremble" and, of course, he did not forget to cite Moses Mendelssohn.[193]

From the political point of view, a radical reform of the status of French Jews was henceforth an accepted fact. The enlightened despot, Joseph II of Austria, had set the example by promulgating successive "edicts of tolerance" for the Protestants (1781) and for the Jews (1783). His brother-in-law Louis XVI instructed Malesherbes to settle the question of the Protestants in 1787, and then entrusted him with the study of the problem of the Jews. This great servant of the crown collected advice from experts such as Lacretelle and Roederer as well as Cerfberr and Gradis (the representative of the Portuguese Jews). He read copiously amongst historical material and concluded that a reform of the Jews was as indispensable as it was difficult. In his opinion, the Jews did not form a state within the State, but a state within States (*imperium in imperiis*). He compared them from this point of view with the Jesuits. As with the Jesuits, "the leaders of this nation come to the help of individuals as much as is necessary to prevent them being driven to leave this religion by despair, but never more than is required for that purpose." He traced back to the prophet Jeremiah and the Babylonian captivity a policy consisting of "riding out the storm, while awaiting the realization of the great dream of the return to the Promised Land, and living amongst the conquering nation without mingling with it and always remaining a foreign nation." But for him there was no question of making the ordinary Jewish people expiate the faults of their leaders: "These unfortunates, who are nevertheless men, would not find asylum anywhere and expulsion would be almost as great a barbarism as the expulsion of the Moors from Spain in 1610."[194]

Malesherbes retired from public affairs in 1788 before he had presented his plan for reform, and the Revolution occurred shortly afterwards. How imminent the emancipation of the Jews seemed, emerges from the imperceptibly insolent tone of a letter Cerfberr addressed to the King:[195]

> Whatever your Majesty's views may be; whether through a
> remnant of sympathy for old prejudices, he only wishes to raise
> the Jews to the rank of citizen by degrees, or whether his
> powerful hand is preparing completely to break the bonds
> which hold this unfortunate people in their wretchedness. . . .

With emancipation on the agenda, the Metz Academy set
a competition in 1785 on the theme: "Are there ways of
making the Jews happier and more useful in France?"—a
statement which postulated that they were neither happy
nor useful. Almost all the ten replies received reflected the
spirit of the Enlightenment, a spirit which believed that all
problems could be solved by enacting good laws, and which
anticipated the centralizing and leveling effect of the Revolution. For example, Abbé Grégoire expressed the hope of the
eradication of "that type of slang, that Teutonic-Hebraic-
rabbinic jargon German Jews use, which only serves to
deepen ignorance or to mask trickery." He then went on to
express a general wish for the "annihilation of provincial
dialects," on grounds of political peace and the "expansion of
enlightenment."[196] But to understand this spirit better it is
important to look a little more closely at the Metz
competition.

The Academy did not find any of the ten treatises entirely
satisfactory. It criticized them for not taking account of all
the "difficulties" regeneration of the Jews posed. These
included *inter alia*:

> the fear of seeing the Jews, whose population is growing with
> stupendous speed, forming inside the kingdom a nation which
> would always be foreign and which, after having taken
> advantage of the freedom of the trades and professions to
> increase its assets, and from the freedom to purchase to sell its
> shares, would end up by invading almost all landed property. . . .

Nonetheless, it noted with satisfaction :[197]

In general, all the treatises that we have received, except for one or two,[198] cite our prejudices against the Jews as the primary cause of their vices and notably the one which we find most disgusting. We make it impossible for them to be honest: how would we wish that they were? Let us be fair to them so that they become fair to us, this is the prayer of humanity and of all reasonable people: everything leads to the belief that the government has realized this and will hasten to accomplish it.

As a result, the Academy shared its prize between three treatises which were published: they were written by Zalkind-Hourwitz, Abbé Grégoire, and the lawyer from Nancy, Thiery.

Hourwitz was a Polish Talmudist who had worked as an old-clothes-dealer in Paris and then become the keeper of the oriental department of the Bibliothèque du Roi. Being in this way emancipated himself, he had drawn apart from his Jewish community: "Everyone who knows me," he wrote, "knows that I am absolutely isolated in France and not in a position to benefit from the advantages that might be granted to my nation there." However, he was bent on defending it and was even the only competitor to plead that his brethren, such as they were, were in no way inferior to the Christians in virtue. He wrote:

The Jews are the most peaceful, the most sober and the most industrious of all peoples; capital crimes are almost unknown among them, and the only vices which they have, in common with other nations, are usury and fraud, and even they are largely the effect of necessity, vengeance and prejudice. ... I defy all the stoics in the world to be more patient and more honest than the Jews if they were in their position.

Hourwitz maliciously quoted the lines by Voltaire—"My crimes are yours, and you punish me for them"—and applied them to the anti-Jewish polemicists:

They exaggerate a Jew's slightest peccadillo and make the

whole nation responsible for it. Moreover, they take the effect as the cause. The Jews, they say, deserve to be oppressed because they are usurers and rogues; instead of saying that they are usurers and rogues because they are oppressed and because all legitimate professions are forbidden them.

From the Jewish people, he moved on to their doctrine, making a distinction between its "philanthropy" and the unscrupulous conclusions that unenlightened rabbis drew from it "through vengeance and despair." The son of a rabbi himself, he knew what he was talking about when he discussed the Talmud. In passing, he issued a warning to the government of the Very Christian King. He noted:

The lies uttered about the Jews provide Pyrrhonism and irreligion with decisive weapons. In fact what belief does History in general deserve, and particularly Biblical History which is the history of the ancient Jews, if the government sanctions so many calumnies against that Bible and so many absurd falsehoods about even modern Jews, if it encourages effrontery to the point of depicting them as a people of Pygmies, who have cross eyes and narrow minds. . . .

This apologist also set out to prove that the "point of honor" was as much cultivated behind ghetto walls as in Parisian salons:

I have still to reply to the third criticism made about the Jews: that they are without ambition and absolutely indifferent to honor and contempt. This criticism is completely unfounded; people of merit are esteemed, the dishonest and ignorant are despised by the Jews as by other nations; they also have their disputes over precedence in the synagogue; although their scholars do not wear doctors' caps, they are no less vain of the fact; some of them chafe at being second in their community, as Caesar at being second in Rome. If this ambition does not lead them to real fame, it is because oppression closes their access to it. . . .

It can be seen that Hourwitz was continually comparing the two societies he knew: the Jewries from which he sprang, and the Parisian world he mixed with. And it was perhaps this dual culture which sharpened his perception and made him a precursor of the Jewish sociologists of future generations. The Metz Academy would not have done too badly if it had awarded him first prize—all the more so, as this skillful dialectician was also an accomplished stylist despite his own apology for his "Sarmatio-French style."[199]

The two other treatises the Academy rewarded[200] had many common features. The lawyer and the priest proved much harder on the Jews than the ex-old-clothes-dealer, describing their depravities in equally dark colors. "Imbecilic diffidence . . . they come before us with a presence clothed in opprobrium and a soul often stained with vice; let us see if there can be hope of developing the germ of the social virtues there . . ." (Thiery). "They are parasitic plants which eat away at the substance of the tree they attach themselves to. . . . If the Jews were only savages, it would be easier to regenerate them . . ." (Grégoire). In a chapter devoted to the Jews' physical constitution, the Abbé examined the causes of their degeneration which, on Buffon's authority, he attributed *inter alia* to their food, notably the consumption of ritually slaughtered meat.[201]

The only virtues the two authors conceded the Children of Israel were domestic virtues, "almost universal with them: concrete kindness towards their needy brethren, a deep respect for the authors of their days; they would be grieved to die without receiving the blessing of their fathers, without giving it to their children" (Grégoire); "It is amongst these people that husbands are still faithful, fathers tender and sentient, sons always respectful" (Thiery).

Neither of them dared dispute the validity of the theological accusation of the deicide. "It is true that this religion teaches us that the Jews, guilty of the greatest crime, have deserved the wrath of the Divinity . . ." (Thiery); "the blood of J . . . C . . . has fallen on the Jews as they desired . . ."

(Grégoire). But both questioned man's right to substitute himself for God in order to punish the Jews. "Is it for us to interpret this order from the Divinity? Has the execution been entrusted to us and would we go so far as to believe that we are the instruments of his vengeance?" (Thiery). And Grégoire goes a long way towards showing the impropriety of such arguments:

> Let us not therefore try to make religion an accessory to a harshness which it rejects; by prophesying the misfortunes of the Jewish nation, the Lord God did not intend to justify the barbarisms of others; and if we pleaded innocent on the grounds that we were instruments of vengeance, in order to fulfill the prophecies, Judas' betrayal would soon have been justified.

With the question of the sacred crime thus out of the way, the two reformers bravely shouldered the responsibility for the Jews' degradation, however serious their sacrilegious crimes might be. It could even be asked if they had not blackened the picture for rhetorical purposes.

> It is we who must stand accused of those crimes so justly blamed on the Jews: it is we who forced them to commit them ... it is to our fathers' barbarous behavior towards them, it is to our own injustice that we must attribute it ... (Thiery).

"If you consider anew the Jews' past crimes and their present corruption, let this be to deplore your work; authors of their vices, be authors of their virtues; discharge your debt and the debt of your ancestors ..." (Grégoire).

But the regenerators were already aware that they had to fight on two fronts. The spirit of the times which allowed them to contest the traditional teaching of the Church had also spread the suspicion that the Jews were "absolutely" evil, that is to say that this was the irrevocable verdict of Nature. This, Abbé Grégoire resolutely denied:

> But the Jews, we are told, are incapable of being regenerated

because they are absolutely depraved . . . this depravity . . . can we believe it is innate? A few peevish philosophers have claimed that man was born evil. Let us correct their education in order to correct their hearts; for a long time it has been repeated that they are men like us; they are men before they are Jews. . . . The Jew is born with the same capacities as ourselves. . . .

Thiery too stigmatized the "senseless men [who] have accused Nature itself: it made a mistake, they say, in forming the Jews, it molded them in filthy mud . . ."; to put such an error forward was to *blaspheme Nature,* he exclaimed. Moreover, the possibility of regenerating the Jews could also be demonstrated by positive arguments. It could be taken as an established fact, "since at Berlin . . . Moses Mendelssohn is rightfully regarded as one of the great philosophers and best writers of this century. . . ." Abbé Grégoire drew an even more spectacular conclusion from the fame of the author of *Phädon.* "The nation has just come into possession of a man of genius, whose place is not vacant, but it has taken seventeen centuries since the historian Josephus to produce Mendelssohn." This was the star argument. The frequency with which it recurred makes it easier to understand the zeal nineteenth-century Jews put into proving their regeneration by distinguishing themselves in all fields of life.

If the priest and the lawyer put forward the same diagnosis, the remedies they proposed differed on one point. Thiery thought it sufficient to emancipate the Jews civilly, without bothering about their religion. He even preferred to see them practicing the Law of Moses, rather than becoming men with neither faith nor Law, "neither Jews nor Christians." Abbé Grégoire, on the other hand, described the Talmud as a "vast reservoir, I almost said a cesspool, where the frenzies of the human mind have accumulated." He wanted to lead them to the Christian religion by kindness, and to this end even proposed re-establishing the practice of compulsory sermons, formerly instituted by Pope Gregory XIII.[202] But all in all, the difference seems minor and, given the similarity of the premises, Grégoire was perhaps doing nothing but drawing the ultimate conclusions. These were the same conclusions at which generations of European Jews later arrived, when they submitted to the ceremony of baptism in order to buy "their admission ticket to European culture" (Heine). It is, in fact, significant that this culture, to express its confident hope in the Jews' improvement, adopted the term *regeneration*, which the science of Descartes and Buffon had borrowed from the language of the Church and which had first really meant the effects of baptism ("regeneration in Jesus Christ").

six

Germany

The good Germany

We have already mentioned the tendency Europeans had in the past to place undue value on Germanic blood, on the basis of obscure recollections of the period of the Barbarian invasions. What gives the phenomenon its full significance is the fact that French or Spanish authors also recognized the pre-eminence of the Frankish or Visigothic races, and this makes it easier to understand the intermittent German megalomania. Obviously east of the Rhine, there were even more of these devotees whose words and dreams were set in the Middle Ages in a rich context of Manichean heresies, daydreams of crusades, aspirations towards universal domination and instigations to massacre and pogrom.[1] These dreams never ceased to stir German life; the most popular seventeenth-century author, Grimmelshausen, gave them a whole chapter in his *Simplicius Simplicissimus*.[2] But if they were perpetuated in this way in the "inner depths of the popular soul," that is to say in the vital areas of feeling which the historian finds it infinitely difficult to penetrate (like a collective unconscious), they are not visible in the pacific Germany of Bach at the beginning of the *Aufklärung* or German Enlightenment. It would be vain to look for their literary manifestations or their political influence at any one of the three hundred German courts of the period, slavishly bowing down to French taste. The country seems to have been passing through a depressive phase in its cyclo-thymic history, on the morrow of the Thirty Years' War.

At that time, chaotic Germany, "without a capital and without capital" (R. Minder), was a backward country. It is generally accepted that not only its fragmentation but also this social and economic backwardness was at the source of the low ebb of national feeling. But every European country was backward as compared with England, the Netherlands and France; and Italy was no less fragmented. In this period the enlightened despots set to work to repair this backwardness, not without some opposition from the champions of the old order. Germany was spared this conflict. On the other hand, its civilization, after moving into the lead in the European advance in the nineteenth century, exploded in the twentieth. If there is any coherent explanation for the German tragedy it should be sought right from the start in the spirit of Lutheranism.

For the philosophical party of the Enlightenment, this spirit was actually synonymous with progress. Mirabeau's comment on a rumor that the King of Prussia wanted to convert to Catholicism could not be more typical. "Heaven preserve mankind from this horrible misfortune!" he exclaimed. "The only leader of the Protestants, that is to say of the party of enlightenment and liberty in Germany, would very soon fall prey to the opposite party!"[3] This opposite party was of course the Church of Rome, frozen in the immobility of its tradition. The Lutheran Church, on the other hand, was wide open to the spirit of the time, since it was free, within the framework of its permanent reform, to develop, philosophize and go forward; it was also free to set up as the obedient servant of the state, notably of Prussia. German Protestant pastors were the first to propagate the new ideas of science and progress and to instill them into their flocks, at the same time as they themselves were revising their theology and introducing high Biblical criticism. What a bold bourgeoisie seized by force in France and

England was professed from the height of the pulpits in Germany by order of the prince.

But just because of this, the intellectual revolution in Germany proceeded with sensible caution; modern enlightenment there remained duly under control, radical tendencies were practically non-existent, only princes dared practice atheism; the mass of the country remained Christian. Transmission took place unimpeded from the despots to the pastors (the pastors, with their large families, provided the personnel for administrative, literary and scientific life),[4] and from the pastors to their flocks. From the time of Luther, obedience has been the national virtue. There is striking testimony to this; Kant's, for example, runs as follows:[5]

The German, of all civilized peoples, adapts himself most easily and constantly to the government under which he lives and is the most remote from the quest for innovation and opposition to the established order. His character is a blend of understanding and phlegm, without either racking his brains over that order which has already been introduced or devising an order for himself. With this, he is precisely the man of all lands and climates, easily emigrates and is not passionately attached to his fatherland. . . .

Madame de Staël, pro-German as she was, nonetheless saw the other side of the coin:[6]

It must be admitted that the Germans today do not have what can be called character. They are virtuous and upright in their private lives, as fathers of families, as administrators, but their gracious and accommodating eagerness for power gives pain, particularly when one loves them. . . . [they] are energetic flatterers and vigorously submissive. They stress their words strongly in order to hide the flexibility of feelings, and utilize philosophical arguments to explain what is least philosophical in the world: the respect for strength and the softening power of fear which changes that respect into admiration. . . .

"The softening power of fear which changes respect into

admiration" is a nice discovery, and it can be seen that Madame de Staël did not lack shrewdness. But the hypocrisy she diagnosed in its turn masked tensions and conflicts arising from the stifling demands of *Pflicht* (duty) and *Sittlichkeit* (morality)—those specific ideas which no translation into any language could render faithfully enough.

Here, we will not need to go further back in German history than the Reformation. Moreover it can happen in the infinitely rich fabric of History that one man places his stamp on a people for centuries, particularly when that man endows it with its common language, as did Luther. In exchange for the beatitudes of spiritual life and the internal kingdom of God, the Reformer preached to his Germans unconditional obedience to Caesar, and the doctrine of the "servile will" from which the requirements of absolute perfection, dear to Leibniz and Kant, developed. This gave rise notably to the concept of the three estates of ethics: the ethics whereby virtue expected its reward on earth ("Judaic ethics"); the ethics which with Christianity arrived at the idea of the immortality of the soul, whereby virtue hoped for reward in the hereafter; and the ethics whereby virtue found its reward in itself, in *Pflicht* duly accomplished. This is a heroic if inhuman code of ethics and Luther was already illustrating it with the fable of the Christian held prisoner by the Turks. It was his duty to obey his new masters blindly even when they ordered him to fight Christians. Ethics like this made the worst cowardice pardonable in the guise of heroism. This is exactly what Kant meant in the *Metaphysik der Sitten,* when he made submission to tyranny an absolute duty,[7] a duty which the Hitler régime would later put to the test. We will come back to these fundamental questions later.

Such might have been the ideological sources of German political irresponsibility. At a psychological level, these stern doctrines reflected the sado-masochistic type of contradictions in the national character, served to justify them and exacerbated them. What we have is a vicious circle which tragically darkened many lives. This is a vast theme with an infinite number of variations, and the comparison between individual and collective tragedy is perhaps questionable, but it is the only one to bring a little clarity into the interpretation of the collective psychology, and thence of historic development. Moreover, German history often takes it upon itself to illustrate the theme and justify the comparison.

The gradual promotion of Frederick II of Prussia to the rank of greatest national hero is an example of this. Never has a monarch shown so great an aversion for his people, its culture and its language. "This nation is coarse, lazy and incapable of being educated," he wrote in his will. He described the works of Goethe and other poets as "disgusting platitudes." As Voltaire was the great love of his life, he filled the Berlin Academy with Frenchmen and wrote only in that language. German posterity repaid this hatred with unfailing love, going so far as to pronounce him a great thinker, "who unfortunately wrote in French." Behind this perverse and complex character, however, as his grotesque counterpart, rose the silhouette of his progenitor the Corporal-King, the bogeyman, that "NCO" commemorated by the statue, "described in school books with amused, fond, respectful sympathy. . . ."[8]

In the eighteenth century, we have not yet reached this point. Before the wars and victories of a violently Germanophobe prince re-awakened Germanic national feeling—a feeling exacerbated as we know by the Napoleonic occupation—the German *Aufklärung* was conspicuous for its complete and quasi-sacrificial cosmopolitanism. Both Lessing and the young Goethe regarded patriotism as a snare, a mental abberation. Other authors thought it had to extend to the dimensions of the planet, as a journal entitled *Der Patriot* explicitly proclaimed.[9] During this depressive phase in national history, the Germans, with infinite good will, wanted to love every man in the world with equal love. But were Jews men? For Lessing, they were men *par excellence* as we will see, but Goethe's cosmopolitanism was limited to *Christian* Europe. Later, in *Wilhelm Meister,* he deliberately excluded Jews from his ideal city, open to men from every country: "We will tolerate no Jew amongst us, for how can we grant him a share of the superior culture of which they deny the origin and traditions?"[10] On the other hand, Schiller, who became the favorite poet of the Polish-Russian ghetto, did not seem to share his great friend's exclusivism.[11] Herder might also be quoted for the end of the eighteenth century. He too was a humanist, but he unwittingly issued this warning to the world:[12]

> Let the historian of humanity take care that he does not choose one people exclusively as his favorite and thereby belittle other peoples to whom the state of their environment has refused good fortune and glory. . . . We can be very happy that a people of such a strong, beautiful, noble culture, of such chaste morals, of so sound an understanding and so upright a temperament as the Germans, and not Huns or Bulgars, occupied the Roman world. But for that reason to regard them as the chosen people in Europe ... would be the ignoble arrogance of a barbarian.

Herder was the great poet of the German *Treue*—that passionate attachment to the person of the *leader,* that *Hörigkeit* or dependence, strengthened by ties of either open or latent homosexuality. His description of the Jews (whom, unlike Goethe, he nonetheless wanted to see assimilated) also anticipated the assertion of the racists of generations to come:[13]

> The people of God, to whom Heaven itself once gave its homeland, has been for centuries, almost from its beginnings even, a parasitic growth on the trunks of other nations: a race of cunning dealers almost throughout the whole world, which despite oppression never yearns for its own honor and dwelling, never for its own homeland.

In the Germany of the Enlightenment, therefore, the

banishment of the Children of Israel seemed to go hand in hand with the awakening of national passions. But in the first half of the eighteenth century, Germany was still feeling the effects of its wars of religion and the Thirty Years' War. It was a tired, humble and benevolent Germany which might be said to be yearning through its novelists and dramatists to love all men, including Jews, with equal love.

The good Jew

Although the thought of the German *Aufklärung* generally drew its substance from its western neighbors, German authors were the first systematically to plead the special case of the Jews. This historical leadership corresponded to the specific nuances in the nature of German cosmopolitanism, but live contact with the Children of Israel certainly contributed greatly towards it. In fact, the descendants of the court Jews made commendable efforts to promote it. In 1745, for example, young Aaron Salomon Gumpertz, a member of the Berlin Gumpertz dynasty, was asking the writer, Gottsched, for permission "to come and graze under your wings, to suck the sweet milk of the sciences ... it is *you* whom we Germans have to thank for so varied intellectual writings."[14] This Jew who declared himself a German and who yearned for the culture of the century was a sign of the times. German authors, for their part, were going against the old conventions or habits of medieval thought and looking for the *man* beneath the Jew.

The first beneficent Jews to appear in literary works of this school saved the Christian heroes from the pitiless clutches of Moors in an interminable Robinson Crusoe-type tale by Schnabel as early as 1731.[15] But however brave they may have been, they asked for payment for their pains. In 1747, the poet, Christian Gellert, described as the *praeceptor Germaniae* at the time, put a group of rich and totally unselfish Jews into his *Swedish Countess*.[16] One of them, who had enormous business dealings stretching from Siberia to Holland, acted as a special good angel to the countess's husband, held prisoner by the Russians. He proved to him "that generous hearts also exist in this people who least seem to have them." And this was the moral: "It is possible that many people who form part of this nation would be better hearted, if we did not force them by our conduct to hate our religion." This was the way in which the first *Aufklärer* shouldered the responsibility for the Jews' degradation.

Later, the majority of German men of letters revived this theme, even if only incidentally, protesting against a condition sanctioned by "barbarous laws." *Der Teutsche Merkur,* under the Francophil Wieland, led a campaign against the Leibzoll, "and this at a few leagues from Berlin, where all they talk about is the rights of man! In France, they write less on the Jews' behalf, but act better ..." (1785).[17] Klopstock, Wieland's great adversary and the first poet of Germany's ancient past, addressed a pompous ode to the Emperor Joseph II at the time of the publication of the Edict of Toleration (1782).[18] But it was primarily on the boards of German theaters that the discussion proceeded.

As early as 1749, Lessing, then barely twenty years old, entered the lists. During the period when Lessing had worked as Voltaire's secretary in Berlin, Aaron Gumpertz was holding the same office with Maupertuis. A friendship between the two men ensued, which seems to have been at the origin of the play *Die Juden,* the first social drama in the German language.

The plot of *Die Juden* is very simple. The *Baron* and his daughter, the *Fräulein,* are attacked by bandits; a noble *Traveler* risks his life to save them. Not knowing how to express his gratitude, the *Baron* offers him his daughter's hand, but the *Traveler* who had hidden his origins till then, hesitates. Here is the dénouement:[19]

Traveler: I am a Jew.
Baron: A Jew! What cruel mischance. . . .

Lisette:	A Jew!
Fräulein:	What difference does that make?
Lisette:	Shush, Fräulein, I'll tell you the difference afterwards.
Baron:	So there are cases when Heaven itself prevents us from being grateful!
Traveler:	It would be superfluous because you wish to be.
Baron:	But I wish to do at least as much as fate allows me. Take all my fortune. I would rather be poor and grateful than rich and ungrateful.
Traveler:	This offer is in vain for the God of my fathers has given me more than I need. As sole reward all I ask is that in future you judge my people more kindly and do not generalize. I did not conceal myself from you because I am ashamed of my religion. No! But I saw that you looked favorably on me but unfavorably on my people. And a man's friendship, be he what he will, has always been inestimable to me.
Baron:	I am ashamed of my behavior. . . . Everything I see of you fills me with rejoicing. Come, we will see to it that the guilty are held in safe keeping. How estimable the Jews would be if they were all like you!
Traveler:	And how praiseworthy the Christians if they all had your qualities!
	[Curtain]

It can be seen how lofty and how refined the feelings of all the characters are. The *Traveler*'s continued concealment might seem surprising, but perhaps it was consistent with the good manners of the time. There is a description in a German newspaper of a Jew at a spa[20]

who actually claimed to be a Christian; he had taken another name, but everyone knew he was a Jew. No one, however, acted as if they knew; he was addressed politely, even amicably, for the Jew was a pleasant man and knew how to behave. . . .

In any case, this detail shows that Lessing was less concerned with pleading the case of the social group formed by
Judaism than with fighting the prejudice whereby all Jews
were by definition bad. His *Traveler* was also rich, like his
predecessors described in the works by Schnabel and Gellert.
Money brought the Children of Israel the respect not only of
princes and officials but also of moralists.

Thirty years later, Lessing took up the theme of the Jews
again in his famous play *Nathan der Weise* who has often
been identified as his friend, Moses Mendelssohn. A defense
of tolerance, this classic play also reflected the spiritual
development of a noble nonconformist, who became a
"Spinozist," a secret atheist at the end of his life. Even on his
deathbed, he yearned to depart for a land where "there
would be neither Christian nor Jew."

In the second half of the eighteenth century, most fashionable German dramatists—Iffland, Kotzebue, the two
Stephanies—were putting "good Jews" on the stage, while
translators of many foreign plays were inserting them, in
order to adapt the original version to contemporary taste.[21]
In German countries, the Jew became the great symbol of
the struggle against prejudice. At the end of the plot, it was
left to one character to point the moral: "Bad luck to those
who make it man's duty to hate men, and who hide from
their like the qualities of the Jew which make him capable of
all human virtues and felicities" (Bischoff, *Judenfeind*, 1780).
In Von Nesselrode's *Der adelige Tagelöhner*, 1774 it was:

> Perhaps all Jews would be honest or the majority would so be, if
> implacable laws did not treat them like cattle and did not
> exclude them from all professions, leaving them nothing but
> usury as a means of subsistence. This Jew Isaac proves that
> Jews too can be honest. ...

More subtle than these conventional remonstrances was
the reply put into the mouth of a generous Jew who rescued
a poor shoemaker from a debtor's prison. The German creditor

urged him to have a Christian heart: "'A Christian heart?' retorted the Jew. 'No, I have a Jewish heart but I am paying, if the gentleman would be good enough to accept this five-gulden note . . .'" (Hensler, *Judenmädchen von Prag*, 1792).

Unwittingly, it can be believed, the author was thus bringing out the semantic ambiguities to which the Jews' own colloquial language sometimes succumbs.

The principal subject of the discussion was therefore the question of knowing whether the Jews were naturally bad or if responsibility for their position devolved on Christian society. These authors seem to be saying: "Make us good laws and we will make you good Jews." There was no shortage of critics to object that the fault lay entirely with the Children of Israel. In this sense, the discussion was already anticipating the polemics of the following centuries.

The first protagonists in this discussion, which began with Lessing's *Die Juden*, were an already famous university professor and an unknown Jewish youth. The latter ended up by incarnating the "good Jew" for the whole body of European public opinion, confirming the fact that nature imitates art. The professor also left his mark on history as we will see later.

Johann David Michaelis (1717–91), an immensely learned theologian, asserted in the *Journal de Goettingen* that no Jew like the *Traveler* could exist. Even mediocre virtue, he explained, was exceptional with a people whose principles and way of life were resolutely immoral. Lessing replied that such Jews really did exist and he was in a position to supply proof of this: had he not just received a letter from a young Jew, filled with the loftiest sentiments? He therefore published this letter which his friend Gumpertz had passed on to him. This was Moses Mendelssohn's entry on to the German literary scene.

He exclaimed in his letter:

Is the cruel judgment of Michaelis justified? How shameful for the human race! And how shameful too for the author!

Is it not enough for us that we must suffer the attacks of the cruel hatred that the Christians have for us, and must this injustice be justified by a slander?

Let them continue to oppress us, let them allow us to live in subjection amidst free and happy citizens, let us be exposed to the scorn and contempt of the whole world; but do not let them try to challenge our virtue, the sole solace for unhappy souls, the sole comfort of the abandoned. . . .

In general, certain human virtues are met with more frequently amongst Jews than Christians. Think of the unutterable horror that they have of murder. You cannot quote a single example of a Jew (except for professional bandits) having killed a man. How easily many a worthy Christian will kill a man for a simple insult. They say this is because of cowardice amongst the Jews. So be it! If cowardice spares human blood, then cowardice is a virtue!

Throughout his life Mendelssohn never ceased to stand as proof of this virtue in the eyes of the world. An exemplary character in every respect, this frail, self-taught hunchback became the leader of the German "philosophical party," while continuing to work in a Berlin silk factory, where foreigners in transit came to drink wisdom from the lips of a pious Jew. It has been said, and it may be true, that enlightened Europe was bestowing its favor not only on his writings but on this paradoxical position. According to Heinrich Heine, Providence in its way had remedied this position by presenting him with a hump so that he was better able to bear his Jewishness. His physique was such that, in the words of one of his visitors, the harshest heart could not help pitying him. But mentally he was endowed with a solidly philosophical temperament; his self-portrait can be believed on that score:

In general, my heart is little accessible to anger, remorse and to other unpleasing emotions of that type. I am only sensitive to tenderness and friendship and then to so moderate a degree that my friends very often accuse me of being lukewarm. But I cannot feign sentiments that I do not feel and I am incapable of lying and pretending, even when they are required by the whims of fashion. . . .

Let us add that, unlike the majority of philosophers whose names have come down to posterity, Mendelssohn married, had children and was able to build up a happy home.

After crossing swords on behalf of his co-religionists in his letter to Lessing, he seemed to lose interest in Judaism. His first work, *Philosophische Gespräche,* also published by Lessing, contained a dialogue in defense of the German culture which Frederick II and his suite were ridiculing. He even had the temerity—he, a *Schutzjude,* a "tolerated Jew," liable to be expelled from one minute to the next—to upbraid the king for his aversion to the German language. This Jew was already showing that he was more German than many a German.

Later, with great skill in method he developed the proofs, dear to the Century of Enlightenment, in favor of religious tolerance, immortality of the soul and the existence of God and a natural religion which permitted every individual to find salvation. His *Phädon,* which ran into seventeen German editions and was translated into a dozen foreign languages, established his fame. But in 1769, his philosophical quietude was broken by the Swiss pastor, Lavater, who took it into his head to convert Mendelssohn. In a publicly issued challenge, he reminded him that even at the level of intellectual interchange he remained a Jew.

In an open letter, Lavater called on him either to refute the proofs of Christianity or, if he were incapable of so doing, to accept baptism "as Socrates would have done." Mendelssohn's philosopher friends pressed him to reply and Lessing urged him to exploit the situation to the full in order to *"écraser l'Infâme."*[22] But the rabbis were asking him to lie low. He chose a middle course and answered Lavater that he had never stopped believing in the truth of Judaism, as his life testified. As for the false belief of Christianity, his position as a Jew prevented him from talking about it publicly.

I wanted to refute the world's derogatory opinion of the Jew by righteous living, not by pamphleteering. However, it is not only my station in life but also my religion and my philosophy that furnish me with the most cogent reasons why I wanted to avoid religious controversy and discuss, in my publications, only those religious verities which are of equal importance to all religions.[23]

Mendelssohn confided the substance of his thoughts in a confidential letter to one of his highly placed correspondents, the Duke of Brunswick. His reason, he wrote, revolted against the mysteries of Christianity, and prevented him believing in original sin. That an innocent man might take upon himself the sin of a guilty one was contrary to divine justice. Moreover, having read the Gospels closely, he had nowhere found that Jesus had exempted the Jews from observance of the Law; but he acknowledged him as a prophet, entrusted with spreading the divine word to all mankind. These views were similar to those John Toland had developed earlier.[24] Mendelssohn was in this way outlining his doctrine of a universal or natural religion, given by God to all men, with the Jews as its priest-nation; hence, the commandments decreed for them.

Meanwhile, the Lavater-Mendelssohn discussion, in which several other philosophers and theologians hastened to join, was firing enlightened Europe. It was translated into French:[25]

The Jewish and anti-Jewish letters have caused such a stir that we think their translation will give pleasure to French readers who will be very happy to see Christian philosophy triumph over a man like Mendelssohn, that Jewish scholar from Berlin.
. . .

So, this frail athlete was promoted to the role of appointed champion of Judaism. He was able to put up a vigorous fight for the rights of his co-religionists, using his philosophical prestige to intervene on behalf of the Jews of Switzerland who were threatened with expulsion, of the Jews of Saxony and of Alsace. This last incident was at the origin of the famous publication *Über die bürgerliche Verbesserung der Juden* which he first thought of writing himself, but then entrusted to his friend Dohm. This book pleaded for the emancipation of the Jews from the political and judicial point of view; Mendelssohn, for his part, undertook to defend it on a higher plane. Thus was born his *Jerusalem, oder über religiöse Macht und Judentum* in which the philosophical Jew once again became a Jewish philosopher. This treatise has kept its place in the history of political philosophy as a plea for the separation of Church and State. It also gave Mendelssohn an opportunity to develop his religious doctrine.

Obviously his principal aim was the granting of civic rights to his brethren. To this end, he boldly advocated a secular state, and consequently the abolition of the political and judicial rights of the Churches. He naturally felt obliged to extend this principle to the Jewish "Church," that is to say to call, on grounds of Reason, for the abolition of the judicial autonomy of the Jewish communities and their formidable weapon, rabbinical excommunication.

It was a painful effort for him to take this step, since by so doing he was going against Talmudic tradition and even seemed to be infringing Mosaic law. Moreover, he was giving his Christian adversaries every opportunity to say that this first step would lead to others and that it was as good as going straight to the baptismal font. Rounding on them, he counter-attacked as follows:[26]

... shall I take this step without first pondering whether it will really extricate me from the state of confusion in which you think I find myself? If it were true that the corner-stones of my house are so out of alignment that the entire building threatens to collapse, would I act wisely if I attempted to save my belongings simply by moving them from the lower to the upper floor? Would I be safer there? Christianity, as you know, is built upon Judaism and would therefore collapse along with it. Thus, when you say that my conclusions undermine the foundations of Judaism, and offer me the safety of your upper floor, must I not suspect that you mock me?

It is interesting to see a man like Mendelssohn following the same line of reasoning here as someone like Fréret. But while the militant atheist proposed a plan of attack, "The first would only have to be destroyed to remove the need to mention the latter,"[27] the Jewish philosopher was inviting his Christian adversaries to join him in defending their threatened religions:

> Surely, the Christian who seriously desires to discover light and right will not challenge the Jew to a fight when their respective truths seem to clash or scripture seems to contradict reason. On the contrary, he will join him in an effort to discover the baselessness of the contradiction. For this is their joint concern. The discussion of their doctrinal differences ought to be postponed until later. Their most important task right now is to join forces to ward off the danger that threatens both of them. They must either discover the fallaciousness of their reasoning or demonstrate that they had merely been troubled by an apparent contradiction.

Mendelssohn was therefore ready to admit the failings of Reason. On other points, too, he stood aloof from the philosophical optimism of the Enlightenment; for example when he challenged the certainties of linear progress and the infinite perfectibility of mankind:

> If you take mankind as a whole, you will not find that there is constant progress in its development that brings it ever nearer to perfection. On the contrary, we see constant fluctuations; mankind as a whole has never yet taken any step forward without soon and with redoubled speed sliding back to its previous position. Most nations remain on the same level of culture for many centuries, in the same twilight, one which seems much too weak for our pampered eyes. Occasionally a dot in a huge mass will start glowing, become a brilliant star, and traverse its course, which after a shorter or longer period,

sets it down once again in or near the place where it had originated. . . . Seen as a whole, however, mankind has clearly maintained virtually the same degree of morality through all fluctuations and periods—the same mixture of religion and irreligion, of virtue and vice, of happiness and misery.

Rabbinic wisdom, that of Ecclesiastes, seems to have invaded this terrain. It might be added that, starting from certain Talmudic hypotheses, Mendelssohn outlined a theory of human alienation on the theme "why man has lost his value for man." His theory, which attributed alienation to the intrusion of technique and the multiplication of signs or symbols which placed a screen between men, seems to anticipate the conclusions of some present-day sociologists on the subject of modern mass communications.[28]

He used these digressions to illustrate his major thesis. He might declare that Jewish theocracy (of which, for him, rabbinic power was only an obsolete remnant) had been abolished since the destruction of the Temple. But he did not cease to insist with the utmost forcefulness upon the maintenance of the observances and ceremonial laws ("revealed law," he specified, and not "revealed religion') which God had ordained for His nation of priests, or "theists," as he put it:[29]

And this unifying bond will, I believe, have to be preserved in the plans of Providence as long as polytheism, anthropomorphism and religious usurpation are rampant in the world. As long as these tormentors of reason are united against us, genuine theists must also create some kind of unifying bond among themselves lest the others gain the upper hand completely. But of what should this bond consist? Of principles and beliefs? We would then get articles of faith, symbols, doctrinal formulas— all shackling our reason. It is of acts that the bond must consist, and of meaningful acts at that—i.e. ceremonial. . . .

Moreover, Mendelssohn considered that even Christian baptism did not in any way absolve a Jew:[30]

I cannot understand how any of us, even if he were to convert to the Christian religion, could believe that he would thereby have appeased his conscience and freed himself from the yoke of the law. Jesus of Nazareth was never heard to declare that he had come to release the House of Jacob from the law. Indeed, he explicitly and emphatically said the opposite and what is more, did the opposite himself. [Cf. Matt. V, 17ff.] Jesus of Nazareth himself observed not only the law of Moses but also the ordinances of the rabbis . . . his entire conduct as well as that of his early disciples is obviously guided and illumined by the rabbinic principle *that anyone not born into the law need not bind himself to the law, but that anyone born into the law must live and die in accordance with it. . . .*

Mendelssohn's opinion of the Jews of his day was in accordance with his original conciliatory position. Even if he was already tending to measure them by the Christian scale of values, his attitude remained indulgent and understanding:[31]

The pressure under which we have been living for so many centuries, has taken all vigor away from our spirit. It is not our fault but we cannot deny that the natural urge to freedom in us has lost all its vitality. It has changed itself into a monkish virtue and expresses itself solely in prayer and suffering, not in action.

In another work, he urged his co-religionists:[32]

Oh, my brothers, hitherto you have felt all too harshly the heavy yoke of intolerance and perhaps thought to find in it a sort of gratification when you were allowed the power to impose on your subordinates a similarly heavy yoke. Revenge seeks its object and if it cannot get at others, then it will gnaw its own flesh. . . . Brothers, follow the example of love, as you have hitherto followed the example of hate! Imitate the virtue of the nations whose lack of virtue you have thought you must imitate. If you wish to be cherished, tolerated and spared by others, then cherish, tolerate and spare each other. Love, and you will be loved!

Needless to say, these prayers and illusions of the Century of Enlightenment were not fulfilled. The "yoke of intolerance" was abolished but its removal did not make the Jews better loved and neither side was content. Mendelssohn's immediate descendants, his own children, were the first to convert, obviously without a moment's thought of perpetuating the ancient observances. On the contrary, they did their utmost by every means within their power to abolish even the memory of them. This accounted for the implacable opinions these rich and enlightened Jews or ex-Jews voiced about their poverty-stricken brethren; but this point will come up again later on.

German philosophy and the Jews

Moses Mendelssohn closes the era of pre-Kantian German philosophy. With his death in 1786, a whole epoch seemed to have ended. Liberated from foreign influences, bubbling with stupendous intellectual activity and evincing originality in every sphere, Germany had regained its self-confidence and henceforth prided itself on being "the land of poets and thinkers." But the days when a man like Lessing pleaded the cause of the Jews were past. Events seemed to suggest that the new sudden awareness was not only reviving national feeling but also arousing hostility towards the Jews. The great philosophers, even more than the poets, men like Herder or Goethe, were dead set against the "Chosen People," leaving no stone unturned to attack them, including the writings of Mendelssohn himself.[33]

Perhaps it is not difficult to understand why. In many respects, classical German philosophy had sprung from Lutheran theology, of which it was a sort of progressive secularization, and we have seen how such a process prepares the ground for anti-Jewish propaganda. To this was added the direct influence of English theology on German religious thought. Add to this the effect of a specific anti-

Semitic tradition, nurtured notably in the German universities (a tradition we described in the first volume of this series as "activated anti-Semitism")[34] and combining, one ventures to say, with consequences logically drawn from Luther's doctrine. It will then be understood why the conceptual structures of men like Kant or Hegel were stained with stupendous anti-Jewish ill-feeling in places.

But before coming on to these intellectual giants, we will return to Johann David Michaelis who paved the way for them as far as our present subject and perhaps others are concerned. It must be said that this great Hebraist was one of the last universal scholars in the seventeenth- to eighteenth-century style. His interest roamed impartially from the functioning of the memory to the mechanism of magnifying-glasses and the invention of fire. As far as ethics were concerned, he seems to have been the first to propound the principle, taken up and expanded by Kant, whereby a lie is a crime in any circumstances, even in matters of life and death. If, for example, an assassin asks you the whereabouts of the victim he is pursuing; "Even in a case like that, the truth must be told and a lie remains a crime."[35]

Here again we find the national cult of obedience, for an infantile irresponsibility can hide behind the categorical imperative of absolute truth. Equally, perhaps only the confused consciousness of a grandiose lie can lead to such an acute nostalgia for truth. As an ironical comment on this national obsession, Goethe made his bachelor in *Faust* say: "In Germany, one lies when one is polite!"[36]

Michaelis was also the first of the Lutheran "rationalist" theologians to subject the Scriptures to verification by Reason, following the English example (he studied in England), and to announce that some parts were worthy of less belief than others. His *Dogmatik* was accepted as authoritative; but it was primarily his *Supplementa ad Lexica hebraica* and his great treatise on Mosaic law which established his international reputation.

On these grounds, he was obviously considered an expert

on the customs and practices of the Jews. As we have seen, his opinion of them was very unfavorable. Moreover it seems that the University of Göttingen, the most famous in Germany, was a veritable hotbed of anti-Jewish propaganda at that time, as the names (now completely forgotten) of Tychsen and Hissmann testify. Either of them could have been amongst the admiring "laymen" who witnessed Blumenbach's demonstration of the peculiar features of Jewish skulls. . . .[37]

Michaelis developed his views systematically—the views of a determined opponent of the emancipation of the Jews—primarily in his criticism of Dohm's *Über die bürgerliche Verbesserung der Juden.* According to him, they were incorrigible and incapable of "regeneration," as much because of their customs as because of their religion. In substance his opposition came under four heads:

1) Jews were vicious and dishonest (he even calculated that they were exactly twenty-five times more so than Christians);
2) they were without honor, and the fact that some of them no longer followed the Mosaic law aggravated this criticism: ". . . when I see a Jew disgracing his religion by eating pig, how can I believe in his promise?";
3) they were worthless as soldiers because of their small stature and also because they refused to fight on the Sabbath; this concern with military value is already characteristic of Germany, and, we think, of Germany alone; finally
4) they did not have a religion in the proper sense since the Mosaic law stipulated how to act and not what to believe. What is expressed in this way is the Lutheran idea of the *jüdischer Glauben,* an erroneous belief which seeks its justification in deeds and not in faith.

It will be noted that the fourth point contains the germ of the three preceding ones: people who do not have a real religion and, which is the same thing, do not believe in a hereafter, are easily dishonest and hold their lives dearer than all else, honor or homeland included.[38]

Views such as these, argued on the basis of Lutheran

theology, gained adherents and inspired following generations to the point where they were reflected in the diatribes
of *Mein Kampf.*[39]

Let us now move on to more illustrious metaphysicians.
With them too, as soon as Jews were mentioned, the seed of
philosophical conjecture was stifled by the chaff of preconceived ideas and emotional outbursts.

For Immanuel Kant also, Judaism was not a religion in the
proper sense, as the law of Moses was only a civil code:[40]

> Judaism is not really a religion at all but merely a union of a
> number of people who, since they belonged to a particular
> stock, formed themselves into a commonwealth under purely
> political laws and not into a church; . . . The proof that Judaism
> has not allowed its organization to become religious is clear.
> *First,* all its commands are of the kind which a political
> organization can insist upon and lay down as coercive laws,
> since they relate merely to external acts; and although the Ten
> Commandments are, to the eye of reason, valid as ethical
> commands even had they not been given publicly, yet in that
> legislation they are not so prescribed as to induce obedience by
> laying requirements upon the *moral disposition. . . . Second,* all
> the consequences of fulfilling or transgressing these laws, all
> rewards or punishments, are limited to those alone which can be
> allotted to all men in this world, and not even these [are
> distributed] according to ethical concepts. . . . Furthermore,
> since no religion can be conceived of which involves no belief in
> a future life, Judaism, which, when taken in its purity, is seen to
> lack this belief, is not a religious faith at all. . . *Third,* Judaism
> fell so far short of constituting an era suited to the requirements
> of the *church universal,* or of setting up this universal church
> itself during its time, as actually to exclude from its communion
> the entire human race, on the ground that it was a special
> people chosen by God for Himself—[an exclusiveness] which
> showed enmity toward all other peoples and which, therefore,
> evoked the enmity of all. . . .

Generations of Kantian Jews have analyzed and interpreted this text. To exonerate their idol to some extent, they

have tried to relate it either to internal Lutheran tradition (Luther, and the rationalist theologians of the *Aufklärung*) or to external sources (Spinoza, via the English deists with whom Kant associated, or Mendelssohn's "Jerusalem").[41] But however important literary influences and sources might have been, they counted for less perhaps than the basic hostility of a thinker who, in various publications and in various places, advocated the euthanasia of Judaism in a manner which could only have been the metaphysical way of crying: "Death to the Jews!"[42] Describing them as "Palestinians," he rails against them in his *Anthropologie* with powerful ill-will:[43]

> The Palestinians living amongst us are, since their exile, because of their usurious spirit not unjustifiably renowned for their deceitfulness, so far as the great majority is concerned. It does indeed seem disconcerting to conceive of a *nation* of usurers; but it is just as disconcerting to conceive of a nation of pure mercantilism, by far the largest part of which is bound together by a superstition recognized by the state in which they live and do not seek any civic honor. But they try to compensate for this lack by the advantages of outwitting the people amongst whom they find shelter and even by deceiving each other. Now this cannot be otherwise in a whole nation of pure merchants as non-productive members of society (e.g. the Jews in Poland). Thus, their constitution, sanctioned by ancient decrees and recognized also by us amongst whom they live (and with whom we have certain sacred writings in common), cannot be nullified without inconsistency even if they do make the slogan "Let the purchaser beware" their highest principle in their intercourse with us.

The Viennese philosopher Otto Weininger (who died in 1904), a master of metaphysical anti-Semitism, regarded this passage as the most anti-Semitic text in world literature. If this assertion can be challenged, if only because world literature is so very rich in this type of text, Kant, like so many other anti-Semites, certainly numbered Jews amongst his best friends. It was his faithful pupil and correspondent

Marcus Herz who introduced his philosophy into Berlin; Lazarus Bendavid spared no efforts to do the same in Vienna; Solomon Maimon, on Kant's own admission, was the man who best understood him; Mendelssohn he considered "the most important man," and he wanted "to have a permanent and intimate relationship with such a man, by nature so kind, so gay and with such a lucid mind. . . ."[44] It should be added that, as a good son of the latter part of the *Aufklärung*, Kant remained an optimist and considered that once rid of their baneful "Judaic spirit" the Jews would be able to mend their ways. His outlook was therefore "Christian" rather than "racist." At the suggestion of his pupil Bendavid, he even advocated the formation of a Judeo-Christian sect, based on both the Torah and the Gospels. But the essential point about this would still be the "euthanasia of Judaism" which he thought would herald the "end of the great drama of religious evolution" and the advent of an era of happiness for all mankind.[45] How strange to find such an eschatological vision, obviously inspired by St Paul and St Augustine, in the great reviver of modern philosophy.

His disciple Fichte, on the other hand, saw the only solution to the problem of the Jews in their expulsion from German lands. "To protect ourselves against them I see no other way than to conquer for them their promised land and see them all there," he wrote in his first important work.[46] He stated as forcibly as possible that their case was hopeless: ". . . But to give them civic rights—I see no means to do that except, one night, to cut off all their heads and give them new ones in which there would not be one Jewish idea." Note that these lines date from the period (1793) when Fichte was describing himself as a revolutionary, even a Jacobin. He therefore evoked the image of a collective decapitation of the Jews even before he urged the anti-French crusade and mystically promoted the Germans to the rank of the only authentic people (*Urvolk*), destined to regenerate the world. In a later work (*Grundzüge des gegenwärtigen Zeitalters*, 1804), Fichte took the views of the most aggressive English deists, like Tindal and Morgan, to their final conclusion.[47] Identifying true Christianity as the "natural religion," he did not find it in a pure state anywhere except in St John, who seemed to him to cast doubts on the Jewish origins of Jesus.[48] The idea of an "Aryan Christ" is thus seen appearing for the first time in the history of European thought. Not content with abusing the Old Testament like his predecessors, Fichte also harshly criticized the major part of the New, notably the epistles of St Paul. "When he became a Christian," he wrote, "Paul still did not want to have been a Jew in error; the two systems had therefore to be joined and adapted to one another." In other words, Fichte thought that original Christianity had been corrupted by its Jewish apostle. He criticized both Protestants and Catholics for being satisfied with[49]

the fallacious fundamentals of the Pauline theory, which, in order to protect Judaism's validity for some time, had to begin from a God who acted arbitrarily; the two parties, completely in agreement on the truth of such a theory, did not entertain the slightest doubt about it and only argued about the best way of keeping the Pauline theory alive and kicking.

Shortly afterwards, in his famous *Reden an die deutsche Nation* (1808), which became the charter of nascent pan-Germanism, Fichte exclaimed: "Christianity, which originated in Asia and became in its corruption thoroughly Asian, which only preached dumb devotion and blind faith, was already to the Romans something alien and exotic. . . ." According to him, only the Germans were qualified to gather "the seed of truth and life of original Christianity."[50] His Nazi exegetists did not have to look too hard at the texts to demonstrate that he was the first prophet of the Nazi *Gottgläubigkeit* and the "Aryan faith," those pillars of hazy Hitlerite metaphysics.[51] From the psychological point of view, some of his writings and comments suggest that he believed that he was destined to fulfill a messianic mission—

to be not only a Christian but a Christ.[52] This Illuminatus might therefore be ranked as one of the family of reformers angling for the role of Messiah and whose anger was directed against the sons of Israel who had usurped this sublime mission. He himself went back to the root, and St Paul became the grandiose prototype of the corrupting Jew. We know all too well how Fichte's glorification of Germanic superiority led him to prepare the ground for the misfortunes of so-called scientific racism, already present in the writings of his contemporaries, Arndt and Jahn.[53] But we will not linger over the psychological case of the weaver's son who became the first great metaphysical prophet of German nationalism. Such interpretations are always labored and hazardous and, in the event, do not seem to serve any purpose, since Fichte's imprecations or heresies, whatever their very personal nuances, are part of the great current of Lutheran theologicophilosophical thought on the subject of the Jews.

The same violence but in a more classical key is also found in the young Hegel. But it must quickly be added that he calmed down in his mature works, where he refrained from abusing the Children of Israel, though he did not abandon his idea of a specific wretched and servile "Jewish consciousness."[54] This idea dated from his youthful theological writings (before 1800) where he developed it forcefully and at length within the framework of a line of thought obscure enough to baffle the best Hegelian exegetists. However, perhaps it would not be wrong if we said that what was involved was simply a secularization of the patristic theme of the transgression and perpetual slavery of the Jews, and if we linked Hegel too, from this point of view, to the mainstream of deists. Discussing the "Spirit of Judaism," he compared Jews to non-Jews and concluded "that general hostility allows nothing but physical dependence, an animal existence, that can only be secured at someone else's expense and which the Jews received as their portion." Obviously, Hegel considered this parasitism a permanent phenomenon, characteristic of both ancient and modern Jewry:

All the conditions of the Jewish people, including the wretched, abjectly poor and squalid state they are still in today, are nothing other than the consequences and developments of the original destiny—an infinite power which it desperately sought to surmount—a destiny which has maltreated it and will not cease to do so until this people conciliates it by the spirit of beauty, abolishing it as a result of this conciliation.

Greek tragedy? That is precisely what the fate of the Jews was not, as far as Hegel was concerned. The Sisyphean state he described, the suffering, the desperate effort and the guilt, was for him the specific state of the Children of Israel, in strong contrast to the state of the rest of mankind. Moreover, the passage might suggest that the Jews were "regenerable," that they retained a hope of salvation. But this hope would be vain as long as they clung to the Mosaic law (we are back to the main thesis of the Fathers of the Church). Hegel multiplied criticism of this law. That it instituted the idleness of the Sabbath, was not the least characteristic one in the eyes of this hard worker:

> The three great yearly festivals, celebrated for the most part with feasts and dances, are the most human element in Moses' policy; but the solemnity of every seventh day is very characteristic. To slaves, this rest from work must be welcome, a day of idleness after six days full of labor. But for living men, otherwise free, to keep one day in a complete vacuum, in an inactive unity of spirits, to make the time dedicated to God an empty time, and to let this vacuity return every so often—this could only occur to the legislator of a people for whom the melancholy, unfelt unity is the supreme reality ... (*dem die traurige ungefühlte Einheit das Höchste ist*).

The Jews were therefore slaves and their law was a law of slaves; they deserved no pity:[55]

> The great tragedy of the Jewish people is no Greek tragedy; it can rouse neither terror nor pity, for both of these arise only out of the fate which follows from the inevitable fault of a beautiful

character; it can arouse horror alone. The fate of the Jewish people is the fate of Macbeth. . . .

Elsewhere, discussing "faith in the divine," the young Hegel found even crueler formulae: [56]

> Spirit alone recognizes spirit. They saw in Jesus only the man, the Nazarene, the carpenter's son whose brothers and kinsfolk lived among them; so much he was, and more he could not be, for he was only one like themselves, and they felt themselves to be nothing. The Jewish multitude was bound to wreck his attempt to give them the consciousness of something divine, for faith in something divine, something great, cannot make its home in a dunghill. The lion has no room in a nest, the infinite spirit none in the prison of a Jewish soul. . . .

As we know, for Hegel, the infinite spirit, after brushing Napoleon with its wings, had chosen Germany, notably Prussia, as its favorite place.

Hegel is a difficult philosopher. He is even generally considered the most difficult of the great philosophers. Amongst other controversial points, exegetists constantly discuss the question of whether he was a believer or an atheist. But this is not very important for our subject because in Germany both religious and anti-religious thinkers tended to take the Jews as their favorite target in an even more marked manner, if possible, than in either England or France.

As far as religious thinkers are concerned, this process is best illustrated by the examples of the theologian Semler (1725–91) and his famous pupil Schleiermacher (1768–1834).

Semler, who is regarded as the founder of historical Biblical criticism, protested against the dogmatic belief that traditional theology put in the Jews' holy books: ". . . because the Jews regard these books as divine and holy, is it right to conclude that other people must also consider them divine, of a superior dignity to their own histories and annals?" This gained added point from the fact that these books told abominable stories, full of threats and curses on other peoples, the like of which God, who loved all men, could never have inspired. Semler was also shocked by the claim to have been chosen, coming from the coarsest of all peoples, and he asked in a manner typical of the progressive theology of the *Aufklärung*:

> ... will they therefore be eternally necessary, these foundations that the incompetent and untutored Jews we know, who cannot even be compared to many honest Greeks and Romans, have adopted under the name of holy Scripture as the true chronicles of their people?

In this connection, he also argued from the Jews' own statements that these books were written for them alone:

> ... that the Old Testament was intended for all mankind, even the Jews do not state; they want to keep these books for themselves alone, in this way to distinguish themselves from the Goyim, whom God would not have judged worthy of happiness.

Semler's reasoning took a gnostic turn as he concluded from this: "For us, for Christians *qua* Christians, it is important to see if the spirit of Jesus Christ lives in these books, before regarding them as forming part of Christian teaching." This spirit, he said, was notably absent from the books of Ezra and Nehemiah: "Christians should take as little interest in the building of the temple, in Jerusalem, and in the work of people like Nehemiah as in what the Samaritans have to say on the subject of their temple of Mount Gerizim."[57]

The logic of these arguments by a rationalist theologian seems impeccable, and the only objection that could be made is that there is no place for logic at the core of religious thought. Moreover, there is no animosity towards the Jews anywhere in it. But the challenge to the canonic validity of the Old Testament was heavy with polemical consequences. For example, it paved the way for Schopenhauer's sarcasm: "The Jews are the people chosen by *their* God, who is the God chosen by *His* people, and this concerns no one but

them and Him." Closer to Semler himself, his pupil Schleiermacher, a romantic and worldly preacher, a regular guest at
the Berlin Jewish salons, drew the following conclusions:[58]

> Judaism is long since dead. Those who yet wear its livery are
> only sitting lamenting beside the imperishable mummy,
> bewailing its departure and its sad legacy. Yet I could still wish
> to say a word on this type of religion. My reason is not that it
> was the forerunner of Christianity. I hate that kind of historical
> reference. . . . Regard only its strictly religious elements. . . . Is it
> anything but a system of universal immediate retribution, of a
> peculiar reaction of the Infinite against every finite thing that
> can be regarded as proceeding from caprice? . . . The belief in
> the Messiah was its highest product, its noblest fruit, but also its
> last effort. . . . This faith has long persisted and, like a solitary
> fruit, after all life has vanished, hangs and dies on the withered
> stem till the rudest season of the year. The limited point of view
> allowed this religion, as a religion, but a short duration. It died,
> and as its sacred books were closed, the intercourse of Jehovah
> with His people was looked upon as ended.

Typically perhaps, the only discordant voice in this
theological concert belonged to a violently anti-rationalist
thinker, Johann Georg Hamann (1730–88), a friend and
philosophical adversary of Kant's. According to experts, his
writing contains curious intuitions into the symbolism of
thought and language, anticipating modern semantics.[59]
"All the hollow discourses on reason," he exclaimed, "are
only empty air: it is language which is its organ and its
criterion." Such remarks could not fail to shock his century;
in any case, his work soon sank into oblivion. This solitary
thinker, for whom faith was the sole source of truth, saw the
Jews as the "genuine original noblemen of the whole human
race and the prejudice of their pride in family and ancestor
is more deeply founded than all the titles of the ridiculous
heraldic style of the chancelleries."[60] Not that he attributed
moral or intellectual pre-eminence over other peoples to the
Children of Israel. It was in the sole name of the Judeo-
Christian revelation that he exclaimed:[61]

Why did God choose this people? Not because of its qualities. Freethinkers may emphasize as strongly as they wish their stupidity and malice in regard to other peoples. Did God not also seek to plant the Gospels through instruments that were equally ignorant and inconsiderable in the eyes of the world? Who can fathom His counsel?

He wrote again:[62]

Jewish history has always been for me the only universal history.... Here there is a fertile field to thresh and flail the blasphemies of our ignorant Hephaistos about Judaism. Every Jew is for me a miracle of all miracles of divine Providence, government and rule—more than Noah's Ark and Lot's wife and Moses' burning bush.

A word must still be said about the anti-Jewish arguments advanced by the militant anti-Christianity party. This party was formed late in Germany, its activity remained unobtrusive and its protagonists were most frequently content to plagiarize English and French authors. The best known philosopher in this context was Hermann Reimarus, whose work was published posthumously and anonymously by Lessing. He adopted an original position in that his criticism and sarcasm were impartially bestowed on Jewish patriarchs and Christian apostles alike and did not even stop at Jesus himself. The two great schools of English deism (which we described above) therefore seemed to be reconciled in his person. At first sight, this would also seem true of Judge Ludwig Christian Paalzow. His *Hierokles* ... (which he also published under the cloak of anonymity) contained an examination of the Christian religion by four characters: the orthodox theologian Less, the rationalist theologians Michaelis and Semler, and Nicolas Fréret, chosen as the harbinger of free thought. More verbose than his three adversaries put together, Fréret emerged victorious at the end of four hundred pages of a discussion in which he incessantly demonstrated the absurdity, intolerance and cruelty of the two Testaments, but primarily of the Old. However, the New was not spared. Fréret said:

> ... since certain theologians state that the Christian religion is based solely on the New Testament and that there is no great need to concern oneself with the divinity of the Old, I would obviously need to embark on an examination of this document. . . .

As a result, he demonstrated that the jealous, morose God of the Christians was not much better than the cruel and vindictive God of the Jews: "I have a horror of reason and I forbid myself to use it. Live in anxiety and fear; and feed on terror, for you know not when the Lord will come. . . ."[63]

But Paalzow later published a book in Latin (*De Civitate Judaeorum*), this time under his own name, directed against the emancipation of the Jews. It contained long translated extracts from J.-B. Mirabaud, notably passages in which the permanent secretary of the Académie française set out to prove that Jews had not been considered base for only eighteen centuries, but were congenitally so and had consequently been despised since time immemorial. He also supported Kant, saying that the Mosaic law was political and not religious, and concluded that there could be no question of welcoming the Jews into the State.[64]

Paalzow's ideas were popularized, in a brisk, racy style, in several booklets by the lawyer Grattenauer, which enjoyed a rapid success in Germany around 1800. For Grattenauer, to talk about emancipating the Jews was "Jacobinism" and "Sans-culottism." They could not be granted civic rights unless their heads were cut off one night and replaced by non-Jewish heads the next, as Professor Fichte had very wisely advocated (it can be seen how the metaphysicians' anti-Semitism spread to the public; this was particularly true of Fichte, who quickly gained a vast audience amongst the young). Otherwise, Grattenauer curiously juxtaposed the criticisms of the Jews that contemporary theology, philosophy and the natural sciences were propounding. Their religion was "finite" and was therefore a superstition (while the Christian religion prescribed faith in the incomprehensible and the infinite and was therefore divine). They were unclean because they never washed; they made money by usury; they were ostentatious and intrusive. They deserved the same treatment as the gypsies. Above all, they stank—a theme to which Grattenauer relentlessly returned, even indicating the nature of the gas (*ammonium pyro-oleosum*) which their race emitted. It was a fact, he concluded, that Germans and Jews faced one another in an implacable war, a "fight to the death."[65]

The success of Grattenauer's pamphlets attracted imitators and emulators. The Jews replied with counter-pamphlets, and the war gathered acrimony until the Prussian government put an end to it in September 1803, by forbidding such documents, whether pro- or anti-Jewish, to be published. Paalzow and Grattenauer remain fairly obscure characters about whom little is known, even though Grattenauer caused a lot of ink to flow in Berlin for a few years. According to some rumors, he ended up penniless and was helped by the Jewish community; others, even more typical, say that he himself was of Jewish origin.[66]

The Berlin Jewish salons

The Jewish colony in Berlin numbered 1,850 members in 1743, and 4,245, or nearly five percent of the population of the capital, in 1777.[67] At the same time as its numbers were increasing, its leading members were growing rich as a result of the wars of Frederick II and the economic expansion of Prussia, and were launching out into all sorts of commercial and manufacturing ventures. They surpassed Christian entrepreneurs both in initiative and wealth. According to Mirabeau, the only millionaires in Berlin were Jews.[68] While the masses, excluded from the guilds and the professions, reduced to small-scale trading and usury, vegetated in devout poverty, these millionaires—the Levys, the Markuses, the Ephraims, the Itzigs—were building sumptuous houses and forming influential connections. High officials and members of the Prussian nobility crowded their receptions. The government granted them a "general lien" which carried with it the grant of all the rights that Christian merchants enjoyed.[69]

Thus a situation which has existed throughout history was legally recognized: a despised class makes up for its inferiority by the power of money. We talked about this phenomenon when we discussed the court Jews and we mentioned it in connection with the "liberated" Jews of medieval Spain.[70] In both these cases, association with the great led the Jews concerned to increase their violations of the Mosaic law, and some of them broke away from it completely. But even then, unless they converted, they remained Jews socially, since there was no "enfranchised" society in which they could integrate. The great new fact of the Century of Enlightenment was that henceforth some Christians also not only deserted but openly challenged their religion. A social stratum, at first only a thin skin, was thus created into which Jews who had broken with Judaism could *assimilate* without becoming Christian, without brutally abjuring the faith of their ancestors, without acknowledging the credo and the God in whose name they were humiliated and persecuted. Moreover their money or their talents, which they did not fail to display, enabled them to play a leading role in this society. This was particularly true in Berlin, a new town, a semi-colonial town, where social and cultural life was low in resources.

This enlightened society, this philosophizing and cosmopolitan stratum, had abandoned the traditional faith in favor of a new cult, that of Reason. This cult too, as we have seen, most frequently implied a very harsh opinion on the subject of the Children of Israel. We have also seen that the Lutheran *Aufklärung*, through the mouths of its theologians and its great philosophers, tended to make its own opinion particularly implacable. (It did, of course, still make the distinction between *Jews,* who seemed to it "regenerable," and *Judaism* which Kant thought required *euthanasia.* But this distinction, so clear-cut in theory, became confused in practice, a confusion already inherent in the ambiguity of the term "Judaism," designating both a religious tradition and a society, an aggregate of men.) Now the Jews who were initiated into Western culture and who were associating with enlightened circles in Berlin hastened to adopt their ideas and opinions. They therefore tended to assess Judaism through the spectacles of the *Aufklärung* : an alienation if ever there was one, they viewed themselves through the eyes of others. They also took a violent stand against the orthodox, that is to say against the mass of Jews, whom they wanted to reform and initiate into the Enlightenment. They were all the more anxious for this as the strong, that is to say, the institutional forms of Jewish solidarity were still in existence : the community, and through it every Jew, was responsible for the offenses and actions of its members, not only morally but also judicially.

To adherents of the ancestral faith, the enlightened Jews were renegades, and rabbis showered them with invective and excommunication. The Jewish *Aufklärung* or *Haskalah,* which orthodox Jews (notably in Poland) called "Berlinism," became for them the worst of heresies. Moses Mendelssohn's attempts to find a point of equilibrium or a compromise between Enlightenment and the tradition of Sinai, were soon left behind. By the force of circumstances, his emulators and descendants in their turn testified against Judaism, that is to say, ultimately against themselves.

They did so in a variety of ways. Moreover, there was a risk that everything they said or wrote would be turned against themselves. Let us first look at the way thinkers and ideologists adapted.

One of the most extraordinary figures on the German philosophical scene at the end of the eighteenth century was the Polish Jew, Solomon Maimon. This son of the ghetto mastered all the arcana of Talmudic thought at a very early age. He then tried to educate himself in "Greek science," his interest stimulated by reading Maimonides (hence his surname). Abandoning wife and children, he went off to philosophize in Germany where he led a vagabond and unedifying existence for the rest of his life. His philosophical output, however considerable, and his criticism of Kant are not of interest to us here. This is by no means true of his most popular book, his *Autobiography*. In many respects, this work suggests Rousseau's *Confessions*, but while the citizen of Geneva aimed at portraying himself completely sincerely, the same purpose pursued by a cynical Jewish philosopher became a statement on Judaism as a whole. This was especially true as Maimon, recalling his youth, gave numerous descriptions of picturesque superstitions and the squalor in which the Polish ghettos wallowed. In this context he lamented his lost youth:[71]

> My life in Poland from my marriage to my emigration, which embraced the springtime of my existence, was a series of miseries with a lack of all facilities for the promotion of culture, and consequently an aimless application of my powers, in the description of which the pen drops from my hands, and the painful memories of which I strive to stifle. The general constitution of Poland at the time; the condition of our people in it, who, like the poor ass with the double burden, are oppressed by their own ignorance and religious prejudices, as well as by the ignorance and prejudices of the ruling classes; the misfortunes of my own family—all these combined to hinder the course of my development and to check my natural disposition. . . .

Maimon's autobiography caused a sensation in Germany. Schiller and Goethe read it with equal delight and Goethe is said to have tried to make his acquaintance.[72]

In his role as a philosopher, however, Maimon proved favorably disposed towards rabbinic moral philosophy, which he compared to true stoicism. He had the obvious

advantage over the great German thinkers of knowing what
he was talking about, and his opinion is worth recording:[73]

> So far as concerns rabbinic moral teachings, then I truly know
> nothing to which objection can be taken, except perhaps that in
> some cases it goes to extremes. It is genuine stocism, but does
> not on that account exclude other useful principles (perfection,
> universal benevolence, etc.). Its holiness even embraces their
> thoughts. In their own way they relate this idea to the following
> verse from Psalms: "Thou shalt have no foreign gods in thee";
> for they ask "what foreign god can dwell in the human heart
> except evil impulses?" They even forbid the deception of a
> pagan, either by deed or word, in a case where he can in fact
> lose nothing, e.g. to use the customary polite greeting "I am
> happy to see you in good health" if it does not express the true
> convictions of the heart. . . . I would have to write a whole book
> if I were to expound all the excellent moral teaching of the
> rabbis. The influence of these teachings in practical life is
> unmistakable. The Polish Jews, who were always allowed to
> engage in all occupations and were not restricted, as in other
> states, to huckstering and usury, are rarely reproached with
> double-dealing. They remain loyal to the country in which they
> live and support themselves in an honest way.

But it was quite exceptional for an enlightened eighteenth-
century Jew to hold such views on the Talmud and its
devotees. More typical was the writing of another philosopher, the Kantian Bendavid, who condemned the rites
and customs of the Jews indiscriminately: "How long will
the excesses of the senseless and shameless ceremonial law
endure?" asked this reformer. "How long will the Jew continue to believe that the heavenly Father will reward him
with a special crown for practicing it?" Moreover, he had
adopted the encyclopedists' theory whereby this law was
only an Egyptian superstition, which the Jews had borrowed
from their masters during their captivity. For the three
thousand years since then, it had not ceased to exert a
disastrous influence on their character. In the Century of
Enlightenment it was preventing them from being benefi-

cent, useful citizens, and such was their egotism, they had even become wolves in their relations with one another:

> The sphere of action of love for one's neighbor was contracting more and more, confining itself to relatives and partners and finally to self. The Jew became an *egoist* and, as the Christian repulsed him while his brethren felt no attraction towards him, he became, what is more serious than being hated, the enemy of mankind or, more accurately, the despiser of mankind.

How could such a lamentable situation be resolved? Conversion to Christianity would settle nothing: "When he has become the despiser of two religions, the Jew emerges from baptism in a worse state than before." Bendavid only saw salvation in the re-education of the Jews in accordance with the dogmas of Reason. Once duly initiated into the Enlightenment, they would realize the absurdity of their superstitions and spontaneously reject them. On himself and on the other already enlightened Jews, devolved the role of instructors and guides in this thankless venture. To be better able to testify on behalf of Reason amongst the Jewish masses, these apostles of Reason also had to forgo the advantages of conversion themselves even if in doing so they ran the risk of genuine martyrdom.[74]

Setting the example, Bendavid himself ran a school for Jews to the end of his life, where not only instruction but also divine worship was carried on in German, and there were numerous attempts of this kind at reform, some more radical than others.

Bendavid's program was a sign of the times. His extreme radicalism could not have better reflected the ambiguous situation of the enlightened Jew, who was trying to persuade his orthodox brethren to leave their state of Jewishness, in order to make his own escape from it more complete. But this state, which had become despicable in his eyes, they delighted in and found glorious. In this way, they compromised and kept a firm hold over the enlightened Jew, who felt that he was their hostage. This situation, pregnant with psychological tension and ambivalence (in this sense Ben-david did not err when he talked about martyrdom) henceforth and as assimilation progressed, marked the lives of Western Jews. Moreover, in the tremendous efforts they made in one way or another to cast off the tunic of Nessus, they showed unprecedented fertility and vitality in all fields of life, which once again contributed to singling them out as "Jews" and to stimulating anti-Semitism.

In the space of the generation which separated the death of Moses Mendelssohn from the Napoleonic occupation, the Berlin Jews, still preserving their legal disabilities which led to an increasing number of conversions, had become lords not only of the financial but also of the intellectual and artistic life of the capital. As a result, they were handled with kid gloves: when Shakespeare's *Merchant of Venice* was presented in Berlin in 1788 the play was preceded by a prologue when the actor playing Shylock assured the Jews that they enjoyed general esteem, and asked them not to take offense at the views his part forced him to voice.[75] Such practices spread to the provinces, where some Jews thought that the golden age had dawned. In 1792, a Jewish writer from Breslau, Moses Herschel, exclaimed:[76]

Thanks to our philosophical century, the age of barbarism has passed away, when one must expect a contemptuous grimace at the mention of the word Jew. The torch of philosophy also illumines with its beneficent light our Silesia, and divine tolerance has made itself at home there. The man who is capable and worthy, whatever his faith and religious opinions, can henceforth lay claim to the affection and respect of those who think differently; he is certain to benefit from it. The Christian and the Jew can love each other with a brotherly love, esteem each other, and honor each other. . . .

To be honest, judging by the press of the period, educated Christians were divided in their views. Some memorialists welcomed the Jewish contribution to the *Aufklärung*,[77] while others were already complaining of being invaded by "that seed of Abraham, as countless as the sand on the sea shore."[78]

In Berlin, it was the fashionable cliques which were dominated by de-Judaized Jews: the backing of a Jewish salon was an unparalleled means of winning fame in the city. Even the intransigent Fichte sought the advantages of such protection: he gave his first Berlin lecture on his "Wissenschaftslehre" in 1800 in Madame Samuel-Salomon Levy's salon.[79] He had been introduced into Jewish circles by Dorothea Mendelssohn, the philosopher's eldest daughter, about whom he wrote to his wife as follows: "Praise of a Jew may seem strange in my mouth, but this woman has destroyed my conviction that nothing good could come out of that nation."[80]

The case of the Mendelssohn family supplies a leading illustration of the shifting destinies of the enlightened and de-Judaized Jews and of their problems, baptism dominant amongst them. Mendelssohn's six children seem to have inherited his character: they remained united throughout their successive doubts and repudiations, and none of them joined the growing flock of anti-Semitic Jews. The arguments for and against conversion at that time are described with total frankness in a letter which one of Mendelssohn's daughters-in-law addressed to a Christian friend in 1799:[81]

Hitherto most converts, through their poor and inconsistent behavior, have cast a kind of contempt on this action, and this also brands the better ones. If somebody emerged who represented a respectable model through unblemished character, through persistence in his hopes and worldliness of conduct (in accordance with which most judgments are determined, sad to say) then a large part of this assertion, which is only too well founded, would disappear. It would be gratifying if this hypocrisy could be dispensed with. But the urge for higher activity than that of a merchant, or a thousand tender bonds in which close contact with members of other religions can involve young minds, do not allow of any other solution. I think that I have never heard your views about this step, they are of great interest and importance to me. . . .

As far as the philosopher's direct descendants were concerned, his youngest son, Nathan, converted to Protestantism and became an official, while the two elder, Joseph and Abraham, remained Jewish and set up a banking firm. Abraham, however, the father of the composer Mendelssohn-Bartholdy, had his children converted, because, as he wrote to his daughter, "Christianity is the religion of the majority of civilized men."[82] His converted brother-in-law, Bartholdy suggested the following argument to clear his conscience:[83]

Do you think you have done something wrong in giving your children that religion which you think the better for them? It is a real tribute which you and we all are paying to your father's efforts for true enlightenment in general, and he would have acted as you have done for your children, perhaps as I have done, for my part. One can remain faithful to an oppressed, persecuted religion; one can force it on one's children in expectation of a life-long martyrdom—so long as one believes it to be the only religion that can save you. But if one no longer believes this; then it is barbarous.

As for Mendelssohn's daughters, one, Recha, of whom little is known, seems to have remained Jewish, while the other two finally turned to Catholicism. The youngest, Henriette, opened a boarding school for Parisian society girls where she held a salon patronized by Madame de Staël, Benjamin Constant and the composer Spontini. Distinguished for her exemplary piety, she later taught Fanny Sébastiani, the future Duchess of Praslin. Dorothea, the eldest sister, had a much more adventurous life. She married the banker, Simon Veit, and had two children, but in about 1795 she left him to throw herself into the arms of the fiery romantic Friedrich Schlegel. For a few years, the couple scandalized Berlin by flaunting their free union, which provided them with the material for two *avant-garde* novels, devoted to their respective partners: Schlegel's *Lucinda* (1799) and Dorothea's *Florentin* (1801). After which, the latter plunged into reading the Bible, "by way of antidote," she wrote to Schleiermacher in November 1802. "I am reading with care both Testaments and feel that even Protestant Christianity is yet purer and to be preferred by far to Catholic. The latter is for me too similar to the old Judaism, and I detest it, while Protestantism seems to me to be the true religion of Christ and the religion of educated people."[84]

In 1804, Dorothea converted to Protestantism which enabled her to regularize her union with Schlegel. The couple then settled in Vienna and a conversion to Catholicism ensued, facilitating the husband's diplomatic career with the Austrian government.

Dorothea and Friedrich met at the leading Berlin Jewish salon held by Henriette Herz, the wife of Dr Herz, a friend and disciple of Kant's. Famous for her statuesque beauty, she made many conquests. Schleiermacher, in particular, adopted her as his "soul-sister," stating that she was "the nearest thing to himself." Platonic or not, their relationship delighted Berlin caricaturists because of the difference in stature between the buxom Jewish Juno and the puny Lutheran preacher. She also was converted in her old age and wrote memoirs in which she describes, not without perspicacity, the reasons for the attraction the Jewish salons exercised on contemporary German youth:[85]

> There, there was no mediation of a tradition, of a culture transmitting itself from generation to generation, keeping pace with the spirit and knowledge of the time; and also none of the prejudice formed by such a train of culture. The lavishness, the arrogance, the transcendence of accepted forms in expression is to be attributed to a similar nature of this spirit and the awareness of this in those women who embodied it. But it was undeniably very original, very powerful, very piquant, very exciting and frequently, with its astounding mobility, of great profundity. . . .

Henriette Herz's salon became the main center of the "League of Virtue" (*Tugendbund*), the name given by antiphrasis to the young Berlin romantic movement. For these young people, moral freedom went hand in hand with the fight against the austere morality personified by the old God of Israel, and in this fight the young generation of enlightened Jews participated with increasing commitment.

Evidence of the deep-seated motives behind this fight and of the horrible fascination their historic past held for these deserters from the ghetto, is supplied by a woman of quite different caliber from Henriette Herz or Dorothea Mendelssohn. Ugly and graceless, Rahel Levin (1771–1832), the daughter of a jeweler, was, according to all her contemporaries, endowed with strange charm and exceptional intelligence. She too held a salon, on the upper floor of the building where her family lived. Her attic room became the hearth of literary life in Germany. Princes, poets and distinguished foreigners passing through, were regular visitors there. There was born the cult of Goethe and there the young romantics pronounced the final death sentence on the cult of Reason. Prince Louis Ferdinand of Prussia, the diplomat Gentz, the Humboldt brothers, Heinrich von Kleist, Adalbert Chamisso, Clemens Brentano, the Tieck brothers were numbered amongst Rahel's friends and admirers. If Henriette Herz was the Madame du Deffand of all philosophic and literary Berlin, Rahel Levin was its Madame de Lespinasse. What makes this comparison all the more justifiable is the fact that salons frequented by intellectual and high-born people, like the Paris salons, were primarily a Jewish institution in Prussia in the last years of the eighteenth century.

As the most recent biographer of this great midwife of German intellects writes, "the central desire of her life had been escape from Jewishness."[86] Her vast correspondence often confirms this obsession and some of her expressions are startling. To her childhood friend David Veit, she wrote:

I have a strange fancy: it is as if some supramundane being, just as I was thrust into this world, plunged these words with a dagger into my heart: "Yes, have sensibility, see the world as few see it, be great and noble, nor can I take from you the faculty of eternal thinking. But I add one thing more: be a Jewess!" And now my life is a slow bleeding to death. By keeping still I can delay it. Every movement in an attempt to staunch it—new death; and immobility is possible for me only in death itself. ... I can, if you will, derive every evil, every misfortune, every vexation from *that*.[87]

The same vehemence occurs in a letter addressed to her brother:[88]

... I do not forget this shame for a single second. I drink it in water, I drink it in wine, I drink it with the air; in every breath, that is.... The Jew must be extirpated from us, that is the sacred truth, and it must be done even if life were uprooted in the process.

After several disappointed love affairs (Count Karl von Finckenstein, Don Raphael d'Urquijo, Alexander von der Marwitz), Rahel Levin converted in 1814 and married the Prussian diplomat and man of letters August Varnhagen von Ense, fourteen years younger than herself. Their marriage was a happy one. On her death bed she forgave herself at last for being what she was and her final words are famous. She marveled:[89]

What a story! I am here a refugee from Egypt and Palestine and find help, love and care with you! To you, dear August, I was sent, through God's guidance, and you to me. With lofty delight I think of my origin and this whole combination of fate through which the oldest memories of the human race are joined to the most modern conditions, the most distant scenes in time and space. What was to me for so long the greatest reproach, the bitterest suffering and misfortune, to be a Jewess, not for anything would I now like to give it up. Will the same thing not happen to me with this bed of suffering, will I not rise once again in the same way and not wish to miss it for anything?

Dear August, what a consoling idea, what a significant comparison!

Judaism, consolation of their ancestors, was thus becoming the very symbol of sickness and torment for Rahel Levin's generation. Her brother, the minor poet Ludwig Robert, himself a convert, outlined a more theological variation on this theme (originally written in sonnet form):[90]

If he is a Jew who, in his mother's womb, was already condemned to a lowly slavish state, who lives an outlaw in his own country, a target for the mud hurled by the mob, when nothing can help, whatever he tries and does, whose cup of sorrows remains full to the brim, contemptuous and shameful, then I am a Jew and know it will always be so.

And if that man is a Christian whose great effort is humbly to bear his earthly cross and to love those who hate him bitterly believing that everything that tears his heart apart has been sent by the Lord to prove him—then I am a Christian, that I can truly say.

While vibrant, sensitive souls were torn in this way, more robust temperaments were trying to escape the suffering of being Jewish by banishing Judaism from their personal lives. This was feasible, given a thick skin and, above all, adequate material means. Conversion, elevation to the nobility, aristocratic marriage, an establishment in Vienna, Paris, London, where it was easier to lose oneself: the descendants of the *nouveaux-riches* Jews of the period dissolved entirely (with rare exceptions, led by the Rothschilds) within the body and notably the aristocracy of the Christians.[91] From a historian's point of view, the conclusion emerges that, contrary to common opinion, Judaism in modern times was certainly not a religion for the rich!

In this context, a word must be said about the two great Viennese salons held by two Berlin Jewesses, the sisters Fanny and Cecily Itzig, married respectively to the Viennese bankers Nathan von Arnstein (or Arnsteiner) and Bernhard von Eskeles. The Arnstein salon, in particular, became the center of all the vanities of the world at the time of the Congress of Vienna, and some of its receptions were said to be even more splendid than the Emperor's.[92] All the diplomats of Europe, nuncios and cardinals included, made it their meeting place and, according to a memorialist, the Tsar, Alexander I, did not think it beneath his dignity to appear there.[93] Fanny von Arnstein, for her part, was such a passionate proponent of Prussian nationalism that, when relations between Prussia and Austria deteriorated, the conflict had repercussions on matrimonial relations and her husband had to dine alone. In fact, criticism of her native land upset her completely and she became so offensive that even Prussian diplomats were embarrassed by her patriotism.[94]

It was she who was said to have introduced the custom of Christmas Eve in the Lutheran style into Viennese society.[95] Although they still did not convert, the Arnsteins and Eskeles's had thus completely broken away from Judaism. Nonetheless the husbands intervened on behalf of the general emancipation of the Jews on one occasion, and above all, however de-Judaized these families were, they remained, in their guests' eyes, very Jewish. Chancellor Nesselrode, who guided Russian foreign policy for forty years, commented: "The amiability of Madame and Mademoiselle Arnsteiner has imbued me with the desire to associate with Jews; if there are many like them, their society is well worth the effort of cultivating."[96] One can see how people who were Jewish in nothing but name, could be the best advertisement. The autocrat of all the Russians may well have been influenced by his Viennese impressions when he began to evince a quite unusual interest in the children of the ghetto at the same time as he was creating the Holy Alliance.[97]

How did one go about shedding one's Jewishness? A case in point is the banker, Salomon Moses Levy, the nephew of Frau Samuel-Salomon Levy who tried to launch Fichte in Berlin. In about 1805, he converted and took the name of

Delmar, an adaptation of his paternal first name (Moses means drawn from the waters). During the French occupation, he set about getting himself made a nobleman, citing the services he had rendered the State. The Prussian officials charged with investigating his claim presented an unflattering portrait, which can be taken for a good likeness:[98]

> Delmar possesses the effrontery characteristic of that sort of person in his intercourse with others who seem to him well-bred and elegant. On the surface, he has a watery veneer of fine culture and also the natural disposition to be a banker in a place like Berlin and the necessary knowledge and skills. But his apparent merit entirely disappears on closer examination.

Delmar then brought the authorities of the occupying power into the affair. The French ambassador, Saint-Marsan, certified that he was a good Prussian:[99]

> I know him intimately because he has done business for the French administration and it is precisely because I have had to recognize that he has always acted with the greatest probity on the one hand and with the sentiments of a good Prussian, a faithful subject of His Majesty, on the other, that I dare to take the liberty of commending him as he deserves. . . .

The French backing proved effective; in September 1810, he received the diploma of Baron (*Freiherr*) Friedrich von Delmar. In gratitude or as a matter of tactics, he chose a French baron's coronet for his coat of arms. Later, his younger brother Karl-August joined the ranks of the Prussian army in the campaigns of 1813–14, and was promoted lieutenant. When peace was restored, Friedrich von Delmar gave up business to try and play a political role. He is seen at the Congress of Aix-la-Chapelle in 1818 keeping open house for diplomats. But his ambitions were probably not satisfied in Prussia. Shortly afterwards, he settled in Paris, where he married a young Englishwoman, Miss Rumbold, and set about breaking into Faubourg Saint-Germain society. His receptions were so sumptuous and his generosity so extensive (except where Jews were concerned) that "even the proudest dowagers and most scatterbrained misses," wrote Heinrich Heine, "stopped making fun of him aloud."[100] He died without issue; Heine's sally has perpetuated the memory of this forgotten character, whom Balzac might well have used as a model.

It was primarily parvenus like this who aroused the wrath of old-established Prussians at the time when Europe was entering the "get rich quick" era. Not that the Christian bourgeoisie with the necessary talents failed to do as much as these Jews but their ascent seemed less spectacular and was less of a shock, probably because there was less to forgive them for. A quotation from a letter which Marshall Gneisenau wrote to Marshall Blücher in July 1818, and which really belongs to later chapters, throws light on this:[101]

> I subscribe with all my heart to what Your Excellency wrote to me on the 10th about the new plans and the Jews. It is the sickness, indeed the rage of the epoch, to overthrow everything old and introduce new legislation. Thereby, and in the course of time, the nobility will be destroyed and in their place Jews and contractors will enter and become our peers of the realm. This Jewish scandal disgusts me, just like the evil-doing of this age when only those people are honored who can make a great display and give great dinners which people attend, however corrupt the host may be. . . .

Nothing is more characteristic than the distinction the old soldier was making between "Jews," specifically designated, and the anonymous Christian "contractors," both of whom were conniving in the "Jewish scandal" of the nascent industrial revolution.

Let us go back to the pre-Napoleonic period. While a growing number of rich Jews were emancipating themselves and only themselves, the Jewish communities were beginning the struggle for the collective concession of Jewish rights. During Frederick II's lifetime, any hope in this direction was useless so that discussion of emancipation was limited to questions of principle. But as soon as his successor Frederick William II came to the throne in 1786, the Berlin community multiplied efforts to get the antiquated and odious régime reformed. A committee was set up, with David Friedländer, a rich and enthusiastic follower of Mendelssohn, its moving spirit. The current atmosphere was favorable: the ideas of Mendelssohn and Dohm had germinated; in Austria and France, Joseph II and Louis XVI were beginning to set the example; and the German Jews seemed to have gained the ear of the new monarch. A government committee was appointed and negotiations opened for a gradual improvement of the condition of the Jews. Immediate enfranchisement was out of the question; the government committee even estimated that it would take two to three generations, sixty to seventy years, before Jews were able to obtain complete equality of rights.[102]

The bargaining between the government committee and the Berlin community went on for ten years and had no positive result. In the government's opinion, it was up to the Jews to make the first move by proving themselves honest and useful subjects. The Jewish delegates objected that to do this, the innumerable disabilities, tyrannies and victimizations which darkened the lives of the Children of Israel had first to be abolished. In 1798, the committee informed the delegates of its final decision. This decision continued to pay lip-service to the great principles of the *Aufklärung*, while reaching conclusions of truly Prussian harshness. It agreed, in effect, that the special laws governing the Jews were harsh and treated them unfairly in relation to other subjects of the State. It added that their repeal would be a credit to mankind and advantageous to bourgeois society. Nonetheless, "in view of the particular character of that nation," it decreed that these be retained in full:[103]

So long therefore as it [the Jewish nation] continues to separate itself from the other inhabitants of the State, not only through its speculative religious opinions but also by practical statutes, customs, habits and decrees, and to cherish a certain national hatred for others; so long as they form, as it were, a special state by virtue of their internal constitution and hierarchy; so long as the education of the great majority is conducted in such a perverted way contrary to the interests of the State; so long as no thorough and general improvement takes place in all these respects, in which only the nation itself can effectively act; so long therefore as the causes remain which have motivated the laws as a means of protection for other citizens, which form the object of the present complaint; the abrogation of these laws is all the less likely to take place, as, on the one hand, experience has not shown that such awkward consequences for the innocent members of the nation, as the petitioners in their representation have sought to show, have in fact really emerged; on the other hand however, the further existence of these laws is yet another reason for the Jews to think towards a solid reform as described above and thereby qualify themselves for complete equality with the other citizens of the State.

On the whole, this decision was consistent with the philosophy of men like Bendavid and other radical reformers.

The expedient of individual conversion remained—and certain delegates had not failed to brandish this threat during the negotiations:[104]

No longer able to endure their condition, they would abandon the religion of their fathers, out of frivolity, perhaps out of despair, and with hypocritical harmful principles and with a corrupt heart insinuate themselves into the larger religious community. The dominant party will of course gain nothing through the entry of such believers but the converts will have attained their end, even at the sacrifice of their moral character.

Sure enough, in 1799, judging that all their efforts to gain admittance to the state were going to continue useless, Friedländer and his enlightened friends tried to approach the Lutheran Church, in order to obtain equality of rights via the expedient of collective conversion. To this end, they issued an appeal, signed by a group of "heads of Jewish families." However, these were men of some position and they had their principles: aware of their responsibilities, they did not want to cheat about their convictions. (In this domain, stricter adherence to principles was demanded of the Jew than of the Christian: the Christian could take his religion lightly without being socially suspect, while the converted Jew was presumed insincere, unless he furnished striking proof to the contrary; a fresh injustice which extended to other fields after emancipation.) Now, these enlightened "heads of families" could quite sincerely state that they had rejected the Talmud and ritualism, that they believed in the immortality of the soul and the infinite perfectibility of the individual, and that they found the eternal truths best expressed in Protestantism. But this still left the mysteries and the dogma—first and foremost the divinity of Christ.

This stumbling block they could not in good faith surmount, and in this they were like so many other Jews in the present and in past centuries who (to go back to the Hegelian formula) "saw in Jesus only the man, the Nazarene, the carpenter's son, whose brothers and kinsfolk lived among them; so much he was, and more he could not be for he was only one like themselves. . . ." Because of this, the "heads of families," in accordance with the teachings of Kant and his pupil Bendavid, suggested the formation of a new Judeo-Christian sect, which they thought ought to take its place in the ranks of the numerous Protestant sects alongside the Socinians or the Unitarians. They declared that they were ready to submit to baptism:[105]

> If the religion of the Protestants prescribes certain ceremonies, then we can well submit ourselves to these as pure forms which are demanded for entry into a society; it being well understood that these ceremonies are only demanded as actions, as customs, to demonstrate that the member admitted has accepted the eternal truths and, as man and citizen, subordinated himself to

the duties flowing from them; but not as a sign that the person who performs these actions admits that he accepts in faith the *dogmas* of the church of this society.

The appeal was personally addressed to one of the leaders of the Lutheran Consistory in Berlin, Pastor Wilhelm Teller, an *Aufklärer* with advanced ideas who had no hesitation in denying the transcendent nature of the revelation of God in Christ in his sermons and writings. However, the reply received from this ultra-rationalist theologian was not encouraging: when faced with Jews, it could be said that he rediscovered greater Christian orthodoxy. While rejoicing to see the "heads of families" abandoning the outdated Law of Moses and while expressing the hope that many of their co-religionists would imitate them, he insidiously asked them:[106]

> You whom the spirit of Christ has already penetrated, why do you also want to benefit from the ecclesiastical repute of those who are baptized in his Name? Does not this spirit give you enough dignity in the eyes of all Christians with higher feelings?

Would they not do better, he added, to stay as they were and devote themselves to the regeneration of other Jews? Having said this, he, for his part, was prepared to grant them baptism; but he laid down conditions and reservations of a practical nature:[107]

> To be Christian you must at least accept the sacraments of baptism and communion and acknowledge the historical truth that Christ is the founder of the most sublime moral religion. It is possible to grant you freedom of religious opinions, which moreover differ within the Church itself, but not as far as the dogmas are concerned. . . . I cannot even tell you in advance if and what civic rights the State will think it has to grant you following your declaration: this is a quite different matter. Protestantism subordinates the Church to the State and the

latter is free to refuse civic rights to any sect, even the Protestant.

Moreover, as the "heads of families" had made their appeal public, voices were raised from all directions shouting them down. Schleiermacher taxed them with hypocrisy, accusing them of being guided by purely material reasons, and he expressed the fear of seeing the Lutheran Church invaded by a sort of "judaizing Christianity."[108]

A well-known scholar, the Swiss physician Jean-André de Luc, the leading advocate of Biblical cosmogony, joined the discussion in about 1800 to express fears of a different sort: by abandoning the Mosaic law, were not the Jews threatening to overthrow the Christian religion as well as their own?[109]

> The privileges which the Jews enjoy in Christian society are based on their profession to acknowledge the divine laws in the Old Testament ... what it is important to note in respect of the Jews is that, as soon as the chain of the Revelations is broken, as soon in fact as they abandon what it is obvious that God himself established, nothing can remain of Christianity but an empty name. . . .

The Jews had therefore to remain integrally Jews, all the more so because there were only too many ungodly men amongst the Christians who "are *born* into the Church: they cannot be rejected without a scandal; and this is a further reason for not admitting people who formally declare that they are of that number—*turpius est ejicere, quam non admittere hostem*" (which is another way of saying that there are two sets of weights and two sets of measures, one for Jews and the other for Christians).

The champion of irreligion, Ludwig Christian Paalzow, joined in the concert, publishing a reply to Friedländer's appeal under the title *Von den Juden* which was a prelude to his treatise *De Civitate Judaeorum*.[110] The "heads of families" petition seemed to be unanimously rejected; at the time, only Immanuel Kant seems to have approved of it.[111]

The collective conversion did not take place. The new Protestant sect was not formed. Once again, the shadow of the Jewish man/god came between Christian and Jew.

PART TWO

EMANCIPATION

seven

The Emancipation

As a bourgeois, industrial and secularized society with a uniform legal system replaced the hierarchical, feudal society of the Middle Ages in Europe, the emancipation of the Jews became inevitable. It was unthinkable that a class of men, who played a leading role in trade and production, should remain subject to a special régime and laws. On the eve of the French Revolution, this emancipation was on its way in all the countries of Western Europe, in the wake of the humanitarian ideas of the period. As far afield as the Tsarist empire, Alexander I would try to improve the position of the dispersed people, even dreaming of setting himself up as their universal protector. But it fell to revolutionary France to offer the world the spectacle of complete emancipation in accordance with the Declaration of the Rights of Man, and this example was followed by most of the other countries when they were under Napoleonic domination. Because of this, all the credit for the emancipation of the Jews was attributed to French revolutionary ideology. This circumstance was probably partly responsible for pushing the Jews into the so-called left-wing camp as and when they became emancipated. Above all, it aroused German national feeling against them from generation to generation and from war to war, heightening that specifically Germanic intolerance.

On the other hand, a number of people were profoundly disturbed by the spectacle of the enfranchisement and rise of the Jews, and the sense of a new and obscure threat revived the medieval legends woven around the "deicidal people." Suitably adapted to the taste of the time—that is to say, secularized and politicized—the final version of them would emerge as "The Protocols of the Elders of Zion." This seems to be the specific root of modern anti-Semitism, against the background of its more general ingredients such as economic jealousies and professional rivalries. We will discuss this later. First we must see how the emancipation of the Jews took place in the major territorial divisions of the continent of Europe and what reactions it aroused.

Emancipation in France

We have already mentioned the work of the Malesherbes committee entrusted by Louis XVI with improving the Jews' position, after having reformed that of the Protestants. "Monsieur de Malesherbes, you have made yourself a Protestant and I am making you a Jew!" legend has it the King said to him. The last vestige of medieval Jewish legislation, the *Leibzoll*, had already been abolished in 1782 (though it continued to exist in Alsace). Louis XVI's edict specified ". . . that it is repugnant to the feelings that we bear towards all our subjects, to allow a tax which seems to degrade mankind to continue in respect of any one of them."[1] This humanitarian edict only aroused opposition from one important quarter, the Parlement de Paris, which refused to register it, considering it "infinitely dangerous in its effects because it would imply public acknowledgment that the Jews have the right to reside in the Kingdom."[2] This should probably be interpreted as a symptom of the specific anti-Semitism of the bourgeoisie, and notably the Parisian bourgeoisie, which we have already mentioned on several occasions.

Then came the calling of the States-General, which has left a vast documentation on the state of public opinion in France on the eve of the Revolution, in the form of the

"Cahiers des Doléances," the complaint books. In provinces which had a Jewish population, these books overflowed with grievances against them, notably in Alsace and Lorraine, where the three estates seemed unanimous, as a good historian tells us: "... the tone alone varies; the clergy sermonize, the nobility is self-assertive, the lawyers quibble. Basically, all agree. The number of Jews has increased excessively and their usury is ruining the population of the countryside. . . ."[3] But it was not only usury: to judge by the example of the book of the clergy of Colmar, the evil went infinitely deeper:[4]

> The Jews, by their harassment, their depredations, the greedy duplicity of which they daily offer such pernicious examples, being the first and foremost cause of the poverty of the people, of the loss of all sense of industry, of the moral depravity in a class formerly renowned for that much vaunted Germanic faith .... [for all these causes] only the eldest son of every Jewish family should in future be allowed to contract a marriage.

Suggestions for more revolutionary and enlightened remedies are found more frequently in the books of the nobility than in the books of the clergy or third estate. The nobility of Toul was a case in point, while the Metz nobles even noted that "all honest means of subsistence are forbidden to the Jews," and asked "that they should be allowed to practice the liberal and mechanical arts, like the rest of His Majesty's subjects."[5] The Paris nobility seem to have had the same idea when they proposed in their book that the lot of the Jews be taken into consideration.[6]

In addition to the positions taken up by the three estates—for the most part hostile—there was also the inarticulate stand adopted by the "silent classes," the "fourth estate," that is to say the mass of the rural proletariat, "whose needs are never known because they are never consulted."[7] In Alsace, they expressed their views against the background of the Great Terror of July 1789, by a wave of pillaging and pogroms, which forced thousands of Jews to seek refuge in neighboring Switzerland.

However, the Jews did not remain passive. They formulated grievances on their own account. But at this period there were several types of Jew in France who had nothing culturally or socially in common other than the fact that they answered to the name of Jews. We have already mentioned the gulf which separated the "Ashkenazim" of the East (the largest group) from the "Sephardim" of the South-west, to whom the Jews of Avignon, called "Papal Jews," were connected. In addition, in Paris at that period, there were several hundred semi-clandestine Jews, already partly won over to the new ideas of the times. The German Jews of the East were sending delegations to Paris, anxious to run with the hares and hunt with the hounds, that is to say to get the restrictive law abolished and still preserve the autonomy of their community, their internal legislation and their orthodox traditions. The "Portuguese" Jews were trying to keep apart from these compromising co-religionists, deliberately disassociating themselves from their representations. In the long run, as the Revolution progressed, it was the action of the small group of Parisian Jews which conquered the reluctance of the Constituent Assembly and tore the great theoretical decision from it.

These ambiguities and contradictions were reproduced in French society at large. If the bourgeoisie, bent on destroying the privileges of the nobility, was speaking and acting in the name of the people, the French Protestants, oppressed by the Church, acted as the first spearhead in the emancipation of the Jews. During the discussion on the Declaration of the Rights of Man, the Protestant spokesman, Rabaut de Saint-Étienne, pleading the cause of his co-religionists, also appealed on behalf of the "people torn from Asia":[8]

... I therefore ask, Gentlemen, for the French Protestants, for all the non-Catholics of the Kingdom, what you ask for yourselves, liberty, equal rights; I ask them for those people torn from Asia, always wandering, always outlawed, always persecuted for the length of eighteen centuries, who would adopt our customs and our habits if they were united with us by our laws, and whose morals we must not criticize because they are the fruit of our own barbarism and of the humiliation to which we have unjustly condemned them!

The theses of the Abbé Grégoire and other "regenerators" of the Jews can incidentally be recognized here.

On December 21–3, 1789, the Constituent Assembly moved on to actual decisions. The total enfranchisement of the Protestants was adopted without difficulty, and at the same time civic rights were granted to actors and even hangmen. Only the Jews were refused them, in the face of opposition from representatives of the clergy and the Eastern provinces. Moreover, even advocates of their emancipation, like Abbé Grégoire or Mirabeau, agreed that the Jews formed a fallen nation, governed by barbarous laws, but, in the great tradition of the Enlightenment, they wanted to reform and regenerate them, while their adversaries hoped to keep them in their former state. A speech by Robespierre at that session nicely summed up the "philosophical" idea: "The Jews' vices are born of the degradation you have plunged them into; they will be good when they can find some advantage in so being!"[9] Clermont-Tonnerre's famous formula did even better: "Everything for the Jews as citizens, nothing as a nation!"[10] In fact, the problem of how to reconcile Talmudic traditions and dispersion with the emancipating ideas of the Enlightenment was difficult, if not insoluble. We have seen the anguish it caused the "good Jew" Moses Mendelssohn.

In the opposite camp, La Fare, Bishop of Nancy, Abbé Maury, the great defender of Louis XVI, and above all the future Montagnard and member of the Directory, Rewbell, deputy for Alsace, were collecting arguments to demonstrate that the Jews were incorrigible, and that any change in their status carried serious risks (the danger of Jewish domination or the danger of a popular outburst).[11] Briefly, one side wanted to raise the Jews up and abolish traditional Judaism; the other to demote the former and maintain the latter. Those two great options recur very often in other countries and at other periods. In the end, the Constituent Assembly passed the following motion by 408 votes to 403: "The National Assembly recognizes that non-Catholics are capable of filling all civil and military offices, except the Jew, on whom it reserves judgment."

However, Jews and Judaism, it cannot be repeated too often, were only words which covered very varied actualities, and their non-Christian status within Western civilization might have been their only common denominator. The "Portuguese," well integrated into the Bordeaux bourgeoisie, maneuvered separately and obtained equal rights a month later, on January 28, 1790. It was not a painless process; that session, which lasted for eleven hours without a break, was the stormiest the Constituent Assembly had ever known. Characteristically, Mirabeau's paper commented on the violent obstruction on the part of representatives of the clergy: "The anti-Judaic party itself was reminiscent of one's image of a synagogue."[12] In fact, the emancipation of the Sephardim was supported, probably decisively, by the Girondins of Sèze, in the name of the town of Bordeaux, while the Alsatian municipalities, notably Strasbourg and Colmar, were opposing emancipation of the Ashkenazim with all their might.[13] Rewbell, for his part, shouted at the top of his voice amidst the uproar: "It is being proposed, Gentlemen, that you declare that the Jews of Bordeaux are not Jews!"[14] The polemics of the time contained arguments which are even more symptomatic of the Christian attitude. Commenting on the session of December 24 (when general emancipation had been deferred), the *Gazette de Paris* exclaimed: "Have we not already on too many occasions forgotten that the King of the French used also to be the Very Christian King? Can he not be King of the French without being King of the Jews?"[15] After the emancipation of the "Portuguese," the paper returned to the attack: "The King of the French should not be King of the Jews!" A curious pamphlet was on sale clandestinely at the Palais Royal at this period; it was entitled: *"Mort et passion de Louis XVI, roi des Juifs et des Français."*[16] Continued agitation and representations on the part of the delegates of the Ashkenazim and the militant Paris Jews caused another moderate paper, *Le Journal de la Cour et de la Ville,* to write on the eve of Easter, 1790: "Their agents should suspend their representations during the week we are about to enter; they should not shut their eyes to the fact that it is full of memories which are unfavorable to them."[17]

Léon Kahn, a chronicler of the first order whose work on *Les Juifs de Paris pendant la Révolution* is still an excellent source book, thought it was legitimate to state that global emancipation only became possible after the king's attempt to flee abroad.[18] This comment is far-reaching. In actual fact, despite the valuable support of the Paris Commune, despite the evidence of a totally enlightened state of mind which the Jews of the capital provided incessantly and copiously,[19] for ten months the Constituent Assembly refused to embark on a re-examination of the question. Everything changed after the famous Varennes affair, that historic accident which destroyed the sacred aura surrounding the Very Christian King of the French, and without which it is hard to imagine his trial and execution, that is to say a basic feature of the French Revolution. On September 27, 1791, before it broke up, the Constituent Assembly provided for total emancipation of the Jews almost unanimously with no serious objections from its few opponents. Regnault de Saint-Jean d'Angély, who was presiding, had cautioned it: "I ask that all those who will speak against this proposal be called to order, for they will be fighting against the Constitution itself."[20] The threat was barely veiled. Times had changed; a new spirit was ruling in Paris, a spirit which would lead to the trial of Louis XVI and the de-Christianization campaigns. It seemed as if the course of events which would later lead to the *regicide* was tending then and thereafter to exonerate the *deicidal* people. Interesting on this score was an anti-revolutionary pamphlet which appeared in 1794, with the suggestive title *Parallèle des Juifs qui ont crucifié Jésus-Christ leur Messie, et des Français qui ont guillotiné Louis XVI leur roi.*[21]

If such an interpretation (bringing in psycho-historical factors which are no less significant however difficult they are to expose) seems hazardous, think of the cleavage in nineteenth-century French society, and the traditional philo-Semitism of a "left" which is only made up of the descendants of the regicides. Was not a fundamental psychological barrier thrust aside when, with great show and extreme solemnity, God's anointed, his earthly representative was put to death? Did it not stimulate those descendants to identify themselves with the descendants of the assassins of God, or to feel that they were accomplices with them and to espouse their cause? The "right-minded" only bewailed the emancipation of the Jews all the more strongly. Commemorating the events of 1789 a century later, Abbé Joseph Lémann, a converted Jew, wrote:[22]

The day of December 23, 1789, was deeply humiliating for our race, but it was sublime in its justice! Yes, the hangman deserved to be reinstated before we were; because the hangman only causes men, the guilty, to die, and we, we have caused the death of the innocent Son of God!

Obviously this psycho-historical aspect of the emancipation of the Jews, however typical, was not the only factor determining the course of emancipation. The case of the Jews can be compared to the colored peoples who were refused rights of citizenship in the same September. And although the Constituent Assembly passed the abolition of slavery on September 28, the morrow of the emancipation of the Jews, it was retained in the colonies, under pressure from the great planters. In this case, prejudice or "physical repugnance" combined with the operation of powerful interests. Where the Jews were concerned, no organized interest of any great extent was involved, given their small numbers, their heterogeneity and their dispersion. In these circumstances, emancipation could be decreed on the basis of purely ideological considerations, as a statement of principle, and, in one sense, its greatness lay in this.

The Jews, notably the Jews of Paris, had worked hard in this matter, which was of vital importance to them. On the other hand, they played practically no part in the French Revolution, and it seems that the majority of Jews in the East remained not only passive but also indifferent, or at least reserved spectators of the discussion which proceeded on the subject of their fate. In this context it is interesting to note that at no time did contemporaries attribute the collapse of the monarchy or the persecution of the Church to a Jewish plot. It was only later, as we will see, that such interpretations sprang up. It is true that people looking for a simple, Manichean explanation, involving a hidden power which acted in the darkness, could turn to the Protestants who were more numerous and more powerful. This opinion was voiced as early as 1790. It was repeated considerably more frequently later.[23]

Jews did not figure amongst either the passive or active actors in the Terror therefore, with a few rare exceptions.[24] But the de-Christianization campaigns naturally brought de-Judaization campaigns in their wake. Listen to *La Feuille du Salut public* thundering against circumcision:[25]

> ... before the error is dissipated, how many children may fall victim to this Judaic observance? This subject, which concerns society, has not yet engaged the attention of our legislators. A specific law is required forbidding the *descendants of Abraham* to circumcise male children. ...

Some rabbis were also prepared to parade their good

citizenship like the clergy and ministers. Solomon Hesse, for example, "Jewish priest in Paris," declared on Brumaire 20, year II, that he "had no other god but the god of liberty, no other belief but in equality" and offered the homeland "galloons woven with the silver from his Judaic ornaments and baubles."[26] Although the Jewish religion was persecuted like the other cults in both Paris and the provinces, it can be assumed that centuries of practice in semi-clandestinity made it easier for its worshipers to escape the Jacobin thunderbolts. However, the distinct impression emerges that the exclusiveness of the cult of Reason redoubled its virulence as far as they were concerned, notably in the eastern departments, fed by the traditional anti-Jewish feeling. Symptomatic of this was a popular booklet glorifying Marat, comparing him to Jesus, "who also fell under the blows of fanaticism, while working with all his might to bring about the salvation of mankind."[27] In the eastern departments an open anti-Jewish propaganda campaign was in process. Baudot, a member of the National Convention and commissary for the armies of the Rhine and Moselle, even proposed a new type of regeneration of the Jews, *regeneration by guillotine*:[28]

> ... everywhere, they put greed in place of love of homeland, and their ridiculous superstitions in place of reason. I know that a few of them are serving in our armies, but while excepting them from the discussion to be opened on their conduct, would it not be proper to turn our attention to a regeneration of them by guillotine?

At the same time (Brumaire, year II), all the Lower Rhine municipalities were ordered

> to collect all Hebrew books immediately, notably the Talmuth, as well as all symbols whatsoever of their cult, in order that an *auto da fé* be made to Truth, on the tenth day of the second decade, of all those books and symbols of the cult of Moses.

It seems that this order was not followed by action because in Pluviôse, three months later, another circular prohibited

citizens who dare to sully the fair name of citizen and combine it with that of Jew, to assemble in their former synagogues and to celebrate their ancient farces there, in an unknown language, with which the general safety might easily be disturbed.

Finally, in Thermidor II, no longer the superstition but the gambling of the Alsatian Jews came under attack, and the municipalities of the district were ordered to "keep a constant eye on these dangerous creatures, who are leeches devouring citizens."

This whole series of orders was signed by Mainoni, the national agent of the Strasbourg district, but they certainly reflected the general state of mind in the Rhine departments. In the month of Brumaire, year II, the Nancy Jacobins laid a decree before their Paris counterparts for the expulsion from France of all Jews living there. The great Parisian club indignantly rejected the suggestion. It was "contrary to justice, to humanity, to the very interests of the country," said Léonard Bourdon (President of the Jacobins' Correspondence Committee), "since at this moment there are at least two thousand Jews in our armies, who are behaving with honor and patriotism there."[29] This did not stop the agitation for expulsion *en masse*. In the month of Thermidor, a member of the National Convention, André Foussedoire, was on a mission in Alsace and was surprised that[30]

people were going so far as to say in meetings of popular societies, that the Jews were all rogues and villains; that they were to be driven out of the Republic within a few days by a decree of the National Convention, and that their debtors were absolved from meeting any obligation to them. . . .

Here again we find the combined grievances of age-old anti-Jewish tradition: superstition and usury. As far as the second of these grievances was concerned, the purchase of national property was increasing demand for the services of Jewish lenders in eastern France. In these circumstances, nothing could have been more in the interest of the *nouveau riche* peasants and bourgeoisie than collective expulsion.

At the other end of France, the Portuguese Jews did not arouse the same recriminations; however, their revolutionary enthusiasm, too, seems to have been fairly lukewarm. Several big Bordeaux merchants and bankers were punished and forced to provide for the wants of the Sans-culottists. The heaviest penalty, 1,200,000 livres, was imposed on the banker Charles Peixotto, "accused of having carried aristocracy so far, even under the *ancien régime,* as to claim that he was descended from the Levi family and was even the first noble in the kingdom as a result. . . ."[31] There was nothing new about these genealogical claims on the part of the Iberian Jews: on the other side of the Pyrenees, the Ha-Levi family, alias Santa Maria, could boast of even more impressive affiliation.[32] According to the Bordeaux chronicler, Detcheverry, "the punishment would have been very much heavier if the Commission had not remembered in time that Peixotto had shown the greatest readiness to buy national property."[33] The Alsatian Jews refrained from buying national property themselves, firstly because of tradition, and also, it may be imagined, because they were sceptical of the prospects of the Revolution. This scepticism seems to have been shared by the great Portuguese Jews, judging by the bargaining they were carrying on with the King's party in Paris and London in 1791–3, for the formation of a sort of autonomous Jewish fief in the Landes, under the suzerainty of the French crown. We only know about this affair from a report by Joseph Fouché,[34] but it might have corresponded to a very long standing scheme, since there was already mention of a "Jewish town" to be created near Bayonne, in a note from Montesquieu.[35] The whole episode revealed a political sense and political aspirations on the part of the Sephardic Jews, totally foreign to the Ashkenazi Jews of the time.

To sum up, the Jews in France, who had some personal reasons for anxiety during the Revolution, did not for the most part evince abounding enthusiasm for it. At first, the emancipation which from the Napoleonic era was to revolutionize the lives of all Jews west of the Vistula, only involved minor changes in the lives of people who had begun by emancipating themselves.

The same seems to have been true in the adjacent lands, as and when the armies of the Republic brought them the revolutionary message. As early as November 1792, General Custine was promising the Jews of the Rhineland an end to their "base servitude": "soon wherever the sacred banners of liberty will fly, no one will weep any longer except slaves and tyrants!"[36] In 1795, the new "Batavian Republic" granted civic rights to all citizens including Jews. Bonaparte, in the course of his campaigns, enfranchised the majority of Jews in Italy, notably in the Papal States. But it would be wrong to say that all the Children of Israel unanimously rejoiced. The proud Sephardim of Amsterdam, particularly, perfectly satisfied with their own individual status, did not stand to gain anything from civic rights, as was demonstrated by the internal conflict and community schisms which ensued. The down-trodden Jews of the Rhineland, like those of Italy, were easier to convince and were henceforth distinguished for their francophilia. In the other Germanic countries, local governments decreed total or partial emancipation of the Jews, equally under French influence. This will be discussed later. The effects of the new French gospel spread as far as distant Portugal where several thousands (two hundred thousand according to Adolphe Thiers)[37] of Marranos or pseudo-Marranos were still subject to the antiquated "purity of blood" statutes. At the time of the French occupation, in 1809, they became the live-wires in the pro-French party, which (again according to Thiers) wanted to offer the crown of the country to Maréchal Junot.

In this way France was established as the protector and emancipator of the Jews over the greater part of Europe.

But, from 1800, France was Napoleon, in whom it saw itself mystically embodied and who "wanted the same thing as the most junior grenadier, but who wanted it a thousand times more"—which sets our study a problem of individual psychology.

At first sight, it really seems that on the subject of the Jew more than on any other, Napoleon was the faithful son of the Revolution and more especially of the Montagne. He tried to "regenerate" the Jews, that is to say to de-Judaize them, and he partly succeeded. His views on the Children of Israel, principally inspired by contemporary deist thought, were not kindly, and enemy of the "ideologists" as he was, he scarcely bothered about the problem of the responsibilities that their debased condition posed, with the result that his opinions placed end to end would provide the material for a small anti-Semitic catechism. They combined old theological prejudice with the nascent scientific superstition: "The Jews are an objectionable people, chicken-hearted and cruel."[38] "They are caterpillars, grasshoppers, who ravage the countryside."[39] "The evil primarily comes from that indigestible compilation called the Talmud, where their true Biblical traditions are found side by side with the most corrupt morality as soon as their relations with Christians are involved."[40] Nonetheless, in his eyes the Jews were a "race" and that race was "accursed":[41]

I do not intend to rescue that race, which seems to have been the only one excluded from redemption, from the curse with which it is smitten, but I would like to put it in a position where it is unable to propagate the evil. . . .

The remedy, in his opinion, lay in the abolition of the race by dissolving it into the Christian race. The task was arduous: ". . . good is done slowly and a mass of tainted blood only improves with time."[42] "When one in every three marriages will be between a Jew and a Frenchman, the Jew's blood will cease to have a specific character."[43]

In actuality, Napoleon ruled the Jews firmly and efficiently. However, his administrative and political plans took into account his visionary dreams, and perhaps also a certain superstitious fear.

At the time of the Egyptian expedition, he issued a proclamation to the Jews, suggesting that they enlist under his colors to reconquer the Promised Land.[44] They remained deaf to his summons. The scheme can be ranked as one of his "eastern mirages," in which he saw himself as the "founder of a new religion, mounted on an elephant, crowned with a turban and bearing a new Koran containing his own message."[45] The attraction the fabulous Orient had for the young Bonaparte has intrigued many of his biographers. Was Sigmund Freud right in attributing one of the sources of this "Egyptian obsession" to an "elder brother" complex in respect of Joseph Bonaparte, which drove Napoleon towards the shores where the Patriarch Joseph made his fortune?[46]

Three or four years later, when he had been appointed First Consul, Bonaparte set about settling the religious question. But the law of Germinal 18, year X, relating to the organization of the Catholic and Protestant religions, left Judaism aside. ". . . as for the Jews," he is reported as saying, "they are a nation apart and their adherents do not mix with any others; we will therefore have time to concern ourselves with them later."[47] The time came under the Empire in the spring of 1806, and it would seem that his first intentions were to deprive them of their civic rights.[48] But the Council of State, composed of advocates of the Revolution (Regnault de Saint-Jean d'Angély, Beugnot, Berlier), was able to exercise a moderating influence. In the end, he decided to sound out the loins and hearts of the Jews first by summoning their representatives to a "General Assembly" in Paris. The delegates' replies to the twelve embarrassing questions they were asked could not have been more satisfactory. Third question: "Do the Jews . . . regard France as their homeland and do they feel under an obligation to defend it?" "Yes, to the death!" cried the Assembly with one voice. But when it came to mixed marriages, which the Emperor wanted the rabbis expressly to recommend (sixth question), the new patriots once more became the stiff-necked people. Without coming into direct conflict with the autocrat, the Assembly skillfully succeeded in evading an answer.[49] On the whole, it survived the examination successfully and made a favorable impression on Pasquier and Portalis, the members of the commission appointed by the Emperor. It was still necessary to find a means of binding the motley Jewish population of the Empire—from the Netherlands to Italy—by the decisions the Assembly adopted. The members of the commission were very surprised to learn that no organized authority existed, no central government, to which all the worshipers of Moses owed allegiance (a surprise still sometimes shared today). It was in these circumstances that the idea was born (its exact author is unknown)[50] of convening a "Great Sanhedrin" in Paris which would furnish a link with the tradition of a government of Israel eighteen centuries before.

The idea immediately fired Napoleon's imagination. Apart from being an instrument for regenerating and keeping the Jews in order, the inspired opportunist thought that he would be able to utilize such an organ for the requirements of his major policies. He perfected the scheme at the same time as the idea of a continental blockade during the last months of 1806. He was probably counting on the pious allegiance of Jewish businessmen to help him to starve England better. The new government of Israel was going to be a faithful replica of the old and would have the same number of members, seventy-one, invested with the same titles. Invitations were sent out beyond the boundaries of the Empire, to all Jewries of Europe. The opening took place on February 9, 1807, amidst great pomp, in the secularized chapel of Saint-Jean, rue des Piliers, renamed rue du Grand-Sanhedrin.[51]

But regeneration of the Jews in this way was alive with disturbing, even provocative associations for Christian feeling. Was not the Sanhedrin the Jewish tribunal that had made the deal with Judas and paid him the thirty pieces of silver? Was it not there that "that scene of unspeakable outrage took place when the Son of God was insulted, covered with spittle and abuse?"[52] Was it not, in a word, the very organ of the deicide? Thenceforth, imaginations ran wild. Anti-Napoleonic propaganda abroad forcefully and fully exploited this theme, which put the final touch to the image of Napoleon, the anti-Christ, as we will see further on. In France, even Catholics who accepted the Republic did not fail to allude to it. "For Christianity, the wretched condition of the Jews is a proof which one would like to make disappear *before its time* ..." protested de Bonald, comparing the Jews' *Sanhedrin* to the philosophers' *Convention.*[53] An anonymous pamphlet which was seized by the police depicted Napoleon as "the Lord's anointed, who will save Israel."[54] But would not the Jews' new Messiah himself be of Jewish origin? This is what *L'Ambigu,* the journal of the French emigrés in London, eagerly asserted, and this imputation too has left its mark on men's memory.[55]

The rapid disbanding of the Sanhedrin suggests that these campaigns made an impression on Napoleon, to the point where he fell prey to a sort of superstitious fear. In fact, this assembly with its ancient name only held a few sessions, when it ratified the decision previously taken by the "General Assembly." On March 9, 1807, a month after its solemn opening, it was dissolved, and there was never any further question of recalling it.

On the reasons for this hasty dissolution, we have the account of the former Minister of the Interior, Count Chaptal. In his *Souvenirs,* he tells how he was present one day at a dinner given by Napoleon. Suddenly, he saw Cardinal Fesch enter[56]

looking very worried, which struck the Emperor: "... What's the matter with you?" he asked. "It's easy to understand what's the matter with me. What's all this about? Do you want the end of the world to come?" "And why?" retorted the Emperor. "Do you not know," answered the Cardinal, "that the Scriptures foretell the end of the world the minute the Jews are recognized as forming a nation?" Anyone else would have laughed at this outburst by the Cardinal. But the Emperor's expression changed and he seemed worried. He rose from the table, went into his study with the Cardinal, and only emerged an hour later. Two days after, the Sanhedrin was dissolved.

The likelihood of this account has been challenged, notably by R. Anchel, in his book *Napoléon et les Juifs.*[57] What is certain is that in various quarters people were trying to dissuade the Emperor from his scheme and create the state of mind that Chaptal described. A Jesuit who accepted the Republic, Abbé Augustin Baruel, a prolific writer who had specialized in the propagation of demonological myths since the Directory, stated that he had passed documents on a Jewish world conspiracy[58] on to Cardinal Fesch and other high dignitaries. Joseph Fouché for his part, on the very morning of the opening of the Sanhedrin, showed Napoleon a note relating to the 1791–3 negotiations between the King's party and the Portuguese Jews, probably in order to make him doubt their loyalty.

Moreover, not only Jews from abroad but also Jews within the Empire failed to show excessive enthusiasm for the institution summoned to govern them, under imperial supervision. As a result, and whatever might have been the reasons for his new change of direction, Napoleon definitively abandoned his great politico-messianic plan. Did he momentarily think of re-establishing the ghetto? Another note by Fouché, commenting on the anxiety of the Paris Jews, might suggest this.[59] But in the end, he contented himself with the so-called "infamous" decree of March 17, 1808, which subjected the Jews to some special laws, varying from department to department. Jews in the Seine and the South-western departments (to which several others were later joined) retained full rights; those in other departments were subject to discriminatory measures which hampered their movements and trading activities. The decree of March 17, which ruined many Jewish families, was motivated by the struggle against usury, but the arduous research into "corrupt practices by the Jews" which the prefects were ordered to undertake on that occasion, once again showed how their bad reputation depended primarily on their Jewishness.

The prefect of Vaucluse, for example, while stating that none of the 631 Jews in his department deserved the title of usurer, wrote:[60]

> I presume that the sort of corrupt practice you are talking about ... is the crime of which the mere name of this people recalls the idea, and which had made them odious for all time, that is to say, usury.

More concisely, the prefect of Mont-Tonnerre stated ". . . that there are no worse Jews in Mayence than some of the Christians."[61] Let us also quote the long report by the prefect of the Seine, Frochot, who made a distinction between *Jews by origin* and *new Jews*, people engaged in *Jewish schemes*:[62]

> ... amongst that host of individuals who have established those scandalous lending firms which the government in its wisdom has just destroyed and whose transactions concealed the most excessively *Jewish* schemes, not a single Jew by origin is to be found. For example, not a single Jew by origin is to be found in that league known in Paris as the *Black Band* which filled the sale rooms in the department of the Seine and near the law courts, pushed out genuine buyers, and monopolized all the estates put up for auction in order to resell them later at higher prices, thereby cheating the government and holding individuals up to ransom. Several Jews by origin have bought national estates like other citizens, for their own enjoyment; but none are known to buy for speculation. And, what is much more certain, with the purchases that they have made, they have been forced, like other honest buyers, to pay tribute to the *new Jews* of the Black Band.

The pen of the high imperial official was thus once again making the distinction dear to the Middle Ages between "Jews" and "judaizing Christians" or "Christian Jews."

Where Jews apparently continued to practice the profession of *Jews* in large numbers, as was the case in the Rhine departments, they generally served as figureheads for Christians who did not dare to judaize openly. The reports from the prefects and mayors point on several occasions to this state of affairs, which the mayor of Metz described as follows:[63]

> The buyers and underwriters of national property sought and found money with Jews. They obtained it at a very high price because, as the Jews had little of it, they became in these transactions the brokers for non-Jewish individuals who wanted to make large profits, while preserving the honest exteriors by which society knew them. The odium thus went to the Jews, and the profit reverted to the others. Moreover, the freedom of trade in money favored usury; usurers are to be found in all classes of Metz society. . . .

However, the members of the Emperor's commission placed the blame solely on the Jews:[64]

> We would say that [the Jews] taught the people they robbed idleness and corruption, while they deprived those they did not rob of their morality. Public notaries led astray by them, employed their services to hide their shameful traffic, and domestic servants and day laborers brought them the price of their services or of their day's work so that they should make it yield like their own deniers. A certain number of Frenchmen thus abandoned the useful professions and became accustomed to living without working, off the profits of usury. . . .

An increasing number of the rising generation of Jews were already distinguishing themselves in some of these "useful professions" the members of the commission are talking about—science and the arts, but above all the army as we will see further on. However, the special laws for Jews continued to exist until the end of the Empire. It fell to Louis XVIII's government to complete the emancipation of the French Jews, by refraining in 1818 from renewing the "infamous decree" of March 17, 1808.[65]

Emancipation in Germany

At the time of the Napoleonic hegemony, the Jews in the various German lands were partially emancipated. Where emancipation was not directly decreed by the French occupation authorities—in the Rhineland for example—it was introduced under their influence or following their example, a shock to the patriotism of not only many contemporaries but also of future generations of Germans who continued to regard it as a measure imposed by "foreign tyranny." German anti-Semitism employed this argument up to the Nazi era. Another distinctive feature of emancipation here was the crucial role sometimes played by certain German "court Jews." Their wealth and influence grew in this troubled period, since money is necessary to wage war, but they could only hope to dispel the opprobrium attached to their Jewishness by cleaning out the Jewries as a whole. However, although the most powerful Jews remained the hostages of the most wretched of their co-religionists in this way, the efforts made to free the latter from their shackles also rested on the particular relationship between the plutocratic leaders of the communities and the Jewish masses. This was a relationship of kings to subjects, kings whose sense of responsibility was developed to the highest point, to the degree to which the external Christian world regarded them as ridiculous monarchs. The vanity of parvenus and the traditional solidarity of the Children of Israel: these were the two major contrasting incentives of the Jewish emancipators.

The most active of them was Israël Jacobson, described by Goethe, an opponent of emancipation, as the "Jewish messiah from Brunswick" or in a play on words, as *jacobin-ischer Israelsohn* (Jacobin son of Israel). Born in Halberstadt in Prussia, Jacobson settled in the Duchy of Brunswick at the end of the eighteenth century, and became the principal financial agent and banker there, in a word, the "court Jew" of Duke Charles-William. His business expanded, and he was soon acting in the same capacity for several princes in the vicinity. As a good son of Mendelssohn's generation, he tried to propagate European Enlightenment amongst the children of the ghetto, as soon as he had the means to do so. In 1801, he opened a model school at Seesen, where poor young Jews and Christians were educated side by side. He endowed it with a capital of a hundred thousand thalers, and it continued to exist until the Hitler era. This attempt at interdenominational reconciliation was not only odious to orthodox Jews. It also incensed a number of Christian priests. One abbé saw it as an indication that "the time is passed when men jealously loved their own religion; faith today is like an old discarded wife who no longer arouses jealousy."[66] But the advocates of tolerance in high society encouraged Jacobson's initiative, and his school was honored with several royal visits. In 1807, he received the title of Doctor *honoris causa* from the University of Τιelmstedt and, a sign of the times, the duke's sister surprised him by crowning him with a laurel wreath, plaited with her own hands.

As early as 1803, Jacobson had secured the abolition of the *Leibzoll* (the capitation tax) on Jews in the Duchy of Brunswick, and, in the following year, he forced the Margrave of Baden to pass the same measure. But he was really able to show his ability both as emancipator and financier under French domination, from 1806. At that time, Napoleon had imposed a tax of over five million francs on the Duchy of Brunswick, which the Christian bankers were unable to get together. They really had no option therefore but to put up with the Jew. The President of the College of Ministers, Henneberg, who found his conditions exorbitant, wrote to his colleagues:[67]

Since the turn that the affair has taken is destined to put us, as well as the whole country, into the hands of Israel, and since every dissenting voice will remain a voice crying in the wilderness, there is nothing we can do but purely and simply to accept his conditions.

True, Jacobson seemed to see things differently. After a discussion when he succeeded in persuading Daru, the French administrator, to give up floating a forced loan, he wrote to Henneberg:[68]

. . . I am so happy to be relieved of an affair that caused me the greatest anxiety and sleepless nights before it was settled; I do not know whether I would have won or lost when it was all finished, for would I not have been denounced by everyone as a usurer keen to make vast profits from the momentary embarrassment of the country. Thanks be to Providence that everything has turned out so happily for the better.

This declaration by a Jew is worth examining, because it epitomizes the vicious circle whereby emancipation was obtained through a financial ascendancy, which disgusted the majority of Christians, and was consequently constantly challenged in Germany. When the Kingdom of Westphalia was created (1807), Jacobson became King Jerome's banker and intimate friend, as he had been Duke Charles-William's, and his possibilities for action increased. As the new kingdom had been organized on the French pattern, he had no difficulty in instituting a régime modeled on the one just established for the Jews in Paris: emancipation on the one hand (but without the restrictions Napoleon imposed in France), a "consistorial" system of government on the other, that is to say the organization of the Jewish religion on the model of the Christian. After Jacobson had secured the position of president of the consistory, he ruled his co-religionists quite tyrannically, modernizing their religious ritual and customs as he pleased. At the same time, he increased initiatives to accelerate emancipation of the Jews in other countries (it was his representations at Frankfurt which inspired Goethe's epigram), even appealing to the Tsar Alexander I. As we saw earlier, he could be considered the first author of the idea of the Great Sanhedrin. "I approach your Majesty's throne with confidence inspired by the great deeds with which you have made the astonished world resound," he wrote to Napoleon. "... Be so gracious, Sire, as to extend your benevolent designs to the Jews who inhabit the countries bordering on the vast empire. ...."[39] It was only too natural that he should have played the French card to the full and, as might be imagined, at the time of the glorification of German nationalist feeling after 1810–12, Germanomane patriots nourished considerable ill-feeling against this "Jacobin son of Israel." But the Nemesis of the emancipation of German Jews also decreed that, in his efforts to be of service to Jerome, who showered him with favors, Jacobson had to purchase property which the king put up for sale by auction, notably six convents which were closed and whose inmates cursed the son of the deicidal race.[70] The description of the anger which later seized the Mecklenburg nobility when Jacobson wanted to buy an estate there for himself in 1816, must be read in Schnee's book. However, he died in peace in Berlin in 1828, covered with honors and wealth. All his descendants converted to Christianity.

This also happened with the descendants of Wolf Breidenbach, another dynamic emancipator whose sphere of action comprised the small principalities of south-west Germany. Unlike Jacobson however, Breidenbach remained an orthodox Jew. Furthermore, he only tried to improve the legal status of the Jews without touching their ritual or customs.

It should be added that while emancipators like Jacobson and Breidenbach were first of all great bankers, other Jewish plutocrats appear to have concerned themselves very little with the emancipation of their brethren. Meyer-Amschel Rothschild for example, at the time when he was laying the foundations of the prodigious family fortune in Frankfurt, does not seem to have taken a large part in the battles the Jewry of the town waged against its bourgeoisie— which ended in the abolition of the ghetto at the end of 1811.

We will not dwell on the evolution of the Jewish régime in the other German countries, some of which (Saxony for example) refrained from any reform at all.[71] Instead, we will concentrate on Prussia, which brings out the dialectic of emancipation in its Christian political perspective particularly clearly. This took the form of an attempt to abolish Judaism which was universally condemned, on the understanding that it would not be possible to get rid of the Jews (in both the financial and the "ethno-religious" sense of the word) in any other way.

On the other hand, this emancipation was obviously in the nature of things, since the time was ripe for the collapse of the old feudal order. In 1807, after the great defeat of Prussia, the king and his government fled to Königsberg, and embarked on a vast program of reform, which is still known by the names of the ministers von Stein and von Hardenberg. It included the abolition of slavery and of the old classes (nobility, bourgeoisie, peasantry), and the acknowledgment of the same rights and duties for all inhabitants, all *Staatsbürger*, of the realm. As a result, the retention of the special regulations for the Jews, and their existence as a separate class of pariahs, became, in the long run, impossible. They either had to disappear or become *Staatsbürger*, "citizens of the State," themselves. At that juncture, as, in fact, at any historical period, there was no shortage of advocates of integral banishment as a solution. They seem to have included Baron von Stein himself who is said to have suggested that Africa be colonized by these "parasitic plants."[72] But a scheme like this was obviously utopian, particularly at a time when the Napoleonic war tax (one hundred and forty million francs for Prussia) was posing problems for the exchequer, which would probably have been insoluble without help from Jews. In addition, some of them were operating as the main suppliers to the French army in the field. Because of this, not only the general situation and the French example, but also pressure from Saint-Marsan, the French ambassador at Berlin[73] (originating, there is scarcely room for doubt, from Jews operating behind the scenes), left no other solution but emancipation, and combined to hasten it.

Moreover, the three large communities of Berlin, Königsberg and Breslau were tireless in their efforts to push the boat, piling representation on representation and bombarding ministers and the king himself with petitions. In summer 1808, Frederick William III instructed the minister von Schroetter, von Stein's right-hand man, to produce a plan of reform for him. Von Schroetter, who shared his superior's views on the Jews, in his turn entrusted the criminal counselor, Brand, with the task. The description of the interview must be read in the Prussian official's memoirs. A minor incident, the grant to a Jew of the right to reside in Königsberg in contravention of the regulations, had provoked a royal remonstrance:[74]

Herr von Schroetter received a disapproving order from the Cabinet and was instructed to revise the existing laws relative to the Jews and to draft a law embodying a new constitution for them. He summoned me ... and blamed me for being the real offender in the incident, gave me the Cabinet order to read and asked me, for he thought the Jews must be well known to me, whether I did not know of means to kill them all off at once but without bloodshed. I replied that I was in possession of an appropriate method of killing, not the Jews, but Judaism, and set myself out to present to him that very day an outline of the law demanded in high places. He received it on October 29 [1808] at the time appointed.

The scheme Brand formulated envisaged a gradual emancipation, and retained the special laws on basic points (exclusion from State service, strict limitation of the number of Jewish merchants, etc.). But this version was criticized as too liberal by the majority of ministers to whom it was submitted for comment. Only the old *Aufklärer* who filled the Ministry of Education advocated immediate and total emancipation. They stressed popular prejudice against the Jews, which they thought was a consequence of the special laws, and they ridiculed fears of Jewish domination as unworthy of Christians. The Minister himself, the great philologist, Wilhelm von Humboldt, thought it useful to show that the destiny of the Jews concealed no mystery. He argued that the national character of the Jews[75]

> ... consists primarily of patriarchal persistence in their original customs and a remarkable power of passive resistance, and, in combination with the Christian ideas according to which Judaism and Christianity from one point of view belong to a single category and from another are divided into two opposing categories, whereby the Jewish people, very unimportant at that time, have received a disproportionate significance—these are the ideas which have made the Jews what they still are amongst ourselves. Their situation therefore belongs to world history in its religious perspective [*kirchlich welthistorisch*] and is such a remarkable phenomenon that some excellent minds have doubted whether it can be at all explained in merely human terms.

This brilliant theory is of purely academic interest. In practice, as a result of the hostility of the other ministers and the lack of enthusiasm of the department, the first reform plan was bogged down in the swamps of administration. Moreover, Prince Karl August von Hardenberg is generally quite rightly considered the real author of Prussian emancipation of the Jews.

An aristocrat who had traveled extensively, he may have owed his benevolent attitude to the Children of Israel to his cosmopolitan education. In addition, at a difficult period in his life, a Jew had appeared to save him from financial embarrassment. The disinterested lender, none other than Israël Jacobson, was far from suspecting that the person indebted to him would, in 1810, become the all-powerful minister of Prussia, and that he would be able discreetly to remind him "that they had known one another for twenty-five years."⁷⁶ Once in power, von Hardenberg worked incessantly for complete emancipation of the Jews, on the principle of "same laws, same liberties, same duties," and in accordance with his theories borrowed from Adam Smith on the reorganization of Prussian trade and finance. He was able to overcome the innumerable objections raised by the administration and by the king himself. In the end, the edict of emancipation, promulgated on March 11, 1812, included only one reservation, article 9 regarding the admission of Jews to State service.

Some of the objections which von Hardenberg swept aside as he proceeded are worth looking at. To de-judaize the Jews more quickly, some ministers suggested that they be forbidden to wear beards. Others called for the abolition of all customs and all religious rites incompatible with Christian practices, that is to say, in practice, the legal abolition of Judaism. Still others suggested that some of the provisions of the old Jewish laws be kept in force, notably the specially harsh punishments for the offenses of receiving and concealing, smuggling and bankruptcy, as well as the principle of the nonadmissibility of their oath in legal proceedings. David Friedländer, the spokesman of the Berlin Jewish community, felicitously expressed the iniquity of this latter proposal:⁷⁷

> In criminal and in civil cases, the oath of a Jew can, may and must have the same validity as the oath of any other man. The Jew is a human being and a citizen as much as anyone else and in his religious ideas there is absolutely nothing which would make his credibility more doubtful than that of a Christian. How often does it happen in criminal cases that Christians declare in court without inhibition that they did not think they had committed a sin if they killed a Jew? What does that prove against the morality of the Christians? These very examples

exist also in civil cases; and the only means to remove such harmful and shameful prejudices from the minds of all religious adherents is equality of the law, the same confidence in everyone, the same punishment for perjurors.

Finally, the Minister of Police, Sack, placed high hopes in the abolition of the very term Jew, which has "become very contemptuous ... in order to inculcate in them a sense of honor which would make them equal to other citizens and raise them in their own esteem. . . ."[78] In support, he recalled the cases of France and Westphalia, where he said that this language reform had helped to bring Jews and Christians closer together, notably in the army. But his advice was not considered. There remained the reservation of article 9, which had been formulated as follows: "As far as the question of knowing to what extent Jews can be admitted to public office and to State service, we reserve the right to settle it later by legislative means." When reaction set in after 1815, this article made it possible to take various discriminatory measures against the Jews, so that they always remained second-class citizens in Germany even in the strictly legal sense.

The question first arose with the Jewish volunteers and ex-servicemen who were hoping to enter State service. The Prussian ministers unanimously refused them this right. However, one of their number, Bülow, the Minister of Finance, suggested making an exception in favor of men who held the iron cross, reckoning that "volunteers of the Jewish religion rewarded with this great distinction can be considered as better than usual in point of morality." But the Council of Ministers was of the opinion that, in the case of a Jew, courage shown on the battlefield did not constitute proof of morality.[79] Moreover, from 1815–16 onwards, the question of revising the edict of March 11, 1812, was raised. Some ministers suggested dividing the Jews into three classes, according to profession and degree of usefulness, and of only allowing members of the first class to retain the benefits of the edict.[80] But this proposal was not adopted. In fact, article 9 was sufficient to exercise a strong restraint on the Jews' newly acquired rights. The idea of "public offices and State service" was very broadly interpreted: it was extended to honorary offices, communal offices, to the various types of teaching, and ended up by encompassing such jobs as communal surveyor, and even hangman. The prevailing atmosphere was even better reflected in a Prussian law promulgated in 1836, forbidding unconverted Jews to give their children usual Christian forenames. The ideology of emancipation hoped to make the Jews the same as Christians, the question of denomination apart. The ideology of the "Christian State" resulted in their being singled out to the point where Frederick William IV could envisage the re-establishment of the ghetto. Criticizing the new tendencies, Stägemann, a member of the old Hardenberg team, wrote to a friend in 1819:

> My Christian evangelical feelings do not allow me to make the Jews suffer, and moreover, I am fundamentally convinced that only complete equality of rights will transform them into Christians. The greater the pressure and contempt, the more they become isolated while still seizing our money.

In another letter, he expressed the same idea slightly differently: "If there had not been the accursed free towns, we would no longer have Jews in Germany in fifty years' time (those of Poland excepted)."[81]

The four "free towns" (Frankfurt, Hamburg, Bremen and Lübeck), dominated by the bourgeoisie, had in fact become the main center of the reaction against emancipation. There, Christian nostalgia for the ghetto was given free play; under pressure from the guilds, the old special regulations were integrally or partially reintroduced. The countries that Napoleon had assigned to the ephemeral Kingdom of Westphalia (Hanover, Brunswick) were equally bent on returning to the old order. In 1815, emancipation seemed to be jeopardized in all Germanic lands. In an attempt to protect the positions gained, the great Jewish bankers besieged diplomats gathered for the Congress of Vienna. The representatives of the free towns for their part did not remain inactive, and the resounding and remunerative arguments, customary at that period, were widely employed on both sides (someone like Gentz even had payment for his good offices stipulated by contract).[82] In the long run, the scales tilted in favor of the Jews, whose cause was taken up by the representatives of the Great Powers. Europe was thus entering upon the Rothschild era, of the alliance between the "concert of the Powers" and the great bank. Admonishing the Frankfurt Senate, a man like von Hardenberg could bluntly write that "in view of the influence that Jewish firms exercise on the credit and trade of the various German states, the question will not escape the attention of the Congress."[83]

In fact, the draft scheme for the confederation of Germanic States was completed by an article which laid down that the rights granted to the Jews in certain countries forming part of the confederation would remain theirs. But at the last minute, the anti-emancipation party succeeded in substituting *by* for *in*, in the text of the article, and this was later used as a legal basis for the free towns and other countries to abrogate an emancipation not promulgated *by* the old restored authorities but *by* the French government. We thus come back to the very special circumstances surrounding the emancipation of German Jews, which coincided with the burst of patriotic anti-French feeling of the "wars of liberation," and with the "germanomane" agitation (*Teutschthümelei*).

Even at the time, there were men who were able to foresee what such a combination of circumstances would mean. The philosopher Friedrich Schlegel, for example, then in the service of the Austrian government, was pointing out as early as 1815 that a general emancipation of the Jews in all the Germanic countries was urgent and indispensable, precisely because it had begun under French oppression. His argument was as follows: if the States and towns repealed emancipation because it had been decreed by the foreign tyrant, this could have serious consequences, "it would mean re-forming a party favorable to the enemy who has fortunately just been beaten"; a party, he added, which was not negligible, with a strength of five hundred thousand active and ambitious men. "If the general principle of repeal were adopted," he asked in conclusion, "should not the Simplon route be blown up because it was built under Napoleon?"[84]

Emancipating tendencies in the Russian Empire

As we know, special regulations for the Jews continued to exist in Russia up to the 1917 revolution. However, various reform projects were envisaged at the beginning of the nineteenth century, and for some time the Tsar Alexander I even played with the idea of universal enfranchisement of the sons of the ghetto. This was at the same period as he was becoming the champion of the Holy Alliance and of pan-European reactionism—which proves that obscurantism and clericalism do not necessarily exclude philo-Semitism. Moreover, the way in which the Russian autocracy approached an apparently insoluble problem throughout successive changes in its political views, does not lack interest for our study.

My first book showed the circumstances in which Jews were forbidden to enter Muscovy in the sixteenth century and how the Reformer-Tsar, Peter the Great, and his successors came to respect this tradition. But conquests and annexation of territory to the west of the Empire brought a larger and larger Jewish population under Tsarist rule. After the partitions of Poland, over half the world population of the Children of Israel had become Russian subjects. Remember that in Poland especially, they formed not only the bulk of the country's bourgeoisie but also part of the urban proletariat, and they also crowded the countryside. Catherine the Great, anxious not to offend the pravoslav population, kept the old prohibitions in force although in her heart of hearts she ridiculed anti-Jewish prejudice. "The entrance of the Jews into Russia," she wrote to Diderot, "might cause great losses to our small merchants, for these people keep everything for themselves; it may be that their return would occasion more recrimination than benefit."[85]

The foundations were thus laid of a territorial limitation which confined the Jews to their "pale of settlement" in the west of the country as long as the Tsarist régime lasted. Jealousy and mistrust soon provoked other measures, notably the plan to clear them out of the villages. Jewish innkeepers in the countryside were in fact accused of spreading drunkenness amongst the peasants and therefore of being the principal cause of their poverty. In practice, they acted as stewards ("agents") or tax-farmers for the landowners, but they were convenient scapegoats for feudal exploitation. (It is interesting to note that the charge of usury was disappearing east of the Vistula to be replaced by that of drunkenness; the Christians really had to have some accusation to level against the sons of the deicidal race.)

In 1799, a famine devastated White Russia, and Paul I ordered an inquiry into its causes. The investigator named by the Tsar was none other than Gabriel Derzhavin, the greatest Russian poet before Pushkin, who had recently been appointed Minister of Finance. Derzhavin's conclusions, developed in a report over a hundred pages long, served as a source of information on the Jews for generations of Russian bureaucrats, and was still considered authoritative at the beginning of the twentieth century.[86]

The report began with a portrait of the Children of Israel, in the style of La Bruyère, seen through the eyes of a cultured Russian noble:[87]

The Yids[88] are clever, perceptive, quick-witted, alert, polite, obliging, sober, modest, simple, not lascivious, etc., but on the other hand, they are unpleasant, stinking, lazy, idle, cunning, covetous, pushful, sly, malicious etc. . . . And besides, so many of them look the same, have the same name, all these Moseses, Abrahams, Leibs, Chaimoviches, Leibevoviches and the like; and they all wear a uniform black dress; the memory is befuddled and the understanding confused when it is a question of counting them or distinguishing them, especially when claims or inquiries are concerned. It is difficult to detect the guilty; all present themselves and no one is the right man. This must also be an example of their cunning.

Derzhavin, in his way, did not fail to describe the Jews' piety:[89]

They pay dearly, ungrudgingly, in order to be able to study their Talmud. I myself saw old men and young bending, shaking and wailing over their books from sunrise to sunset. They consider themselves far superior to all others. As a consequence, in order not to display their humiliation, for nobody will they remove the skull-caps they wear on their heads.

These are quite Voltairean tones. And Derzhavin gave even greater proof of his enlightenment when he challenged the story of the ritual murder, or when he seemed to be attributing the Jews' shortcomings not to their nature, but to the régime of plutocratic oppression in the communities or *Kahals*:[90]

Their poor, which are the larger part, live in extreme deprivation and hardship. It is horrible to look at them. On the other hand, the rich members of the communities live in affluence; they maintain in their hands dual authority, religious and civil, and exercise great power over their people.

In conclusion he implacably decreed:[91]

In accordance with these earlier and more recent views on the Yids and varied opinions concerning them, I find: their schools are nothing more than a nest of superstition and hatred for Christians; the communities are a dangerous state within the State, which a well-organized political body is not obliged to tolerate; their *Chirems* [excommunications] are an impenetrable sacrilegious cover for the most terrible abuses committed to the detriment of the community and the individual. . . . Their leasing and tax farming, inns, factoring, trade and all their other institutions and activities observed above are nothing more than subtle devices in the guise of benefit and service to others, to seize their property.

Moreover, with the exception of Nota Chaimovich, a rich supplier to the army and a Jewish proponent of Enlightenment, Derzhavin noted that all the sons of Israel he had consulted showed hostility to changes in the established order. He therefore, in a manner characteristic of the period of enlightened despotism, suggested "bringing them under the authority of the absolute power and for this to weaken their fanaticism and bring them imperceptibly to a right system of instruction, whilst in no way diverging from the principle of the toleration of different beliefs."[92]

In conclusion, he drew up a program of reform, which provided for the introduction of civic status for the Jews, their abandonment of their traditional costume, the abolition of the autonomy of the *Kahals,* the transformation of the "agents" and innkeepers into craftsmen and agriculturalists, and the transfer of some of them to the steppes of "New Russia" to the exclusion of the purely Russian provinces "so that they should not corrupt the inhabitants there." But in his opinion, the spread of Western education was still the essential precondition for the Jews' improvement. The experience of past centuries had shown, he wrote, that neither kindness and mercy, nor contempt and oppression had been able to open up the hearts of the Jewish people to Christian princes. But the Jew Mendelssohn, "famous in German lands for his knowledge," had recently gone about it in a different way:[93]

In order to expose the superstition of misguided zealots of his faith, that is to say the deceived deceivers, he has taught some of his brethren the pure Jewish language[94] and, by translating the

Scriptures into everyday German, he has made ordinary people read them. They have been understood, the veil has fallen and the reign of the Talmuds has ended. Since then, the numbers of erudite Jews, second to none amongst the most learned men in Europe, have multiplied on German soil. . . .

Derzhavin therefore set about drawing up an education program; he advocated that children only be allowed to study in religious schools (*heders*) up to the age of twelve, and that above that age attendance be made compulsory at establishments where European education would be dispensed by Jewish teachers educated in Germany.

Paul I was assassinated in 1801 before he had time to study these proposals. However, his successor, Alexander I, set up a "Committee for the Reorganization of Jewish Life" within the framework of the vast scheme of liberal reform he adopted at the beginning of his reign. The Committee included Derzhavin and followed the broad lines of his program. In 1804, a law considerably restricted the auto-nomy of the *Kahals*, allowed young Jews to attend schools and universities, and made the teaching of European languages compulsory in Jewish schools. On another count, Jews were given the right to settle in the provinces of "New Russia"; but to balance this, even in the "pale of settlement," the law decreed their expulsion from the countryside. This deracination, which involved about a third of Polish-Russian Jews, had great economic and social consequences for them.

The measure was to come into force in 1807 and 1808. The date coincided with the war of 1807, marked by the battles of Eylau and Friedland, as well as with the opening of the "Great Sanhedrin" in Paris. Now this action by Napoleon, the "anti-Christ," produced very complex reactions throughout the world, which will be discussed later. They were particu-larly pronounced in Russia. Amongst other fears, the Russian government was disturbed to see Jews *en masse* joining the enemy camp. The Tsar convened an inter-ministerial com-

mittee to study the new situation. The committee was of the
opinion that the expulsion should be suspended and the Jews
warned of the French Government's intentions. Instructions
were therefore sent to the governors of the "pale of settlement," recommending them to confirm the idea amongst the
Jews that Napoleon and his entourage of Jewish emancipators were working for the destruction of the ancestral
faith.[95]

In these circumstances, rabbinic orthodoxy and the power
of the *Kahals*, which the Russian autocracy was seeking to
destroy, became its best allies. The majority of Talmudists
and cabalists, eagerly scanning the meaning of the apocalyptic conflict between the emperors of the *Goyim*, "between
Gog and Magog," prayed for victory for Alexander, more
propitious, they thought, to hastening the coming of the
Messiah. Their calculations and mystical views will be
discussed later. At a more political level, the famous *tzaddik*
Schneer-Zalman argued as follows:[96]

If Bonaparte is victorious, the wealth of the Jews will increase
and their position will improve, but on the other hand, their
hearts will move away from their heavenly Father; but if our
Tsar is the victor, the hearts of the Jews will draw closer to our
heavenly Father, but on the other hand, the poverty of Israel
will worsen and its degradation on earth will be more
pronounced.

(It could not be said that history has proved this prognosis
wrong.)

Whether because of primeval patriotism, superstitious
hopes and fears, or calculations, Polish-Russian Jews proved
devoted and useful collaborators for the tsarist forces when
the Great Army passed near to their homes in 1812, spying
on the French, and feeding Russian partisans. The Tsar of all
the Russians expressed his good will towards them, praised
their loyalty and promised a delegation from the *Kahals* that
he would improve their lot, when hostilities had ended.[97]

He was then entering his pietist and reactionary phase, when he dreamed of being the regenerator of a unified and purified Christianity. To Europe, he issued the message of the Holy Alliance in the name of the universal brotherhood of kings and peoples. At the same time, he was trying to unite all the subjects of his Empire in a sort of evangelical ecumenism. Taking his advice henceforth from German mystics (Mme de Krüdener, Jung-Stilling, Baader), he was infatuated, in Joseph de Maistre's opinion, with "the chimera of universal Christianity and of the uniformity of all Christian sects, all considered equally good."[98] He appointed as Minister of Public Education and Religion his childhood friend, Prince Alexander Golitzin, a reformed Voltairean, instructing him to work for the well-being not only of Christians of different faiths but also of infidels. The powers concentrated in Golitzin's hands were unprecedented: "... in a certain sense," wrote a recent historian, "he was patriarch, pope, financial secretary, chief rabbi and mufti in one man."[99] The golden age seemed to have dawned for all nonpravoslavs in Holy Russia; and perhaps the Jews benefited from it more than anyone else. The old plans for reform were abandoned and there was no longer any question of inculcating them with Western enlightenment. In fact, philosophy had become the great enemy at this period. Censorship hunted down all books which "were inconsistent with Christianity." Metaphysics, political economy and geology were banished from university syllabuses "as contrary to the Holy Scriptures."[100] (Let us note in passing that the rabbinical authorities practiced this sort of persecution very often in the ghetto.)

The great thing at this time was propagation of the Bible, through the efforts of a "Bible Society" formed on the English model, to which the Tsar belonged and which he richly endowed. Defenders of the established order saw in all this the dangerous seeds of anarchy. The French ambassador, La Ferronays, wrote:[101]

... this Bible Society, which is only tending to make Protestantism universal, must give birth to ideas of freedom in men
accustomed to regard their emperor as the supreme head of a
religion which teaches them nothing but submission and
respect; nonetheless, it is this powerful medium, this salutary
prestige that they want to destroy.

The fears of the orthodox clergy were even stronger: ". . . the
enemies of Russia," stated a clandestine tract, "have convinced Alexander that he, the savior of Europe, is summoned to abolish the differences between the various religions, so that there should be only one single minister, and
one single flock. . . ."[102] Joseph de Maistre, if we may quote
him again, shared this view: ". . . it seems obvious," he
reported, "that the Bible Society is only a Socinian machine,
set up to overthrow all ecclesiastical society."[103]

The Tsar thus combined the most unbridled obscurantism
with the tendency to take the message of the Gospels literally. The Jews enjoyed the advantages of a favorable régime
during the second half of his reign. A rudimentary form of
elected representation, the "deputation of the Jewish
people," was even instituted at St Petersburg. Even more
remarkably, Alexander wanted to extend his solicitude to
Jews in other countries. In 1816, he took up the cudgels on
behalf of the Jews of Lübeck, when the Senate of the town
expelled them and he also intervened on behalf of the Frankfurt Jews.[104] Then came the dream of improving the position
of all European Jews by international emancipation, and he
attempted to persuade the concert of the great powers to
enact it.

The idea was suggested to him by Lewis Way, an English
missionary, who devoted his life to the enfranchisement of
the Biblical people, with an eye to their subsequent
conversion.[105] Way came to Russia in 1817, had several
interviews with the Tsar and left an enthusiastic description
of him.[106]

It was not an audience of a private man with an Emperor, but rather a most friendly exchange of views of a Christian with a fellow Christian. What genial condescension, what an inviting smile, what an open heart, what fiery words and what love; almost, or rather complete and absolute, divine love! It was the spirit of God which manifested itself in this memorable interview.

As a result, the Tsar asked Way to draw up a draft plan for the emancipation of the Jews by the great powers, a plan which the Russian delegation presented to the Congress of Aix-la-Chapelle (1818). Way envisaged immediate and general emancipation. He argued:[107]

> . . . It is vain to invite them to become Christians without treating them as men and brothers . . . civil and political existence; free re-integration; return into the bosom of the great social family, it is this that seems to constitute the essential prerequisite to the complete regeneration of the Israelites, and to their reception into the flock of Jesus Christ and their reunion with the house of God. . . .

It is interesting to see how Way directly related emancipation or *regeneration* of the Jews to their conversion, that is to say the disappearance of Judaism. We have already pointed out that, in the final analysis, this was the acknowledged or unacknowledged object of almost all the emancipators. It seems true to say that the Christian method had the advantage of frankness and clarity, not to mention logic, over the various "philosophical" methods. This did not, as we have said already,[108] mean that the Christian method was not closely copied from the philosophical—to the point where Capodistrias, the Russian delegate charged with defending the project at the Congress, could confuse Way with Christian Dohm, the old apostle of secular emancipation.

The question came up on the agenda on November 21, 1818, on the eve of the closing of the Congress. The records make laconic mention of Capodistrias's speech. He ". . .

submitted for examination by the Congress a detailed memorandum concerning the position of the Jews, which had been
sent to the Emperor Alexander by Dohm, 'Minister of the
Gospel.' " The author set out warmly to defend the parity of
rights of the Israelites with the Christians, and proposed that
the Congress proclaim the following principles:[109]

> 1) Israelites and Christians should enjoy exactly the same civil
> and secular immunities, and
> 2) The Governments must instruct the clergy and most particu-
> larly the bishops to preach the greatest tolerance towards Jews.

This latter point is not lacking in significance. But Way's
plan enjoyed no better fate than other grandiose schemes the
Tsar championed (European federation or the collective
secular pact guaranteed by the great powers) and which the
Congress dismissed for fear of Russian hegemony in
Europe.[110] The same day, a protocol signed by the representatives of the five powers announced:[111]

> Messieurs their Lordships of Russia have conveyed the attached
> document relating to a reform in the civil and political legisla-
> tion concerning the Jewish nation. The conference, without
> absolutely sharing all the views of the author of this piece, has
> given credit to the general tendency and the praiseworthy aim
> of his propositions. MM. their Lordships of Austria and Prussia
> have declared themselves ready to give any information on the
> state of the question in the two monarchies that might serve to
> solve a problem which must concern both the statesman and
> the friend of humanity.

This was the diplomatic death certificate of a plan which
seems much less utopian in retrospect than the other daydreams of the pious autocrat. One might think, in fact, that
an international statute relating to the Jews was no more
unrealistic than the agreements on the abolition of the slave
trade or piracy, adopted at the same period.

Alexander continued to play with the idea of a Christian

regeneration of the Biblical people for some time. "The Emperor is doing a lot to make much of the Jews," stated La Ferronays in April, 1820. "Prince Golitzin is taking particular care of a certain Biblical rabbi who is probably involved in the great work."[112] But the Jews cherished in this way showed no inclination to let themselves be converted. A society of *Christian Israelites* (that synonym for *squared circle*, according to de Maistre)[113] only recruited a few dozen members. On the other hand, a new Judaizing sect, the "Subbotniki," who claimed kinship with the Mosaic faith, considerably increased its following amongst the Russian peasantry at that time. The religious authorities attributed this advance to Jewish proselytism and dealt severely and relentlessly with that "sect of Yids."[114] This affair probably contributed to a change in Alexander I's attitude, basically comprising the loss of his pious illusions and the darkening of his humor which continued to the end of his life. At the Congress of Verona in 1822, he politely got rid of Lewis Way, who had come along to remind him of his promises.[115] In the same year, Prince Golitzin fell into disfavor, and was replaced by a protégé of the famous Arakcheev. The old plan for the expulsion of the Jews from the countryside came out of its pigeon-hole. It came into force in 1824, a prelude to the judeophobic policy which marked the reign of Nicholas I and his successors. The paradox of a Romanov who had looked kindly upon the Children of Israel was over within the space of a few years.

eight

Effects of Emancipation

The Jews' point of view

Today, the vast majority of Jews regard the seclusion of the ghetto with horror. Only a few so-called anachronistic grouplets (Mea Shearim in Jerusalem is the best known) retain a nostalgia for its confinement, which they say is consistent with Israel's mission. This horror is easily projected on to the past, with the result that there is a general tendency to think that the Jews greeted their emancipation enthusiastically. Moreover, numerous documents seem to justify such a view; in fact, the Jewish proponents of emancipation, who led campaigns in the press and multiplied petitions, have, one might say, retrospectively stifled the voices of their adversaries.

The truth was curiously more complex, varying, as we have already shown, from country to country and Jewry to Jewry. In France, the Portuguese Jews, already very assimilated in practice, almost unanimously rejoiced at their emancipation. But the Jews in Comtat-Venaissin (the district of Avignon) proved more reserved: some of them did not even want to give up their ancient symbol of dishonor, the "yellow hat."[1] We have also said that the Jews of Paris were already relatively liberated. However, a report by the Prefecture of Police in 1809 suggested that there were some, particularly amongst the "lower classes," who did regret the old order. ". . . What will seem strangest, although completely true, is that it is precisely amongst this wretched horde that the individuals are most scrupulously attached to the rites and practices of their religion. . . ."[2] It was thus the poorest Jews who fell into this category, and the same observation emerged from a report on the state of mind of Alsatian Jewry which Laumond, Prefect of the Bas-Rhin, sent to Paris in 1800. Noting that the Revolution had slid over the masses without altering their mental habits and that ancestral prejudices were still as flourishing on the Jewish as on the Christian side, he wrote: "Nevertheless, I am excluding the wealthy classes who are repudiating the prejudices of the populace in almost every country."[3] He went on:

> As for the Hebraic mob, it continues to wallow in the same ignorance and the same lowliness as before. Its religious principles, which in some way separate it from the rest of the nations, and which nothing up till now has been able to eradicate, are an almost insuperable obstacle to the *rapprochement* that the public good would require.

Curiously enough, he did not think it was the rabbis' fault; they were "generally quite enlightened and well-meaning men, for whom I have nothing but praise." The blame lay with their "fanatical flocks," determined to make the Talmudists pay dearly for the "slightest divergence." In short, the Alsace Jews

> . . . cannot lose the idea that they are foreigners everywhere, and this old prejudice will prevent them thinking of settling permanently for a long time to come. Exceptions to this general attitude on the part of the Jewish people are rare. Perhaps it will require centuries before they can unhesitatingly decide to regard themselves as a real part of the great family.

However, Laumond remained optimistic: ". . . with time, their wretched prejudices will certainly die out; and after that, less harried by public contempt, they will attach themselves to the soil which feeds them. But they are still a very long way from this happy conversion." Note that this excellent

republican administrator does not use the word "regeneration," generally employed, but the even more expressive one
"conversion."

In the German lands, the picture is also varied and sometimes contradictory. In the Rhineland, where emancipation
was directly decreed by the French, only a section of the
Jews voted for annexation to France: nonetheless there were
more Jewish than Christian francophiles. The emancipating
party or, what was almost the same thing, the francophile
party, seems to have collected the majority of votes at
Frankfurt and Hamburg—not surprisingly, as they both held
rich Jewish communities settled in towns dominated by the
Christian bourgeoisie. In Prussia, too, "enlightened" Jews
had been lording it since Moses Mendelssohn's time.[4] But
judging by certain documents, their opponents suffered no
shortage of arguments. For example, the reformist rabbi Saul
Lewin, in his book *K'tav Yocher*, featured an orthodox
melamed who was hostile to innovations which threatened to
rob him of his livelihood. He also hoped that Jewish persecution would redouble in intensity and he put his faith in the
hatred of the nations as the only thing capable of increasing
the virtues and sanctity of the Chosen People. . . .[5]

A series of government reports are available for the
Austrian Empire and these sound the same tune as Prefect
Laumond's. The announcement of the convention of the
Great Sanhedrin filled the Vienna Cabinet with anxiety, and
governors were requested to inform themselves of the state
of mind of the Jews. The results of their investigations were
on the whole satisfactory and Emperor Francis was able to
conclude that "as far as the zealous Talmudists were concerned, there was absolutely nothing to fear, and that the
Congress of Paris [sic] could only influence those who
belonged to the fashionable classes and who wanted to be
thought enlightened." Now, only a minority of the Jews of
Vienna and Trieste formed part of the "fashionable" classes,
and were anxious to be thought enlightened. The Jews in
Bohemia, Moravia and Hungary completely satisfied the

authorities. The Jews in Galicia seemed even more loyal: according to the governor, von Urményi, "they were all absolutely stupid and attached to the Torah and the Talmud" and regarded the Sanhedrin as "the tomb of Judaism."[6]

As we have seen, this was also the attitude of the Jews in Poland and Russia, although in their case the judgment should perhaps be qualified. In practice, some Polish Talmudists, loyal to their country to the last gasp, were placing their hopes on its definitive revival and, consequently, on victory for Napoleon. The varied factors which determined the Jews' political choices certainly included attachment to the country they had settled in.

It is now important to see what emancipation meant to the great masses of Jews in reality. Perhaps this question can best be clarified by looking at it from the angle of the complete change in their politico-legal position.

From this point of view, the anti-Jewish polemicists or emancipators, who claimed that the Jewish communities formed a state within the State, were not wrong. Throughout their lives the Jews within the ghetto were dealing with Jewish authorities who embodied both the coercive and protective powers of a State for them. The communal oligarchs (generally "emancipated *avant la lettre*" characters) formed a screen which divided them off from the Christian authorities whom they tended in practice to regard as a foreign and hostile power. Because of this, the mass of the people of Israel really constituted a nation *sui generis,* a well integrated nation, and one which defined itself as such in relation to the other nations of the world. Humiliated and persecuted, the Jews of the ghetto knew distinctly what they were.

The cornerstone of the emancipators' plan—the abolition of communal autonomy—aimed at changing this radically. As a child, the Jew had to attend a public school. As a young man, he had to do his service in the army. As an adult, he was no longer subject to a rabbinical tribunal, no longer needed to fear the thunderbolts of excommunication, and so on. On the one hand, he was in actual fact "emancipated," since he was now withdrawn from the paternalist power of rabbis and plutocrats, at the same time as he was relieved of his disabilities. But on the other hand, from then on and for all his life he had to face the Christian authorities directly, and these authorities were assumed to be antagonistic. This can be regarded as the cause of the fear which the new order first aroused and of the general hostility to emancipation.

True, its advantages, notably in the everyday struggle for existence, the abundant opportunities it offered to make money or a career, fairly quickly brought about a change of attitude. Where the fathers remained antagonistic or sceptical, it was the sons who became the advocates of emancipation. The rebellion against parental authority hastened the revolt against rabbinical government. In the space of one or two generations, almost all Jews on both sides of the Rhine were coming round to the new ideas and the process was later repeated in Eastern Europe. But an implacable condemnation of the Jews was still inherent in the code of values of Western society. The former son of the ghetto was assured that henceforth he was a citizen like everyone else, simply a citizen "of the Israelite faith," a man and not a Jew. But he felt that things were not so simple, that a man could not cease to be a Jew while he still remained Jewish. And amongst the various observations or experiences of all types which strengthened this feeling, the rise of anti-Semitism, which we will be considering further on, played a preponderant role.

This gave birth to psychological conflict within the emancipated Jew who henceforth tended to judge himself by the standards of the predominantly Christian society, to see himself as others saw him. Sometimes he may have overestimated himself, but he more often indicted himself and the two attitudes could easily go hand in hand. "The Jews' patriotism consists of self-hatred," noted the Jewish philosopher, Theodor Lessing, completing without contradicting the formula of the anti-Semitic philosopher Schopenhauer: "... the Jew's homeland is other Jews." It is useless to add that it is wrong to generalize, that psychological conflicts like these were already perceptible inside the ghetto, and that innumerable Jews in modern times, who have not attracted attention and whose simple, integrated lives have left barely any written trace, escaped them. In a word, our means of investigation are very inadequate to clarify an extremely complex psycho-historical process, with its constant interaction between individual psychology in depth and the phenomena of collective or social psychology. The fact remains that the principal Jewish personalities of the first post-emancipating generations most frequently took pleasure in vying with one another in their anti-Semitism, whether they resorted to the Christian religion (like Friedrich Stahl) or irreligion (like Karl Marx). The more sensitive approach of certain poets enabled them to supply less conventional answers to the situation and to determine its true aspect for posterity.

No one at the time could do this better than Heinrich Heine (1799–1856). His irony spared neither Judaism, "that misfortune, that family illness of German Jews," nor its disloyal servants, like the Marquis Gumpelino, "deserter from Jehovah's bodyguard," and his valet Hyacinth, "the Rothschilds' *famillionaire*." In *articulo mortis* his tune changed:[7]

> Now I see, the Greeks were only beautiful adolescents, the Jews on the other hand were always men, strong and unyielding, not only in the past, but until today, despite eighteen centuries of persecution and hardship ... martyrs, who have given the world a God and a code of morality, and who have fought and suffered on all the battlefields of thought.

His less sophisticated rival, Ludwig Börne (1786–1837), let off the customary shafts at the Talmud, but praised its devotees or ex-devotees: "You are thirty million Germans and you do not add up to thirty. If there were thirty million Jews, the world would be theirs!"[8] The inconsistency inherent in belittling Judaism while praising the Jews, that is to say in criticizing a culture while vaunting its products, was taken to its extreme by another writer from the Frankfurt ghetto, the Alsatian, Alexandre Weill (1811–99). His furious hatred of the Talmud and rabbinical government did not prevent him announcing[9]

> that more ingenuity, more spirit was expended in one day in the Jews' street in Frankfurt than in all the rest of Germany in a year ... for centuries, this street represented a civilized life, amidst barbarism, where in an oppressed society, faith, charity and justice reigned. ...

The list of inconsistencies and contradiction of this type in the post-emancipating generation could easily be lengthened. Men like Adolphe Crémieux in France or Gabriel Riesser in Germany, who were able to maintain a reserved and dignified attitude, were in the minority.

Other Jewries caught up in the wheels of change nearer to the present time have produced memorialists who have recalled the conflict in even more evocative ways. To the Mediterranean Jew, Albert Cohen, Judaism is a mysterious oubliette, a dark basement which his hero "Solal" frequents and secretly loves. The image was the same but the plus sign was reversed with the Russian Jew, Osip Mandelstam:

> All the elegant mirage of St Petersburg was merely a dream, a brilliant covering thrown over the abyss, while round about there sprawled the chaos of Judaism—not a motherland, not a house, not a hearth, but precisely a chaos, the unknown womb world whence I had issued, which I feared, about which I made vague conjectures and fled. ...

Unraveling the thread of his childhood memories, Mandelstam goes on to evoke his Jewish teacher:[10]

> There was one striking thing in that teacher, although it sounded unnatural: The feeling of national Jewish pride. He

talked about Jews as the French governess talked about Hugo and Napoleon. But I knew that he hid his pride when he went out into the street, and therefore did not believe him.

Another image, by the writer David Scheinert, is the "small Jewish lodger" permanently in residence even inside Jews who are entirely detached from ancestral tradition or communal life. But the great name of Kafka is a reminder that this type of conflict has acquired universal resonance at the present time: that is to say that the Jews' alienation might only be an extreme case of the tensions engendered by technological civilization, and that its counterpart should be identifiable amongst other human groups.

A comparison has sometimes been made between the situation of the Children of Israel and the American Negroes. Alexis de Tocqueville once wrote about the Negro:[11]

> He has been told from the moment he was born that his race is intrinsically inferior to the Whites, and he is not far from believing it: he is therefore ashamed of himself. He discovers a trace of slavery in his every feature and, if he could, he would joyfully agree to repudiate himself entirely. . . .

Nowadays, if one of their spokesmen is to be believed, these Negroes themselves are no longer very sure what they are: "I am ready to bet that over half of the black population would find deep psychological difficulties in answering the apparently simple question: 'Who am I and what am I?' "[12]

The translation from hierarchical to democratic society (tolerant and leveling) poses serious psychological problems for all its members. Obviously the newly enfranchised and therefore unwelcome groups live through these problems particularly acutely.

A situation like this exacerbates the wish for prestige, the desire to make oneself accepted (esteemed and loved) by the new society. These aims can be pursued in different ways according to the temperament of each individual, his social position and the circumstances of the case, but whichever means is selected, money opens all doors, if not all hearts. It is the "answer to everything" (as Ecclesiastes already noted), and acts as a common denominator. In bourgeois society particularly, it is the universal symbol of success. Having ever excelled in the pursuit of wealth, the emancipated Jews redoubled their zeal in this direction and the political and economic turmoil of the period facilitated many spectacular ascents. However, by making money they were behaving, from the Christian's point of view, in a *Jewish* way. To find favor in their eyes, it seems that it was necessary to put aside their primeval instincts and prove themselves in a different way. In France, Napoleon undertook to put them through a probationary period before granting them complete equality of rights.

Questionnaires were sent out to the Prefects: Were the Jews performing their military duties in a becoming manner? Were they practicing useful skills and professions? Were they making their children attend public schools? How were they behaving generally? The Prefects' replies show the efforts the Children of Israel were expending to win the good opinion of authorities and public. The Prefect of the Rhône was ironical on this score: "... it must be believed," he wrote, "that they are feeling the effects of the air they breathe, what I mean is that they share the feelings of probity which distinguish Lyon in Europe as a commercial center."[13] The Prefect of the Seine painted an enthusiastic picture of their rapid progress. He wrote:[14]

It is common knowledge in all Paris that the Jews of that capital, freed from the fetters which have for so long hampered them in the exercise of their industry, with the hope held out of being raised to the rank of other citizens, only took advantage of their first moments of enfranchisement to prove that they were worthy of it. ... For example, they are to be seen lining up under the colors, cultivating science and the arts, embracing professions, establishing useful institutions, and indulging in speculations distinguished by honor and probity. ...

No deserter or defaulter is known amongst the Paris Jews,

and a few heads of families of that nation can boast of having two or even three sons serving under the colors. Nearly two hundred Jewish children are at present apprenticed to various craftsmen. Some are known to be studying medicine, jurisprudence, painting, metal engraving, engraving on fine stones, and clock and watch making, and a few have succeeded in these professions and are making them their vocation. At the various Paris secondary schools, at the one in Versailles, at the Polytechnic school and in several boarding schools, the young Jews of Paris are to be found devoting themselves to the study of various skills which can prepare them for useful and honorable professions in the exercise of which they will no longer be exposed to either the criticism of their co-citizens or the censure of government. . . .

As a result, in June 1808, the Jews of Paris were excluded from the application of the "infamous decree." But it remained in force in most departments. Jews in the provinces, notably Alsace, earnestly requested individual exclusions, supported by testimonials certifying that far from being usurers, "vampires taking advantage of the distress of their co-citizens,"[15] it was common knowledge that they were charitable and generous men. The Central Consistory also multiplied reports to the government, quoting their soldiers and writers, their craftsmen and their dancers at the Opera[16] as arguments in favor of the Children of Israel.

In short, the Jews had to give clear proof that they possessed the human and national attribute (good Frenchman, good German, etc.), which was presumed to be natural and innate in Christians, by doing more and better than the others. They had to clear themselves of a presumption to the contrary: and it was the demands of this demonstration or exoneration which henceforth spurred on the most gifted of them to their spectacular achievements. This later led to a new outburst of criticism, writers and ballerinas provoking anti-Semitic propensities just as much as usurers and second-hand dealers. But the first generation of emancipated Jews were far from suspecting this vicious circle.

To enter high society, they first had to go through public school—the *via dolorosa* for many Jewish children, leaving its mark on them for the rest of their lives. At the peak of his achievements, Adolphe Crémieux recalled his past:[17] "... I could not cross the streets of my native town without receiving some insult. What battles I waged with my fists!" (To correct the effects of this recollection, the statesman immediately added: "Oh well, in a few years time, I finished my studies in Paris, and when I returned to Nîmes in 1817, I was called to the bar and I was no longer a Jew to anyone!" Nîmes society was thus tactful enough not to see the Jew in Crémieux. This perhaps is the secret of French tolerance.) It can be assumed that the Provençal writer Frédéric Mistral's description of those childish battles of fifty boys against one in *Nerto* were based on childhood memories:[18]

Lou *pecihoun*! Lou *capeu jaune*! A la jutarié! Que s'encaune! Cinquanto enfant ié soun darrié; E d'un pouceu, per trufarié. Simulant éli l'auriheto, Em'un gueiroun de sa braieto, Ié crido lou vou d'esparpai: "Vaqui l'auriho de toun pai!"

Everything suggests that a similar routine of bullying was just as common in eastern France. The rabbi of Metz, J.-B. Drach, described his brother's childhood:[19]

... his school mates ... followed [him] when the class came out, showering him with abuse, and stones and what was worse, rubbing his lips with lard. Despite the heads of the school who brought their authority to bear on more than one occasion, these persecutions continued until my brother had distinguished himself by his progress and the prizes he obtained at the end of every year; he is now one of the best miniaturists in his province.

Rabbi Drach, for his part, tried to complete his regeneration by converting to Catholicism when he had reached mature years. But as a general rule, conversion seems to have been relatively rare in France (there are no statistics available). In any case, it never acquired the character of an epidemic and the fact that there are today a thousand or so Jews at the most originating from Comtat-Venaissin (Avignon) for example, as compared with nearly three thousand at the time of emancipation, is rather the result of cumulative individual defections over the generations.[20]

It is true to say that the successive governments of France, if not French society as a whole, were the only ones in Europe to take emancipation entirely seriously. After the Restoration, all legal discrimination against Jews actually disappeared there.

In Germany, on the other hand, the most prestigious positions of authority and command—consequently the least "Jewish," and therefore the most passionately desired by numerous Children of Israel—always remained barred to "citizens of the Mosaic faith." As a result, there was an epidemic of conversions at the beginning of the nineteenth century. The immediate pretext for it might have been the desire to practice a liberal profession or to enter into State service. But the name it was given, *Gefallsucht* (desire to please), suggests that thirst for Christian love and esteem was its general and deep-seated cause.

In fact, there were very mixed motives behind these conversions. David Mendel, a grand-nephew of Moses Mendelssohn, who became the prince of Protestant church historians under the name of Johann Neander (1789–1850), received a call from God at the age of seventeen. Sincere conviction also seems to have presided at the baptism of Julius Jolson (1802–61), infinitely better known as Friedrich Julius Stahl, the name by which he gained his reputation as the great master of Prussian conservative thought. We have seen how Felix Mendelssohn-Bartholdy's father intended to pay tribute to Christian civilization when he had his children baptized; this was already a much less serious attitude to religion.

The case of Heinrich Heine is already too well known. A friend of his, Eduard Gans (1798–1893), a comrade-at-arms in a circle for reviving Jewish culture, suddenly converted in order to obtain a chair of philosophy at the University of Berlin. (Gans was also a friend of Hegel's, and the master of Karl Marx (1818–83), who was himself baptized at his father's wish when he was seven years old.) Heine flung an angry couplet at Gans :[21]

> *Und du bist zum Kreuz gekrochen,*
> *Zu dem Kreuz, das du verachtest. . . .*

and shortly afterwards followed his example, so that he could register at the Hamburg bar, where he never practiced. "Admission ticket to European culture," he said ironically, and also: ". . . if the law authorized the theft of silver spoons, I would not have converted!" His rival, Ludwig Börne, who converted in order to be able to run a newspaper, was no less casual in his comments on the sacrament of baptism. "The three drops of water that were administered to me were not even worth the small amount of money they cost me."

Rahel Varnhagen-Levin stated that half the members of the Berlin Jewish community had already converted in 1823.[22] Nonetheless German history, which was so deeply stamped by the names we have just mentioned, has recorded them as Jews. Amongst the famous men of that generation, only Giacomo Meyerbeer did not convert, perhaps out of affection for his aged mother,[23] and also perhaps because "with the good fortune to have talent, he combined the talent to have good fortune," as Berlioz said of this millionaire.[24] However, he was a very complex character, as his most recent biographer reveals, and his wealth provoked abundant jealousy which caused him suffering. In any case, this "defamed musician" remains an exception from the point of view that concerns us.[25]

Sincere in their own fashion, some of them did not even

pretend to sincerity in their convictions. Others, while becoming practicing, even convinced Christians, kept their "small Jewish lodger" at the bottom of their hearts. His presence can be illustrated by the example of one of the sons of the emancipator, Breidenbach, who became director of the Department of Education at Hesse after his baptism. A Jewish teacher who came to see him to ask for a transfer, told how his first reception was hostile: "You Jews give us too much work," his co-religionist said to him. Nonetheless, he gave him permission to return in a month's time. On the appointed day, Breidenbach was not to be found in his office. The applicant went to his home to try his luck. This time, he was warmly received: the master of the house took him into a room where two candles were lit, and said: "Today is the anniversary of my father's death. Here is a sum of money for *kaddish* [the prayer for the dead] to be said for him. And here is your transfer order." History does not and cannot tell us what the real relationship of Breidenbach junior to the God of the New Testament was. In any case, the form his filial piety took was of a type to offend the rabbis as much as the priests at that time.[26]

The mass of German Jews, without going as far as the baptismal font, could not fail to be impressed by the conversion of so many rich and brilliant personalities, some of whom, as we have seen, even completed their de-Judaization by changing their names. Examples like these reinforced the effects of the abolition of rabbinic government. German Jewry was rapidly broken up into, firstly, the converted of all faiths, secondly, the indifferent who had completely discarded ancestral observances, thirdly, the advocates of a reformed Mosaism, and finally, the block of loyal followers of the Talmud. The greater number of them already wanted to be German first: "In general, what the Jews in Prussia are pressing for is to be Prussians and nothing more," noted Alexandre Weill in 1844.[27] Even those who prided themselves on their loyalty to Jewish tradition had greater Germanization of the Jews in mind. It was typical that the founder of the "science of Judaism," Leopold Zunz, was diverted to his historical research by the desire to prove that medieval Jews generally had Christian first names and used local dialects for worship.[28] "The German Jew thinks in an essentially German way on all questions of intellectual and social life," noted the famous Catholic theologian, Ignaz Döllinger, in 1857 : [29]

> ... and as our culture, our civilization have issued from Christianity and are colored by Christian influences, then he cannot avoid, however averse he may otherwise be to Christianity, thinking and therefore acting in a Christian way, consciously or unconsciously.

In fact, what we have here is a new generation of Marranos, its major difference from the victims of the Inquisition lying in the distinction between shame and the desire to be loved on the one hand, and fear on the other. Like the "new Christians" of the Iberian peninsula, these Jews, even when converted, remained Jews socially in the eyes of the Christians—Jews, as we will see, liable to arouse greater anti-Jewish passion than the traditional sons of the ghetto. At the beginning of the twentieth century, the great economist Werner Sombart was lamenting on behalf of his statistics that "men appear on the scene as Christians, who in reality are Jews. They or their fathers were baptized, that is all."[30] But as early as 1832, the militant Jew Gabriel Riesser (1806–63) saw further ahead: "Believe me," he warned the neo-Marranos, "hate like the angel of death can find its man, it can recognize him by whatever name he calls himself...."[31] Yet, even this practicing Jew admitted that his love was divided between the God of Israel and a new foreign goddess. Had he not chosen as his motto: "We have a Father above, and we have a mother: God, father of all beings, and Germany, our mother on earth"?[32]

Thus, the psychological conflict which afflicted people like Rahel Levin was becoming the lot of a growing number of

Jews. To be honest, it is difficult to know what term to use to designate a community whose leaders had renounced the Mosaic faith. We have seen how German Judaism had become a family misfortune, even a disease for Heine. In Alexandre Weill's opinion, it was in process of becoming "a Christian sect."[33] The problems of semantic identification reflect the confusion reigning amongst the former children of the ghetto, who were themselves no longer very sure what they were. For the most part, it could be said that the only identity they recognized was a negative one: ". . . we are people who are not old-Christian Germans." They conscientiously aped German behavior and vied with each other in patriotism, even in their synagogal worship, but Germany already seemed to be replying: "You are what you are not."

One of the results of the German type of emancipation was thus to give the age-old Judeo-Christian dialectic a new turn: henceforth it is by copying the Christian that the Jew compares himself to him. Heine's ironic genius gives him the last word (but the beauty of the lines remains untranslatable):[34]

> For a thousand years and more we have borne with each other in brotherly fashion; you allow me to breathe; I allow you to rant and rage. But now and then, in dark times, a strange feeling overcame you and you stained your loving, pious paws with my blood. Now our friendship is firmer, and firmer every day; for I also began to rant and rage and almost became like you.

But one of the first pioneers of socialism in Germany, Moses Hess, was already, after clearing the way for Marx and Engels, choosing a different route in preference to conversion: the road to political Zionism, that privileged solution to the neo-Marrano psychological conflict.

The non-Jews' point of view

As emancipation had profoundly changed the attitude of

Jews both towards non-Jews and towards themselves, it might be assumed that by a reverse process, the majority society would find itself equally affected, and even experience a sort of parallel development in the image it formed of the Jews, if not of itself. On the other hand, this society was passing through an exceptionally disturbed phase in its history, since the questioning of traditional beliefs and ideas, in conjunction with the rise of the bourgeoisie, had had repercussions on political and social structures and precipitated a general conflagration. After that, many intellectuals were looking for a simple and coherent explanation of the apocalyptic spectacle Europe had offered since 1789, and since the Jewish people were both authors, bearers and principal actors in the Holy Scriptures, their enfranchisement could not fail to be reflected in the various explanatory schemata suggested. The tenor of these eschatologies might therefore provide us with a first clue in a study of the Christians' reactions to emancipation.

But it is also true that the principal theories of this type were originally formulated well before the events they claimed to explain. The age of incredulity, that is to say the Century of Enlightenment, was also, as we know, an age of extreme credulity. Once the yoke of the Church had been shaken off and theological discipline relaxed, the field was clear for new revelations to compete with the Judeo-Christian revelation. There had always been an abundant supply of prophetic personalities. They were henceforth able to recruit followers at their leisure, and found chapels, conventicles and religions (from this point of view, the worship of the goddess of Reason might be regarded as nothing but the triumph of the most radical of all the heresies which were found in profusion at the time). At the lowest level of pure charlatanism, men like Cagliostro or Saint-Germain gleaned easy success practicing the arts of magic. At the highest, mystical stage of millenarianism, people like Swedenborg or Saint-Martin, following on from Jacob Boehme, were engaged in an exercise in depth. The first category—

the men of action—may have infatuated their contemporaries, but the second, the men of meditation, deeply influenced the attitude of later generations via romanticism and philosophy.

Like Boehme before him, Swedenborg glossed the two Testaments abundantly; that is to say if references to the Jews are as frequent in the one as in the other. It should be noted that Jacob Boehme (1575–1625) developed extremely benevolent views on the Children of Israel—typical of Christians at any period (but particularly today) who have studied and thought about the Epistle to the Romans. Notably, he foretold the imminent restoration of the Chosen People.[35] Very different was the view of Emmanuel Swedenborg (1688–1772) who was famous as a scholar in Stockholm and London, before he became even more so as a prophet, carrying on big business with spirits. Not only did he resolutely deny the possibility of any such reintegration but his glosses and visions had led him to the conclusion that the Jews had always been a despicable and idolatrous nation, attached to the material things of this world, incapable by nature of perceiving the divine message (the great deist thesis is recognizable here):[36]

... The character of this nation is such that, more than the other nations, they worship externals [i.e. tangible objects] as well as idols, and that they want to know absolutely nothing about internals [i.e. spirituality]; in fact, of all the nations, they are the most miserly, and greed like theirs, which consists of loving gold and silver as gold and silver and not for some purpose, is the most worldly affection ... one must see clearly by this how mistaken are those who think that this nation will be chosen anew, or that the Church of the Lord will pass into them anew. ...

The spirits had informed Swedenborg that the Scriptures had been misread hitherto, for the "restoration of Israel" should be understood as the restoration of true Christians. In fact, this restoration had already taken place, since the Last

Judgment had already been held in 1757. At it, he, Swedenborg, had been entrusted with the task of building the new
Jerusalem, and those who hearkened to his words formed the
camp of the chosen.[37]

The philosopher Karl Jaspers, who studied the Swedish
prophet from the psychiatric angle, saw him as a clear case
of schizophrenia. "Swedenborg's obsession," he wrote, "can
be understood as the result of a religious tradition, as well as
of the subjects which conditioned his thought before his
illness. ..."[38] As far as the subjects were concerned, his
views on the Jews were no different from those of the English
deists, to which he thus gave the seal of prophetic revelation.
As far as the tradition is concerned, it is not uninteresting to
note that this son of a Lutheran bishop was using the same
image as Luther when he announced "that one would
convert stones rather than them [the Jews] to faith in the
Lord."[39] He might also be compared with the reformer in
the evocative power of his style, and also in his use of
scatological description where Jews were concerned. After
visiting it, he described the hell which was set aside for them
"as if you were there." It was

> a town to which they flock, crowding up together; but this town
> is foul and covered with filth, consequently it is called the
> *defiled Jerusalem*. There, they run about in the mud and in filth
> above their heels, moaning and lamenting.

All they have for food there is filth or worse, "cadaverous
matter, putrid, excremental, and stercoral, foul and urinous."
Other Jews, however, wandered outside the *defiled
Jerusalem*:[40]

> ... those are Jews wandering about like that, uttering threats to
> kill, massacre, burn, roast alive, and this to everyone they meet,
> even to Jews or friends. From this, I could learn their character,
> although they dare not show the world what they are.

Swedenborg was probably the first modern author to talk

about the Jews' "true nature." If he was mad, his madness found numerous followers, and, as we have said on many occasions, this sort of passion against the Chosen People is frequently found in specific gentiles who feel that they have been called to break the insolent monopoly of this people, and supplant their message. Nothing is more typical of this than Swedenborg's animosity towards the apostle Paul. During his explorations into the hereafter, the intrepid visionary even found that the other apostles also kept away from this Jew.[41]

Similar ideas were expressed by Claude de Saint-Martin (1743–1803), "the unknown philosopher," and probably the most influential occultist of the following generation. He also dealt with the problem of the "restoration of the Jews" which, he inferred from their books, would be fatal to the gentiles, and contrary to the well-known decrees of Providence. "If the Jews were brought back as a national body in this world, no one could hope for eternal salvation, because the divine circle of the supreme operations would thereby be fulfilled and closed in time." It should be noted that this argument seems to date from the period when Bonaparte issued his "Zionist" proclamation to the Jews at the time of the Egyptian campaign, thus setting himself up as their Messiah. Let us add that, unlike Swedenborg, Saint-Martin was grateful to the Jews, whose crime was "inestimably useful" to the gentiles : ". . . . the blood which they have laid to their charge was spirit and life." He also offered them the solace of baptism; Catholic universalism seems to have been a thing of the past by then.[42] Elsewhere, the "unknown philosopher" drew a parallel between the French and the Jews, which illustrates certain of the expectations of the period:[43]

> ... the French might be regarded as the people of the new law, as the Hebrews were the people of the old law. There should be nothing surprising about this selection, despite our crimes and

brigandage. The Jews who were chosen in their day were no better than the French. . . .

The revolutionary triumphs, followed by the Napoleonic triumphs, obviously gave a powerful impetus to eschatological conjecture, and the subject of irreligion triumphant was added to the theme of the eternal mysteries of existence. The uneasy questionings of this period were formulated by Joseph de Maistre, principal author of the "providential theory" of the Revolution.[14]

I understand nothing, that is the great byword of the day. . . . How then (people are crying out from all sides) do the guiltiest men in the world triumph over the world! A terrible regicide has all the success that those who committed it might expect! Monarchy is torpid throughout Europe! Its enemies are even finding allies on the thrones! The wicked succeed in everything. There is a *satanic* quality about the French Revolution which distinguishes it from anything that has been seen and perhaps from anything that will be seen. . . .

An early answer was to indict the Protestants (either led by Satan, or as an autonomous and fully responsible faction). The theory of the "Protestant conspiracy" could be supported by the pro-revolutionary sympathies of the majority of members of the Reformed Churches, old scapegoats of the Very Christian kings, and above all by the fact that the main bankers to the monarchy, like the Minister Necker, were in fact of Protestant origin. But "capital" or "capitalism" had not yet been absorbed into contemporary customs as a great explanatory principle, so that the Protestant conspiracy theory rapidly faded before another, perhaps less plausible in our post-Marxist eyes: secret societies formed by anti-Christian sects.

Here we will ask the reader for a moment's care. "Secret societies" have been promoted to the rank of a vital historical factor, particularly in relation to 1789, an honor they certainly do not deserve (although research is, by definition difficult). On the other hand, belief in the omnipotence of these societies had an incontestable influence on Western historical development, notably during the first half of the twentieth century. Even so, these beliefs still had to be able to crystallize around some pretext or news item, opportunely supplied by fanatics or humbugs *playing* at secret societies— perhaps an indispensable condition for the birth of great myths of this type, and in this sense, there would not in fact have been smoke without fire. This was the way in which the principal authors (the Frenchmen Augustin Barruel and Joseph de Maistre; the Englishman Robison; the German Göchhausen) were able to attribute the revolutionary apocalypse to the triad "illuminism—freemasonry—philosophy," with the emphasis particularly on the first.

The affair of the Bavarian order of the Illuminati bears a curious resemblance to the news item from which Dostoievsky took the material for his *Demons*. The unfrocked Jesuit, Adam Weishaupt, claimed that he was leading a conspiracy on a European scale intended to destroy all States and set up a universal republic. He was believed and thrown into prison. It should be noted that the affair took place a few years *before* 1789, and imagination or art seemed to be anticipating nature.[45] Freemasonry in the eyes of these philosophers was associated with Illuminism. As for "philosophism," although the principal authority on the subject, Abbé Barruel, thought that, in the persons of Voltaire, d'Alembert and Frederick II of Prussia, it had woven a carefully drawn-up plan, it had a far more significant effect than the other two occult categories as we know, even in the absence of such a plan. Moreover, certain forgotten authors carried the search for causes even further: as early as 1794, a priest instructed by Pius VI to write the history of the "French persecution" listed "ingenious inventions" such as balloons and "Montgolfiers" amongst subversive factors.[46]

The Jews were not forgotten amidst all this. But it is interesting to note that during a preliminary period which lasted until 1806, anti-revolutionary polemicists only attributed to them an incidental and passive role; they were pawns being used by the great conspirators for their machinations, or foils which showed up their baseness better. For example, in 1786, the German, Göchhausen, one of the first great anti-Illuminist propagandists, drew attention to the Judaic connection with Masonry:[47]

> No order bears more revealing marks or *birthmarks*—let me emphasize this very appropriate word—than the symbolism of Masonry, which is centered on the purest Jewish hieroglyphics. All its implements, cloths, institutions, instructions, as well as its history—it has been published—are a heap of Hebraic imagery. The Jewish Solomon is one of its supreme masters and his temple is the basic allegory of it.

Genuine Masons, for their part, were emphasizing this genealogy. One Karl Leonhard Reinhold (Brother Decius) reminded his brethren in 1788 that the "Great Architect of the Universe" was none other than Jehovah and that it was their duty to build not just any sort of temple, but actually the "Jews' destroyed temple, the temple of the religion on which the common faith of Christians is based." This did not imply any special affection on his part for the first builders of this temple; quite the reverse.[48]

Abbé Barruel also attributed Judaic descent to Freemasonry. But he primarily criticized the philosophical conspirators for having wanted to enfranchise the Jews "in order finally to separate the people from their religion," by giving the "lie to the God of the Christians and his prophets." He supported this contention by referring to the correspondence between Voltaire and Frederick II,[49] but this first version did not assume that the Children of Israel, left outside the conspiracy, were actually working for their restoration and the downfall of the Church themselves.

To sum up, before Napoleon convened the Great Sanhedrin, contemporaries scarcely thought of ranking the Jews amongst the evil powers, bent on harming Christianity. In the past, the deicidal people may have been accused of trying to destroy it with magical processes and every type of spell, but these legends had lost all credence with the moderns. For them, even Satan was henceforth apparently obliged to take the natural laws into account and to carry out, in conjunction with his agents, a strategy dictated by political facts.

The new move by the "enemy of Europe" (already promoted to the rank of ogre or Anti-Christ by his detractors) gave new food for thought and revived old fears. Imaginations worked feverishly and the chancelleries exploited this fever. "Jews have never been talked about so much as now," wrote a Parisian newspaper in 1806. "All Europe seems to be in a state of suspense about the motive which has led to their summons, as well as about the result of their assembly. . . ."[50] The "suspense" was not confined to Europe. In 1806–7, in the remote United States of America, a distant spectator of the European psychological conflict, a polemic divided public opinion: was Napoleon a general benefactor, *Judaeorum salvator, Europae pacifactor* and *humani generis benefactor,* or had he been bought by Jewish money? Was he by any chance a Jew himself, as was claimed in certain quarters?[51]

These latter arguments, frivolously advanced on the other side of the Atlantic, were developed very vehemently in Europe. We have mentioned the concern which gripped the Austrian government when the convention of the Great Sanhedrin was announced and it can be imagined that if the news was not exploited for purposes of political propaganda, it was in order not to aggravate relations with Napoleon. Such considerations did not affect Russia which was in open conflict with France. At the beginning of 1807, the Holy Synod ordered a proclamation to be read in all Russian churches accusing the Emperor of having concluded a sacrilegious pact with the Jews:[52]

In order to complete the degradation of the Church, he has

convened the Jewish synagogues in France, restored the rabbis to their dignity, and laid the foundations of a new Hebrew Sanhedrin, the same infamous tribunal which once dared to condemn Our Lord and Savior Jesus Christ to the cross. And now he is daring to bring together all the Jews whom the anger of God had dispersed over the face of the earth, and launch all of them into the destruction of the Church of Christ, in order, Oh unspeakable presumption, greater than any heinous crime, that they should proclaim the Messiah in the person of Napoleon.

The Roman Catholic archbishop also published a pastoral letter attributing blasphemous intentions to the Emperor of the French.[53] Political propaganda tried in this way to pluck the strings of national mystique.

It fully succeeded, to judge by the space that contemporary Russian newspapers gave to the subject of Napoleon the Anti-Christ, or Napoleon the Jews' Messiah,[54] and the mystical francophobia of Russian society continued to grow up to the patriotic war of 1812. Pierre Besouhoff's cabalistic calculations when he formed the plan to assassinate Napoleon in Tolstoy's *War and Peace*, are classical literary evidence of this state of mind.

The most influential source of inspiration for these millenarian hypotheses were the German theosophists, continuing the tradition of Swedenborg and the "unknown philosopher." Could the Napoleonic adventure be anything but the final struggle between Good and Evil, the age of the Great Trial when the Beast would reign? And if the Corsican usurper was not the Anti-Christ in person was he not at least *Panaleon*, the destroyer, and the *Apollyon* or Black angel foretold in Revelation (IX, 11)? In this case, his antagonist Alexander could only be the White or Sacerdotal angel. This is suggested by the most influential of the Tsar's mystical devotees, Johann Heinrich Jung-Stilling, whose most recent biographer (Professor Max Geiger) tells us "that he exercised a direct and determining effect on the course of historical development."⁵⁵ Jung-Stilling's eschatology was kind to the Jews, even if they were in his opinion "completely immoral and depraved."⁵⁶ Unlike Swedenborg and Saint-Martin, he in fact thought that Israel would have to gather in the flesh in the Promised Land and rebuild the Temple, on the eve of Parousia:⁵⁷

> Now imagine Palestine, lying as it were in the middle between Asia, Africa and Europe, at the eastern end of the Mediterranean Sea, in contact with every country by sea and land, and think of the most industrious and active of all nations—for that is the Jewish—and now this nation, in glowing love for God and Christ, full of burning zeal to win all mankind for Christ. . . .

Even so, the damned people first had to be converted. But this theosophist, on the basis of information on symptoms of this conversion supplied by the old apostle Lavater, saw it making headway everywhere with emancipation. In every continent, he noted "a lively animation and fermentation amongst the Jews, the beginning of a leaning towards Christ, as well as serious preparations for going to the Promised Land." His information came from mysterious sources, whose revelations he confided to his diary using secret writing. For example, after the convening of the Great Sanhedrin, he received a visit "from an important man whose father was an emir in Syria":⁵⁸

> He told me that his father belonged to the society which held its meetings in Jerusalem on the mountain of The Temple. This society was none other than the Old Sanhedrin which had never yet entirely died out; it consists of apparent Jews, who are, however, secret Christians and are only waiting for a sign from the Master to gather Israel from the four winds and lead it back to Christ and to its homeland.

The messenger, about whom Jung-Stilling supplies no further details, must either have been a convert or a charlatan, probably both. And this leaves room for a certain amount of reflection on the secret sources of theosophic inspiration: was there a Jewish humbug lurking in the shadows behind many of the mystics of this genre?[59] In any case, it shows how prophetic passion could lead, through some obscure choice, to love as well as hate, to "philo-Semitism" as well as "anti-Semitism," the common factor being a constant awareness of the destiny of the Biblical people.

Without lingering over Jung-Stilling's many German emulators, of whom the Catholic philosopher, Franz von Baader, was the most prominent and remains the best known,[60] let us move on to Great Britain, traditional home of apocalyptic exegesis and sworn enemy of the Ogre. By virtue of this coincidence, the English millenarists too were not only devoting themselves to public obloquy of Napoleon Bonaparte, they were also formulating views which varied greatly, according to circumstances and temperament, on the Jews.[61] But it can also be noted that this sort of prophecy did not require any special political conditions, since half a century later over fifty English and American authors happened to resume the work independently of one another, and discover that the Anti-Christ had already made his appearance in the form of Napoleon III, and that he had already contracted his alliance with the Jews![62]

England was also the main center of propaganda by French *émigrés*, dedicated, like all *émigrés*, to acting as agitators and sources of political ferment. Their principal organ, *L'Ambigu*, devoted a dozen articles in 1806–7 to the Great Sanhedrin, taking Napoleon to task on every count (October 20, 1806):

> ... is he claiming to pass himself off and be acknowledged by them [the Jews] as the Messiah they have waited for, for so long? This, time will tell. Nothing remains for us but to see this Anti-Christ struggle against the eternal decrees of the Divinity: this must be the last act of his diabolical existence.

More soberly, another polemicist recalled Jewish enthusiasm at the time of Sabatai Zvi, quoted Bossuet and warned Europe (December 10, 1806): ". . . the author wished to clear his conscience towards Christian governments and people; if they neglect to take prompt and effective counter-measures, they will recognize the consequences too late." A Vienna correspondent described the Jews as a "plague which is gnawing the entrails of the Austrian monarchy" (July 20, 1806). Nostradamus's prophecy was also used on October 20, 1806, and a month later, *L'Ambigu* revealed the crux of the enigma to its readers: the usurper was himself a Jew, whether his family "was descended from the Jewish race" or whether his "light-hearted mother Laetitia Fesch had given birth to him after having practiced the same hospitality towards some descendant of Israel at Ajaccio as Rahab towards Joshua's spies at Jericho." This second version must have been propagated at the time of the Egyptian campaign, since in May, 1799, a friend wrote to Jung-Stilling (always well informed) that the "man of sin" was born of adulterous intercourse between an oriental princess and an "important" Jew.[63]

But it was in France itself that the subject of the Great Sanhedrin was exploited most originally. While de Bonald and other Catholic publicists were embarking on a new campaign against the emancipation of the Jews, Abbé Barruel (who meanwhile had rallied to the imperial régime and become canon of Notre Dame) sounded the alarm in government circles. Like Jung-Stilling he too had his mysterious informants, one of whom, Simonini, an "Italian soldier," had come forward to betray world Jewry's plans to him. Before he acted, Barruel took the precaution of finding out from Pope Pius VII how much of this he should believe. The Pope is said to have informed him that everything pointed to the truth of Simonini's information.[64] This was an important matter. Having succeeded in worming his way into a close relationship with the great Tuscan Jews, Simonini had learned that Israel's age-old dream was on the point of coming true. All the evils which Christianity was suffering were thus finally explained. It was Jews who had founded the sect both of the Freemasons and of the Illuminati. It was they again who were to be found behind all anti-Christian sects. Other Jews were passing themselves off as Christians in order "better to deceive their world." In particular, they were working to infiltrate into the Catholic Church, with the result that, in Italy alone, over eight hundred ecclesiastics, including a few bishops and cardinals, were actually working on their behalf. As for the conspirators' final goal, it was nothing less than "to be the masters of the world, to abolish all other sects in order to make their own reign supreme, to make as many synagogues as there were Christian churches, and to reduce the remaining Christians to slavery."[65]

However serious this information was, Abbé Barruel refrained from making it public, from fear, he said, of provoking a general massacre of the Jews. In order "to prevent the effect that the Sanhedrin might have," he judged it more effective to give a discreet warning to Joseph Fouché and Cardinal Fesch, the police and the Church. Consequently, he claimed the credit "for the abrupt conclusion of the Great Sanhedrin, which the Emperor dismissed without having obtained any positive result."[66] That, therefore, is how Jewry found itself associated with Freemasonry, Illuminism and "philosophism," in the capacity of a great instigator of war and revolution—and on this occasion as a leading actor in the vast conspiracy attributed to it. Perhaps what we have here was the primary source of the *Protocols of the Elders of Zion*. Barruel, whose work was translated into all the major European languages, may have refrained from publishing his ultimate revelation during his lifetime but others did it for him. In particular, it can be recognized in Joseph de Maistre's warning to the Tsar in about 1810:[67]

The Jews . . . deserve particular attention from all governments, especially the government of Russia which has many of them within its bosom; there is nothing surprising in the fact that the great enemy of Europe favors them in such an obvious fashion; they already have vast properties at their disposal in Tuscany and Alsace; they already have a capital at Paris and another in Rome, whence the head of the Church has been driven. Everything leads to the belief that their money, their hatred and their talents are in the service of great conspirators. The greatest and most deadly talent of this accursed sect, which makes use of everything to achieve its ends, has since its origins been to utilize even princes in order to destroy them. Those who have read the necessary books of this type know the skill with which they were able to place men who share their views in positions close to princes.

These themes were to be a rich source of anti-Jewish propaganda half a century later. But from this period, the Christian theosophists were joined by a few neo-pagan theosophists who disparaged both Jews and Church. Men like Azaïs were describing them as a "truly ignoble and vicious people," or, with Quintus Leclerc, labelling them "the most atrocious of all peoples."[68] In short, the varied processes which led to this line of thought, against the background of the Napoleonic epic, from the Egyptian campaign to Waterloo, were as numerous as they are difficult to trace. The Italian scholar, R. de Felice, points out an Italian pamphlet published in Venice in 1799.[69] We have exhumed a German booklet dated 1816, *Das Judenthum in der Maurerey*:[70]

> ... Although Napoleon be isolated on his rock in the ocean, his Jewish confidants are holding the threads of a conspiracy which extends not only to France, but also to Germany, Italy, Spain and the Netherlands, and whose goals consist of nothing less than world revolution. ...

In the same category can be ranked *Der sarmatische Lykurg*, a curious utopia published by Franz von Spaun, as a warning against the "philanthropic delirium" of emancipation which ran the risk of leading to the advent of "circumcised kings on the thrones of Europe."[71]

Anti-Semitic propagandists in the second half of the nineteenth century did not fail to use all these sources. But, characteristically, the Jews, dissociated from Napoleon, then had to act alone in pursuit of world domination. *"Habent sua fata fabulae"*: Napoleon, Messiah of the Jews, was a myth which died as quickly as it was born—and we have only been able to reconstruct it by going back to the original sources. For later generations of Europeans, the great captain emerged as a brilliant Aryan hero. (Moreover, the Nazis also tried to take him over, after he had been duly "germanized.")[72] And he did not easily fit into the role of a leader of a shady conspiracy. As for his Semitic origins, for the same reasons, they could only gratify a certain Jewish attitude found amongst men like Disraeli, the principal Jewish authority for the racial interpretation of history, as we will see later. Elsewhere, east of the Vistula, the Jews ended up cultivating the memory of the "liberator of Israel," whose portrait decorated many a Jewish home in the nineteenth century.

If we have spent longer perhaps than necessary amongst the occultists and mystics, on the borderline of charlatanism, it is because we believe that these visionaries, whatever their intuitions and deep-seated convictions, possess very sensitive antennae to catch both the hopes and fears of the common run of worshippers. Numerous other famous or obscure contemporaries, more sober of temperament, were equally disturbed by the spectacle of the emancipation of the Jews and without shouting "conspiracy!" conjured up the specter of Jewish domination. In 1806 for example, de Bonald quoted J. G. Herder, to predict ". . . that the Children of Israel who form a state within the State everywhere, would manage by their systematic and rational conduct to reduce the Christians to nothing more than their slaves."[73] Chateaubriand thought that the Sanhedrin "was the result and resulted . . . in world finances falling to the Jews' stalls and thereby created a fatal subversion."[74] In 1808, a sub-prefect, du Gard, summarized the import of the discussion: "It would be better to expel the Jews from Europe, than be expelled by them."[75] In Balzac's time, other witnesses who will be quoted later thought that the Jews had won the round. Let us therefore try to throw some light on the deeper reason for these misgivings.

It is necessary to go back to the socio-economic disturbances of the period and to the new reign of money. Herder (whom de Bonald misquoted) criticized Christian negligence in this context:[76]

> Thus where there are Jews, the betterment must begin with dishonorable Christians who misuse the Jews. A ministry where the Jew counts for everything, a house in which the Jew holds the keys to the wardrobe or the whole cash desk, a department or commissariat where Jews conduct the main business, a university where Jews as brokers and money-lenders rule the students, are undrainable Pontine marshes. Political conversion begins at the wrong end if it aims at the Jew, not the Christian.

De Bonald himself indicted the Jews "who have spread that acquisitive spirit in Europe which has made such strange headway amongst Christians."[77] Here Marshal Gneisenau's "Jews and contractors" thus put in an appearance (to become "our peers of the realm").[78] Here we have the European élite taking fright at the disappearance of the old hierarchical order, and the nobility, not long since the Jews' best support, beginning to rally to the new anti-Semitic camp. "Christians can be cheated by Jews," protested de Bonald again, "but they must not be controlled by them, and this subordination offends their dignity, even more than the Jews' greed harms their interests."[79] It is therefore not a question of "economic anti-Semitism"; far from it. At any period, this concept has only expressed a superficial approach, even in cases when cut-throat competition seems to be involved. Georges Bern-

Christian imagination as avenging specters, once they had been released from their chains. It was probably these new fears which de Bonald was expressing in his great article *Sur les Juifs*: [90]

> And let there be no mistake about it, the Jews' domination would be harsh, like that of so many peoples who have been enslaved for a long time and who find themselves on a level with their former masters; and the Jews, all of whose ideas are corrupted, and who despise or hate us, would find terrible examples in their history. . . .

Outside the unusual case of the Jews, the great social and political phenomena of the nineteenth century—the rise of nationalism and racism—might have been partly due to Western man's hidden need to erect new partitions and new hierarchies after the disappearance of the old hierarchical barriers. We will be returning to this later. In 1835 Alexis de Tocqueville wrote: [91]

> The White no longer clearly sees the barrier which should separate him from a degraded race, and he keeps away from the Black all the more carefully because he is afraid that the day will come when he will intermingle with him.

This comment can be applied equally to our problem. The anguish of no longer being differentiated from the Jew, of intermingling with him (at the extreme, of being a Jew oneself), in a standardized world, from which God is beginning to disappear and where many Christians feel themselves adrift, would therefore be a deep-seated and specific factor in modern anti-Semitism. While to the sociologist, the moralist and the experienced politician, it constitutes a dangerous social disease, the psychologist can do nothing, it would seem, but note the alleviating effect of such a defense mechanism on the mind. As a regressive phenomenon, it is also selective because it only appears in its dynamic and irresistible form in certain types of men. The difference

anos later talked about this in his essay defending Drumont "from an excuse invented to satisfy society hungry for logic." [80] In the same book, he deplored "the terrible uniformity of customs" at a period "when everything seems to be sliding along a sloping surface with a speed which increases daily." [81] Perhaps certain remarks by Goethe will help us to understand better how this should be interpreted.

Painting an idyllic picture of the customs of yesteryear at the end of his life, Goethe stressed the advantages of "the diversified subordination which, from the highest to the lowest, from the *Emperor to the Jew,* seemed to unite rather than divide individuals, and favored general well-being." [82] Thus, in the poet's opinion, what cemented society and favored general well-being, was the set place, traditionally assigned to each individual, on whichever social rung he found himself. Is this not the problem of personal identity, set against the background of the early stages of the leveling process? In a society in process of democratization, where the *Emperor* is knocked from his zenith and the *Jew* no longer chained to his nadir, the traditional framework of reference is found to be false; this was indeed "disorder worse than injustice." At the announcement of any change brought forward in the law relating to the Jews, Goethe flew into a rage: "The most serious and most disastrous consequences are to be expected . . . all ethical feelings within families, feelings which rest entirely on religious principles, will be endangered by these scandalous laws," he exclaimed, suspecting a maneuvre by the "omnipotent Rothschild." [83]

Perhaps Goethe is expressing the whole of Western Christian tradition here. What then was the psychological reality of the millennial idea of the "witness-people," a people whose "probative value" and usefulness (unlike pagan peoples) Church scholars unanimously extolled? What was the psycho-religious function of these so-called deicidal infidels, whose very existence was considered an offense, but who nonetheless were covered by canonical immunity and, according to the Apostle, brought salvation? At the time of the first emancipation campaign, a Roman apologist proclaimed: "A ghetto of Jews is better proof of the religion of Jesus Christ than a whole school of theologians."[84] Why? Would the answer not be the role they played as an indispensable reference group, enabling Christians to know themselves as Christians and to incarnate good by contrast with evil, just as so many theologians think that the very existence of evil is explained by its role in revealing good?

Various indications suggest that, even today, the Jews have not ceased to exercise this unrewarding function: certain discussions on the "schema on the Jews" at the Ecumenical Council in 1963–5, for example. The passage in this schema explicitly exonerating the people of Israel of the deicide was omitted, we are told, at the request of the bishops of oriental countries who were afraid that their worshipers would interpret it as a denial of Christ's divinity.[85] The religion of these simple folk therefore seems to rest on the Jewish *felix culpa*; rehabilitate, "regenerate" the Jews, and you plunge them into agonies of doubt, of tottering faith; they no longer know where they stand, *who* they are. Outside the theme of the deicide and in an even clearer fashion, the Protestant sociologist Bernhard Olson wrote in a book published in 1963 that a Christian "cannot know who he is and what his role consists of until he understands who the Jew is and what is Israel's role." In this context he did not fail to regret that, instead of an "identifying mirror," the Jew had acted as a foil for the Christians.[86] But has not this role played its part in the mental equilibrium of innumerable Christians? And did not the emancipation of the Jews, in other words, the distortion, or even the extinction of the age-old image, the divergence which arises between the symbol and the reality, did this not sow obscure terrors—if the Jew is no longer a Jew, who am I and whence cometh my salvation—did not this result in a fresh outbreak of hatred, precisely because of emancipation?

Side by side with this specific sort of mechanism (symmetrical in relation to the Jews' great removal from their

usual surroundings), other processes were und ing into play, acting in an opposite direction, to the scheme of the ideologists of emancipa walls of the ghetto were broken down, the school and in the army relinquished, in th comrades, at least some of the mysterious disturbing aspects that every society tends t knows nothing about and who cultivate differ page of Balzac's *Illusions perdues* nicely reflec attitude, consisting, when you come to think forth taking the Jew for what he has become a old prejudice:[87]

... Lucien asked himself what was the motive royal intrigues. He answered in the first place sense: the Spanish are generous. The Spaniard the Italian is a poisoner and jealous, as the frivolous, as the German is frank, as the Jew is Englishman is noble. Reverse these statements! the truth. The Jews have cornered the gold, they *Diable*, they act *Phèdre*, they sing *William Tell* sion pictures, they build palaces, they write l wonderful poetry, they are more powerful th religion is accepted, finally they give credit to the

Liberal publicists of the day, notably Benja expressed similar views[88] and examples of attitude could certainly be found in other cou But every type of document consulted to clarif of the Christians' emotional reactions to Israe tion most frequently seems to give a quite diff particularly in Germany. Describing the rise 1819, Ludwig Börne spoke of the "inexpli inspired by Judaism, which "like a ghost, like murdered mother, accompanies Christianity fro laughing derisively."[89] But the eternal victim who were also deicides, that is to say mystica and infanticides, became infinitely more th

between anti-Semitism and medieval Judeophobia from which it is descended, can be seen. In the first place, Judeophobia placed Jewry as a whole on one side and all Christianity on the other; then, this confrontation or age-old "cold war," with its economic sub-structure, was also a conflict of interests between two socio-religious groups, and finally, each of them, within the framework of its traditions and its way of life, ultimately profited by it and found psychological satisfaction in it. But with the great changes in the modern world, this rule was broken. Reluctantly deprived of their accustomed role, the majority of Jews were resigning themselves to "assimilating" with the Christians, to regarding them as brethren, and they were therefore trying—to the terror of a large part of the latter—to erase the frontier which divided them from each other. However, other Christians, following the example of men like Balzac, did not appear to see anything wrong in admitting the former children of the ghetto into their society. The different attitudes are primarily determined by the emotional conditions of individual equilibrium, by the "personality" of each person, and a portrait of an anti-Semite begins to take shape in this way. Then again, the period was propitious for the exacerbation of hatred and "racial" or "ethnic" prejudice. All the social factors or "anomy" which sociologists regard as necessary (and sometimes sufficient) conditions for these tensions seemed united: at the same time as customs were becoming uniform, "vertical mobility" was increasing and urbanization accelerating. But to the extent that resentment chooses the Jews for its focus, the old religious myths are always involved.

In Germany, the revolution in customs was even reflected in certain turns of phrase, which functioned as alarm bells for champions of the old order. These champions showed their concern in official documents. Thus, when the von Hardenberg reforms were promulgated in 1811, the Prussian nobility protested against the abolition of its privileges in the following terms :[92]

... Already we are no longer given the name that belongs to us, and this applies also to our domains, because it is thought too fine for us. The draft edict speaks of "landed estates, known as noble lands." The Jews, on the other hand (to give an example), they too are no longer called by their name, but for a contrary reason, i.e. because it is considered too vile for them. In the decree which authorizes them to acquire lands they are termed "those who profess the Mosaic religion."

The Jews if they are really true to their faith are the necessary enemies of every existing state (if they are not true to their faith they are hypocrites) and have the mass of cash in their hands. So soon as landed property will have sunk to such a level that they can acquire it advantageously it will at once pass into their hands, *they* will become, as landowners, the chief representatives of the state and so our old honorable Brandenburg Prussia will become a new-style Jewish state [*ein neumodischer Judenstaat*].

The original draft of the protest mentioned the "new Jerusalem." This theme of the judaization of Christian lands was exploited by various romantic writers and became a literary convention in Germany, since possession of the maternal soil is a powerful symbol. Achim von Arnim devoted a novel, *Die Majoratsherren* (1820), to the subject. In it, he traces the decline through Jewish greed, of a family of good and old descent. He depicts the specter of Christian servitude in these terms: "... Eventually, the town came under the domination of foreigners, the hereditary fiefs were abolished and the Jews left their narrow streets, while the whole continent was incarcerated like a criminal caught in the act. ..."[93] Von Arnim showed an obsession with the Jew in his daily life as well as in his work.[94] As early as 1809, he had founded a patriotic society in Berlin, the *Deutschchristliche Tischgesellschaft*, to which "Jews and Philistines did not have access": "... not Jews, or converted Jews, or the descendants of Jews." His brother-in-law, Clemens von Brentano, primarily famous for his tales haunted by malevolent Jews, spoke to the members of the *Tischgesellschaft* about the Jewish essence: "It is what every Jew would give anything in the world to get rid of, except money."[95] Unlike Jews, Philistines were judged incapable of discerning who they were, and the definition von Brentano gave was not clear. Marshall Gneisenau's "Jews and contractors" again come to mind; whatever the terminology adopted, it was always "Jews and Co.," the head lighting the way and the tail with the vague contours of an ill-starred comet. On the other hand, Bettina von Arnim, Clemens's temperamental sister, a talented novelist and an outstanding personality herself (she was Goethe's Bettina-child) belonged to the aggressive minority which appears at all times in all places to oppose the compact majority and champion the Jews' cause. When she was twenty years old, she was surprised in the middle of Berlin one day, broom in hand, in the process of cleaning out the hovel of a poor, sick Jew.[96] She pleaded the cause of emancipation in her novels and semi-fictional dialogues.[97] It is a pity that there is apparently no trace of the discussions that must have broken out on this burning issue between sister and brother, and husband and wife.

We are luckier with another famous couple, whose epistolary polemic on the subject of the Children of Israel throws light on the contradictions and ambiguities inherent in such a debate. It began at the time of the Congress of Vienna, between Wilhelm and Karoline von Humboldt. This exemplary couple were often separated because of the husband's political career and his travels. Both of them had attended Henriette Herz's salon in Berlin in their youth and von Humboldt had even started learning Hebrew there. We have already mentioned his emancipating convictions.

The polemic began suddenly at the beginning of 1815, when there was some question in Berlin of war with Saxony. Describing the emotion which had gripped the capital, Karoline noted on January 3, 1815, that panic was spreading

more amongst the class of the lowly-minded, if I can express myself thus, of usurers and Jews. There are also Christian Jews. About Jews. Well-informed people maintain that all the money of the country, all its resources, are in their hands and that, if we preserve peace, the first thing must be to ease the lot of the countryman, the peasant as well as the noble.

Without completely contradicting her, Wilhelm replied that the evil was not due to the emancipation of the Jews:[98]

... I approve the edict. It is in all reason impossible to allow the old differences between Jew and Christian to exist for ever and increase prejudices even more ... [but] I firmly believe ... that we perhaps failed to do things that should necessarily have happened at the same time as the edict.

Begun in this way, the polemic carried on for over a year, leading each protagonist solemnly to state his position. Wilhelm, for example: "With me, these ideas go back to my youth: when we were still children, Alexander[99] and I were regarded as the great knights-errant of Judaism" (June 4, 1815); "I will never drop either my childhood friends or the Jews!" (March 22, 1816). Karoline retorted: "You boast about never dropping the Jews. This is your only fault I know of. You are too indifferent to them. But indifference is not in the Jews' nature." After which, while still storming against the mercantile spirit and the cowardice of these "stigmata of the human race" (who, she states, already own three out of every four mansions in Berlin), she reproaches her husband for his formal tone and the rigidity of his principles (March 29, 1816). The husband's character and the Jewish question curiously overlapped in the conjugal correspondence.

While correcting Karoline's fantastic information and commenting ironically on her passion, Wilhelm sometimes gave way to curious reflections. As early as January 17, 1815, he confessed: "I am working with all my might for the granting of civic rights to the Jews, so as not to have to attend their salons out of generosity. Furthermore, they do not like me at all," he added. It will be agreed that the remark does not indicate immoderate affection for the objects of his solicitude. In particular, he openly showed his aversion to his wife's great friend, Rahel Varnhagen-Levin, avoiding the company of this famous blue-stocking as much as possible. Even more remarkable is his letter of April 30, 1816, which he hoped would end the discussion. In it, he made what was in effect an *amende honorable* :

> ... basta, as you say, for this subject will never be exhausted. I do not compare Adelheid's[100] hatred of the Jews with yours. The former I can well imagine. It has everything that New Christians really have. ... But I also only really like the Jews *en masse*; *en détail*,[101] I avoid them as much as possible. Varnhagen has returned with his wife. ... I have visited her, and will leave it at that. She has become terribly ugly. One will never understand why this happens to some people. ...

However, von Humboldt did come to evince sympathy for certain Jews *"en détail."* For example, in London in 1818, he obviously enjoyed the company of Rothschild, who had helped him to negotiate a Prussian state loan. He invited him to dinner, and told his wife about it the next day:

> Yesterday Rothschild dined with me. He is a very rough and quite uncultivated man but very intelligent and with a real genius for money. Several times he administered a delightful snub to Major Martens who also dined here and was praising everything French. Amongst other things Martens was lamenting in stupidly sentimental tones the misfortunes of war and the many who never returned. "Ach," said Rothschild, "if the people hadn't all died, you, Major Martens, would probably still have remained a drummer." You should have seen Martens's face!

Even more informative is a long letter dated June 4, 1815, which described how an old Talmudist had tried to bribe him, to make him kindly disposed to the Jews. The story also throws some light on the diplomatic practices of the Congress of Vienna:

I have noticed for some weeks that the patrons of Judaism are growing and as Gentz was at their head, the reason was soon clear. From von Hardenberg of Hanover I learnt for certain that he had even concluded a written contract! No offers were made to me but an old man from Prague whose nature greatly appealed to me, for he does not belong to the new-fashioned Jews, came to me several times and commended the matter to me.... Yesterday the old man came again, thanked me infinitely and offered me as a present three rings, emeralds set with large diamonds, adding that if I did not want them I could have at my disposal more than 4,000 ducats on his account. Of course I rejected both and you cannot imagine the surprise of the man, when I told him without affectation or phrase-making that what I had done I had done purely for the sake of the Jews, that I would take nothing in return. ... The old Jew would not be satisfied and now has the idea of having a silver service made for me, to send me in a year's time. I told Gentz that in ten years I would still take nothing. ... Gentz ... held forth at length ... that this was to him an insoluble riddle in me...

It can be seen therefore how a complex personality like Wilhelm von Humboldt, who had made emancipation one of the guiding principles of his life, reserved his sympathy for the so-called typical Jews, corresponding to the image that a Christian aristocrat could form of a Jewish financier. On the other hand, the hot-headed Karoline, who proclaimed her hope "that in fifty years the Jews would be exterminated, as Jews" (March 29, 1816), numbered "the new type" of de-judaized Jews amongst her dearest friends, people like Rahel Levin, Dorothea Schlegel-Mendelssohn, or Dr Koreff—and declared her affection for them in hyperbolic terms.[102] It could perhaps be said that she was proving more logical than her husband. In any case, the Jews seem to have provoked feelings as contradictory as they were powerful in both von Humboldts, and it remains an open question which was the more anti-Semitic of the two.

Nor is judgment easy in the case of Friedrich Gentz, one of the best political brains of the period. In the matter of the

Jews, this "secretary of Europe" followed simple principles: to squeeze as much money out of them as possible and to say as much in their favor as possible. Before becoming the Rothschilds' official mouthpiece,[103] he had been an assiduous guest at Jewish salons in Berlin and Vienna. But this is how he expressed himself on the subject in private:[104]

> Intelligence—that is the mortal sin of the Jews. All of them are more or less intelligent; but only let one be born in which a spark of heart, a spark of true feeling can be found. The curse pronounced on them, and it pursues them to the ten-thousandth generation, is that they can never leave the sphere of intelligence, in the narrower meaning of the word, to their own detriment and that of the world, but must make endless circles in it until their black souls descend into hell. That is why the monsters are at home everywhere where intelligence, stupid and criminal intelligence arrogates the right to govern alone; born representatives of atheism, Jacobinism, Enlightenment and so on. No Jew has yet believed seriously in God! No Jewess—I make no exception—has ever known real love! All the misfortune of the modern world, if it is traced to its furthest roots, comes manifestly from the Jews, they alone made Bonaparte emperor; only they struck the North of Germany with such a shameful blindness that Villiers's prize-winning book is accorded canonical authority!—But enough of these cannibals! . . .

A curious philippic! Some of the themes of nascent romanticism, dear to people like Rahel Levin, can be recognized in it, as well as the ideas peculiar to Barruel and his emulators, which were beginning to spread throughout the West. But Gentz's fury seems only half feigned, and though he may not have seriously believed in the planetary maleficence of the Jews "who have struck the North of Germany with . . . blindness," he gives the impression that he would not have been sorry to think so.

In any case, as far as personal letters and diaries are available (normally they are only available where highly placed or famous personalities are involved), in which the authors expressed themselves freely without worrying what people would say, they frequently evinced a predilection for Jews who respected the old rules and kept in their place as Jews.

The young Bismarck was an example of this. In 1847, at the United Prussian Diet, he took up de Bonald's dogmatic argument (but, sign of the times, with oratorical caution): [105]

I admit that I am stuffed full of prejudices which, as I say, I have sucked in with my mother's milk and I cannot argue them away; for if I imagine myself as representative of the sacred majesty of the King face to face with a Jew whom I am to obey, then I must confess that I would feel myself deeply depressed and bowed down, that I would be bereft of the joy and righteous sense of honor with which I am now concerned to fulfill my duties towards the state. I share this feeling with the mass of the lower strata of the people and am not ashamed of this company.

Shortly afterwards, Bismarck praised the old man Rothschild of Frankfurt in a letter to his wife: ". . . I like him, just because he is only a Jewish trader [*Schacherjude*] and because at the same time he is a strictly orthodox Jew, who touches nothing offered at dinner and only eats *kosher*."[106] The sympathy here therefore sprang from the double possibility of placing a distance between the Jew and himself. However, this great realist advised that "Jewish mares" should be mated with "Christian colts" and held out the hope of good results from this cross-breeding (but he hesitated to give his sons such advice).[107] "There are no bad races," he said, while still assuming a radical difference between them and relying on his flair to recognize a Jew from a distance.[108] Alongside Bismarck, we might mention the first king he served, Frederick William IV, who, at the beginning of his reign, in 1842, wanted to grant the eternal people a single favor by re-establishing the ghetto in Prussia.[109] This mystical prince talked about emancipation with quite Goethian horror. He wrote to a friend:[110]

> The contemptible Jewish clique strikes daily by word and example at the root of the German character; it does not (unlike myself) want to distinguish between the estates which alone can form a German nation; it wants to throw all the estates together.

With time and the progress of assimilation, the theme of the individual noxiousness of the invisible Jew became a favorite argument for militant anti-Semites. Drumont, for example:[111]

> ... every Jew one sees, every professing Jew is relatively harmless, he is sometimes even estimable; he worships the God of Abraham, this is a right that no one would dream of disputing, and as one knows what is believed on this score, it is possible to supervise him. The dangerous Jew is the shadowy Jew. ... This is the dangerous animal *par excellence* and at the same time the uncatchable animal ... he is the most powerful trouble-making element the earth has ever produced, and he thus passes through life with the joy which awareness of having, in various ways, harmed Christians, gives Jews.

In Germany, the term "civilized Jew" (*Zivilisationsjude*) had acquired insult-value equivalent to "ferment of decomposition" in the anti-Semitic polemic at the beginning of the twentieth century.[112] The final word has been said by Hitler: "The Jew is always settled in our midst, but it is simpler to fight him in flesh and bone than in the form of an invisible demon."[113]

The mass of the ordinary people, who Bismarck said shared his ideas, only rarely expressed them articulately. But in 1819, Germany, as well as certain adjacent countries, was the scene of a popular disturbance, which can be regarded as the expression by these masses of their feelings and resentments towards the Jews.

To transgress the existing order, the people normally need

encouragement from influential or literate men. Behind the 1819 pogroms in Germany lay the nationalist glorification of the "wars of liberation," primarily cultivated by professors and students. Side by side with the philosopher Fichte, it is appropriate to mention propagandists such as Ernst Moritz Arndt and Friedrich Jahn. The first, Arndt, a fierce gallophobe, advocated a system of watertight bulkheads between the peoples of Europe which even the doctrinaire racists of the Third Reich found too rigid. The second, the famous "father of gymnastics" (*Turnvater Jahn*), stated that crossbred peoples, like hybrid animals, lost their "strength of national production." He also proclaimed that the Poles, the French, the clergy, tramps and Jews were the curse of Germany—which made a lot of curses for one country.[114]

People like Arndt and Jahn only attacked the Jews when the opportunity offered. Other agitators specialized in this field, and particularly after 1814, when ideologists of liberation and ex-servicemen were faced with the reactionary realities of the Holy Alliance instead of seeing the flowering of Germanic freedoms which they had fought for. High amongst these freedoms figured the liberty of being able to send the Jews back to the ghetto, wiping emancipation off the board. Ludwig Börne made the following comment on these ambitions:[115]

Amongst the Germans who blamed Napoleon alone for all the tyranny under which they suffered ... the urge to freedom and hatred for the French united in one sentiment. And as man misunderstands or despises the good that enemies offer, so what was worthy of respect brought by French legislation into Germany was misunderstood or despised. Thus after the expulsion of the French, the civil freedom of the Jews, granted by the French, began here and there to be looked on as something dangerous. In addition, the Jews were considered friends of French rule because, though they were no less oppressed than the other Germans, they had found some recompense for their hardship. It is forgivable if an uncomfortable feeling turns us against those who draw advantage from the source of our sufferings—I mean, it is a forgivable *weakness*.

A man like Börne was trying to understand and to excuse his compatriots, but other emancipated Jews virulently attacked the prevailing state of mind. Saul Ascher, an otherwise mediocre publicist, undertook to defend the *Aufklärung* of yore in a pamphlet which he entitled *Die Germanomanie*. The title of the book and some of the arguments used—like the appeal to the authorities to maintain public order— threw fuel on the fire of Germanomania and anti-Jewish passion.

From 1814, inflammatory writings blossomed by the dozen, both by hack writers of the lower orders and famous scholars. Without wasting time on the first category, a few words are required on the second. The most famous was the Kantian, Jacob Fries (1773–1843), a pupil of Fichte and leader of the philosophical school which was claiming to reduce physiology to mechanics. In his pamphlet on the "Jewish danger," he called for "the radical extermination of the caste of Jews."[116] (Later, he justified himself by stating that what he had in mind was Judaism not the Jews.) Fries was also the only professor to honor with his presence the famous Wartburg festival (1817), when excited students threw books they regarded as reactionary on the fire, including Ascher's *Germanomanie*. Amongst Fries's emulators mention can be made of Professor Ruehs of Berlin, a pupil of the imaginative Meiners,[117] and Dr Köppe whose booklet laid down this concise principle: "Educated Jews are a cosmopolitan rabble, who must be tracked down and expelled from everywhere."[118]

Gradually, the repercussions of this agitation reached the masses, who moved into action in the summer of 1819.

We have talked about the ideas the instigators propagated but we have not said anything yet about the vested interests which flew to their aid. Germany was in the throes of an economic crisis; the end of the continental blockade made it possible to import English merchandise and a number of manufacturers found themselves ruined; many peasants were likewise in debt. The Jewish moneylender was still a familiar figure in town and countryside. The trading guilds as always wanted to evict Jewish craftsmen. On another score, the possibility of governmental and police provocation intended to distract the people from any liberating aspirations cannot be excluded. This was the opinion of a French observer,[119] and it was also classic pogrom tactics. The police reports on the other hand accused libertarian Germanomanes of having intended to toss the Jews "like a balloon, into the hands of the people, to see how far the overheated plebs could be pushed, in view of the other disruptions."[120] Explanatory factors are, as can be seen, manifold if not contradictory. Perhaps it would be more prudent to stick to the diagnosis of the Prussian historian, von Treitschke. In the context of the anti-Jewish troubles he talked of "the prodigious emotion aroused by the wars of liberation, which brought all the secrets of the German soul out into the open."[121]

Whatever their origins, the troubles began at Würzburg, at the beginning of August, 1819, and immediately spread through German towns and countryside, leaving out the kingdom of Prussia where the proverbial order was maintained. Anti-Jewish excesses likewise occurred in Bohemia, Alsace, the Netherlands and Denmark. Unknown missionaries traveled through towns and larger villages, stirring up the populace. The rioters' war cry was "Hep! Hep!" Intellectuals interpreted this as a contraction of *"Hierosolyma Est Perdita,"* thought to be the cry of the Crusaders in 1096. Improbable in itself, this version shows that in Germany, the memory of the persecutions which took place in 1096 had not been lost. The contemporary press gives detailed descriptions of the riots, which generally began when a crowd formed and Jewish passers-by were molested. Then, to shouts of "Hep! Hep!" the mob, armed with axes and iron bars, repaired to the Jewish district or street to engage in systematic pillage. Often the synagogue, sacked from top to bottom, was the first objective. But though there were acts of violence in plenty, assassinations were rare. In some cases, the police intervened immediately; in others, they turned a blind eye. In a few towns, a delegation from the bourgeoisie presented itself to the authorities the next day to demand the expulsion of the Jews, whose presence had lit the fuse. These details all leave the impression of a certain degree of organization and of a preconceived plan.

The prevailing atmosphere in August, 1819, in Berlin— where, moreover, the disturbances were nipped in the bud by the efforts of the Prussian police—emerges from the following description. It also shows how an old Jew could bow his head under the storm (*La Renommée*, Paris, September 3, 1819):

September 3, Prussia: the excesses which have been committed against the Jews in several towns in Germany have given rise to fear amongst the Israelites in this capital; there have even been some small scenes here already. A few of the Jews' enemies paid a fair number of ne'er-do-wells to cry Hep! Hep! under the windows of the country house of a banker of that nation.

An old Israelite pedlar of ribbons and pencils was chased by delinquents in the street which echoed with the ominous cry; he made the best of it like a man with a sense of humor and continued on his way laughing and even shouting Hep! Hep! incessantly himself, but having taken it into his head to peer into a shop and shout inside, a woman who happened to be on the threshold dealt him a violent box on the ears, to which he immediately replied with another. A police employee, who was within call, took him under his protection and, to get him out of reach of the ill-treatment to which he was still exposed, conducted him to the police station. . . . The famous Hep! Hep! has already caused some tumultuous scenes in several public places. It is greatly feared that there were more serious disorders on the occasion of the "Catch of Strahlau," a festival which took place on August 24.

In the other regions of Germany, the disorders were more serious, without being comparable to the Russian pogroms or the medieval persecutions, since little blood was shed. Nonetheless, the Jews were painfully surprised to see cordial neighbors or erstwhile customers, axes and crowbars in hand, swoop down on their shops and homes; to see, mystery of pogroms, yesterday's friends "making them dance in another way."[122]

A movement towards emigration ensued—to the United States, and also to France which welcomed the refugees with open arms. Even the powerful Frankfurt Rothschilds, whose bank narrowly escaped being sacked, also thought of leaving Germany.[123] The ministers of the Holy Alliance were aroused and, in view of the shortcomings of numerous municipal authorities, Metternich ordered Austrian troops to intervene when necessary. At the same time, he announced severe measures to be taken against student guilds and revolutionary agitators.

In a letter to her brother, Rahel Varnhagen-Levin mentioned "Fries, von Arnim, von Brentano and their like," in connection with these events. Further on, she wrote:[124]

> I am infinitely sad as never before. On account of the Jews. They want to keep them; but for torment, for contempt, for swearing at ... for kicking and throwing downstairs.... The hypocritical new love for the Christian religion (may God forgive me my sins), for the Middle Ages, with its art, poetry and horrors, inflames the people, reminded of old experiences, to the horror to which it can still be inflamed....

Her psychological analysis did not lack shrewdness; in simple terms, Rahel was bringing out the Jews' "functional significance" as scapegoats of Christianity. Her husband viewed the matter with a more political eye, and blamed the Children of Israel for having thrown in their lot with those in power:[125]

> The persecution of the Jews in our towns is a horrible phenomenon. The authorities do not show themselves so impressive as in

Hamburg. In Heidelberg the town director Pfister is firmly held guilty, in Karlsruhe gentlemen of quality are said to have joined in the attackers' cry of Hep! From the universality of these attacks on the Jews it can be seen that those people are wrong who imagine that our political fragmentation is an obstacle to general popular movements. The greatest unity of the Germans can be recognized in the feelings which they express about their condition. But these assaults on the Jews are a beginning of such events which will later bring them all equality of rights with the Christians by way of the people. People advise the Jews to follow the liberals. Hitherto they look on themselves more as belonging to the people with power.

Once again, certain enlightened Jews sought to reform their brethren; it was the disturbances of 1819 which stimulated Gans and his friends to found their "Association for the culture and knowledge of the Jews."[126] But it was in vain that growing numbers of them were active in the liberal or progressive party; anti-Jewish riots broke out anew in Germany in 1830, 1834, 1844 and 1848.[127]

PART THREE

THE RACIST REACTION

After all, even if it were proved that there never was an Aryan race in the past, we want there to be one in the future: for men of action, this is the crucial aspect.

(H. S. Chamberlain, ed., *Foundations of the Nineteenth Century*, London, 1927.)

As long as the Jews actually lived under a special legal régime, they were regarded, in good theological doctrine, as possessing all the attributes of human nature, and the curse hanging over them as being only an expiation, from the point of view of Christian anthropology. It was when they were emancipated and able to mix freely in bourgeois high society that the curse became, under the terms of the new so-called scientific anthropology, a biological difference or inferiority and that the despised class became an inferior race. It was as if the badge or conical hat of yore were henceforth carved, "internalized" into their flesh, as if Western opinion could not dispense with a definite distinction and that this distinction became an *invisible essence* once the *visible symbols* identifying the Jew had been erased.[1]

The last part of this book will study the rise of modern anti-Semitism, a passion which scorns all theology, and seeks the reasons for its existence in science. This pursuit has led us to investigate the real sources of the "Aryan myth" which not so long ago was taught as a subject in schools and formed part of the intellectual equipment of the nineteenth-century European, sometimes to the point where Jews were the first to agree that they were inferior to "Aryans."[2] We know the consequences of this myth but its origin has been very inadequately explored. The territory involved is in many respects dangerous, situated in a sort of no-man's-land between the history of ideas, political history and anthropology. Although a few good books[3] have made a historical record out of an imposture which dominated European scientific thought for several generations, no attempt has, to our knowledge, been made to analyze adequately the deep-seated reasons for its irresistible success. It seems to me that the perspectives which the study of the history of anti-Semitism opens on the development of the European attitude make it possible *ipso facto* to fill this gap by at least revealing the secrets of the birth of a modern myth. A question like this obviously deserves an immense amount of research into background material which we cannot undertake within the framework of the present book. However, I hope one day to be able to devote myself to it and I regard the ideas which follow as the first stages in such an investigation (cf. *The Aryan Myth: A History of Racist and Nationalist Ideas in Europe*, L. Poliakov, London, 1974).

What deep-seated reasons drove nineteenth-century Europe fantastically to choose for itself an Indo-Persian ancestry? Let us first note that such a choice could not be a matter of indifference, that it was attended by strong emotional echoes. Did it not involve the question of the origins of Western man, the "where do I come from?" which is a prelude to the "what am I?" And so we come back by this route to the problem of Western-Christian identity which has already been considered.

The age-old tradition of the European peoples clashed with the teaching of the Church on these points from century to century. The Church, though unspecific in this particular case, nonetheless attributed to them a vaguely "Jewish" descent, in the sense that it made the whole human race go back to the original couple Adam and Eve, in the same way as it awarded Hebrew the rank of the primitive universal language, preceding the "confusion of Babel." The cradle of mankind was immutably placed in the fabulous Orient, where once the Garden of Eden was situated and where Noah and his three sons had set foot after the Flood. Europeans were generally supposed to be descended from Japhet. Thus, in this ontogenic way as well, the "Jew" assumed his old role of "father," whether under the features of Adam, the universal progenitor, or Shem, the eldest brother.

The new myth of the Aryans implied, it should be noted, the loss of this role, and in this sense it also marked, or symbolized, liberation from the ecclesiastical yoke, the end of the "age of faith" ("Judaism loses, as it were, in veneration, what the Jews gain in political freedom," noted a contemporary).[4] In addition, the new age, the age of science, went through a deist stage in the beginning. It is typical that the idea of India as the cradle of "natural religion," even of mankind, spread in the second half of the eighteenth century, even before the relationship between European languages and Sanskrit was discovered.[5] Moreover, this relationship had already been established on several occasions in the past, when the time had not been ripe, and the discovery had fallen into oblivion. Things had changed in 1786 when the Englishman William Jones pointed out the structural affinity which exists between Sanskrit, Greek, Latin, "Gothic" and "Celtic" in his *Asiatic Researches*. In so doing, he thought he could attribute pre-eminence to the Indian language, "a wonderful structure, more perfect than that of Greek, richer than that of Latin, and more exquisite than that of either."[6] Contemporary philosophy gave this opinion a favorable reception and it was taken up and amplified by the Schlegel brothers, the founders of indology in Germany. In about 1805, Friedrich Schlegel wrote that the Indian language was "older than the Greek or Latin languages, not to mention German or Persian. . . . Indian is distinguished," he added, "by its depth, clarity, calm and its philosophical turn"; he also inferred that Indian was "the oldest of the derived languages," the closest, consequently, "to the primitive language from which all languages are descended."[7] (Friedrich Schlegel therefore retained the idea of one "primitive language" from Christian anthropology but, as a product of his time, chose a different one from Hebrew.) In the same book, the idea already occurs of "colonies" of Indians settled in Europe from time immemorial. August Wilhelm Schlegel revived one of Leibniz's ideas about the use of philology in the study of the origin of peoples, and also dealt with the "origin of the Hindus," and proclaimed the superiority of their language over the Semitic languages.[8] At the same period, the philosopher Schelling was criticizing the imperfections of the Holy Scriptures, which in his opinion, did not stand comparison "in truly religious content" with the Indians' sacred books.[9] "There was a sort of intoxication at that time," wrote a historian of Gobinism a century later. "Modern civilization thought it had rediscovered the family deeds, lost for centuries, and Aryanism was born. . . ." (In a note, he added, nostalgically perhaps: "Today, the scientific world has changed, it is stated that European culture is autochthonous. . . .")[10]

The Schlegel brothers as well as Schelling were still confining themselves, in the main, to philological and philosophical territory, and Friedrich Schlegel, like Herder before him, refused to extend the concept of *races* to mankind (while Schelling was suggesting limiting its application to the "degraded" non-European races).[11] But during this first decade of the nineteenth century another German philologist, J. C. Adelung, referring to geographers like Pallas, de Pauw and Zimmermann, openly annexed anthropology to his discipline. The way in which he did this revealed particularly clearly how the "Aryan myth," in process of taking preliminary shape, was modeled on the "Biblical myth" while trying to free itself from it.

In the introduction to his essay on comparative grammar, the famous *Mithridate*, Adelung noted that in effect Asia had always been regarded as the cradle of mankind. But what part of Asia was involved? Account had to be taken of the unanimous opinion of scholars that the "primitive people" could only have been formed on mountain peaks where the flood waters had first subsided. Adelung consequently thought that he could name the exact place. It could only be Kashmir, which was known to combine all the splendors of the Garden of Eden, as Moses described it, "everything that the most luxuriant fantasy can possibly conceive, as the highest ideal of all sensual delights." He therefore developed this comparison of Eden and Kashmir at length and added a further proof: [12]

> Even the people are distinguished above all other Asians. They have nothing of Tatar or Mongol culture, which is characteristic of Tibetans and Chinese; but they are of the finest European forms, and in spirit and wit surpass all Asians.

He went on to tell the story of the first human couple and its descent, as he imagined it. It can be seen, therefore, that Adelung remained faithful to Christian anthropology and only departed from it on one essential point. The "original couple" was no longer the Adam and Eve of the Bible; its habitat was transferred from the Middle East to India; it spoke an Aryan language (*avant la lettre*) and it possessed "the finest European forms."

After Adelung, let us pause a moment at an author who is forgotten, the German, Johann-Gottfried Rhode, who may have invented the word and idea "Aryan" in its modern meaning.[13] In 1820, intending to study the origins of culture and language, Rhode turned to the *Zend-Avesta*, in other words the revelation of Zoroaster. He considered this sacred book of the Medes and Persians to be a more reliable source than the other writings of great antiquity. Unlike the Mosaic account, it never invoked miracles, and Zoroaster took his stand only "on the inner strength of truth."[14] In addition, Zoroaster's account seemed to him to be corroborated by the vague pieces of information about the ancient race of Aryans supplied by Herodotus and Diodorus.[15] Comparing the two revelations, Rhode concluded that Zoroaster was superior and earlier than Moses: according to him, Moses was either inspired directly by Zoroaster, or "from a common source."[16] Some aspects of his description of the moral beauty of the *Zend-Avesta* already seem to have Nietzschean nuances:[17]

> Man must be pure, holy and like God; truthful and just in his actions, gentle and gracious in his sentiments and above all grateful for every act of benevolence shown to him! In the face of such sentiments, which the law commands and presupposes, can a murder take place? Thus the law does not even make mention of this crime. The servant of Ormuzd does not need this law.
>
> How strange it is likewise that amongst all these laws there is not one relating to interest and usurers. . . . Even the oath is not known to the legislator and his people, for neither in the law nor in all the Zend scripture is there the slightest reference to it. Each word is an oath and every breach of one's word is looked on and punished as perjury.

Elsewhere, Rhode disputed the validity of the prevailing views which, since Anquetil du Perron and Herder, had located the historical cradle of the Medes and Persians in the Caucasus. He, for his part, transferred it to the high plateaux of central Asia and considered that its inhabitants would have left in the wake of some natural cataclysm.[18] Finally, on the basis of the description of paradise which Ormuzd was said to have offered his people (a paradise which he therefore substituted for the Biblical Eden), he thought he had discovered a geographical nomenclature there enabling him to reconstruct "the onward march of Aryan conquest."[19] On many points, this completely forgotten author blazed the trail for the Aryans' triumphal march.

Everything, therefore, indicates that Europe was looking for new ancestors though still bound by certain traditional ideas. The relationship between this ambition and the deist polemic against the Old Testament Jehovah can be seen, and the distinction men like Rhode made between Mosaism based on miracles, and Zoroastrianism resting only "on the inner strength of truth," was typical. Nonetheless, right through the first half of the nineteenth century, scholars continued to measure time on the Biblical yardstick. Not all of them may have followed medieval chronology which placed the birth of Christ in the year 4004 of the Creation, but all remained convinced that mankind had only existed for a few millennia. This conviction certainly delayed the birth of the archaeological sciences (one only has to think of the disappointments of people like Lyell and Boucher de Perthes) and therefore provided additional reasons for situating the cradle of mankind in Asia whence it would have "colonized" Europe late in the day. Another pioneer of indology, F. A. Pott, thought that mankind had obviously followed the sun in its upward march: "*ex oriente lux,*" and Asia was for him the playground and gymnasium of its first physical and spiritual exercises.[20] But why did it emigrate to the northern countries? Jakob Grimm, in his famous *Geschichte der deutschen Sprache,* said that populations were set in motion "by an irresistible instinct the cause of which remains concealed from us."[21] The scholarly world's reluctance to admit that the European might quite simply be a native of Europe, the hostility which met any hypothesis of this sort,[22] is an additional indication of the paralyzing influence of accepted ideas, even when ostensibly they took the opposite point of view from Biblical cosmogony.

A more radical rupture with Biblical cosmogony was presented by the polygenist theories which had been popular since the Century of Enlightenment. Following Voltaire, Goethe had adopted these views, and the arguments he put forward to support them showed an underlying "anti-Judaic" motivation. What Goethe did was first to justify his convictions by personifying nature, whose *spirit,* according to him, was not economical but on the contrary, lavish :

I must speak against this opinion (that nature in her productions went to work extremely economically). I maintain that nature always shows herself plentiful, indeed wasteful, and that it is far more sensible to admit that instead of one single miserable pair she has allowed mankind to go forth by dozens, indeed by hundreds. When the earth had thriven to a certain point of ripeness, the waters had run off and the dry land was sufficiently green, there came the period for the creation of man and men arose everywhere through the omnipotence of God where the ground permitted, and perhaps first of all on the heights.

Goethe then advanced another argument. It took the form of a witticism but it revealed an underlying motive for the choice which the majority of European scholars were making towards the middle of the nineteenth century:[23]

The Holy Scriptures, to be sure, speak only of one human pair whom God created on the sixth day. But the gifted men who designed the word of God, which the Bible delivers to us, had first of all to do with their chosen nation, and so we will in no way dispute with it the honor of its descent from Adam. But we others as well as the Negroes and Laplanders and slender men, who are handsomer than all of us, had certainly other ancestors; for as the worthy society will certainly admit, we are differentiated from the true descendants of Adam in a quite manifold manner, and they, especially as regards money, are in front of us all.

It was therefore important for Goethe "really to differentiate himself from the true descendants of Adam," a task which European, notably German, authors, set about in innumerable ways, when dealing with the origins of mankind. Gustav Klemm, for example, the author of a popular *Allgemeine Cultur-Geschichte*, was already in 1843 distinguishing between an *active* (virile) race and a more primitive *passive* (feminine) race:[24]

In the meantime another race had matured in the highlands of the Himalayan regions ... in its heart the urge to unceasing creation, thought, research, poetry. .... This tribe did not live in valleys and plains but in the rough hills, at first a hunting people, then robbing, boldly and arrogantly attacking its passive neighbors.

This was already striking the very pugnacious note found in Wagner's writing at this period and which he developed in music. But the confused identification of "youth" or "aggressiveness" and "perfection" or "valor" can be seen in the most serious scholars. To the great indologist Lassen, for example, "the Aryans form the most completely organized, the most enterprising people; it is therefore the youngest, the earth only having produced the most perfect species of plants and animals later. . . ." Lassen was already comparing Aryans to Semites from this point of view in about 1845:[25]

> . . . Amongst the Caucasian peoples we must award the palm to the Indo-Germans without a doubt. This is not fortuitous but we believe that it springs from their higher and more comprehensive talents. History shows that the Semites do not possess the harmonious balance of all the powers of the soul, in which the Indo-Germans excel.

The Semites' principal failings, according to Lassen, were their total philosophical mediocrity and their egotistical religious fanaticism.[26] Thus, in 1845, the last cornerstone of the myth was laid.

But there were still the blacks, that is to say, the "Hamites." The new academic anthropology remained dependent on the old on one other point; it adopted the division of mankind into three great races, an echo of the myth of Noah's three sons. This has been noted in Cuvier.[27] It is remarkable to observe in this context that Biblical terminology was also still generally employed, since blacks and Jews, the lowly races, were styled "Hamites" and "Semites." But for themselves, the Europeans, who had chosen noble descent, objected to the designation, however logical, of "Japhetites" with its Old Testament odor. They chose to be *Aryans* probably because the term was supposed to come from the same root as *honor* (*Ehre*). These sorts of ideas spread remarkably rapidly and were immediately applied in the most varied fields, including the vital realm of religion. As early as 1853, Wagner, that spokesman for the nineteenth-century, was writing "that primitive Christianity" had been tainted by its mixture with Judaic dogmas, and that "this Christianity was only a branch of venerable Buddhism."[28]

It might be asked yet again if, taking the state of scientific knowledge at the time into consideration, there were positive justifications for the great "Aryan theory." But no attempt to find them has produced anything except the discovery of the family of Indo-European languages, that "discovery of a new world" (Hegel). Even people like Cuvier distinguished the main branches of the races by the "analogy of languages."[29] Voices were rarely raised against this confusion. It is also noteworthy that the loudest protest, which came from Alexander von Humboldt, was at the same time directed against the division of races into "superior" and "inferior."[30] The tendency became increasingly pronounced after the Napoleonic storm, and before Darwin arrived on the scene, the question of European origins became the private preserve of philologists, subject to the "tyranny of the Sanskritists." Moreover, it was the most famous of them, the Germano-English Max Müller of Oxford, who made the use of the term "Aryan" acceptable in academic circles. His lectures to the London Royal Society in 1858–61, which recalled the triumphant advance of the Aryans towards the North Cape and the pillars of Hercules, are still famous. His retractions and warnings, after 1872, made less of an impression, and it was in vain that at the end of his life he declared that the term *Aryan race* was as unscientific as *dolichocephalic* grammar.[31]

European ethnocentrism, which had perverted nascent anthropology since the Century of Enlightenment, grew to tremendous proportions in the era of romanticism and nationalism. It orientated scholarly thought and was a primary factor in the conception of academic theories and classifications. It was in this atmosphere that a mystical tri-partition was formulated: the Aryan, or real man, was defined by comparison with both brother Shem, the Jew, half-man, half-demon, and brother Ham, the black, half-animal, half-man. Philosophers in their turn produced a multitude of these sorts of hierarchies. Even men like Hegel, however anti-racist in principle,[32] paid tribute to it when describing the character of the Negro. "There is nothing harmonious with humanity to be found in this type of character," he wrote:[33]

> The Negro ... exhibits the natural man in his completely wild and untamed state. We must lay aside all thought of reverence and morality—all that we call feeling—if we would rightly comprehend him; there is nothing harmonious with humanity to be found in this type of character.... The Negroes indulge, therefore, that perfect *contempt* for humanity, which in its bearing on Justice and Morality is the fundamental characteristic of the race. They have moreover no knowledge of the immortality of the soul.... Cannibalism is looked upon as quite customary and proper.

Professional scholars did not care about the immortality of the soul, but their views on the race of Ham were, if possible, even harsher. According to Cuvier's brief description[34]

> the Negro race is confined to the south of the Atlas; its skin is black, its hair fuzzy, its skull compressed and its nose squashed; its projecting snout and thick lips visibly connect it with monkeys; the small tribes of which it is composed have always remained barbarous.

The great precursor of transformism, the Englishman Lawrence, expanded on the Negroes' moral and intellectual imbecility at greater length:[35]

> ... they indulge almost universally in disgusting debauchery and sensuality, and display gross selfishness, indifference to the

pains and pleasures of others, insensibility to beauty of form, order and harmony, and an almost entire want of what we comprehend altogether under the expression of elevated sentiments, manly virtues, and moral feeling.

Is it surprising if "race" was soon raised to the rank of the great mover in human development, supplanting Providence? Recent historians (principally historians of anthropology) who have tried to find out the real reasons for the "catastrophic confusion" (Wilhelm Schmidt)[36] between races and languages, between history and anthropology, but primarily between a philosophy choked with theological residue and science, often refer to the letter-program which William Edwards sent to Amédée Thierry in 1829. In it, he proposed investigating "to what extent the distinctions which the historian establishes between peoples correspond to those of nature," and to examine the concordance between *the historic races and those that natural science acknowledges.*[37] These ideas were already in the air everywhere at that time. The novelist Walter Scott was interpreting English history "racially," in the light of the wars between Saxons and Normans, well before the historians, the Thierry brothers, and the naturalist, Edwards. Thus, racial science drew its inspiration from romantic daydreams—and "since the battles of Leipzig and Waterloo, the soil of Europe was super-fertile in the generation of races."[38] The process of generation was spontaneous, and Germany, as the names and texts quoted above show, was the main laboratory. In France, ideas of this type were discussed in around 1820 in a côterie created by a certain Roux-Bordier who (like Walter Scott) had associated a great deal with German authors. Its members included the poet Ballanche, as well as the famous Ampère. In 1821, Ampère wrote to Roux-Bordier:

I have an excessive desire to learn about the work you are doing with Gasparin on races. How do you establish that I am Scandinavian? According to your previous letters, it seems to me that I would at least have to be a good gentleman to be this, but that a lowly scholar, an obscure nobody, can only be a Celt, an Arab, etc. Is it because I have grey eyes that I belong to the race you are so proud of?

A letter from Roux-Bordier informs us that he too had a horror of the Old Testament:[39]

The history of the would-be people of God is nothing other than a frightful tissue of infamous, base and cowardly deeds, beginning with the sacred King David himself. . . . Do you not agree with me that the Christians were very wrong to sanction all the enormities the Bible contains? Enormities of a kind to pervert the judgment and sear the hearts of our children?

The major deist theme can be recognized here (the obscure Roux-Bordier was also expounding a new universal religion, based on purified and de-judaized Christianity). This theme acted as an implicit philosophy for nineteenth-century myth-perpetuating anthropology which achieved its final and deadly form in twentieth-century German national-socialism. The latter did nothing but follow the former through to its logical conclusion: it can be asked in retrospect whether the death sentence on European Jewry was not signed at the moment when the West decided to establish a new genealogy for itself, and the Jews were deprived of their ancient role, "losing in veneration what they gain in political freedom," as Capefigue had written in his *Histoire philosophique des Juifs*.

Can we say today that the Aryan myth has run its course? Under the Hitler régime, it came to be incarnated in tragic reality, since the Aryans, in their security, stood in as sharp a contrast with the hunted Semites throughout Europe as life with death, cradle with grave. It has been said that in this sense, Nazism was a desperate attempt positively to demonstrate the truth of the Aryan myth, and that this attempt was crowned with success, for "that this illusion of anti-Semitism which before had only psychological and compensating significance, should become a truth, an indisputable reality ... a matter of life and death is worth more than one Jew."[40] Today, the German government services in charge of reparations for the victims of Nazism still have the classification—not so long ago "non-Aryan"—of *Jewish persons of the Christian faith*. It can therefore be said that the effects of racial legislation have not yet all disappeared. But are not human races, to the extent that they exist, primarily a psychological and social reality, born of the irresistible wish-to-be-different of societies, peoples and ethnic groups?

nine

England

Jews in Walter Scott and Disraeli

We have not yet talked about England in our discussion of emancipation. In fact, the Jews there had enjoyed a similar status to Catholics and other "non-conformists" since the eighteenth century, with the result that their disabilities were limited to exclusion from political and honorary offices. Moreover, the Jews involved were principally Portuguese, who were already strongly Westernized, as we have already said.[1] The basic point at issue was eligibility for the House of Commons which was granted to English Catholics in 1829 (Roman Catholic Emancipation Bill). The enfranchisement of the "papists" seemed to promise a similar concession for the *followers of Moses,* but this met much stronger resistance, so that political battles on the subject went on for nearly a quarter of a century. The analogy with France (where the Jews were emancipated in the wake of the Protestants) is obvious, and also emerges in several details: like the young Constituent Assembly of 1790, the venerable House of Commons in 1854 was the scene of an unparalleled "tumult" on the subject of the Children of Israel, which an English newspaper did not fail to compare with "the conduct of worshippers in a synagogue, and we know what that means."[2]

Nonetheless, once they had been acquired, the political rights of the Jews in Great Britain were never again questioned, in the same way as the Jews there were spared the crises and anti-Semitic campaigns which raged practically everywhere in Europe in the second half of the nineteenth century. For Gladstone, an uprising against the Jews in his homeland was as improbable as an uprising against the gravity of the earth. Not that the universal prejudice had been dissipated there. The Chosen People created the same feelings of unease in England as elsewhere, and numerous publicists there developed corresponding themes from generation to generation. But their writings did not create a political movement, or combat organizations or defense leagues, in other words, collective and organized panic. The low ebb of English anti-Semitism has been explained by religious affinities ("two peoples fed on the Old Testament"), or historical affinities ("the cult of ancestral tradition"), or the similarity of economic ethics ("two nations of shopkeepers holding trade in high esteem") or again English idiosyncrasy (Albion's "pride" and "insolence"). On this last point, it must indeed be admitted that the morbid fear of the "Jewish invasion" was incompatible with the glorious self-confidence of Queen Victoria's subjects, lords of the seas and international trade.[3] Whatever the significance of these diverse factors, the originality of the English, often described as philo-Semitic, was expressed in very varied ways. It must primarily be related to the respect for traditional hierarchies in a country where the population never came under the spell of revolutionary myths. Because of this, the British Jews for their part showed no inclination to ally their political interests with those of the "left" or the "working classes" (Disraeli was not the only Jewish champion of Conservatism: three of the eight Jewish members elected to the House of Commons in 1868 belonged to the Rothschild dynasty).[4]

Britain defended the interests of the dispersed nation on many occasions during the nineteenth century. From this point of view, 1840 is a date to remember, for the "Damascus affair" (which will be discussed later) marked the beginning of this protective relationship as well as creating a new awareness amongst the emancipated Jews of Europe. Political calculations within the framework of the "Eastern Question" were partly responsible for British policy, and the same might be said of the various schemes to re-establish a Jewish state in a half-political, half-eschatological perspective which British writers, prelates and even statesmen had been discussing since Lewis Way's day.[5] But in what other Christian state could a politician proclaim from the height of the parliamentary rostrum that the Jews were a superior race, an "aristocracy of nature" without such a provocative statement preventing him from becoming Prime Minister and founder of the British Empire? It is through the curious figure of Disraeli that the originality of the relationship between England and the Jews can best be understood.

However, we have said that the Jews aroused the same reaction on this side of the Channel as elsewhere. Such feelings of hostility and contempt, when not externalized, are best revealed in artistic creation. Now, throughout the evolution of means of expression and literary styles, the image of the Jew in Shakespeare's homeland showed little variation and remained dominated by the grandiose figure of Shylock. It is true that, as elsewhere in Europe, the conventional type of "good Jew" flourished on theater stages there at the end of the eighteenth century, but this didactic device (ridiculed by the satirist William Cobbett)[6] was only employed by now forgotten minor authors.

The great creative artists remained fascinated by that implacable figure in the *Merchant of Venice,* whose resentment gave way to the unprovoked maleficence of the child-tormenter, *Fagin,* in Dickens. More subtle and more remarkable is the way in which Walter Scott treated the Jewish theme.[7] In *Ivanhoe,* his most popular novel, the Jewish race (represented by Isaac and his daughter Rebecca) in the first place formed a complete contrast with the Christian race. Second, the Christians themselves were engaged in a secular conflict slowly hammering out the course of English history, since "four generations had not sufficed to blend the hostile blood of the Normans and Anglo-Saxons."[8] These two races equally appeared to have nothing in common except their aversion for the Children of Israel. Finally Isaac and Rebecca also stood in contrast with each other: less sanguinary than Shylock, the father was nothing more than a contemptible scoundrel, while the daughter combined the most sublime virtues with radiant beauty, and her perfection was further emphasized by the trials and misfortunes to which Scott condemned her. This distribution of characteristics, which only accentuated the lights and shades in the medieval image of the Jew,[9] could not have suited the Romantic muse better and it turned almost immediately into a literary convention. During 1820 alone, no less than four English playwrights placed the Jewish heroes of *Ivanhoe* on the stage,[10] while in France, Chateaubriand tried to explain "why the women of the Jewish race are more beautiful than the men" in an essay on *Walter Scott et les Juives*.[11] He finds an interesting explanation for this phenomenon: the Son of God was denied, martyred and crucified by the men alone, while "the women of Judea believed in the Savior, loved him, followed him, comforted him in his afflictions."

This theory is not completely confirmed by the account in the Gospels. On the other hand, it does pinpoint the "Oedipean" psychological truth of 'anti-Semitism which regards only the Jewish male as dangerous and ugly—the castrating father cannot in fact be anything but masculine. Deprived of a penis, the Jewish woman does not share in the "curse of the race" and her innocence even makes her particularly desirable. In this context, Chateaubriand set out to interpret Christian tradition by referring to the Woman of Bethany, the good Samaritan, and the adorable Magdalene thanks to whom, he concluded, "the reflections of some beautiful beam will have remained on the foreheads of Jewesses." The beauty of Jewesses, often described as divine, was · also a recognized idea of the Romantic period ("heavenly beauty," wrote Michelet with all the seriousness in the world,[12] and "pearl of the Orient"), while her misfortunes added the role of a "violated goddess" or a "sexual symbol" to her other attractions.[18] Rarely, I believe, has the explosive mixture of religion, eroticism and archaic anguish which is the basis of anti-Semitism, been so clearly revealed as in the forgotten commentary by the author of *Le Génie du Christianisme.*

Scott's attitude to this type of phantasm also appears in his novel *The Surgeon's Daughter.* This time, the plot is contemporary. The beautiful and unfortunate *Zilia Monçada,* a modern version of Rebecca, has been seduced by a Christian aristocrat and her love is thwarted by a cruel and fanatical father. *Richard Middlemas,* the bastard son she brings into the world, becomes a thorough blackguard, an adventurer and wanderer. He, in his turn, seduces an innocent Christian girl (as if he were forced to revenge his mother's outraged virtue?). His baseness is emphasized by the virtues of his friend *Adam Hartley* who possessed "an open English countenance of the genuine Saxon mould." After causing his parents and the touching *Menie Grey* immeasurable suffering, the saturnine hero is crushed by an elephant which "put an end at once to his life and to his crimes." Breaking away from the old theme of guilty Jews and innocent Jewesses, this is historically the first lesson in the dangers of a "mixture of blood."

With the emancipation of the Jews and their entry into society, the Jewish woman became an original, and in a way autonomous, phenomenon in European cultural life. Her curious charm was exercised in various ways. In real life, in Germany or Austria, she acted as the "midwife of ideas"; this was the case of the great Jewish ladies of Berlin and Vienna. In the intermediate zone between life and imagination, she distinguished herself in the theatrical world, like the sublime Rachel and Sarah Bernhardt in France. Finally in England, from *Jessica* to *Rebecca,* she appeared as a seductive phantom. It would seem that these various gradations are governed by the intensity of the reactions her male partner aroused, ranging from open to latent anti-Semitism.

In about 1750, a Jewish merchant from Ferrara, Benjamin Disraeli, settled in London to trade in coral there. His son Isaac turned to literature and earned a respectable reputation with his essays and short stories, some of which had the distinction of being translated into French.[14] Displaying all the qualities of an accomplished gentleman, Isaac associated with the great men of his day in London and Paris: amongst others, he dined with Lord Byron and the Thierry brothers. In England, baptism was not an indispensable "admission ticket to European culture," and although Isaac Disraeli left the synagogue and had his children converted in 1817, this followed a misunderstanding with his co-religionists. His defection did not prevent him publishing *The Genius of Judaism* anonymously in 1833. It consisted of a defense and illustration primarily of Spanish Judaism, which already suggests the influence of the new ideas about the individual "geniuses" of peoples or races. The work, which displays a solid Jewish culture, was immediately translated into German.)[15]

His son Benjamin was born in 1804 and was first educated at an English boarding school where he seems to have suffered his share of insults from his Christian schoolfellows, all the more so as a rabbi came on Saturdays to instruct him in the Law of Moses. But instead of leading up to the celebration of the *bar mitzvah*, when he had completed his thirteenth year in 1817, his religious education culminated in Anglican baptism. This, as might be imagined, did not strengthen his respect for the established religions.

Intelligent and ambitious, he then, like a Jewish Julien Sorel, dreamed of conquering a hostile world. One can picture the adolescent with black curls, fascinated by Israel's past splendor, plying his father with questions. It was to his father that most of his love went (his mother hardly counted as far as he was concerned; this would seem to have augured well both for his loyalty to ancestral tradition and his dreams of future glory). Following his father's example, he first tried his hand at literature. Composed after a journey to the East, his *Alroy* (1833) expressed, he noted in his diary, his "ideal ambition," that old Marrano dream: to re-establish a Jewish state.[16] But his "active and real" ambitions as a Jew converted to Anglicanism were political and worldly. For a few years he adopted the manners of a dandy, following the example of the famous Brummel, and shone in the salons. Then he was elected to the House of Commons. But there, he immediately came up against the suspicions and obstacles inevitable for a man of unaristocratic origins and born a Jew to boot. This latter handicap was aggravated by a name which rang out like a challenge, and an oriental appearance which was no less unusual in England at that time.

The peculiar circumstances of their birth normally drove ambitious young Jews at that time to deny an "otherness," which they wanted to reduce to a simple difference in faith. It was in this way that the Jewish St-Simonians in France and the Jewish forerunners of the "Young Germany" were "anti-racists" *avant la lettre,* doing battle in the various liberal parties. In England, the liberal historian Macaulay developed this type of argument when he advocated Jewish rights in 1831. He compared "Jewishness" to "red hair," an unimportant accident of birth.[17] The young Disraeli's great originality was to take the opposite line, a line which was only practicable in eccentric England. Convert that he was, he used the fact that he belonged to the Chosen People as a basis for demanding preferential treatment and the political promotion of his brethren.

After his entry into political life, Disraeli set out his vision of the world together with his plan of action in his "political trilogy" of novels (*Coningsby,* 1844; *Sybil,* 1845; *Tancred,* 1847). The specific case of the Jews had no connection with the conditions of the English working classes or the duties of the Church, but it was not the problem which interested him least. As a preliminary, he had taken a great deal of trouble to inform himself on the anthropological ideas of the time, and this enabled him to classify the "Semites," Jewish or Arab, as members of the "Caucasian race."[18] "All is race: there is no other truth" was a leitmotif of his trilogy. Although this idea was already in the air as we have seen, he was the first Englishman to make it the cornerstone of a political vision as well as an explanatory principle. But contrary to the predominant views on Germanic pre-eminence, already propagated on this side of the Channel by men like Carlyle or Thomas Arnold,[19] it was the "Semites" whom he promoted to the rank of an "aristocracy of Nature." The insolence of this lesson was increased by the mouthpiece he adopted: *Sidonia*, a Jew whose wisdom was only matched by his wealth (he is, the critics tell us, "Disrothschild," that is to say a compound of Disraeli senior and the Rothschild wealth). *Sidonia* acts as mentor and instructor to *Coningsby* and *Tancred*, revealing to these young English aristocrats the secrets of Semite supremacy, based on the cult of purity of race. To *Lord Coningsby*, he makes statements like this:[20]

... The fact is, you cannot destroy a pure race of the Caucasian organization. It is a physiological fact. ... And at this moment, in spite of centuries, of tens of centuries, of degradation, the Jewish mind exercises a vast influence on the affairs of Europe. I speak not of their laws, which you still obey; of their literature, with which your minds are saturated; but of the living Hebrew intellect. You never observe a great intellectual movement in Europe in which the Jews do not greatly participate. The first Jesuits were Jews; that mysterious Russian diplomacy which so alarms Western Europe is organized and principally carried on by Jews; that mighty revolution which is at this moment preparing in Germany and which will be, in fact, a second and greater Reformation, and of which so little is as yet known in England, is entirely developing under the auspices of Jews, who almost monopolise the professorial chairs of Germany. ...

But Disraeli was not satisfied with populating Spanish monasteries and German universities with camouflaged Jews, that is to say, Marranos. He also claimed the greatest historical characters for the race: Kant, Mozart, and even Napoleon, not to mention minor heroes like Massena or

Soult. This mystification naturally cut both ways and the argument could equally be used to demonstrate the Jews' corruptive power: a weapon later employed by anti-Semites in every country in the way we know so well, and which is still in use today.[21] On the other hand, the proponents of pan-Germanism used the method of unauthorized naturalization on an even vaster scale, claiming the whole pantheon of great men from Giotto to Pasteur. On all these points, Disraeli was a precursor, and perhaps a creative thinker.

In *Tancred,* his own favorite work, he took these provocative themes even further, without even bothering about a pseudonym; for here it is the author himself who glorifies the "Semitic spirit" and ridicules the "civilization of the Franks":[22]

> . . . some flat-nosed Frank, full of bustle and puffed up with self-conceit (a race spawned perhaps in the morasses of some Northern forest hardly yet cleared), talks of Progress!
>
> The European talks of progress, because, by an ingenious application of some scientific acquirements, he has established a society which has mistaken comfort for civilization!

Further on, it is *Tancred* who in his turn humbly agrees that he is descended "from a horde of Baltic pirates," a race which would probably have "perished in mutual destruction" if they had not been enlightened by the "spirituality of the Semites!"[23]

Disraeli propagated this virulent racism throughout his life, not only in his popular novels but also in a purely political profession of faith, *Lord George Bentinck* (1851), where Chapter XXIV is devoted to a defense of the Jews. On the morrow of the revolution of 1848, the future Lord Beaconsfield saw Israel as the secret and efficient cause of European subversion, and the stupid Christian oppressors had only themselves to blame. Why did they not understand that it was unnecessary to drive the chosen race to desperation? In fact:[24]

Destruction of the Semitic principle, extirpation of the Jewish religion, whether in the Mosaic or in the Christian form, the natural equality of man and the abrogation of property, are proclaimed by the secret societies who form provisional governments, and men of Jewish race are found at the head of every one of them. The people of God co-operate with atheists; the most skilful accumulators of property ally themselves with communists; the peculiar and chosen race touch the hand of all the scum and low castes of Europe! And all this because they wish to destroy that ungrateful Christendom which owes to them even its name, and whose tyranny they can no longer endure.

When the secret societies, in February 1848, surprised Europe, they were themselves surprised by the unexpected opportunity, and so little capable were they of seizing the occasion, that had it not been for the Jews, who of late years unfortunately have been connecting themselves with these un-hallowed associations, imbecile as were the governments, the uncalled-for outbreak would not have ravaged Europe. But the fiery energy and the teeming resources of the children of Israel maintained for a long time the unnecessary and useless struggle.

"Secret societies" and "Jewish race"; these ideas, dear to the nineteenth century, were underwritten in this way by an epigone of the Marrano irony. However, although it is difficult to think that Disraeli believed everything he wrote, his apologetics display a curiously strong passion, particularly in *Tancred,* when he thrashes weak and shameful Jews who deny or conceal their origins.[25] His sincerity is even better demonstrated by the astonishing speech in 1847 when, staking his political career, he demanded the admission of Jews to the House of Commons, not on the basis of some abstract principle of tolerance or equality, but as a privilege due to the people of God:

On every sacred day you read to the people the exploits of Jewish heroes, the proofs of Jewish devotion, the brilliant annals of past Jewish magnificence. The Christian Church has covered every kingdom with sacred buildings, and over every

altar ... we find the tables of the Jewish law. Every Sunday—
every Lord's day—if you wish to express feelings of praise and
thanksgiving to the Most High, or if you wish to find expression
of solace in grief, you find both in the words of the Jewish poets.
... All the early Christians were Jews. The Christian religion
was first preached by men who had been Jews until they were
converted; every man in the early ages of the Church by whose
power, or zeal, or genius, the Christian faith was propagated,
was a Jew. ...

These words sent a buzz of indignation through the
benches. Disraeli went even further:[26]

In exact proportion to your faith ought to be your wish to do
this great act of national justice. If you had not forgotten what
you owe to this people, if you were grateful for that literature
which for thousands of years has brought so much instruction
and so much consolation to the sons of men, you as Christians
would be only too ready to seize the first opportunity of meeting
the claims of those who profess this religion. But you are
influenced by the darkest superstitions of the darkest ages that
ever existed in this country. It is this feeling that has been kept
out of this debate; indeed, that has been kept secret in yourselves—enlightened as you are—and that is unknowingly influencing you as it is influencing others abroad. ...

So spoke Disraeli: as a Jew proud of his origins to the
point of megalomania, and in no way afraid of shocking his
Christian adversaries who, like Gladstone, were criticizing
him "for not having one drop of English blood in his veins."
On this subject André Maurois in his *Disraeli* (where he took
care not to overemphasize his hero's judeomania, like all
Disraelian biographers) showed remarkable intuition when
he compared Disraeli to his great rival. Gladstone, he wrote,
"saw climbing over against him a hostile and bizarre figure
. . . despite himself he took it as the measure of his own
success, and *deemed himself outstripped by all if he were
outstripped by Disraeli.*" Disraeli would thus have served as
a measuring-rod, an existential guideline to Gladstone—a

traditional role for the Jew. But, writes Maurois further on, Disraeli displayed a sort of timidity, which "prevented him from ever finding real pleasure in the society of men. *To feel himself their equal, he needed to be their Chief*"[27] (that is to say, to feel the equal of the English). Rarely, in our opinion, has the strangeness of the relationship between Jew and Christian, and the deep-seated reason which forces the first to do his utmost to do "more and better" than the second, been described so felicitously, unobtrusively and succinctly.

Certainly English public opinion, with a few exceptions, had very little taste for Disraeli's judeomania. Carlyle waxed indignant at his "Jewish jackasseries" and asked "how long John Bull would allow this absurd monkey to dance on his chest?"[28] He also described him as a "cursed old Jew who is not worth his weight in cold lard."[29] A certain Professor Wilson (Christopher North) replied to *Coningsby* with an *Anti-Coningsby,* published in 1844.[30] Thackeray parodied it in *Punch* in a minor masterpiece of British humor, entitled *Codlingsby*. In it, *Sidonia's* role as instructor is taken over by *Mendoza*, a descendant of *Rebecca*, with whom *Sir Wilfrid Ivanhoe* has contracted a marriage beneath his station. (It is the only "blot upon the escutcheon of the Mendozas.") Mendoza reveals to *Godfrey de Bouillon, Marquis of Codlingsby,* the mysteries of Semite blood. Everyone is secretly Jewish—from the Pope downwards: " 'Hush!' said Rafael, leading him from the room. '*Au revoir,* dear Codlingsby. His Majesty is one of *us,*' he whispered at the door; 'so is the Pope of Rome; so is . . .' a whisper concealed the rest."[31] In the scientific world, a Professor Robert Knox, in *The Races of Man*, severely criticized Disraeli, while literally paraphrasing his doctrine:[32]

Nevertheless, that race in human affairs is everything, is simply a fact, the most remarkable, the most comprehensive, which philosophy has ever announced. Race is everything: literature, science, art—in a word, civilization, depends on it.

Once this principle had been laid down, the conclusions that the obscure professor drew from it expressed the Western state of mind infinitely better than the theses defended by the famous statesman. These were notably refuted in the following terms:[33]

> A respect for scientific truth forbids me refuting the romances of Disraeli; it is sufficient merely to observe here that, in the long list of names of distinguished persons whom Mr Disraeli has described as of Jewish descent, I have not met with a single Jewish trait in their countenance, in so far as I can discover; *and, therefore, they are not Jews,* nor of Jewish origin. . . .

The antithesis is worthy of the thesis, and the tones are very much those of modern anti-Semitism. Elsewhere, the Jews and the author of *Coningsby* are taken to task jointly:[34]

> But where are the Jewish farmers, Jewish mechanics, labourers? Can he not till the earth, or settle anywhere? Why does he dislike handicraft labour? . . . the real Jew has no ear for music as a race, no love of science or literature; he invents nothing, pursues no inquiry; the theory of *Coningsby* is not merely a fable as applied to the real and undoubted Jew, but is absolutely refuted by all history.

However, Lord Beaconsfield's supreme fame rapidly obliterated England's memory of the polemics which had surrounded Disraeli. His admirers and biographers either keep quiet about his racial theories or treat them as a practical joke or a whim. "It is curious to note," writes Raymond Maître, "that most critics question Disraeli's seriousness and sincerity on this point. They regard it either as an incoherency or as a symptom of mental derangement, or most often as a practical joke: 'the most extraordinary joke that Disraeli ever dared perpetrate.' "[35]

This sort of humor was not understood on the continent. It is noteworthy that Disraeli, one of the authors whom the

Anglo-Saxon public of his time most enjoyed and who is still read today,[36] has been very little translated in Europe. This did not prevent his racial theories being taken much more seriously there than in his own country. There have even been attempts to show that the Comte de Gobineau borrowed the main part of his political philosophy from him.[37] It is in fact probable that these two sparkling conversationalists were introduced in 1841 in Paris (where Disraeli associated with the Thierry brothers and de Tocqueville). The *Essai sur l'inégalité des races humaines* was conceived after this date and some of its descriptions of "races," both "English" and "Jewish," bear strong resemblances to the corresponding treatment in the Disraelian political trilogy.[38] But questions of priority or reciprocal influences like these are hard to solve, particularly when an "idea in the air" exercises an intellectual fascination in the way politico-racial determinism did in the second quarter of the nineteenth century. It is easier to produce examples of the use which anti-Semitic and racist propaganda later made of the ideas which issued from the famous Jew. In France, Gougenot des Mousseaux and Édouard Drumont both became his ingenuous disciples. *Le Juif, le judaïsme et la judaïsation des peuples chrétiens* contains several pages of Disraeli in translation with favorable comments.[39] *La France juive* quotes him in thirteen different places, and his theories are discussed, notably in the context of the "Semitism" of various historical characters.[40] But as far as the special case of Napoleon was concerned, Jules Michelet was already welcoming and supporting the views of the "spiritual Englishman M. Disraeli": "The love of hoarding too, so many millions piled up in the cellars of the Tuileries, also indicates the Marrano."[41]

The various arguments of this type were revived by most French anti-Semitic authors before 1914, particularly when they were anglophobes—which was commonly the case. In Germany, Ludwig Schemann (the apostle of Gobineau) and Houston Stewart Chamberlain both compared the great Jew who had been the first to proclaim the importance of race to the shabby cohort of Jewish "anti-racists."[42] Hitlerite propaganda, on the other hand, obviously made him the symbol of an England governed by Jews. This resounding name therefore lent itself to very different types of exploitation, and probably aroused anti-Semitic susceptibilities in innumerable ways from 1845 to 1945 and perhaps even later.[43] It is difficult to measure this sort of effect precisely, since we are in the realm of so-called invisible forces and hidden influences which the initiated surround with secrecy. But it would appear that the author of *Coningsby* and *Tancred* was an unavowable source of inspiration to generations of anti-Semitic hoaxers, falsifiers and illuminati, and that he was all the more easily believed and imitated, if not plagiarized, in that his spectacular career seemed to illustrate the validity of his theories. These theories in their turn rested on his familiarity with Marrano tradition which burned with its last brilliance in his person, often considered enigmatic. In his day, was not a Duke of Naxos[44] for the Ottoman Empire what Lord Beaconsfield became for the British?

ten

France

The Jews' entry into society

As early as 1816, a contemporary was rejoicing in the new era: "We see the Israelites by our side; we talk to them, they share our burdens, our sacrifices, our pleasures, our vigils, our fears, our hopes; why? Because they enjoy the same rights. . . ."[1] In fact it seemed as if nothing but outward prejudices should any longer separate Jews from Christians. As all careers were henceforth open to them, they were already to be seen, noted Benjamin Constant in 1818, "figuring honorably in the administration, no longer avoiding the military profession, cultivating science, and teaching it. . . ."[2] Unlike what would occur beyond the Rhine, this first generation did not produce any absolutely leading figure (with the exception perhaps of Rachel). However, the sons of Israel were making names for themselves as second strings, like the Halévy brothers, or men like Léon Gozlan or Alexandre Weill acting or writing for the theater, joining the Saint-Simonian movement in force, and cultivating the art of war—in a way which was perhaps typical of French Jewry.[3] As for the second generation, in Alfred de Vigny's opinion, it had nearly reached "the summit in everything, in business, letters and particularly the arts and music, rather than the fine arts."[4] In other words there was not just the Rothschilds and the bank. And already the problem of the Israelites' uncertain identity posed by emancipation was being reflected in literature: in 1840 an anonymous author expressed his anguish cloaked in a romantic and medieval plot in the style of the time:[5]

> And if, to avoid a cursed fate,
> I finally desert my outlawed race,
> The Christian will point a finger at me astounded
> At my change and will cry: behold the Convert!
> ... And are you surprised at my intense sadness?
> Jews, Christians, I hate you! A curse on you all.

However, with the Restoration, bourgeois opinion under an orderly government seemed favorably disposed to the Children of Israel. A country which was aspiring to order and legality was afraid of controversial subjects. Every symptom of persecution or discrimination immediately found critics on the watch, particularly amongst the Protestants, rich, active and—they too—collectively traumatized. On the subject of the fraudulent baptism of a Jew, the specter of the Dragonnades was resurrected: "Has the edict of Nantes been revoked for a second time, and are we destined to see a return of the time when missionaries carried off the children of Protestants and Jews and had them brought up in convents?"[6] Denouncing the persecution of the Protestants of the Cévennes, Benjamin Constant's plea covered "the other religion, much more cruelly persecuted for two thousand years, which, as an inevitable consequence of this unfair curse, seemed imbued with hatred and hostility towards the social order which condemned it."[7] In return, the historian Léon Halévy promised that if a Jew "was summoned to the legislature ... he would side with the defenders of our liberties and sit on those benches from which the Benjamin Constants, the Gautiers and other Protestants so eloquently defend the cause of their constituents of all religions."[8]

But the Jews now had advocates of their own. Adolphe Crémieux for his part proclaimed that the old hatreds had had their day. "You are no longer the same, they are no longer the same, their change is remarkable, yours is no less so . . .".[9]

> Cast your eyes over this France, homeland of all liberal feelings; see the Israelites launching into all the honorable careers and distinguishing themselves by all the virtues which make good citizens. ... Let men cease therefore to make the name of the Jewish nation echo within their boundaries, if indeed the Jews can be regarded as a nation at all since they have the good fortune to be blended into the great family of the French people.

The name of Adolphe Crémieux symbolized the success of emancipation in France. In 1830, Gans (Karl Marx's Berlin teacher) noted, with a twinge of envy, that Crémieux "shone, thanks to the fame of his knowledge, his ability and, a third point which is honored here, namely that he is a Jew."[10] *Here,* was the salon of the Marquis de Lafayette thronged with Parisian and international high society.

Even more significant of the eclipse of anti-Jewish prejudice in the enlightened and propertied classes of the period, is an argument used by Victor Schoelcher to show the inanity of anti-Negro prejudice: "Amongst Europeans, something of this feeling exists between us and our hired servants, as once between Catholics and Jews, as still today between Russian and Polish nobles and their serfs. . . ."[11]

The case of the Jews was quoted here as an example of a past prejudice. The feeling that still existed affected serfs or hired servants: this was indeed the society that Balzac described, where money was king. Now, all French Jews were not rich, far from it, and it was the most wretched of them who formed the stumbling block to collective entry into society and the nation. To transform them into so-called useful citizens, into "Israelites," the consistories Napoleon had inflexibly organized spared no effort, multiplied schools, scholarships and centers for apprenticeships. If there was one point on which the communities remained loyal to their old ancestral practices, it was their plutocratic structure: a sniper, the mathematician Olry Terquem, described French Judaism in 1836 as a "vast commercial confederation, in the context of a religion": "Have money and you become a notable; with gold you reach the consistories; diamonds, and you attain the Central Consistory. . . ."[12]

Because of this, supreme leadership of French Judaism quite naturally fell to the richest Jew, the Austrian consul (he was never naturalized in France), James de Rothschild *primus inter pares* of the five famous brothers, "Chief Rabbi of the Right Bank," according to Heinrich Heine,[13] "unquestionably the high priest of Judaism," according to that other *enfant terrible*, Alexandre Weill.[14]

"Kings of the Jews, and Jews of the Kings", the Rothschilds were firstly the court Jews of the Holy Alliance of kings. But the Rothschildian phenomenon consisted of much more than that. At a time when the banks, by the expedient of public credit, "are taking the lead in the states" (Stendhal), the bank belonging to the sons of the Frankfurt ghetto became the arbiter of the political as well as the financial situation on many occasions. In Paris, the firm "played a much more significant role than governments, with the exception of the English cabinet" (Chancellor Metternich).[15] "Viceroy and even King of France," exclaimed the wife of the Russian chancellor, Nesselrode, more bluntly, after dining with James de Rothschild.[16] Financial circles, for their part, reckoned that a large transaction only had a chance of succeeding in Europe with Rothschild collaboration.[17] In the eyes of contemporaries, their power had become "a sort of fate which it was hard to escape," as their best historiographer wrote recently.[18] Adversaries of the established order could enjoy themselves to the full. In his *Briefe aus Paris*, Börne was the first to comment ironically on this "Jewish domination":[19]

Rothschild has kissed the Pope's hand. . . . Order has at last been restored such as God intended when He created the world. A poor Christian kissed the Pope's feet and a rich Jew kissed his hand. If Rothschild had received his Roman loan at 60% instead of 65% and so been able to send the Cardinal-Chamberlain ten thousand ducats more, then he would have been allowed to embrace the Holy Father. Would it not be the greatest boon for the world if all kings were chased off their thrones and the Rothschild family installed in their place?

Good or ill, the joke had some justification, since the Rothschilds took pains to prevent senseless carnage. Peace was the great byword of the bank; a peace which weighed with the full weight of its gold, "binding Europe so that nothing can shift,"[20] and which it succeeded in preserving until the middle of the century. If blood did not flow in Europe, its concealed domination served some purpose there. But needless to say, contemporaries did not intend to pay such a price for peace. In 1842, Michelet wrote:[21]

Dismal mediator of nations who speaks the language common to them all, gold, and thereby forces them to agree amongst themselves. . . . They will not imagine, for example, that there are ten thousand men in Paris, ready to die for an idea. . . .

In itself, the famous family personified the bogey which the de Maistres and the von Arnims had flourished not so long ago. It appeared to justify the gloomy prophecies of men like Barruel, or the megalomania of those like Disraeli. "And let us not thank the Jew for the peace he gives us," protested Toussenel; "If it was in his interest for war to be waged, war would be waged."[22] Even if the Rothschilds' desire for peace may have been based on their wish for the smooth running of their business, it was still consistent with the pacific and cosmopolitan tradition of the ghetto. "What is the good of quarreling? Russia is a long way away . . .", Nathan in London wrote sententiously to Salomon in Vienna, in 1829; and James in Paris in 1830: "We will do the impossible to maintain peace. . . ."[23] A little further on we will see how he contributed to preserving it at the time of the great

Eastern crisis in 1840, and how international conflict was preceded by a debate on the Jews' ritual crimes.

Rothschilds' peace or *pax judaica*? Despite the super-abundance of Rothschildian literature, it is not easy to answer this question, for the lack of information on the purely Jewish aspect of their policy makes it difficult to form an opinion. "To the historian, the Rothschilds as *bankers* appear more typically bourgeois than Israelite," Jean Bouvier recently wrote.[24] But where does the banker stop and the man begin? One of the reasons, and not the least important, for the power of the firm lay in the wonderful understanding between the various national branches, cemented by an inbreeding which was both Jewish and Rothschildian, marriages outside the family only being contracted as a last resort. Rothschilds first? But plutocrats, whatever may be said about them, also have a homeland. Suitably adapted, a statement of faith by an American who was head of General Motors before he became Defense Secretary, can be applied to the five brothers, so that it might be assumed that, "what was good for the Rothschilds was good for Israel."[25] Working for their own glory, they probably thought that they were enhancing the reputation and serving the interests of their co-religionists to the same extent.

Although the subject of the Rothschilds has been a source of inspiration for generations of anti-Semitic propagandists, it is worth noting that the major witnesses of the period partially or even entirely dissociated Rothschilds from Jews. For Balzac, Nucingen, "the profiteer," that is to say Baron James, was first and foremost an Alsatian, and his tone was proverbially Germanic.[26] Heine, not without a twinge of irony, placed Rothschild amongst the glories of Germany.[27] Stendhal, who depicted the Baron in the form of Leuwen senior, de-judaized him completely and gave him a half-Dutch origin.[28] Altogether, these contemporaries saw the Rothschilds more as foreigners than as Jews. It can also be said that they were in their way fulfilling one of the wishes of the emancipators, by seeing the foreigner in the Jew, rather than the Jew in the foreigner. This was an additional symptom of an apparently favorable climate, which made it possible for some authors to write that anti-Semitism was unknown in France, or that it remained "underground," before the great outbursts at the end of the nineteenth century.[29] Even the anti-Rothschildian polemicists in their way dissociated the bankers from the Children of Israel: the pamphleteer, Mathieu-Dairnvaell, wrote in *Rothschild, ses valets et son peuple*: "I bear no grudge at all against the Jews whom I regard as my brethren. ... I bear a grudge against those I call Jews. ..."[30] Reservations of this type were also typical of all manner of works in which the authors were afraid that they had overdone their disparagement of the Jews and apologized for it in a note or in some other way. Michelet usually adopted this process. After a historical portrait of rarely equaled violence ("The Jew, the unspeakably foul man. ... Humiliation after humiliation, and there they are on the throne of the world ..."),[31] he praised the "famous Jews" from Meyerbeer to Rachel who "have really rehabilitated them." Even more indicative was the case of his former secretary, Toussenel, who attacked the Jews in his *Juifs, rois de l'époque* without the slightest reservation. In a preface, his publisher wanted to apologize in his stead "for having indicted the Jewish race."[32] These considerations and circumspections allowed the Jews to hope that the old prejudices would end by dying out of their own accord.

However, these prejudices appeared forcefully on the occasion of certain repercussive incidents. When a Jew found himself in the center of a scandal, it immediately became a Jewish scandal, and all the Children of Israel were encompassed in the same censure. This occurred in 1832, when the Duchesse de Berry, betrayed to Louis Philippe's government by the convert Simon Deutz, was arrested. The Holy See had recommended this adventurer to the Duchesse, but the censure (principally voiced by Chateaubriand and Victor Hugo) went to the synagogue. Chateaubriand evoked the ghost of Judas Iscariot: "Let the descendant of the Great Traitor, let Iscariot into whom Satan had entered, *intravit Satanas in Judam,* say how many pieces of silver he received for the deal. . . ."[33]

Hugo employed the more modern image of the wandering Jew—and if Deutz had apostasized, it was because he was worse than a Jew:[34]

> He is not even a Jew! He is a filthy pagan,
> A renegade, the disgrace and outcast of the world,
> A foul apostate, a crooked foreigner. . . .
> Move on, wandering Jew. . . .

Börne, for his part, noted the act with very typical black humor: "One does not understand why this Jew turned Catholic, he could just as well have become a scoundrel by remaining a Jew."[35] Only Alexandre Dumas made some attempt to give Deutz a fair hearing.[36] Even today, historians like André Castelot regard him as a *traitor* and a *Jew,* as circumstances require.[37]

The Deutz episode remained primarily symptomatic. The Damascus affair in 1840 had deep international repercussions. By an accident of history, the concert of the powers, including Russia under Nicholas I, then took Jews persecuted by agents of the French government under its protection, but it was no accident that in the era of nationalism, such a situation provoked a temporary incompatibility between the status of Jew and Frenchman.

The year 1840 marked the acute phase of the Eastern crisis, in which France supported the viceroy of Egypt, Mehemet Ali, as opposed to the rest of Europe, which was favorable to the Sultan. Minor history then took a hand in major events. In the partly Christian town of Damascus, in February 1840, a Capuchin monk, Father Thomas, mysteriously disappeared. The French consuls, Ratti-Menton and Cochelet, attributed this disappearance to the Jewish community and instituted proceedings against its notables, on a charge of ritual murder. After long torture, some succumbed, others apostasized, still others made false confessions. Now, two of these notables happened to be Austrian subjects. The Austrian consuls, Merlatto and Laurin, tried to get their nationals out of trouble. The governments of both sides, under Metternich and Thiers respectively, took their agents' part, and this clash became an episode in the trial of strength which brought France and the other great powers into conflict. It served, in fact, as a sort of prologue to it. The atmosphere in Europe grew heated over the affair: in Syria, the representatives of England, Prussia and Russia went to the help of their Austrian colleagues; the question of the human sacrifices that the Talmud was thought to prescribe was openly discussed in the capitals.

In Paris, the Council of Ministers was not very interested in knowing whether Christian blood was an ingredient in the cooking of unleavened bread. What did matter to Thiers was that his bluff in proclaiming his intention of defending Mehemet Ali to the end should not be called, which was why he made common cause with his consuls. His principal antagonists, Crémieux, Fould and Rothschild, were bound by a different solidarity. The documents[38] suggest that Baron James and his brothers felt vitally concerned with the fate of their Syrian co-religionists (this side of the Germanic "profiteers" totally escaped Balzac). As Thiers proved intractable in an interview with James, the latter, as he wrote to his brother Salomon, wanted to resort "to the omnipotent medium here, namely the help of the newspapers,"[39] but for once the remedy failed, all the more so as patriotic fervor was beginning to rise in Paris. A governmental organ (*Le Messager*) was instructed to write that the superstitions of oriental Jews prescribed ritual murder and that their co-religionists would do better to keep quiet.[40] Perhaps Thiers believed this: what could he know about Judaism? Heinrich Heine criticized his glaring ignorance: "The most distressing thing that the bloody Damascus question has brought to light is that ignorance of eastern affairs which we observe in the present President of the Council of Ministers. . . ." He continued with customary lucidity:[41]

> . . . a glaring ignorance which might one day make him commit the most serious mistakes, when it will no longer be this small bloody question of Syria, but really the major bloody world question, the fatal and inevitable question that we call the Eastern question which will have to be solved.

Thiers was in fact being increasingly hoist with his own petard and was playing the bully. On the subject of the "major question," he wrote to Guizot: "We are nine, you ten, the king eleven. All of us together should be enough. Let us not be afraid and go forward as a man. The interest in France is extraordinary."[42] As for the "minor question," he counterattacked from the height of the rostrum in the Chamber:[43]

> You are protesting in the name of the Jews, and I am protesting in the name of a Frenchman. So may I be allowed to say: an extremely honorable thing has come to pass for the Israelites. When the facts were known, they were aroused in all Europe, and they have brought to this matter an enthusiasm, an ardor which does them great honor in my eyes. And if they will allow me to say so, they are more powerful in the world than they pretend to be, and at the present time, they are protesting to all the foreign chancelleries. They are putting extraordinary enthusiasm into it, an inconceivable ardor. It takes courage for a minister to protect his agent attacked in this way. I believe that I have shown some firmness in this affair, and I have had to. . . .

Shortly afterwards, Thiers spoke to the Chamber of Peers in even more treacherous terms: "Should I not believe M. Cochelet's word, rather than that of a sect which I respect for its energetic efforts to vindicate itself, but which after all is itself a party to the suit?"[44] Endorsed by the President of the Council, propagated by him at his daily press conferences,[45] against the background of the bellicose mood of the French, the bloody story was sprawled over all the newspapers, including, lamented the *Archives israélites*, "those most devoted to the ideas of progress and liberalism."[46] As for those whose "political and religious opinions had remained most retrogressive,"[47] they vied with each other in citing a *raison d'État et d'Église.* "If one wants the Jews to be innocent," wrote the *Gazette de France,* "one will have to accuse Moslems and Christians; this is a sad alternative." According to *La Quotidienne,* "even their innocence would be a matter for more than serious care; it is easy to accuse the whole human race of imbecility to explain its hereditary animadversion to the nation of shopkeepers."[48] There were as many reasons for condemning the Jews as there were newspapers. Only two Paris papers defended them: *Le Journal des Débats,* devoted to the Rothschilds, and *L'Espérance,* because of Protestant solidarity. What could readers think, faced with the almost total unanimity of the press? "Who can say how much semi-dormant loathing, how many odious conjectures have been re-awakened . . ."[49] exclaimed *L'Espérance.* "During the sorry Damascus episode," wrote the *Archives israélites* two years later, "did none of your friends say to you, laughing the laugh that bruises the soul: 'I don't want to dine with you in case you serve me a Father Thomas cutlet!'" Nothing could have hurt the Jews more than this very Parisian and slyly menacing humor which Heinrich Heine also noted when talking about Thiers's treachery. "To hear him talk, one might end up by actually thinking that the Jews' favorite dish was Capuchin friars' meat."[50]

In the other Western countries, and especially in Great Britain, public opinion was hostile to France and because of this, tended to espouse the cause of the Jews. The Jews, anxious to clear themselves of an ignominious suspicion, saw the problem only from its Jewish angle, and were therefore the only ones to worry about its basis, rather than its repercussions and political exploitation. This state of affairs showed how, struggling for their security and their honor, they could be brought in to serve the cause of truth;

the Damascus affair was the first great modern example of this. Organizing themselves on an international scale for the first time since their emancipation, the Jewish notables met in London. Crémieux, the delegate for France, exclaimed: "France is against us!"[51] In the situation, he, therefore, seemed to feel more of a Jew than a Frenchman, and on this point at least, Thiers's attacks had some justification. One of the English notables, Bernard van Oven, suggested that all the rabbis of Europe be made solemnly to swear that the Jewish religion did not prescribe human sacrifice.[52] It was finally decided to delegate a mission to the Sultan and Mehemet Ali, composed of Crémieux, Moses Montefiore and the orientalist, Munk. It actually set out on a frigate put at its disposal by the British government. But the fate of the Jews of Damascus still hung on the upshot of the international crisis. This ended with Thiers's resignation—which did not appear unrelated to a representation by James de Rothschild to Louis Philippe. Revenue had just fallen, peace was preserved. Did the Rothschilds force Thiers's dismissal and so facilitate the peaceful solution of the conflict? Did they then set to work to have an international conference convened to save France's injured self-respect?[53] This is major history which every historian interprets in his own way, according to his conception and the documents available. Jewish history has noted that the Jews were rehabilitated after Mehemet Ali's capitulation and that the matter of the bloody rites of the Talmud and of "Father Thomas" cutlets was no longer referred to in Paris. But it had been a sharp warning, and the intrigue hatched by the obscure Count of Ratti-Menton served as a starting point for the formation of international organizations for the defense of the Jews, beginning with the *Alliance israélite universelle*.[54]

Ghosts from the past: the wandering Jews

In 1842, the French electorate returned three Jews to the

Chamber: Crémieux, Cerfberr and Fould. The *Archives israélites* was jubilant: "Who is talking about disagreements? They are no longer possible in France after a result like this, there are no longer religious differences amongst us, no longer hereditary hatreds, no longer beliefs which kill! Fanaticism is in ruins, persecution is dead, superstition has vanished!"[55] In another article, the review beseeches "the literary marshals commanding the great army of the press" to discard the adjective *Jewish* for ever: [56]

> Not that we blushed for our beliefs . . .—God forbid!—but because in France, in 1842, the adjective *Jewish* is devoid of meaning; because the Jew, as the dictionary of the Academy knows him, becomes rarer every day; because the Jew whose soul is in Jerusalem and his body in France, scarcely exists any longer in our day; it is because the *Jewish* nation no longer exists on French soil. . . .

It was the romantic movement, and its leading authors, whom the *Archives israélites* accused of perpetuating a "word which is a permanent weapon against us":

> Everyone of them at least once in his lifetime is determined to cut himself a doublet in Middle Ages style and, when their imagination runs dry, they knock up a history of the Jews. There is not a novelist, a would-be short story writer, not the most wretched manufacturer of feuilletons who has not got a fantastic picture of the Jews of yore in his bag, an account of our past misfortunes, a version of our naïve legends. It might be said that since our great historic shipwreck, the poorest scribbler has a claim on our wreckage.
> Do you like the Jew? he turns up everywhere.
> At the theater, from Shakespeare to Scribe; in novels, from Ivanhoe to Paul de Kock; in the newspapers, ever since there have been writers to perpetrate feuilletons and a public which is willing to swallow a lengthy daily rigmarole; everywhere in fact, in this world of printed paper . . . crack, a Jew is knocked up for you as an egg would be fried. . . . Heaven preserve you from these gentlemen's local color!

This is valuable evidence. But it was in vain that the *Archives israélites* tried "to tell these writers that they are caricaturing us, that they are disfiguring us and that they are dressing us up wrongly in antiquated finery." The worst, in the eyes of the review, was yet to come, because in 1844 *Le Constitutionnel* began publication of the famous *Juif errant* (or *Wandering Jew*) by Eugène Sue.

Let us remember that although the subject dated from the Middle Ages, the popular legend of the wandering Jew had spread in Europe in the sixteenth century, and that it was at the beginning of the nineteenth that it gained universal notoriety and appeared in major literature. Goethe, Schubart, A. W. Schegel, von Brentano, Chamisso and Gutzkow in Germany, Byron, Shelley and Wordsworth in England, tackled the subject at that period. In France, the popular version in ballad form seems to date from around 1800.[57] In 1833, Edgar Quinet made *Ahasvérus* the slightly confused Promethean or Faustian symbol of toiling, suffering mankind. Sue gave his character the same significance. This, the *Archives israélites* could have claimed, was to do their co-religionists too great an honor. It also, of course, went against the popular meaning of the myth embodied in "the image of the Jewish people, driven from their home for having repudiated Christ, wandering across the world since then and, despite persecution, always keeping a well-stocked purse" (Gaston Paris).[58] What made this all the more interesting was that the legend followed the teaching of the Church on its essential points: the idea of eternal testimony borne by the witness-people, as well as of the fall from grace of the elder brother, since the wandering Jew, wandering like Cain, was also marked by a similar sign on the temple.

Cain he certainly was, "vagabond and fugitive upon the face of the earth," but minus the crime perhaps. Like the people he personified, the wandering Jew could blame himself for nothing but his loyalty to the ancient Law, or his unbelief; if he "irrationally" refused to help Jesus on the

Way to Calvary, it was because he saw him as the "magician," the "criminal." Listen to the ballad:

> Churlishly, rebelliously,
> I said to him irrationally
> Get you gone, criminal
> From outside my house,
> Move on, get going
> For you shame me.

Moreover, the wandering Jew repented and yearned with all his being to expiate his crime: would he have been touched by divine grace? He called Jesus *my Savior*:

> It was a cruel presumption
> Which caused my misfortune;
> If my crime is expiated,
> I would be too fortunate:
> I have treated my Savior
> Too harshly.

On all these points, he formed a contrast with Judas Iscariot, whom he replaced as a personification of the Jewish people in modern times. What did this new image mean and why did the substitution occur?

It will be noticed that the legend spread after the expulsion of the Jews from Spain, when the refugees, the Marranos, dispersed throughout Europe, were in effect free, and that its fascination increased in the nineteenth century, with the general emancipation of Western Jews. Might not the metamorphosis of the Jewish myth from Judas to the wandering Jew be interpreted in the light of the change in the Jewish situation? Judas, in the Christian imagination, was a traitor, an unspeakable being, who in the collective person of the Jews, suffered well-deserved punishment in the shape of the ghetto, the badge, all the forms of social and legal ostracism. The wandering Jew, on the other hand, if he had acted like a Jew, had no fault other than his unbelief; a fault which he deeply regretted, even yearning to become Christian (perhaps the legend in its way reflected the Marrano psychological conflict). The enormity of his punishment, contrary to all spirit of justice, and even less consistent with the moral teaching of the Gospel, has often been the subject of puzzled reflection. It can be seen how the new symbol linked up with the new reality: no special laws, no theologically motivated punishment, no crime committed with deliberate intent, but a Jewish guilt which continued to exist, a mysterious and diffuse guilt, an even more tragic condition, an implacable curse, which it might be said no longer depended on what the Jew *did* but on what he *was*, on his very essence, his *nature*. In short, the new symbol seemed in its way to illustrate the transition from theological to racial anti-Semitism.

But let us go back to Sue's *Juif errant* and his innumerable offspring. For innumerable they were: in France alone, even before Quinet and Sue, Béranger had created a wandering Jew who, "with an inhuman laugh," "outraged the scarcely breathing Man-God," while Gérard de Nerval was translating Schubart's macabre *Juif errant*. At the end of 1834, Quinet's generous and universalist wandering Jew was the source of inspiration for a publication in the same vein: *Le Juif errant, journal*, a monthly progress report. It explained itself in its first number:[59]

The wandering Jew! at this name, the whole world stops and bows down in terror before the majesty of God: children, peasants, noblewomen. . . .

The wandering Jew, according to the orthodox priest, is the Jewish race, eternally dispersed amongst the nations, without merging with them, without becoming a sister to them, alone amongst the peoples of the earth, thus fulfilling the prophecies of the divine curse. . . According to us, he is mankind which is traveling onwards, he is progress which is moving forwards, and that is why we have taken for our banner this title which is both popular and symbolic of the future. . . .

This was also Eugène Sue's image of the wandering Jew. This humble craftsman, who doomed all craftsmen who followed him, all the damned of the earth, "to eternal suffering," was also known to have been an instrument in the service of an anti-Jesuit war machine. His success equaled *Les Mystères de Paris*—which accounts for his innumerable descendants. They began the following year, with *La Juive errante* by Léon Lespès, a gluttonous daughter, who really had nothing Jewish about her except the title. (That sort of title really was good for sales.[60] The *Archives israélites* was in no way exaggerating.) Then in 1847, in the "Bibliothèque des Légendes," Collin du Plancy brought out a *Juif errant* sanctioned by the archbishop and conspicuous for his passionate impenitence, slitting the throats of Christian children and shattering crucifixes on the way.[61] The year 1848 saw the blossoming of a new *Juif errant* in the form of a revolutionary periodical, whose existence was as ephemeral as its precursor's in 1833.[62] In the same year, the *Juif errant* (Sue's) was put on the stage at the Ambigu-Comique; and the turn of the Opéra came in 1851, with music by Halévy, and words by Scribe and Saint-Georges. This was a maleficent Jew, whose own son froze "with terror at the sight of him":

Ahasvérus (to his children) :   Fear nothing!
                                   The blood they want to shed, my
                                   children, is mine!
Léon : No, no! I want none of your terrible help!
          It is you who brings misfortune on our heads! Go hence!
Théodora (to Léon):   Do not be deaf to his grief!
Ahasvérus (with despair): Oh inflexible decree!
Léon : Your name, your cursed name freezes me with terror![63]

This particular Jew survived the Last Judgment on the stage of the Opéra. In the same year, Alexandre Dumas, during his exile from Brussels, tackled an even more stupendous *Juif errant*:[64]

[a] Christian and evangelical Jew ... from Byron without

doubt, of eternal consolation . . . the future, the world, as it will be in a thousand years—Siloö, second son of God—the last day of the world—the first day of the planet which must follow it.

All in all, a galactic wandering Jew, but only two volumes saw the light of day, instead of the twenty or twenty-five anticipated, the imperial censor having forbidden an undertaking which its author intended to be both a universal and a supernatural history of mankind.

There was also the image of the wandering Jew: an artistic picture with Gavarni (Sue's illustrator) and Gustave Doré, who illustrated sumptuously Pierre Dupont's poem; or a popular image, with the twenty-five engravings of Épinal which the art historian Champfleury listed for the years 1800–60.[65] The fascination the modern archetype of the Jew exercised over both élite and masses can be seen. "It is a name linked forever to that of Christ, to a name as well known as Mohammed or Napoleon" (1834, *Le Juif errant, journal*). "Of all the legends which have taken root in the mind of the people, that of the wandering Jew is certainly the most persistent" (1869, Champfleury). In 1893, Dr Henry Meige, a student of Charcot's, undertook to explain the legend medically: he and his patron had had the opportunity of observing neurasthenic or vagabond Jews and he devoted his doctoral thesis to this subject, coming to the following conclusion: "The wandering Jew therefore exists today; he exists in the form he had taken on in past centuries. . . . Nervous pathology produced Cartaphilus, Ahasuerus, Isaac Laquedem in the same way as the patients whose history we have just traced."[66] This "entry of the wandering Jew into the Salpêtrière" is indeed the supreme sanction. Nonetheless, unlike his English and German counterparts, no great French writer let himself be tempted by the theme which depicts the Jew on to whom Jesus would have unloaded his cross—which might be explained by the national sense of moderation, rather than by chance.

The focus on the man who reviled Christ could only vary within certain limits inside the framework set by the legend; at the most, the emphasis could change from the hardships at one moment of time depicted by some authors, to the eternal expiation drawn by others. The medieval Jew left romantic imaginations much greater latitude, a latitude which most frequently acted to his disadvantage, like the contemporary Jew, whose powers of fascination drew this comment from Börne: "Some people criticize me for being a Jew, others praise me for so being, still others forgive me for it, but all of them are conscious of it."[67] It remains for us to cast an eye over the image of the Jew depicted by the great creative artists of the period.

Victor Hugo proved quite ferocious before he reached mature years. A text written in his earliest youth (1819) clearly showed Voltairean or deist influence: the massacres perpetrated by the crusaders were justified not by the deicide, but as a "bloody reprisal for the Biblical massacres committed by the Jews." However, the young Hugo concluded with an expression of regret for the religious apathy of his contemporaries. "Today, there are very few Jews who are Jewish, very few Christians who are Christian. People no longer despise, no longer hate, because they do not believe. It is an immense misfortune."[68] Behind the grandiloquence of the "young Jacobite" can one not glimpse an undertone of the alarm that the emancipation of the Jews had aroused in the most varied circles? Later, in *Cromwell* and *Marie Tudor*, Hugo depicted quite alarming Jews. *Rabbi Manassé ben Israël* (who negotiated the return of the Jews to England) showed a thirst for Christian blood (*Cromwell*, act IV, scene 5):

Of the two rival parties, what does it matter which succumbs?
Christian blood will flow in waves.
I hope so anyway. That is the best thing about plots.

This rabbi certainly earned the reproach of "foul Jew,

deicide, Barrabas," that *Cromwell* threw in his face, just as the maxims "Jew who speaks, Mouth which lies" and "Lying and stealing, it is all the Jew" which Fabiani applied to the Jew *Gilbert* in *Marie Tudor* (first day, scene 6) also all seemed justified to the spectator. But these are only the stock dramatic civilities in use by the young romantics, and the poet who "passed away surrounded by Jews,"[69] according to Drumont, had previously made an *amende honorable* to Israel in his *Torquemada* (1882).

Lamartine seems, at first sight, to form a contrast to the young Hugo rather as Rousseau contrasts with Voltaire. In his *Voyage d'Orient*, he proclaimed his love for the Jews, one of those "poet nations ... who have idealized politics and made the divine principle predominant in the life of peoples," and like Rousseau, he voiced Zionist and providential hopes:[70]

> Such a country, populated once more by a young, Jewish nation, cultivated and watered by intelligent hands, made fertile by the tropical sun ...—such a country, I say, would still be the Promised Land today, if Providence returned it a people and the policy of rest and liberty.

This is the tone of the *Vicaire savoyard,* and shortly afterwards Lamartine added the episode of the Jewish pedlar to his *Jocelyn*:

> The poor pedlar died last night.
> No one wanted to give the planks for his coffin;
> The blacksmith himself refused a nail:
> "It's a Jew," he said, "come from I don't know where,
> An enemy of God whom our land worships
> And who, if He returned, would outrage him again. ...
> And the wife of the Jew and his small children
> Vainly implored the passers-by for pity.

The priest *Jocelyn* reads the lesson to his parishioners : "I put the Christians to shame for the harshness of their soul."

The fable he tells them brings out their better feelings. "This moral drama brought back their souls and they were competing for the wife and child."[71]

Other authors did not commit themselves on the destinies of Israel, and the Jews who appeared episodically in their writings gave no indication of their personal feelings: perhaps they had none. An example of this was Alfred de Musset, who depicted a Jewish old-clothes man, *Munius*, in *L'Habit vert*, an old rogue diddled in his turn by the grisette *Marguerite* and her friends.[72] Another example was Stendhal, whose *Le Juif (Philippo Ebreo)* was primarily a man telling the author about his adventurous life. This marvelous Stendhalian summary appeared in the account: " 'This is the life I led from 1800 to 1814. I seemed to have God's blessing.' And the Jew bared his head with *tender respect*." In George Sand, *Les Mississipiens* contained a gambler of Law's time, *Samuel Bourset*, an imaginary nephew of the famous financier, Samuel Bernard, whom the novelist, like generations of historians, wrongly thought was Jewish.

There were swarms of Jews in Balzac's world, sketched from life, and often identifiable (*Nucingen* was Rothschild; *Nathan*, Gozlan; *Dr Halpersohn*, Dr Koreff[73] or Dr Knothé).[74] One can count about thirty, all in all. The courtisan and the "sublime" beauty were not absent from the list, nor was the crafty art dealer, *Magus*, or the plain usurer *Gobseck*; but their creator displayed no prejudice towards them. This was not true of some of his characters. *Lady Dudley*, receiving the writer *Nathan*, said to her friend: "There are, my angel, pleasures for which we have to pay highly" (*Le Lys dans la vallée*). The student, *Juste*, "told in 1831 what was going to happen and what has happened: assassinations, conspiracies, the reign of the Jews" (*Z. Marcas*). Balzac himself noted the rigidity of provincial ostracism (*Louis Lambert*):[75]

Mlle. de Villenoix's origin and the prejudices against Jews which are preserved in the provinces, did not allow her, despite her fortune and that of her guardian, to be received in that absolutely exclusive society which rightly or wrongly is called the nobility.

But the provincial bourgeoisie must have been no less exclusive, notably at Lyon, where a native writer (Fleury la Serve) noted that "Judaism is condemned from afar, suspected, avoided more than elsewhere."[76]

We have already had occasion to mention Chateaubriand twice. This Breton gentleman had vowed a stubborn hatred for the Jews, sometimes rejoicing in the fall of the *torturers of Christ* ("mankind has put the Jewish race in quarantine, and this quarantine, proclaimed from the height of Calvary, will only end with the end of the world"), sometimes envying their prosperity:

Happy Jews, crucifix dealers, who rule Christianity today. . . . Ah! if you wanted to change skins with me, if I could at least slide into your strongboxes, rob you of what you have stolen from gilded youth, I would be the happiest of men.

The contradiction between these two passages from *Mémoires d'Outre-Tombe*[77] could only be removed by attributing supernatural powers to the Jews; it would seem that Chateaubriand ascribed the failure of his political career to the Rothschilds.[78] These feelings were, as we have already said, typical of a nobility which could not reconcile itself to the new social order. This class bitterness is also found in Alfred de Vigny, but complicated by his eccentricities and the flaws in his character, and assuming an almost obsessional form with this bitter thinker. Although his stage Jew (*Samuel Montalto* in *La Maréchale d'Ancre*, "rich and miserly, humble and treacherous") might only have been the counterpart of Hugo's *Manassé ben Israël* and his numerous rivals, his *Journal d'un poète* contained a number of passages which revealed this obsession.[79]

In Jewish men, whosoever they might be, Vigny consistently saw the Jew first, the man afterwards. "Heine is

Jewish. . . ." Then followed the description of this "cold and wretched" character whom Vigny did not like (1832).[80] "Spinoza is Jewish. . . ." There followed a summary of the "system" of the *Ethics* (1833).[81] In 1847, Vigny noted an "astonishing fact: M. Halphen (Jewish) has been appointed mayor of the second district of Paris."[82] The *Journal d'un poète* also supplied abundant information on the way Vigny viewed the world. This was a terrible world, where everything was going from bad to worse: "Paris, sad chaos, early gave me the sadness it bears within itself, and which is the sadness of an old town, at the head of an old social body" (1847).[83] "The bourgeoisie is mistress of France, it dominates it in length, breadth, and depth" (1842).[84] "Man is turning back into a monkey" (1851).[85] "The ancients had the advantage over us of not knowing about printing" (1839).[86] In a world like this, what was the lot of the Comte de Vigny, who was, he tells us, "oppressed since childhood"? Note: "On a thousand occasions in my life, I saw that the nobles in France are like colored people in America, persecuted to the twentieth generation."[87]

Moreover, this world was totally Jewish. Vigny's thoughts that we have on this subject were either his personal opinions or a writer's notes for a future book, but it is not always easy to make a distinction between the views of the man and their transformation by the artist. Is this Vigny's proverbial resignation? He spoke of this "judaization" without acrimony (as early as 1822 he exclaimed in *Hélène*: "To the sons of Judas everything is allowed"),[88] but this only makes his evidence more striking. First and foremost, the Jew was the instigator of the July revolution:

The Jew paid for the July revolution because he handles the bourgeoisie more easily than nobles—the Jew pays Prospero— This Jew is beautiful, fat, pale, happy and getting the better of Christians who worship the golden calf in all lands.

In the last chapter he tells us that the Grand Turk and the

Pope both received him equally well and that he bought one cross from the Emperor and the other from a King. "The world is his. When he wishes, duchesses do the honors at his salons, and Christian barons are his humble servants . . ." (April 22, 1837).[89]

At this period, Vigny was beginning the great work he was planning. From May to September, 1837, he wrote a fragment of it—*Daphné*—in which the action took place under Julian the Apostate. One gets the feeling that, at that time, he was fascinated by the timeless character of the Jewish financier, incarnated in 1837 in the Rothschilds (July 20, 1837):[90]

> *Daphne. Thought-mother.*
> "Let them alone," says Libanius.
> But the Jewish *Banker* smiles at these efforts and says:
> "Jehovah has not abandoned his eternal people. He has given me the royalty of wealth and the understanding of affluence, which is the scepter of the world."
> A Jew at this very moment rules over the Pope and Christianity; he is paying sovereigns and buying nations. *King of credit* and major *gold movements.*

This was, of course, Rothschild. He mentioned him by name later on, imagining a way in which "Mlle Rothschild" might be able to evade her father's last wishes.[91] Other plans dated from 1840: then, the Jewish banker was "a rich, benevolent, quite good-natured banker" who "gathers his four children together to know if he will make his youngest grandson a Christian. It is easier for him to catch Christians in his net if he is their brother."[92] The proceedings, it might be said, seemed natural to Vigny. However, he was not unaware of the fact that these Jews, these bankers, were most frequently only hoping to assimilate, since in 1842 he imagined this starting point :[93]

> An honorable Jewish banker endowed with all the personal virtues, has become so French that he no longer practices his religion . . . imitating Jean-Jaques, [he] wanted to let his son reach the age of manhood before choosing a religion. . . .

Nonetheless, the Jewish kingdom, of which all the Jews were nothing but maintainers and profit-takers, was an established fact for Vigny. For example, a few days later, he noted: "Luxury. The Jewish banker, the millionaire, is king of the world. 'What do you think of my dominion?' he says to his son."[94] He justified this dominion a few weeks later under the title *Des Juifs et de l'esprit juif* (July 13–14, 1842):[95]

> Dr Black:[96] "Who says that this Jew is wrong? Is Europe, is, in fact, the world, anything but a Jewish kingdom? Since men have been writing, they have been complaining of greed: Orpheus says this, Homer says that and Juvenal: 'We are in the ninth age,' etc., and gold is always king. Let us try and see if the fault does not lie with the first man to create this symbol of exchange and [illegible] the proletariat also. That done, the Jew invents the bill of exchange; he is still master of it. He does not believe in the divinity of Christ, you say, but you do not believe in it either."

A benevolent note on the "oriental, fiery race" of Jews is dated March, 1856:[97]

> *Note on the Jews*—This oriental, fiery race, direct descendants of the patriarchs, filled with all the knowledge and all the primeval harmony, has superior aptitudes which lead it to the top of everything in business, letters, and above all the arts and music rather than the other fine arts. Barely *one hundred thousand* Israelites are settled in the midst of *thirty-six million* Frenchmen and they ceaselessly take the first prizes at schools. Fourteen of them at the *École Normale* took the first places. It has been found necessary to reduce the number of them allowed to compete in public examinations.

At that period, Vigny had made friends with the convert Louis Ratisbonne, whom he later appointed executor of his will; friendships based on attractions of this kind were, we know, frequent occurrences. Similarly, no acrimony towards the Jews is perceptible in a note of 1839 on the poet's romantic sadness:[98]

Stello sought in infinity a resting point on which to settle his ever-wandering thoughts. An ineffaceable impression of sadness made him look everywhere for someone as sad as himself, and thinking that the memory of the greatest griefs of the world would abate the sense of his own, he began to think of the people who had best understood the sadness of life: the Jews....

Thus, to "abate his sadness," it is in the Children of Israel that Stello, that is to say Vigny, seeks a fixed resting point for his *wandering thoughts*. Once again, it is the witness-people who serve both of them as a reference point in their distress: "We and the Jews." This fundamental comparison is even more obvious in the completed fragment of *Daphné*, which Vigny was still thinking about resuming two years before his death.[99] There, the contrast was marked in the following way: on one hand, the *others*, the gentiles, *Julian the Apostate* and his pagan or Christian friends, *Libanius*, the philosopher, or *St John Chrysostom*, who make speeches, struggle and suffer; on the other, the narrator, the young Jewish merchant, *Joseph Jechaïah*, impassive observer of these speeches, struggles and suffering, an identification by the author therefore if not actually a conscience. Moreover, *Joseph Jechaïah* was no ordinary merchant: he associated on an equal footing and as a cultural equal with the emperor and his circle; and, a philosopher himself, could not "prevent himself admiring the way in which all the changes in idolaters inevitably resulted in an increase in our power over the world."[100]

Right through the narrative, there are only ineffable feelings, only the throbbing anxieties of the august protagonists for the human future—was it better for mankind to be Christian or pagan?—and the philosophical Jew even seemed to share these feelings and anxieties. But right at the end, after the "stupid and ferocious" Christians had massacred the pagans and sacked their temple, *Joseph*

Jechaïah bought the pagans' treasure from them dirt cheap, and threw off his mask:[101]

> This could rebuild a good part of the Holy Temple of Solomon. So, thanks to our perseverance, our holy nation is digging a mine filled with gold under the feet of all the nations of the earth, where they will be buried, will become our lowly slaves and recognize our indestructible power. Praise be to the God of Israel!

The shrewd observer therefore was nothing in fact but an Elder of Zion.

Man is both an angel and a beast. Today we know[102] that while he was carving his character for posterity in his "ivory tower," the poet was denouncing prominent members of his circle whom he suspected of republican sympathies to the imperial police. In the figure of the treacherous *Joseph Jechaïah*, Count Alfred de Vigny perhaps succeeded in producing one of the most extraordinary self-portraits.

Future threats: the Socialist movements

While men like Chateaubriand and even Vigny were using the old arguments from the Catholic arsenal against the Jews, the Church refrained from conducting a campaign against them during the first half of the nineteenth century. Was this because the memory of the Revolution and the Voltairean attacks was still too painful? The fact remains that hardly any members of the clergy figure amongst the anti-Jewish polemicists of this period. The only notable exception was the Italian Abbé Chiarini, professor of Oriental Antiquities at Warsaw, who published his *Théorie du judaïsme appliquée à la réforme des Israélites de tous les pays de l'Europe*[103] in 1829 in Paris, at Emperor Nicholas I's expense. The work, which stirred up the old stories of ritual murder and well-poisoning, caused quite a stir, and the

Archives israélites ranked its author amongst the great historical slanderers of Judaism.[104] He suggested an original method of regenerating the Jews, or rather, as he wrote,[105]

> two different methods, but almost equally reliable, and simple and new as well: by Hebrew taught systematically and by the translation of the Talmud ... so as to make this formless chaos, this receptacle of errors and prejudices, where all the dreams of fanaticism crowd in delirium, publicly explode.

This original scheme failed on the untimely death of Abbé Chiarini in 1832.

Otherwise, Catholic specialists in anti-Judaism were recruited from amongst converted Jews. Abbé Drach and the Ratisbonne brothers were joined by Cerfberr de Medelsheim, Louis Ratisbonne's cousin, whose pamphlet *Ce que sont les Juifs de France* (1842) sold twenty thousand copies and seems to have caught Vigny's attention.[106] But there is another reason why he deserves to be rescued from oblivion. There are features in his work which portray a society: if this author is to be believed, the Jew, under the July monarchy, could only have access to virtue and religion once he had made his fortune:[107]

> ... Although as a rule the German Jew dies in final impenitence, it does sometimes happen that he mends his ways, particularly when he has made his fortune. These Jews are then genuinely good and noble; they do good unostentatiously, live without display and without arrogance; they give their children a solid and liberal education; they are useful citizens and the homeland can depend on them in time of danger; they are frank and loyal, recognize the errors of their nation, and as no personal benefit then forces them to conceal their feelings, they acknowledge the truth and almost all are becoming Christians.

It is all the easier to understand why at that period the great anti-Jewish campaigns came from quite a different quarter. But right through Western history, any scheme for a radical reorganization of society has taken account of the multiform image of the Jew, sometimes by cloaking itself in the messianism of Israel, more often by tending to make the Jew an anti-symbol. The phenomenon is demonstrated particularly clearly in the case of the French socialist movements.

Directly descended from the Enlightenment, Saint-Simon does not seem to have been personally concerned with the question; only a few, not very prominent, lines on the subject can be found in his writings.[108] But his few disciples included two young Jews, Léon Halévy and Olinde Rodrigues, and when the Saint-Simon movement sprang into life after his death, many sons of Israel were amongst its active members and sympathizers. The doctrine, which gave trade and banking a place of honor, had the ingredients to attract the hereditary experts in these professions, disorientated by emancipation, and probably also looking for new methods of penetrating society. The alliance between young Jews and Saint-Simonism found its expression not only in the latter's philo-Semitism but also, as far as any eschatological pretensions the sect had, in an expedition to the East in search of a "Mother" who would be both universal and Jewish.[109] The alliance helped to make public opinion identify Saint-Simonians with Jews, but there were more deep-seated foundations for this. The outcome of the Saint-Simonian adventure is well known, and also the way in which not only the Pereire brothers, but also the Talabot brothers, Michael Chevalier and the leader of the sect, Enfantin himself, found their niches in banks and on boards of directors. A story which Taxile Delord quotes, was current in the financial world at that time: " 'You will not succeed,' someone said to an industrialist who was setting up a big business, 'you have no Jews on your board.' 'Don't worry,' he replied, 'I have two Saint-Simonians.' "[110]

Other observers took a more tragic attitude. This tirade in Capefigue's *Histoire des grandes opérations financières* is suggestive and shrewd in its way:[111]

Why deny it? We are right in the middle of a Saint-Simonian and Jewish society. Attempts to avoid it have been in vain; it is everywhere. When the magistrature, with that noble and holy dignity which characterizes it, had condemned the leaders of the Saint-Simonians (today rich and promoted to high positions) to imprisonment in 1832, it had foreseen the society that these doctrines would create in the world: the family goes; property crumbles away; people leave the countryside for the cities, the small towns for the large; machines create a dismal slavery; railroads a monotonous numbness, a Babylonian existence which no longer offers any distraction but the narcotic smoke of a new opium.

Numerous equally terrified contemporaries described as *Jewish* the irreversible changes in the modern world, prophetically discerned by Saint-Simon and his followers. The other socialist doctrinarians, hostile to the Industrial Revolution, voiced the popular protest more faithfully, and, helped by sectarian rivalry, the majority of them were anti-Semitic to a more or less pronounced degree.

First and foremost amongst them was Charles Fourier. Whatever may have been the debatable sources of his inspiration (Swedenborgian Illuminism which had its French center in Lyon,[112] or the working men's fraternities, the "Poor of Lyon"[113]), this erstwhile commercial traveler faithfully expressed the old guild claims with regard to the Jews. In 1808, the recriminations of eighteenth-century merchants were flowing from his pen,[114] and a conventional lower-middle-class mentality was emerging when he made himself the spokesman of the threatened competitors, in his "fable of the Jew Iscariot and the six Christians":[115]

The Jew Iscariot arrives in France with a hundred thousand pounds in capital which he gained from his first bankruptcy: he sets up as a merchant in a town where there are six accredited and respected rival firms. To take away custom from them, Iscariot begins by selling all his goods at cut prices; this is a sure means of attracting the mob; Iscariot's rivals soon start shouting; Iscariot smiles at their complaints and cuts prices even further.

Then the people exclaim in admiration: long live competition, long live the Jews, philosophy and fraternity; the price of all goods has fallen since Iscariot arrived; and the public says to the rival firms: "It is you, gentlemen, who are the real Jews, and who want to make too much money. Iscariot is an honest man, he is content with a modest profit, because his household is not as splendid as yours." In vain do the old traders point out that Iscariot is a rascal in disguise who will sooner or later go bankrupt; the public accuses them of jealousy and calumny and buys from the Israelite more and more. . . .

The fraudulent bankruptcy is not slow to come, and "Iscariot disappears with his portfolio to Germany, where he has sent his merchandise bought on credit." But what is more, he gradually involves the six Christian firms in his downfall and "this is the way that the establishment of a vagabond or a Jew is enough entirely to disorganize the body of merchants in a large town and force the most honest people into crime."

Is it surprising that the villain of the fable is called Iscariot? One always comes back to the fact that economic resentment was fed by theological resentment: did not Fourier (in his *La Fausse industrie*) claim to be a "social interpreter come after Jesus"?[116]

John the Baptist was the prophetic precursor of Jesus. I am his prophetic postcursor, foretold by him and completing his work of rehabilitating men in the industrial sector alone ... this office of prophet which has fallen to me was not a personal mission given to a chosen person, like John the Baptist's, but a competitive mission, a career open to all. . . .

Moreover, this prophet had lived in contact with real life and was not unaware that in France, usury was practiced by Christians, "natives of the country" as he put it. But in his eyes, Jewish usury was more dangerous, and the emancipation of the Jews all the more ill-omened. Once the Jews had really spread in France, he wrote in 1808, the country "would no longer be anything but one vast synagogue, for if the Jews held only a quarter of the properties, they would have the greatest influence because of their secret and indissoluble league."[117] In 1821, emancipation was still a scandal to him, worse than "the advance of the mercantile spirit" and the "industrial scandals":[118]

> To these recent evils, all circumstantial evils, let us add the most shameful, the admission of the Jews to citizenship. It was therefore not enough for the *civilized* world to ensure the reign of deceit; it has to summon help from the nation of usurers, the *unproductive patriarchalists*. The Jewish nation is not civilized, it is patriarchal, having no sovereign and believing all deceit to be commendable, when it is a question of cheating those who do not practice its religion.

If there were some honest Jews, wrote Fourier again, they only showed up the vices of the sect more sharply.[119] Another proof of dishonor was its refusal to break bread and salt with Christians (probably nothing could shock this amateur *bon vivant* more). Here, Fourier had another anecdote:[120]

> One day, the President of the Great Sanhedrin was invited to dinner with the arch-chancellor; he confined himself to sitting down at table and drinking; he refused to eat any of the dishes, because they were prepared by Christians. Christians have to be very patient to tolerate such impertinence. In the Jewish religion it denotes a system of defiance and aversion for other sects. Now, does a sect which wishes to carry its hatred as far as the table of its protectors, deserve to be protected? Does not a refusal to eat on the part of the leader of the Jews prove that all the dishonor they are criticized for is a reality, including the principle that robbing a Christian is not stealing?

There was hardly one of Fourier's works that did not contain its share of anti-Jewish attacks, with the exception of his last book, *La Fausse industrie* (1838). At the end of his life, he probably hoped to interest Rothschild in his ideas: in any case, he compared him to Ezra and Zerubbabel, and even offered him the throne of David:[121]

> The restoration of the Hebrews would therefore be a fine prize for MM. de Rothschild; they could, like Ezra and Zerubbabel, lead the Hebrews back to Jerusalem and re-establish the throne of David and Solomon there, to found a Rothschild dynasty upon it. The omen seems a dream and nothing is easier to bring about in six months under the protection of all the monarchs. . . .

Fourier's disciples did not lay down their arms after his death. At the time of the 1848 revolution, *La Démocratie pacifique* wrote: "The presence of M. Crémieux at the Ministry of Justice is a serious danger. . . . Sincerely republican Israelites, enemies of favoritism and cliques, will not be offended when we say: France has just made a Revolution, not a sabbath!"[122] Later, during the Dreyfus affair, the Fourierist *Rénovation* gave vent to frenzied anti-Semitism.[123] We can also evoke the shade of Dostoievsky who kept nothing of his Fourierism after he had rejected all he had once held dear, except its judeophobia: on this point, the roads from Damascus have rarely been followed right to the end.

Dispersed in Fourier, the attack was concentrated in *Les Juifs, rois de l'époque* (1844) by his disciple Toussenel. Before this work was supplanted by *La France juive* it was a classic which Drumont had hoped only to equal.[124] Its principal historical interest lies in the light it throws on the use of the term "Jew," at a time when it was beginning to be used as a battle cry. Toussenel could not be more explicit on the subject:[125]

> I call by this despised name of Jew every trader in cash, every unproductive parasite, living off the substance and work of others. . . . And when one says Jew it also means Protestant, and it is inevitable that the Englishman, the Dutchman and the Genevan, who learn to read the will of God in the same book as

the Jew, profess the same contempt as the Jew for the laws of equity and the rights of the workers.

Further on, the circle seemed to be enlarged to include *foreigners* in general.[126] Attacking England especially, Toussenel reached the point, on the subject of the opium trade, of implicating the Pope who "has himself held his peace. The God of the Gospels has not had a vicar on earth for too long! The vicar of Christ [the Pope] is an old man who borrows from the Jews. . . ."[127] And very many of the chapters in *Les Juifs, rois de l'époque* do not involve the Jews at all.

Toussenel's true purpose was to denounce the rule of money, as the sub-title of the book, *Histoire de la Féodalité financière*, indicates. He even expressed his satisfaction that, thanks to the Jews, he could attack this feudal system openly:[128]

> Praise be that the supreme Providence ordained that the mercantile feudal system should have as its primary sponsors the children of Israel, the unregenerated sons of those Pharisees and scribes who put Christ on the cross, so that the Christian world should immediately recognize the *Infâme* by nothing but the contamination of his name!

Elsewhere, he acknowledged that "glorious names of artists and scholars have sprung up from amongst the descendants of Israel in recent times."[129] He even took Rachel under his special protection, at a time when *Le Journal des Débats* and *Le Commerce* were bent on destroying her.[130] In his attack on the actress in *Le Commerce*, Petrus Borel had begun by making Racine "shake very painfully on his pedestal" and ended by brandishing the threat of the times:[131]

> when that race, once exiled and burned, will so have decimated and subjected us that our towns will no longer have anything more than a Christianery in a small corner of the suburbs . . . as in the Middle Ages they each had a Jewry.

Despite the fact that Borel had protested against the out-dated prejudice in *Dina ou la belle Juive* (1833), he can be said to have had much more of the makings of a genuine anti-Semite than Toussenel.

The Christian Socialist Pierre Leroux, whose article published in 1846, was also called "Les Juifs, rois de l'époque"[132] was less dogmatic. With Leroux, the Jew became the ambivalent symbol of the human race:

> Taking us to the root of all the evils which afflict mankind in all its members, we will say that if the evil, in a certain specific form, is more particularly displayed by this people, it is not because the evil, in this same respect, is particularly in this people, and attacks it alone: the evil attacks all men to different degrees.

Leroux might talk about the "terrible predestination attached to this people," but he did, on the other hand, envisage the loftiest destinies for it :

> ... we will not always see that unsightly countenance it has today. It will recapture a more cheerful, younger, smiling countenance; it will cease to look like the Jew Shylock; and I hope to see it resurrected in the features of the Nazarene whom the Jews have crucified and whom they are still crucifying today by gambling and capital.

Like Toussenel, Leroux cited linguistic practices as evidence:

> We are talking about Jews like the Academy!
>
> The academy makes the following remarks on the word Jew in its dictionary: *Jew*: this word is not included here as the name of a nation, but because it is employed figuratively in a few phrases in the language. For example, a man who lends usuriously is called a Jew. . . . It is applied in familiar speech, to anyone who shows great greed and eagerness to profit from it.

"It is the *Jewish spirit* that we resent," continued Pierre

Leroux, "it is certainly not the Jews as a collection of individuals nor any individual Jew." Not even the Rothschilds, he added in substance. Reading statements like these makes one wonder if the emotional indictment of the term "Jew" was not even more powerful a century ago than it is today, and it can be seen that the Academy only defined its symbolic and pejorative meaning.

Codified by the dictionaries, such an indictment justified the campaigns against the Jews' ascendancy, but these campaigns also expressed deep-seated and permanent historical factors. They were an echo of the campaigns by the popular preachers of the Middle Ages, mendicant monks or heretical fraternities, who, quoting the message of the Gospels, had once aroused a Christian people, hungering for justice, against the usurious deicides. The religious undertones of the socialist movements emerge particularly clearly in the light of these old anti-Jewish agitations. However, times had changed; the anti-Semitic component was no longer inevitable and, despite the Rothschild phenomenon, several early socialists, like Étienne Cabet, Constantin Pecqueur, Louis Blanc and Auguste Blanqui refrained from emphasizing such arguments, probably because their understanding had not been clouded by the historical legacy of Christianity.[133] Even within the bosom of the Fourierist movement, active members like Victor Hennequin and Jean Czynski were anxious to defend the Jews.[134] As we have already noted,[135] a subtle personal coefficient henceforth entered the general equation, perhaps with decisive effect. It can be said that anti-Semitism became individualized, internalized; like religion, it became a private affair. But this affair easily assumed immense proportions: as with Pierre Proudhon.

For this influential French socialist thinker, the Jew was the *evil element, Satan, Ahriman,* and he was perhaps the first in France to see this element incarnated in a race, the race of Shem. This is how he developed the concept:[136]

The Jew is by temperament unproductive, neither agriculturalist nor industrialist, not even a genuine trader. He is an intermediary, always fraudulent and parasitical, who operates in business as in philosophy, by forging, counterfeiting, sharp practices. He only knows the rise and fall of markets, transport risks, uncertainties of returns, hazards of supply and demand. His economic policy is always negative; he is the evil element, Satan, Ahriman, incarnated in the race of Shem.

If Proudhon's Jew was completely free to exercise his maleficent influence in the contemporary world, it was because this world was profoundly depraved. Moreover, it was under the heading of *Décadence* that the revolutionary in his main work (*De la justice* ...) accused the Jews of having "made both the high and the low bourgeoisie, throughout Europe, like themselves."[137] We can recognize the argument de Bonald put forward in 1808[138] and Proudhon may perhaps have been directly inspired by it. In fact, on the subject of decadence, he called Napoleon and Chateaubriand, the "hero and the poet," as witnesses; but in vain "did Napoleon try to re-awaken religious feeling by the Concordat ... it turned out that he had brought the soul of a Christian back into the body of an unbeliever."[139]

The attempt to fight against "the sovereigns of the period" seemed to Proudhon even more vain, at the point to which things had come; "absolutely no purpose would be served today by expelling them."[140] Proudhon diagnosed the decadence of this period by numerous symptoms—his list included the decrease in the height of conscripts, and the degeneration of the equine races.

This pessimistic tone, these illusions and these fixed ideas already suggest modern anti-Semitism, and in Germany, men like Richard Wagner would later say as much or more. What was remarkable about Proudhon was the confusion between theology and racism. For him, the Jews had placed themselves "outside the human race" by rejecting Christ.[141] His theology became less banal when (in *De la justice*) he compared *Jewish polytheism* with *Indo-Germanic mono-theism*: Did not the Scriptures refer to Jehovah as "Lord of Lords" or "God of Hosts"?[142]

> It is a hierarchized polytheism.... Monotheism is so little a Jewish or Semitic idea that the race of Shem can be said to have been repudiated by it, rejected; this is what the declaration of the apostles to the Jews, unyielding in their particularism is expressing: *"Since you spurn the word of God,* of the universal God, *we pass on to the gentiles.* Monotheism is a creation of the Indo-Germanic spirit; it could only have come from there...."

This was the way in which the new racial anthropology, formulated principally in Germany, was employed in a global vision of the world. Even so, Proudhon was toning down his real feelings, for the ones he confided to his *Carnets* were hardly publishable:

> The Jews, unsociable, stubborn, infernal race. First authors of that maleficent superstition called Catholicism, in which the furious intolerant Jewish factor always prevails over the others, Greek, Latin, Barbarian, etc., and has long tortured the human race. ... The influence of the Jewish element in Christianity is thus explained by the character of that nation: a fine subject for history to deal with.

He (like Voltaire) forgot his anti-clericalism when faced with the Jew:

> When Crémieux speaks from the tribune on a question which involves Christianity, directly or indirectly, he is careful to say: *your* faith, which is not mine; your God, your Christ, your Gospel, your brethren in the Lebanon. All Jews do this; they agree with us on all points, in so far as it is to their advantage; but they are always careful to exclude themselves—they sit on the fence! I hate this nation.

After which Proudhon moved on to the question of female pay, which he wanted to reduce: ". . . it is good that the woman should feel the man's superiority and that her feeling of receiving protection and devotion to her weakness and her charms, should be combined with her love." But the Jews held no hidden charms for him: moreover, a few months later he sketched out a program of action, similar to the one carried out in Europe in the second quarter of the twentieth century:[143]

> *Jews.* Make a provision against that race, which poisons everything, by butting in everywhere, without ever merging with any people.—Demand its expulsion from France, except for individuals married to Frenchwomen.—Abolish the synagogues, allow them to enter no employment, finally proceed with the abolition of this religion. Not for nothing have the Christians called them deicides. The Jew is the enemy of mankind. That race must be sent back to Asia or exterminated.

These furies of Proudhon are not adequately explained by Fourier's influence, or his differences with Marx (whom he described as the "tapeworm of socialism"),[144] even less by his theological studies or his rural origins. Perhaps all these had a cumulative effect and perhaps historians who wanted to see this apostle of the middle classes as an *avant la lettre* fascist are not wrong (we are not going to enter this debate). His other hates and fears furnish a guide to a better understanding. He included the foreign invasion in his list of symptoms of France's decadence in *De la justice . . .:*[145]

> While the Jews are taking possession at all points, of banking, credit, interest, reigning over industry and holding property by mortgage, armies of German, Belgian, English, Swiss, Spanish workers are replacing French workmen in industry and already invading the countryside.

He wrote to Pierre Leroux on similar lines: "I want my nation returned to its primitive nature, once and for all free from all exotic belief, from all alienogenic institution. The Greek, Roman, Barbarian, Jew, English have influenced our race quite long enough. . . ."[146]

France for the French? The xenophobe in Proudhon spoke even louder in an unfinished, posthumous work, *France et Rhin*:

French Nationality. Invaded by the English, Germans, Belgians, Jews, etc. The Declaration of the Rights of Man, the liberalism of 1789, 1814, 1830 and 1848 has only benefited foreigners. What does governmental despotism matter to foreigners? They do not belong to the country; they only enter it to exploit it; thus it is in the government's interest to favor foreigners, whose race is imperceptibly driving out our own.

There followed the plan of a work to be written:[147]

A few, strongly emphasized pages on the Jews.—a freemasonry throughout Europe.—A race incapable of forming a State, ungovernable by itself, is wonderfully in agreement about exploiting the others. Its analogues in the Bohemians, the Polish *émigrés*, the Greeks and all who wander.

This work was never to see the light of day: Proudhon seemed to have been obsessed all his life with the idea of writing a book about Jews, either ancient or contemporary, and although he was able to revise his judgments on so many other points, he always remained consistent on the subject of anti-Semitism. We could also take a look at Proudhon the anti-Protestant, who went to the lengths of justifying the repeal of the Edict of Nantes.[148] But it is primarily the fanatical anti-feminist who is worth looking at.

In *De la justice* ... Proudhon attacked the emancipators "who persist in making woman other than what we want her. . . . Man will master and woman will obey. *Dura lex sed lex.*"

The complete human being, adequate to fulfill his destiny, I am talking about physical appearances, is the male, who by his virility attains the highest degree of muscular and nervous tension which his nature and his ambition require, and thereby the maximum results in work and battle. Woman is a diminutive man who is lacking an organ to be able to become anything but an ephebe.

What would happen to civilization if this being, deprived of the *organ*, enjoyed full rights? A castrated world, a world of eunuchs.

> To put [women] on a par with us, the strength and intelligence in us would have to be rendered useless, the progress of science, industry, work halted, mankind prevented from developing its power in a masculine manner, its body and soul mutilated, its destiny belied, nature driven back, all for the greatest glory of that poor little soul of woman who can neither compete with her companion nor follow him.

Further on, to defend masculine privilege, Proudhon referred to the supreme values which justice, virile dignity and chastity were for him:

> Chastity is thus a corollary of justice, the product of male dignity, the principle of which, as has been explained earlier, exists, if it exists at all, in a much weaker degree in women. With animals, it is the female who seeks out the male and signals to him, and it must be admitted that it is no different with woman as nature places her and society secures her. The only difference between her and other females is that she is permanently on heat, sometimes her whole life through. To say she is a *coquette* puts the whole thing in a nutshell. In the fields, in the town, everywhere where little girls and little boys mix together in their games, it is almost always the lust of the former which provokes the coldness of the latter. Which men are most lascivious? Those whose temperaments most closely resemble woman's.

In short, woman is "unproductive by nature, sluggish, without skill or understanding, without justice and without modesty," and she is even "a sort of middle point between him [man] and the rest of the animal kingdom."[149]

Obsession with women, obsession with Jews: everything suggests that the subjection of the one and the expulsion of the other took on a related significance for Proudhon. In fact, this revolutionary behind his own times, this man of violence, can be seen as a precursor of the *authoritarian personality* of the twentieth century. Research in depth into this human type present in our midst has made it possible to establish, to a more or less pronounced degree, connections between anti-Semitism, an exaggerated interest in sexual matters, authoritarian aggressiveness, a conventional mind and certain other characteristics.[150] It also starts a train of thought leading on to J.-P. Sartre's *Portrait d'un antisémite*, where a personality of this type is described with the force and economy of means only found with a great literary talent. But perhaps France is a particularly favorable land for grasping the *homo antisemiticus* in his pure state, precisely because in its very differentiated intellectual climate, men of this stamp stand out more sharply than in other countries, notably Germany. Faced with Jews, their cognitive faculties cease to function normally. Fourier asserted that he was speaking from experience: "I speak with full knowledge, having lived with them for a long time."[151] Proudhon claimed even longer knowledge of them: "H. Heine, Alexandre Weill and others are only secret spies; Rothschild, Crémieux, Marx, Fould, evil, irascible, envious, bitter, etc. beings who hate us."[152] A process of projection (in the psychoanalytical sense) if ever there was one, which shows us a Proudhon whom Proudhon did not know, and in Vigny too, we saw how the "Jew" he carried within himself masked the man he saw before him. But it is a fact that in France in the first half of the nineteenth century, this process was a factor in the formation of political opinion particularly on the part of the social reformers.

eleven

Germany

Arndt, Jahn and the Germanomanes

The phenomenon of the cult of the Germanic race which surged up in Germany at the beginning of the nineteenth century has no analogy in any other country. None of the varieties of European nationalism which were beginning to compete with each other at the time assumed this biologically orientated form. Between 1790 and 1815, with practically no transition, writers moved on from the idea of a specifically German mission to the glorification of the language, and from there to glorification of German blood, within the framework of a particularist "counter-messianism" which formed a counterpart to French universalist messianism. The fact is that the drama of the French Revolution remained as the basis of the twentieth-century German tragedy, everything, or almost everything in the field which concerns us having been said beyond the Rhine over a century before the Hitler movement was born.

On the plane of racist anti-Semitism, the Germanic obsession with purity of blood led to condemnation of the Jews even in the absence of a specific hatred. It produced the German prototype of the patriot who was not subjectively an anti-Semite but who was hostile to Jews because he professed the myth of race. Henceforth, he took his place alongside the prototype of the international anti-Semite whose personal image of the universe was peopled with Jews. The arrival of the new prototype was announced in the writings of the two great apostles of Germano-Christian racism, Ernst Moritz Arndt and Friedrich Ludwig Jahn. It has recently been said that these two agitators "mark the first appearance of the lower middle class in German nationalism."[1] Moreover, neither of them was of pure German stock, since Arndt was a Swedish subject at first, while Jahn, as his name indicates, was of distant Czech extraction.[2] Perhaps this fact speaks volumes about one of the factors in Germanic prophetism; over the generations, its great harbingers have sprung from all points of the European compass.[3] Of the two, Arndt (1768–1860) is still the best known, and it was primarily he whom the Nazis saw as their great ideological precursor. Arndt's texts which they quoted firmly backed up this relationship; all the more remarkable is the comment by one of his post-Hitlerite apologists, who wrote that "his personal evolution reflects the particular path taken by German national sentiment."[4] But the Arndt who interests us here is not the man who dreamed of a Germany encompassing Alsace, Switzerland and the Netherlands, nor even the one who praised the child's aggressive instincts. We are concerned with the Arndt who, according to Baron Stein (whose secretary he was), apparently seemed to belong "to a tribe of American savages and had the nose of a hound to smell out differences of blood."[5] And it was in blood that Arndt imagined that the pre-eminence of the German "people of light" (*Lichtvolk*) was rooted. For this pious Lutheran, they were the only people to possess the genuine divine spark. He wrote:[6]

> I do not think I am mistaken in stating that the powerful and ardent wild stock called German was the good species into which the divine seed could be implanted to produce the most noble fruits. The Germans, and the Latins impregnated and fertilized by them, are the only ones to have made the divine germ flower, thanks to philosophy and theology, and as rulers to animate and guide . . . the surrounding peoples, belonging to foreign species.

But *Teutschkeit,* "German-ness," primarily distinguished by
its simplicity, sense of liberty, and honesty, had to be protected from all foreign contamination, notably from the
French *Welschheit,* which "attacks the most noble seed like
a narcotic poison."⁷ Moreover, throughout his long life,
Arndt never ceased to advocate the battle against a mixture
of bloods, or "degeneration," and to demand watertight com-
partments between peoples, which his Nazi commentators
had great pleasure in demonstrating were much narrower
and divided-off than those of Hitlerite doctrine and legislation. What Arndt did was to identify the human races with
nations and he therefore distinguished between a German,
French, Italian or Russian race, all of which, he announced,
perpetuated themselves in the same way as the different
canine or equine races. To show the ill effects of a mixture of
races, he referred to experiments by English stock-breeders.
Some of the hypotheses of the anthropology of the Enlightenment, rapidly taken to the extreme in the German
climate of the time, seem to be recognizable in all this, but
Arndt himself quoted quite different sources. He thought
that he could rediscover the cult of the purity of blood in the
ancient Germanic tribes that Tacitus described, and as a
Protestant who was well acquainted with the Old Testament,
he also supported his theory by recalling the anger of the
Almighty against "the sons of God who saw that the
daughters of man were beautiful" (Genesis, VI, 1–6). The
Flood, in his eyes, was thus only a just punishment for the first
"degeneration."

Jewish blood seems to have been no worse and no better
than any other foreign blood in Arndt's estimation. Although
he strongly protested against the admission of the Polish
Jews, "that wound and plague," into Germany, his views were
not so far removed from those of the emancipators when he
expressed the hope that the Jews in Germany would rapidly
disappear once they were converted. "Experience shows," he
wrote, "that as soon as they abandon their disconcerting laws
and become Christian, the peculiarities of the Jewish

character and type rapidly grow indistinct and by the second generation, it is difficult to recognize the seed of Abraham."

To the German, the name of Arndt primarily recalls the poet who (together with H. von Kleist, T. Körner and M. von Schenkendorf) called his people to arms, urging them to drive out or massacre the foreign tyrant. But the idea of "impure blood," blood which was required to water the furrows on both sides of the Rhine, in Germany quickly became that of inferior blood. This transition took place all the more easily perhaps in that the Germans had scarcely been aroused to a state of war-like excitement when they were confronted with the realities of peace and the emotion had to be expended entirely in the irresponsible realm of imagination. The fact is that, after 1815, Germanomania insidiously encroached, even invading school textbooks. An example of this is Kohlrausch's *Teutsche Geschichte* which was used in Prussian schools until the end of the nineteenth century. It too referred to Tacitus to glorify the virtues of the German people, "that vessel chosen by God for the preservation of his teaching," and compared their purity with the degeneration of Jews, Greeks and Latins. For men like Kohlrausch, as well as Fichte or Arndt, the Germans were the chosen people of the New Alliance whom Luther had made aware of its mission. But the collective Messiah devoted to the service of mankind, depicted by the preceding generation of theologians, became a proud and triumphant Messiah once embodied in race and blood.[8]

The Romantic writings of the period reflected the idea of the Germans as the chosen people in innumerable ways: poets like Novalis and Hölderlin expressed it in their fashion,[9] while the names of Adam Müller, Görres and his friend Perthes are a reminder that it did not come to a halt at the denominational frontier.[10] With Fichte, it was wrapped up in metaphysics, while Friedrich Ludwig Jahn (1778–1852) gave it a more direct, more brutal form. Furthermore, this apostle of physical culture was able to propagate a folklore and create a popular movement which foreshadowed many aspects of the Nazi paramilitary organizations.

He was a curious character, this *Turnvater Jahn*, the "father of gymnastics." Even his life story and his style suggest the Führer of the Third Reich, despite his relative tolerance of Jews. The son of a pastor, he early on displayed a quick-tempered, unstable personality and an unwillingness to study. Sent down from one university after another, he led a wretched, vagabond existence until the age of twenty-five. Throughout his life, he flaunted a coarseness (consistent in his eyes with German straightforwardness); one story showed him being shocked by a reproduction of the Sistine Madonna, which he considered indecent, and expanding on this theme in barrack-room style. The bizarre apparel he affected and which he described as "old-German costume" was on a par with his other eccentricities.[11] The first book to bring him popular acclaim, the *Deutsches Volkstum* (1810), was inspired by the Prussian disaster of 1806. In it, in a very personal style, stuffed with neologisms of his own invention (like the term *Volkstum* itself), he developed a program for national revival by means of the elimination of all foreign, notably French, influences. To this end, not only the arts and literature, but language as well had to be expurgated. Foreign first names, including those of Biblical origin, had to disappear. Popular entertainments had to be regulated. And for every act of daily life however unofficial, like attendance at church, Germans of both sexes had to wear the *Volkstracht*, the popular costume, as Jahn described it (green for little girls, red for virgins, blue for married women, brown and silver for matrons, and orange and white for prostitutes).[12] Obviously the fight against the foreign menace entailed a barrier against foreign blood, and this, on pain of the extinction of the German people. Indeed,[13]

> hybrid animals have no real capacity for reproduction; similarly, mongrel peoples have no national survival of their own ... he who strives to bring all the noble peoples of the

world into one herd runs the risk of ruling over the most
despicable outcasts of the human race.

This was therefore the same veterinary philosophy as Arndt's
but developed with more vitality. While glorifying the
German race, Jahn did not dispute the merits of other
peoples, provided they were free from all mixture. What was
an abomination in his eyes was the "sin against the blood,"
copulation contrary to nature, and its traces were not erased
down to the thousandth generation. On this subject, his style
reached untranslatable heights of Germanomane invective.[14]
This pastor's son prophesied that God drew away his hand
from "crossbred peoples" and he did not fail to cite Moses
and Nehemiah. That was why he advocated that Germans
who married foreigners should forfeit their civic rights.
No specific animosity towards the Jews can be discerned but
he obviously forbade his compatriots to marry "Rachels."[15]
In another context, the only authentically pure and noble
peoples that Jahn recognized were the ancient Greeks, and
the Germans who had taken their place. These were
the two holy peoples of the earth, and the Germans
were the sole heirs to the spirit of "original Christianity."[16]
Jahn's views on questions of international politics were all as
expeditious. "Frontiers or natural divisions exist and they can
be discovered by a rapid glance at a geographical map of
Europe"; monster-states like Portugal, which (the metaphor
was borrowed from Arndt) was a cancer on the body of
Spain, had to be abolished.[17] Jahn may not be the only
European of his time to praise the advantages of war, but
he found particularly forceful formulae for it. Elected to the
German parliament in 1848 when he was an old man, he
wrote: "What I do know is that a long period of peace gives
birth to internal discords and quarrels which undermine our
national strength. What we lack is the iron yoke of war, the
steel antidote of weapons," and he described his contemporaries as "vermin engendered by a long peace, a species born
of a totally rotten situation."[18] To complete the picture,

there was his concern for animals which we will also find in other famous Germanomanes; Jahn even called for police protection for cockchafers.[19]

This was Jahn the writer, whom nineteenth-century Germany, from Gervinus to von Treitschke, spoke of with irony or embarrassment[20] and whose madly prophetic stature would be discovered in our time. The man of action was revealed in 1813–14, when he created a commando unit (the *Lützower Freikorps*) to attack the French. True, he proved a deplorable soldier, only agreeing, it seems, to fight the enemy in hand to hand combat with an axe. But, with the figure of a Hercules, he was a good trainer of men, and once peace was restored, these qualities enabled him to propagate the cult of gymnastics throughout the country (*Turnen,* the word which describes gymnastics in Germany, is one of the neologisms he invented). As he understood it, physical culture should contribute to the moral improvement of the Germans; it should, in the words of one of his disciples, permit "a gradual elevation of the people towards the highest destiny of man, as a result of the development of all the faculties of body and soul that God has given to it."[21] In actual fact, the gymnastic societies, which claimed nearly six thousand adherents in 1818,[22] became political conventicles, led by Germanomane anti-establishment students, and served as nuclei for the new student guilds (*Burschenschaften*). Jahn, who had become a national hero at the end of the war, exercised a curious hold over this world, "an agonizing power," in the words of a contemporary.[23] He also liked to train his followers in tremendous forced marches, on the lines of the future *Wandervögel* ("migratory birds"). Jews were not excluded from them; at the time of the epic of the "Lützow-commando unit," a Jew named Simoni even served as Jahn's orderly.[24] But the atmosphere could not have been particularly favorable to them. Wolfgang Menzel, a gymnast who later became a famous literary critic, described a typical incident in this context. During a particularly hard expedition under a torrid

July sun, most of the marchers had given up and no more than ten or so were left. One of them

> a tall but somewhat frail Berlin Jew held back at a milestone and could move no further. Jahn furiously bore down on him, threatened to kill him with an axe, and made such an unnecessary row that I could stand it no longer. Now he turned on me, but I held my ground and declared that I would take charge of the very womanish and pitifully whining Jew although I did not have a farthing. . . .

(Each marcher actually had to hand over his money to the treasurer of the band.) Menzel therefore stayed with his protégé, however pitiful he might have thought him. An hour later, they set out on the march again and were pleasantly surprised to see the gymnasts lined up at a corner of the road; "the old Jahn in front, who received me with words of praise and, in his honorable way, made full amends, for he was always regretful when he went too far in the heat of the moment."[25]

Throughout the episode, there is an atmosphere of the male solidarity of the gymnasts, of masculine fraternities or so-called élite troops, grouped behind a well-loved leader. Another of Jahn's disciples who also achieved notoriety later, the historian Heinrich Leo, spoke of the pleasure of inflicting physical pain on himself: "The sight of my own new scars has something exalting about it for me, when I see beads of blood form on my flesh. . . . There is nothing more beautiful than a new triangular scar."[26] Other gymnasts set themselves other ascetic exercises.[27] But the leader himself, an obdurate brawler, seems to have preferred inflicting physical pain on others.

He was a disturbing character, this *Turnvater*. Von Treitschke wrote that he wanted to drive the enemy out of Germany with a heave of the stomach.[28] But in the event, the farce came over a century before the grand tragedy; or to quote Heine: ". . . little puppies that run around in the empty arena, barking and snarling at one another until the hour shall arrive when the gladiators appear."[29] The chief puppy is still in many respects a difficult person to classify. Is this because his life story and his historical role were not studied seriously at the time and it was not until the advent of national socialism that his significance burst out into the open? Shortly before Hitler came to power, a German historian wrote of Jahn in a university review: "In our conception today of the problem of the leader, scientifically and as a matter of experience, that is precisely what we would expect."[30] Ten years after the Führer's defeat, an educationalist attempted to defend the *Turnvater* in the East German schoolmasters' journal.[31] It cannot be denied that Jahn had a sort of genius. The inventions and folkloric terms he endowed his country with are innumerable. The gymnasts rallying cry, *Gut Heil!*, which foreshadowed the Hitlerite *Sieg Heil!*, for example. Another of his inventions was the red-black-gold colors of the Lützow commandos, which he claimed were "old-German." They were adopted by the 1848 parliament (the "Frankfurt Parliament") and have finally become the national colors of both West and East Germany.

This was the man who was the idol of the "gymnasts" and the Germanomane students, the most vital elements of a youth which, after 1815, dreamt of the unification of the homeland and waxed enthusiastic over the magic words "liberty" and "revolution." The universities, particularly those with Protestant allegiances, were the principal centers of political agitation in Germany. But paradoxically the program of these early German revolutionaries was already reactionary. They were aggressive and chauvinistic. They drew their inspiration from an imaginary past. An allegedly Germanic purity and chastity took the place of a moral ideal for them. Commenting on this "gloomy enigma" at the time, Görres noted that the revolution had already been carried out in Germany, and that it had been carried out "from above":[32]

In Germany it was not the Third Estate that made the revolution but governments under the protection of a foreign power [Napoleon's] . . . . With us it is the supporters of a despotism who use Jacobin forms and practices, whereas some of the friends of freedom defend the principles of the French reactionaries. That is the confusion which presents the foreign observer with a puzzling problem. . . .

It was indeed an enigma. People like Jahn considered themselves liberals persecuted by a reactionary government, but liberals who entered German history in this capacity; ideologists of popular sovereignty like Rottek (1775–1840) or Dahlmann (1785–1860) were scarcely less exclusive than he on the subject of the Jews.[33] Karl von Rottek particularly, who opposed the granting of political rights to Jews, left them with the memory of a bitter enemy.[34]

The German liberals were notably aiming at restoring university morals. Arndt and Jahn, each in his own way, had formulated programs for reorganizing student associations with this end in view, and the new *Burschenschaften* were trying to put them into practice. Arndt's program was not only more radical; it was also more exclusive, since it barred Jews from entry into the guilds. This question gave rise to great discussion in the various *Burschenschaften*. According to von Treitschke, their members "thought they were a new Christian knighthood and in this respect showed an intolerance towards the Jews reminiscent of the time of the Crusades." In the end, it was agreed that each *Burschenschaft* would decide its own policy. It is curious to note that it was the most active and radical guilds which coupled their dreams of direct action with an emphasis on the importance of religious life and practices and a refusal to accept Jews as members. The Giessen *Burschenschaft*, under the influence of the "German Robespierre," Karl Follen, was a case in point.

It was easier to get unanimity on the subject of anti-French feeling. The first statutes of the Jena *Burschenschaft*, regarded as the mother of the new guilds, stipulated that these "eternal enemies of the German name" would never be able to regain admission to its ranks. These statutes said nothing about Jews. The Kantian philosopher J. F. Fries, who came to Jena to teach in 1814, preceded by a solid reputation as a Jew-baiter—"all Jewry is shaking," wrote Goethe, "for its most ferocious enemy has just settled in Thuringia"—succeeded in procuring a corresponding revision of the statutes.[35]

Jahn and Fries were the moving spirits behind the famous Wartburg festival in October 1817, intended to commemorate both the tricentenary of the Reformation ("internal liberation") and the tenth anniversary of the battle of Leipzig (political liberation of the Germans). On this occasion, delegations from fourteen mainly Protestant universities converged on Jena to found the *Allgemeine deutsche Burschenschaft*. After a solemn procession, followed by a divine service, a group of Jahn's followers organized an *auto da fé* of books or objects regarded as anti-German and reactionary: administrative statutes lay side by side at the stake with a corporal's baton; the queue of a wig with Saul Ascher's *Germanomanie*—which may throw some light on the nature of these early German libertarian aspirations.[36] "They probably burned my *Germanomanie*," wrote Ascher, "because I said in it that all men are made the same way as Germans, and that Christianity is not a German religion."[37] This comment by an otherwise mediocre author foreshadowed the debunking function which so many of his famous co-religionists beyond the Rhine would later perform.

Jahn had become the main center of student political agitation at that time but the spirit which had prevailed at the Wartburg *auto da fé* was cultivated by active minorities at all the universities. A Heidelberg student, the future theologian Richard Rothe, described this state of mind in 1818, in a letter to his father, which is all the more remarkable in that its author was only nineteen years old:[38]

The people in Jena want a Christian-German *Burschenschaft*

but we had always wanted till then a general one in the strictest sense of the word and we therefore decided to give entry to Jews and foreigners as to anyone else if they had acquired academic rights through matriculation. Thereupon the *Germans* —there were about twenty of them—flew into a terrible rage. . . . Since then they form a sect in the *Burschenschaft* and at general meetings are mainly distinguished by forming a perpetual opposition and are of a different opinion from the rest of the *Burschenschaft*. They keep strictly together and have a way of their own. They are great gymnasts, that one must grant them, go in for dueling, rarely laugh (and in that they are like the Trappists), go around in German coats with downcast glances and in semi-mourning (for Germany's distress) like souls in torment. . . . They are not too keen on their studies and act as if they have found the philosopher's stone, and meditate on how they will one day (perhaps even today?) become Germany's saviors and redeemers.

It brings to mind Heine's student of Göttingen crying out in a tavern "that the torture of Conradin of Hohenstaufen must be avenged in the blood of the French." This was the way in which the early active minorities advocating racist pan-Germanism made their presence felt at the German universities. In 1819, the assassination of the writer Kotzebue by a student, Sand, was met by repressive measures and their agitation was restricted. Arndt was deprived of his professorial chair; Jahn was accused of high treason and imprisoned in a fortress. Their ideas only gained more ground. The discussion on the concept of the purity of the German race was resumed in the *Burschenschaften* in the second half of the century, and after 1918, almost all of them were excluding "non-Aryans" from membership. Even German professors, Max Weber noted in 1919, henceforth told their Jewish students: *lasciate ogni speranza.*[39]

The detour of economic anti-Semitism

We have seen that the emancipation of the Jews in the

German States was incomplete. In some lands, their situation was almost unchanged. In the Kingdom of Saxony, for example, where their numbers were far too small for the government to bother to legislate on their behalf, they remained governed by the old feudal laws until 1848. Elsewhere, the rights granted in 1800–15 were challenged: Prussia after King Frederick William IV came to the throne in 1840, was the most remarkable example of this.

Frederick William had taken part in the "war of liberation" as a young man and he held fast to the romantic and Germano-Christian ideals of his generation. Friedrich Carl von Savigny, the famous legal historian who was entrusted with his political education, could only have strengthened his convictions; he had after all, and as early as 1815, compared the Jews to Roman *peregrini* and demanded the restoration of the special regulations governing them.[40] (The thinkers of the German historical school stood high amongst the partisans of a return of the ghetto. Heine mistrusted the members of this school as "gendarmes and police".)[41] Drawing his inspiration from ideas of this sort, Frederick William IV marked his joyful accession to the throne by, *inter alia,* bestowing the Iron Cross on Jahn and restoring Arndt, now an old man, to his university chair. On the other hand, he wanted to institute a régime for the Jews to correspond with their so-called supernatural destiny. He therefore decided to exempt them from military service, to keep them definitively out of public office and to form them into a "separate nation" under his special protection. In this way, he thought he was "obeying the decrees from on high and proving to the Jews the benevolence of which they are the object."[42] But the Jewish communities implored the king to exercise his benevolence in some other way, and the protestations of patriotism[43] ("We would no longer be true Prussians if we were exempted from serving in the army") helped to make him abandon this utopian project.

This shows the precarious state of emancipation in Germany, where measures excluding the Jews from positions of influence and authority were always maintained. As a result, the Children of Israel were channeled even further into the occupations to which their past predisposed them, and the new promises of the Industrial Revolution led them. Trade, finance and the liberal professions—these were the realms in which they exercised their talents.

To what extent did they contribute to Germany's economic rise? The very fact of emancipation makes it difficult to answer this, since administrative documents relating to the activities of the ex-"Jewish nation" in the nineteenth century are not available. Historians today are doing their best to clarify the question (the disappearance of the Jews has stimulated research of this type in Germany). They quote disparate facts and suggest names: in this way, for example, it emerges that thirty of the fifty-two banking firms which existed in Berlin in 1807 belonged to Jews.[44] What also emerges is that Jewish bankers, led by the omnipresent Rothschilds, were the principal promoters of public credit, at the time when the practice of state loans was becoming general, and that other sons of the ghetto were the moving spirits behind branches of new activities such as railroad building or the German textile industry (one of them, Liebermann, could boast to Frederick William that he had "expelled the English from the Continent"). Later their spirit of initiative worked wonders in the non-ferrous metals trade, the creation of an electrical industry and in establishing big stores, nearly eighty percent of which remained a Jewish monopoly in Germany until 1933. The exploitation of the mining basin of Upper Silesia was also to a major extent due to Jewish entrepreneurs. On the other hand, the Ruhr industrial empire with its dependencies in the Saar, was built solely by Christian ironmasters, and this would also seem to be the case with the chemical industry—although this was still a typically "new" branch of activity. It would be as easy to multiply examples of such disparities, as it would be difficult to suggest a coherent explanation for them. Moreover, these facts only have a marginal interest as far as our subject is concerned. In any case, they are a reminder that in a liberal and capitalist régime (which its main critics described as "Jewish" at the time), the religion of the economic operator loses its significance and that although certain past specializations may continue to exist, new specializations seem to take place at random. Added to this is the trend towards concentration and the rise of joint stock companies with their interwoven interests, so that in the long run it becomes impossible to distinguish between "Jewish" and "Christian" business.

But at the dawn of the Industrial Revolution, extra-economic factors were making the economic role of the Jews in Germany as elsewhere, and perhaps more than elsewhere, appear more important than it was. For example, there was their rush to the large towns and their concentration in the wealthy residential district within these towns, where they showed a certain propensity for displaying the external symbols of their success, like individual mansions and horse-drawn carriages. The continued existence of the old occupations of shopkeeper, pedlar and money-lender had the same effect, and the new professions of advocate or notary, doctor or pharmacist also multiplied the valuable services Jews were rendering Christians. In addition, Jews were still numerous in the villages in the nineteenth century, notably in Bavaria and Württemburg, where they acted as intermediaries between countryside and town, many-tentacled and mysterious, easily personifying domination.[45]

All these factors contributed to strengthen the impression of a Jewish invasion or annexation, an impression which rested on less fragile foundations in Germany than in the other Western countries. Some statistical data are available on this subject for the beginning of the twentieth century, which reflect the end of the development process and can therefore be used to determine ideas about its beginning. What notably emerges from these data (collected by Werner Sombart)[46] is that in 1900, Jews, comprising nearly one percent of the German population, supplied twenty-five percent of members of boards of directors and fourteen percent of the holders of positions as managing directors in industrial and financial enterprises. It can be supposed that some of these captains of industry might have preferred to satisfy their ambitions in offices which were closed to them within the general staff and diplomatic corps for example, or in the high administration.[47] Their relegation to the economic sphere contributed in its turn to strengthen the impression that they had climbed to their positions as "Jews" and not as "managers" or "bankers." As for the body of Jews as a whole, tables drawn up by Sombart show that they were on an average six or seven times richer than their compatriots, in other words they held six to seven percent of the nation's wealth in their hands.

These were the sources, half-real, half-imaginary, of economic anti-Semitism, a phenomenon which, if it deserves its name, only deserves it in modern times to the extent that Jews were better than non-Jews in the roles of financiers and entrepreneurs or in the practice of the so-called liberal professions. Taking Europe as a whole, such superiority was particularly pronounced at the beginning of industrialization at the time of the "capitalist take-off" which coincided with Jewish emancipation. The traditional jealousies of the Christian guilds were then aroused by the liberation of the men of the ghetto, whose competition became even more redoubtable to them. There is no doubt that their conniving lay behind many an anti-Semitic campaign and that many a pamphlet was manufactured to order; but intrigues and provocations of this type, plotted in secret, are difficult to trace. However, the anti-Jewish disturbances of 1819, which were followed by police investigations, reveal bourgeois agitation, against the background of the crisis which struck the nascent German industries after peace was restored. For example, it appears that employers bought drinks for workmen and apprentices and incited them against the Jews; innkeepers were even said to have distributed weapons; at Würzburg, where the disturbances began, provocation was so obvious that the government threatened to suppress the guilds.[48]

Similar occurrences are found in Russia, a century later. The Soviet economist and statesman, M. I. Kalinin, has described them:[49]

> A Jewish family, barely emerged from the ghetto, naturally becomes better fitted for the struggle for existence than the cultured Russian families, who have obtained rights not by open competition but as a sort of birthright. It is the same for the merchants. Before being able to embark on the high road of capitalist exploitation, the Jew has had to pass through the hard school of the struggle for existence. The only ones who could leave the ghetto, where thousands of small merchants and craftsmen heatedly competed for custom amongst themselves, were Jews who had evinced specific talents for making money by means of utilizing surrounding conditions honestly or dishonestly. It is obvious that these Jews outstripped by a whole head the Russian merchants who had not been educated in such a hard school. This is why in the eyes of Russian merchants and members of the liberal professions, in the eyes of the bourgeoisie in general, the Jews were regarded as terribly dangerous competitors.

This was therefore, as we have said, a general phenomenon in Europe, but one which became particularly pronounced at a given stage in socio-economic development. It is also important to note that in practice Christian merchants had everything to gain by the disappearance of the Jews, while the mass of the people could only lose by it. Remember what Charles Fourier wrote:[50]

> ... the people exclaim in admiration: "Long live competition! long live the Jews, philosophy and fraternity! the price of all goods has fallen since Iscariot arrived"; and the public says to the rival firms: "It is you, gentlemen, who are the real Jews!"

But these were very gullible people. Let us therefore look more closely at the idea of "economic anti-Semitism"—that "socialism of imbeciles" as it has often been called, which in its most common meaning encompasses the covetousness and blind fury of the Christian people as a whole.

Whatever the meaning, and whether it be "rational" (as with merchants) or "irrational" (as with customers), economic anti-Semitism remains rooted in theology and only continues to exist by virtue of it, since without the theology, propertied Jews would only have been money-grubbers like any other money-grubber. "Where there are no Jews, Christians judaize far worse . . ." Bernard de Clairvaux was already pointing out.[51] What is true in the distant past seems to be reproduced along the generations like a compulsive repetition. Historically, the Jew's theological function preceded and determined his economic specialization, and it is the composite image resulting from these two functions which continued to single him out as a Jew within the new bourgeois society. It is the first function which is relevant in relation to anti-Semitism. And it is infinitely Protean. We have seen, and will see again, how it could be wrapped up and masked, as in the West the Jew, whatever his own personal belief, served as evidence against contradictory beliefs which reared their heads. That is why a history of anti-Semitism is first and foremost a theological history, however entangled it may be with economic history.

For example, it would be impossible to isolate the Frenchmen's resentment of the Rothschild hegemony from the emotion aroused by the Damascus ritual murder affair; but this is the type of passion which has from generation to generation caused the banker Jews to be discerned in the Jewish bankers. This eternal interaction, or this ancient lineage, can be traced even better in modern Germany. In fact, the Jews, while continuing to figure prominently as formidable business competitors in the new bourgeois and chauvinistic world, became the appointed enemies of the convictions this world professed and which it raised to the rank of supreme values. They became so, in an even more expressive manner than formerly—some as ideologists, others (more numerous) merely by their presence, and without really understanding how. It was primarily in this capacity of appointed enemies that they exercised a strong influence on Germanic destiny, which brings us back to the core of our own subject.

Börne and Heine: young Germany or young Palestine?

A now forgotten champion of the people, Ludwig Börne, born Loeb Baruch, would probably have entered history as the Mazzini of Germany if the republican and revolutionary mystique had caught on more there. During his lifetime, he was the acknowledged philosophical leader in liberal circles: he was the "Börne oak" to Friedrich Engels, "a morsel of world history" to Heinrich Laube. Later, only the Swiss Jakob Burckhardt and Gottfried Keller cultivated his memory.

Born in the Frankfurt ghetto in 1785, this brilliant pamphleteer was the son of an already liberated court Jew who, in his old age, "was happy to read what his son wrote, but would rather it had not been written by his son."[52] He had the advantage of a philosophical education, attended Henriette Herz's salon in Berlin, followed Schleiermacher's courses and fell in love with Germany. Nevertheless, at the time of the Great Sanhedrin, he made Napoleon his idol, comparing him to Moses and Christ.[53] Later, however, he changed his tune and shared the patriotic ardor of "the war of liberation." But he never lost his love for a France which had liberated the Children of Israel. He praised the spirit and talents of his ex-co-religionists, and was delighted with their rapid infatuation with Western ideas and fashions.[54] Judaism to him was nothing but an "Egyptian mummy which only looks as if it is alive, but whose corpse refuses to decay."[55] In other words, the only future he saw for his brethren was within a regenerated, free and fraternal Germany. Men like Arndt or Jahn were also dreaming of a

Germany like this, but they had a different conception of it. A patriot like Börne could only serve a party which did not challenge his role as a patriot and a German, and if this did not exist, found another party. In this way a dialectic peculiar to German history entered the scene and Friedrich Schlegel was right when he predicted that the anti-emancipating campaigns would end up by dividing Germany into two opposing factions.[56]

At the time when this division was taking shape, Börne was candidly stating his conviction that he was a better German patriot than the rest, precisely because he had been born in the ghetto. As early as 1808, he noted: "I am glad I am Jewish: this makes me a citizen of the world, and I do not have to be ashamed of being German."[57] To Germans who found such an aphorism profoundly irritating, he later replied that they were only slaves: "Is not Germany the ghetto of Europe? Do not all Germans wear a yellow ribbon on their hats? You will become free *with* us or you will *not* become free."[58] And he expounded the "divine grace" of being Jewish, explaining it as follows:[59]

... I can appreciate the undeserved good fortune of being a German and a Jew at the same time, to strive for all the virtues of the Germans and yet not share in any of their defects. Yes, because I was born a slave I love freedom more than you. Yes, because I have come to know slavery I understand freedom better than you. Yes, because I was born without a country, I desire a fatherland more ardently than you.

This whole-hearted follower of the Enlightenment therefore made no distinction between the liberation of the Germans and the emancipation of the Jews. Again on this subject, he wrote:[60]

In order to help them, their cause must be brought into harmony with justice and the claims of universal freedom. They must be spoken of as opportunity offers, unexpectedly, so that the uninvolved reader is forced to occupy himself with them;

because he finds them on his path. I also think it would in this
way be easier to defend the Jews.

Börne did in fact refer to the Jews in every context, if not out
of context—claiming their "right to hate,"[61] after a performance of *The Merchant of Venice* in Frankfurt; noting the
fatal conjunction of Judeophobia and Francophobia at the
time of the 1819 disturbances; rejoicing at seeing the European balance preserved as a result of the efforts of Jewry in
1868;[62] criticizing the Germans for wanting "as in an opera,
a chorus singing in unison, wearing the same uniform; they
only wanted Germans straight from the forests of Tacitus;
with red hair and light blue eyes. The swarthy Jews stood
out displeasingly. . . ."[63]

This sort of apologetics could only stir up Germanomane
furies to white heat, and obviously the first argument that
Börne's adversaries employed was to counterattack the Jew.
As he himself noted, "as soon as my enemies felt that they
were sinking before Börne, they found an anchor in
Baruch."[64] The critic Wolfgang Menzel, who was his ally at
first, reproached him "for writing in French," and for doing
so because he could not forget the humiliations that he had
suffered in the role of a Jew.[65] Another critic spoke "of the
numerous and unpleasant failings of this Asiatic, which cannot disappear with baptism."[66] He was criticized for hating
Germany and for having hatred in his blood. Karl von Sim-
rock, the translator of the *Niebelungen,* used himself as an
example to give weight to this criticism: "When I look at
myself, I see clearly that if I had not been expressly enjoined
to love all men fraternally, I would have had to hate your
people." From this he concluded that this people, propelled
by its tribal spirit, could only hate the Germans.[67] Shortly
after Börne's death, the "Young Hegelian" *Hallische Jahrbücher* described him as the "Ham of the German people";
"as a true fanatical Jew, he only knows hatred, his mind is
nothing but a joke."[68] As Börne saw it, "they are all
bewitched by this Jewish magic circle, no one can get

out."[69] This circle made the name Baruch-Börne a symbol and probably enlarged it to more than life-size.

This function as a symbol, or more exactly as an anti-symbol, is even more pronounced in the case of his great rival Heinrich Heine. Perhaps no man has so accurately perceived and expressed the impasses and hazards of emancipation. When Heine wrote that he "had found his marching orders for life in his cradle," he summed up in a striking formula the factors which led Börne and himself to serve in the same party and attack the same injustices. Otherwise, the two men formed a contrast between the passionate convictions of the champion of the people and the poet's ironic genius and soul-searching. Heine has often been criticized for taking nothing and no one seriously. On closer inspection, his personal letters show that he made an exception for the old-style patriarchal Jew. He accused his own generation of "not having the strength to wear a beard, fast, hate and endure hatred" like its ancestors of the ghetto,[70] as if he were fascinated by these grandiose parental images. The frequency of this theme in his letters and also in his writings, suggests a conscience tortured by a "betrayal complex" particularly after his baptism. Heine did not spare his peers ("deserters from the old guard of Jehovah"), starting with himself—did he not exclaim on the morrow of his conversion, that henceforth he was abominated by both Jew and Christian alike? But he exercised his gifts of prophetic sarcasm primarily at the expense of Germans who were born baptized. Although as a Jew he could only bear a deep-seated hatred towards the followers of the cult of the Germanic race, he differed from men like Börne or Ascher in his ability to see clearly and far ahead, in his presentiment of the tragic outcome of this cult and in foreseeing singularly acutely the turn twentieth-century history would take. He did so in his poems—where the satire often becomes scurrilous: for example, when a goddess at the end of *Wintermärchen* makes him inhale the odors of the German future, and he swoons in the cesspool,[71] or in his essays where he draws in the contours of this future more precisely:[72]

> Christianity—and this is its fairest service—has to a certain degree moderated that brutal lust of battle, such as we find it among the ancient Germanic races, who fought, not to destroy, nor yet to conquer, but merely from a fierce, demoniac love of battle itself; but it could not altogether eradicate it. And when once that restraining talisman, the cross, is broken, then the smoldering ferocity of those ancient warriors will again blaze up; then will again be heard the deadly clang of that frantic Berserker wrath, of which the Norse poets say and sing so much. The talisman is rotten with decay, and the day will surely come when it will crumble and fall. Then the ancient stone gods will arise out of the ashes of dismantled ruins, and rub the dust of a thousand years from their eyes; and finally Thor, with his colossal hammer, will leap up, and with it shatter into fragments the Gothic Cathedrals.
>
> And when ye hear the rumbling and the crumbling, take heed, ye neighbors of France, and meddle not with what we do in Germany. It might bring harm on you. Take heed not to kindle the fire; take heed not to quench it. Ye might easily burn your fingers in the flame. Smile not at my advice as the counsel of a visionary, warning you against Kantians, Fichteans, and natural philosophers. Scoff not at the dreamer who expects in the material world a revolution similar to that which has already taken place in the domains of thought. The thought goes before the deed, as the lightning precedes the thunder. German thunder is certainly German, and is rather ungainly, and it comes rolling along tardily; but come it surely will, and when ye once hear a crash the like of which in the world's history was never heard before, then know that the German thunderbolt has reached its mark. At this crash the eagles will fall dead in mid-air, and the lions in Africa's most distant deserts will cower and sneak into their royal dens. A drama will be enacted in Germany in comparison with which the French Revolution will appear a harmless idyll. To be sure, matters are at present rather quiet, and if occasionally Germans here and there rant and gesticulate somewhat violently, do not believe that these are the real actors. These are only little puppies,

that run around in the empty arena, barking and snarling at one another, until the hour shall arrive when the gladiators appear who are to battle unto death.

This warning was addressed to the French. It had been written in Paris, where Heine had settled and where, to the indignation of the Germanomane party, he did his best to work for a Franco-German reconciliation. But his talents as a Cassandra were not only exercised in connection with the national socialist episode: he predicted the Communist epic, as the outcome of a world war, and the establishment of the Stalinist church several years before the publication of the Communist Manifesto.[73] He also expressed the hope that his grandchildren would be born into the world with very thick skins.

Heine's clairvoyance, which can still give subtle intellectual pleasure today, could only exasperate the greater number of his compatriots, to the point where a genuine "Heine case" grew up as the years went by, a thorn in the side of Wilhelmian Germany. But it was impossible to leave the poet of the *Lorelei* out of national history; as that Germany was apt to do with Börne. At least the German cities agreed not to erect a monument to this Jew, this ingrate, who "never stopped spitting on his homeland" (von Treitschke).[74] Particularly determined opposition came from Düsseldorf, Heine's birthplace. When his centenary was approaching, Elizabeth of Austria, who was an admirer of his, wanted to make the erection of a monument compulsory and the debate turned into a minor *affaire d'état*.[75] In the end, the Empress had to resign herself to erecting the statue, which she had ordered and which found no takers, in the garden of her palace on the island of Corfu, whence it was later banished by William II. In 1906, an influential literary critic, Adolf Bartels, published an indictment of the poet's misconduct under the title of *Heinrich Heine: auch ein Denkmal*[76] which already criticized his lyrical style in the light of his Jewish blood. Finally, in 1913, the town of

Frankfurt found its own way of ending the debate by erecting a group to Heine's *muse*, as the man was declared unworthy of public homage. But the debate is not closed, and Heine is still a controversial poet in Germany today.[77] The flames of these civic passions found additional fuel in the writings of militant Jews. As early as 1878, von Treitschke, who popularized the formula "the Jews are our misfortune." was criticizing the historian Graetz for having glorified Börne and Heine, who "like kings" acted as mentors to the "German Michael," rousing him from his sleep. Nothing could be more indicative than Graetz's embarrassed reply, explaining that the incriminating passage dated from 1868, when it was still legal, even customary, to call the Germans "Michael"; "the glorious victories as well as the unification and the restoration of Germany, due to inspired leadership, took place later."[78] After 1870–1, it had become even more difficult to be a Jew in Germany.

Heine and Börne have entered German literary history as the two leaders of the "Young Germany" movement. The other members of this group—Gutzkow, Laube, Wienbarg, Mundt—were authors whose revolt was primarily directed against the moral and domestic structure, and whose work notably advocated "the emancipation of the flesh." Almost all of them had been influenced by Rahel Varnhagen-Levin —Mundt even described this Jewess as the "mother of Young Germany."[79] All these emancipators were enveloped in the same condemnation. The Germanomane critic, Wolfgang Menzel, who denounced their movement to the authorities, called it "Young Palestine," a "Jewish republic of vice of the new firm Heine and Co."[80] The censorship decree, which imposed an interdiction on these writers in 1835, put their allegedly Israelite blood on the list of charges against Gutzkow, Wienbarg and Mundt[81]—which shows once again the significance the Jewishness of Heine and Börne assumed in these German politico-literary conflicts.

Karl Gutzkow, the most important author of the "Young Germany" movement, wrote that they had a resounding success with youth, and yet they did not please, "they occupied the mind and did not win hearts, but it needed two Jews to overthrow the old ideology and shake all illusions."[82] He also noted that "Christians' repulsion for Jews was a physical and moral idiosyncrasy as hard to fight as the repugnance some people have for blood or insects."[83] But Gutzkow, an erstwhile *Burschenschaftler*, could have cited himself as an example. After he had become a rebel, did he not write that the "eternal Jew" had been guilty of crimes against mankind far worse than the one for which he was wrongly blamed? These consisted of particularist egoism, "nihilist materialism" and literary mercantilism. The term "ferments of decomposition" was already flowing from his pen. This emancipator again blamed the Jews "for believing that the sun, the moon and the stars, everything, only moves and only turns for emancipation; Goethe, Schiller, Herder, Hegel should be judged solely by what they thought on the subject of emancipation."[84]

Heinrich Laube was at first more benevolent. In his main work, *La Jeune Europe*, the Jew Joel fought for universal freedom but found it unrewarding. Although he had "repudiated the Jew in himself," Christians continued to repudiate it, so that he decided to "become a Jew again" and even to become a pedlar.[85] But later, Laube, whom Meyerbeer had accused of plagiarism, also came to the conclusion that the Jews were "of a completely different eastern nation," whose "deepest maxims of existence are flagrantly repugnant to us."[86] Here, he was probably expressing the common conviction of the contemporary German republic of letters. As the present-day German sociologist, H. P. Bahrdt, writes, "for the literarily cultured public, the ideas of 'Jew' and 'Jewry' had ceased to designate concrete social figures; they were generally used only symbolically."[87] Gutzkow's "eternal Jew" could not be a better illustration of the statement. It is interesting to note in this context that, unlike the theme of the Jew in English or French literature, the Jew in nineteenth-century German literature has never tempted an academic in search of a subject for a thesis,[88] surely because the results of the research would be both distressing and monotonous. Only authors whose names have been swallowed up in oblivion would emerge as favorably disposed towards the Jews. The research might also cover so-called low-brow literature, which does not figure in textbooks of literary history, but is a better reflection of public taste than the rest. In this domain, the Jews in Stieber's *Secrets of Berlin* vied in villainy with those in Bass's *Mysteries of Berlin*,[89] and if Karl Spindler's romantic *Jew* (1828) still corresponded to the prototype of *Ivanhoe, The Pious Jew* (1844) by his collaborator, Wilhelm von Chézy, is already an Elder of Zion, working for emancipation as a better means of enslaving the German people.[90]

As far as better-quality authors were concerned, they seemed to have shot their bolt after the emancipation of the Jews. Men like Jean-Paul Richter may have tried to learn rabbinical wisdom and regretted that they did not know Hebrew,[91] but Ludwig Tieck declared in 1835 that the Jews "are a foreign element in the State; in German letters, where they have been dominant since Rahel, Heine and Börne, their influence has been more harmful than beneficial."[92] The following year, Karl Immermann, who was one of the first to admire Heine's lyrical genius, published his novel *Die Epigonen* which devoted several chapters to the new generation of Jews. It began with a surprise for the readers: the character he introduced "wears a jacket with an open collar, as prescribed by Jahn; long blond curls fall from his head; beautiful blue eyes shine in his frank and open face." This sympathetic individual presented himself as a victim of reactionary persecution, a survivor from Metternich's prisons. But a few pages further on, we learn that the self-styled freedom fighter is only a highway robber, a Jew disguised as a German: the frank countenance is only a mask, the blond hair—a wig![93] Immermann then gave numerous descriptions of the customs and costumes of the "Egyptian knighthood," as he styled the Jews, and came to the following conclusion: "The Jew remains Jewish and the Christian must be specially on his guard particularly when he seems pleasant. They are all freed slaves, humble and crawling when they want to get something, haughty when they have obtained it."[94]

But many German Jews were hardly less severe on themselves, and leading figures sometimes evinced astonishing changes of front. Ferdinand Lassalle (1825–64), born of a still orthodox family, was an example of this. An adolescent at the time of the Damascus affair, he dreamt of becoming the avenging messiah of the Jews:

> Faint-hearted people, you deserve your fate! The worm wriggles when it is crushed under foot but you, you flatten yourself still further! You do not know how to die, to destroy, you do not know the meaning of righteous revenge, you cannot die with the enemy, tear him to shreds while dying! You were born for slavery!

Shortly afterwards, he voiced his hope of seeing the hour of vengeance near at hand, and declared his thirst for Christian blood. He was not slow to change his ambitions and opinions, and when his restless life made him the messiah of the German working classes, his fury seemed to turn solely against his brethren: "I do not like the Jews at all, I even detest them generally."[95] Karl Marx, who detested them even more, nonetheless dubbed him a "Jewish Negro" and even wrote to Engels that Lassalle was the curious product of cross-breeding between Blacks, Jews and Germans.[96] Such passions and such abjurations, crowned by such successes, could only single out or isolate the Jews even further in Germany, where Jewish exclusivism found ample sustenance in Germanic exclusivism.

The route from emancipating universalism to nationalist particularism could vary. This was the case with Moses Hess (1812–75), the "communist rabbi," who brought the message of Karl Marx and was Friedrich Engels's first teacher.[97] He too professed the prevailing Christian concepts on the subject of Jews, adapted in Hegelian style. They were, he wrote, nothing but soulless mummies, phantoms lingering in this world, and he compared the Christians' humanist God to the nationalist God of Abraham, Isaac and Jacob (*Die europäische Triarchie,* 1841). In 1845, probably under Marx's influence, he found even more powerful formulae:[98]

> The Jews, whose world-historical task in the natural history of the animal world was to develop the beast of prey out of humanity, have now at last fulfilled this vocation. The mystery of Judaism and Christianity has become visible in the modern Judeo-Christian world of shopkeepers.

When he too was later exiled to Paris, Hess sought truth in the positive sciences of the day, immersed himself in books on anthropology and, working henceforth with the concepts of "Aryan" and "Semite," which he had acquired, thought that he had found the primary cause of the "class struggle" in the "race struggle." In this way, spurred on by the spirit of the times and the anti-Semitism around him, he became a nationalist at the end of his life, a "Jewish Germanomane" to use his own expression. For him, as for his adversaries, it was "race" which made the Jew. In 1862, in *Rom und Jerusalem,*[99] his last book, the precursor of Marx became the doctrinarian of political Zionism, the precursor of Herzl. So the route that this John the Baptist followed seems to anticipate the path which twentieth-century history would force upon German Judaism.

Needless to say, his Jewish contemporaries did not listen to Hess, in fact he terrified them. Other people, today forgotten, were expressing their dominant inclinations better, notably their patriotic conformism to which even practicing Jews henceforth paid tribute. The middle way between rabbinical orthodoxy and the social revolution can be symbolized by Gabriel Riesser (1806–63) who tried to turn his individual circumstances into a representative case.

Although his future as a jurist was jeopardized by his Jewishness, he refused to convert or to find some compromise with
injustice. Instead, he fought for a general reform of the laws
in a homeland that he wanted to see unified. The journal he
founded to fight on two fronts—against discriminatory
practices and against false conversions—bore the provocative title *Der Jude*. Elected to the Frankfurt parliament in
1848, he spoke loudly and clearly in favor of the equality of
all Germans. He became its vice-president and was a
member of a delegation which offered the German crown to
the King of Prussia. Later, he became the first Jewish judge
in Germany. Von Treitschke cited this famous Jew as an
example "of a German man in the best sense of the word,"
and made a deliberate distinction between him and Börne,
Heine and the other oriental "ferments of decomposition."
This nationalist, therefore, was drawing a line between one
Jew and another, as was customary at the time. But
obviously, to earn the right to be described as a German
man, a Jew had to give proof of qualities which few non-
Jewish Germans could claim.

The atheists' crusade

> These doctors of the Revolution and their relentlessly deter-
> mined disciples are the only people truly alive in Germany
> and the future belongs to them.
>
> *Heinrich Heine*

Meditating on the boldness of Germanic philosophy and
citing himself as an example, Heine, at the end of his life,
warned his friends Ruge and Marx, as well as Daumer,
Feuerbach and Bruno Bauer against the "self-deification of
atheists."[100] In 1840–50, German metaphysicians were openly
challenging the existence of God; on this issue, "young Hegelians" shouldered arms three-quarters of a century after the
French materialists of the Enlightenment. We are not going
to spend time on the causes or significance of this time-lag. It

is sufficient for our purpose to note that every criticism of the Christian God was a challenge to the people who were called as witnesses for the defense, and that the men to whom Heine's warning was addressed were in constant occupation of the public prosecutor's seat. They therefore deserve attention.

The eldest of the five, Georg Friedrich Daumer (1800–75), is currently the least well known but not the least interesting. He personally represented the past rather than the future. Daumer was a poet and theologian, a pupil of Hegel's, and he is typical of the excesses employed by German idealists seeking to capture the absolute and put it into a system.[101] He never succeeded in completing this, and probably lacked the necessary seriousness; but he too wanted to abolish the reign of the Son, or theology, and establish in its stead that of the Spirit, or Germanic philosophy. Under attack from orthodox ministers, he let himself be carried away by polemic, and with the years his hatred of the Christian's man-God went on increasing. He vented it in pseudo-scientific pamphlets which gave free play to a new type of Biblical criticism, backed up by immense reading. Under his pen, primitive Christianity finished up by becoming a confraternity of cannibals; he thought that he had penetrated its last stronghold in his work, *Die Geheimnisse des christlichen Alterthums* (1847).

According to this document, Jehovah and Moloch were one and the same at first, and Easter was "the solemn festival when the Semites sacrificed children."[102] But the Hebrews purified their cult in the most distant times, and introduced offerings of animals. However, "a sect which did not cease to perpetuate the old cannibalistic horrors" continued to exist in their midst. Jesus was the leader of this clandestine sect; if he mistrusted Judas it was because he felt that Judas was spying on him. The two men came face to face at the Last Supper, which was, for Daumer, an anthropophagous ceremony:[103]

Jesus discovers that Judas is dangerous from the fact that the latter does not participate at all or only participates incompletely in this very special meal. To test the judgment and spirit of this false apostle, he makes him taste a morsel of the dishes which the other does not want and which he can only swallow with disgust and horror. After this scene, Judas, profoundly distressed and indignant, hastens to expose what has happened under cover of silence.

The mysteries of Christianity are thus explained:[104]

it follows ... that the idea of the human victim, sacrificed to God, is the fundamental idea of Christianity. ... How so? You no longer know therefore that it teaches the bloody sacrifice of the body of its God? Once at Golgotha in the original, and an infinite number of times in imitation?

And Daumer runs over the crimes of past centuries which he sees as so many Christian ritual murders: "Innumerable are the kidnappings of children in the Middle Ages and we will not be mistaken in attributing the greater part of them to religious superstition."[105]

To which he added: "the psychological and physical mortifications, the inquisitions of the orthodox faith, the scaffolds, stakes, Saint Bartholomew massacres, trials for sorcery, massacres of the Jews."[106]

He also made use of the old legends, and the Pied Piper of Hamelin became purveyor of fresh flesh to the Church.[107] As Daumer's excellent biographer, Mme Kühne, noted, *"Die Geheimnisse des christlichen Alterthums* demonstrated the havoc that can be wrought by the speculative idealist method and what happens when an author gets used to working with vague suspicions instead of precise proofs."[108]

The *Secrets* were taken seriously in their day, notably in German revolutionary circles. Hermann Ewerbeck, the Paris leader of the communist "League of the Righteous," hastened to translate them into French and to introduce them as one of the highspots of German philosophy.[109] In London, in

November, 1847, Karl Marx devoted a report to Daumer's ideas, which he regarded as "the last blow dealt to Christianity" and consequently, the confirmation of his own eschatological hopes. A curious personal note suggests that he too had thought of this exegesis; he added, in fact, that Protestantism had transposed human sacrifice "to spiritual man" and had, as a result, "moderated the thing slightly."[110] Arnold Ruge, who visited Daumer at Nuremberg in 1844, was very impressed by the man. "How rarely one sees such men! I am putting off my departure so that I can go on listening to him . . . his expression, his features, his movements, his lively conversation are worth it. . . ." Daumer's great concern, he said, was to "abolish religion" by spreading his discoveries outside scholarly circles, direct to the people.[111]

But the life of this champion of idealistic blasphemy was tragic. His was only a *succès de scandale* and the people did not follow him. Reviled by the churches, ill and alone, he finally abandoned hope of the advent of the reign of Spirit or the Germanic mission. He then felt drawn to Judaism, writing in 1849: ". . . that it constituted a contradiction of Christianity, namely the first and the most immediate, and that it did all it could to prevent such a great misfortune [Christianity] from issuing forth from its bosom and spreading."[112] In around 1855, he drew up an anthology of *Die Weisheit Israels,* and even wanted to join the Frankfurt Jewish reform community; but the Jews did not want to have anything to do with him.[113] He ended up seeking refuge in the bosom of the Catholic Church where he did not find peace.

Daumer for his part thought of himself as a deist in quest of true religion, not as an atheist. If his deism developed unusually aggressive forms, the sharp edge of this aggressiveness was directed entirely against the dominant religion and society. He only seems to have criticized the Jews when the nature of his task made it inevitable: how can Jesus or his apostles be exposed without demonstrating the maleficence of those particular Jews or their modern emulators? And to this end, he drew on every type of ancient and

modern document in order "to instruct philosophy on historical facts"—as he wrote to his great friend Ludwig Feuerbach
in 1842. The letter reflects prejudices which are less aberrant
than they seem, since every anti-Christian crusade from the
Voltairean campaigns to the Soviet polemic, has experienced
their like. It is worth quoting:

> It seems to me absolutely necessary that philosophy should be
> provided with more historical material in order to attain fully
> its objectives; my aim is to provide this material. I have
> come across wondrous secrets. Amongst the Jewish sects, as far
> as I know them, the Karaites are pure of all atrocities, and
> worthy folk. But the Rabbanites and Talmudists, the Sabbatians
> who border on Christianity, and the Hassidic sects who are so
> numerous in the Slav lands, have their bloody mysteries. . . .
> Christianity also, which is a kind of Sabbatianism and
> Hassidism of earlier times, long performed human sacrifices. . . .
> The bones of the sacrificial victims were preserved and
> worshiped in the churches as relics, as was the case with us in
> Nuremberg. . . .

Daumer predicted that "a terrible light" would one day be
cast on all this. He promised to reveal "unheard of things," to
show how far "the negative and abstract foundation on
which everything rests" (that is to say the bloody cult of
Moloch) remained the real basis of the Judeo-Christian
revelation. He ended his long letter abruptly by telling his
friend that he had just explored an old Jewish cellar and
underground oven and had found bones there; any comment
seemed futile.[114]

Needless to say, although Daumer distinguished between
enlightened Jews, whose prototype was Judas, and cannibal
Jews, whose prototype was Jesus, he found followers who
hastened to set lucubration back on its feet. There was, in the
first place, his pupil Friedrich Wilhelm Ghillany (1807–76),[115]
a Nuremberger like himself and, to start with, a theologian as
well. But at Daumer's instigation, it seems, he left his post as
pastor and also set out to expose the Jews' cannibalism

during the years which followed the Damascus affair.[116] In his opinion, evidence of this "molochism" was provided not only by the ritual murder of Jesus but also by the ritual murders the Jews did not cease, he thought, to commit in the Germany of his day, having neither forgotten nor learned anything:

> How can political rights be granted to such men, who adhere so rigidly to old inhuman prejudices, who regard us as impure, like serfs and dogs, just as their ancestors did, even if they do not flaunt it to our face. It is men such as these who claim full civil rights, the right to exercise functions of government, to become the superiors of Christians, judicial and administrative officers!

Anti-French feeling comes to light:[117]

> Shall Germany also be deformed by that hybrid culture such as we find in France? Has modern history any more repulsive phenomenon than those French Jews who, now French, now Jews again, publicly flatter the great nation but at home and in the synagogue pray for the establishment of a Jewish kingdom?

Hitlerite propaganda glorified both master and pupil; a book by one R. W. Stock, published by Stürmer editions in 1939, gave them a leading place and saw both of them as great precursors.

Did Daumer also influence Feuerbach (1804–72) whose philosophy he wanted to instruct in historic facts? A close friendship existed between the two men: *Das Wesen des Christentums* (1840), Feuerbach's main work, contained a reference to the "unmasked Judaism" of Eisenmenger, one of Daumer's major sources; the text also permits such an assumption. In it, Feuerbach taxed the Jews with egoism—a classic theme notably developed by Hegel—and also attributed to them an enlarged "stomach sense" and a gastronomic craving for God, which might be an echo of Daumer's "molochism." It is true that the Fathers of the Church were already talking about Jewish gluttony. Whatever the case, the following is the passage:[118]

The Jews have preserved themselves until today in their uniqueness. Their principle, their God is the most practical principle in the world—egoism, indeed egoism in the form of religion. Egoism is the God who never allows his servants to fall into disgrace. Egoism is essentially monotheistic for it only has one thing—itself—as its objective. Egoism brings together, concentrates man on himself. It gives him a firm, solid vital principle. But it makes him theoretically limited, because of indifference to everything that does not directly refer to the welfare of the self. Science only originates therefore, like art, from polytheism, for polytheism is the open, unresentful feeling for everything that is beautiful and good, without differentiation; the feeling for the world, for the universe. . . .

The Greeks contemplated nature with the theoretical senses; they heard heavenly music in the harmonious course of the stars. From the foam of the ocean, the producer of all things, they saw nature emerge in the shape of Venus Anadyomene. The Israelites, on the other hand, only opened their gastric senses to nature. They only enjoyed nature through their palate. They only became aware of God through the enjoyment of manna. . . . Eating is the most solemn act or even initiation into the Jewish religion. In the act of eating the Israelite celebrates and renews the act of creation. In eating, man declares nature to be a nullity in itself. When the seventy elders climbed the mountain with Moses, then "they saw the God of Israel . . . they stayed there before God; they ate and they drank" (Exodus, XXIV, 10–11). The sight of the highest being therefore only aroused their appetite.

It seems that, in the case in point, the theology of the founder of atheist humanism rested on the unconscious association of the modern accusation of materialism (the Jew, a limited being, who is indifferent "to everything that does not directly refer to the welfare of the self"; taste is considered a material sense) with the old accusation of deicide or ritual murder ("they only became aware of God through the enjoyment of manna," which means unleavened bread which means Christian blood). Perhaps the famous Feuerbachian maxim *Der Mensch ist, was er isst* might equally be ascribed to a reminiscence of the oral stage. We will not linger over these transports, in case we lose our footing and let ourselves be carried out into deep water. Correctly interpreted however, they might reveal the most secret cannibal projection of the anti-Semitic mechanism. Let us stay on *terra firma* and move on to other crusades of the atheism that Heine was talking about.

It is remarkable that Heine did not mention David Friedrich Strauss whose *Life of Jesus* (1835) reduced the gospel story to a myth and marked an epoch in the history of atheism. Would this have been because Strauss maintained complete scholarly objectivity and refrained from value judgments on Jews or anyone else? But the polemics his work unleashed did produce innumerable value judgments and were at the origin of the Young Hegelian campaign; Ruge, Bauer and Marx were in the forefront of this conflict.

Arnold Ruge (1802–80) was a former Germanomane *Burschenschaftler* who had been involved in a conspiracy and spent several years in prison. Freed, he converted to Hegelianism in 1833. In the absence of philosophical talents, he possessed a lively pen and was temperamentally a live-wire and organizer.[119] In 1838, he founded a review, the *Hallische Jahrbücher*, which became the organ of the "Young Hegelians," that is to say the radical wing of a school which, like its master, expected salvation from Prussia. This Prussia, wrote Ruge, was[120]

> so deeply rooted in Germanism that it was prevented, by that very fact, from opposing the tendency to the free forms of State. ... It is only by realizing all the consequences of Protestantism and also of constitutionalism that Prussia will be able, with Germany, to accomplish its high mission and fully achieve the concept of the absolute State.

For Ruge, as for the rest of the young Hegelians, it was understood that such a state, like the philosophy, must be atheist; but he was not the only polemicist of this type to "rediscover" his faith when he was dealing with Jews, "these maggots in the cheese of Christianity," he wrote, "who are so unutterably comfortable in their reflective and stock-jobbing skin that they believe in nothing and precisely for this reason remain Jews."[121] Ruge, for his part, believed in a philosophy which he thought could only be atheist. The man really seems to have belonged to the species of atheist which "believe that they do not believe."

When the *Hallische Jahrbücher* was later banned, Ruge tried to revive it under the title of *Annales franco-allemandes,* in Paris in 1843. A curious letter to his mother showed him facing up courageously to the difficulties of emigration. He wrote that he had started a bookshop and was hoping that his friend Karl Marx would come into partnership with him:[122]

> I myself cannot avoid becoming half a trader, which is something I had never expected. ... I am obliged to note that the Jews could only continue to exist thanks to trade. This was always their lot and it is instructive that they now have the whole world in their pocket.

The quarrel with Marx intervened and Marx then became "a skunk and a shameless Jew" (October 6, 1844). Another letter (May 27, 1845) contained a reference on the subject of the practice of socialism, to "a community of atrocious Jewish souls."[123] From 1850, Ruge lived in England where he continued to practice political journalism. Abandoning philosophy, he became the defender of Bismarck's unified Germany which granted him an annual "honorarium" of three thousand marks in 1877.[124]

Bruno Bauer (1809–82) was a philosophical brain of a different caliber. He began as an orthodox Protestant theologian but also converted to Hegelianism and lost his faith. The critical study of the Gospels that he then embarked on, remains, in Albert Schweitzer's opinion, "the most inspired and complete catalog ever to be drawn up of the difficulties the life of Jesus poses."[125] In Berlin, in 1836–40, Bauer was the life and soul of the *Doktorenklub* which could boast Karl Marx as its fiery Benjamin. The varied plans for the future which they drew up together in 1841 included the publication of a review entitled *Archives of Atheism.*[126] This friendship also broke up shortly afterwards following a quarrel which Marx has immortalized in *Die heilige Familie* and *L'Idéologie allemande.* These disparaged Bauer's thought;[127] nonetheless, the system he had formulated by combining Hegel's dialectic with Fichte's philosophy of the ego, foreshadowed many elements of the early eschatology of communism. For him too, history was a series of revolutions or catastrophes; the last, which would precede the coming of a golden age for mankind, would be "terrible, even more awe-inspiring than the one which marked the birth of Christianity," he wrote to Karl Marx in April, 1840. "The future appears so certain that one could not doubt it for a moment. . . ."[128] For him, the hour of this "final struggle," as a result of which victorious Reason would sign God's death certificate, had already come in 1843.[129]

In the conclusion of his main work of Biblical criticism, Bauer summed up his philosophy of history:[130]

In the religions of antiquity, essential interests conceal and veil the depth and horrors of alienation: the perspectives of nature are full of charm, the bonds of family have their sweet grace, the folk-interest gives to the religious spirit a fiery tension with the powers that it reveres. The fetters that man's mind bore in the service of these religions were wound round with flowers. . . . As the flowers withered in the course of time, the charms were broken by the power of Rome and the vampire of spiritual abstraction [Christianity] completed the task. It sucked sap and juice, blood and life to the last drop from humanity. Nature and art, family, people and state were absorbed and on the ruins of a world that had disappeared the enervated ego remained to itself, as the sole force. After its enormous loss the ego could not at once re-create from its depth and universality, nature and art, people and state. The great and mighty work that now took place, the only task that preoccupied the ego was the absorption of everything hitherto existing in the world. The ego was now the all and yet it was empty. ... It saw in the Messiah the guarantee of its continued existence, who only represented what in reality the ego itself was, i.e. the universal power, but that power which it was in fact, in which all the sights of nature and the moral prescriptions of the spirit of family, people and of political life and the view of art have collapsed.

The historical starting point for this revolution was present in the national life of Judaism for in its religious consciousness, nature and art were already throttled.

Nonetheless, for Bauer, the "spiritual abstraction" of that "vampire" Christianity was an advance on Judaism, "the expression of a new and loftier stage of the universal Conscience" and it is precisely because it was an advance, or a "better approximation to the Truth," that it was dialectically at the origin of an "alienation of the human ego" which Bauer described in the terrifying tones which we have just instanced.[131] Thus "the broad outlines of a picture of bourgeois society were drawn up, as it has been sketched out by the social critics of the time," noted a commentator in 1963.[132] However, how can we fail to identify Bauer's transition from "natural religion" to the bliss of the "universal Conscience" via the "spiritualist abstraction," with the trinity "Reign of Father," "Reign of Son," "Reign of the Spirit," which goes back to the Joachimites and the religious Franciscans?

Deprived of his university chair in 1841, Bruno Bauer's aggressive enthusiasm redoubled. His first blow, *Die Judenfrage*, was oblique. Polemicizing against the emancipation of the Jews, he said that "his conception of Judaism was going to seem even harsher than the one people had so far been used to hearing from opponents of emancipation."[133] In fact, he criticized the Jews "for having made their nest in the pores and interstices of bourgeois society,"[134] of being the craftsmen of their own misfortunes, since they remained Jews. The "tenacity of the Jewish national spirit," he attributed to the absence of a faculty for historical development, consistent with the completely "ahistoric" character of this people and due to its "oriental essence"[135] (an idea of Hegel's is recognizable here). The Jews' crime lay in "not recognizing the purely human development of history, the development of the human conscience."[136] Having finished with Judaism, the book turned to a criticism and reinterpretation of Christianity within the framework of the Hegelian categories:[137]

> It is true that Christianity is the completion of Judaism ... but this completion is, as we have shown above, at the same time and necessarily the negation of the specific Jewish essence. But those Christian theologians deny this negation, the thoroughgoing negation of the essence of the Old Testament, because they do not wish to admit that the divine revelation in its progress through world history has ever progressed.... These Jewish Christians do not want any development, any history, any negation of the old and it is a matter of indifference to them whether they make Judaism Christian or Christianity Jewish. All the more is it a matter of indifference because they can in any case only make it a Jewish Christianity.

Bauer also opposed the emancipation of the Jews in a society where all men were enslaved by religion and needed to be emancipated. "We must first become free ourselves before thinking about inviting others to liberty. . . . Only a free world can hope to liberate the slave from prejudice." Moreover,[138]

> it is a deceptive state of affairs if the Jew is theoretically excluded from political rights, whereas in practice he possesses a vast power and exercises in a general way a political influence which is denied him in detail. The Jew who, in Vienna for example, is only tolerated, determines through his financial power the fate of the whole Empire. . . .

Bauer also dared the limited, uneducated "Jew" to refute Eisenmenger's *Das entdeckte Judentum* and write a "Christianity unmasked" to set beside this classic of anti-Judaism.[139]

Immediately afterwards, Bauer began to write this treatise himself. Published in Zurich in 1843, *Das entdeckte Christentum* was confiscated and pulped by the cantonal authorities. Its violence is confirmed by a letter which the author sent his publisher in February, 1843:[140]

> The publication being very extremist—in it, I demonstrate that religion is the hell of the hatred of mankind, and that God is the great provost of this hell—you can, if you wish, put the name of another firm and not your own on the cover. I have already introduced the title, *Das entdeckte Christentum*, in advance in my *Judenfrage*, which has just appeared. . . .

It seems that Bauer was informing the Jews that a "Christian stage," in other words, baptism, was a necessary preliminary to their emancipation.[141] However, in the same year, another crusader of atheism succeeded in publishing and distributing extracts from *Das entdeckte Christentum*.[142] This was none other than Wilhelm Marr, the future doyen of German racist anti-Semitism and the alleged inventor of the actual term "anti-Semitism." At this period, he was serving in the socialist ranks and popularizing Feuerbach at his own expense.[143] Bauer's ideas developed on very similar lines to Wilhelm Marr's or Ruge's. This rebel, of whom as early as 1845 Marx was saying "that his belief in Jehovah had been transformed into belief in the Prussian state,"[144] later became a doctrinarian of German conservatism and served under Bismarck. But as far as the Jews and the sources of Christianity were concerned, his theology did not change between 1840 and 1880.[145]

This leaves Karl Marx (1818–83). He immediately went one better than his older confrère and, in his turn, published a *Judenfrage*, in which Bauer's corrupted but still "Christian" world became "Jewish." In it, Marx was already drawing a distinction between theory and *Praxis*: ". . . in its perfected practice, the spiritual egoism of Christianity necessarily becomes the material egoism of the Jew."[146] The work was divided into two parts. In the first, which was theoretical, he polemicized with his ex-friend, showing that it was futile to try and suppress religion before the axe had been applied to the roots of society and state. *En passant*, he explained to the Jews that the political emancipation they required was not human emancipation since it did not necessarily de-judaize them.[147] In the second part, Marx attacked the society of his day with the utmost violence, denouncing it as entirely Jewish, since it was entirely dominated by money. He was therefore using words in their derived or conventional meaning, caring as little about the human reality of the followers of Moses scattered over the world, as men like Ruge and Bauer—or Alphonse Toussenel whose *Les Juifs, rois de l'époque* dated from the same year, 1844.

Resounding phrases emerged from the fog of Hegelian dialectic:

> Let us not seek the secret of the Jew in his religion, but let us seek the secret of religion in the real Jew. What is the profane basis of Judaism? *Practical* needs, *self-interest*. . . . Very well: in ridding itself of *huckstering* 'and *money*, and thus from real and practical Judaism, our age would emancipate itself. . . . We discern in Judaism, therefore, a universal *anti-social* element of the *present time*, whose historical development, zealously aided in its harmful aspects by the Jews, has now attained its culminating point. . . . The Jew has emancipated himself in a Jewish manner, not only by acquiring the power of money, but also because *money* has become, through him and also apart from him, a world power, while the practical Jewish spirit has become the practical spirit of the Christian nations. The Jews have emancipated themselves in so far as the Christians have become Jews. . . . In North America, indeed, the effective domination of the Christian world by Judaism has come to be manifested in a common and unambiguous form; the *preaching of the Gospel* itself, Christian preaching, has become

an article of commerce. . . . The Jew, who occupies a distinctive place in civil society, only manifests in a distinctive way the Judaism of civil society. . . . What was, in itself, the basis of the Jewish religion? Practical need, egoism. The monotheism of the Jews is, therefore, in reality, a polytheism of the numerous needs of man, a polytheism which makes even the lavatory an object of divine regulation. . . . Money is the jealous god of Israel, beside which no other god may exist. Money degrades all the gods of mankind and changes them into commodities. . . . The bill of exchange is the real God of the Jew. His God is only an illusory bill of exchange. . . . That which is contained in an abstract form in the Jewish religion—contempt for theory, for art, for history, and for man as an end in himself—is the *real, conscious* standpoint and the virtue of the man of money. Even the species-relation itself, the relation between man and woman, becomes an object of commerce. Woman is bartered away. The *chimerical* nationality of the Jew is the nationality of the trader, and above all the financier. The law of the Jew, which is without basis or reason, is only the religious caricature of morality and right in general. . . . Jewish Jesuitism, which Bauer discovers in the Talmud, is the relationship of the world of self-interest to the laws which govern this world, laws which the world devotes its principal arts to circumventing. . . . Christianity issued from Judaism. It has now been re-absorbed into Judaism. From the beginning, the Christian was the theorizing Jew; consequently, the Jew is the practical Christian. And the practical Christian has become a Jew again. . . . It was only then that Judaism could attain universal [*allgemeine*] domination. . . . As soon as society succeeds in abolishing the *empirical* essence of Judaism—huckstering and its conditions —the Jew becomes impossible. . . . The *social* emancipation of the Jew is the emancipation of society from Judaism.

Marx wrote *Die Judenfrage* during the winter of 1843–4, partly at Kreuznach, partly in Paris. It dated from the crucial year in his life, which saw his marriage, his exile and his conversion to communism. The work already seemed to foreshadow the *Idéologie allemande* which he later described as "an examination of philosophical conscience."

In his prophetic wrath, he castigated the world of his day, utilizing the terminology it had manufactured itself. It can be supposed that the Jews, whom he only knew through a few bourgeois examples, seemed as blameworthy to him as this world. The subject of the book, the method it employed, and even its title, had been dictated to Marx by Bauer whom, in his polemic passion, he was trying to surpass. He too criticized even more violently a bourgeois society which both of them identified with Judaism. But the descendant of a line of rabbis had a second motive unknown to the ex-theologian which can legitimately be recognized as a more secret motive, pursued by an inverse approach and dictated by a different passion. By identifying Judaism with this society, by magically transforming all other Jews into money-grubbers, was this penniless Jew, converted at the age of seven, not unconsciously trying to stress his distance from Judaism, to produce his certificate of non-Jewishness, to show an alibi for which, particularly at this time, so many of his co-religionists were yearning in vain?[148]

And yet, a curious phrase in *Die Judenfrage* stands out from the remainder of the book and seems at first glance to contradict this interpretation. The question occurs of the Jew's real mission: ". . . when the Jew recognizes his *practical* nature as invalid and endeavors to abolish it, he begins to deviate from his former path of development, works for general *human emancipation* and turns against the *supreme practical* expression of self-estrangement."[149] This is a curious pronouncement, redolent perhaps of an involuntary admission. Was Marx offering himself as a wildly over-demanding example to those Jews? And this was the man who refused to acknowledge himself a Jew throughout his life, who, despite the evidence of his eyes, pretended not to know of the existence of Jewish socialism,[150] and who only used the word to denounce capitalists or to abuse his enemies.

In fact there is also Karl Marx's private correspondence in which the term "Jew," coupled with harsh invective, is often applied to Jews who have happened to displease him, and to them alone:[151] "The Jew Steinthal, with the bland smile . . ." (1857); "The cursed Jew of Vienna [Max Friedländer] . . ." (1859); "The author, that pig of a Berlin journalist, is a Jew by the name of Meier . . ." (1860). His doctor was described as a Jew because he was pressing for payment (1854). Even worse if the Jew were a banker: Bamberger formed part "of the Stock Exchange synagogue of Paris"; Fould was a "Stock Exchange Jew"; Oppenheimer was "The Jew Süss of Egypt." As for Lassalle, "the shape of his head and his hair show that he is descended from the Negroes who joined Moses' flock at the time of the exodus from Egypt," or else he was "the most barbarous of all the Yids from Poland,"[152] or again he was Lazarus the leper, who, in his turn, was "the primitive type of Jew." However, when Marx was taking a cure at Karlsbad, he struck up a friendship with the aggressive Jewish historian Graetz and inscribed his copy of *Das Kapital*, "To Monsieur Professor Heinrich Graetz, a token of friendship and esteem."[153] Not that he had studied his work; this sort of history did not interest him; he preferred to ignore it. His reading notes for 1852 show that when he was studying a treatise on general history (the *Allgemeine Culturgeschichte* by Wachsmuth), he avoided the chapter on the Jews.[154]

Karl Marx's promethean—or paranoid—temperament is a known fact; the demiurge decided from on high who was a Jew and who was not; the philosopher did what he liked with this term charged with age-old scorn. What we said when we were discussing Voltaire might perhaps be applied to the revolutionary Messiah, contemptuous of the old God of Israel. In the alchemy of anti-Semitic passion, the imagination (blaming oneself for acting like a Jew, while competing with Jews, identifying negatively with them—the case of Voltaire) or the reality (to be a Jew by birth and no longer wish to be one—the case of Marx) can lead to similar precipitates. But in the second case, the reaction can be even more explosive, since reality comes to the aid of imagination. This gives rise to additional incentives and tensions: to converts particularly, it is even more important to prove to themselves and to others that they are not Jews. In the case we are studying, Marx's friends and disciples themselves, each in his own way, drew attention to his Jewishness. His son-in-law, Dr Lafargue, even thought he could recognize the Jewish race in the proportions of Marx's body.[155] Because of this, anti-Semites of Jewish descent lack the safety net which enabled a man like Voltaire, faced with a Jew, to rediscover that he was a "very Christian gentleman." Simulation is futile; the blows fall on the person who is dealing them, victim and executioner cohabit inside the same skin; to Jews, anti-Semitism can offer only moderate pleasures.

We are not going to dig more deeply into these quicksands of individual psychology. It has already been done; in fact everything touching on Karl Marx has been the subject of innumerable publications, and a lot of ink has also been expended on his anti-Semitism.[156] Last of all, a psychoanalyst, Arnold Künzli, has devoted a total of over eight hundred pages to him, interpreting the founder of Marxism in the light of little Karl's childhood conflicts from which he thought his "Jewish self-hatred" (*jüdischer Selbsthass*) derived.[157] Moreover, we have seen to what extent de-judaized Jews of the time had a tendency to testify against themselves. Karl's father, the gentle *Aufklärer* Heinrich Marx, seems to have been no exception. But to go from here to the claim that the liberated slaves had "attained universal domination," involved crossing a bridge, handling a terminology, which had until then remained the domain reserved to Christians, like the French utopian socialists or the visionaries of German Romanticism. Marx drew from all these sources; what erupts on to the historic scene is Jewish anti-Semitism,[158] characterized by its excesses and expressing itself in the hyperboles we have already found amongst men who have left their stamp on Western history.

All in all, Marxist anti-Semitism, more than any other, seemed to be supra-determined, fed by numerous currents, of which the later ones are not necessarily the most

important. After the conflicts of early childhood—a childhood which remains curiously undocumented—after the
Catholic school at Trier and the shameful Jews of Berlin,
there were the attractions of Hegelianism and the activist
environment of the sect. There was also—unforgettably—
Hegel himself. Georges Cottier wrote:[159]

> Marx initiated a phenomenology of Judaism which is not with-
> out great similarity to what the young Hegel wrote about
> Abraham in his youth. . . . If Marx did not know Hegel's youth-
> ful writings, he is familiar with *Phänomenologie* where their
> spiritual tone is faithfully transmitted. . . .

Lastly, there was Bauer's *Judenfrage*. What Marx added to it
by his criticism paradoxically remains the best, for however
unpleasant his logorrhea may be, it seems already pervaded
by the spark that Engels would later relight; the germ of an
economic and social critique is perceptible in it.

It could be said that with this book Marx squared urgent
accounts with his past, his mother, Bauer and in the end with
himself. His tone did actually begin to soften in the following
year. In *Die heilige Familie*, a new attack on Bruno Bauer
("Saint Bruno"), there was still mention of a "modern world
which is Jewish to the most intimate places of its being."[160]
The *Thèses sur Feuerbach*, where his new philosophy took
off from the ground ("philosophers have only interpreted the
world in different ways; what is important is to transform
it"), described the bourgeois *Praxis* of "dirty Jew"
(*schmutzig-jüdisch*).[161] Later, these tones became barely
perceptible. Until his death, Karl Marx talked contemptu-
ously about Jews in his correspondence ("Ramsgate is full of
fleas and Jews," 1879)[162] and demagogically in *Das Kapital*
("the capitalist knows that all merchandise . . . is money,
internally circumcised Jews"),[163] but he now only talked
about them rarely and marginally. It was as though, once he
became "an economist in the strict and scientific meaning of
the word" (Raymond Aron), he gave up rousing this particular phantasm.

The other phantasms remained. There was still, for example, a historiosophy "set on its feet again" but with the apocalyptic visions of the young Hegelians forming a substratum. Marx never dropped this revolutionary and Christian messianism, incorrectly described as Karl Marx's "Jewish messianism,"[164] that expectation of the last days or the final struggle. This eschatology was even responsible for the far-reaching effect of Marxist scientific thought. It seems that there was even more: was not a vision which set out, like the old scholastics, to pierce the final mysteries of existence, led on precisely because of this to embrace social life in its totality, to bring out the historic dimension, to unveil the mutability and the relativity of institutions and régimes?[165]

Marx's youthful metaphysical aspirations and intuitions never ceased to inspire his socio-economic criticism in one way or another. For example, the millenarianist heresy was at the origin of the constitution of a theory of sociology. Science advanced on impossible dreams. As with Kepler or Newton, metaphysical theories sought strict proof for themselves. As usual, there were more false ones than true; but that is how things are in this world.

And just as naturally, the weapon with which Marx sought to wound contemporary society was immediately turned against himself. His favorite correspondent on the *Neue Rheinische Zeitung,* which he edited at the end of the revolutionary year of 1848, was Edward Tellering.[166] Tellering wrote to him from Vienna:

> What you can call bourgeois are here the Jews who have taken over the democratic leadership. These Jews are ten times more despicable than the West European bourgeoisie. . . . If we win, again it will only be common Jews, with their cowardly speculative spirit, robbing democracy of all respect amongst the people, who will profit, leading us into all the degradations of a bourgeois government. . . .

The revolution having failed, Tellering tried to put himself at the service of the Prussian government. To make more of an *amende honorable* he published an anti-communist booklet in 1850:

> It is well known that the vengeance of the Jew goes further and is the most irreconcilable. . . . Marx, the future German dictator, is a *Jew*. In 1848 I forced him to attack the Jews in his journal. He bit his lips and did so because his other collaborators also hit out at the Jews. Now the vengefulness in his heart begins to stir up in reaction against me. . . .

The booklet was entitled: *Foretaste of the Future German Dictatorship of Marx and Engels*. Others followed and the wave of authors went on increasing. Tellering's pamphlet was only a foretaste.

The case of Richard Wagner

> Wagner is a neurosis
>
> *Nietzsche*

Many artists have wanted to be prophets but Wagner alone was recognized as such by his country and the entire Western world. It is therefore not solely as a musician that he concerns us but as a musician who played a part in shaping yesterday's world politically.

Everything about his case is exceptional; starting with the insoluble problem of his origins. It will never be known if he was the son of the Saxon official Karl Wagner or the actor Ludwig Geyer, whose name he bore until he was fourteen. There is even less chance of ever knowing if Geyer was of Jewish origin[167] as was often claimed. Viennese humorists were dubbing the composer "Chief Rabbi of Bayreuth" during his lifetime.[168] But on this unverifiable question, we prefer Solomonic scepticism[169] to Nietzsche's passionate denunciation. Moreover, this sort of problem is not in itself important to our subject. On the other hand, what can contribute a great deal towards it is what the people concerned thought about it themselves and what became their subjective truth. Now Wagner was certainly inclined towards the "Geyer hypothesis" and therefore thought he was the child of an adulterous union. Did he also believe that Geyer (which means *vulture* in German) was a Jew? This seems equally probable, and if so, the hermit of Sils-Maria would have got his suspicions from the original source, which would explain the confidence he displayed.[170] But once again we have a dilemma.

Whether he was simply a bastard or the bastard son of a Jew is not fundamental since if the Jew is a bastard for the anti-Semitic unconscious, the converse can be true, in so far as the persecuted bastard resembles the Jew (both are vagabonds "without hearth or home"). We refer to what we said in the last chapter: in these matters, it is the imagination, "the psychological reality," which takes precedence. At the most, it can be asked whether, taking into account the action of the collective imagination, Wagner (which means *blacksmith*) would have become exactly what he did for Germany, if his name had been *vulture*.

In his autobiography, which tells us that Wagner, in childhood, was known by this doubly equivocal name (a *Geyer* is already almost an *Adler*—eagle—Nietzsche exclaimed),[171] he also describes how Ludwig Geyer consoled his mother for her husband's infidelities. He talks about him affectionately, sometimes calling him his step-father, sometimes his father, as if he was doubtful about his own identity.[172] These *lapsus calami* in a man who is producing a self-portrait for eternity, seems evidence of the origin of a neurosis which almost all Wagner's biographers bring out, after their fashions and whatever their piety towards the sacred monster: a demanding, excessive, purely Wagnerian neurosis.

Let us quote the testimony of his leading French apostle, Édouard Schuré:[173]

. . . the slightest contradiction provoked his unparalleled anger. Then came tiger-like leaps, bestial roars. He paced the room like a caged lion, his voice became almost raucous and expelled words like cries, his speech hit out at random. He then seemed like an unleashed element of nature, something like an erupting volcano. With this went bursts of impetuous sympathy, moving bouts of pity, excessive tenderness for men he saw to be suffering, or animals and even plants. This violent character could not see a bird in a cage; a cut flower made him grow pale, and when he found a sick dog in the street, he took it home. Everything about him was gigantic and excessive. . . .

Do not certain aspects of this portrait, notably in the first part, bring to mind a more recent German idol? But it is the love of animals which is the significant clue, and as he himself wrote to Mathilde Wesendonck, the slaughter of a chicken awoke old obsessions in Wagner:[174]

The terrible scream of the animal, and the pitiful weaker wailing during the act of violence, entered my soul with horror. Since then I have never again rid myself of that impression, that I have already experienced so often. It is terrible on what an infinite abyss of the most cruel misery our existence, that always in the main craves for enjoyment, is based.

With Wagner, obsession with castration ranked with death agony, and also with passionate love, and its stormy and tantalizing liaisons,[175] with an unbridled taste for luxury that his biographers describe in their various ways. He himself justified this to his friend Liszt by his genius as an artist and a magus:[176]

I cannot live like a dog; I cannot sleep on straw and drink bad whisky. I must be coaxed in one way or another if my mind is to accomplish the terribly difficult task of creating a non-existing world.

He later peopled this grandiose world he had created with Aryans and Semites, an imposture on the Wagnerian scale.

Everything about him was spectacular: the awakening of his
anti-Semitic rage, which holds a place in the history of music
and in the history of Germany, would deserve another in
psychology textbooks. This rage burst into the open in 1850
when Wagner was thirty-seven; until then, he himself
informs us, he had worked for complete emancipation of the
Jews.

In 1837, as an unknown artist, he had formed a relationship with Meyerbeer, twenty years his senior and, at the
time, king of European opera. At first, he made him his
artistic, German and universal god. In an early letter, he
wrote to him:[177]

> Here it would in any case be most inappropriate for me to burst
> forth in clumsy eulogies of your genius, only so far as to say that
> I saw in you the complete problem solved of the German who
> made his own the qualities of the Italian and French schools,
> and made the creations of his genius universal.

In an article he compared him to Glück, Handel and
Mozart:[178]

> Above all, it must never be overlooked that they were Germans
> as is he. . . . The peculiar, characteristic features of the Germans
> burden Meyerbeer also. Meyerbeer was so German that he soon
> trod in the footsteps of his old German predecessors. These
> crossed the Alps with the full vigor of the North and
> conquered fair Italy. . . . Meyerbeer retained his German
> heritage, the *naïveté* of sentiment, a chaste inventiveness . . . an
> unblemished conscience. . . .

When Wagner left to make his fortune in Paris in 1839,
Meyerbeer helped him with real generosity, introduced
him to musical circles and lent him money. The irresistible
young musician accepted it as his due: could he conceive of
a better foster-father than a rich and amiable Jewish composer—whose name even rhymed with Geyer? Besides, he
declared to Meyerbeer that his only hope of salvation was
from him:[179]

I implore you to show me the way to the hearts of the Paris public through recommendations and support. . . . with all my sins and weakness, hardship and grief I respectfully commend myself to you, praying for release from all evils through God and yourself. If you remain kind to me, then God is also close to me. . . .

However exaggerated they may have been, at first these effusions really seem to have corresponded to feelings of sincere gratitude, which are reflected in the entry for June 1840 in his private diary.[180] But the nature of Wagner's character, and also perhaps the Parisian intrigues, could not allow the idyll to last, and while Meyerbeer continued to fulfill his function as an efficient patron, his protégé soon reached the point of displaying very clear duplicity. Here, it is the correspondence with Robert Schumann which is revealing. At the end of 1840, Wagner was still pro-Meyerbeerian: "Don't let Meyerbeer be criticized: I owe him everything and especially my almost-celebrity."[181] Such debts easily became intolerable: at the beginning of 1842 the tone had completely changed: "Halévy is frank and honest and not an intentionally sly deceiver like Meyerbeer. But don't abuse him! He is my protector and—joking aside —a pleasant man!"[182]

Wagner is therefore not yet consciously anti-Semitic: but he is already anti-Meyerbeerian and—he is prudent. Sufficiently so for Meyerbeer to continue to work on his behalf, to mount *Rienzi* in Dresden and *The Flying Dutchman* in Berlin. Wagner thanked him publicly in the first edition of his *Autobiography* and in a letter of February, 1842: "In all eternity I will never be able to say anything to you but thanks and thanks again,"[183] while he wrote to Schumann that the work of his benefactor was a "spring whose mere smell repels me at a great distance."[184] He continued to enjoy his hospitality and to accept the services he rendered; his forbearance is astonishing. In December, 1845, he expressed surprise at the cordiality and interest that Mme Meyerbeer was showing in him.[185] Always impecunious, he asked for fresh financial aid in the fall of 1848.[186]

After he had failed in Paris, Wagner directed the Dresden Opera from 1842. This is the revolutionary and "Young Hegelian" period of his life: he read Feuerbach, made friends with Bakunin, wanted to link the future of his art to the German political future and, in spring 1849, took part in the Saxon revolution. (A curious episode shows him as a prudent revolutionary, knowing when to stop. At the crucial point in the uprising, this impetuous individual let his wife Minna keep him under lock and key.)[187] He later emigrated to Switzerland where he wrote his main theoretical treatises in 1849–51. During this exile, he studied the Germanic and Germanomane myths; thereafter he set the philologists' and the metaphysicians' theories to music with the far-reaching effects we know. "The Wagnerian names, the Wagnerian music," recalled Georges Dumézil in 1939, "inspired the German troops in 1914 to 1918 at moments of sacrifice and defeat even more than at moments of triumph. The Third Reich did not have to create its basic myths. . . ."[188] But before breathing life into these dreams, Wagner explained his plans.

In his first book[189] he proclaimed that legend was truer than history and gave a summary of the so-called Aryan theory of the origin of mankind:

> . . . upon this island, i.e. these mountains, we have to seek the cradle of the present Asiatic peoples, as also of those who wandered forth to Europe. Here is the ancestral seat of all religions, of every tongue, of all these nations' Kinghood. . . .

He then concentrated particular attention on the Frankish people and the legend of the *Niebelungen*: "Research has shown the basis of this saga, too, to be of religio-mythic nature: its deepest meaning was the ur-conscience of the Frankish stem, the soul of its royal race . . . compelling respect. . . ."[190]

Later, he resurrected the old god Wotan or rather he thought he could identify Wotan with the Christians' God; God the Son, let it be noted, rather than God the Father:[191]

> The abstract Highest God of the Germans, Wotan, did not really need to yield place to the God of the Christians; rather could he be completely identified with him: it was sufficient to strip off the physical trappings with which the various stems had clothed him in accordance with their idiosyncrasy, their dwelling place and climate.... But that one native stem-god, from whom the races all immediately derived their earthly being, was certainly the last to be given up: for in him was found the striking likeness to Christ himself, the Son of God, that he too died, was mourned and avenged—as we still avenge Christ on the Jews of today. Fidelity and attachment were transferred to Christus all the easier, as one recognized in him the stem-god once again. ...

But Wagner too had something to avenge: his childhood, his poverty, and his failures; or the favors accepted from the Jew Meyerbeer and his own soft-soaping? It can be assumed that this latter objective was not the least pressing, even if, prudent as ever, he published his treatise on *Das Judentum in der Musik* under cover of dual anonymity: he signed it with a pseudonym and he did not attack Meyerbeer by name but via Mendelssohn-Bartholdy and the Jews in general. In June, 1849, he confided his intentions to Liszt:[192]

> ... I want money as much as M, or really more than M, or else I must make myself feared. Well, money I have not, but a tremendous desire to practice a little artistic terrorism. Give me your blessing, or, better still, give me your assistance. Come here and lead the great hunt; we will shoot; and the hares shall fall right and left. ...

The following year, he put his plan into practice. Three themes were interwoven in *Das Judentum in der Musik* which, of all his books, aroused the greatest interest and was also the most influential.[193] By way of introduction, Wagner made the apology necessary for an ex-revolutionary who intended henceforth to come to terms with established authority and tradition—an extra reason for choosing the Jews as scapegoats (or hares, as he put it in his letter to Liszt). He explicitly renounced any "aspiration to social liberty":[194]

> Even when we strove for emancipation of the Jews however, we were more the champions of an abstract principle than of a concrete case: just as all our liberalism was a not very lucid mental sport—since we went for freedom of the Folk without knowledge of that Folk itself, nay, with a dislike of any genuine contact with it—so our eagerness to level up the rights of Jews was far rather stimulated by a general idea, than by any real sympathy. . . .

What it was—and this is the second theme of the book— was that Jews dominated a degenerate society, and more especially the art of that society:

> We have no need first to substantiate the be-Jewing of modern art; it springs to the eye, and thrusts itself upon the senses. . . . But if emancipation from the yoke of Judaism appears to us the greatest of necessities, we must hold that the most important thing is to prove our forces for this war of liberation. . . .

Depressing images followed:

> Only when a body's inner death is manifest do outside elements win the power of lodgment in it—yet merely to destroy it. Then indeed that body's flesh dissolves into a swarming colony of insect-life; but who, in looking on that body's self, would hold it still for living?

But although the corrupting Jew moved on from triumph to triumph like this, his case was no less tragic. Wagner set out to describe it: this is the third theme of *Das Judentum in der Musik* in which venom does not exclude lucidity:

> The cultured Jew has taken the greatest pains to strip off all

the obvious tokens of his lower co-religionists: in many cases he has even held it wise to make a Christian baptism wash away the traces of his origin. This zeal, however, has never gone so far as to let him reap the hoped-for fruits: it has conduced only to his utter isolation, and to making him the most heartless of all human beings; to such a pitch, that we have been bound to lose even our earlier sympathy for the tragic history of his stock.

Nothing good could come from a Jew like this, doubly maleficent and sterile in Wagner's eyes since he had "broken all links with his own race." Even men like Mendelssohn-Bartholdy whose talent he, privately, rated very highly[195] had never been able "to call forth in us that deep, that heart-searching effect which we await from Art." But the most treacherous thrusts were aimed at Meyerbeer:

Whoever has observed the shameful indifference and absent-mindedness of a Jewish congregation, throughout the musical performance of Divine Service in the Synagogue, may under-stand why a Jewish opera-composer feels not at all offended by encountering the same thing in a theater audience, and how he can cheerfully go on laboring for it; for this behavior, here, must really seem to him less unbecoming than in the House of God. . . . In general, the uninspiring, the truly laughable, is the characteristic mark whereby this famed composer shews his Jewhood in his music. From a close survey of the instances adduced above—which we have been able to discover by seek-ing to justify our indomitable objection to the Jewish nature—a proof emerges for us of the *ineptitude of the present musical epoch.* . . .

"Judaism is the evil conscience of our modern civilization," Wagner concluded, and he evoked the wandering Jew, who has no salvation to expect except the grave. Adopting a threatening tone, he urged the Jews: ". . . one thing only can redeem you from the burden of your curse: the redemption of Ahasuerus—going under!" It is on these lines that the pamphlet ends; from first to last, no mention had been made of Meyerbeer's name.

The following year, in *Oper und Drama*, Wagner incidentally attacked Meyerbeer by name and put forward a new argument:

> As a Jew, he owned no mother tongue, no speech inextricably entwined among the sinews of his innermost being: he spoke with precisely the same interest in any modern tongue you chose, and set it to music with no more concern for its idiosyncrasies than the mere question of how far it was ready to be a pliant servitor to Absolute Music.

To put it more concisely, others were to say after him: "When a Jew speaks in German, he lies!"

In his autobiography, Wagner stated that *Das Judentum in der Musik* stirred up a Jewish conspiracy against him, with Meyerbeer at its head. He attributed all the criticism, all the intrigue, all the blows of fate that he experienced after 1851 in his eventful life to this conspiracy:[196]

> The stir, nay, the genuine consternation, created by this article defies comparison with any other similar publication. The unparalleled animosity with which, even up to the present day, I have been pursued by the entire press of Europe can only be understood by those who have taken account of this article. ...
> This fury, however, assumed more the character of slander and malice, for the movement against me had meantime been reduced by a great connoisseur in such things, Meyerbeer, to a clearly defined system, which he maintained and practised with a sure hand until his lamented death. ...

Here therefore was Wagner in the throes of a persecution mania; here, once the act of aggression had been committed, he had become a perfect anti-Semite. In 1853, Liszt described their mutual friend's new obsession to Princess Wittgenstein:[197]

> ... He flung his arms round my neck, then he rolled on the ground, caressing his dog Pepi and talking nonsense to it, in

between spitting on the Jews, who are a generic term with him, in a very broad sense. In a word, a grand and grandissimo character, something like Vesuvius. . . .

Some twenty years later, the Gobinist Ludwig Schemann gave a more detailed account of Wagner's transports:[198]

His laments at the unutterable misery wrought by the Jews against our people culminated in the description of the fate of the German peasant who would soon no longer own a square inch of his own soil. . . . I have never seen him exhibit such a flare-up of holy wrath; after his last words, quite beside himself, he flung himself out into the winter night, and only returned after an interval, when the paroxysm had died down, together with his Newfoundland dog who had in the meantime wearied him into a state of mad repose.

It is worth noticing how dogs proliferate in the background of these diatribes: whether it be Pepi, the poodle, or the faithful Newfoundland. However, other letters and other evidence show that Wagner, who was a remarkable psychologist (Thomas Mann even compared him to Sigmund Freud),[199] was very conscious of the advantages to be reaped from his mania. Subjective advantages (to Liszt, 1851):[200]

I felt a long-repressed hatred for this Jewry, and this hatred is as necessary to my nature as gall is to the blood. An opportunity arose when their damnable scribbling annoyed me most, and so I broke forth at last. . . .

But also objective advantages, enhanced reputation (to his niece Franziska in the same year):[201]

Through the stupidity of Meyerbeer, who recently hired an army of scribblers, I have suddenly become famous in Paris or at least very interesting. . . . The prospects of a terrible but important and uncommonly successful battle with Meyerbeer excites my—let us call it, malice.

The lucid Wagner who appears here was only wrong on one count: Meyerbeer never started anything whatsoever against his former protégé: he made it a matter of principle not to reply to the attacks and he was resigned to the anti-Semitism around him. Nonetheless, even at the human level, he remains historically the loser, the "shifty customer."[202] (As if he had resigned himself to the fact in advance, Meyerbeer wrote to Heinrich Heine in 1840 that "99 percent of readers are anti-Semites, that is why they relish and will always relish anti-Semitism, as long as it is administered to them with a little skill.")[203]

Likewise, the "Jews" of the time never started anything either against the composer or against the pamphleteer. On the contrary, they continued to supply his most loyal supporters and friends. Sheltered by the musical veil, under the slogan of "art for art's sake," the dialectic of anti-Semitism in all its purity could have free play.

Whatever the reasons, in the realm of fine arts, it was primarily as musicians that the emancipated Jews excelled. As early as the dawn of the nineteenth century, they became interpreters and composers. There is nothing surprising in the fact that the mastermind of *The Ring*, that Wagner, the inspired entrepreneur, should have utilized their talents. What becomes significant, in the event, is the frequency with which he did so. Wagner's partiality for Jewish interpreters was well known: "Why didn't your father and mine have us circumcised at the proper time?" the orchestral conductor, Hans von Bülow, comically exclaimed to a colleague.[204]

"Many of my best friends are Jews"; Wagner always followed this golden rule of erstwhile anti-Semitism. But this guilty preference or alibi was not purely one-sided: psychologically, the advantages easily became reciprocal. The extreme example of this sort in the Wagnerian entourage was the virtuoso Joseph Rubinstein. Their liaison opened with a letter which the musician sent from his native Ukraine to the author of *Das Judentum in der Musik* telling him that he approved of it on all counts and that the only choice left him therefore was suicide or redemption at the hands of the Master. Wagner agreed to act as his paternal patron, welcomed him into his household in 1872 and made him his favorite pianist: visitors to the house listened to the airs of *Siegfried, Wotan,* the *Valkyries* interpreted in their arrangement for the keyboard by this Jew. His devotion to Wagner knew no bounds and his death left him so bereft that he committed suicide on his Master's grave. "He could not bear what all the Master's followers bore: to survive him," commented Wagner's official biographer.[205]

Another pianist, Karl Tausig, a pupil of Liszt's, is not mentioned as a Jew in this biography, written under Cosima Wagner's supervision; its authors confine themselves to an allusion to "his confused origins." The thing was that Tausig, who was also a man of action, was the great artisan of the Bayreuth project; the Wagnerians probably felt that it was important to spare him posthumously.

Also a Jew was the tenor Angelo Neumann, Wagner's favorite Lohengrin and Siegfried; when he became a theatrical manager, he obtained the Master's promise of the world rights of *Parsifal,* outside Bayreuth.[206] After the artistes and impresarios, come the admirers and patrons. Wagner had so high an opinion of the music critic Heinrich Porges that he brought him to Munich in 1864 and wanted to engage this "doyen of Wagnerians" as his secretary.[207] The business affairs of the *Patronatsverein* in Bayreuth were administered by a certain banker Cohn,[208] and the composer himself agreed that it was Jews who clapped his operas most loudly.[209]

Were they trying to assert their German-ness more strongly in this way? Herein lies one of the sources of the attraction that the anti-Semite can have for the assimilated Jew. In the Jew's eyes his enemy seems invested with a special function: to present him with a certificate of patriotism, if not of non-Jewishness. The temptations can become subtle: witness the thoughts which a still traditionalist Jew, the novelist

Berthold Auerbach, confided to a relation after having read *Das Judentum in der Musik*:[210]

> The thing is more dangerous and more poisonous than it appears and cannot be shrugged off by saying: it will pass, people will soon see that Wagner was only writing through malice and jealousy. No, there is something else in it that must be fully recognized and brought to the surface. ... What Wagner wrote about Mendelssohn's music I have in part always felt myself. ...

Auerbach added that this music lacked character, and he only made an exception for *Walpurgis Night* and the *Midsummer Night's Dream*. Was he speaking solely as a musician or was he simultaneously awarding himself a diploma as a good German?

Let us now look at the Wagnerian side of the affair. His anti-Semitism went on growing until his death, and found increasingly violent expression. Before coming on to his writing and secondary manias, let us note that he rejoiced when he learned of Meyerbeer's death in 1864,[211] and that he showed no regret when fire broke out during a performance of Offenbach at the Ringtheater in Vienna in 1882, causing the death of over eight hundred spectators, Christian and Jew alike:[212]

> ... but men are too bad for one to be moved if they perish in masses. The people sitting in such a theater are the most worthless. If miners in a colliery are buried alive, then I am heart-broken and outraged. ...

The same year, he declared: "That mankind is nearing its end is not by any means impossible ... if our culture is collapsing, there's no harm in that; but if it collapses through the *Jews*, that's a disgrace."[213] Let the world collapse, but let it collapse through Wagner!

Why do anti-Semites enjoy the ignominious society of Jews? Probably for a variety of reasons, which may include the generosity they are thus displaying on one hand; but the essential benefit must be the parade of the Aryan splendor in front of the obsequious Semites and, in the final analysis, of themselves. To dominate the Jews is to place oneself above the most astute of all peoples, to surpass the supermen, who have been able to bestialize, to castrate the Aryans: "We are sheep and have taken everything over from the Jews,"[214] Wagner said again, shortly before his death.

As a tyrant, he enjoyed playing a cat-and-mouse game with the "Jew." At the peak of his fame, he entrusted the direction of *Parsifal*, his "German-Christian sacred theatrical work" (*christlich-germanisches Weihefestspiel*), to the orchestral conductor, Hermann Levi, whom he described as his "plenipotentiary" and even his *alter ego*.[215] He wanted to convert him to Protestantism but he also congratulated him on having kept his name completely intact.[216] A temporary difference of opinion arose just before the first night of *Parsifal*, which speaks volumes on the nature of the relationship.

About the middle of June, 1881, Wagner received an anonymous letter from Munich begging him not to let his work be directed by a Jew who, it insinuated, was involved in an illicit relationship with Cosima.[217] The Wagner couple were expecting Levi to dinner that day. The husband placed the letter on a table in the room kept for Levi.

Now Levi was late. Wagner was waiting for him at the door, watch in hand, and said to him in a stern voice: "You are ten minutes late! Unpunctuality comes immediately after infidelity!" He then added: "Now, let us go and dine— no, first read the letter I have ready for you."

At table, Levi, upset by the letter, sat in silence. Wagner asked him why he was so quiet. Levi answered that he did not understand why Wagner had made him read the letter instead of tearing it up immediately. He received the following reply:

I am going to tell you. If I had not shown the letter to anyone, if I had torn it up, perhaps something of its contents would remain in me, but this way, I can assure you that I will keep not the slightest memory of it.

Without taking his leave, Levi returned to Bamburg where he earnestly asked Wagner to release him from the direction of *Parsifal*. Wagner answered by telegram, "Dear friend, you are very seriously requested to return as quickly as possible: this most important business must be brought to a successful conclusion." Levi insisted on resigning and then received a letter containing the following phrases :

My very dear friend, I have every respect for your sensibility; however in this way you are not making things easier either for yourself or for us. It is just because you look at yourself with such a gloomy eye that we might be gripped with anguish in our relations with you. We are completely in agreement to tell this sh. . . to the whole world but this also requires that you do not abandon us and do not let people suppose still more absurdities. For the love of God, come back immediately and learn to know us better! Do not give up any of your faith, but take courage from it!—perhaps a great turning point in your life will come—but in any case you are the leader of my orchestra for *Parsifal*.

This could be Wagner's great ploy: a sadistic desire to humiliate; a conciliatory and sentimental mood; and above all, the desire to bind himself even more closely to his victim. Levi went so far as to agree that *Das Judentum in der Musik* had been dictated by noble idealism. The same year, he wrote to his father, a rabbi:[218]

One day posterity will recognize that he was as great a man as an artist, as his own friends already know. His struggle against what he calls "Judaism" in music and literature is equally explained by the most noble motives.

After the death of this loyal Wagnerian, H. S. Chamberlain gave him an appreciative notice in the *Bayreuther*

Blätter. After stating his merits as an exceptional Jew, he concluded that his problem, seemingly insoluble in real life —that is to say, his awareness of the stigma of his race— especially suited him to express *Parsifal's* desperate quest, as an artist.[219] But it was, as we shall see further on, as if Wagner's son-in-law stopped midway in the argument.

The bibliography on Wagner comprises over forty-five thousand titles, only surpassed, it seems, by Jesus Christ and Napoleon. No other artist has stirred up the masses so much; neither has any been so hated.

He was the great disappointment of Nietzsche's life; Nietzsche, after having liked him very much, urged the Germans to protect themselves against him "as against a disease" (*The Case of Wagner*). "Wagner was something complete; he was complete corruption; Wagner was the courage, the will, the *conviction* of corruption." And Nietzsche declared war "on the cretinism of Bayreuth—and, incidentally, on German taste." (One example would do: did not Edmund von Hagen, in his aphorisms on Wagner, describe his idol as "omnipotent, Sophocles and Plato, Shakespeare and Bacon, Schiller and Kant, Goethe and Schopenhauer in one man, dominating the world.")

Thomas Mann, who also fell under the Wagnerian spell, first saw him as the creator of myths. In 1933 he wrote:

> When one hears it, one seems to believe that the music was only created to serve a myth and that it can set itself no other task. Wagner's music is psychology, symbol, mythology, bombast— everything, but not music in the free and pure sense. . . .

In 1940 he said: ". . . I have so loved that work that even today I am deeply stirred whenever a few bars of music from it impinge on my ear." But he thought that this work, "created and directed against the entire culture and society dominant since the Renaissance, emerges from the bourgeois humanist epoch in the same manner as does Hitlerism," and that it was "the exact spiritual forerunner of the 'metapolitical' movement today terrorizing the world." An intensely German work to an exemplary degree, he added again.[220]

But Wagnerism, like Hitlerism, was a European phenomenon as well. In France, there were the crazes for Baudelaire, Barrès and Proust, the symbolists and the *Revue wagnérienne,* "the homage rendered since childhood at the altar of the god Richard Wagner" which Lévi-Strauss speaks of.[221] The passage of time and, even more, the Hitler ordeal have gradually toned down opinions on an art form which wanted to be the music of the future and which has orchestrated a bloody past. "There is no doubt that this thoroughbred German, this genius who was so authentically Germanic," wrote Henri Lichtenberger at the end of the last century, "has found a perfect spiritual homeland with us . . . we respect him as one of the most noble heroes of modern Germany and of art of all time."[222] Half a century later, in around 1944, Marcel Beaufils noted:[223]

> Wagner is going to affect the Frenchman, as he is going to affect the German and at curiously contradictory levels. It seems that this man, with his own temperament, was able to release others': the temperament of his race for a long time, of foreign races for generations.

Even more recently, in 1960, Marcel Schneider agreed that Wagner was great but with a greatness which, just because it was "sacred," exposed him to hatred and raillery:[224]

> Deceit and ill faith can be scented and there is nothing more shocking than a false prophet who uses the enthusiasm of his worshipers for personal ends, than the ridiculous magus who turns the sacred to criminal use. It is, however, to this idea of religious mystery that one must return to understand the apotheosis that Wagner experienced at the end of his life. It cannot be explained in any other way. When religion has lost its prestige, men expect the artist to replace the priest. . . .

On the other hand, the Third Reich fêted Wagner even

more than the Second, and regarded him as a precursor and initiator. The whole climate of opinion concurred to this end, but it was more particularly the doing of one man. One of Adolf Hitler's childhood friends states that he "looked for much more than a model and an example in Wagner. He literally appropriated Wagner's personality as if he wanted to make it an integral part of his individuality."[225] The diagnosis does not appear exaggerated when applied to a man who, in his youth, divided his century into people who were Wagnerians and those who "had no special name" (cf. Hitler's *Table Talk*).[226] In his own particular way, Alfred Rosenberg seems to be saying the same thing:[227]

> But the essence of all the art in the West became manifest in Richard Wagner; that the Nordic soul is not contemplative, that it does not go astray in individual psychology but willingly experiences the laws of the cosmos and the psyche and shapes them intellectually and architectonically.

But perhaps Wagner had no better exegetist than Wagner himself.

Throughout his life, he explained himself on the subject of his work in which he was trying to blend music, thematic action and ideology into an indissoluble unity. After the Zurich period, most of his writing on art, politics and other subjects, was done at Bayreuth, at the end of his life. His anti-Semitism was unflagging; with time, he became gloomier. He wrote to the King of Bavaria, Ludwig II, in 1881:[228]

> I regard the Jewish race as the born enemy of pure humanity and everything that is noble in it; it is certain that we Germans will go under before them, and perhaps I am the last German who knows how to stand up as an art-loving man against the Judaism that is already getting control of everything.

(Which did not prevent him from comforting his impresario Angelo Neumann when he was exposed to the anti-Semitic disturbance in Berlin in the same year, from criticizing the anti-Semitic campaign on that occasion, and from speaking of "absurd misunderstanding"—this too was Wagner.) Schopenhauer's pessimistic arguments were enriched by Gobineau's on racial decadence. "Plastic demon of mankind's decadence" was how he described the Jew in a work entitled, not perhaps irrelevantly, *Erkenne dich selbst* (*Know Thyself*). Here he attributed to the "Jew" a maleficent superiority, and astonishing successes. He ascribed not only the invention of money, worse, of paper money, a "diabolic plot," to him but, at the extreme, also all Western civilization which "is a judaico-barbaric jumble" and in no way "a Christian creation." This power on the part of the Jew seemed to Wagner to be inherent in his blood, and so powerful that "even mixing does not harm it; man or woman, if he marries into races most foreign to his own, he will always produce a Jew."[229]

This is a fundamental theme of Nazism, from which Nazism drew the conclusions which we know all too well. With Richard Wagner, it was interwoven with vegetarianism, which Hitler also followed. Wagner explicitly related "the forbidden taste of animal flesh" to "the fact that the Jewish God found Abel's fatted lamb more savory than Cain's offering of the produce of the field."[230] In his eyes, consumption of animal flesh was a major cause of mankind's decadence. He developed this view particularly in *Religion und Kunst* (1880).

According to the terms of Wagnerian theory, men in the golden age of yore lived, innocent and happy, on high Asiatic plateaux. After innumerable vicissitudes, which he related in detail,[231] they became carnivores and cannibals. The final stage on this journey from Aryan vegetarianism to Jewish cannibalism was "a Parisian slaughterhouse during its early morning traffic." Wagner tended to condemn the murder of an animal more harshly than that of a man.

Towards the end of his life, he was attracted by the figure of Christ, but he invented a form of Christianity to suit himself. In fact, he thought that the Last Supper meant the return to primitive innocence, and was intended to symbolize respect for animal life and therefore vegetarianism. On this basis, the bread and wine had taken the place of flesh and blood: the Apostles were intending to commemorate the Savior and seal the New Alliance in this way. But as the Church had rapidly become "judaized," this symbolism of primitive Christianity had been completely obliterated.[232]

However it may be with these theological fantasies, which on closer examination emerge as the exact reverse of Daumer's fantasies,[233] the fact that Wagner situated his slaughterhouse in Paris has a significance of its own. Almost as fascinated by the French as by the Jews, he jeered coarsely at these "semiticized Latins" in his *Eine Kapitulation* on the morrow of the surrender of Paris in 1871; nonetheless, however "turbulent" they were, in his eyes, they were still "the gods and masters of the world."[234] This also seems very German; but the ambivalence here was still kept within bounds, or, in other words, the attraction was less repressed.

Wagner, who was not a systematic doctrinarian, barely bothered with other "inferior races," Slavs and Blacks. As for the women who loved and helped him so much, they symbolized in his work the romantic idea of the "eternal feminine," in the two forms of the immaculate Mother of God and the genetrix, Venus, or of "nature" as opposed to "spirit." What he had to say about this discursively was interrupted by his death in February, 1883; it does not seem that the essay on the "feminine element in the human being" that he had sketched out, would have advocated anti-feminism in Proudhon fashion.

The particular feature in Wagner, therefore, which seemed to go hand in hand with hatred of the Jews, was love of animals. In his operatic works, both *Lohengrin's* and *Parsifal's* swans incarnated innocence and purity—the purity, as he wrote to Mathilde Wesendonck, from which he drew all his strength :[235]

I tell you this—only the feeling of my *purity* gives me this power: I feel myself *pure*: I know in the very depths of my being that I have always worked for others, never for myself; and my constant sufferings are my witnesses. . . .

The sufferings of this egotist also included an obsession with pollution which his books (notably the work he regarded as the most important: *Heldenthum und Christenthum*) revealed in two forms: contamination by Jewish blood and contamination by animal flesh. It was to a combination of the two that he tended to attribute Western decadence:[236]

It certainly may be right to charge this purblind dullness of our public spirit to a vitiation of our blood—not only by departure from the natural food of man, but above all by the tainting of the heroic blood of the noblest races with that of former cannibals now trained to be the business agents of society.

He saw no remedy for this decline except "divine purification" by[237]

. . . the partaking of the blood of Jesus, as symbolized in the only genuine sacrament of the Christian religion. . . . That would have been the antidote to the decline of races through commingling and perhaps our earth had brought forth breathing life for no other purpose than that ministrance of healing.

What then was this religion? What was this *Aryan Mystery of Bayreuth,* which some exegetists thought held the elements of the "old Aryan religion"?[238] These phantasms occurred again in another publication, where Wagner, fighting against vivisection, went even further.[239] He first warned that what we are debating here "is the most earnest concern of humanity." He then gave a summary of his main theory:

When first it dawned on human wisdom that the same thing breathed in animals as in mankind, it appeared too late to avert the curse which, ranging ourselves with the beasts of prey, we seemed to have called down upon us through the taste of animal food: disease and misery of every kind, to which we did not see mere vegetable-eating men exposed. The insight thus obtained led further to the consciousness of a deep-seated guilt in our earthly being. . . .

Would the murder of the animal be mankind's original sin? Here, Wagner seems curiously close to Sigmund Freud, who thought that "murder of the father" was at the origin of the feeling of guilt and totemic sacrifice. For this was what really seemed to be involved for Wagner:

Races drawn to rawer climates and hence compelled to guard their life by animal food, preserved till quite late times a feeling that the beasts did not belong to them, but to a deity; they knew themselves guilty of a crime with every beast they slew or slaughtered, and had to expiate it to the god: they offered up the beast, and thanked the god by giving him the fairest portions of the spoil. What here was a religious sentiment survived in later philosophers, born after the ruin of religions, as an axiom of humanity. . . .

The crime he was protesting against was all the more horrible in his opinion because the animal seemed to him morally superior to man, notably because of its "devotion true till death." He attributed other virtues to it—sincerity, simplicity, the impossibility of lying. Here, too, he ended up by evoking the expiatory death of Jesus, but the powers of evil had regained the upper hand, Christianity had become judaized: "The Pentateuch has won the day, and the prowling animal [that is to say, man] has become the 'calculating' beast of prey . . ."

In a letter which he addressed to E. von Weber, the president of the anti-vivisectionist league, Wagner advised him to take a strong line, and bethought himself anew of the Jews:[240]

Even today it would do no harm for example if the Jews learnt to be afraid, whereas they are daily becoming more insolent.

Likewise the gentleman-vivisectionists must learn fear, learn to fear for their life, *i.e.*: they must think they see the people with sticks and clubs before them.

Here again the Jews are cited as an example, in a way which is reminiscent of Marshall Gneisenau's "Jews and contractors" and Clemens von Brentano's "Jews and Philistines"; other people at this juncture were talking about "Jews and Freemasons." But we think that we have collected sufficient data to be able to come to a conclusion, in the way that the inspired artist seemed to be suggesting when he wished he were "conscious of the unconscious" (*Der Wissende des Unbewussten*).

The Wagnerian neurosis was, in the first place, a sign of the time, a form of *"mal du siècle."* It was—excessive with Wagner as with the rest—"the suffering of the artist"; it could therefore be cultivated and exhibited to advantage, just as his anti-Semitic component only expressed one of the prevailing ideologies of the period. The real disease, the narcissistic wound, remains. On this plane, this neurosis, like any other, prolongs the conflict of early childhood into adult life, a conflict complicated with Wagner by his dual and uncertain paternity. As the conflict was not resolved, the father image was split in two, and all the composer's emotional attachments remained marked by this schism: friends, patrons became the good and loving father figure, a Geyer to whom he devoted a grateful memoir; enemies and rivals became extensions of the threatening and castrating father—Geyer in his mother's bed, Geyer the intruder, the Jew—whom he hated, whose memory he sought to repress, but with whom he also continued to identify in the depth of his unconscious.

Wagner's conversion to anti-Semitism can be thought to have put some balm on the wound. It enabled him to square this old account at least to some extent. Henceforth, he seemed to feel, in his own way, that he was a father, a leader, and he ordered his life accordingly; he no longer played the rebel; he acquired an audience, disciples; he, in his turn, dominated. But the wound continued to exist, the soul remained mutilated and, on close examination, this misanthropist only had real affection for people he held entirely under his thumb. This was for several years the case with Nietzsche. In 1872, he wrote to the young philosopher who laid himself at his feet, that he was, after his wife Cosima, his sole gain from life; apart from them, there was only his dog Fidi; his flesh and blood children, Siegfried and Eva, did not figure in this existential balance sheet.[241]

Dogs and Jews thus marked out the artist's emotional life and he probably associated the one with the other in the depths of his unconscious; note the two obsessions with pollution by flesh (animal) and blood (Jewish). Similarly, he extended the feelings of affection he had for animals, to servile Jews, castrated by him, men like Joseph Rubinstein or Hermann Levi, Wagner's human dogs, animated objects, subject to his complete control—pleasures of revenge, repulsion metamorphosed into attraction. This sort of transference has also been observed in the Nazi killers, great animal lovers, who also lavished affectionate benevolence on the Jewish slaves allocated to their personal service. These are typical of the workings of the anti-Semitic psyche which in addition deliberately attributes everything it dreads and would like to ignore in itself, to the object of its passion, by the process of projection. In Wagner's case, this was a devouring greed, hunger for money and hunger for blood, both conceived as unclean, and easily connected; in other words, the "Jew" in himself. But this particular demon cannot be taken in, especially in such a clear-sighted character as Wagner, and this hunger cannot be assuaged; the wound remains incurable, the suppressed hate persists; this gives rise to guilt feelings, observed in the form of contamination, and the hope of redemption by the blood of the Savior, which once again, with the renovator of old myths, reflects hunger for blood, the avenging impulse.

This precious blood forms the core of the mystical plot of

Parsifal, the sacred work of Bayreuth, the apotheosis, product of a quarter of a century of thought. It is the blood which will cure the wound of King Amfortas, whom Wagner invested with all his anxieties. He is known to have taken the theme from the legend of the Grail, modifying it in his own way, on the assurance that its medieval author had misunderstood it.[242] Some of these alterations enable us, in the light of his relationship with Hermann Levi, to add one or two final touches to this character study.

Some of the liberties which he took with the theme of the Grail surprised or shocked many critics. King Amfortas, "a figure of tremendous tragic interest," he wrote as early as 1859,[243] became the central character in the plot. The Last Supper—Catholics particularly criticized this—was a sort of vegetarian banquet. And above all, Good Friday was the absolute opposite of a funeral festival. "Happy every creature, all that open and soon die, for redeemed nature decks itself in innocence on such a day!" This was the famous *Good Friday Spell*; he sent the score of it to Hermann Levi in February, 1879. The package was accompanied by a letter full of enigmatic allusions, which H. S. Chamberlain published in the *Bayreuther Blätter* in 1901, together with some thirty other letters Wagner had written to Levi. But the first sentence of this particular 'letter was replaced by omission marks: [244]

Dear Friend,
(My wife is never tired of talking to me of your kindness in respect of her and I must therefore thank you with an autograph that you will be able to copy for your collection.) What I have to tell you will not mean much unless the expression of my great joy over you means something. With this estimate of my "joy" I would not like to be thought presumptuous as if there were any value when I rejoice. But there are here at bottom serious and deep secrets and the person who would bring them in full to the light of reason, would for example acquire in my "joy over you" a good support for a construction of future configurations of human affairs, amongst the noble harmony of

which to find ourselves purified again would seem to us both not altogether without consolation.

Social metaphysics!

Thank you once again. Warmest greetings from your very devoted

RICHARD WAGNER

Bayreuth, February 27, 1879

The first sentence can be assumed to have been omitted out of respect for Cosima Wagner, or even at her request; she would have thought it important to keep her distance from the agreeable Jewish orchestra leader. But there is still the rest of the letter which did not seem in the least subversive to Wagnerians and which is important to us. What were those "serious and deep secrets" which Wagner humorously mentioned to Levi when sending him the *Good Friday Spell*? What was the mutual "purification" which he foresaw? What were those "social metaphysics"? Moreover, why was he so persistent about converting Hermann Levi and living in communion with him?[245] Why did he describe him as his *alter ego* and set such store by *Parsifal* being conducted by this son of a rabbi?[246] The exact nature of the Wagner-Cosima-Levi relationship also needs to be examined more closely. The two parts of the letter, the omitted sentence and the remainder, might be connected in various ways.

Here, we are brought back to the "Geyer Question." If Wagner the anti-Semite secretly thought that he was a Jew, he would not have expressed himself any differently, and this would have been his "wound of Amfortas," that mysterious malady, that anguish he described to the King of Bavaria.[247] But beyond that, a supplementary theory can be sketched out, relating to one source of the Wagnerian myth of *Parsifal*, which was probably obscure to the artist himself.

In the course of an ironical account of Meyerbeer's sentimental enthusiasms, Wagner once described him as a "modern redeemer, lamb of God expiating the sins of the world."[248] In this context, an indignant Catholic critic, Father T. Schmid, raised the question of whether *Parsifal*, which contains a great deal about the Redeemer and the Redemption, were not a sacrilegious farce, a parody of the Passion.[249] He listed Wagner's heresies and asked if his art did not bear the shibboleth "*Mysterium, Babylona magna, mater fornicationum et abominationum terrae*" on its brow.[250]

Perhaps there was no need to be so ambitious. While Wagner's admirers were claiming that, inspired by the Holy Spirit, he had rediscovered the true meaning of the Last Supper,[251] it can be assumed that a better source of his inspiration lay in anti-Semitic literature. Not surprisingly, he was an assiduous reader of this and occasionally found fault with it. For example, he criticized Wilhelm Marr for superficiality, and Eugen Dühring for his vulgar style.[252] But *The Jew of the Talmud* by Father A. Rohling, Professor of Theology at the University of Prague, met with his entire approval. This treatise, which contained a great deal about ritual murder, helped him to bear the eczema he was suffering from in 1880, and he was dumbfounded by the "curious practices of the Jews."[253] It can be assumed that in his day he had read Daumer's *Die Geheimnisse des christlichen Alterthums*.[254] Think of his emotion—what the psychologist would call "reactive make-up"—when a chicken was killed. Whether he was accusing the Jews of cannibalism or yearning for redemption through the blood of the Savior, this fascination with innocent blood appeared. Now, what purpose did Christian blood serve for the Jews according to the dictates of anti-Semitic tradition? There are multiple variations: to commemorate the passion of Christ in bitter hatred; to consecrate unleavened bread; to salve the wound of circumcision; to remove the *foetor judaicus*; for men to stop menstrual blood or to cure some other unmentionable disease.[255] In any case, this blood must preferably be procured on Good Friday. The Jews are supposed to rejoice on that day; this myth died hard, as a comment that Proust put into the mouth of the Baron de Charlus showed.[256]

Did Wagner's creative genius become intoxicated with these themes? Was it for him an obscure question of erasing the stigmata of Geyer, of exorcizing this old specter? Was it the "Jew" in him—and as he saw the Jew in himself—which yearned for this cure by redemption by Christian blood and rejoiced in Good Friday? Was this the final meaning of *Parsifal* (not understood by Wagner himself); a ritual murder, a vast frenzied farce, conducted, orchestrated by his "other self," the rabbi's son, Hermann Levi?

However that may be, this is the path a theologian must follow if he wants a clearer understanding of the reasons which make anti-Semitism the worst abomination for a Christian, since it is the converse of the eucharistic mystery.

CONCLUSION

At first glance, the term "survival" in the anthropological sense, seems the most salient characteristic of modern anti-Semitism, for it was propagated at the time when the Jews of Western Europe were tending to abandon both their historical particularism and their own culture. At a social level, nothing henceforth seemed to separate them from Christians; they professed the same values and often went so far as to form the same opinions of themselves as the bourgeois society with which they were trying to integrate. But this society remained hostile to them and this hostility was even becoming more marked. Prejudice and hatred were particularly pronounced in the middle classes and amongst the clergy, but they extended to an aristocracy which had recently been relatively favorable to the Jews, and they were displayed, sometimes with the utmost violence, by the doctrinarians of nascent socialism. It was therefore not a question of an economically determined "class phenomenon." The conflict was regarded as racial, but if contemporaries formed an imaginary image of a Jewish race, they did so because a theologically condemned caste already existed.

In an attempt to make this phenomenon intelligible, we first set out to examine the positions in relation to the people of the Bible adopted by the great ideologists, who shook established belief and order. These positions were variegated, sometimes even contradictory. But they all, each in his way, anticipated the future while paving the way for it.

Voltaire, for example, seemed to emerge as the apostle of a new faith, trying to break the prophetic monopoly of the Jews; the eccentricities of his character must have contributed to making him the prototype of the modern anti-Semite. On the other hand, certain themes and probably certain motivations of future philo-Semitism were combined in Jean-Jacques Rousseau. The English deists and the French encyclopedists appeared to be responsible for the scheme to discredit established belief by discrediting the witness-group of the Jews or challenging them. They therefore were *anti-Jewish*, hostile to a belief, and not *anti-Semitic*, enemies of a hypothetical essence. Nonetheless, the theoretical distinction, clearcut in principle, easily became confused in practice. The early stages of the science of man favored the confusion. For this science, with its tendency to take a globally negative view of everything except the white men of Europe (with the Negro well to the fore), condemned the so-called degenerate races more than the so-called superstitious beliefs, the men more than the ideas. The desire of the universalist humanism of the Enlightenment to liberate the children of the ghetto was based on this sort of conception. Their emancipation was conceived as *regeneration*; to become fully a man, the Jew had to abandon not only his historical particularism but also his habits or way of life. From this period, in the France of the Enlightenment, the line which separated anti-Judaism from anti-Semitism became tenuous to the point of imperceptibility.

We then moved on to the Germany of the poets and thinkers and, particularly in connection with the latter, emphasized the peculiarities of a national history which, within the framework of the Protestant *Aufklärung*, allowed the transition to the modern world to be effected without violent rupture or a break in continuity. As a result, the harsh criticism of Judaism and the Jews made by Kant and Hegel, prolonging Lutheran tradition, was more directly descended than elsewhere from its medieval sources. On the whole, Luther and his descendants, both theological and philosophical, certainly talked no differently from the Fathers of the Church on the subject of the Jews' guilt and error. On the other hand, the rootedness of the Jews in Germany and the economic role they played there, especially at court, stirred up particular animosity towards them.

We came then to the problems created by the emancipation of the Jew which was proclaimed by the French Revolution and carried out in different Western countries with varied success. But in nearly all these countries, the liberation of the pariahs aroused not only complaints and recriminations, but also superstitious anxieties, of which we have tried to give numerous examples. Paradoxically, the Jews' efforts to assimilate, that is to say, to cease to be Jews, often had the opposite effect, notably in Germany. The more like the Christians they became, the more mysterious, elusive and frightening they appeared. The conclusion is unavoidable: if the despised class turned into an inferior race instead of disappearing once it had been suppressed by law, it did so because it had a psycho-social function to fulfill, because Christianity in some way needed the Jews, to make a favorable comparison between itself and them. Their success in different spheres of life, the sight of despised money-grubbers raising themselves to the highest social positions, increased the tension and resentment which followed on their liberation. The idea of a Semite race, therefore, seemed to be destined to fill a social void created by emancipation, a void which was so distressing that certain visionaries were already going to the lengths of attributing the revolutionary upheavals of the period to the Jews. The shadow of the Elders of Zion was silhouetted on the horizon. Nothing epitomized all these contradictions better than the correspondence between the Humboldts: the wife displaying virulent *avant la lettre* anti-Semitism and lavishing friendship on de-judaized Jews: the husband, a great humanist and great ·emancipator, but more tolerant of orthodox than "new style" Jews; all the ambiguities of anti-Semitism were brought together here.

It was against this background that the great emancipation scheme came under attack. What is more, the phenomenon of racist reaction contributed to maintaining the bonds of ancestral solidarity amongst emancipated Jews and to perpetuating their feeling of a Jewish identity which even baptism could not entirely obliterate. The reaction against emancipation invented the concepts which suited the new age of science, and in order to separate itself from the Jews, concocted a specific genealogy called the "theory of Aryanism." This theory, taken as authoritative throughout Europe, was an international creation; but anti-Jewish feeling developed in a different way in different countries.

In Great Britain, for example, it was only revealed in literature. This country did not experience anti-Semitic agitation: no ideologist here took it into his head to attribute the evils of the Industrial Revolution to the Jews. France, where the romantic socialist movements, each in its own fashion, exaggerated the medieval myths, was another story; the Jewish danger was used as a bogey both by the champions of the fallen nobility and the exploited masses, both by Chateaubriand and de Vigny and by Fourier and Proudhon. It is remarkable to see how their views converged to an almost identical point on this subject. Anti-Semitism already seemed to be sketching in a link-road between otherwise incompatible positions.

But it was Germany which was the choice terrain for the anti-Jewish passion of the new era after the Napoleonic turmoil. We tried to make a distinction between the rise of a specifically Germanic racism, which decreed the congenital superiority of its followers over other human groups, and the anti-Jewish reaction common to all Europeans.[1] On the morrow of 1815, the combination of circumstances resulted in the development of an early "purity of race" program by the various agitators forming the extreme wing of youthful German nationalism; the following century would see it translated into fact. A similar climate of ideas condemned the German Jews to become rebels and critics, to fight against accepted ideas and to incarnate everything universal *par excellence* in German culture. The contradictions inherent in their position—epitomized by Heine—stimulated their intellectual fertility and made them play the revolutionary role we know; a handful of Judeo-German thinkers were to a large degree responsible for the fact that the great ideas of the future were formulated in the heart of Europe. Meanwhile, German philosophy, in an extension of the campaigns of the encyclopedists, in its turn undertook the demolition of established beliefs, with a view to a better future. This time, numerous Jews took part in the campaign, and it was within this framework that the Jewish anti-Semitism of men like Karl Marx reared its head. But it is by examining the case of Richard Wagner that we have tried to bare the final sources of anti-Semitic passion. If, as Nietzsche prophesied or Thomas Mann diagnosed, the great creator of myths paved the way for fascist Europe and Hitler's Germany, from the psychological point of view, his pleasure in anti-Semitism flowed from the same source as the anguish of feeling that he was Jewish, and the religion of *Parsifal* seemed to be fed by the phantasm of the ritual murder.

Can we go further? Can we, through Wagner's conception of the Last Supper, however heretical it might be, expose a very secret, and all the more powerful source of medieval orthodox Judeophobia? To attempt this archaeological reconstruction, let us recall the link between the accusation of deicide and the eucharistic sacrament which commemorated the Last Supper, that is to say Christ's offer of his body of a man-God.

From generation to generation and from communion to communion, this supreme sacrament, the sacrament of the mystical union in Christ, set the community which fed on the flesh and blood of its Lord against the people so suggestively named the "witness-people." These were the people who excluded themselves from the feast, placed themselves outside the sacred bond, and therefore disputed its significance, and in this way condemned themselves to their role as scapegoats. However, the Church taught its worshipers that they too were guilty of the death of Christ, that they too had crucified the man-God who had sacrificed himself for them. But on whom did this guilt, emphasized by medieval piety and art with all the suggestive power we know, more easily fall than on the legendary murderers whose outrageous crime, far from being attenuated by the Christian assumption of responsibility, was indefatigably remembered because of it? It was primarily in this way that religious feeling changed to hatred for the deicidal race. It was in this way that the Jews became, in the medieval imagination, butchers of children and profaners of hosts. A direct connection can in fact be seen between the propagation of legends of their ritual murders and profanations in the twelfth and thirteenth centuries and the propagation and dogmatic sanction by the church of the idea of Jesus as actually present in flesh and blood in the consecrated host.[2] Miracles describing the Child Jesus rising victoriously from hosts profaned by Jews[3] can therefore be regarded as an echo of the first miracle of the host, which caused the festival of the Holy Sacrament to be instituted. Ritual murder trials likewise grew up in the twelfth century and multiplied in the thirteenth; the institution of the wheel-shaped badge, the burning of the Talmud and the expulsion of its disciples are all symptoms of this rise of Christian anti-Semitism.[4] This ominous evolution in its turn contributed to relegating the sons of Israel to the reviled profession of usury.[5] They thus appeared as universal malefactors who butchered Christians by sucking not only their blood but also their money. Foreigners everywhere, because they were driven out of everywhere, wandering without hearth or home, natural associates of the Devil, initiated into the magic arts of medicine and the mysteries of finance, they henceforth combined all the qualities required to act as targets for the Christian's sacred hatred.

The ancient deicide accusation was fundamental to all this, but it must be realized that this motive, however coherent, was kept alive by a different guilt. This was the guilt which the accusers were casting off when they identified themselves by the consumption of flesh and blood—that is to say by the realistic means of an introjection—with the man-God who had taken the sins of the world upon his shoulders. Moreover, the transfer of guilt in this manner is sketched out by certain Fathers of the Church as early as the first centuries of Christianity; this appointment of the Jews as scapegoats therefore seems to have been an essential and specific cause of Christian anti-Semitism; the other charges seem only to be extensions of it or sequels to it.[6] In addition, the divine blood which lay at the Jews' door was still that of a Jewish king, descended from David. In this way the butchers of Christian children remained associated with the God of grace of the New Testament, while incarnating the God of vengeance of the Old. This is perhaps the final ambivalence of anti-Semitism.

In modern times this anti-Jewish passion is kept alive by actions and reactions, by processes which we have tried to clarify. How many sceptics or doubters, how many champions of irreligion or of purified religion found, like Voltaire, that they were good Christians and good Catholics when they came face to face with a Jew. It can be noted in this context that very many heritages or survivals of this type of emotional pre-disposition "imbibed at the mother's breast" still exist. The means whereby they are transmitted are still not entirely understood. In Catholic France prejudices of this kind still linger against Protestants, those other victims of erstwhile persecution and hereditary enemies of yore; the Jews' identity in this sense was much more pronounced, and their efforts to modify or even obliterate it only aggravated Christian prejudice more. Moreover, while the ancient teaching of contempt, in its orthodox form or in various heretical disguises (like Wagnerian mythology), went on, the old religious passions continued to have their effect, converging with those of the new crusade by atheists. A large number of nineteenth-century ideologists thus payed their tribute to a tradition which Charles Maurras described as the "anti-Semitic genius of the West."

The sociologist could follow up another specific determinant of anti-Semitism of a supra-individual nature: namely the effect exercised by language which remained constant in a world in process of rapid evolution. The active indictment contained in the word "Jew" and those which are associated with it, also in some way "imbibed at the mother's breast," remained immutable. As a result, to confused contemporaries, distressed or even suffering from loss of status because of the economic and social upheavals, the world seemed to have become "Jewish," just when the Jews were doing their utmost not to be Jewish, at least in the pejorative, traditional and medieval sense of the term. Still, in order to do this, they had to pursue their eminent role in commerce and finance; but Jewish bankers and entrepreneurs remained Jews who engaged in banking and entrepreneurial functions; the order of the wording defined and judged them not by what they actually did (by their conduct) but by what they were reputed to be (by an imaginary essence). On this subject, texts are scattered at various places over this book in which contemporaries bring in the words *Jew* and *Judaism* to designate the criteria of evil. In our opinion, one cannot overestimate the influence of the active indictment inherent in a language colored with Judeophobia which took shape and manufactured its means of expression (perpetuated even today) in a monolithically Christian Europe. These means, too, connect modern anti-Semitism with medieval theology.

The well-known difficulty of giving an adequate definition of the Jew today might arise from the same source. Theories born of Christian civilization have postulated categories of religion or faith, and nation or nationality. Judaism, which was conceived in pre-Christian times as a particularist community with a universal ethical vocation, "which has its dwelling apart,"[7] cannot be integrated globally into either of these two categories. In the nineteenth century, it was considered—and considered itself—a "faith" in the West of Europe, and a "nationality" in the East. But the language of the Polish-Russian Jewries was already completing this definition by adding the curiously strong concept of *yiddishkeit*, that is to say of an attitude peculiar to Jews. The idea of a "Jewish race" was thereafter unanimously rejected both on grounds of the progress of anthropology and for peremptory reasons of an extra-scientific nature. Today the substitution of the idea of "Jewish specificity" or of "Jewishness" is sometimes suggested. The latter, from the point of view of Western analytical reason, runs the risk of being tautological since the Jew is defined by a Jewishness which in its turn is defined by the Jew, or by a Jewish attitude, the elements of which are unknown except that they are inherent in the Jew.[8] However, this definition has the advantage of putting the accent on the uniqueness of the phenomenon within Western civilization (it is a reminder that in the nature of things the destiny of the Jews—the "Jewish fact"— is without parallel there).[9]

Lastly there is the idea of a "Jewish community," a concept which is most frequently challenged by non-practicing Jews and more generally by atheists of all affiliations, because of its religious connotations. Nonetheless, just because of this, it places the emphasis, not unfelicitously in our opinion, on humanitarian interests and ethical aspirations (turning moreover easily into claims and accusations against the surrounding world) which is characteristic of the Jewish attitude or even the "Jewish soul." But however that may be, all these difficulties and contradictions would really seem to be due, in the final analysis, to a way of thought and terminology formed in a society where the Christian was the rule and the Jew was the exception. Marginal in relation to language as in relation to society, he did not fit into the usual categories. Obviously neither the *Yiddish* of Eastern European Jewries nor the *Ladino* of Mediterranean Jewries, which reflected the methods of Talmudic thought on this point in their structures, experienced these difficulties.

The origin of the Jewish fate and the uniqueness of the Judeo-Christian relationship make the question of anti-Semitism difficult to understand, protect it from generalizations, and will probably lead for a long time to come to the short-circuiting of sociological interpretations by mystical interpretations, as much from habits of thought as from desperation. Sociology comes back into its own more easily in aberrant cases, which shock accepted ideas and lead to real questions being posed. In the present instance, such aberrant cases do exist. It is easy to say that anti-Semitism is eternal and intrinsic to Judaism, but it was nonetheless non-existent in the Far East. Moreover, it was this fact which at the time suggested the theory with which I began my research. The Jewries of China and India, I wrote some fourteen years ago,

> have not shocked the world by a history of torment and massacre, nor expiated its imperfections, they have never played a role disproportionate to their numbers, or distinguished themselves in intellectual or economic activities, nor have they assumed any role other than their own.

This observation led me to conclude that "faith in the divine destiny of the Jews has been an important influence on their truly strange fate."[10] I meant by that the centuries-old interaction within the limits of the monotheist religions, between the followers of the mother-religion and those of the daughter-religion. This interaction is much more pronounced in Christianity than in Islam. Such an approach made it possible to interpret the anti-Semitic phenomenon in a way which in my opinion had the additional advantage of cutting short "supernatural" interpretations of it. It could reasonably be attributed to psycho-social tensions acting at the combined levels of a theology, which singled out the Jews, and an economy within which they consequently played an eminent role. A thesis on economic history devoted to the function of the Jews in medieval society seemed to me to confirm the accuracy of my initial hypothesis. In fact, this work led me to conclude that the secret of the Jews' professional specialization was to be found in Christian religious thought and awareness rather than in the congenital aptitudes which there was a tendency to attribute to them and which, on further thought, are nothing but the "racial features" of the anthropology (plus preconceived ideas) of the recent past.[11]

The case of the Jews in the non-anti-Semitic society of the Far East contrasts with the case of the anti-Semitic society—despite the absence of Jews—of modern Spain. This other aberrant case shows how the phenomenon is perpetuated after Jews have disappeared, but also how it finally dies out. In this instance, the first stage in the process begins with the religious unification of Spain (the expulsion of the Spanish Jews in 1492) which first gave rise to the phenomenon of crypto-Judaism; the "Marranos" preserved their existence in secret within families for several generations and it was only at the beginning of the eighteenth century that the persecutions of the Inquisition seemed to have lost their object. But their shadow persisted and thus it was that during a second stage, which overlapped with the first but also stretched over some two centuries, one part of Catholic Spain persecuted the other, reputed to be of Jewish descent and therefore "impure." The conflict between "old" and "new" Christians was the same type of phenomenon as the conflict between "Aryans" and "Semites" in nineteenth-century bourgeois Europe, even if the minority exposed to the contempt and injustice was uniformly Catholic in one case, diversified, as we have seen, in the other. The conduct of the majority was anti-Semitic on both occasions. On the side of the minority, the corresponding reactions maintained an attitude which has still not completely died out; reminiscences still persist in varied forms in the Balearic Islands as well as Portugal.[12]

The similarities stop there. It would be futile in our opinion to try to draw any lessons whatsoever relating to our contemporary world from this. The decline in anti-Semitism since the first half of the present century is explained by other causes. Let us give a brief summary of them in all their heterogeneity. The racial persecutions of the Hitler régime, which were already spreading to other human groups after they had begun with the Jews, aroused unanimous reprobation, and the racism, with which anti-Semitism is generally identified, has been surrounded with a sort of taboo. The Christian Churches particularly condemned it thereafter. The change in the attitude of the teaching relating to the Biblical people, culminating in the decisions of the Ecumenical Council in 1965, is in this sense a symptom and a promise for the future (which must be related to the general evolution of religious psychology and thought). This censure of anti-Semitism, propagated by the élite, is therefore acting from the top downwards. But from the bottom upwards, a new image of the Jew could be said to be spreading, inspired by the youthful folklore of Israel and by the plain fact of the existence of the State. He is no longer a bastard without hearth or home; he is no longer the wandering Jew; the features of a soldier-farmer blur those of a rapacious Shylock. In this way, the play of the collective imagination backs up the action taken by the moral conscience of the West. But beyond these new predispositions which result from the historical situation, there is an additional factor which arises from the evolution of its psychological components.

Today, the Jews are no longer accused of weaving a permanent plot against mankind, of unleashing revolutions and historical catastrophes. They are no longer attributed with supernatural powers. Any display of fanatical or "paranoid"[13] anti-Semitism by an individual which, as we have described, had such a hold on certain leaders of nineteenth-century thought, is dismissed by public opinion as a freak or even a psychosis. Even half a century ago, a puerile myth like the "Elders of Zion," was taken seriously not only by anti-Communist Russians or nationalistic Germans, but by certain ruling circles of the victorious Entente.[14]

This is what would be unthinkable today. In the final analysis, this return to common sense reflects the great changes in the Western world. Everything suggests, in fact, that the Jews jar far less and shock less in an industrialized society like our own, henceforth accustomed to be what the destiny of the West has made it, accustomed to urbanization, to the accelerated rhythm of existence, in short to its own changes. The wandering people, for their part, has been involved in this sort of cycle for a long time. Many of its features—urbanization,[15] frequent change of horizons[16]—had been familiar to them since the beginning of the dispersion. This gave rise, *inter alia*, to their traditionally sharp critical sense and their natural gift for de-mystification. But in this respect as well, the contemporary world, sceptical of ideologies, resigned to its disenchantment, is no longer roused or is less roused by a critique of values until recently described as "Jewish", just as the cult of material well-being which characterizes our affluent civilization was reputed to be "Jewish." Thus, if this civilization has ceased to endure the criticism of being "Jewish" on one account or another, in the long run it is because the change in the modern world, which has become permanent, henceforth forms part of the everyday environment and is accepted by custom. In this sense, our suggestion can be illustrated more clearly, if we venture to say that our life too has actually become "Jewish" in the anti-Semitic meaning of the term, and even that the world will go on "becoming Jewish" wherever technical and liberal society grows up.

In these circumstances, it seems that anti-Semitism no longer constitutes a threat capable of tearing the social body apart. What remains is the underlying attitude and its interaction with a Jewish attitude still traumatized by the memory of the Hitler persecutions.

This "Jewishness" was revived in 1967, on the eve of the Six Days War, by the threat of destruction which seemed for a few days to hover over the State of Israel. Against the background of general and confused emotion, these events provoked unexpectedly violent reactions amongst Jews in the diaspora, leading to a sense of awareness similar to the feeling which recently accompanied the anti-Semitic campaigns. The disillusioned words of a Jewish critic: "The State of Israel is the new religion of the Jews," can demonstrate how strong certain passions are. But the almost holy atmosphere which surrounded the rediscovery of the Wailing Wall shows the complexity of the problem. Finally, it can also be said, thinking of a certain vicious aphorism of yore, that the Jews' patriotism obviously no longer consisted of self-hatred.[17] In any case, the widespread idea that the existence of a Jewish state would lead to a future where the end of the dispersed Jewish people would be more or less in sight seems, as far as man can see, to have been refuted. At the very least, the diagnosis was premature, and the question-mark that the sociologist Georges Friedmann added to the title of his book proved very largely justified.[18] It is also worth reflecting on the contrast between these reactions and the anti-Zionist convictions of preceding generations, notably amongst French Jews. But where the fathers feared the least suspicion of dual allegiance and the challenge of their patriotism, the children primarily appear obsessed by the memory of those fathers who perished in the gas chambers. In addition, Israel gives them an image of themselves corresponding to the one emanating from it throughout the world and which, simply because it is a national image, is not the anti-Semitic image of the Jew. The play of mirrors therefore offers them psychological security. However, these Israeli allegiances have not failed to arouse censure, and critics coming face to face with Jews have sometimes found that they are patriots of their respective countries, as in times of old. Moreover, the Israeli victory in 1967 exacerbated official anti-Semitism in the so-called Socialist countries; and in a more subtle fashion it also propagated in certain circles in Western countries anti-Zionist sentiments which are not always easily distinguished from anti-Semitism pure and simple.

Historians are not prophets, and I will refrain, finally, from making any prognosis. Only the future will show if, and to what degree, a hatred of the Jews, justified theologically until the French Revolution and "racially" until the Hitlerite holocaust, will have a third incarnation under a new "anti-Zionist" guise.

NOTES

Foreword

(1) Religious sociology only acknowledges practicing Jews, that is to say a minority.

(2) An economic history of European Jews in the nineteenth century is theoretically possible, but it would require extremely extensive research into the archives used for general works of economic history, and it would in addition pose hazardous problems of identification, as well as the problem of converted Jews. It is not surprising that no serious work of this type exists, as opposed to the often excellent works dealing with earlier centuries.

(3) *Annales*, XXII (1967), p. 656. In the same journal a few years ago Father Alphonse Dupront devoted a memoir to the "Problèmes et méthodes d'une histoire de la psychologie collective," a history which included that "of the collective psyche" or the collective memory. Amongst other subjects for research, M. Dupront suggested the establishment of an "inventory of the manifestations of irrational forces (panics, epidemics, psychoses, acts of witchcraft) throughout the medieval and modern West." (*Annales*, XVI (1961), pp. 3–11.)

1 The Jews of Europe in the Eighteenth Century

(1) Joseph Addison in *The Spectator*, September 27, 1712.

(2) Dr Schulz, *Voyages . . .*, quoted by Max Grunwald, *Spinoza in Deutschland*, Berlin, 1897, p. 288.

(3) E. Bodemann, *Kurfürstin Sophie von Hannover, Briefwechsel mit ihrem Bruder*, Leipzig, 1889, p. 369.

(4) Isaac Pinto, *Réflexions critiques sur le premier chapitre du VIIe tome des œuvres de M. de Voltaire*, in *Lettres de quelques Juifs . . .* by the Abbé Guénée, Paris, 1821, Vol. I, pp. 12 ff.

(5) Léon Poliakov, *Les Banquiers juifs et le Saint-Siège du XIIIe au XVIIe siècle*, Paris, 1965. (English translation, *Jewish Bankers and the Holy. See*, London, forthcoming.)

(6) *Ibid.*, "Bibliographie."

(7) Herbert Lüthy, *La Banque protestante en France . . .*, Paris, 1959, Vol. I, p. 28.

(8) I refer to this in *Les Banquiers juifs . . .* (especially pp. 100-8).

(9) Cf. "Notes on the struggle against famine in white Russia, and the reorganization of the life of the Jews"; *Works of Derzhavin* (in Russian), St Petersburg, 1878, Vol. VII, p. 278. In 1773, the

governor of the province of Mohilev described the same state of things as follows (*ibid.*, p. 334):

> . . . they are in debt to everyone from whom they can borrow anything at all and eventually deliberately make themselves bankrupt; they seek out every means to incur debts and thereby force themselves to be tolerated. They borrow money by various means and if the creditor does not have confidence in one of them, then their whole community borrows, in appearance but not in reality.

(10) Cf. *Les Banquiers juifs* . . ., p. 148.
(11) A Feilchenfeld, "Die älteste Geschichte der deutschen Juden in Hamburg," *M.G.W.J.*, XLIII, 1889, pp. 279 ff.
(12) Cf. Léon Poliakov, *History of Anti-Semitism*, Vol. I, *From the Time of Christ to the Court Jews*, New York, 1965, pp. 233-4.
(13) Cf. *Les Banquiers juifs* . . ., pp. 50, 293.
(14) L. de Bonald, "Sur les Juifs," *Mercure de France*, XXIII, 1806, pp. 249-67.
(15) *Praesertim Viennae ab opera et fide judaeorum res saepius pendent maximi momenti*; quoted by W. Sombart, *The Jews and Modern Capitalism*, New York, 1962, p. 97.
(16) Summarized from the account by Selma Stern, *Der preussische Staat und die Juden*, Tübingen, 1962, Erster Teil, Die Zeit des Grossen Kurfürsten und Friedrichs I, Chapter 1, pp. 11-15.
(17) Stern, *op. cit.*, Zweite Abteilung, *Akten*, No. 27, pp. 33-4.
(18) Cf. Heinrich Schnee, *Die Hoffinanz und der moderne Staat*, Berlin, 1953, Vol. I, pp. 54-5.
(19) Stern, *op. cit.*, *Akten* (1. Die Zeit des Grossen Kurfürsten und Friedrichs I; 2. Die Zeit Friedrich Wilhelms I).
(20) *Ibid.*, Vol. 2, No. 267, pp. 330-1.
(21) *Ibid.*, Vol. 2, No. 18, pp. 27-31. ("Gegenvorstellung der sämtlich vergleiteten Judenschaft hiesiger Königl. Residentien contra einige unruhige Krämer unter Namen sämtlicher deutschen und französischen Handelsleute daselbst und deren ungegründete Klagen.")
(22) *Ibid.*, Vol. 1, No. 121, pp. 108-9.
(23) *Ibid.*, Vol. I, pp. 113-15, 126.
(24) Stern, *op. cit.*, 2/1, pp. 9-10.
(25) Schnee, *op. cit.*, Vol. I, pp. 189-90.
(26) Sombart, *op. cit.*, p. 45.
(27) *Ibid.*, p. 23, quoting a senate investigation: ". . . they are increasing in numbers. There is no section of the great merchant class, the manufacturers and those who supply commodities for daily needs, but the Jews form an important element therein. They have become a necessary evil."
(28) Cf. Wilhelm Treue, "Die Juden in der Wirtschaftsgeschichte des rheinischen Raumes," in *Monumenta Judaica*, Cologne, 1962, p. 428. For the inscription "kein Jud' und kein Schwein darf hier nicht hinein," see the contemporary Zalkind-Hourwitz, *Apologie*

des Juifs en réponse à la question: Est-il des moyens de rendre les Juifs plus heureux et plus utiles à la France?, Paris, 1789, p. 63, note. The Frankfurt authorities maintained the prohibition until the beginning of the nineteenth century, despite protests from rich Jews; cf. Georg Liebe, *Das Judentum in der deutschen Vergangenheit*, Leipzig, 1903, pp. 113-14.

(29) As we know Goethe was a native of Frankfurt. In his old age he recalled his impressions of the ghetto (Liebe, *op. cit.*, p. 114):

> Among the weighty matters that preoccupied the boy and also the young man was particularly the state of the Jews' town, really called the Jews' street because it hardly consists of anything more than a single street which in former times had perhaps been squeezed in between the ditches and the city wall. . . . The confinement, the dirt, the swarm of people, the accent of an unpleasant tongue—all made a disagreeable impression, even if one only looked in when passing by the gate. It took a long time before I ventured in alone and I did not return easily, since I had escaped so many people untiringly intent on haggling, either demanding or offering.

(30) *Ibid.*, p. 34.

(31) *Ibid.*, p. 115.

(32) *Über die bürgerliche Verbesserung der Juden,* by C. W. Dohm, Berlin, 1781, p. 17.

(33) The biography of Alexander David of Halberstadt, according to Schnee, *op. cit.*, Vol. II, pp. 88-100.

(34) *The Life of Glückel of Hamelin, written by herself,* Beth-Zion Abrahams, ed. and trans., London, 1962, p. 80. See Poliakov, *From the Time of Christ to the Court Jews,* pp. 230–1.

(35) Schnee, *op. cit.*, Vol. III, p. 72.

(36) *Ibid.*, Vol. III, pp. 102-4.

(37) *Ibid.*, Vol. III, pp. 35-8.

(38) *Ibid.*, Vol. II, pp. 241-5 and 289.

(39) *Ibid.*, Vol. II, pp. 235-6, describes Voltaire's speculations in Germany, according to F. Költzsch, "Kursachsen und die Juden in der Zeit Brühls," thesis, Leipzig, 1929.

(40) Liebe, *op. cit.*, p. 114.

(41) Cf. Maurice Aron, "Le Duc Léopold de Lorraine et les Israélites," *Revue des Études Juives (in future R.E.J.)*, XXXIV, 1896, pp. 107-8.

(42) The quotations which follow are taken from the remarkable study by N. Roubin, "La vie commerciale des Juifs comtadins en Languedoc au XVIIIe siècle," *R.E.J.*, XXXIV-VI, 1896-7, pp. 75-89, 91-105, 276-93.

(43) Léon Brunschvicg, "Les Juifs en Bretagne au XVIIIe siècle," *R.E.J.*, XXXIII, 1896, p. 111.

(44) Cf. Roubin, *op. cit.*, p. 80.

(45) *Ibid.*, pp. 91-8.

(46) *Traité commun des flefs,* by M. Götsman, former councillor on

the Supreme Council of Alsace, Paris, 1768, Vol. II, pp. 317-18.

(47) *Requête des marchands et négociants de Paris contre l'admission des Juifs*, Paris, 1765. This memorandum became a "classic" of anti-Jewish polemic in France, at the end of the eighteenth century; furthermore, it was reissued in 1790, when the Constituent Assembly envisaged the emancipation of the Jews. Some of Goulleau's formulae are worth quoting:

> ... the Jews can be compared to wasps who only break into hives to kill the bees, open their stomachs and draw out the honey in their entrails. ...
> ... they are particles of quicksilver, which run about, wander, and when they reach the slightest slope, join together into a main block. ...
> As for the Jews of Bordeaux, "they were Jews in Portugal, they turned Christian there, they arrived in France as Christians, and there they became Jews; what a people!"

(48) *Annales*, by Linguet, criticizing a decree made by the Paris Parlement on July 21, 1777, London, 1777, Vol. II, pp. 99-125.

(49) Book of complaints of the second-hand hosiers of Montpellier, quoted by Roubin, *op. cit.*, p. 87.

(50) Cf. Pierre Grosclaude, *Malesherbes, témoin et interprète de son temps*, Paris, 1961, Vol. II, p. 645.

(51) Prince Eugène went to hunting parties organized by the Viennese court Jew, Wolff Wertheimer; cf. H. Schnee, Vol. III, p. 243. Maurice of Saxony estimated that only Jewish purveyors were able to provision his armies in a fitting manner. In 1727, he addressed this note to a lieutenant of the Paris Police (cf. Léon Kahn, *Les Juifs de Paris au XVIIIe siècle*, Paris, 1894, p. 106):

> Monsieur, Mister Salomon promises to become a very honest man, nay even a good Catholic; he has done me a service, and gratitude commits me to desire that you should have indulgence for his Jewishness; he is still employed on my business for a few days, therefore I beg you to give him respite or pardon. There is nothing more for me to do but to thank you again for the goodness you have had in this respect, and to assure you that no one could be more perfectly your humble and very obedient servant, Monsieur, than Maurice of Saxony.

(52) *Oeuvres choisies, littéraires, historiques et militaires du maréchal prince de Ligne*, Geneva, 1809, Vol. I, pp. 53, 65.

(53) Kahn, *op. cit.*, pp. 74 ff.

(54) *Ibid.*, p. 94.

(55) *Mémoire pour un Nègre et une Négresse qui réclament leur liberté contre un Juif*, Paris, 1776 (Bibliothèque Nationale, Paris, 4 Fn. 8377). The style of the document is a remarkable illustration of French feeling at the end of the *ancien régime*:

> Two slaves have the good fortune to land in France. They have learned that the air breathed there is that of Liberty. Their souls destroyed by the harshest slavery, are opened up

to the sweetest hope. . . . These unfortunates begin to feel
that liberty is the first of the rights of man and also the most
precious of his possessions. . . . Their position is terrible. It
is humanity itself which offers them to justice. . . .

(56) Cf. the letter of congratulation from Voltaire to Le Moyne des
Essarts, the lawyer defending the two blacks (October 18, 1776).

(57) Cf. Poliakov, *History of Anti-Semitism*, Vol. I, pp. 203-9.

(58) *Ibid.*, Vol. II, *From Mohammed to the Marranos*, New York, 1973.

(59) *The Spectator*, September 27, 1712; cf. M. F. Modder, *The
Jews in the Literature of England*, Philadelphia, 1939, pp. 46-7.

(60) G. M. Trevelyan, *English Social History*, London, 1946, pp. 32-3,
394. Cf. also in the same context, *The Cambridge History of
British Foreign Policy*, London, 1919, Vol. I, p. 3, as well as
A. E. Bland, P. A. Brown, R. H. Tawney, *English Economic
History, Select Documents*, London, 1946, pp. 4 ff.

(61) Modder, *op. cit.*, pp. 50-76.

(62) The description of the anti-Jewish agitation of 1753 which follows
is taken from Cecil Roth's *History of the Jews in England*,
Oxford, 1949, pp. 212-21.

(63) Letter quoted by Roth, *ibid.*, p. 217 note:
The world will not hear the truth, and the proof is very
evident from this abominable spirit that rages against the
Jews. I expect they will shortly be massacred. . . . We now treat
the Jews just as the Mohammedans treat the Christians.

(64) Cf. the obituary notice in "Bell's Life," September 3, 1836
(quoted by Albert M. Hyamson, *The Sephardim of England*,
London, 1951, p. 216):
It has long been admitted that no pugilist that ever existed
so completely elucidated or promulgated the principles of
boxing as Mendoza. Dan . . . may be said to have been the
first "great master" of pugilistic science in this country; and
to have introduced a system of attack and defence at once
new and imposing.

(65) We are dealing here, of course, with popular sentiment. On the
political plane, there were anti-Jewish campaigns in the
Catholic press in Italy after the suppression of the Papal States,
and there was above all the tragic interlude of Mussolini's state
anti-Semitism, after the creation of the "Axis" in 1938.

2 The United States of America

(1) In some American states, legal discrimination outlived the
formation of the United States. For example, in North Carolina
and New Hampshire, the exclusion of Jews and Catholics from
certain public offices was only abolished in 1868 and 1876
respectively. In Maryland Jews and Quakers only obtained the
right to vote in 1825.

(2) Quoted by R. Learsi, *Israel, A History of the Jewish People,* New York, 1949, p. 399.

(3) Cf. *The Jews of the United States, A Documentary History,* L. Blau and Salo W. Baron, eds., Vol. I, General Introduction, p. xxi, New York, 1963.

(4) Alexis de Tocqueville, *Democracy in America,* London, 1946.

(5) "We hold these truths to be self-evident, that all men are created equal, that they are endowed by their Creator with certain unalienable rights: that among these are life, liberty, and the pursuit of happiness."

(6) De Tocqueville, *op. cit.*

(7) W. Sombart, *The Jews and Modern Capitalism,* New York, 1962, p. 50. We know that, according to Sombart's thesis, the Jews were the real creators of capitalism; therefore he attributes to them a decisive influence on the American way of life, without perceiving that entirely original features, such as the perceptive de Tocqueville described nearly a century earlier, were involved.

(8) De Tocqueville, *op. cit.*

(9) See, for example, the articles "Anti-Semitism" in the *Jewish Encyclopaedia,* 1901, and in the *Encyclopaedia Britannica,* 1910.

(10) The number of Jews in the United States was about 50,000 in 1850, 275,000 in 1880, 1,100,000 in 1900, and 3,800,000 in 1925 (in 1960, it was around 5,300,000).

(11) The history of Jews in America began as a dream. For in the heart of a hunted and pursued man the dream of sanctuary always exists. It is the spark that keeps him alive in the midst of terror. Fenced in physically by ghetto walls, hemmed in spiritually by proscriptive laws and the hatred of his neighbors, the Jew of the age of exploration and discovery dreamed of a sanctuary, an island to which to escape from the persecution and darkness that surrounded him. . . .
This is the beginning of an article "History of the Jews in the United States" in a recent American Jewish encyclopedia (*The Jewish People, Past and Present,* New York, 1955, Vol. IV. The idea of a Jewish experience, unique of its kind, is well conveyed by the title of a recent essay by Rabbi Stuart E. Rosenberg, *America is Different,* New York, 1964).

(12) Blau and Baron, *op. cit.,* Introduction, p. xxxv.

(13) Rosenberg, *op. cit.,* p. 257.

3 The Men of the Ghetto

(1) Selma Stern, *Der preussische Staat und die Juden,* Tübingen, 1962, II/1, p. 168.

(2) Cf. M. Kayserling, *Moses Mendelssohn, Sein Leben und Wirken,* Leipzig, 1888, p. 522.

(3) *Mémoire sur les Juifs du prince Ch. de Ligne, ed. cit.,* p. 49.

(4) *Apologie des Juifs en réponse à la question: Est-il des moyens de rendre les Juifs plus heureux et plus utiles à la France?,* by M. Zalkind-Hourwitz, a Polish Jew, Paris, 1789, p. 20.

(5) *Ibid.,* p. 67.

(6) Cf. Léon Poliakov, *History of Anti-Semitism,* Vol. I, *From the Time of Christ to the Court Jews,* New York, 1965, p. 143.

(7) Van De Brande, *Voyage en Languedoc,* Montauban, 1774, 110.

(8) "The Jew loves money and fears danger. . . ."

(9) In the Austrian Empire, the Jews had to pay a special tax to marry in the eighteenth century; likewise in Prussia, where this tax consisted of purchasing a very expensive porcelain service from the State factory. At Frankfurt, they could not marry under the age of twenty-five, etc.

(10) Cf. Karl Thieme. "Der religiöse Aspekt der Judenfeindschaft" in *Judentum; Schicksal, Wesen und Gegenwart,* Wiesbaden, 1965, Vol. II, p. 609.

(11) Cf. Luke II, 42-8: "and when he was twelve, they made the pilgrimage as usual . . . and after three days they found him sitting in the temple surrounded by the teachers, listening to them and putting questions, and all who heard him were amazed at his intelligence and the answers he gave."

(12) In her *Life* Glückel of Hamelin writes that she continued to earn her own living until an advanced age, in order not to become a burden on anyone else. *The Life of Glückel von Hamelin,* Beth-Zion Abrahams, London, 1962, p. 150:

> . . . my fortune grew less and less. My business was large, for I had extensive credit with Jews and non-Jews. I afflicted myself: in the heat of summer and in the snow of winter I went to fairs and stood there in my shop all day; and though I possessed less than others thought, I wished to be always held in honour and not, God forbid, dependent on my children, sitting at another's table. It would be worse to be with my children than with strangers, in case, God forbid, through me, they sinned. This would be worse than death to me.

(13) Zalkind-Hourwitz, *op. cit.,* p. 33.

(14) *Ibid.,* pp. 29-30.

(15) ". . . out of all peoples you shall become my special possession; for the whole earth is mine. You shall be my kingdom of priests, my holy nation" (Exodus XIX, 5-6); "You shall be holy to me, because I the Lord am holy. I have made a clear separation between you and the heathen, that you may belong to me" (Leviticus XX, 26); ". . . a people that dwells alone, that has not made itself one with the nations" (Numbers XXIII, 9); "When you say to yourselves, 'Let us become like the nations and tribes of other lands and worship wood and stone,' you are thinking of something that can never be" (Ezekiel XX, 32). See

also Chapter VIII of Samuel I, where the Jews undertake to force the hand of God in order to have a king to judge them and lead them to war, "like other nations."

(16) We have tried to throw some light on the specific machinery of the relationship between the Jews and their environment in the conclusion of our book on the Jewish money trade. The following is a vital extract (Léon Poliakov, *Les Banquiers juifs . . .*, Paris, 1965, pp. 295-300):

"Let us consider the great actor in human geography, 'man,' molded by the environment that his ancestors have created," (P. George) and let us ask what is the environment and what are the ancestors when that man is a Jew. We immediately come up against a curious discrepancy. In a given area (Middle East, Maghreb, Europe), the Jews' genetic ancestors are, as we now know, of the same stock as the population living in the same environment. But Jewish tradition enjoins its worshipers to disclaim both these ancestors and this environment. The population, notably when it is Christian, shares the belief that the Children of Israel are descended from the "patriarchal race." In this way we immediately note the intrusion of a joint resistance which forms a barrier between the Jews and the natural framework. Certainly, in any human group whatsoever, a "human environment" comes between the individual and this framework. But in the case of the Jews, the actual barrier erected by man's social nature is reinforced by a theoretical psycho-religious barrier, created by the particular nature attributed to the Jews, since it is their dis-identification or religious separation from the "autochthonous" human environment which identifies them as what they are. As a result, their natural framework is, from a spiritual point of view, a *two-fold* one.

The very real and very tangible one they live in, they tend to be the first to regard as a land of exile, a place of punishment, not a protective, foster-homeland. The host country, for its part, excludes them and, notably in Christian Europe, goes so far as to forbid them to own landed property, that is to say to take possession of the soil. The other framework which, very incompletely, plays this maternal role for them spiritually, is only a memory, but one they cultivate with obsessive fervor and all the hypnotic power inherent in the ritual and observances of Judaism. It even seems that this power and fervor are going to increase as the time-lapse since the legendary weaning widens. However, the fact that the word for a *man* in ancient Hebrew is *adam*, and the word for land *adama*, does not fail to suggest the emotional, almost erotic, nature of the roots sunk in a native soil. (In another connection, it can be asked if Jewish tradition would have been enough to preserve the Jews their identity, that is to say to prevent their fusion with the host nations in the melting pots of the Christian West, had it not been for the immense credit which the tradition, and consequently the identity, enjoyed with these nations.)

As a result of this two-fold character, the Jews' civilization is, as we have seen, a dual civilization: they have two sets of first names (that is to say, two forms of identification); they follow two different calendars simultaneously. They write from left to right in Latin letters when they are addressing Christians, and from right to left when they correspond with one another in Hebrew (but smatter it with words borrowed from the language of the country). Amongst themselves, they speak the language of the country they inhabit (but stuff it with Hebrew terms). They are permanently tempted to lay down integral roots in the host country (where their settlement often preceded the formation of an autochthonous people). The Italian Jews of the Quattrocento, which we studied, are a typical case from this point of view. When one Ismael Laudadio da Rieti told the messianic agitator Reubeni that Jerusalem held no attraction for him because he felt that things could not be better for him than in Siena, it would be wrong to interpret this solely as a banker's *ubi bene, ibi patria*. It has been said, and it may be true, that the Jew's attachment to the country he lives in can reach unparalleled intensity, just because possession is incomplete; it is in fact, challenged both by Jewish tradition and Christian attitudes which concur on this point.

Confining ourselves to the case of Jews settled in the West where, as we have tried to show elsewhere, certain articles of the Christian faith in a strange way helped them to keep their sense of identity, we note that, depending on the country and situation concerned, it was sometimes relations with the host country, sometimes those with the Promised Land which were in the foreground of their collective consciousness. But neither relationship was ever completely on top. This resulted in their secular split into two "basic personalities" in cultural-anthropological terms, or the conflict between two "mother figures" (in pyscho-analytical terms). This split, this constant tossing between two frameworks or sets of emotional ties—and in the last analysis between two identities—can be thought to lie at the root of the proverbial "Jewish restlessness." We will not attempt to express this very vague and quasi-metaphysical idea in precise terms. It will be sufficient to point out the relationship between such an unusual insertion into the existing order, and all the Jews' emotional and intellectual characteristics. We therefore believe in the first place, that this state of conflict is responsible for both the economic vitality and the cultural fertility which they have evinced in the dispersion. Of course, account must also be taken of super-determination which played its part in a variety of ways: "restlessness" grows in proportion to persecution which can only cause stress; the culture was historically bolstered up by the compulsory religious instruction to which the "fathers of the Talmud" were already subjecting their flock.

Thus quasi-physical roots in a country were, in the case of the Jews, replaced by a complex collection of ideas, a doctrine whereby taking root becomes an eschatological event, which it is incumbent on the "Chosen People" to hasten. It is not surprising that Jewish historians almost always postulate, even if implicitly, an *"idée-force"* as a basis for the preservation of Judaism, and that their philosophy of history is, explicitly or not, a voluntarist philosophy, and that, in a variety of ways, as we have frequently shown in the present book, it gives such great importance to man's ability to choose between good and evil, that is to say to free will (for non-Jews in the same way as Jews), given its full dignity as a factor in history. . . . Here therefore we have a whole gamut of unique characteristics which were making the Jews different—some originating in the distant past, others since the first millennium of the present era. (The hatred and persecution to which they were exposed, probably derived from here in various ways. The psycho-analytical school has not failed to bring out the manifold and powerful symbolism of the Jew, who at different levels is said to be deicidal, or God the repressive Father, or a bastard without hearth or home. His Exile was a punishment imposed by the Almighty—probably such an admission of auto-culpability stimulated the indictment by the peoples they lived among.)

To what extent did such characteristics predispose the Jews to excel in intellectual and commercial activities? In any case, one can see the innumerable difficulties inherent in the comparative method and, ultimately, its inadequacy. . . .

(17) Letter from Moses Mendelssohn to the Benedictine monk Winkopp, July 28, 1770 (cf. M. Kayserling, *op. cit.*, p. 269).

(18) *Licht und Recht, Von dem Zustand und Tractament der Juden,* n.p., 1704.

(19) Cf. G. Liebe, *Das Judentum in der deutschen Vergangenheit,* Leipzig, 1903, p. 120.

(20) *Mémoire d'un enquêteur dépêché par Noailles en prévision de la création d'un mont-de-piété.* Bibliothèque Nationale, Paris, MS. Fr. 113666-7.

(21) This is the context (cf. "Voyages," in the edition of Montesquieu's *Oeuvres complètes* by M. A. Masson, Paris, 1950-5, Vol. II, p. 1290):

Nothing I had been told about the greed, knavery, swindling of the Dutch is exaggerated: it is the pure truth. I do not think that, since a famous man called Judas, there had ever been Jews more Jewish than some of them.

(22) A remark by the "repentant servant" in Lessing's play *Die Juden*, 1749

(23) Cf. S. Dubnov, *Modern History of the Jewish People*, Paris, 1933, Vol. 1, p. 108.

(24) Dubnov, p. 412.

(25) Cf. Robert Anchel, *Napoléon et les Juifs, Essai sur les rapports de l'État français et du culte israélite de 1806 à 1815*, Paris, 1928, pp. 226-9.

(26) *Ibid.*, p. 412.

(27) This comment was made in a university thesis (which we hope will be published shortly) by Sister Marie-Louise Gabriel (London): "The portrait of the contemporary Jew in English and German fiction and drama from 1830 to 1880."

4   The English Deists

(1) "The Fox and the Grapes" (*Fables, Book XII*, 169).

(2) Cf. V. Monod, *Dieu dans l'Univers; essai sur l'action exercée sur la pensée chrétienne par les grands systèmes cosmologiques depuis Aristote jusqu'à nos jours*, Paris, 1933, p. 178.

(3) "An historical account of two notable corruptions of Scripture." (This work by Newton was only published in 1737.)

(4) See particularly *Christianity Not Mysterious . . .* , 1696, and *Nazarenus, or Jewish, Gentile and Mahometan Christianity*, 1718, by John Toland (1670-1722).

(5) *Ibid.*, pp. 77, 84.

(6) *Ibid.*, preface, p. vi.

(7) *Reasons for Naturalizing the Jews in Great Britain and Ireland, on the Same Foot with All Other Nations, Containing also a Defence of the Jews Against All Vulgar Prejudices in All Countries*, London, 1714.

(8) *Ibid.*

(9) A *Confutation of the Reasons for Naturalizing the Jews, Containing the Crimes, Frauds and Insolencies, for which They were Convicted and Punished in Former Reigns*, London, 1715.

(10) *Memoirs of the Life and Writings of Mr. William Whiston, written by himself*, London, 1753.

(11) Cf. Norman Torrey, *Voltaire and the English Deists*, Yale, 1930, p. 109, and Preserved Smith, *The Enlightenment 1687-1776*, New York, 1962, p. 419, quoting *Alciphron* by Bishop George Berkeley.

(12) *Christianity as Old as Creation . . .* , London, 1731, pp. 239-42.

(13) Thomas Morgan's best known book is *The Moral Philosopher*, in

a Dialogue between Philalethes, a Christian Deist, and Theophanes, A Christian Jew, London, 1737; obviously the deist philosopher triumphed over the "Judeo-Christian" defender of orthodoxy. Not having been able to consult this book in Paris, I have extracted the above quotation from another book by Morgan: *A Brief Examination of the Rev. Mr. Warburton's Divine Legation of Moses . . . ,* London, 1741, pp. 158, xiv.

(14) Cf. Julius Guttmann, *Kant und das Judentum,* Leipzig, 1908. According to Guttmann, Kant's ideas on Judaism and the Jews were borrowed from Chapters III, V and XVII of the *Tractatus Theologico-Politicus,* which Morgan is also said to have used.

(15) See below, pp. 139, 140.

(16) Warburton's argument is reminiscent of the second story in the Decameron: "Abraham the Jew, stimulated by his friend Jeannot, goes to Rome and, seeing the depravity of the Clergy, returns to Paris and becomes Christian." In Rome, Abraham notes that, from the way in which it is conducted, the Church should collapse immediately—its age-long survival makes him believe in miracles, and, consequently, in the truth of Christianity. On the origins (Eastern) of this theme, cf. L. Poliakov, *From Mohammed to the Marranos, History of Anti-Semitism,* Vol. II, London, 1974.

(17) This slogan was borrowed from the couplet by E. W. Ewer, "How odd of God to choose the Jews." Cf. the Jewish apologetic book by Lewis Browne, *How Odd of God,* London, 1935, and also an anti-Semitic pamphlet by D. Reed (without place or date, but later than 1942), of the same title.

(18) Woolston pretended to defend the methods of allegorical symbolical exegesis (which go back to Origen) against those of textual exegesis. His real intentions did not come to light for a long time; cf. Torrey, *op. cit.,* pp. 59-108.

(19) This passage is a burlesque exegesis of Exodus VIII, 12-14:
> . . . and Moses appealed to the Lord to remove the frogs which he had brought on Pharaoh. The Lord did as Moses had asked, and in house and courtyard and in the open the frogs all perished. They piled into countless heaps and the land stank . . .

For Woolston, the frogs "typified" the Jews. T. Woolston, *The Old Apology for the Truth of the Christian Religion Against the Jews and Gentiles Revived,* London, 1705, pp. 124-8.

(20) Torrey, *op. cit.,* pp. 175-98.

(21) *Letters on the Study and Use of History by the late, Right Honourable Henry St. John Bolingbroke,* Edinburgh, 1777, p. 85.

(22) Torrey, *op. cit.,* p. 145.

(23) *Letters . . . , op. cit.,* p. 93:
> . . . If the foundations of Judaism and Christianity have been laid in truth, yet what numberless fables have been invented

to raise, to embellish, and to support these structures, according to the interest and taste of the several architects? That the Jews have been guilty of this, will be allowed: and, to the shame of Christians, if not of Christianity, the fathers of one church have no right to throw the first stone at the fathers of the other.

(24) *Reasons for Naturalizing the Jews in Great Britain* . . . , Chap. VIII:

I am not ignorant how much the world is govern'd by prejudices, and how farr some, who would not be counted of the vulgar, are yet sway'd by vulgar errors. One of the most general is the prevailing notion of a certain genius or bent of mind, reigning in a certain Family or Nation. That there is in reality such a Bypass frequently observable, I go not about to deny; but only maintain that it wholly proceeds from Accident, and not from nature. The different methods of Government and Education are the true springs and causes of such different inclinations all over the world; as it demonstrably appears from the progressive changes which alterations in those two main points have affected in most countries, both of the modern and ancient times. Compare the present Greece and Italy with the past; or even old England with the new, and you can doubt of the matter no longer. I reject not all that is attributed to the climate; but as Government and education even get the better of that, so it is frequently changed by the inhabitants, and has been so far for many ages by the Jews. . . .

(25) For example, in his letter to a young Catholic, Albert Burgh: *The Correspondence of Spinoza,* translated and edited with introduction and annotations, by A. Wolf, London, 1928, p. 353:

As to what you add about the common consent of myriads of men, and of the uninterrupted succession of the Church, etc., this is the same old song of the Pharisees. For these, also, with no less confidence than the adherents of the Roman Church, produce their myriads of witnesses, who relate what they have heard about, with as much pertinacity as do the witnesses of the Romans, just as if they themselves had experienced it. They trace back their lineage to Adam. They boast with equal arrogance that their Church maintains its growth, stability, and solidarity to this very day, in spite of the hostility of the Heathen and the Christians. Most of all do they take their stand on antiquity. They declare with one voice that they have received their traditions from God Himself, and that they alone preserve the written and unwritten word of God. No one can deny that all heresies have left them, but that they have remained constant for some thousands of years, without any imperial compulsion, but through the mere power of superstition. The miracles which they relate are enough to weary a thousand gossips. But what they chiefly pride themselves on is that they number far more martyrs than any other nation. . . .

(26) Some information on this subject appears below, Part III (The Racist Reaction).

(27) This has been established with the aid of Voltaire's "Carnets" by Torrey, *op. cit.*, 1930.

5   France in the Enlightenment

(1) Letter to Mme de Grignan, June 26, 1689. From this letter it emerges that the Queen of France had wanted to convert the Jews when visiting Avignon. I would like to thank the unknown friend who kindly pointed out this fact to me.

(2) *L'Histoire des Juifs, réclamée et rétablie par son véritable auteur, M. Basnage, contre l'édition anonyme et tronquée qui s'en est faite à Paris chez Roulland, 1710*, Rotterdam, 1711, preface, p. 16.

(3) Paul Hazard, *La Crise de conscience européenne, 1680-1715*, Paris, 1961, p. 96.

(4) See *Dictionnaire historique et critique* by Pierre Bayle, notably the articles entitled "Barcochébas" and "Acosta."

(5) *Commentaire philosophique sur ces paroles de Jésus-Christ: Contrains-les d'entrer, ou Traité de tolérance universelle*, Rotterdam, 1713, Vol. II, p. 377. This treatise was composed immediately after the repeal of the Edict of Nantes. Elsewhere, Bayle expanded his arguments for tolerance towards the Jews (Vol. I, p. 377):

> Let us endeavor to clarify this point as briefly as possible, and first of all, as far as the Jews are concerned, one is convinced, even in the countries of the Inquisition like Italy, that they should be tolerated. They are tolerated in several Protestant states, and every reasonable person is horrified at the way they are treated in Portugal and Spain. It is true that much of it is their fault; because why do they stay in the guise of Christians, and with a horrible profanation of all the sacraments, when they can go and practice Judaism openly elsewhere? But this fault does not excuse the Spaniards' cruel laws and still less the rigid execution of these laws. In the second place, as far as the Mohammedans are concerned . . . .

(6) *L'Histoire et la Religion des Juifs depuis Jésus-Christ jusqu'à présent. Pour servir de supplément et de continuation à l'histoire de Joseph*, M. Basnage, Rotterdam, 1707, Vol. 1, preface.

(7) Basnage, *op. cit.*, The Hague ed., 1716, Vol. V, pp. 179-80):

> Most of the parables found in the Talmud are *different from those in the Gospel* and *almost always have a different*

purpose. Is not the one about the workers who go late to the vineyard clothed in ridiculous circumstances and applied to the Good Rabbi who worked on the law more in twenty-eight years than another did in a hundred? A collection has been made *of Greek thoughts and expressions* which have some connection with those used in the Gospel. Is this grounds for saying that Jesus Christ copied Greek writings? It could be said with all the more probability since these authors conceived and published their works before Jesus. However, this would obviously be untrue. *It is said that these parables were current amongst the Jews before Jesus Christ taught.* But on what is this based? One must guess, in order to have the pleasure both of making the Pharisees original scholars and Jesus Christ a copyist *who borrowed what was finest and most delicate in the others*!

One might ask who Basnage was alluding to when he spoke of those who sought to make "the Pharisees original scholars and Jesus Christ a copyist." In his day, such views might have been current amongst certain "enlightened" rabbis in Holland.

(8) M. Huber, *Le Monde fou préféré au monde sage, en vingt-quatre promenades de trois amis, Criton (philosophe), Philon (avocat). Éraste (négociant),* Amsterdam, 1731, Vol. I, pp. 167, 175.

(9) Cf. Espiard de la Cour, *Oeuvres mêlées . . .,* Amsterdam, 1749, p. 22. "M. de Saumaise declared *in articulo mortis* to a friend who asked him what were his own thoughts in this last moment, that if God required a creed the Jewish religion was the true one."

(10) *Lettres choisies à M. Simon,* Amsterdam, 1730, Vol. 1, Letter XXXVII, p. 316.

(11) D. Hume, *Dialogues Concerning Natural Religion,* London, 1779, p. 89.

(12) On the role Chaix and La Chapelle played in d'Argens's literary apprenticeship, see the thesis by E. Johnston, "Le Marquis d'Argens, sa vie et ses œuvres," Paris, 1928, p. 33.

(13) See Voltaire's correspondence under "d'Argens" and also his letter to Frederick II of February 1, 1772, on the subject of the Marquis's widow: "This Dame Isaac is a virtuoso. She knows Greek and Latin and writes her own language in a way which is not commonly found."

(14) *Mémoires pour l'histoire des Sciences et des Beaux-Arts (Journal de Trévoux),* July, 1736, part 1, pp. 1350-63.

(15) D'Argens was to insert the following dedication at the beginning of Vol. III of *Lettres juives* (1738 edition):

I dedicate it to you *gratis,* without hope of any return. What costs nothing is always perfectly well received, particularly by you Israelites. There would thus be a type of disgrace if you find fault with a book which is henceforth going to make you known to all Europe. It is true that your nation is generally as little interested in praise as it is greedy for money . . . .

(16) Voltaire to d'Argens: letters February 2, 1737 and December, 1736.

(17) *Lettres chinoises*: Letters 120, 123, 124, 128, 129 (The Hague, 1750, Vol. V, pp. 23-143).

(18) Cf. Paul Vernière's reflections, "Montesquieu et le monde musulman, d'après l'Esprit des lois," *Actes du congrès Montesquieu*, Bordeaux 1955, p. 175.

(19) In Montesquieu's *Pensées*, the following idea occurs:
    . . . The law of Moses was very crude. "If a man beats his slave and he dies under his hand, he will be punished; but if he survives one or two days, he will not be, because it is his money." What sort of people is this where the civil law needs to relax natural law!

(20) *Oeuvres complètes*, published under the guidance of M. A. Masson, Paris, 1950-5, Vol. II, pp. 582-4.

(21) *Ibid.*, Vol. II, p. 273.

(22) *Ibid.*, Vol. II, p. 139:
    The Jews, solely by their enthusiasm, defended themselves against the Romans better than all the other peoples who were swallowed up in that Empire. . . . A sign that intolerance is a dogma of the religion of the Jews is that in Japan, where there are (I believe) seventy sects, there is no dispute between them as to pre-eminence.

(23) *Ibid.*, Vol. II, p. 37.

(24) *Ibid.*, Vol. III, pp. 421-2.

(25) *Ibid.*, Vol. II, pp. 114, 118.

(26) *Ibid.*, Vol. II, p. 107.

(27) *Ibid.*, Vol. II, p. 262.

(28) To the Duc de Nivernais: defense of *L'Esprit des lois* before the Commission of the Index.

(29) *Oeuvres meslées, contenant des pensées philologiques et quelques poésies* by M. E. /spiard/D./e.L./a/C./our/. On the subject of this Burgundian family, see the *Dictionnaire généalogique* by La Chesnaye-Desbois, Amsterdam, 1749.

(30) See my book on the Jewish bankers in Italy (*Les Banquiers juifs et le Saint-Siège du XIIIe au XVIIe siècle*, Paris, 1965), Chapter XII ("Le cas singulier de Venise").

(31) *Les Intérêts de la France mal entendus dans les branches de l'agriculture, de la population, des finances, du commerce, de la marine et de l'industrie*, by M. le Chevalier Goudar, Vol. I, pp. 421-30, Amsterdam, 1756.

(32) *Chimki, histoire cochinchinoise, qui peut servir à d'autres pays*, by Abbé Gabriel-François Coyer, London, 1768, pp. 60-2. This pamphlet borrowed most of its ingredients from *Mémoire sur le*

corps des métiers, by the physiocrat Simon Clicquot-Bervache, 1758.

(33) This is obviously the *Requête des marchands et négociants de Paris contre l'admission des Juifs,* quoted above, pp. 28, 29.

(34) Henri Labroue, *Voltaire antijuif,* Paris, 1942.

(35) In *Instruction du gardien des capucins de Raguse à Frère Pediculoso* . . . , 1768. In the *Dictionnaire philosophique,* art. "Ezekiel" Voltaire gave another adaptation of this chapter:

> A mother had two daughters, who parted with their virginity very early in life; the name of the elder was Aholah, and of the younger Aholibah: . . . Aholah doted on young lords and captains, and rulers; she committed whoredom with the Egyptians in her youth. . . . Aholibah her sister was more corrupt in her whoredoms than she, with captains and rulers clothed most gorgeously, horsemen riding upon horses, all of them desirable young men; she has discovered her nakedness, she has increased her whoredoms, she has eagerly sought the embraces of those whose member is as the member of asses, and who shed their seed like horses. . . .

(36) *Profession de foi des théistes.*

(37) We have used the J. Benda–R. Naves edition, 1936, which follows the 1769 edition of the *Dictionnaire* for our analysis.

(38) . . . What is very odd is that there is never any mention of the question of torture in the Jewish books. It is truly a pity that so gentle, so honest, so compassionate a nation did not know this means of finding out the truth. The reason for this, in my opinion, is that they did not need it. God always made it known to them as to his cherished people. . . . thus torture cannot be in use with them. This was the only thing lacking in the customs of the holy people.

(39) Good-day, Job, my friend. You are one of the oldest characters mentioned in the books; you were no Jew: we know that the book which bears your name is older than the *Pentateuch.* . . . It is obvious that this book is about an Arab who lived before the time at which we place Moses . . . what demonstrates that this fable cannot be about a Jew is that there is mention of three constellations which we today call the Bear, Orion and the Hyades. The Hebrews have never had the slightest knowledge of astronomy; they did not even have a word to express this science; everything touching on the intellectual arts was unknown to them, even the word geometry.

The Arabs, on the contrary, lived under canvas, being continually in a position to look at the stars, and were perhaps the first who fixed their years by inspecting the sky.

A more important observation is that there is only mention of a single God in this book. It is an absurd error to have imagined that the Jews were the only people to have recognized a single God; this was the doctrine of almost all the East, and the Jews in this were nothing but plagiarists, as they were in everything. . . .

(40) Moland, XIX, pp. 511-41. The article "Jews" does not figure in the Benda–Naves edition of the *Dictionnaire*.

(41) *Dictionnaire philosophique*, art. "Job" (cf. the note above).

(42) *Essai sur les mœurs*, Chap. VIII.

(43) *Lettre au Cardinal Dubois, et mémoire joint,* May 28, 1722, XXXIII, 66:

Monseigneur, I am sending your Eminence a small report of what I have been able to unearth concerning the Jew of whom I had the honor to talk to you. If your Eminence considers the matter important, dare I point out to you that a Jew, not being of any country except the one where he makes money, can just as well betray the king to the emperor as the emperor to the king? I am very much mistaken if this Jew will not easily give me his cipher with Wilar and give me letters for him.

(44) Letter, December 15, 1773, XLVIII, 522.

(45) L. de Bonald. *Sur les Juifs*, article reprinted by the *Ambigu*, London, XIV, 1806, pp. 3-22.

(46) *C. W. Fr. Grattenauers erster Nachtrag zu seiner Erklärung über seine Schrift wider die Juden*, Ein Anhang zur fünften Auflage, Berlin, 1803, p. 75.

(47) *Oeuvres choisies . . . du prince de Ligne*, Vol. I, Geneva, 1809, p. 48.

(48) Isaac Pinto, a Portuguese Jew, had written *Réflexions critiques sur le premier chapitre du VIIe tome des œuvres de M. de Voltaire* (I quoted an extract from it at the beginning of this book) and had sent them to Voltaire, together with the following letter:

If I had to address myself to anyone but yourself, Monsieur, I would find it very embarrassing. It is a question of bringing to your notice a criticism of one place in your immortal work; I, who am its greatest admirer, I, who am fit only to read it in silence, to study it and to hold my peace. But as I admire the author even more than I admire this work, I think him a great enough man to forgive me this criticism in favor of the truth which is so dear to him, and which has perhaps only escaped him on this single occasion. I at least hope that he will find me all the more pardonable as I am acting on behalf of a whole nation, to which I belong and to whom I owe this defense.

I had the honor, Monsieur, to see you in Holland, when I was very young. Since then, I have steeped myself in your work which has always delighted me. It has taught me how to fight you; it has done more, it has inspired me with the courage to admit it to you.

My sentiments of esteem and veneration exceed any words, etc. etc.

Voltaire replied (July 21, 1762, XLII, 181):

The lines you are complaining of, Monsieur, are violent and unfair. There are amongst you men who are very educated and very worthy of respect; your letter quite convinces me of this. I will take care to make an insertion in the new edition. When one is wrong, one must make amends; and I was wrong to attribute to a whole nation the vices of several individuals.

I will say to you with the same frankness, that many people cannot tolerate either your laws, your books or your superstitions. They say that your nation has at all times done a lot of harm to itself and to the human race. If you are philosophical, as you appear to be, you will think like these men but you will not say so. Superstition is the most abominable scourge of the world. It is superstition which, at all times, has caused the slaughter of so many Jews and Christians. It is superstition which is still sending you to the stake with otherwise estimable peoples. There are aspects of human nature which are infernal; but decent people passing by the Grève where people are broken on the wheel, order their coachmen to drive faster, and seek distraction at the Opéra from the awful spectacle that they saw by the way.

I might be able to argue with you about the sciences which you attribute to the ancient Jews and show you that they knew no more about them than the French at the time of Chilperic. I might be able to make you agree that the lingo of a small province, mixed with Chaldean, Phoenician and Arab, was as poverty-stricken and crude a language as our ancient Gallic. But I would perhaps annoy you and you seem to me too much of a gentleman for me to wish to displease you. Remain a Jew since you are one. You will not slaughter forty-two thousand men for not pronouncing *shibboleth* correctly, nor twenty-four thousand men for having slept with Midianites. But be philosophical, that is the best that I can wish you in this short life.

I have the honor, Monsieur, to be, with all the sentiments that are due to you, etc. etc.

VOLTAIRE, Christian gentleman in ordinary
of the chamber of the Very Christian King.

It was around this correspondence that the Abbé Guénée built his *Lettres de quelques Juifs portugais, allemands et polonais à M. de Voltaire*, published in Paris in 1769 and reissued on several occasions.

(49) In 1746, Voltaire obtained (J. Donvez, *De quoi vivait Voltaire*, Paris, 1949, p. 126)

the office of gentleman in ordinary in the King's Chamber. This office was a very good investment, not so much because of the 1600 livres that it brought him in annually but because he was able to re-sell it for 30,000 livres in 1749; by a special favor, he retained the title which he very proudly flaunted to the end of his life and which he was able to turn to good use when the occasion arose.

(50) XLII, 184.

(51) VIII, 415.

(52) "The unfortunate fathers of your religion, the Jews, are burning in Spain, reciting the same prayers as those who tore them to shreds . . ." (*Aline et Valcour*). The great specialist and editor of de Sade's work, M. Gilbert Lély, has been good enough to confirm that there is no other mention of the Jews in it.

(53) Cf. the series *The Studies in Prejudice*, New York, 1949-51, and notably *Anti-Semitism and Emotional Disorder* by N. W. Ackerman and M. Jahoda, and *Dynamics of Prejudice* by B. Bettelheim and M. Janowitz, as well as *The Authoritarian Personality* by T. W. Adorno, *et al.* This latter work is generally regarded as one of the classics of American social psychology; cf. comments by J. Meynaud and A. Lancelot, *Les Attitudes politiques*, Paris, 1962, pp. 78-84.

(54) XXVIII, 320.

(55) Letter to the Duc de Richelieu, June 8, 1744 (XXXVI, 305).

(56) Letters to La Harpe (XLVIII, 16) and Marquis d'Argens (XXXVII, 467).

(57) Cf. the article "Joseph" in the *Dictionnaire philosophique*:
The history of Joseph, considered only as an object of curiosity and literature, is one of the most valuable monuments of antiquity which have reached our times . . . in almost every part it is of admirable beauty and the conclusion draws forth tears of tenderness. It exhibits a youth in his sixteenth year, of whom his brothers are jealous. He is sold by them to a caravan of Ishmaelite merchants. . . . This history has every interesting ingredient of an epic poem; the sublime, the marvelous, the exposition, connection, discovery and reverse of fortune.

(58) XIX, 527.

(59) For the formation of Voltaire's mind and attitudes, see the major work by M. René Pomeau, *La Religion de Voltaire*, Paris, 1954, which I have used as a starting point for the present chapter.

(60) *La Vie de Voltaire*, by M. the Abbé Duvernet, Geneva, 1786, pp. 112, 313-15:
. . . He was only three years old and he already knew the whole *Moïsade* by heart. It is rare that, in the course of a lifetime, a man is not what his early education has made him. As few people know this *Moïsade*, we have transcribed it. . . .

(61) *La Henriade*, fifth canto (VIII, 140-1).

(62) *Ibid.*

(63) *An Historical Commentary on the Works of the Author of the Henriade*, in *The Works of the Late M. de Voltaire*, translated from the French, Vol. I, London, 1780, p. 93.

(64) Cf. Voltaire's evocation of the "chamber of meditations": "It is thus that in former times one emerged from the Jesuits' chamber of meditations: The imagination is inflamed by these objects, the soul becomes terrible and implacable" (*Avis public sur les Calas et les Sirven*, XXV, 527).

(65) The broadness of the Jesuit outlook stretched a very long way at the beginning of the eighteenth century. For example Father Louis Lecomte glorified the "natural religion" of the Chinese (*Nouveaux mémoires sur l'état présent de la Chine*, 1698-1700, Vol. II, p. 98):

> In the wise distribution of the graces which the divine grace has made amongst the Nations of the world, China has no cause to complain since there is none which has been more constantly favored. . . . China has preserved for over two thousand years the knowledge of the true God and has practiced the purest maxims of morality, while Europe and almost all the rest of the world was wrong and corrupt.

See also the liberties that the popular *Histoire du peuple de Dieu* by Father Berruyer takes with the Old Testament; or in another sphere, the praise of Pierre Bayle by the *Journal de Trévoux*, April/June, 1707, pp. 693-706.

(66) "First Letter," article "Jews," in the *Dictionnaire philosophique*, XIX, 526.

(67) Cf. Gustave Lanson, "Voltaire et son banqueroutier juif en 1726," *Revue latine*, 1908.

(68) "First Letter" above, and Beuchot's note that "The verses quoted here only appeared for the first time in the London edition, 1728." The d'Acosta family were included among the subscribers to this edition.

(69) *Voltaire's Notebooks*, Bestermans, Geneva, 1952, pp. 31, 233.

(70) I, pp. 67 ff. (*Commentaire historique . . .*). A million livres is equivalent to over sixteen million new francs! On the Pelletier-Desforts lottery, see J. Donvez, *Voltaire financier*, Paris, 1949, pp. 37-56.

(71) Cf. above, p. 25. Frederick II regarded the Hirschel business as "the case of a rogue who wanted to cheat a swindler.'

(72) Donvez, *op. cit.*, pp. 59, 69.

(73) *Journal de la traité des Noirs*, presented by Jehan Mousnier, Paris, 1957, p. 13.

(74) Donvez, *op. cit.*, p. 175.

(75) Cf. his letter to Frederick II (June 8, 1770, XLVII, 102):

> Why do you not take charge of the vicar of Simon Barjone [the Pope] while the Empress of Russia dusts down the vicar of Mohammed? You two would then have purged the world of two strange follies. I had earlier formed these great hopes of you; but you have been content to mock Rome and me, go straight for the main chance, and be a very prudent hero.

(76) XXVII, 112.

(77) Quoted by Pomeau, *op. cit.*, p. 353.

(78) XLIV, 361.

(79) " . . . tell him truly that he is the hope of our small band and the man of whom Israel expects the most. He is bold but not at all reckless . . . " (A. Thiérot, November 19, 1760, XLI, 69).

(80) Cf. Léon Poliakov, *History of Anti-Semitism*, Vol. I, *From the Time of Christ to the Court Jews,* New York, 1965, p. 224.

(81) Letter to Mme Du Deffand, 1770 (XLVII, 93).

(82) *Essais historiques et critiques sur les Juifs ou Supplément aux mœurs des Israélites,* by the Abbé Fleury, Lyon, 1771, Part I, p. 216.

(83) *Apologie des Juifs . . . ,* p. 57, note.

(84) *Dictionnaire philosophique,* art. "Arius."

(85) *Dialogues, Oeuvres complètes,* Paris, 1865, Vol. IX, p. 3.

(86) "The Creed of a Savoyard Priest," from *Emile or Education* by Jean-Jacques Rousseau, Barbara Foxley, trans., Everyman Library, London, 1933:

> When I yield to temptation, I surrender myself to the action of external objects. When I blame myself for this weakness, I listen to my own will alone; I am a slave in my vices, a free man in my remorse; the feeling of freedom is never effaced in me but when I myself do wrong, and when I at length prevent the voice of the soul from protesting against the authority of the body.

(87) *Profession de foi du Vicaire savoyard,* Paris, 1914, letter to M. de Franquières and P. Moultou, 1769; cf. P.-M. Masson, *La Religion de Jean-Jacques Rousseau,* Paris, 1916, II, pp. 246-7.

(88) In Rousseau, "The Creed of a Savoyard Priest."

(89) In his *Lettre à Mgr de Beaumont, archevêque de Paris,* in which he protested against the condemnation passed on *Émile* (of which as we know the *Profession de foi . . .* formed part).

(90) *Journal inédit du duc de Croy,* by le vicomte De Grouchy and P. Cottin, Vol. III, Paris, 1907, p. 15.

(91) Cf. *Essai sur l'origine des langues,* Chap. IX ("Formation des langues méridionales").

(92) *Considération sur le gouvernement de Pologne et sur sa réformation projetée en avril 1772,* Chap. II ("Esprit des anciennes institutions").

(93) On the subject of the racial origin of the Jews, see Poliakov, *From the Time of Christ to the Court Jews,* Appendix A.

(94) These two unpublished pages by Jean-Jacques Rousseau, preserved in the public library at Neuchâtel (*Cahiers de brouillons, notes et extraits,* no. 7843) have been mentioned by Pierre-Maurice Masson in his critical edition of the *Profession de foi du Vicaire savoyard,* Paris, 1914, p. 375, note 1. Masson gave a partial transcription of it in *La Religion de Jean-Jacques Rousseau,* Paris, 1916, II, p. 240. I would like to thank the distinguished archivist of the Neuchâtel library, M.-J. Biadi, who

has been so good as to send me a photocopy of these two pages.

(95) *Journal inédit du duc de Croy, loc. cit.*

(96) *Profession de foi . . . , ed. cit.*

(97) Letter to P. Moultou, February 14, 1769.

(98) Letter to M. de Franquières, 1769 (according to the text given by P.-M. Masson in his critical edition of the *Profession de foi . . . , p. 525*).

(99) *Rêveries . . . , Oeuvres*, Paris ed., 1865, Vol. IX, p. 341.

(100) *Ibid.*, Vol. X, p. 228 (letter to Voltaire, June 7, 1760).

(101) *Rêveries . . . , p. 345.*

(102) B. Bouvier, "Notes inédites de Voltaire sur La Profession de foi du Vicaire savoyard," *Annales de la Société Jean-Jacques Rousseau*, I, 1905, pp. 272-84.

(103) C. Maurras, *Les Monod peints par eux-memes* (Chap. XXIII: "Idées françaises et idées suisses") in *L'Action française* (bimonthly bulletin), I, 1899, pp. 321-2.

(104) Cf. *Correspondance inédite*, ed. A. Babelon, Paris, 1931, Vol. II, p. 212.

(105) Diderot is alluding here to a cabalistic concept relating to a "pre-Adamic" or Idumaean humanity, composed solely of men; what is concerned therefore is homosexual love.

(106) This merchant was called Vanderveld; cf. *Voyage en Hollande* by Diderot, *Oeuvres complètes* (ed. Assézat Tourneux), Vol. XVII, p. 494. The episode has been clarified by T. Reinach, "Les Juifs dans l'opinion chrétienne aux XVIIe et XVIIIe siècles . . . ," R.E.J., VIII, 1884, pp. 141-2.

(107) *La Promenade du Sceptique ou Les allées, ed. cit.*, Vol. I, pp. 171 ff.

(108) Cf. *Diderot et Catherine II*, by M. Tourneux, Paris, 1899, pp. 298-9.

(109) *Ibid.*, pp. 532-5.

(110) The following are the original and the published texts respectively of this passage (according to Jacques Proust, *Diderot et l'Encyclopédie*, Paris, 1962, p. 542):

> . . . All that can be reasonably said on this subject is that the talmudists have made comparisons similar to those of Jesus Christ, but that the way that this obscure and fanatical Jew applied them, and the lessons he drew from them generally, have a more serious character than the use of these similes and parables made by the authors of the Talmud.
>
> . . . all that can be reasonably said on this subject, is that the talmudists have made comparisons similar to those of J.C. but the way that the Son of God applied them, and the lessons drawn from them are always beautiful and sanctifying, whereas the others almost always apply them in a puerile and frivolous way.

(111) Tourneux, *op. cit.*, pp. 200-3.

(112) Masson, *Oeuvres complètes*, Vol. II, p. 97.

(113) " . . . it must only be borne in mind that the idea of a divinity necessarily degenerates into superstition. The deist has cut off a dozen hydra heads: but the head he has left it will reproduce all the others" (*Diderot et Catherine II*, p. 307).

(114) Proust, *op. cit.*, p. 295 ("La critique de la morale chrétienne").

(115) Towards the end of his article, Faiguet does not fail to mention the medieval usurers, but he does so in two lines:

> . . . in this case, one must always assume an iniquitous deal, prejudicial to the public and to individuals, of the type that was made in France in former times by Italians and Jews . . . in a word, the usury of Jews and Lombards, who grew fat in those days on the poverty of France. . . .

(116) Tourneux attributes this article to Diderot and it appears in his classic edition of the *Oeuvres complètes*. According to M. Jacques Proust, the attribution is erroneous (cf. *Diderot et l'Encyclopédie*, year II, p. 536).

(117) For details of Voltaire's collaboration in the *Encyclopédie*, see R. Naves, *Voltaire et l'Encyclopédie*, Paris, 1938; on the subject of the article "Messiah", cf. pp. 27-32 and Appendix IV.

(118) Ira O. Wade, *The Clandestine Organization and Diffusion of Philosophic Ideas in France from 1700 to 1750*, Princeton, 1938 (Conclusion, p. 269):

> The greatest single influence exercised upon the writers of the period is that of Spinoza, so great is his influence that one is tempted to see in the whole movement a gigantic manifestation of Spinozism triumphant over all other forms of thought.

(119) "Lettre de Thrasybule à Leucippe," *Oeuvres complètes* of Nicolas Fréret, Paris, year VII, Vol. XX, p. 99 (the italics are mine).

(120) *La Moïsade*, ibid, Vol. XX, p. 267.

(121) *Lettre to M. * * * sur le Juifs' où il est prouvé que le mépris dans lequel la nation juive est tombée, est antérieur à la malédiction de Jésus-Christ . . .* , Mixed dissertations on various subjects (by J.-B. Mirabaud, Amsterdam, 1740, Vol. 1, p. 164).

(122) *Ibid.*, p. 171.

(123) *Ibid.*, p. 185.

(124) The phrase appears in contemporary memoirs. For example, the Swiss, Meister, described the d'Holbach establishment as "one of the sweetest hospices of the initiates of the *Encyclopédie*, and their most famous synagogue." (Cf. René Hubert, *D'Holbach et ses amis*, Paris, 1928, especially p. 49.)

(125) Quoted by Pierre Naville, *D'Holbach*, Paris, 1942, p. 49.

(126) *Ibid.*; see the bibliography drawn up by Naville, pp. 405-20.

(127) Cf. Chapter IX of the *Code de la nature* by d'Holbach.

(128) See for example the Utopian society that Diderot describes in his *Supplément au voyage de Bougainville*. There, the cruel bonds of monogamous marriage are broken, at the same time

as the prohibitions on adultery and incest are abolished: men and women change partners "every month." But women who are sterile (temporarily or permanently) are excluded from the joys of love, and the women that the men are vying for are the "fertile Venuses," those who hold promise of "an increase of fortune for the household and of strength for the nation"; in other words, the aim of the sexual act remains the same as that of the Church. Many other examples from eighteenth-century utopias could be quoted; they are generally characterized by an encroaching regulation, notably of sexual life, claiming as its authority a nature which legislates instead of God. On this subject cf. Jean Ehrard, *L'Idée de nature en France dans la première moitié du XVIIIe siècle,* Paris, 1963, Vol. II, pp. 768 ff.

(129) The method consisting of attacking the Church using the Jews' arguments was not new and, in the eighteenth century, the pattern had been set by John Toland; see above, p. 60. A treatise by Anacharsis Cloots, published in London in 1780, *La Certitude des preuves du mahométisme,* continues the process under the pretext of a defense of Islam. The long note on pp. 76-85 states:

> The people of God have all the appearances in their favor: a pure and holy law, derived with their opponents' consent, from the Almighty, whose will is unchanging; books inspired by the Supreme Being, which make no mention of the future destruction of the oldest religion in the world; on the contrary, these books are filled with flattering words which promise that it will last for ever. In a word, the Jew alone possesses all the advantages of *Tradition*; the objections of Christians and Mohammedans turn to dust when the rabbi takes up the weapon of overwhelming *Tradition.* All the interpretations of the Bible by Christian and Moslem scholars, all the miracles that they attribute to *Jesus* and *Mohammed,* the prophecies they apply to them, are chimeras, dreams, absurd stories, when the *Tradition* of the Jewish Church makes its voice heard; it is an unshakable chain, a thread nothing can break. It is really thought to be even more terrible against the Nazareans than against the Islamites because of the place where the alleged gospel farce was enacted. Even a Jew of very mediocre abilities can emerge successful from an argument against these two sects. "I fall back," he says, "on our Tradition; I am using the same arguments and the same weapons that they use against the opponents that they have inside their own beliefs. They cannot deny me something from which they themselves draw so much benefit, and to which they accord so much authority! Thus I am using our tradition as an impregnable rampart: I compare the authority of the Rabbis

to that of the Popes or the Muftis and the Talmud to the books of their early Scholars. . . ."

(130) *L'Esprit du judaïsme ou Examen raisonné de la loi de Moïse et de son influence sur la religion chrétienne,* translated from Collins's English version by Baron d'Holbach, London, 1770. But this book is not by Collins, who never published anything like it. Perhaps the real author is d'Holbach himself? For the above quotations, see pp. 10, 167, 170 and 201.

(131) From *D'Holbach, textes choisis,* ed. P. Charbonnel, Paris, 1957, Vol. I, pp. 108, 115, 172.

(132) *Tableau des saints ou Examen de l'esprit, de la conduite, des maximes et du mérite des personnages que le christianisme révère et propose pour modèle,* London, 1770, pp. 90-2.

(133) Charbonnel, *op. cit.,* p. 80.

(134) *Ibid.,* p. 106, note 1.

(135) Poliakov, *History of Anti-Semitism,* Vol. II, *From Mohammed to the Marranos.*

(136) Remember the passages Tacitus devotes to the Germans' courage and loyalty (*Germany,* Chap. XIV):

When the battlefield is reached, it is a reproach for a chief to be surpassed in prowess; a reproach for his retinue not to equal the prowess of its chief: but to have left the field and survived one's chief, this means life-long infamy and shame; to protect and defend him, to devote even one's own feats to his glorification, this is the gist of their allegiance: the chief fights for victory, but the retainers for the chief.

But over and above the cult of the chief, Tacitus attributed an unmixed racial purity to the Germans (*Germany,* Chap. IV):

Personally I associate myself with the opinions of those who hold that in the peoples of Germany there has been given to the world a race untainted by intermarriage with other races, a peculiar people and pure, like no one but themselves; whence it comes that their physique, in spite of their vast numbers, is identical: fierce blue eyes, red hair, tall frames, powerful. . . .

(137) Cf. J. Ridé, "La fortune singulière du mythe germanique en Allemagne" (*Études germaniques,* XXIV, 4 1966) where the popularity of Tacitus in Germany is explained in the light of the peculiarities of national history from the sixteenth century.

(138) The visionary Michelet made this comment: as a nineteenth-century man, he concluded that Germany was a race while France was a nation: "Germany has given its Suevians to Switzerland and Sweden, to Spain its Goths, its Lombards to Lombardy, its Anglo-Saxons to England, its Franks to France. It has named and replenished all the populations of Europe." (*Introduction à l'histoire universelle,* L. Fèbvre, ed., Paris, 1946, pp. 118-37).

(139) Cf. T. Simar, *Étude critique sur la formation de la doctrine des*

races au XVIIIe siècle et son expansion au XIXe, Brussels, 1922, pp. 22-30, and R. Aron, *Les Grandes étapes de la pensée sociologique*, Paris, 1967, pp. 72-3, note 19.

(140) Ehrard, *op. cit.*, Vol. I, pp. 42-4.

(141) *Histoire de l'ancien gouvernement de la France* . . . , by the late M. le Comte de Boulainvilliers, Amsterdam, 1727, Vol. I, pp. 26, 36.

(142) "De l'origine des Français et de leur établissement dans la Gaule," 1714; *Oeuvres complètes* of Fréret, Paris, year VII, pp. 1-227, Vols. VI and V, pp. 155-367.

(143) *Qu'est-ce que le tiers état?* (1789).

(144) Starting with Charles Darwin, who remarked: "It is immaterial whether one designates the varied human varieties by the name of races or whether the expressions 'species' and 'sub-species' are employed although this latter expression appears more suitable." Today, some anthropologists advocate excluding the term race from scientific language.

(145) The *Encyclopédie* gives the following two definitions of *Race*:

Race (geneal.): extraction, descent, lineage; which means as much the ancestry as the descendants of the same family; when it is noble, this word is synonymous with birth. . . . See *Birth, Nobility*, etc.

Race (Maréch.): means specific species of some animals, particularly horses. . . .

In the article "Negroes," they are described as a *variety* or *species*; the word *Race* in this article is used to designate the human race in its entirety, a meaning that Maupertuis was giving it in his *Vénus physique* as early as 1745. On the whole, the *Encyclopédie* passes severe judgment on the Negroes both physically and morally (Negroes, *nat. hist.*):

Not only does their color distinguish them, but they differ from other men in every feature of their faces, wide, flat noses, thick lips and wool in place of hair, appearing to constitute a new species of man. If one moves away from the Equator towards the Antarctic pole, the black becomes lighter but the ugliness remains: there are also those objectionable people who inhabit the southern point of Africa. . . .

Negroes considered as slaves.

Characters of the Negroes in general. If by chance one meets decent people amongst the Negroes of Guinea (the greatest number are always vicious), they are mostly inclined to libertinage, to vengeance, to theft and to lying. Their obstinacy is such that they never admit their fault, whatever punishment they are made to undergo; even the fear of death moves them not at all. . . .

(146) Cf. *Ideen zur Philosophie der Geschichte der Menschheit*, IV, 5: "Girgen wir wie Bär und Affe auf allen Vieren, so lasset uns

nicht zweifeln, dass auch die Menschenrassen (wenn mir das unedel Wort erlaubt ist) ihr eingeschränkteres Vaterland haben und nie verlassen würden."

(147) See *Littré, Race* . . . 5: "It sometimes means a class of men resembling each other either by profession, habits, or inclinations; in this meaning, it has something ironic, even abusive about it. . . ." Likewise, the *Dictionnaire de l'Académie française*: "*Race* also means a class of men practicing the same profession or having common inclinations or habits; in this meaning, it is always to be taken amiss. . . ."

(148) *Telliamed ou Entretien d'un philosophe indien avec un missionnaire français* . . . , Amsterdam, 1748 ("Sixième journée").

(149) *Traité de métaphysique* (1734); Moland, XII, 210, cf. also *L'Essai sur les mœurs*, Chap. CXLVI.

(150) In his old age, Goethe recalled Buffon's influence in Germany as follows (Review of the *Principes de philosophie zoologique de Geoffroy de Saint-Hilaire*, Paris, 1830):

> In the very year when I was born, 1749, Count Buffon published the first part of his *Histoire naturelle* and aroused much interest amongst the Germans who were at that time very susceptible to French influence. The volumes followed at yearly intervals and so the interest of a cultured society accompanied my development. . . .

(151) *Histoire naturelle, générale et particulière avec la description du Cabinet du Roy*, Paris, Vol. II ("De l'âge viril," pp. 518-35).

(152) *Histoire naturelle* . . . , Paris, 1766, Vol. XIV, pp. 311-74.

(153) "Seconde partie, contenant une dissertation sur l'origine des Noirs," 1745.

(154) *Histoire naturelle* . . . , Paris, 1749, Vol. III, pp. 374-5.

(155) *Ibid.*, p. 377.

(156) *Supplément au voyage de Bougainville.*

(157) *Voyage en Laponie*, by J.-F. Régnard, ed. Lepage, Paris, 1875; *Relation d'un voyage dans la Laponie septentrionale.* . . . , by Maupertuis *Oeuvres de Monsieur de Maupertuis.*

(158) We also know the vogue enjoyed in the eighteenth century by the myth of the "Noble Savage," whose virtues were suggested as a model for Europeans. But what was involved here was primarily a process of social criticism and this type of vindication did not gain the adherence of the precursors and founders of anthropology. It can be believed that their essential faith in their science involved a positive prejudice in favor of the society within which this science was developing. Whatever the case, all the scientific writings or scientific claims of the time are characterized by the idea of the superiority, in the wide sense, of European man.

(159) *Ideen zur Philosophie der Geschichte* . . . , VI, 4.

(160) Article "Irreligious."

(161) On Buffon's religion, see the conflicting opinions of Jean Piveteau, in his edition of the *Oeuvres philosophiques,* Paris, 1954 (Buffon a believer or a deist) and of Jacques Roger, *Les Sciences de la vie dans la pensée du XVIIIe siècle,* Paris, 1963, especially p. 558 (Buffon as an atheist).

(162) Note to the tenth edition of the *Systema Naturae,* 1754.

(163) Preface to the *Fauna Suevica,* by Linnaeus, 1746.

(164) *Histoire naturelle . . . ,* Paris, 1753, Vol. IV, p. 384. At this point, Linnaeus, who adapted his classification in successive editions of his *Systema . . . ,* had not yet grouped man, monkeys and lemurians in the "Primates"; that is why Buffon attacked him obliquely and, as it were, in advance.

(165) Louis Daubenton, *Exposition des distributions méthodiques des animaux quadrupèdes* in the *Oeuvres complètes de Buffon,* ed. Lamouroux, Paris 1824, Vol. XVI, p. 168.

(166) "Nouvelles observations sur l'épiderme et le cerveau des Nègres," by M. Meckel, *Mémoires de l'Académie royale des Sciences et Belles-Lettres de Berlin,* XIII, 1757, p. 71.

(167) *Oeuvres de Pierre Camper . . . ,* Paris, 1903, Vol. II, pp. 449-76 ("De l'origine et de la couleur des Nègres").

(168) Having dissected several Negroes, Soemmering concluded "dass im allgemeinen, im Durchschnitt die afrikanischen Mohren doch in etwas näher ans Affengeschlecht als die Europäer grenzen." (Samuel-Thomas Soemmering, *Über die körperliche Verschiedenheit des Mohren vom Europäer,* Mainz, 1784, p. 32.)

(169) Roger, *op. cit.,* pp. 683-748.

(170) C. Meiners, *Grundriss der Geschichte der Menschheit,* Lemgo, 1785, pp. 69, 76-7.

(171) J.-J. Virey, *Histoire naturelle du genre humain,* Paris, 1801, Vol. I, pp. 145-7.

(172) *Ibid.,* Vol. II, pp. 119-20.

(173) *Ibid.,* Vol. I, pp. 184, 413.

(174) On Saumarez, see A. de Quatrefages, *Rapports sur les progrès de l'anthropologie,* Paris, 1867, p. 306:

> The idea of cranial capacity and the differences it presents between races is not new in science. In this connection Saumarez had compared the skull of a Negro with those of thirty-six Europeans, and he found that it contained less water. Virey and Palissot de Beauvois had repeated the experiment. . . . The result of these first experiments had been to show that the skull of a Negro has a smaller capacity than a European's. . . .

(175) "Von den verschiedenen Racen der Menschen," 1783; *Bestimmung des Begriffs einer Menschenrace,* 1785.

(176) "Von den verschiedenen Racen der Menschen," in *Der Philosoph für die Welt,* Carlsruhe, 1783, II, p. 105:

> Herr Maupertuis's proposal to bring up a naturally noble breed of men in some territory or other, in whom understand-

ing, ability and uprightness would be heritable, was based on the possibility of carefully eliminating degenerate births, and eventually creating a lasting family strain. This is a proposal that is certainly in my opinion feasible but is prevented by the wiser ways of nature because it is precisely in the mixing of evil and good that lie the motives which call into play the slumbering powers of humanity and force it to develop all its talents and to approach the perfection to which it is called.

(177) J. F. Blumenbach, *De l'unité du genre humain et de ses variétés,* Paris, 1804, pp. 285, 299-300.

(178) J. F. Blumenbach, *Decas quarta collectionis suae cranorum diversarum gentium illustrata,* Gottingae, 1790, p. 10. The claim or hope of finding specific characteristics in the skulls of Jews persisted up to the time of the Third Reich, when German scholars embarked on various comparative studies of this type.

(179) Blumenbach, *De l'unité du genre humain . . . ,* p. 207.

(180) *C. W. Fr. Grattenauers erster Nachtrag zu seiner Erklärung über seine Schrift wider die Juden,* pp. 29-30.

(181) Cf. below, p. 226.

(182) Erich Voegelin, *Die Rassenidee in der Geistesgeschichte von Ray bis Carus,* Berlin, 1933. I am grateful to Voegelin for putting a copy of this book at my disposal as it is now unobtainable.

(183) Blumenbach, *De l'unité du genre humain . . . ,* p. 115.

(184) *Dissertation sur la tolérance des protestants, en réponse à deux ouvrages, dont l'un est intitulé l'Accord parfait, et l'autre, Mémoire au sujet des mariages clandestins des protestants en France,* n.p., n.d. (probably published around 1760), pp. 22-3.

(185) *Essai sur la régénération physique, morale et politique des Juifs,* Metz, 1789, p. 132:

> But we are going to be told the Protestants will demand the same privileges. We have laid down the principles, and although we would draw the same inferences in their favor, the faithful Catholic and the dutiful citizen will easily be recognized in the humble writer who offers his ideas with diffident circumspection, and never made the arrogant claim to dictate laws to the supreme authority.

(186) *Rapport sur la réclamation des Juifs portugais* (who were claiming the right to settle in the French colonies) submitted to M. de Sartine, Minister of the Navy, in July 1776; cf. *Collection de mémoires et correspondances officielles sur l'administration des colonies . . .* by V.-P. Malouet, former administrator of the Colonies and of the Navy, Paris, 1802, Vol. I, pp. 120-7.

(187) *The Spirit of Laws,* XV, 5 ("Of The Slavery of The Negroes").

(188) *Plaidoyers,* Brussels, 1775; *Plaidoyer pour Moïse May, Godechaux et Abraham Levy, Juifs de Metz, contre l'hôtel de ville de Thionville et le corps des marchands de cette ville.* The Jews were asking for admission to the guild of merchants; they lost the case, but were determined to have their lawyer's speech

published. Pro-Jewish writings, by Isaac Pinto and Israël Valabrègue, had previously appeared in 1760-70, but the publication of this speech is the first manifestation of the campaigns on behalf of "Teutonic" Jews (from Alsace and Lorraine).

(189) On Cerfberr, see *Notes et documents concernant la famille Cerfberr*, by Roger Levylier, Paris, 1902, Vol. I.

(190) *L'Esprit des lois mosaïques*, by M. Senger, Bordeaux, 1785; this work only being—as Senger indicated in a "prefatory note"—a summary of the treatise by the German orientalist; and *Instruction salutaire adressée aux communautés de l'Empire par le célèbre Harwic Wesely, Juif de Berlin, traduit en français en l'an 1782* (new edition in 1790).

(191) Cf. Comte de Mirabeau, *De la monarchie prussienne sous Frédéric le Grand*, London, 1788, Vol. VI, p. 46, note 1.

(192) L.-S. Mercier, *L'An deux mille quatre cent quarante, rêve s'il en fût jamais*, 1786 edition, Chap. LXXIX ("Jews"). This utopia seems to us the first to project the ideal régime in time (and space), foreshadowing contemporary science fiction. It is interesting to add that in a note to his chapter on "The Jews," Mercier voiced his admiration for the Mosaic law and was surprised to see it practiced, paradoxically, by the vilest people on earth.

(193) *Lettre sur les Juifs à un ecclésiastique de mes amis, lue dans la séance publique du musée de Paris, le 21 novembre 1782* by M(onsieur) le B(aron) C(loots) Du V(al) De G(râce), Berlin, 1783, p. 37 (M. Court de Gébelin's reply), pp. 50 ff. (Second letter from the author to M. Court de Gébelin).

(194) Summarized from the account by Pierre Grosclaude, *Malesherbes, témoin et interprète de son temps*, Paris, 1961, Vol. II, Chap. X; *La question juive*, 1788, pp. 631-49.

(195) Document quoted by Levylier, *op. cit.*, p. 21.

(196) *Essai sur la régénération . . .*, pp. 160-1:
France embraces perhaps eight million subjects, some of whom can barely stammer a few mispronounced words or a few disjointed phrases in our idiom; others are completely ignorant of it. It is known that in many places in Lower Brittany and beyond the Loire, the clergyman is still forced to preach in the local dialect, on pain of not being understood if he speaks French. The government does not know or does not feel how much the annihilation of dialects means to the expansion of enlightenment, to the purified knowledge of religion, to the easy execution of the laws, to national happiness and to political peace.

(197) A. Cahen, "L'émancipation des Juifs . . . et M. Roederer," *R.E.J.*, I, 1880, pp. 102-4.

(198) *Ibid.*, pp. 63-104. An attorney to the Metz Parliament had sent a letter to the Academy in which he proposed to deport all the

Jews to Guiana. On the other hand, a long treatise by a Benedictine monk recalled the usefulness to the Christian church of their abasement and suggested forcing them to harvest honey and wax, "considering their decided taste for these substances." The authors of all the other treatises, including three ecclesiastics, proved advocates of the emancipation of the Jews.

(199) *Apologie des Juifs en réponse à la question: Est-il des moyens de rendre les Juifs plus heureux et plus utiles à la France?*, by M. Zalkind-Hourwitz, Polish Jew, Paris, 1789.

(200) *Essai sur la régénération physique, morale et politique des Juifs*, by M. Grégoire, parish-priest of the diocese of Metz, Metz, 1789; *Dissertation sur cette question: Est-il des moyens de rendre les Juifs plus heureux et plus utiles à la France?*, by M. Thiery, lawyer to the parliament of Nancy, Paris, 1788.

(201) *Essai sur la régénération* . . . , p. 49:

3. The use of badly chosen, badly prepared foods. It is proved by experience that this cause makes for prompt degeneration of the human species, and the authority of M. Buffon gives new weight to this assertion; now it is a fact that, for fear of eating blood, the Jews squeeze almost all of it out of their meats and thereby remove much of the nourishing juices. We are assured that in certain countries they use little salt; their dishes must then have an unhealthy quality and render digestion difficult. . . .

(202)   Full religious freedom granted to the Jews will be a great step forward towards reforming them, and I dare say towards converting them; for truth is only persuasive in so far as it is sweet . . . ; in 1584, Gregory XIII ordered hebdomadal instruction for the Jews. Various sovereigns have decreed the same; this custom of preaching to them, which has lapsed in Hesse, in the principality of Colemberg, and at Metz, continues in Italy. The success with which Father Marin preached controversy to the Hebrews of Avignon is known. To force the Jews to be instructed is not the same as forcing them to convert, and I would be inclined to believe that to subject them to hearing a few discourses, is not contradicting the rights of humanity; or else convince me that the State cannot force its subjects to acquire enlightenment.

6 Germany

(1) On this subject, see Norman Cohn's book, *The Pursuit of the Millennium*, London, 1957, notably Chap. V ("Manifestos for a future Frederick").

(2) Chap. IV, *Jupiter speaks in front of Simplex about the German hero who will inspire the world with peace* (*Der abenteuerliche Simplicissimus*):

I will give up Greek so as to speak nothing but German. And, as the crowning touch to my favors, I will give the Germans, as I once gave the Romans, dominion of the world . . . . I will raise up a German hero who will accomplish his task with the blade of a sword. . . .

. . . I then asked my Jupiter what the Christian kings would then do and what role they would play in this vast scheme. He replied:

Those of England, Sweden and Denmark, who are of German origin and blood; those of France, Spain and Portugal, whose countries were formerly conquered and governed by old Germans, will receive their crown, their kingdom and the territories in it that they have annexed from the German nation, in the form of fiefs. And then an eternal and unalterable peace will reign amongst all the people of the world.

(3) Comte de Mirabeau, *De la monarchie prussienne sous Frédéric le Grand,* London, 1788, Vol. V (6), p. 11.

(4) Robert Minder, *Allemagnes et Allemands,* Paris, 1948, p. 94:

. . . swarming families of pastors, schoolmasters, organists, teachers, doctors, judges, intellectuals of all orders. At least two-thirds of the writers of classical German literature have been sons, grandsons, nephews or descendants of pastors, often pastors themselves.

(5) Immanuel Kant, *Anthropologie,* Part II.

(6) Madame de Staël, *De l'Allemagne.*

(7) Kant, *Metaphysik der Sitten,* I, "Rechtslehre," ed. Leipzig, 1838, pp. 153-4:

There is therefore no legitimate resistance by the people to the legislative ruler of the state; for only by submission to his legislative will is a lawful condition possible. There is therefore no right to insurrection (*seditio*), still less to revolt (*rebellio*), least of all against him, as an individual (*monarch*), an attempt on his person, even on his life (*monarchomachismus sub specie tyrannis*) under the pretext of the abuse of his power (*tyrannis*). The slightest attempt at this is high treason (*proditio eminens*) and the traitor of this type, as one who seeks to destroy his country (*parricida*), cannot be punished with less than death. The ground for the duty of the people to endure even an abuse of the supreme power that is thought intolerable lies in the fact that its resistance to the highest legislation can itself never be considered other than as a breach of the law, even as destructive of the whole legal order.

(8) Minder, *op. cit.*, p. 134. For Frederick's Germanophobia see Pierre Gaxotte, *Frédéric II,* and above all the book which caused a scandal in its day, by Werner Hegemann, *Fredericus oder das Königsopfer,* Berlin, 1924.

(9) Lessing:

> The reputation of being a patriot would be my last ambition, if patriotism must teach me to learn to forget that I must be a citizen of the world . . . at the very most, I see in it a heroic weakness which I can well do without.

Goethe:

> What good are these vain efforts to bring back to life a feeling which we can no longer experience, which only existed, which only exists amongst certain peoples, at specific moments in history . . . God preserve us from patriotism, as the ancient Romans knew it!

Right from its first issue *Der Patriot* proclaimed: " . . . I regard the whole world as my homeland, yes, as a single city, and I consider myself the relation and co-citizen of all men." (Quoted by L. Lévy-Bruhl, *L'Allemagne depuis Leibnitz,* Paris, 1907, pp. 147, 245, 248.)

(10) *Wilhelm Meisters Wanderjahre,* Book III, Chap. XI (the speech by Friedrich).

(11) Cf. Ludwig Geiger, *Die deutsche Literatur und die Juden,* Berlin, 1910, pp. 125 ff.

(12) *Ideen zur Philosophie der Geschichte der Menschheit,* Book XVI, Chap. XII.

(13) *Ibid.,* Book XII, Chap. III ("The Hebrews").

(14) This grandiloquent letter by the young Gumpertz has been published by M. Kayserling, *Moses Mendelssohn, sein Leben und sein Wirken,* Leipzig, 1888, pp. 15-18.

(15) Ludwig Schnabel, *Die Insel Felsenburg,* 4 Vols., 1731-43.

(16) Christian Gellert, *Das Leben der schwedischen Gräfin von G...,* 1747.

(17) Wieland's *Der Teutsche Merkur,* 1785, Vol. I, p. 285 (quoted by Henri Brunschwig in his thesis: "La lutte pour l'émancipation des Juifs de Prusse," Paris, 1946).

(18) Quoted by G. Liebe, *Das Judentum in der deutschen Vergangenheit,* Leipzig, 1903, p. 120:

> Wen fasst des Mitleids Schauer nicht, wenn er sieht, Wie unser Pöbel Kanaans Volk entmenscht! Und thut der's nicht, weil unsre Fürsten, Sie in eiserne Fesseln schmieden? Du lösest ihnen, Retter, die rostige, Engangelegte Fessel von wunden Arm, Sie fühlen's glauben's kaum. So lange, hat's um die Elenden hergeklirret. . . .

(19) *Die Juden,* a play in one act by Lessing, 1781.

(20) *Deutsches Museum,* Leipzig, 1782, I, 337 (quoted by H. Brunschwig in his thesis, see above).

(21) This was notably the case with the *Mercure galant* (or *La Comédie sans titre* by Boursault, which became *Die Heirat durch das Wochenblatt,* 1788) and the *Joueur* by Regnard (which became *Das Spielerglück,* 1790). Likewise, the German adaptation of *The Jew* by Cumberland (*Der Jude,* aus dem

englischen, 1798) was enriched by a tirade against the special laws which weighed on the Jews, which did not exist in the original. (On this subject, see Herbert Carrington, "Die Figur des Juden in der dramatischen Literatur des XVIII Jahrhunderts," thesis, Heidelberg, 1897.)

(22) Letter from Lessing to Mendelssohn, January 9, 1771:

> One more thing I ask of you—if you reply, do so with every possible freedom, with every conceivable emphasis. You alone in this matter must and can speak and write in that way; and you are therefore infinitely more fortunate than other honest people who cannot further the overthrow of the most despicable structure of nonsense except by pretending to establish it afresh.

(23) Mendelssohn's first reply to Lavater, December 12, 1769.

(24) See above, p. 60.

(25) *Lettres juives du célèbre Mendelssohn, philosophe de Berlin, avec les remarques et réponses de Monsieur le docteur Kölbele et autres savants hommes . . .* , Frankfurt and the Hague, 1771.

(26) *Jerusalem and Other Jewish Writings* by Moses Mendelssohn, Alfred Jospe, trans. and ed., New York, 1969, p. 58.

(27) See above, p. 118.

(28) *Jerusalem . . .* , pp. 74-5:

> At first, it was explicitly forbidden to add anything in writing to the laws which Moses had recorded for the people in accordance with God's instructions. According to our rabbis, you are not permitted to write down what has been transmitted orally. It was only much later that the heads of the Synagogue decided, albeit with considerable reluctance, to grant permission—which had by then become necessary—to record some legal traditions in writing. They called this permission "a destruction of the law," saying with the Psalmist, "It is time when for the sake of the Lord the law *must* be destroyed."
>
> Yet this development was not in harmony with the original intent. The ceremonial law itself is a living kind of script, as it were, stirring heart and mind, full of meaning, stimulating man to continuous contemplation . . . .
>
> The ready availability of books and other printed material, whose number has enormously increased since the invention of the printing press, has changed man radically. It has revolutionized human thought and knowledge. This development has, of course, been beneficial and contributed to the improvement of mankind—something for which we cannot be grateful enough to Providence. But like every good thing that happens to man on earth, it also has some evil side-effects, partly owing to abuse and partly to the inevitable limitations of the human condition. We teach and instruct each other through writings; we get to know nature and men only from

writings; we work and relax, edify and amuse ourselves through writings. The preacher no longer talks with his congregation—he reads or recites a written essay: and the teacher reads his written notes from the lectern. Everything is reduced to the dead letter: the spirit of living dialogue no longer exists anywhere. We love and vent our anger in letters, quarrel and become reconciled in letters; our social contacts are maintained by correspondence; and when we do get together, we know of no other entertainment than games and reading aloud.

As a result, a man has lost almost all value in the eyes of his fellow men. We do not seek personal contact and interchange with a man of wisdom, for we can find his wisdom in his writings. . . . In one word: we are *literati*, men of letters. Our whole being depends on the printed word, and we can no longer comprehend how mortal man can educate and perfect himself without books.

(29) Letter to Herz Homberg, September 23, 1783.
(30) *Jerusalem* . . . , p. 105.
(31) Letter to an unknown noble correspondent, January 26, 1770.
(32) Mendelssohn's preface to the German translation of the *Vindiciae Judaeorum*, by Manasseh ben Israel (*Gesammelte Schriften* . . . , *ed. cit.*, p. 202).
(33) The way in which Kant and, after him, Hegel, took Mendelssohn's *Jerusalem* . . . as their authority to deny Judaism the dignity of a religion, has been well brought out by Nathan Rotenstreich, *The Recurring Pattern, Studies in Anti-Judaism in Modern Thought*, London, 1963, pp. 45, 52-3.
(34) Cf. Léon Poliakov, *History of Anti-Semitism*, Vol. I, *From the Time of Christ to the Court Jews*, New York, 1965.
(35) Kant expanded his views on truth and falsehood in *Metaphysik der Sitten* (II, "Sittenlehre"), but, primarily, see his 1797 book, *Über ein vermeintes Recht, aus Menschenliebe zu lügen*, where he argues from the above example, recognizes Michaelis's prior claim and adopts his views.
(36) "Im Deutschen lügt man, wenn man höflich ist" (*Faust*, line 6771).
(37) Cf. above, p. 138.
(38) "Orientalische und exegetische Bibliothek," Vol. XIX, Frankfurt am Main, 1782.
(39) Adolf Hitler, *Mein Kampf*, Chap. XI:

For here also everything is borrowed, or rather, stolen—precisely by virtue of his own being the Jew cannot possess a religious organization for he lacks idealism in any form and thereby the belief in the beyond is quite alien to him. But from the Aryan standpoint a religion cannot be conceived which lacks conviction in a life after death in one form or another. In truth, the Talmud is not a book of preparation for the life beyond but only for a practical and tolerable life in this world.

(40) I. Kant, *Religion Within the Limits of Reason Alone*, New York, 1960, pp. 116-17.

(41) Cf. for example Hermann Cohen, "Innere Beziehungen der Kantischen Philosophie zum Judentum," *Jüdische Schriften*, Vol. 1, Berlin, 1924; Julius Guttmann, *Kant und das Judentum*, Berlin, n.d.; A. Lewkowitz, *Das Judentum und die geistigen Strömungen des 19. Jahrhunderts*, Breslau, 1935.

(42) Kant speaks of the euthanasia of Judaism either in relation to the birth of Christianity (Judaism has therefore been dead for eighteen centuries), or with reference to the reform of contemporary Judaism (it is therefore destined to die shortly). On this subject, see Nathan Rotenstreich, *The Recurring Pattern, Studies in Anti-Judaism in Modern Thought*, pp. 38-40.

(43) Cf. *Vermischte Schriften*, ed. Félix Cross, Leipzig, 1921, pp. 389-90.

(44) Letter from Kant to his pupil Marcus Herz, August 20, 1777; cf. *Gesammelte Schriften, Akademieausgabe*, Vol. X, p. 211. Cf. also Kant's letters to Mendelssohn (Vol. X, pp. 70, 346) as well as Kant's book about him published shortly after his death, *Qu'est-ce que s'orienter dans la pensée?*, ed. A. Philonenko, Paris, 1959, pp. 60, 82.

(45) I. Kant, *Streit der Fakultäten*, Part I:

One can regard very favorably the idea expressed by a good mind belonging to this nation, Lazarus Bendavid, publicly to accept the religion of Jesus (probably with its vehicle, the Gospels). . . . clearly, the Jews must be left with the freedom to interpret the Torah and Gospels, in order to be able to distinguish the way in which Jesus spoke as a Jew to Jews from the way in which he spoke as moral teacher to men in general. The euthanasia of Judaism is the pure religion of morality, with the abandonment of all old doctrines, of which some must still be retained in Christianity (as the Messianic belief); a sectarian difference which eventually must also disappear and thus bring back, at least in the mind, that which is termed the conclusion of the great drama of religious evolution on earth (the return of all things) when there is only one shepherd and one flock.

(46) J. G. Fichte, *Beiträge zur Berichtigung der Urteile über die französische Revolution*, 1793. (Cf. C. Andler, *Le Pangermanisme philosophique*, Paris, 1917, pp. 8-11.) Fichte, primarily basing his arguments on the idea of the social contract, defended the right of the French to alter their constitution and from there moved on to plead the right of the citizens of a country to secede. This gave him the opportunity to protest against "The state within the State" which, according to him, the Jews formed. He specified that he had nothing against their belief

but against their "hatred of the whole human race":

> Throughout almost all the countries of Europe there is spreading a mighty hostile state that is at perpetual war with all other states and in many of them imposes fearful burdens on the citizens: it is the Jews. I do not think as I hope to show subsequently that this state is fearful not because it forms a separate and solidly united state but because this state is founded on the hatred of the whole human race. . . . In a state where the absolute monarch cannot take from me my paternal hut and where I can defend my rights against the all-powerful minister, the first Jew who likes can plunder me with impunity. This you see and cannot deny, and you utter sugary words of tolerance and of the rights of man and civil rights, all the time wounding in us the primary rights of man. You could not do enough to satisfy the kind indulgence for those who do not believe in Jesus Christ, with all titles, dignities and positions of honor which you give them, while you publicly scorn those who only believe in him differently from you, and take away their civil honor and the bread they have honorably earned. Do you not remember the state within the State? Does the thought not occur to you that if you give to the Jews who are citizens of a state more solid and more powerful than any of yours, civil rights in your states, they will utterly crush the remainder of your citizens?

This philippic was followed by the suggestion of conquering Palestine on behalf of the Jews which we have quoted in the text.

(47) Cf. above, pp. 64-5.
(48) *Grundzüge des gegenwärtigen Zeitalters,* ed. 1946, pp. 98-9, 209-11:

> Es gibt nach unserem Erachten zwei höchst verschiedene Gestalten des Christentums: die im Evangelium Johannis, und die beim Apostel Paulus. . . . Was das Historische anbelangt, ist ihm [Johannes] seine Lehre so alt, als die Welt und die erste ursprüngliche Religion; das Judentum aber, als eine spätere Ausartung verwirft er unbedingt, und ohne alle Milderung. . . . Es bleibt auch bei diesem Evangelisten immer zweifelhaft, ob Jesus aus jüdischen Stamme kam, oder falls er es doch etwa wäre, wie es mit seiner Abstammung sich eigentlich verhalte. . . . Paulus, ein Christ geworden, wollte dennoch nicht unrecht haben, ein Jude gewesen zu sein; beide Systeme mussten daher vereinigt werden und sich in einander fügen. . . .

> There are in our opinion two very different forms of Christianity: That in the Gospel of John and that in the Apostle Paul. . . . So far as the historical aspect is concerned, John's teaching is as old as the world and the first original

religion; but he unconditionally projects Judaism as a later degeneration and without any palliative. . . . In the case of this evangelist it is always doubtful whether Jesus was of Jewish origin, or, if this was in fact so, how matters stood in regard to his origin. . . . Paul, having become a Christian, did not wish to be in error in having been a Jew; both systems must therefore be united and adapted to each other.

(49) *Ibid.*, p. 104 (223).

(50) *Reden an die deutsche Nation* (Sixth Speech).

(51) Cf. Ludwig Roselius, *Fichte für heute*, Berlin, 1938.

(52) Cf. A. Philonenko, *La Liberté humaine dans la philosophie de Fichte*, Paris, 1966, p. 15.

(53) See below pp. 380-91.

(54) Hegel dealt with Judaism in *Lectures on the Philosophy of Religion, Phenomenology of Mind* (London, 1964) and *Philosophy of History*, particularly in the following passages:
1) But because the servile consciousness rests obstinately on its particularity, and because its particularity has been taken up into the unity immediately, it is exclusive, and God is . . . the exclusive Lord and God of the Jewish people. It need not surprise us that an Oriental nation should limit religion to itself, and that this religion should appear as absolutely connected with its nationality, for we see this in Eastern countries in general. . . . Still this exclusiveness is rightly regarded as more striking in the case of the Jewish people, for such strong attachment to nationality is in complete contradiction with the idea that God is to be conceived of only in universal thought, and not in one particular characterization. . . . The Jewish God exists only for Thought, and that stands in contrast with the idea of the limitation of God to the nation. It is true that amongst the Jewish people, too, consciousness rises to the thought of universality, and this thought is given expression to in several places . . . so now this limitation is explained for us from the nature of the servile consciousness; and we see too, now, how this particularity arises from the subjective side. . . . (*Lectures on the Philosophy of Religion*, Rev. E. B. Spiers and J. Burdon Sanderson, trans., Vol. II, London, 1895, pp. 208-10.)
2) Just so it may be said of the Jews that it is precisely because they stand directly before the door of salvation, that they are and have been the most reprobate and abandoned:— What the nation should be in and for itself, this, the true inner nature of itself, it is not conscious of being, but puts away beyond itself. By this renunciation it creates for itself the *possibility* of a higher level of existence, if once it could get the object thus renounced back again to itself, than if it had never left its natural immediate state of existence— because the spirit is all the greater the greater the opposition

out of which it returns into itself; and such an opposition the spirit brings about for itself, by doing away with its immediate unity, and laying aside its self-existence, and separate life of its own. But if such a consciousness does not mediate and reflect itself, the middle position or term where it has a determinate existence is the fatal unholy void, since what should give it substance and filling has been turned into a rigidly fixed extreme. It is thus that this last stage of reason's function of observation is its very worst, and for that reason its complete reversal becomes necessary. (*Phenomenology of Mind*, J. B. Baillie, trans., London, 1964, p. 367.)

3) The Jews possess that which makes them what they are, through the *One*: consequently the individual has no freedom for itself. Spinoza regards the code of Moses as having been given by God to the Jews for a punishment—a rod of correction. The individual never comes to the consciousness of independence; on that account we do not find among the Jews any belief in the immortality of the soul; for individuality does not exist in and for itself. But though in Judaism the *Individual* is not respected, the *Family* has inherent value; for the worship of Jehovah is attached to the Family, and it is consequently viewed as a substantial existence. But the State is an institution not consonant with the Judaistic principle, and it is alien to the legislation of Moses. In the idea of the Jews, Jehovah is the God of Abraham, Isaac, and Jacob; who commanded them to depart out of Egypt, and gave them the land of Canaan. The accounts of the Patriarchs attract our interest. We have seen in this history the transition from the patriarchal nomadic condition to agriculture. On the whole the Jewish history exhibits grand features of character; but it is disfigured by an exclusive bearing (sanctioned in its religion), towards the genius of other nations (the destruction of the inhabitants of Canaan being commanded even)—by want of culture generally, and by the superstition arising from the idea of the high value of their peculiar nationality . . . (Hegel, *Philosophy of History*, p. 197).

(55) *On Christianity, Early Theological Writings,* by Friedrich Hegel, T. M. Knox, trans., New York, 1961, pp. 193-4, 204-5.

(56) *Ibid.*, p. 265.

(57) J. S. Semler, *Abhandlungen von freier Untersuchung des Canon,* Halle, 1776, Part I, pp. 32, 89, 102, 103.

(58) Friedrich Schleiermacher, *On Religion*, English translation, London, 1893, pp. 238-40.

(59) Cf. Isaiah Berlin, *The Age of Enlightenment*, New York, 1956, pp. 271-5. The English philosopher writes:

One need not accept Hamann's theological beliefs or his anti-scientific bias to realize the depth and originality of his ideas about the relations of thought, reason, semi-inarticulate emotional (and spiritual) life, the cultural institutions in which this last is embodied, and the languages and symbolisms of mankind. . . . Hamann deserves an act of belated homage in the twentieth century, whose most revolutionary philosophical innovations he did something to anticipate.

(60) "Golgotha und Scheblimini," *Werke*, J. Nadler, ed., Vol. III, p. 309. I would like to thank Professor Helmut Gollwitzer of the University of Berlin who was kind enough to send me this quotation as well as those which follow.

(61) "Biblische Betrachtungen," J. Nadler, ed., I, II.

(62) *Briefwechsel* IV, S. Hensel, ed., p. 147.

(63) *Hierokles oder Prüfung und Verteidigung der christlichen Religion, angestellt von den Herren Michaelis, Semler, Less und Fréret*, Halle, 1785, pp. 285, 311.

(64) From an unpublished thesis by H. Brunschwig ("La lutte pour l'émancipation des Juifs en Prusse," Paris, 1946). *De civitate Judaeorum* is said to be an expanded version of the pamphlet *Von den Juden* which Paalzow published in 1799 (and which I have not been able to consult).

(65) *Wider die Juden, Ein Wort der Warnung an unsere christliche Mitbürger* (5th ed., Berlin, 1803); *Erklärung an das Publikum über meine Schrift: Wider die Juden* (4th ed., Berlin, 1803); *C. W. Fr. Grattenauers erster Nachtrag zu seiner Erklärung über seine Schrift Wider die Juden* (5th ed., Berlin, 1803).

(66) Cf. the thesis by H. Brunschwig (see above), p. 90, and the anti-Semitic dictionary *Sigilla Veri* ("Semi-Kürschner"), Erfurt, 1929, Vol. II, p. 809.

(67) Heinrich Schnee, *Die Hoffinanz und der moderne Staat*, Berlin, 1953, Vol. I, p. 190.

(68) Comte de Mirabeau, *De la monarchie prussienne sous Frédéric le Grand*, Vol. V (6), p. 42.

(69) Schnee, *op. cit.*, Vol. I, p. 186.

(70) Cf. Poliakov, *History of Anti-Semitism*, Vol. II, *From Mohammed to the Marranos*, New York, 1973.

(71) *The Autobiography of Solomon Maimon*, London, 1954, p. 62.

(72) Cf. H. Grätz, *Geschichte der Juden*, Leipzig, 1870, Vol. XI, p. 151.

(73) "Bref exposé de la religion juive," in *Salomon Maimons Lebensgeschichte*, Appendix I, pp. 349-50.

(74) Cf. A. Lewkowitz, *Das Judentum und die geistigen Stromungen des 19. Jahrhunderts*, Breslau, 1935, pp. 66-71.

(75) From S. Dubnov, *Histoire moderne du peuple juif*, Vol. I, Paris, 1933, p. 29:

Intelligent people in Berlin are beginning to think more highly of Mendelssohn's co-religionists; today we are seeing that this people (whose prophets and early laws we honored) is capable of producing great men in both the sciences and the arts. Can we want to afflict such a people with our jibes? No, we cannot want to do this. We also represent Christian rogues. We blame the oppression and cruelty which prevail in convents. In *Nathan der Weise*, the most disagreeable role falls to the Christians. In the *Merchant of Venice*, this role falls to the Jews. . . .

(76) Quoted by Max Brod, *Heinrich, Heine*, Amsterdam, 1935, p. 162.

(77) K. Boettiger exclaimed in 1797 (K. Boettiger, *Literarische Zustände und Zeitgenossen*, Leipzig, 1838, II, pp. 102 ff.):

Yes, things have reached such a point that very often the Christians, particularly in matters of taste and the prevailing philosophy, soak their dark little lamp in the oil of the Jewish brokers of light. Previously the pretty Jewish women were able to determine matters of make-up and fashion only in Berlin. But for some time now they also hold the initiative in judgments on the most subtle syllogism, the wittiest comedy, the most accomplished actor and the best poem.

(78) J. F. Unger, *Jahrbücher der preussischen Monarchie unter der Regierung Friedrich Wilhelm des Dritten*, Berlin, 1798, II, p. 23. The Berlin dandies and young scholars who have no access to people of quality or do not seek it, turn for a substitute to the rich Jewish houses. The cultured members of this nation form a special class which is currently acquiring more influence than its baptized fellow-citizens would readily concede. If among the seed of Abraham which is as ever as numerous as the sand on the sea-shore, some fine speculative minds have distinguished themselves, then that is still very few amongst a huge number and they are inexpressibly proud of this. They never forget that they have had a Moses Mendelssohn, and Jews and the friends of the Jew still bow before this light whilst hundreds of equally deserving scholars, which are not however so rare, are forgotten.

(79) Schnee, *op. cit.*, I, p. 220.

(80) Cf. B. Hagani, *L'Émancipation des Juifs*, Paris, 1828, p. 138.

(81) S. Hensel, *Die Familie Mendelssohn, 1729 bis 1847*, Berlin, 1911, p. 95.

(82) *Ibid.*, p. 112.

(83) *Ibid.*, p. 105.

(84) Cf. Franz Kobler, *Juden und Judentum in deutschen Briefen aus drei Jahrhunderten*, Vienna, 1935, p. 134.

(85) J. Furst, ed., *Henriette Herz, ihr Leben und ihre Erinnerungen*, Berlin, 1850, p. 121.

(86) Hannah Arendt, *Rahel Varnhagen, The Life of a Jewess*, Richard and Clara Winston, trans., London, 1957, p. 176.

(87) *Ibid.*, p. 4.

(88) *Ibid.*, p. 97.

(89) Quoted by Brod, *op. cit.*

(90) Quoted from A. Eloesser, *Vom Ghetto nach Europa*, Berlin, 1936, p. 82.

(91) See the heavily documented conclusions in the book by Schnee, *op. cit.*, Vol. III, pp. 220, 266.

(92) Cf. S. W. Baron, *Die Judenfrage auf dem Wiener Kongress*, Vienna, 1020, p. 127, quoting a report by the Viennese police.

(93) In his work (see above) p. 125, S. W. Baron, on the basis of the reports of the Viennese police, disputes the fact, first stated by M. Bermann, *Konzert bei der Baronin Fanny von Arnstein*, Vienna, 1855.

(94) The Prussian consul Friedrich-August Stägemann wrote (quoted by Baron, *op. cit.*, Vol. I, p. 137):

> It is often said that Jews have no homeland. But Madame d'Eskeles goes into a trance when anyone says anything against Prussia, and Madame d'Arnstein is offensive to people and gets very upset. Humboldt says that she is compromising us with her unbridled patriotism.

(95) *Ibid.*, p. 127, quoting a letter from Prince Radziwill.

(96) *Lettres et papiers du chancelier comte de Nesselrode*, Vol. II, p. 153.

(97) On Alexander I's philo-Semitism, see below, pp. 250 ff. His whole entourage in Vienna frequented the Arnstein salon; cf. Baron, *op. cit.*, p. 125.

(98) Cf. Schnee, *op. cit.*, Vol. I, p. 236.

(99) *Ibid.*, p. 237 (in French in the text).

(100) *Ibid.*, p. 229:

> A former Prussian contractor who, in a pun on his Hebrew name Moses (meaning "drawn from the water," in Italian "del Mare") has taken the corresponding but more sonorous name of Baron Delmar, founded here some time ago an educational institution for impoverished young nobles, for which he allocated more than one and a half million francs, a noble deed that was esteemed so highly in the Faubourg St Germain that even the proudest dowagers and the youngest girls no longer make open fun of him. Has this nobleman of the tribe of David ever given a single penny to a collection for Jewish interests?

(Heine was alluding to the collection made after the Damascus affair (1840), to which reference will be made later.)

(101) Cf. Kobler, *op. cit.*, pp. 209-10.

(102) Ismar Freund, *Die Emanzipation der Juden in Preussen*, Berlin, 1912, Vol. I, p. 49.

(103) *Ibid.*, p. 75.

(104) *Ibid.*, p. 65.

(105) Quoted from S. Dubnov, *Weltgeschichte des jüdischen Volks*, Vol. V, Berlin, 1928, p. 204.

(106) *Beantwortung des Sendschreibens einiger Hausväter jüdischer Religion an mich den Probst Teller*, Berlin, 1799, p. 21.

(107) *Ibid.*
(108) Dubnov, *op. cit.*, p. 206.
(109) J.-A. de Luc, *Lettres sur le christianisme* . . . , Berlin, 1801, p. 122, and *Correspondance entre M. le Dr. Teller et J.A. de Luc*, Hanover, 1803. De Luc also published a *Lettre aux auteurs juifs d'un mémoire adressé à M. Teller*, Berlin, 1799, which I have not been able to consult.
(110) Cf. the unpublished thesis by Henri Brunschwig, "La lutte pour l'émancipation des Juifs en Prusse," p. 83. I have not been able to consult this booklet by Paalzow.
(111) Cf. Rotenstreich, *The Recurring Pattern* . . . , p. 40, referring to the interpretation of Hermann Cohen, *Kants Begründung der Ethik*, Berlin, 1910, p. 196.

7 The Emancipation

(1) Cf. David Feuerwerker, "L'abolition du péage corporel en France," *Annales*, XVII, 1962, p. 867.
(2) *Ibid.*, p. 870.
(3) Maurice Liber, "Les Juifs et la convocation des états généraux, 1789," *R.E.J.*, LXIII-LXVI (1912-13); LXIII, p. 194.
(4) Quoted by P. Goubert and M. Denis, *1789, Les Français ont la parole, cahiers des états généraux*, Paris, 1964, pp. 195-6.
(5) Liber, *op. cit.*, pp. 196-9.
(6) *Ibid.*, p. 209.
(7) Goubert and Denis, *op. cit.*, p. 226.
(8) Quoted from Léon Kahn, *Les Juifs de Paris pendant la Révolution*, Paris, 1899, p. 17.
(9) Robespierre's speech to the National Assembly, session of December 23, 1789, *Moniteur*, December 23-5, 1789.
(10) What Clermont-Tonnerre actually said during his speech was: "Everything must be denied to the Jews as a nation. and everything granted to them as individuals; they must not form either a political body or an order in the State; they must be individual citizens."
(11) An analysis of the speeches by the adversaries of emancipation will be found in Kahn, *op. cit.*, pp. 30-45. See also the arguments by Curé Thiébault, the Member of the Constituent Assembly for Metz, who published a memoir in October, 1789, aimed at refuting the grievances of the Jews in the East:
> How can you ask to live and reside amongst us thus, you who are forbidden by your law to reside amidst idolaters? . . . How can you think of settling in our midst by buying land here? Is not your demand a formal infraction of the letter of your law, is it not in culpable opposition to its spirit?
Rewbell, on the other hand, was appealing to "progressive" arguments when he wrote to Camille Desmoulins (cf. C.

Hoffmann, *L'Alsace au XVIIIe siècle,* IV, pp. 517-19):
> I doubt whether anyone in the whole Assembly is more tolerant than I am. . . . What do you think of individuals who want to become Frenchmen and still have Jewish administrators, Jewish notaries, the lot, exclusively; who want to have different laws on inheritance, on marriage, on guardianship, on majority, etc., from French citizens, their neighbors. . . . You see it is not I who am excluding the Jews; they are excluding themselves. . . .

(12) *Le Courrier de Provence,* no. 99 (cf. Kahn, *op. cit.,* p. 74).
(13) S. Dubnov, *Histoire moderne du peuple juif,* Paris, 1933, Vol. I, pp. 118-19.
(14) Kahn, *op. cit.,* p. 70.
(15) *Ibid.,* pp. 44, 80.
(16) *Ibid.,* p. 64.
(17) *Ibid.,* p. 94.
(18) *Ibid.,* p. 110.
(19) See the classic works of Jewish history. In particular, dozens of Parisian Jews enrolled in the National Guard. The newspapers of the day praise their good citizenship and their "dejudaization." For example, *Le Journal général de France,* April 2, 1790:
> They are no longer those pig-headed men *dura cervice*: they no longer have that obstinacy and the tenacity in their religious opinions which used to characterize them; they are giving up without scruple those practices which we regarded as trivial and ridiculous, and which they regarded as sacred and very necessary for their conscience.

Or *La Feuille de Paris,* 24, Brumaire, year II:
> Is it possible? Even the Jews have become reasonable. The circumcised people, that hard people who, our priests told us, had been stricken with eternal blindness, that nation, separated from all nations, is becoming enlightened and reconciled with us by its wisdom and generosity.

(20) Kahn, *op. cit.,* p. 110.
(21) Cf. A. Pichault, *Une Exécution révolutionnaire en 1794 à Mons,* "Messager des Sciences historiques de Belgique," 1842, pp. 10 ff. The author, Charles-Louis Richard, was guillotined at Mons in 1794.
(22) Abbé Joseph Lémann, *La Prépondérance juive,* Paris, 1889, p. 131.
(23) Cf. the documents and pamphlets which Kahn quotes, pp. 48-9.
(24) Jacob Pereyra, the Frey brothers, the Calmer family (cf. Kahn, *op. cit.,* pp. 236-93).
(25) *Ibid.,* p. 191.
(26) *Ibid.,* p. 190.
(27) Quoted by M. Jean Bruhat, "Divinités de la Raison," in *La Naissance des dieux,* Paris, 1966, p. 219.

(28) Cf. Moïse and Ernest Ginsburger, "Contributions à l'histoire des Juifs pendant la Terreur," *R.E.J.*, XLVII, 1903, pp. 283-99. (Likewise for the quotations which follow.)

(29) Kahn, *op. cit.*, p. 168.

(30) *Pétition à la Convention pour les citoyens ci-devant juifs de Strasbourg* by Foussedoire, published by M. and E. Ginsburger, *op. cit.*, pp. 296-7.

(31) Quoted by Kahn, *op. cit.*, p. 234.

(32) Cf. Poliakov, *History of Ant-Semitism*, Vol. II, *From Mohammed to the Marranos*, New York, 1973. The Santa Maria family, which was descended from the converted rabbi Samuel Ha-Levi, was admitted to the advantages of "pure-blooded" Christian in the sixteenth century because it was supposed to belong to the same family as the Holy Virgin.

(33) A. Detcheverry, *Histoire des Israélites de Bordeaux*, Bordeaux, 1850, p. 101.

(34) This report by Fouché is not without interest for the history of pre-Zionist aspirations and schemes. It was dated February 11, 1807, and contained the following fundamental passages (cf. E. d'Hauterive, *La Police secrète du Premier Empire, Bulletins quotidiens adressés par Fouché à l'Empereur*, Paris, 1922, Vol. III, p. 152):

> Although the following information is not of recent date, it may be useful to set it down or recall it here, as the details of it are correct. In February, 1793, the council of the Comte de Lille, who was calling himself regent of the kingdom at that time, discussed a plan for an agreement suggested by the Jews. It involved ceding them the bay of Arcachon and all the lands of the territory between Bordeaux and Bayonne, to be held by them in ownership, under the suzerainty of the crown. . . . The Jews would offer twenty-five million, five in cash at the time the project was adopted; another five million in bills payable within a year, and supplied under the guarantee of the Dutch and Portuguese synagogues; the fifteen million remaining to be payable at the time of possession. After quite lengthy deliberation by the Comte de Lille's council the scheme was rejected after opposition from the bishop of Arras on religious grounds, and because such an infraction of the laws of the kingdom relating to the Jews could not be made in a time of regency.

(35) Cf. above, p. 83.

(36) Kahn, *op. cit.*, p 319.

(37) A. Thiers, *Histoire du Consulat et de l'Empire*, Paris, 1851, Vol. XI, pp. 69-72. The figure may have been exaggerated. The history of the Marranos of Portugal has still to be written!

(38) Cf. Robert Anchel, "Napoléon et les Juifs," Paris, 1928, p. 63, note 5.

(39) Cf. François Piétri, *Napoléon et les Israélites*, Paris, 1965, p. 54.

(40) Anchel, *op. cit.*, p. 93.
(41) *Ibid.*
(42) *Ibid.*, p. 241.
(43) Cf. P. Sagnac, "Les Juifs et Napoléon, 1806-8," *Revue d'histoire moderne et contemporaine*, II, 1900-1, p. 613.
(44) On the birth of this scheme, see A. S. Yahuda, "Conception d'un État juif par Napoléon," *Évidences*, May-June, 1951, pp. 3-8.
(45) *Ibid.*, p. 3.
(46) This interpretation was developed at length by Freud, notably in his letters to Arnold Zweig and Thomas Mann; cf. E. Jones, *Sigmund Freud . . .*, London, 1957, Vol. III, pp. 203-4, 492-3.
(47) Anchel, *op. cit.*, p. 42, note 2.
(48) This was P. Sagnac's opinion in his study, see above, pp. 474-5. See also point 3 of a note dictated by Napoleon in March, 1806 (Anchel, *op. cit.*, p. 78): " . . . to date from January 1, 1807, Jews who do not possess property will be subject to a tax and will not enjoy the right of citizenship. . . ."
(49) It replied
    that religious law only absolutely prohibited marriage with the seven Canaanite nations, Amon and Moab (in the past) and idolaters (in the present); that modern nations are not idolaters, since they worship a single God; that several mixed marriages had taken place, at different periods, between Jews and Christians in France, Spain and Germany; but that the rabbis would be no more disposed to bless the marriage of a Christian with a Jew or a Jew with a Christian, than the Catholic priest would consent to bless similar unions.
(50) Robert Anchel, whose thesis "Napoléon et les Juifs," remains the most erudite work on the subject, seems to attribute (pp. 187-8) the idea of the Great Sanhedrin to Napoleon himself. According to Georges Wormser, one of the directors of the *Consistoire central israélite*, it was suggested by Abraham Furtado, leader of the "enlightened" Jews in the General Assembly (cf. G. Wormser, *Français israélites . . .*, Paris, 1963, p. 23). Perhaps, however, its parentage should be attributed to Israël Jacobson, the "Court Jew" of King Jerome of Westphalia, who, in August, 1806, addressed a letter to Napoleon. The following are its most important passages (quoted by Heinrich Schnee, *Die Hoffinanz und der moderne Staat*, Berlin, 1953, Vol. II, pp. 130-2):
    . . . Be so gracious, Sire, as to extend your benevolent designs to the Jews who inhabit the countries bordering on the vast empire. If your Majesty limits his benefits to those of my brethren who are his subjects, how much would they still not have to desire? . . . The German Jew would be happy if he were allowed to earn his living honestly, to enjoy rights of citizenship, and if his religion were given a form and a procedure which would be consistent with the exercise of all

the duties of the citizen without separating him from his law. But this goal would require 1. the establishment of a Jewish supreme council, presided over by a patriarch, and with its seat in France; 2. the division of the whole community into districts, each of which would have its own individual synod, which would decide all matters relating to religion and would appoint rabbis under the supervision of the French government and the Jewish supreme council. . . .

(51) For anything about the Sanhedrin, see particularly R. Anchel's thesis; the change in the name of the rue des Piliers is mentioned by Count Thibaudau, *Le Consulat et l'Empire* . . . ("Empire," Vol. III), Paris, 1835, p. 203.

(52) Abbé Joseph Lémann, *Napoléon Ier et les Israélites, la prépondérance juive* . . . , Paris, 1894, pp. 110-13.

(53) L. de Bonald, "Sur les Juifs," *Mercure de France,* Vol. XXIII, pp. 249-67.

(54) D'Hauterive, *op. cit.,* Vol. III, p. 142.

(55) See below, pp. 278, 282, 330 ff.

(56) Cf. *R.E.J.,* Vol. XXVI, 1892, p. 316.

(57) Anchel, *op. cit.,* p. 217, notably pointing out that Napoleon was in East Prussia on that particular day.

(58) See below, p. 283.

(59) D'Hauterive, *op. cit.,* Vol. III, p. 284.

(60) Archives nationales, Fo 19-11010 (Vaucluse).

(61) Piétri, *op. cit.,* p. 136.

(62) Anchel, *op. cit.,* pp. 361-2.

(63) *Ibid.,* p. 401, where there are numerous other quotations of the same type.

(64) Cf. Archives nationales, sub-series AF IV (State Chancery), 300, do. 2150.

(65) Cf. F. de Fontette, "L'article 4 du décret "infâme" de 1808," *Mélanges René Savatier,* Paris, 1965, pp. 277-90.

(66) Schnee, *op. cit.,* Vol. II, p. 118, cf. the chapter "Der geheime Finanzrat Israel Jacobson, der Vorkampfer der Judenemanzipation," from which we have taken the main details of Jacobson's life (Vol. II, pp. 109-54).

(67) *Ibid.,* p. 128.

(68) *Ibid.,* p. 130.

(69) *Ibid.,* p. 131.

(70) *Ibid.,* pp. 137-9.

(71) An excellent account of the variations in the status of the Jews in the different German lands in 1800-15 will be found in S. W. Baron, *Die Judenfrage auf dem Wiener Kongress,* Vienna, 1920, pp. 9-23.

(72) For Baron Stein's attitude see Baron, *op. cit.,* notably his quotation of an ironic letter from Humboldt to his wife (who hardly shared his emancipating views) (p. 33):

Your tirade at the Jews, dear soul, is divine; I would like to make it known to Stein, who freely shares your views but suggests even more heroic methods as a solution, for he wants to settle them on the north coast of Africa.

(73) Cf. Ismar Freund, *Die Emanzipation der Juden in Preussen*, Berlin, 1912, Vol. I, p. 198.

(74) *Ibid.*, pp. 126-7.

(75) *Ibid.*, Vol. II (*Urkunden*), pp. 269-70.

(76) *Ibid.*, Vol. I, pp. 428-30 (letter from Jacobson to von Hardenberg, February 14, 1811).

(77) *Ibid.*, Vol. I, p. 182.

(78) *Ibid.*, Vol. I, p. 182.

(79) *Ibid.*, Vol. I, p. 232.

(80) *Ibid.*, Vol. I, pp. 236-8.

(81) Baron, *op. cit.*, pp. 89-90, note 56.

(82) *Ibid.*, pp. 173-5, quoting a letter from W. von Humboldt to his wife in which he described the various methods of corruption at the Congress of Vienna.

(83) *Ibid.*, p. 87.

(84) Cf. Paul Busch, *Friedrich Schlegel und das Judentum*, Munich, 1939, Annex I (article by Friedrich Schlegel in *Oesterreichischer Beobachter*, March 2, 1815).

(85) Cf. J. Hessen, *Law and Life. The History of the Restrictive Laws governing the Life of the Jews in Russia* (in Russian), St Petersburg, 1911, pp. 18, 181, note 7.

(86) *Ibid.*, p. 45.

(87) *Works*, by Derzhavin, St Petersburg, 1878, Vol. VII (*On the Jews*), pp. 280, 288.

(88) Derzhavin used the pejorative term "Yid" although Catherine the Great's government had advocated replacing it by "Yevrei" (cf. Dubnov, *op. cit.*, Vol. I, p. 356).

(89) *Ibid.*, pp. 281, 282.

(90) *Ibid.*, p. 283.

(91) *Ibid.*, p. 290.

(92) *Ibid.*, p. 291.

(93) *Ibid.*, p. 327.

(94) This should probably be regarded as a printing or copying error and be read as "pure German language."

(95) Hessen, *op. cit.*, p. 47; Dubnov, *op. cit.*, Vol. I, p. 375.

(96) Dubnov, *op. cit.*, Vol. I, p. 382.

(97) Declaration by Alexander I on June 29, 1814; text in Hessen, *op. cit.*, pp. 56-7. The Tsar is said to have made similar remarks to the English missionary John Patterson; according to Patterson "Emperor Alexander has been particularly interested in their [the Jews'] favor from their fidelity to him in the time of the French invasion." (Quoted by Max Kohler, *Jewish rights at the Congresses of Vienna and Aix-la-Chapelle*, The American Jewish Committee, New York, 1918, p. 91.)

(98) *Correspondance diplomatique de Joseph de Maistre*, Paris, 1880, Vol. II, p. 311.

(99) E. Benz, *Die abendländische Sendung der östlich-orthodoxen Kirche*, Wiesbaden, 1950, p. 5.

(100) Cf. A. Koyré, "Un chapitre de l'histoire intellectuelle de la Russie: la persécution des philosophes sous Alexandre Ier," *Le Monde slave*, 1926 (IV), pp. 90-117.

(101) Quoted by Maurice Paléologue, *Alexandre Ier, un tsar énigmatique*, Paris, 1937, p. 266.

(102) Cf. Peter von Goetze, *Fürst Alexander Nikolajewitsch Galitzin und seine Zeit*, Leipzig, 1882, p. 109.

(103) *Correspondance diplomatique de Joseph de Maistre*, Vol. II, p. 118.

(104) Cf. Baron, *op. cit.*, pp. 190, 197.

(105) On Lewis Way, see James Parkes, "Lewis Way and his Times," *Transactions of the Jewish Historical Society of England*, XX, 1964, pp. 189-201.

(106) Quoted by Kohler, *op. cit.*, p. 88.

(107) Cf. Parkes, *op. cit.*, p. 197 (quoted in French).

(108) See above, pp. 142-56.

(109) F. de Martens, *Recueil des traités et conventions conclues par la Russie avec les puissances étrangères*, St Petersburg, 1885, Vol. III, p. 298.

(110) Cf. Maurice Bourquin, *Histoire de la Sainte-Alliance*, Geneva, 1954, pp. 219-37.

(111) Parkes, *op. cit.*, p. 199 (quoted in French).

(112) Quoted by Constantin de Grunwald, *Alexandre Ier, le tsar mystique*, Paris, 1955, p. 282.

(113) *Correspondance diplomatique de Joseph de Maistre*, Vol. II, p. 362.

(114) Cf. Dubnov, *op. cit.*, Vol. I, pp. 594-7. On the link between the Judaizing heresies of the fifteenth to sixteenth centuries and the Russian anti-Jewish tradition, see my *History of Anti-Semitism*, Vol. I, *From Roman Times to the Court Jews*, London, 1974, pp. 275-82.

(115) Cf. Kohler, *op. cit.*, p. 88, note 10, quoting Miss Drusilla Way's recollections.

8 Effects of Emancipation

(1) Cf. J. Bauer, "Le chapeau jaune chez les Juifs comtadins," *R.E.J.*, XXXVI, 1898, pp. 53-64.

(2) Robert Anchel, "Napoléon et les Juifs," Paris, 1928, p. 360.

(3) *Statistique du département du Bas-Rhin*, by Citizen Laumond, Prefect, Paris, year X, pp. 198-206.

(4) A. Kober, "The French Revolution and the Jews in Germany," *Jewish Social Studies*, VII/4, 1945, pp. 291-321.

(5) Quoted by J. Meisl, *Haskalah, Geschichte der Aufklärungs-bewegung unter den Juden in Russland,* Berlin, 1919, pp. 21-2 and 206.
(6) Cf. N. M. Gelber, "La police autrichienne et le Sanhédrin de Napoléon," *R.E.J.,* LXXXIII, 1927, pp. 1-27, 113-35.
(7) "*Geständnisse,*" 1854.
(8) *Pensées,* by L. Börne, Alexandre Weill, trans., *Ludovic Börne,* Paris, 1878, p. 65.
(9) A. Weill, *Ma Jeunesse,* Paris, 1870, Vol. III, pp. 7-8.
(10) Osip Mandelstam, *The Noise of Time,* cf. *Commentary,* New York, October, 1965, pp. 37-41.
(11) Alexis de Tocqueville, *De la démocratie en Amérique,* J.-P. Peter, ed., Paris, 1963, p. 181.
(12) Louis-E. Lomax, *La Révolte noire,* Paris, 1963, p. 13.
(13) Quoted by Anchel, *op. cit.,* p. 386.
(14) Archives nationales, Fo 19-11,010.
(15) Cf. the dossier of Jacques Javal (A.N., Fo 12-1565 (10). Asking the Emperor for an individual exclusion, Javal, at his request, attached nine testimonials issued by officials of the departments of Vosges and Haut-Rhin.
The attorney of the Épinal Magistrates Court testified that:
M. Javal . . . has the reputation of being a man of honor and probity; that he is intimately known to the under-signed; that, far from being one of these vampires taking advantage of the distress of co-citizens, he has often distinguished him-self by acts of generosity and benevolence. . . .
The mayor of Rambervilliers testified:
that he has done a number of acts of charity to the needy in the commune and round about, without distinction as to religion, that he has not indulged in any gambling whatsoever, that he has even helped his friends liberally and from his own purse, that no complaint of usurious lending has been lodged with us about him, that he has always been a good citizen, that he has deserved the esteem and even respect of all honest people, that his departure from this town to fix his abode at Colmar was seen with sorrow. . . .
(16) The piece of paper on which I made a note of these reports by the Central Consistory does not indicate the classifications of the A.N. dossier in which I found them.
(17) Speech by Crémieux to the General Assembly of the Alliance Israélite Universelle; *Archives israélites,* Vol. XXVIII, 1867, p. 13.
(18) Piece of rag! Yellow hat! To the Jewry! let him hide! Fifty children are after him; And mockingly with a pig. Simulating an ear with a corner of their flies, the volley of idiots shout at him: "This is your father's ear!"
(19) *De l'harmonie entre l'Église et la Synagogue* . . . , by the Chevalier J.-B. Drach, Paris, 1844, Vol. I, p. 36.

(20) Cf. M. Roblin, *Les Juifs de Paris*, Paris, 1952, pp. 61, 89.

(21) *And you have crawled towards the crucifix,*
The crucifix that you despised. . . .

(22) Carl Cohen, "The road to conversion," *Leo Baeck Yearbook*, VI, 1961, p. 264.

(23) Cf. Hermann Mendel, *Giacomo Meyerbeer, eine Biographie*, Berlin, 1868, p. 5.

(24) Quoted by Lionel Dauriac, *Meyerbeer*, Paris, 1913, p. 49.

(25) Cf. Heinz Becker, *Giacomo Meyerbeer, Briefwechsel und Tagebücher*, Berlin, 1960-7, Vols I and II, and *Der Fall Heine-Meyerbeer*, Berlin, 1958.

(26) From H. Schnee, *Die Hoffinanz und der moderne Staat*, Berlin, 1953, Vol. III, pp. 153-4.

(27) A. Weill, "De l'état des Juifs en Europe," *La Revue indépendante*, XVI, 1844, p. 506.

(28) Cf. S. Dubnov, *Histoire moderne du peuple juif*, Paris, 1933, Vol. I, p. 525 and Max Brod, *Henri Heine*, Amsterdam, 1935, p. 206.

(29) Cf. Hans Lamm, *Von Juden in München*, Munich, 1958, pp. 109-10.

(30) W. Sombart, *The Jews and Modern Capitalism*, New York, 1962, p. 30.

(31) Cf. Erich Lüth, "Gabriel Riesser 1806-1863," *Tribüne*, Frankfurt am Main, 11/5, 1963, p. 10.

(32) "Einen Vater in den Höhen, eine Mutter haben wir; Gott, ihn, aller Wesen Vater, Deutschland unsre Mutter hier." (Cf. F. Kobler, *Juden und Judentum in deutschen Briefen aus drei Jahrhunderten*, Vienna, 1935, pp. 231 ff.)

(33) Weill, *op. cit.*, p. 517.

(34) Fragment "An Edom" (September, 1824).

(35) Cf. his commentary on the sons of Noah (Genesis IX, 20-29), in *Mysterium Magnum*, Chap. 34.

(36) *Arcana Caelestia quae in Scriptura Sacra, seu Verbo Domini sunt in mundo spirituum . . .*, by Emmanuel Swedenborg, Paris, 1843, no. 8301.

(37) On Swedenborg, see August Viatte, *Les Sources occultes du romantisme*, Paris, 1928; Jacques Roos, *Aspects littéraires du mysticisme philosophique et l'influence de Swedenborg . . .*, Strasbourg, 1951 and above all, Ernst Benz, *Emmanuel Swedenborg*, Munich, 1948.

(38) Karl Jaspers, *Strindberg et van Gogh, Hölderlin et Swedenborg*, Paris, 1953, p. 189.

(39) Swedenborg, *Arcana Caelestia . . .*, *ibid.* Cf. Luther in the preface to *Schem Hamephoras*: " . . . it is as easy to convert a Jew as to convert the Devil, for a Jew . . . a Jewish heart are hard as a stick, as stone, as fire . . . . " (See Poliakov, *From Roman Times to the Court Jews*, p. 219.)

(40) Swedenborg, *Arcana Caelestia . . .*, no. 940, Vol. II, pp. 87-8.

(41) Cf. Benz, *op. cit.*, p. 499:

So berichtet [Swedenborg] 1749 in der anderen Welt sei es eine bekannte Tatsache, dass die Briefe des Paulus nicht den "inneren Sinn" besässen. Die unersättliche Eigenliebe, die ihn von seiner Bekehrung beherrscht habe, sei auch nachher nicht von ihm gewichen, sie habe sich nur ins Geistige verkehrt, nunmehr wollte er der Grösste im Himmelreich sein, und die Stämme Israels richten. Weiter berichtet Swedenborg, in seinen Visionsserlebnissen habe er haüfig feststellen können, dass die übrigen Apostel dem Apostel Paulus im Himmel die Gemeinschaft verweigern, und ihn nicht als einen der Ihrigen anerkennen wollten.

(42) *De l'esprit des choses* . . . , by the unknown philosopher, Paris, year VIII (1800), pp. 248-52.

(43) *Ministère de l'Homme-Esprit*, 1802 (quoted by A. Tanner, *Gnostiques de la Révolution, Claude de Saint-Martin*, Paris, 1946, p. 208).

(44) J. de Maistre, *Considérations sur la France*, p. 6.

(45) On Weishaupt and the Illuminati, see R. Le Forestier, *Les Illuminés de Bavière et la franc-maçonnerie allemande*, Paris, 1914, and Jacques Droz, *L'Allemagne et la Révolution française*, Paris, 1949, pp. 402-5.

(46) *Mémoires pour servir à l'histoire de la persécution française, recueillis par les ordres de Notre Très Saint-Père Pie VI*, by Abbé d'Auribeau d'Hesmivy, Rome, 1794. This book mentions (Vol. I, p. 244)

ingenious inventions (balloons, Montgolfiers, magnetism, mesmerism, etc.), or rather ancient discoveries revived in our day with the intention of persuading the people that several miracles on which the religion of Jesus Christ is unshakably based should be attributed to natural causes. . . .

(47) E. A. A. Göchhausen, *Enthüllung des Systems der Weltrepublik*, Rome, Leipzig, 1786, p. 398.

(48) *Die Hebräschen Mysterien oder die älteste religiöse Frey-maurery*, by Brother Decius, Leipzig, 1788, p. 17; for disparagement of the Jews, see especially pp. 28, 56.

(49) *Mémoires pour servir à l'histoire du jacobinisme*, by Abbé Barruel, 2nd ed., Hamburg, 1803, Vol. I, pp. 146-8, and also (for the Jewish inspiration behind Masonic symbolism), Vol. II, pp. 253-4.

(50) "Mélanges de philosophie et d'histoire," *Annales catholiques*, Paris, 1806, Vol. I, p. 226.

(51) "Napoleon I as the Jewish Messiah; some contemporary conceptions in Virginia," by Joseph J. Shulim, *Jewish Social Studies*, VII(3), pp. 275-80.

(52) Cf. Anchel, *op. cit.*, pp. 221-2.

(53) Cf. the article "Napoleon Bonaparte," by J. Hessen, in the

Russian *Jewish Encyclopedia*, St Petersburg, 1910, Vol XI, p. 513.

(54) *Ibid.*

(55) Max Geiger, *Aufklärung und Erweckung, Beiträge zur Erforschung Johann Heinrich Jung-Stillings und der Erweckungtheologie*, Zurich, 1963, p. 262.

(56) Cf. "Szenen aus dem Geisterreiche," scene XI, in *Johann Heinrich Jungs . . . sämmtliche Werke*, Vol. II, Stuttgart, 1841, p. 169.

(57) Geiger, *op. cit.*, pp. 221-2.

(58) Letter to his friend Hess, December 28, 1809, quoted by Viatte, *op. cit.*, Vol. II, p. 56.

(59) The case of a cabalistic Jew, Ephraim Hirschberg, who was in contact with Claude de Saint-Martin and abundantly supplied theosophic circles with pieces of humbug, has been described by Gershom Scholem, "Ein verschollener jüdischer Mystiker," *Leo Baeck Yearbook*, Vol. VII, 1962, pp. 247-78.

(60) Baader is said to have shared Saint-Martin's ideas on the Jews; cf. E. Benz, *Die abendländische Sendung der östlich-orthodoxen Kirche*, p. 598.

(61) Cf. James Parkes, "Lewis Way and his time," *Transactions of the Jewish Historical Society of England*, XX, 1964, pp. 189-201.

(62) Cf. M. Baxter, *Louis-Napoleon the destined monarch of the world and personal Antichrist, foreshown in Prophecy to confirm a seven-years Covenant with the Jews . . .* , Philadelphia, 1863, where the author after stating his own thesis lists the works of fifty-seven authors who have arrived at the same conclusions (pp. 175 ff.).

(63) Cf. Geiger, *op. cit.*, p. 331.

(64) Simonini's report has been published by Father Grivel in the Catholic review *Le Contemporain*, Vol. XVI, 1878, pp. 49-70, together with other notes by Barruel. Barruel notably wrote: " . . . His Holiness wrote to me through M. the abbé Testa, his secretary, that everything pointed to the truth and probity of the man who had revealed to me everything he said that he had witnessed." (*Souvenirs du P. Grivel sur les PP. Barruel et Feller*, p. 62.)

(65) *Ibid.*, pp. 58-62.

(66) *Ibid.*, p. 62. Abbé Barruel concluded:
In order to understand this hatred the Jews have for the kings of France, it is necessary to go back to Philip the Fair, who, in 1306, drove them out of France. . . . From there, in the process of time, common cause with the Templars . . . .

(67) *Oeuvres complètes*, by J. de Maistre, Lyon, 1884, Vol. VIII, p. 336 ("Quatre chapitres sur la Russie").

(68) Viatte, *op. cit.*, Vol. II, Appendix I ("Illuminés et Juifs," pp. 277-8).

(69) *Memorabili avvenimenti successi sotto i tristi auspici della*

Repubblica Francese; cf. Renzo de Felice, *Storia degli ebrei italiani sotto il fascismo*, Turin, 1961, p. 41.

(70) This booklet is often quoted in Nazi literature; for example, in Adolf Rossberg, *Freimaurerei und Politik im Zeitalter der französischen Revolution*, Berlin, 1942, p. 231. Its author, Johann Christian Ehrmann, is said to have been an Illuminatus himself.

(71) *Der sarmatische Lykurg, oder Über die Gleichstellung der Juden . . .* , Nuremberg, 1811; cf. R. W. Stock, *Die Judenfrage durch fünf Jahrhunderte*, Nuremberg, 1939, pp. 347-51.

(72) For example, in Philipp Bouhler, *Napoleon, Kometenlaufbahn eines Genies*, Munich, 1941, p. 332:

> That the Corsican, who was born of a noble family in north Italy, was descended from the Langobards, is a statement which, although it cannot be completely proved, has a number of arguments in its favor. What is certain is that his domination was exercised in a spirit of Germanic democracy.

Bouhler was the head of Hitler's personal chancellery.

(73) L. de Bonald, "Sur les Juifs," p. 21.

(74) Chateaubriand, *Mémoires d'Outre-Tombe*.

(75) S. Posener, *Adolphe Crémieux*, Paris, 1933, Vol. I, p. 9.

(76) Herder, *Adrastea . . .* , Part 2, Stuttgart, 1829, pp. 229-30 ("Bekehrung der Juden").

(77) De Bonald, *op. cit.*, p. 19.

(78) Cf. above, p. 204.

(79) De Bonald, *op. cit.*, p. 20.

(80) G. Bernanos, *La Grande peur des bien-pensants, Édouard Drumont*, Paris, 1931. This is the passage (pp. 212-13):

> For years and years, Millot, a jeweler by profession, gravely explained to the dumbfounded audience, Jewry had ruined him as a result of competition from paste jewels. Only, well before he had made his comical statement, everyone had understood that this was nothing but an excuse invented to satisfy society hungry for logic, and that, jeweler or not, Millot had hated the Yids, in exactly the same way as the roaming, chimerical, Parisian cur, so friendly with its comrades, hates the noiseless calculating cat whose way of life remains incomprehensible to it.

(81) *Ibid.*, pp. 39, 45.

(82) Goethe, *Dichtung*, book VII, Mayer, ed., Vol. XIX, pp. 284-5.

(83) Cf. L. Geiger, *Die deutsche Literatur und die Juden*, Berlin, 1910, pp. 94-5.

(84) Cf. Léon Poliakov, *Les Banquiers juifs . . .* , Paris, 1965, pp. 281 ff.

(85) Father G. Baum, one of the advisers on the subject at the Council, wrote ("Commentary on Part 4 of the declaration *Relationship of the Church to Judaism*," by Gregory Baum,

O.S.A., Centre for Biblical and Jewish Studies, London, *Bulletin*
8/1966):

The phrase really was taken out because this was the wish
of the near eastern bishops. Even some non-Roman Churches
of the near East joined this plea. Why? It was claimed that
people could interpret the Church's denial that the Jews are
guilty of deicide as a sign that the Church no longer
acknowledged the divine sonship of Jesus Christ. . . .

(86) Bernhard E. Olson, *Faith and Prejudice*, Yale University Press,
1963, pp. 23-4:

A conception of the spiritual status and role of the Jew
becomes essential to the Christian's comprehension of his own
mission. For he cannot know who he is and what his role
consists of until he understands who the Jew is and what is
Israel's role.

Further on, talking about Christian teaching: "As such, Jewish
figures can serve only as a foil for the Christian—and not as a
mirror to show the Christian to himself—because the Christian
understandably cannot identify with them", pp. 228.

(87) *Illusions perdues,* Club français du Livre, ed., 1962, Vol. IV,
p. 1067.

(88) Cf. below, p. 338.

(89) L. Börne, "Für die Juden," *Sämtliche Werke*, Düsseldorf, 1864,
Vol. I, p. 873.

(90) Article quoted, p. 21.

(91) A. de Tocqueville, *De la démocratie en Amérique*, J.-P. Peter,
ed., Paris, 1963, p. 191.

(92) Cf. *Friedrich August Ludwig von der Marwitz, ein märkischer
Edelmann im Zeitalter der Befreiungskriege*, F. Meusel, ed.,
Berlin, 1908-13, Vol. 11/2, pp. 20-1 ("Politische Schriften und
Briefe").

(93) *Die Majoratsherren*, Mayer, ed., Vol. II, pp. 246-86.

(94) Cf. von Arnim's letters, quoted by Hans Uffo Lenz, *Das
Volkserlebnis bei Ludwig Achim von Arnim*, Berlin, 1938,
pp. 94-5.

(95) "Der Philister vor, in und nach der Geschichte": discourse given
by C. von Brentano to the *Tischgesellschaft* in March, 1811,
Berlin ed., 1905.

(96) Letter from Bettina to Clemens, around 1802; cf. Franz Kobler,
*Juden und Judentum in deutschen Briefen aus drei Jahrhunder-
ten*, Vienna, 1935, p. 166.

(97) Notably in *Goethes Briefwechsel mit einem Kinde*, in *Die
Günderode* and in *Gespräche mit Dämonen*, the main works by
Elisabeth Bettina von Arnim.

(98) *Wilhelm und Karoline von Humboldt in ihren Briefen*, Anna
von Sydow, ed., Berlin, 1907-13, 7 vols; the polemic on the
Jews is in Vols IV and V.

(99) Alexander von Humboldt, the famous naturalist and traveler and Wilhelm's youngest brother.

(100) Adelheid was the Humboldts' daughter; thirteen years old, she had just taken her first communion.

(101) In French in the text.

(102) In 1798, Karoline von Humboldt wrote to Rahel Levin (cf. Kobler, *op. cit.*, p. 205):

> . . . I cannot and will not abandon the hope that I will one day live with you. To me it seems we belong to each other for ever. . . . Of him, I can only say that I love him as nobody has ever loved anyone else. . . .
>
> Here, my love, I am leaving only two people who cost me infinitely much to leave—Dorothea Schlegel for I feel myself loved by her and Dr Koreff. . . .

(103) Amongst others, Gentz had written a long article on the Rothschilds for Brockhaus's encyclopedia. In it, he attributed their success not only to their material means, but also to spiritual qualities "which have disarmed jealousy and paralyzed the tongue of slander," etc. (Cf. *Ungedruckte Denkschriften, Tagebücher und Briefe von Friedrich von Gentz*, Mannheim, 1840, Vol. V, pp. 113-22, "Biographische Nachrichten über das Haus Rothschild.")

(104) Cf. Kobler, *op. cit.*, pp. 149-50 (letter from Gentz to Brinkmann).

(105) *Fürst Bismarck's Reden*, Stein, ed., Leipzig, I, pp. 24-5.

(106) Cf. Otto Jöhlinger, *Bismarck und die Juden*, Berlin, 1921, p. 18.

(107) *Ibid.*, p. 27.

(108) *Ibid.*, pp. 27, 94, 189. "Die [Juden] Frage ich nicht nach den Glauben, denen sehe ich es an," said Bismarck.

(109) See below, p. 392.

(110) Quoted by Golo Mann, *The History of Germany since 1789*, translated by Marion Jackson, London, 1968, p. 69.

(111) *La France juive*, ed. Paris, 1943, Vol. I, p. 322.

(112) For example, the term *Zivilisationsjude* was used in this sense by Ernst Jünger; cf. Eva Reichmann, "Diskussionen über die Judenfrage 1930-1932," in *Entscheidungsjahr 1932*, Tübingen, 1965, p. 515.

(113) Conversation with Rauschning; cf. *Tribüne*, Frankfurt am Main, 1964, p. 1055.

(114) Cf. below, pp. 380-91.

(115) Börne, *op. cit.*, Vol. I, p. 875.

(116) J. Fries, *Über die Gefährdung des Wohlstandes und Charakters der Deutschen durch die Juden*, Heidelberg, 1816. Other anti-Jewish pamphlets also issued from this philosopher; on this subject, see E. Sterling, *Er ist wie Du*, Munich, 1954, pp. 163, 226.

(117) See above, pp. 135, 136.

(118) Regierungsrat Köppe, *Die Stimme eines preussischen Staatsbürgers in den wichtigsten Angelegenheiten dieser Zeit*, 1816. A

bibliography of the anti-Semitic writings of this period will be found in Sterling, *op. cit.*, pp. 224-32.

(119) M. Moureau attributed the 1819 troubles to the fact that the government wanted to compromise the representative régime the Jews desired, in the eyes of the people. (Moureau [de Vaucluse], *De l'incompatibilité entre le judaïsme et l'exercice des droits de cité* . . . , Paris, 1819, p. 9.)

(120) Cf. Sterling, *op. cit.*, p. 182.

(121) H. von Treitschke, *Deutsche Geschichte im 19. Jahrhundert*, Leipzig, 1886, Vol. II, p. 417. This historian was the principal ideologist of "liberal anti-Semitism" in about 1875; see Walter Boehlich, *Der Berliner Antisemitismusstreit*, Frankfurt am Main, 1965.

(122) Alexandre Weill, in *Ma jeunesse* (*op. cit.*, I, pp. 53-62), has given a vivid account of the pogrom which nearly broke out in the village of Sufflen in Alsace, where he was born; but after intervention by the mayor the crowd which had gathered served as a pretext for a country ball. The amazement of the Jews, assailed by their neighbors, can be found again in eye-witness accounts of Russian pogroms; see particularly J. Svirsky, *The Story of My Life* (in Russian), Moscow, 1947.

(123) Cf. Kobler, *op. cit.*, pp. 210-11.

(124) Letter quoted in H. Grätz, *Geschichte der Juden*, Vol. XI, pp. 365-6.

(125) Letter of September 3, 1819; cf. *Briefwechsel zwischen Varnhagen von Ense und Oelsner*, Stuttgart, 1865, Vol. I, pp. 299-300.

(126) Cf. Geiger, *Geschichte der Juden in Berlin*, 1871, p. 175.

(127) Sterling, *op. cit.*, p. 180.

Part Three   The Racist Reaction

(1) Cf. in this context the interesting comments by M. Louis Dumont, whose study "Caste, racisme et 'stratification,'" relates Western racism to the dualistic tradition of Christianity (L. Dumont, "Caste, racisme et 'stratification,'" *Cahiers internationaux de sociologie*, XXIX 1960, p. 109):

It can be noted that, in certain circumstances which should be specified, a hierarchical difference continues to be set up, but that this time it is attached to somatic characteristics, the cast of features, color of skin, "blood." These distinctive characteristics were probably always there, but they have become the essence. How can this be explained? Here, it can be recalled that we are heirs to a dualistic religion and philosophy: the distinction between mind and matter, between soul and body impregnates our whole culture, and the popular mentality in particular. It was as if the egalitarian-identitarian frame of mind lay inside this dualism, as if, with equality and identity relating to the individual *souls*, the distinction could no longer be attached to anything but the body. . . .

(2) In 1892, Salomon Reinach, in a work on *L'Origine des Aryens*, noted in the form of an introduction: "We have been raised, on our college benches, on the idea that the civilizations and races of Europe had their cradle in the central plateau of Asia. . . ." In my next book, I will deal with the astonishing ascendancy that the "Aryan myth" exercised over minds at the end of the nineteenth century. Here, a single witness will be enough. In 1895, during a discussion on the "anti-Semite question" in the Chamber of Deputies, Alfred Naquet said that (cf. official records of the session of May 27, 1895): "the Jews . . . have been enfranchised by what you will permit me to call the Aryan European fertilization. . . . I who am a Jew and not an anti-Semite, think . . . that in the beginning, in Palestine, there was an inferiority on the part of Jews compared with the Aryan race."

(3) In French, we can mention the old book by S. Reinach, *L'Origine des Aryens, Histoire d'une controverse* (Paris, 1892). The wealth of documentation in T. Simar's *Étude critique sur la formation de la doctrine des races au XVIIIe siècle et son expansion au XIXe siècle* (Brussels, 1922) is still unequaled. R. Gérard's thesis, "L'Orient et la pensée romantique allemande," Paris, 1963, gives new insight into the origin of the "Aryan idea" in the eighteenth century.

Apart from Isaac Taylor's *The Origin of the Aryans. An Account of the Ethnology and Civilisation of Prehistoric Man*, London, 1890, works in English on the subject frequently consist of brief summaries in the many histories of anthropology and sociology; the best work of this type remains L. L. Snyder, *Race, A History of Modern Ethnic Theories*, New York and London, 1939. Hannah Arendt's *The Origin of Totalitarianism*, New York, 1951, contains some interesting views in Chapter VI, "Race Thinking before Racism."

There are also two valuable studies by a German Catholic philosopher (which have passed by unnoticed because of the date of their publication): Erich Voegelin, *Rasse und Staat*, Tübingen, 1933, and *Die Rassenidee von Ray bis Carus*, Berlin, 1933. One might also add Wilhelm Schmidt, *Rassen und Völker in Vorgeschichte und Geschichte des Abendlandes*, Lucerne, 1946. ·

(4) M. Capefigue, *Histoire philosophique des Juifs*, Paris, 1833, p. 13.

(5) Herder particularly was responsible for spreading this idea; cf. R. Gérard, "L'Orient et la pensée romantique allemande," pp. 57-60 *et passim*.

(6) Cf. T. Benfey, *Geschichte der Sprachwissenschaft und oriental-ischen Philologie in Deutschland*, Munich, 1869, pp. 347 ff.

(7) *Über die Sprache und Weisheit der Indier*, by Friedrich Schlegel, Vienna, 1808.

(8) A. W. Schlegel, "De l'origine des Hindous," *Essais littéraires et politiques*, Bonn, 1842, pp. 439 ff.

(9) F. W. von Schelling, *Über das Studium der Theologie*, *Sämtliche Werke*, Stuttgart, 1859, Vol. V, p. 300.

(10) Ernest Seillière, *Le Comte de Gobineau et l'aryanisme historique*, Paris, 1903, p. xxiv.

(11) Cf. Hermann Blome, *Der Rassengedanke in der deutschen Romantik und seine Grundlagen im 18. Jahrhundert*, Berlin, 1943, pp. 95, 168.

(12) *Mithridates oder allgemeine Sprachkunde . . .* , Johann Christoph von Adelung, Part I, Berlin, 1806, Vol. I, pp. 8 ff.

(13) *Die heilige Sage und des gesamte Religionssystem der alter Baktrier, Meder und Perser, oder des Zendvolkes*, J. G. von Rhode, Frankfurt am Main, 1820. This book earned Rhode the appointment of doctor *honoris causa* at the University of Jena.

I have not met the term Aryan, used in its modern sense, in works prior to 1820. It is true that I have not read everything!

(14) *Die heilige Sage . . .* , p. 29:

Folgenden Unterschied zwischen Zoroaster und Moses müssen wir noch berühren. *Moses* bewies—wenigstens nach der Form, wie wir jetzt seine Schriften besitzen, die Göttlichkeit seiner Sendung, und die Wahreit seiner Offenbarung, durch eine Menge Wundertaten; *Zoroaster* kennt keine Wunder: die innere Kraft der Wahreit ist alles, worauf er sich beruht.

We must still mention the following difference between Zoroaster and Moses. *Moses* proved—at least in the present form of his writings—the divine nature of his mission and the truth of his revelation through a mass of miracles. *Zoroaster* has nothing to do with wonders. All he relies on is the inner power of truth.

(15) *Ibid.*, p. 65.

(16) *Ibid.*, pp. 455-61.

(17) *Ibid.*, pp. 441-2.

(18) *Ibid.*, p. 97.

(19) Cf. Michel Bréal, "De la géographie de l'Avesta," *Mélanges de mythologie et de linguistique*, Paris, 1882, p. 180.

(20) F. A. Pott, *Etymologische Forschungen*, I, p. xxi, quoted by O. Schrader, *Sprachvergleichung und Urgeschichte*, Jena, 1883, p. 11. It was through another book by Pott, entitled *Die Ungleichheit menschlicher Rassen . . .* that Richard Wagner learnt of the work of Gobineau, who was thus promoted to posthumous glory in Germany. (Cf. "Lettres de Cosima Wagner à Gobineau," *Revue hebdomadaire*, Paris, July 23, 1938.)

(21) Schrader, *op. cit.*, p. 13.

(22) Cf. Taylor, *op. cit., passim.*

(23) J. P. Eckermann, *Conversations with Goethe,* R. O. Moon, trans., London, 1950. (Interview with the naturalist von Martini, October 7, 1828.)

(24) Gustav Klemm, *Allgemeine Cultur-Geschichte der Menschheit,* Leipzig, 1843, Vol. I, p. 202.

(25) Christian Lassen, *Indische Alterthumskunde,* Bonn, 1847, Vol. I, p. 414.

(26) *Ibid.,* pp. 414 ff.

(27) Cf. Earl W. Count, "The evolution of the race idea in modern Western culture, during the period of the pre-darwinian XIXth century," *Transactions of the New York Academy of Sciences,* XXIX, 1946, pp. 139-65.

(28) Letter to Liszt, June 7, 1855.

(29) Cuvier, *Le Règne animal . . . ,* Paris, 1817, Vol. I, pp. 94-5 ("Variétés de l'espèce humaine").

(30) A. von Humboldt, *Kosmos,* Stuttgart, 1845, Vol. I, p. 345.

(31) On the adoption of the term *Aryan,* see M. Müller, *Essays,* Leipzig, 1879, Vol. II, pp. 333 ff. ("Arisch als ein technischer Ausdruck"). Müller first proclaimed his warning during a lecture at Strasbourg on May 23, 1872 ("Über die Resultate der Sprachwissenschaft").

(32) See Chapter VI of *Phenomenology of Mind,* which has been pointed out to me in this connection by my friend Alexandre Kojeve.

(33) *The Philosophy of History,* by Georg Wilhelm Friedrich Hegel, J. Sibree, trans., New York, 1944, pp. 93-5.

(34) Cuvier, *Le Règne animal . . .*

(35) *Lectures on physiology, zoology, and the natural history of man . . . ,* by W. Lawrence, F.R.S., London, 1819, p. 476; Count, *op. cit.,* p. 154, describes this author as the "greatest anthropologist between the time of Kant and Darwin."

(36) W. Schmidt, *Rassen und Völker in Vorgeschichte und Geschichte des Abendlandes,* Lucerne, 1946, p. 120.

(37) *Des caractères physiologiques des races humaines considérés dans leur rapport avec l'histoire.* Letter to M. Amédée Thierry, author of *Histoire des Gaulois,* by W. F. Edwards, Paris, 1820.

(38) The metaphor comes from Bruno Bauer. An old friend of Karl Marx, he is all the more valuable as a witness in that he had become one of the main doctrinarians of the pan-Germanist idea at this period. In the context of the quotation, Bauer was criticizing Disraeli's political ideas (*Disraelis romantischer und Bismarcks socialistischer Imperialismus,* Chemnitz, 1882, p. 60):
Disraelis Marotte von seiner Race steht nicht allein. Seit den Schlacten von Leipzig und Waterloo war der Boden Europas überfruchtbar in der Erzeugung von Racen, von denen jede sich der höchsten. Leistung und Bestimmung im

Fach der Moral, des Glaubens und Denkens rühmte, so dasse den Anderen immer nur das Nachsehen blieb. . . .

Disraeli's obsession with his race is not unique. Since the battles of Leipzig and Waterloo the soil of Europe has been super-fertile in the generation of races, each of which has prided itself on the highest achievement and vocation in the sphere of morality, faith and thought, so that all that others could do was look on. . . .

(39) Cf. H. Viatte, *Claude-Julien Bredin (1776-1854). Correspondance philosophique et littéraire avec Ballanche,* Paris, 1958 (Introduction).

(40) Margherita von Brentano, "Die Endlösung. Ihre Funktion in Theorie und Praxis des Faschismus," in *Antisemitismus, Zur Pathologie der bürgerlichen Gesellschaft,* Frankfurt am Main, 1965, p. 61.

9   England

(1) Cf. above, p. 34.

(2) *Standard,* London, July 22-3, 1854.

(3) Cf. H. Meyer-Cohen, *Die Juden im heutigen England,* Berlin, 1890, p. 20: "Der Engländer ist wirtschaftlich zu gebildet, als dass man ihm vorlügen dürfte, er werde von einem Handvoll Juden beherrscht. Er wäre auch zu stolz, etwas Derartiges zu glauben. . . . " This little book by a contemporary contains a number of pertinent comments.

(4) Baron Lionel de Rothschild for the City of London, Baron Mayer de Rothschild for Hythe, and Nathaniel Mayer de Rothschild for Aylesbury; cf. C. K. Salaman, *Jews as They Are,* London, 1885, p. 90.

(5) Cf. above, p. 251.

(6) Cf. *Political Register,* by W. Cobbett, 1818, p. 522.

(7) On the image of the Jew in English literature, notably in Dickens and Scott, see the major work by Edgar Rosenberg, *From Shylock to Svengali, Jewish Stereotypes in English Fiction,* London, 1961.

(8) *Ivanhoe, A romance,* 1831, p. 2.

(9) Cf. Poliakov, *History of Anti-Semitism,* Vol. I, *From the Time of Christ to the Court Jews,* New York, 1965. Rebecca's undeserved misfortunes having provoked numerous protests from readers, Scott had to apologize to them for not having been able to give her as a wife to Ivanhoe; cf. *Introduction to Ivanhoe,* 1831.

(10) Alfred Bunn, *Ivanhoe, or the Jews of York*; T. John Dibdin, *Ivanhoe, or the Jew's Daughter*; W. T. Moncrieff, *Ivanhoe, or the Jewess*; George Soane, *The Hebrews.*

(11) Chateaubriand, *Oeuvres complètes,* Paris, 1861, Vol. XI, pp. 764-6.

(12) In Vol. VIII of *L'Histoire de France* ("Renaissance").

(13) J.-P. Sartre, *Réflexions sur la question juive.* The theme of the Jewess in literature has been dealt with by M. Bloch, *La Femme juive dans le roman et au théâtre,* Paris, 1892, and in the recent (1964-65) unpublished work by A. Pessès, "L'image du Juif dans la littérature romantique française."

(14) *Trois nouvelles d'I. Disraeli,* translated from the English by Mme Collet, Paris, 1821.

(15) Cf. *Im Vaterhause Lord Beaconsfields* by Dr A. Jellinek, Vienna, 1881, p. 30.

(16) *Mutilated Diary,* September, 1833.

(17) Thomas B. Macaulay, "Civil disabilities of the Jews," *Edinburgh Review,* January, 1833.

(18) Cf. Raymond Maître, *Disraeli, homme de lettres,* Paris, 1963, p. 206, note.

(19) Cf. Frederic E. Faverty, *Matthew Arnold the Ethnologist,* Evanston, 1951 (Chap. II, "The Teutomaniacs").

(20) *Coningsby,* Bradenham edition, London, 1927, p. 264.

(21) "Mouscou 66," by Jean Neuvecelle, *France-Soir,* August 10, 1966:

> "Picasso is Jewish! You didn't know? Cézanne was too. And Kandinsky. Not to mention Chagall, of course. When the latter was people's commissar at Vitebsk, he did everything to silence the revival of Russian painting which began in the nineteenth century: he was at the head of the great conspiracy!" These statements figure in a report on the Soviet Union which came to our attention by chance when we were writing these lines; they were made by a representative of the "Stalinist opposition."

(22) *Tancred,* Bradenham edition, London, 1927, p. 233.

(23) *Ibid.,* p. 440.

(24) *Lord George Bentinck, A Political Biography,* London, 1905, p. 324.

(25) *Tancred, op. cit.,* p. 394:

> "But the Mesdemoiselles Laurella were ashamed of their race." They also believed that, thanks to progress, a respectable Hebrew, particularly if well dressed and well mannered, might be able to pass through society without being discovered, or at least noticed. Consummation of the destiny of the favourite people of the Creator of the universe!

(26) Cf. Monypenny and Buckle, *The Life of Benjamin Disraeli . . . ,* London, 1929, Vol. I, pp. 884-5. On the subject of this speech, Disraeli's biographers comment "Disraeli's argument was very distasteful to the House. There were cries of Oh! Oh! at intervals, and many other signs of general impatience. . . . Disraeli sat down without a cheer and amid cries of Divide."

On the other hand, Disraeli senior said next day that this speech was the most important ever to be pronounced in the House of Commons.

(27) André Maurois, *Disraeli, A Picture of the Victorian Age,* Hamish Miles, trans., London, 1927, pp. 229, 245.
(28) *Ibid.,* p. 178.
(29) Maître, *op. cit.,* p. 98.
(30) *Ibid.,* pp. 14, 29 (notes).
(31) *The Works of William Makepeace Thackeray,* London, 1880, Vol. VI, pp. 478-88.
(32) *The Races of Men: A philosophical enquiry into the influence of race over the destinies of nations,* by Robert Knox, London, 1850 (2nd edition, 1862). Preface, p. v. Emerson had a high regard for this book and found it "loaded with striking and unforgettable truths" (cf. Faverty, *op. cit.,* p. 17).
(33) *Ibid.,* p. 208.
(34) *Ibid.,* pp. 194-5.
(35) Harrison, 1894; cf. Maître, *op. cit.*
(36) Cf. Maître, *op. cit.,* p. 424, Appendix II ("L'œuvre de Disraeli et le public anglais contemporain").
(37) Carl Koehne, "Disraeli als Vorläufer und Anreger Gobineaus, Untersuchungen . . . ," *Archiv für Rassen- und Gesellschaftsbiologie,* XVIII, 1926, pp. 370-96.
(38) *Ibid.,* pp. 379-80, the tables of concordances drawn up by Carl Koehne.
(39) *Le Juif, le judaïsme et la judaïsation des peuples chrétiens,* by the Chevalier Gougenot des Mousseaux, 2nd ed., Paris, 1880, pp. 386-92, 354. ("The work that we are taking the liberty of translating, bears the signature of that Prime Minister of Great Britain from whom, in the preceding chapter, we have made a short and vital borrowing," etc.)
(40) Those to whom the Jews are hostile, wrote Drumont, "are thwarted in everything, as Disraeli explains so well; defamed, demoralized, they do not know whom to blame. . . ." Elsewhere: "For twenty years the Semites have pulled, as Disraeli said, the strings of secret diplomacy. . . ." And again, "Disraeli, who was an expert, has wonderfully depicted them on many occasions, mysteriously engaged in the common work. . . ." (*La France juive,* ed. Paris, 1943, Vol. I, pp. 49, 110, 333).
(41) It is unnecessary to recall that Michelet was not very fond of Napoleon. He wrote (*Histoire du XIXe siècle,* ed. Paris, 1880, Vol. III, p. 340):

> These sudden transitions from theatrical grandeur to trivial baseness probably put him on a footing with the mediocre actors of Italy who do not know the art of the skillfully contrived transition. However, in my first volume I set out the reasons which place him in contrast with Italy, above all the indifference to beauty and complete prosaicness of a character

in no way sympathetic to the fine arts. I have said that a spiritual Englishman, Monsieur Disraeli, would like to think him a Jew by origin. And as Corsica was in former times peopled by the Semites of Africa, Arabs, Carthaginians or Moors, Marranos the Spaniards say, he seems to belong to them rather than to the Italians. The love also of hoarding, so many millions buried in the cellars of the Tuileries, also indicates the Marrano.

(42) "Vor allem aber hat ein grosser seinen kleineren Stammes-genossen das Konzept gründlich verdorben: Benjamin Disraeli . . ." (L. Schemann, *Die Rasse in den Geisteswissenschaften, Studien zur Geschichte des Rassengedankens*, Berlin, 1938, p. 24). "In Tagen, wo so viel Unsinn über diese Frage geredet wird, lasse man sich von Disraeli belehren . . ." (H. S. Chamberlain, *Die Grundlagen des XIX. Jahrhunderts*, ed. Munich, 1919, p. 322).

(43) It can be said that the Disraelian practical jokes were hard to kill. The doctoral thesis submitted by Raymond Maître in 1962, to which I have referred on several occasions, was still defending the theory of Immanuel Kant's "Semitism!" (p. 193, note 13.) Moreover, if M. Maître does not take the Disraelian doctrine of race seriously, he takes his stand on the contemporary and quite as fantastic one produced by Ernest Renan (p. 119). On that score, he speaks of "the absence of subtlety and suppleness which seems to characterize the Semitic spirit," of "the sort of moral laxity which makes the Semites profoundly indifferent to the choice of means," etc.

(44) On the character of Joseph Nassi, Duke of Naxos, see Poliakov, *History of Anti-Semitism*, Vol. II, *From Mohammed to the Marranos*, New York, 1973.

10 France

(1) M. Bail, *Des Juifs au XIXe siècle*, 2nd ed., Paris, 1816, p. 17.

(2) *La Minerve française*, Vol. III, 1818, p. 543.

(3) An author noted this in 1860 (Dr Gallavardin, *Voyage médical en Allemagne*, Paris, 1860, p. 125):

Generally one is accustomed to believe that the Jews are unsuited to military service, for which, it is said, they have a great repugnance. However, everything proves the contrary, in our country at least. In fact out of four thousand pupils admitted to the Polytechnic School since 1830, over a hundred belong to the Israelite religion. Thus, while the Israelite population forms barely a four-hundredth part of our population, its members figure in the military schools in the proportion of a fortieth.

(4) Cf. below, p. 362.

(5) *Chrétiens et Juifs,* a play in five acts, by M. * * * , Épernay, 1840. The plot of this drama is placed in the fourteenth century, but the modern allusions are perfectly transparent.

(6) *La Renommée,* June 16-17 and July 9, 1819 (cf. S. Posener, *Adolphe Crémieux,* Paris, 1933, Vol. I, pp. 70-2).

(7) *La Minerve française, loc. cit.*

(8) L. Halévy, *Résumé de l'histoire des Juifs modernes,* Paris, 1827, p. 319.

(9) Crémieux voiced this plea in 1826 and 1827, in order to obtain the abolition of the *more judaico* oath, the last remnant of the old special regulations for Jews; cf. Posener, *op. cit.,* p. 83.

(10) Eduard Gans, "Paris im Jahre 1830," *Rückblicke auf Personen und Zustände,* Berlin, 1836, p. 75.

(11) Victor Schoelcher, *De l'abolition de l'esclavage,* 1840; cf. *Esclavage et colonisation,* E. Tersen, ed., Paris, 1948, p. 70.

(12) O. Terquem (Tsarphati), *Huitième lettre d'un Israélite,* Paris, 1836; cf. Posener, *op. cit.,* Vol. I, p. 179.

(13) Heine, *Lutèce, lettres sur la vie politique, artistique et sociale de la France,* Paris, 1855, p. 65 (letter, May 27, 1840). The "Chief Rabbi of the left bank" was the banker, Fould; Heine was referring to the two Paris-Versailles railroads.

(14) A. Weill, "De l'état des Juifs en Europe," *Revue indépendante,* XIV, 1844, p. 481.

(15) Metternich to the ambassador Apponyi, December 11, 1845; cf. Jean Bouvier, *Les Rothschild,* Paris, 1960, p. 52.

(16) Nesselrode, *Lettres et papiers . . . ,* Vol. VIII, p. 91.

(17) Mirabaud Papers, letter from a banker in Geneva, November 30, 1835, quoted by Bertrand Gille, *Histoire de la maison Rothschild,* Geneva-Paris, 1965, Vol. I, p. 491.

(18) B. Gille, in his major history already mentioned, p. 486.

(19) L. Börne, *Briefe aus Paris,* 1830-3, 72nd letter (January, 1832).

(20) Gille, *Histoire de la maison Rothschild,* p. 486.

(21) Jules Michelet, *Journal,* Frankfurt, July 21, 1842, Vol. I (Michelet's reaction to his visit to the Rothschild bank).

(22) A. Toussenel, *Les Juifs, rois de l'époque,* 1845, 4th ed., Paris, 1888, Vol. I, p. 12.

(23) Letters quoted by Bouvier, *op. cit.,* pp. 80 and 92.

(24) *Ibid.,* p. 2.

(25) "What is good for General Motors is good for America." The words are attributed to the Secretary of State for Defense, Wilson, a colleague of President Eisenhower's.

(26) Albert Pessès points out that the Jewish aspect of Nucingen becomes gradually more pronounced from *Père Goriot* (1834) to *Splendeur et misère des courtisanes* (1843) via *La Maison Nucingen* (1838); cf. his thesis (unpublished) "L'image du Juif dans la littérature romantique française," Paris, 1964-5, p. 74.

(27) "Wir Deutschen sind das stärkste und das klügste Volk. Unsere Fürstengeschlechter sitzen auf allen Trönen Europas, unsere

Rothschilds beherrschen alle Börsen der Welt, unsere Gelehrten regieren in allen Wissenschaften . . . " (*Zur Geschichte der Religion und Philosophie in Deutschland, Erstes Buch*).

(28) Cf. Bouvier, *op. cit.*, p. 49.

(29) Cf. for example, Rabi, *Anatomie du judaïsme français*, Paris, 1962, p. 48: "The work of Balzac is proof that anti-Semitism in France, during the first fifty years of the century, was, at the most, underground."

(30) Cf. Pessès, *op. cit.*, p. 126.

(31) Similarly, see Michelet's revealing note in *La Bible de l'humanité* (ed. 1864, p. 303): "Nothing has given me more pain than this chapter, I love the Jews. . . . And yet, how can one keep quiet? . . . The Jew throughout the world has been the best slave, the support even of his tyrants."

(32) See Toussenel's preface to the fourth edition of his book (1888 ed., Vol. I, p. xxxii):

    . . . it is not I who, in the early editions of this book, appeared to be begging the public's pardon for indicting the Jewish race. . . . I leave the responsibility for the act of contrition and the excuses to the publishers of the *librairie sociétaire*. . . .

(33) *Mémoire sur la captivité de Madame la duchesse de Berry*, by M. de Chateaubriand, Paris, 1833, p. 72.

(34) V. Hugo, "A l'homme qui avait livré une femme, " 1832 (in *Les Chants du crépuscule*).

(35) L. Börne, *Briefe aus Paris*, November 20, 1832 (cf. *Gesammelte Schriften*, 1834 ed., Vol. XIII, p. 23).

(36) Dumas's account contains the arguments in defense of Deutz as well as the repercussions of the affair. It first appeared in 1833 under the signature of General Dermoncourt and under the title *La Vendée et Madame*. Cf. *Madame dans la cheminée*, by A. Dumas, Jacques Suffel, ed., Paris, 1942.

(37) Cf. André Castelot, *La Duchesse de Berry*, Paris, 1963, p. 251 ("le Juif") and p. 253 ("le traître").

(38) Published in 1926 by N. Gelber, the documents of the state archives of Vienna relating to the Damascus affair notably include two letters from James de Rothschild to his brother Salomon (whose daughter he had married): cf. "Oesterreich und die Damascusaffaire im Jahr 1840, nach bisher unveröffentlichen Akten," *Jahrbuch der Jüdisch-Literarischen Gesellschaft*, XVIII, 1926, pp. 21-64.

(39) "Bei solchen Umständen blieb uns nur das hier allmächtige Mittel übrig, nämlich die Zeitungen zu Hülfe zu nehmen . . ." James to Salomon, May 7, 1840 (*ibid.*, p. 241).

(40) *Ibid.*

(41) Heinrich Heine, June 3, 1840; cf. *Lutèce* . . . , Paris, 1855, p. 79.

(42) Thiers to Guizot, ambassador in London, July 31, 1840; quoted by Charles Pouthas, "La politique de Thiers pendant la crise orientale de 1840," *Revue historique*, 182, 1938. Cf. also F.

Charles-Roux's harsh judgment on Thiers's irresponsible policy, in *Thiers et Méhémet Ali,* Paris, 1951.

(43) Thiers's reply to Fould's question, June 2, 1840; cf. Posener, *op. cit.,* Vol. I, p. 225.

(44) Chamber of Peers, session of July 10, 1840; *ibid.,* p. 233.

(45) H. Heine, *Lutèce . . . ,* p. 74 (letter of June 3, 1840).

(46) "Horrible accusation contre les Juifs de Damas," *Archives israélites,* I/1840, p. 165.

(47) *Ibid.*

(48) *Gazette de France,* April 10, 1840; *La Quotidienne,* May 7, 1840; cf. Posener, *op. cit.,* pp. 207, 215.

(49) Quoted from the *Archives israélites,* I/1840, p. 220.

(50) Heine, *Lutèce . . . ,* p. 78.

(51) Cf. Dubnov, *Histoire moderne du peuple juif,* Paris, 1933, Vol. I, p. 747, as well as Posener, *op. cit.,* Vol. I, pp. 230-9.

(52) Cf. L. H. Loewenstein, *Damascia, Die Judenverfolgung zu Damascus,* Frankfurt am Main, 1841, p. 229.

(53) Cf. the information on the Rothschilds' role in the solution of the 1840 crisis in Gille, *op. cit.,* p. 304.

(54) Cf. the history of the foundation of the *Alliance israélite universelle,* Posener, *op. cit.,* Vol. II, pp. 134 ff., as well as N. Leven, *Cinquante ans d'histoire, l'Alliance israélite universelle (1860-1910),* Paris, 1920, p. 67.

(55) *Archives israélites,* III, 1842, p. 362 ("Les députés israélites, MM. Cerfberr, Crémieux et Fould").

(56) *Ibid.,* pp. 147-55 ("Les complices d'un adjectif").

(57) Cf. Gaston Paris, "Le Juif errant" (extract from the *Encyclopédie des Sciences religieuses*), Paris, 1880, pp. 16-17.

(58) *Ibid.,* p. 18.

(59) *Le Juif errant, journal,* monthly progress report, December, 1834, p. 2. Only three installments of this review appeared.

(60) *La Juive errante,* Paris, 1845 (2 vols). The work was published by Lespès under the pseudonym of Marquise de Vieuxbois. It relates the loves and adventures of a courtesan, the "Padouna"; it remained unfinished, so that the "mystery of the heroine's birth" was unsolved; perhaps the author intended to make her Jewish by birth.

(61) *Légende du Juif errant,* by J. Collin de Plancy, Paris, 1847. Work sanctioned by Mgr the bishop of Chalois.

(62) This periodical, which does not appear in the catalog of the Bibliothèque Nationale, is mentioned by Champfleury (J. Husson), *Histoire de l'imagerie populaire,* Paris, 1869, p. 4.

(63) *Le Juif errant,* opera in five acts (act IV, second tableau, scene V).

(64) Letter from A. Dumas to his English publisher, Sinnett, March 26, 1852 (cf. C. Crivel, "Notes sur Alexander Dumas d'après des documents nouveaux," *La Revue indépendante,* July, 1902, p. 332).

(65) Champfleury, *op. cit.*, pp. 95-104.

(66) Henry Meige, "Étude sur certains névropathes voyageurs. Le Juif errant à la Salpêtrière," Paris, 1893, p. 61. This doctoral thesis in medicine was defended on July 13, 1893, before a jury chaired by Charcot. It was typical of the mythology of the period. Dr Meige stated in principle: "Almost all legends originate in popular observation bearing on material facts"; that is why he was led to think that the wandering Jew might well be only "a sort of prototype of the Israelite neuropaths wandering through the world" (pp. 8-9).

(67) *Briefe aus Paris,* 72nd letter, January, 1832.

(68) "Journal des idées, des opinions et des lectures d'un jeune jacobite de 1819" (*Littérature et philosophie mêlées*).

(69) *La France juive,* ed. 1934, Vol. I, p. 106.

(70) *Voyage en Orient, Oeuvres complètes,* 1861 ed., Vol. I, pp. 65, 307.

(71) *Jocelyn,* ninth installment. This episode was not to everyone's taste. For example, the *Annales de Philosophie chrétienne* (March 31, 1836) commented:

> To want to have a Jew buried by a Catholic priest, is to go against all conventions. To suppose that there are in our time Christians as fanatical as to drag a Jew's corpse like a dog's to crevices in a rock is a calumny.

(72) Furthermore, *L'Habit vert* was written by Musset in collaboration with Émile Augier, who seems to have been the main craftsman of the two.

(73) Karoline von Humboldt's friend (cf. above p. 296); this identification was suggested by M. A. Pessès in his thesis mentioned above.

(74) Mme Hanska's doctor; the identification was suggested by M. M. Bouteron, in the La Pléiade edition of the *Comédie humaine* (Vol. I, p. xxix).

(75) On the subject of "Balzac and the Jews" see the thesis by M. A. Pessès already mentioned, as well as Rabi, *op. cit.*, pp. 43-8 ("Balzac témoin").

(76) (F. la Serve, "Les Juifs à Lyon," *Revue du Lyonnais,* 1838, p. 343.) In 1838 Fleury la Serve wrote:

> Of all the towns in France ours is unquestionably the most tenacious of its prejudices and, as Lyon is universally Catholic, it follows that Judaism is condemned from afar, suspected, avoided more than elsewhere. This almost general caution of the Catholics, and the national spirit of the Jews, confine the latter to their own sphere and scarcely allow any but purely commercial relations between the two religions. . . .

(77) *Mémoires d'Outre-Tombe,* centenary edition, Paris, 1948, Vol. IV, p. 401 (September 17, 1833).

(78) Cf. the note by M. Levaillant, Vol. IV, p. 395 in the edition cited above.

(79) The fascination that Jews and Judaism held for Vigny has been glimpsed by Georges Bonnefoy in his thesis "La pensée religieuse et morale d'Alfred de Vigny," Paris, 1945, pp. 291-7:

> Vigny can only envisage the "wisdom" of the Jews with irony and alarm: would the greed for gold go hand in hand with unbelief in Christ? What is the permanent function of this race of important materialists if not to humiliate Christians, unfaithful to their Christianity? . . . He is certainly obsessed by the new power of these materialistic kings, whom moreover, the Christian has not the right to blame for anything.

(80) *Journal d'un poète*, cf. *Oeuvres complètes* of Alfred de Vigny, La Pléiade ed., Vol. II, p. 947:

> Heine is Jewish. He has come to see me several times—I do not like him—I find him cold and wretched. He is one of those foreigners who, having missed fame in their own country, want to give the impression of it in another.

(81) *Ibid.*, p. 994:

> Spinoza was Jewish (Portuguese) and his first name was Baruch. His system is as follows: "One substance in nature—one, eternal, independent, indivisible and simple; modified in extent it produces all bodies, in thought all intelligences." Atheism and pantheism united. *Everything is God* and *God does not exist* as an intelligent and independent being. "Died February 11, 1677."

(82) "Supplément au Journal d'un poète," in H. Guillemin, *M. de Vigny, homme d'ordre et poète*, Paris, 1955, p. 101.

(83) *Journal d'un poète*, La Pléiade ed., Vol. II, p. 1258.

(84) *Ibid.*, p. 1163.

(85) *Ibid.*, p. 1286.

(86) *Ibid.*, p. 1119.

(87) *Ibid.*, p. 1298.

(88) *Helena, Oeuvres*, ed. cit., Vol. I, pp. 286-7:

> They were all Jews. . . . They were counting the pile of gold which had fallen into their hands. The swords of Damascus which the soldier admires, and the soft woven clothing from Kashmir, the Christian chalices, the necklaces, the crescents, these rings, innocent ornaments of the ear: For everything is permissible to the sons of Judah, as everything is admissible to their treasuries. . . .

> On this subject, G. Bonnefoy, in his thesis mentioned above, expresses surprise as to "why, towards the end, [Vigny] introduced Jews sharing Christian and Moslem gold indiscriminately, and in fact nothing calls for their presence at that point" (p. 78).

> In *Daphné*, Vigny powerfully developed the theme of the Jews as omnipresent profiteers. See below.

(89) *Ibid.*, p. 1061.

(90) *Ibid.*, p. 1069.

(91) *Ibid.*, p. 1178:

> To end up with Mlle Rothschild's trick. Her father had mentioned in his will that she would have his millions if she married a man of her religion. The young thing meets a fine officer in the Horse Guards in the country. They fall in love, she consults an attorney and says to him: "But I am a Jewess and if I marry him, I lose all my fortune." "No, no, there is a way." She marries. Her father's attorneys tell her: "But you have no right to anything."—"Yes, Monsieur, read the will. It says, 'If she marries a man of her religion.' On Monday I became a Christian. He is a Lutheran Christian. I married him on Tuesday. I am all right." As English law abides by the letter, she had her fortune.

(92) *Ibid.*, p. 1143.

(93) *Ibid.*, p. 1176.

(94) *Ibid.*, p. 1179.

(95) *Ibid.*, p. 1183.

(96) "Dr Black" is the cold rational intelligence, in no way inhuman but led, by the professional practice of inquiry into causes, to find the reason for things" (Fernand Baldensperger).

(97) *Ibid.*, p. 1321.

(98) *Ibid.*, p. 1123.

(99) *Ibid.*, p. 1363 ("Plan de Daphné").

(100) *Ibid.*, p. 798. The Jew in *Daphné* came to life again in an unpublished text, in about 1840, when he exclaimed: "At present you deny that Jesus Christ was God. We have known it for eighteen hundred years. Kneel down then and ask pardon." (Cf. Bonnefoy, *op. cit.*, p. 74, note 26.)

(101) *Daphné*, La Pléiade ed., Vol. II, p. 854.

(102) Thanks to documents published by M. Henri Guillemin, in the first chapter of *M. de Vigny, homme d'ordre et poète*, Paris, 1955.

(103) *Théorie du judaïsme appliquée à la réforme des Israélites de tous les pays de l'Europe*, by Abbé Louis Chiarini, Paris, 1829.

(104) *Archives israélites*, III/1842, p. 633: "You were once called Wagenseil, Eisenmanger, Chiarini, etc."

(105) *Théorie du judaïsme*, Vol. II, p. 197, and Vol. I, p. 6.

(106) Bonnefoy, *op. cit.*, p. 297, note.

(107) A. Cerfberr de Medelsheim, *Ce que sont les Juifs de France*, 2nd ed., Paris, 1844, pp. 64-5. The work was also translated in England and Germany.

(108) *Oeuvres de Saint-Simon et d'Enfantin*, Paris, 1865-78, Vol. XIX, p. 178; quoted by the historian of Saint-Simonism, Georges Weill, "Les Juifs et le saint-simonisme," *R.E.J.*, XXX-XXXI, 1895, pp. 261-73:

> This people, melancholy, reserved, devoured by a pride inspired in it by its super-terrestrial nobility and by the

humiliation in which it has been forced to live, consoles itself for the one by the other, and returns the contempt it receives from its idolatrous neighbor a hundredfold. This deep-seated frame of mind has not yet been destroyed; in his universal captivity, from all sides reduced to the level of the brute beast, the unyielding Israelite says in his heart: I am the man of God.

(109) Cf. S. Charléty, *Histoire du saint-simonisme,* ed. Paris, 1965, p. 179.

(110) Cf. G. Weill, *op. cit.,* p. 272.

(111) *Histoire des grandes opérations financières,* by M. Capefigue, Paris, 1858, Vol. III, p. iii.

(112) In Flora Tristan's opinion (*L'Émancipation de la femme . . . ,* Paris, 1846, quoted by M. Bourgin, *Étude sur les sources de Fourier,* Paris, 1905, p. 32):
Swedenborg, by the revelation of the communications, pointed the way to the unity and the universality of science, and suggested this beautiful system of analogies to Fourier. . . . Fourier wanted to bring Swedenborg's heavenly dream into being and transformed the convent of the Middle Ages into a phalanstery.

(113) In Michelet's opinion, "Fourier dreams *L'Harmonie.* . . . But nothing has more effect on him than the burning environment of Lyon, its working men's fraternities. Socialism was there at his hearth, and already old with the Waldenses of Lyon, the poor of Lyon" (*Histoire du XIXe siècle,* Paris, 1880, Vol. I, p. 3).

(114) See above, pp. 27, 28.

(115) *Théorie des quatre mouvements et des destinées générales,* Leipzig, 1808, pp. 327-31.

(116) *La Fausse Industrie morcelée, répugnante, mensongère . . . ,* Paris, 1836, pp. 484-6.

(117) *Théorie des quatre mouvements . . . ,* p. 357, note. It is worth noting that this threat should have been stirred up by Fourier on the eve of the meeting of the Great Sanhedrin.

(118) *Le nouveau monde industriel et sociétaire, Oeuvres,* 1841 ed., Vol. VI, p. 421.

(119) *Publication des manuscrits de Charles Fourier,* Paris, 1852, Vol. III, p. 34.

(120) *Ibid.,* Vol. II, p. 226.

(121) *La Fausse Industrie . . . . ,* p. 660.

(122) Quoted by Posener, *op. cit.,* Vol. II, p. 63.

(123) Cf. the book which we have found valuable on very many subjects, by E. Silberner, *Sozialisten zur Judenfrage,* Berlin, 1962, p. 36.

(124) "Pamphlet, philosophical and social study, the work of a poet, of a thinker, of a prophet, Toussenel's wonderful book is all this at once, and my sole ambition, I admit, after long years of literary

labor, would be that my book might take its place beside his in the libraries of those who would understand the causes which have brought ruin and shame to our country." (*La France juive, ed. cit.,* Vol. I, p. 346.)

(125) A. Toussenel, *Les Juifs, rois de l'époque,* 4th ed., Paris, 1888, Vol. I, pp. xi, xv.

(126) *Ibid.,* p. 42 ("But I ask you what does it do for them, these English, these Genevans, these Jews, all these foreigners, that France should be bled white?").

(127) *Ibid.,* p. 66.

(128) *Ibid.,* p. xxiv.

(129) *Ibid.,* p. xxxi.

(130) *Ibid.,* Vol. II, p. 15:

> The feuilleton [in the *Journal des Débats*] which I am tired of having heard for such a long time called witty, had also in times past embarked on the destruction of Mlle Rachel. . . . Mlle Rachel is an incomparable actress, who has resurrected Racine and Corneille, and who, by her wonderful diction, has revealed unsuspected marvels of harmony in the masterpieces of the masters of the stage!

(131) *Le Commerce,* July 15, 1844. Cf. M. A. Pessès's thesis (see above) p. 119.

(132) Pierre Leroux, "Les Juifs, rois de l'époque," *La Revue sociale,* January, 1846. In 1866, Leroux expanded the same concepts in an appendix to his play *Job.* Cf. Silberner, *op. cit.,* pp. 44-5.

(133) Cf. Silberner, *op. cit.,* pp. 43, 53, 65.

(134) *Ibid.,* pp. 39-40.

(135) See above, p. 291.

(136) Pierre-Joseph Proudhon, *Césarisme et christianisme,* Paris, 1883, Vol. I, p. 139.

(137) *De la justice dans la Révolution et dans l'Église, Oeuvres,* ed. 1935 vol. IV, p. 458.

(138) See above, p. 286.

(139) *De la justice . . . ,* pp. 451-2.

(140) *Ibid.,* p. 458.

(141) P.-J. Proudhon, *Jésus et les origines du christianisme,* Paris, 1896, p. 122:

> . . . the faith of Jesus has conquered the world; the emperors have become Christian; and nothing would have prevented there being Jews amongst them if the Jews themselves had had the faith, if they had not placed themselves, by their messianic obstinacy, outside the human race.

(142) *De la justice . . . , ed cit.,* Vol. I, p. 445.

(143) *Carnets de P.-J. Proudhon,* P. Haubtmann, ed., Paris, 1960-1, Vol. II, pp. 23, 52, 151, 337.

(144) *Ibid.,* p. 200.

(145) *De la justice . . . , ed. cit.,* Vol. IV, p. 458.

(146) Quoted by Henri de Lubac, *Proudhon et le christianisme*, Paris, 1945, p. 68 (December 7, 1849).
(147) *France et Rhin*, Paris, 1867, p. 258.
(148) Cf. H. de Lubac, *op. cit.*, pp. 123 ff.
(149) *De la justice . . .* , ed. *cit.*, Vol. IV, pp. 179-215 ("La femme").
(150) T. W. Adorno, *et al.*, *The Authoritarian Personality*, New York, 1950.
(151) *Publication des manuscrits de Charles Fourier*, Vol. III, p. 34 ("Questions de morale et politique commerciale").
(152) *Carnets de P.-J. Proudhon*, Vol. II, p. 338.

11 Germany

(1) Cf. Harry Pross, *Dokumente zur deutschen Politik 1806-1870*, Frankfurt, 1959, pp. 78-9.
(2) Jahn wrote that his ancestors had emigrated from Bohemia at the time of the Thirty Years' War; cf. *Deutsches Volkstum*, ed. Reclam, Leipzig, n.d., p. 22.
(3) The Frenchman Gobineau, the Englishman H. S. Chamberlain, the Balt Alfred Rosenberg, the Austrian Hitler, etc.
(4) Walter Bussmann, "Ernst Moritz Arndt," *Das Parlament*, March 9, 1960, pp. 141-6.
    We must also mention the study by Ernst Weymar which appeared under the same title in the issue of May 18, 1960, of *Das Parlament*, in which the author brings out the "pre-racist" aspect of Arndt's thought.
(5) Quoted by Hermann Blome, *Der Rassengedanke in der deutschen Romantik und seine Grundlagen im 18. Jahrhundert*, Berlin, 1943, p. 297. This author described Arndt as "prime champion of a racial and hygienic 'Kulturpolitik' " (p. 309).
(6) Quoted by Weymar, *op. cit.*, p. 322.
(7) The summary of Arndt's ideas on anthropological subjects given below follows Weymar, *op. cit.*, and *Das Selbstverständnis der Deutschen*, Stuttgart, 1961, pp. 41-8. Cf. also G. Illgen, *Die Anschauungen Ernst Moritz Arndts über Volk und Staat*, 1938.
(8) On the subject of Kohlrausch's textbooks, see the remarkable study already mentioned by Weymar, *op. cit.*, pp. 19-41 (Chap. 1: "Die christlich-germanische Sendung"). The transition by Lutheran thinkers from the "servant Messiah" (as is still found in Herder and Schleiermacher) to the "triumphant Messiah" has been studied by Gerhard Kaiser, *Pietismus und Patriotismus im literarischen Deutschland*, Wiesbaden, 1961 (cf. Chap. XI: "Völkerfamilie oder Sendungsidee").
(9) Cf. the writings and poems of Novalis and Hölderlin, quoted by Jacques Droz, *L'Allemagne et la Révolution française*, Paris, 1949, pp. 459-75 and 486-8.

(10) Adam Müller: "The great federalism of the European peoples, which will come about one day, as true as we live, will still carry the German colors; for everything that is great, profound or eternal in European institutions is German" (*Elemente der Staatskunst*, 1809, quoted by Kaiser, *op. cit.*, p. 220). Görres: "As Judea once was, so Germany is at present, the holy land, where religion builds its temple. It is the Germans whom it behoves to be the priests of the modern period, the Brahminic class" (*Fall der Religion und ihre Wiedergeburt*, 1810, quoted by Gérard, *op. cit.*, pp. 171-2). Perthes: "We Germans, we are a chosen people, a people representing mankind, and for whom everything becomes an affair of general interest. Never has this people whom we are, been purely and simply national." (Letter to Görres, 1808, quoted by M. Boucher, *Le Sentiment national en Allemagne*, Paris, 1947, p. 79.)

(11) There are few serious works on Jahn and, as far as we know, no recent ones. We have used the one by Edmund Neuendorff, *Geschichte der neueren deutschen Leibesübung . . .*, Vol. II, "Jahn und seine Zeit," Dresden, n.d. The episode of the Sistine Madonna, told by the Prussian pedagogue Henrich Steffens, is described on p. 489.

(12) *Deutsches Volkstum*, ed. Reclam, Leipzig, n.d., pp. 194-5.

(13) *Ibid.*, p. 40.

(14) The following is a sample (*Werke zum deutschen Volkstum*, 1833; cf. Jahn, *Werke*, 1885, Vol. II, p. 560):

> Im Mittelalter gleichen die Mangvölker [the "crossbred peoples," notably the French] einem Mischsud, schäumen wie Most und toben im wilden Drunter und Drüber, bis die widerstrebenden Urteile sich zersetzen, auflösen und endlich wie Quenckbrei vereinen. . . . Mangvölker fühlen ewig die Nachwehen, die Sünde der Blutschande und Blutschuld verfolgt sie, und anrüchig sind sie immerdar auch noch bis ins tausendste Glied. . . .

(15) That is to say, Jewesses (cf. *Werke*, II, p. 827).

(16) *Deutsches Volkstum*, p. 38.

(17) *Ibid.*, p. 48.

(18) Letters quoted in *Geschichte der neueren deutschen Leibesübung*, II, p. 403.

(19) Cf. C. Euler, *Fr. L. Jahn, Sein Leben und Wirken*, Stuttgart, 1881, p. 131.

(20) "In Jahn we see everything that the Fichtes and the Arndts have done and advised to be done to favor the development of the character and freedom of Germany, distòrted to the point of caricature . . ." (Gervinus, *Histoire du XIXe siècle*, Paris, 1864, III, p..145). This is the dominant tone, and von Treitschke, in his *Deutsche Geschichte*, has devoted pages of ferocious humor to Jahn. But in the twentieth century, whatever the author's political religion, the tone ceases to be ironic. Today, notably

in the German Democratic Republic, it is often openly enthusiastic; there, Jahn is on the way to becoming a popular "great ancestor."

(21) Franz Passow, *Das Turnziel*, Breslau, 1818, p. 65.

(22) Cf. Neuendorff, *op. cit.*, Vol. II, p. 304.

(23) Evidence by the educationalist Henrich Steffens; cf. Neuendorff, *loc. cit.*

(24) Cf. O. F. Scheuer, *Burschenschaft und Judenfrage, Der Rassenantisemitismus in der deutschen Studentenschaft*, Berlin, 1927, p. 8, note 10.

(25) Wolfgang Menzel, *Denkwürdigkeiten*, Leipzig, 1887, p. 11–12.

(26) Heinrich Leo, *Meine Jugendzeit*, Gotha, 1880, p. 62.

(27) Cf. E. Schuppe, *Der Burschenschaftler Wolfgang Menzel*, Frankfurt am Main, 1952, p. 17.

(28) H. von Treitschke, *Deutsche Geschichte im neunzehnten Jahrhundert*, Leipzig, 1882, Vol. II, p. 387.

(29) See below, pp. 402-3.

(30) Carl Brinkmann, "Der Nationalismus und die deutschen Universitäten im Zeitalter der deutschen Erhebung," *Sitzungsberichte der Heidelberger Akademie der Wissenschaften*, 1932, p. 67.

(31) Cf. Willy Schröder, "Das pädagogische Vermächtnis Jahns," *Deutsche Lehrerzeitung*, no. 34, 1955, p. 3.

(32) Quoted by Golo Mann, *The History of Germany since 1789*, Marion Jackson, trans., London, 1968, p. 58.

(33) Cf. Brigitte Theune, "Volk und Nation bei Jahn, Rotteck, Welcker und Dahlmann," *Historische Studien*, 319, 1937.

(34) When the anti-Semitic agitation began in unified Germany in 1879, the old novelist Berthold Auerbach wrote to a friend: "Isn't it terrible that everything must start all over again? For fifty years Hofacker at Stuttgart and Rotteck at Karlsruhe have besmirched the Jews. This gives me no peace . . ." (cf. Kobler, *Juden und Judentum in deutschen Briefen*, Vienna, 1935, p. 270).

(35) See Brinkmann, *op. cit.*, H. von Treitschke, *Deutsche Geschichte . . . , vol. cit.*, and O. F. Scheuer, *Burschenschaft und Judenfrage.*

(36) Cf. Franz Schnabel, *Deutsche Geschichte im neunzehnten Jahrhundert*, Freiburg, 1933, Vol. II, pp. 245-8.

(37) Saul Ascher, *Die Wartburg-Feier . . .* , Leipzig, 1818, p. 34.

(38) This long letter has been published in full by Scheuer, *op. cit.*, pp. 17-19.

(39) Max Weber, *Wissenschaft als Beruf*, cf. R. Aron, ed., *Max Weber: le savant et le politique*, Paris, 1959, p. 61.

(40) Friedrich Carl von Savigny, *Vom Beruf unsrer Zeit . . .* , ed. Heidelberg, 1840, p. 175.

(41) "Geh nicht nach Norden. Und hüte dich von jenem König in

Thule, Hüt' dich vor Gendarmen und Polizei, Vor der ganzen historischen Schule" (*Wintermärchen*, Chapter XXVI).

(42) Cf. correspondence in the *Journal des Débats*, Paris, March 10, 1842.

(43) Collective petition from the Jewish communities of Prussia, quoted by S. Dubnov, *op. cit.*, Vol. I, pp. 454-5.

(44) The data on the economic role of the Jews in Germany which follow have been taken from the study by Ernst Fraenkel, "Der Beitrag der deutschen Juden auf wirtschaftlichem Gebiet," *Judentum, Schicksal, Wesen und Gegenwart*, Tübingen, 1965, pp. 552-600, and in the more heavily documented study, which however primarily concerns the Weimar Republic, by Esra Bennathan, "Die demographische und wirtschaftliche Struktur der Juden," *Entscheidungsjahr 1932*, Tübingen, 1965, pp. 87-131.

(45) Cf. H. P. Bahrdt, "Gesellschaftliche Voraussetzungen des Antisemitismus," *Entscheidungsjahr 1932*, p. 141.

(46) Sombart, *op. cit.*, pp. 122 and 177-86.

(47) In other fields, notably teaching, a *numerus clausus* was observed, easily degenerating into actual exclusion (for example, in primary teaching in Prussia). Cf. E. Hamburger, "Jews in public service under the German monarchy," *Leo Baeck Yearbook*, Vol. IX, 1964, pp. 206-38.

(48) Cf. the data collected by Sterling, *op. cit.*, pp. 168, 218.

(49) M. I. Kalinin, *Jewish Agriculturalists in the Union of the Peoples of the USSR* (in Russian), Moscow, 1927, pp. 26-7.

(50) Cf. above, p. 368.

(51) I refer to this subject in my book, *Les Banquiers juifs et le Saint-Siège . . .*, pp. 29, *passim*.

(52) Quoted by Joseph Dresch in his edition of L. Börne, *Études sur l'histoire et les hommes de la Révolution française*, Paris, 1952, p. 12.

(53) "Moses, Christ and Napoleon form the holy triad of History," (*Aphorismen*, 1808-10; cf. *Sämtliche Werke*, 1964 ed., Vol. I, p. 141).

(54) *Ibid.*, pp. 14 ff ("Bemerkungen über die neue Stättigkeits- und Schutzordnung für die Judenschaft in Frankfurt am Main . . .").

(55) *Ibid.*, p. 163 (*Aphorismen*, 1808-10).

(56) Cf. above, pp. 243-4.

(57) *Ibid.*, p. 145.

(58) Quoted by Helmut Bock, *Ludwig Börne, Vom Gettojuden zum Nationalschriftsteller*, East Berlin, 1962, pp. 105 and 422.

(59) *Briefe aus Paris*, 74th letter (February 7, 1832).

(60) *Ibid.*, 103rd letter (February 2, 1833).

(61) "Der Jude Shylock im Kaufmann von Venedig," *Sämtliche Werke, ed. cit.*, I, pp. 499-505.

(62) "Das europäische Gleichgewicht wird von der Judenschaft erhalten. Sie gibt heute dieser Macht Geld, morgen der andern, der Reihe nach allen, und so sorgt sie liebevoll für den

allgemeinen Frieden . . . " (*Aphorismen und Miszellen*, 1828, *ed. cit.*, Vol. II, p. 306).

(63) *Für die Juden, ed. cit.*, Vol. I, p. 876.

(64) Cf. F. Kobler, *Juden und Judentum* . . . , Vienna, 1935, p. 277.

(65) H. Bock, *Ludwig Börne* . . . , pp. 392-9.

(66) Quoted by L. Marcuse, "Ludwig Börne," *Tribune*, Frankfurt am Main, VI/1963, p. 614.

(67) Quoted by Bock, *op. cit.*, p. 450.

(68) *Hallische Jahrbücher*, II, 1839, p. 1347.

(69) *Briefe aus Paris*, 74th letter.

(70) Letter to I. Wohlwill, April 1, 1823. "We are no longer strong enough to wear a beard, to fast, to hate and out of hatred to endure . . . , " he added. He often went back to this subject in his letters to his close friends, particularly at the end of his life. To his brother Max, he wrote in May, 1849 (cf. Kobler, *Juden und Judentum*, pp. 215, 230-1):

> Our fathers were tough. They humbled themselves before God and were therefore so obstinate and defiant towards men, towards the powers of this world. As for me, I was brazen towards Heaven and humble and cringing towards men—and that is why I now lie underfoot like a crushed worm. Glory and honor to God in the highest!

(71) *Wintermärchen*, Chap. XXVI.

(72) Heine, *Prose Writings*, Havelock Ellis, ed., London, n.d.

(73) Cf. the texts collected and accompanied by a commentary by Golo Mann, *Deutsche Geschichte des 19. und 20. Jahrhunderts*, pp. 161-70 ("Heinrich Heine").

(74) *Deutsche Geschichte im neunzehnten Jahrhundert*, Leipzig, 1885, Vol. III, p. 420.

(75) The discussions about Heine's monument have been described by Paul Arnsberg, "Heinrich Heine als linksintellektuelles 'Anti-Symbol,'" *Tribüne*, Frankfurt am Main, VI/1963, pp. 643-57.

(76) Adolf Bartels, *Heinrich Heine: auch ein Denkmal*, Dresden, 1906.

(77) "Es scheint nicht ganz zuffälig, wenn Heine auch heute noch in Deutschland als Dichter umstritten ist, während das Ausland ihm einen Platz neben Goethe zuordnet, ja, ihn dem Weimarer Olympier gelegentlich sogar vorzieht." (Heinz Becker, *Der Fall Heine-Meyerbeer*, Berlin, 1958, p. 23).

(78) W. Boelich, *Der Berliner Antisemitismusstreit*, Frankfurt am Main, 1965, p. 52.

(79) Cf. J. Dresch, *Gutzkow et la Jeune Allemagne*, Paris, 1904, p. 155.

(80) Cf. H. Bock, *Ludwig Börne* . . . , p. 383.

(81) Cf. H. H. Houben, *Jungdeutscher Sturm und Drang*, Leipzig, 1911, p. 96, quoting the Bavarian government's interdiction decree, but the preliminaries are said to have been due to Metternich himself.

(82) *Jahrbuch der Literatur,* I, 1839, p. 14; cf. Dresch, *op. cit.,* pp. 64-5.

(83) Cf. Sterling, *Er ist wie du,* p. 114.

(84) K. Gutzkow, *Julius Mosens Ahasver* (followed by a *Nachtrag* polemic in which he maintains and specifies his theory on the Jews); *Vermischte Schriften,* Leipzig, 1842, Vol. II, pp. 115 ff., 171 ff.

(85) Cf. the unpublished thesis by Marie-Louise Gabriel, "The portrait of the contemporary Jew in English and German fiction and drama from 1830 to 1880," p. 21.

(86) Cf. Sterling, *op. cit.,* p. 206, note 103, referring to Laube's *Dramatische Werke,* 1847, p. 21.

(87) "[Hierzu trug bei] dass gerade die Begriffe 'Jude' oder 'Judentum' für die literarisch gebildete Offentlichkeit den Charakter der Bezeichnungen anschaulicher, sozialer Gestalten verloren und sich nahezu ins 'Symbolische' verflüchtigt hatten" (Hans Paul Bahrdt, "Gesellschaftliche Voraussetzungen des Antisemitismus," *Entscheidungsjahr 1932,* p. 149).

(88) The exception being the comparative thesis quoted above by Marie-Louise Gabriel. The work by Ludwig Geiger, *Die deutsche Literatur und die Juden,* Berlin, 1910, is only a collection of essays.

(89) Cf. Geiger, *op. cit.,* p. 22.

(90) Cf. the work by Marie-Louise Gabriel, p. 57 and particularly p. 206.

(91) Cf. his correspondence with his Jewish friend Emmanuel Osmond (Kobler, *op. cit.,* pp. 150-1).

(92) Cf. R. Koepke, *Ludwig Tieck . . . ,* Leipzig, 1855, Vol. II, p. 214.

(93) K. Immermann, *Die Epigonen, Familienmemoiren . . . ,* Düsseldorf, 1836, Vol. II, pp. 208 ff.

(94) *Ibid.,* p. 344.

(95) In French in the text. Cf. E. Silberner, *Sozialisten zur Judenfrage* (Chap. "Lassalle," pp. 160-80).

(96) *Ibid.,* p. 137.

(97) On September 2, 1841, Hess wrote to his friend Auerbach:
> He is the greatest, perhaps the one genuine philosopher now alive. . . . Dr Marx, the name of my idol, is still very young (no more than about twenty-four) and will give the *coup de grâce* to medieval religion and politics. He unites the most profound philosophical earnestness with the most biting wit: imagine Rousseau, Voltaire, Holbach, Lessing, Heine and Hegel fused into one person, not thrown together—and you have Dr Marx.

(98) Cf. Silberner, *op. cit.* (Chap. "Hess," pp. 181-97).

(99) M. Hess, *Rom und Jerusalem,* Leipzig, 1862, pp. 31, 39.

(100) Cf. the preface to the second edition of Vol. II of his works (*Zur Geschichte der Religion und Philosophie in Deutschland*), in which he describes his friends as *gottlose Selbstgötter.* I have

not been able to consult this edition, which Mme Kühne quotes (see following note).

(101) The life and works of G. F. Daumer have been studied in the remarkable thesis by Agnes Kühne, *Der Religionsphilosoph Georg Friedrich Daumer, Wege und Wirkungen seiner Entwicklung,* Berlin, 1936; the thesis is all the more remarkable in that Mme Kühne was not afraid to be subtly ironical on the Nazi "Volkschristliche deutsche Bewegung" (pp. 86-7). It is principally from this work that we have borrowed the data on Daumer given below.

(102) G. Friedrich Daumer, *Die Geheimnisse des christlichen Alterthums,* Hermann Ewerbeck, trans., in *Qu'est-ce que la Bible d'après la nouvelle philosophie allemande,* Paris, 1850, p. 57. This translation is abridged in various places but I have not been able to consult the original German text.

(103) Quoted by Kühne, *op. cit.,* pp. 70-1.

(104) Ewerbeck translation, pp. 64, 70.

(105) *Ibid.,* p. 124.

(106) *Ibid.,* p. 56.

(107) *Ibid.,* pp. 130-3.

(108) Kühne, *op. cit.,* p. 73.

(109) *Qu'est-ce que la Bible* . . . ; cf. also Ewerbeck's preface to *Qu'est-ce que la religion d'après la nouvelle philosophie allemande,* Paris, 1850.

(110) Marx said (Karl Marx, Friedrich Engels, ed., MEGA," I, 6, pp. 640-1):

> All the writings hitherto directed against the Christian religion were limited to proving that it was based on erroneous foundations, e.g. that the authors copied each other; but the practical cult of Christianity had not yet been studied. We know that the supreme element in Christianity is human sacrifice. And now Daumer shows, in a recently published work, that Christians have in effect cut men's throats, eaten human flesh and drunk human blood. . . . Human sacrifice was holy and really existed. All Protestantism did was to transpose it to spiritual man and moderate the thing slightly. . . . This history, as Daumer expounds it in his work, gives the final blow to Christianity. This makes us certain that the old society is approaching its end and that the structure of falsehood and prejudice is collapsing.

(111) Arnold Ruge, *Zwei Jahre in Paris, Studien und Erinnerungen,* Leipzig, 1842, Vol. I, pp. 6-12.

(112) *Die Religion des neuen Weltalters,* Hamburg, 1849; cf. Kühne, *op. cit.,* p. 96, note 12.

(113) *Ibid.,* pp. 96-7. *Die Weisheit Israels* by Daumer was published by L. Hirschberg, Berlin, 1924.

(114) *Ausgewählte Briefe von und an Feuerbach,* W. Bolin, ed., Leipzig, 1904, Vol. I, pp. 96-8.

(115) These data on F. W. Ghillany come from R. W. Stock, *Die Judenfrage durch fünf Jahrhunderte,* Nuremberg, 1939, pp. 391-427.

(116) See above, pp. 345-9. Daumer's writings might also have been influenced by the Damascus affair, but his views took shape before it broke out in 1840.

(117) Cf. Stock, *op. cit.,* p. 413.

(118) L. Feuerbach, *Das Wesen des Christentums,* Chap. XII (for greater clarity, we have reversed the order of the two paragraphs of the quotation).

(119) The life of Ruge is taken from W. Neher, *Arnold Ruge als Politiker und politischer Schriftsteller,* Heidelberg, 1933, and H. Rosenberg, "Arnold Ruge und die Hallischen Jahrbücher," *Archiv für Kulturgeschichte,* XX, 1930, pp. 281 ff.

(120) "Europa im Jahre 1840," *Hallische Jahrbücher,* III, 1840, p. 691.

(121) "Die Düsseldorfer Malerschule . . . ", *Hallische Jahrbücher,* II, 1839, pp. 1596-8.

(122) *Arnold Ruges Briefwechsel . . . ,* Nerrlich, ed., Berlin, 1886, Vol. I, pp. 332-3.

(123) " . . . da Marx ein ganz gemeiner Kerl und ein unverschämter Jude ist . . . eine andere Praxis des Sozialismus als die Gemeinschaft dieser greulichen Judenseelen und ihrer Genossen gab es doch wahrlich und gibt es noch jetzt in Paris nicht" (*ibid.,* pp. 367, 396).

(124) Cf. W. Neher, *Arnold Ruge als Politiker und politischer Schriftsteller,* p. 225.

(125) A. Schweitzer, *Geschichte der Leben-Jesu-Forschung,* Tübingen, 1933, p. 161.

(126) Cf. A. Cornu, *Karl Marx et Friedrich Engels . . . ,* Paris, 1953, Vol. I, p. 267.

(127) Cf. Horst Stuke, *Philosophie der Tat . . . ,* Stuttgart, 1963; 2. *Bruno Bauer und die Begründung der Philosophie der Tat im philosophisch-politischen Radikalismus* (pp. 123-87). In the long note to pages 127-30 where Bauer's works are listed, Stuke examines the reasons why historians of Marxism dislike this philosopher.

(128) Letter of April 5, 1840; cf. Cornu, *op. cit.,* p. 166.

(129) Stuke, *op. cit.,* p. 158, quoting *Das entdeckte Christentum,* by Bruno Bauer, 1843.

(130) B. Bauer, *Kritik der evangelischen Geschichte der Synoptiker,* Leipzig, 1841, Vol III, pp. 309-10.

(131) Cf. Stuke, *op. cit.,* as well as Cornu, *op. cit.,* pp. 157-61.

(132) Stuke, *op. cit:,* p. 150.

(133) B. Bauer, *Die Judenfrage,* Brunswick, 1843, p. 3.

(134) *Ibid.,* p. 9.

(135) *Ibid.,* p. 11.

(136) *Ibid.,* p. 21.

(137) *Ibid.,* pp. 79-80.

(138) *Ibid.*, p. 114.
(139) *Ibid.*, pp. 84-7 ("Das entdeckte Judentum und Christentum").
(140) Cf. Ernst Barnikol, "Bruno Bauers Kampf gegen Religion und Christentum und die Spaltung der vormärzlichen preussischen Opposition," *Zeitschrift für Kirchengeschichte*, XLVI, 1928, pp. 1-28.
(141) We have not been able to consult *Das entdeckte Christentum*, published with a commentary by E. Barnikol in 1927. In the *Grundriss der Geschichte der Philosophie* (Berlin, 1870, Vol. II, p. 666), J. E. Erdmann said of this document: "Im wesentlichen führt es denselben Gedanken durch, dass dem Christen am Nächsten gelegt sei, sich zur Freiheit der Atheisten zu erheben, während dem Juden kaum etwas übrig bleiben möchte, als durch jenes [das Christentum] hindurchzugehen."
(142) These extracts were published by W. Marr under the title *Das entdeckte und das unentdeckte Christentum in Zürich und ein Traum. Eine Bagatelle, Auszüge aus der in Zürich konfiszierten Bauerschen Schrift enthaltend und dem christlichen Bluntschli gewidmet vom Antichrist.* Cf. Barnikol, *op. cit.*, p. 15.
(143) Wilhelm Marr, *Das junge Deutschland in der Schweiz*, Leipzig, 1846, p. 180.
(144) *Die heilige Familie.*
(145) Cf. B. Bauer, *Christus und die Caesaren. Der Ursprung des Christentums aus dem römischem Griechentum*, Berlin, 1879, as well as the article "Bauer" by E. Barnikol in *Handwörterbuch für Theologie und Religionswissenschaft*, Tübingen, 1957, Vol. I, pp. 922-3). ("Der radikale Atheist wirkte nach 1848 als konservativer Politiker und Mitglied der 'Kreuzzeitung' und galt als der geistige Schöpfer des konservativen Staatslexikons Wageners. Zugleich trat er als entschiedener Antisemit auf.")
(146) *Early Writings*, T. B. Bottomore, trans. and ed., London, 1963, p. 39.
(147) *Ibid.*
(148) Here, we are following a view developed by Arnold Künzli in his *Psychographie* of Marx (*Karl Marx, Eine Psychographie*, Zürich, 1966, p. 209; cf. also p. 551):

> ... so long as he identified "the Jew" with that human type and that system of society through whose fanatical condemnation and hostility he had made himself a name in the world, he possessed—so he hoped at least—an alibi for his own "no longer being a Jew." If "the Jew" was a capitalist, then it was impossible for Karl Marx to be a Jew. Marx must therefore have experienced the emergence of a Jewish socialism as a vexation for thereby the legitimacy of his system, into which he had, after a successful and radical operation, forced Judaism, was made questionable and his alibi destroyed and he himself again brought into association with his Judaism.

(149) *Op. cit.*, p. 34.
(150) Cf. E. Silberner, *Sozialisten zur Judenfrage*, pp. 138-40 ("Anfänge des jüdischen Sozialismus").

I only discovered the study by Gérard Lyon-Caen, *Lecture de la "Question juive,"* when this volume was going to press. In it, he writes (*Archives de la philosophie du droit*, Paris, No. XII, 1967, "Marx et le droit moderne," pp. 1-11):

. . . it was therefore a question of saying to the Jews: be revolutionaries, you have no other choice, if you insist on emancipating yourselves as citizens and as men. . . . The Jew must be more than assimilationist or irreligious; he must be revolutionary.

In conclusion, Lyon-Caen makes the following comments on the book:

It must not be concealed: this text is violent and explosive. To say that it was at the origin of modern anti-Semitism would very certainly be excessive. But to put forward the theory that it encouraged certain anti-Semitic currents in capitalistic countries or even in countries which were freed from capitalism seems hard to dispute.

(151) The quotations which follow are taken from Silberner, *op. cit.*, pp. 136-48. ("Private Ausserungen") and from Künzli, *op. cit.*, pp. 214-15, with references to support them.
(152) "Der ungriechischste aller wasserpolackischen Juden" (which implies "the contrast between 'Athens' and 'Jerusalem' ").
(153) Silberner, *op. cit.*, pp. 115, 319-20.
(154) Künzli, *op. cit.*, p. 210.
(155) This description by Dr Lafargue is quoted by F. Mehring, *Karl Marx . . .*, Leipzig, 1933, p. 549:

Er war auch in der Tat sehr kräftig, seine Grösse ging über das Mittelmass, die Schultern waren breit, die Brust gut entwickelt, die Glieder wohl proportioniert, obgleich die Wirbelsäule im Vergleich zu den Beinen etwas zu lang war, wie es bei der jüdischen Rasse häufig zu finden ist.

Similarly, Freiligrath ("Oberhaupt der Synagoge"), Borkheim ("Germane jüdischer Herkunft"), Hyndman ("It is very obvious that Marx was a Jew . . . "); cf. Künzli, *op. cit.*, pp. 196-7.
(156) It seems that the first author to stress the question of Marx's anti-Semitism was the future Czech statesman, Thomas Masaryk; cf. *Die philosophischen und soziologischen Grundlagen des Marxismus*, Vienna, 1899, p. 454.
(157) *Karl Marx, Eine Psychographie;* in particular Künzli brings out Marx's resentment of his mother.
(158) However, there was the case of Baruch Spinoza in the seventeenth century; cf. Poliakov, *History of Anti-Semitism*, Vol. II, *From Mohammed to the Marranos*, New York, 1973.
(159) Georges M. Cottier, *L'Athéisme du jeune Marx, ses origines hégéliennes*, Paris, 1959, pp. 229-31.

(160) *Die heilige Familie.*
(161) *Theses on Feuerbach,* thesis I.
(162) Silberner, *op. cit.,* p. 138.
(163) *Ibid.,* p. 125 (*Das Kapital,* Vol. I, Chap. IV: Marx retained this metaphor and others like it in the three editions of Vol. I published during his lifetime).
(164) In an extremely broad way, all "messianism" (both that of the Enlightenment, for example, and *a fortiori* that of the millenarianist movements of the Reformation) can be described as "Jewish" since an attempt to trace its origins necessarily ends up by going further and further back towards the Apocalypse and the Jewish prophetic books. But when Marx's "Jewish messianism" is referred to, it is his family origins that are in mind. Now, according to all we know about his family environment and education, no rudiment of Jewish tradition was inculcated into him in childhood. Later, as we have seen, he deliberately avoided the study of Jewish history. Therefore, at first glance, how would Marx's messianism be more Jewish than his friend Bauer's, the "Messiah of atheism" (without bringing in Jungian-type unverifiable hypotheses whereby Karl Marx could have inherited messianism from a "collective unconscious" or some other chain process of this type)?

However, a broad relationship between Marx's Jewishness and the perspicacity of his social criticism can be established in an intellectually satisfying way. Certainly, the Jews did, in fact, generally play the role of pioneers in the human sciences (unlike the natural sciences), and certain branches of knowledge—notably sociology and depth psychology—were to a major degree formed by them. In the main, this was due to their social marginality, their distance from the object they were studying; within Christian society, every Jew was potentially a critic of established values and ideas.

From this point of view, it can in effect be stated that his original environment predisposed Marx, more than any other thinker of the Hegelian pleïad, to become the sociological and economic genius that he was. It is therefore Marx the sociologist who would be "Jewish," in the sense in which it is generally understood, and not Marx the prophet. It is only by this means and by noting that Old Testament prophetism involved a sort of social criticism, that Karl Marx's Judaism can be related to the historic role he exercised. It can also be added that social criticism played a much larger part in the sociology of the past than in contemporary sociology.
(165) This idea has been particularly upheld by Jean Marchal; cf. *Deux essais sur le marxisme,* Paris, 1955, pp. 17-82 ("Le marxisme comme conception générale de l'Homme et du Monde"). Almost half a century ago, the English economic

historian Tawney was already describing Karl Marx as the "last of the scholastics."

(166) Cf. W. Blumenberg, "Eduard von Müller-Tellering, Verfasser des ersten anti-semitischen Pamphlets gegen Marx," *Bulletin of the International Institute of Social History*, III/1951, pp. 178-97.

(167) In 1912, one Otto Bournot devoted his doctoral thesis to Ludwig Geyer. Using the Saxon parish archives, he was able to go back to his great-grandfather, Benjamin Geyer, who was organist at the church of Eisleben at the end of the seventeenth century. The study of successive birth certificates made it possible for him to conclude that all the ancestors of Ludwig Geyer had belonged to the Evangelical church and to state that "the possibility of Geyer paternity involves nothing unfavorable, as regards opinions that can be formed of the artistic work of Bayreuth" (O. Bournot, *Ludwig Heinrich Christian Geyer*, Leipzig, 1913, p. 13). Wagnerians could thus be reassured; but the fact remains that Wagner himself did not possess this information; he could hardly think of undertaking an investigation into the origins of his stepfather. Moreover, such investigations always remain unreliable.

(168) Viennese humorists waxed equally ironical about "Kosher Valkyries"; cf. Ernest Newman, *The Life of Richard Wagner*, New York, 1942, Vol. II, pp. 612-13.

(169) Proverbs, XXX, 18-19:

> Three things there are which are too wonderful for me, four which I do not understand: the way of a vulture in the sky, the way of a serpent on the rock, the way of a ship out at sea, and the way of a man with a girl.

(170) These questions have been studied by the Wagnerian, Ernest Newman, who has been able to establish that the rumors relating to Wagner's Jewish origins were propagated following a note Nietzsche inserted in *Der Fall Wagner* ("Is Wagner German? . . ."). Newman has equally assumed that the suspicions formulated by Nietzsche rested on confidences which Wagner is said to have made to him at the end of 1869 (cf. Newman, *op. cit.*, pp. 608-13, "The Geyer Question").

(171) *Adler* is a common surname for German Jews. This is also true of other bird names (*Sperling, Gans, Strauss* and, generically, *Vogel*), and *Geyer* obviously has the same figurative meaning in German as vulture in English: a rapacious and usurious man—which could only strengthen suspicion relating to the origin of Richard Wagner's stepfather.

An additional determining factor in the Wagnerian "Geyer complex" might be reluctantly suggested. Yet it can be assumed that the composer, great reader and great imaginative personality as he was, knew of the Egyptian myth which several Greek authors relate, whereby procreation by vultures excludes male intervention. They are therefore "father-less" birds, i.e. "bastards": perhaps this theme had made an impression on the adopted son of "Geyer" whose name he bore? In any case the coincidence is curious. The symbolism of the vulture also, as we know, forms the central theme of the essay that Freud consecrated to the case of Leonardo da Vinci.

(172) Cf. Richard Wagner, *Mein Leben,* Munich ed., 1963, pp. 10, 12, 13, 87 and 265 (alternation of terms *stepfather* and *father*).

(173) E. Schuré, "Souvenirs sur Richard Wagner," in *Richard Wagner, son œuvre et son idée,* Paris ed., 1930, p. xlii.

(174) Letter, October 1, 1858; from *R. Wagner an Mathilde Wesendonck,* 5th imp., Berlin, 1904.

(175) "Wagner was to scorn the opinion of society by falling in love with rich women and living off the generosity of their husbands" (M. Schneider, *Wagner,* Paris, 1960, p. 30).

(176) Letter, January 15, 1854.

(177) Letter, February 4, 1837, from Königsberg; cf. J. Kapp, "Wagner–Meyerbeer, Ein Stück Operngeschichte," *Die Musik,* XVI/1, 1923, pp. 25 ff.

(178) This article remained unpublished until 1911, when it appeared in J. Kapp's "Richard Wagner und Meyerbeer," *Die Musik,* X/14, 1911, pp. 84 ff.

(179) Kapp, "Wagner–Meyerbeer . . . ," p. 32 (letter, January 18, 1841).

(180) Paris, June 23, 1840; cf. *Lettres françaises de Richard Wagner,* Paris, 1935, p. 56:

> Any improvement can only depend on lucky events, and amongst the latter I must count the people on whom I base my hope and who, with no personal interest, would do something for me: a hope which would be humiliating if I had to be convinced that I only counted on alms. Fortunately, I am obliged to agree that people like Meyerbeer and Laube would do nothing for me if they did not believe that I *deserve* it. Despite this, weakness, whim, chance can influence these people and alienate them from me. This is a terrible thought.

(181) Letter, December 29, 1840 (cf. Maurice Boucher, *Les Idées politiques de Richard Wagner,* Paris, 1947, p. 57).

(182) Cf. J. Kapp, "Wagner–Meyerbeer . . . ," p. 37 (letter, January 5, 1842).

(183) Cf. J. Kapp, "Wagner–Meyerbeer . . . ," p. 80.

(184) Cf. J. Kapp, *Musik* XVI/1, p. 38 (letter, February 25, 1843).

(185) Cf. J. Kapp, "Wagner–Meyerbeer . . . ," p. 39.

(186) Cf. Heinz Becker "Giacomo Meyerbeer," *Leo Baeck Yearbook,* IX (1964), pp. 178-201 (p. 189). It emerges from Meyerbeer's diary that he refused the requested loan (1,200 thalers).

(187) Hugo Dingen, *Richard Wagners geistige Entwicklung,* Leipzig, 1892, Vol. I, p. 184:

> On the Monday Wagner again sent a letter from the Kreuzturm to his wife with a request for two bottles of wine.

Frau Wagner became alarmed and asked the messenger whether Wagner was by himself up in the Kreuzturm. When this was denied and names like Bakunin were mentioned, she sent neither wine nor tobacco but a letter that Wagner should come home at once, otherwise she would leave home. At once Wagner abandoned his observation post and returned to his house where his wife kept him imprisoned through a wise concealment of the door key.

(188) Georges Dumézil, *Mythes et Dieux des Germains,* Paris, 1939, p. 156.

(189) *Die Nibelungen, Weltgeschichte aus der Saga, Wagner's Prose Works,* W. Ashton Ellis, trans., London, 1897.

(190) *Ibid.,* Vol. 7, p. 260-6.

(191) *Ibid.,* p. 287.

(192) Letter to Liszt, Paris, June 5, 1849 (from *Correspondence of Wagner and Liszt,* Francis Huefler, trans., New York, 1897, p. 27).

(193) Cf. H. S. Chamberlain, *Richard Wagner, sa vie et ses œuvres,* Paris, 1900; according to Chamberlain, "one of the favorite periphrases to designate Richard Wagner, is 'the author of *Das Judentum in der Musik.*'" In 1935, the publisher of the *Lettres françaises de Richard Wagner* (Julian Tiersot) voiced this opinion: "His writings against the Jews appeared scandalous in their time; today they are authoritative."

(194) *Wagner's Prose Works,* Vol. III, p. 80.

(195) Various places in Glasenapp's biography reflect Wagner's high opinion of Mendelssohn. He particularly admired the *Hebrides* overture (Carl F. Glasenapp, VI, p. 320):

> Das ist enorm schön, geisterhaft! . . . Bei der *Sommernachts-traum-Ouverture* muss man bedenken, dass ein Fünfzehn-jähriger sie geschrieben hat, und wie formvollendet ist das schon alles. . . . Aber wie stümperhaft kam ich mir vor, als junger Mann, nur vier Jahre jünger als Mendelssohn, der ich erst mühsam anfing Musik zu treiben, während jener schon ein fertiger Musiker war und auch als gesellschaftlicher Mensch die anderen völlig in die Tasche steckte. Ich wusste damals nichts besseres zu tun, als—in meiner *Columbus-Ouverture*—ihm nachzuahmen, was ich freilich seitdem glücklich verlernt habe. . . .

(196) Richard Wagner, *My Life,* London, 1911, p. 566.

(197) Letter, July 3, 1853 (F. Liszt, *Briefe an die Fürstin Carolyne Sayn-Wittgenstein,* ed. La Mara, Vol. IV, Leipzig, 1899).

(198) Ludwig Schemann, *Neue Erinnerungen an Richard Wagner,* Stuttgart, 1902, pp. 46-7.

(199) Thomas Mann, *Leiden und Grösse Richard Wagners* (1933); cf. *Adel des Geistes,* Stockholm, 1945, p. 406.

(200) *Correspondence of Wagner and Liszt.*

(201) Cf. Kapp, "Wagner–Meyerbeer . . . ," p. 42.

(202) Cf. for example, René Dumesnil, *Richard Wagner*, Paris, 1954, pp. 20, 76, 79.
(203) Quoted by Heinz Becker, *Der Fall Heine-Meyerbeer*, Berlin, 1958, p. 21.
(204) Quoted by E. Newman, *The Life of Richard Wagner*, Vol. IV, p. 643, note.
(205) Glasenapp, *op. cit.*, Leipzig, 1907, Vol. V, p. 34.
(206) Cf. Angelo Neumann, *Souvenirs sur Richard Wagner*, Paris, 1908, pp. 331 ff.
(207) On Heinrich Porges, see Glasenapp, *op. cit.*, Vol. III, 1, pp. 106-7, 110, 117, 447-8, and Vol. VI, pp. 508-9.
(208) Glasenapp, *op. cit.*, Vol. II, 1, p. 392.
(209) *Oeuvres en prose de Richard Wagner*, Paris, Vol. IX, p. 108.
(210) Letter to J. Auerbach, March 12, 1869; cf. F. Kobler, *Juden und Judentum . . .*, pp. 330-1.
(211) Cf. the postscript by M. Gregor-Dellin to his edition of Wagner's autobiography (*Mein Leben, ed. cit.*, pp. 888-9).
(212) Glasenapp, Leipzig, 1911, Vol. VI, p. 551.
(213) *Ibid.*, p. 435 (Wagner had just become acquainted with the pessimistic theory of Count Gobineau with whom he struck up a friendship shortly afterwards).
(214) *Ibid.*, p. 721. (Wagner was inquiring why the Hindu concept, whereby understanding is man's "sixth sense," was not more common in Europe—"Woran es läge, dass diese einmal gewonnene Erkenntnis wieder verschwinden könne?—Daran, dass wir Schafsköpfe sind und alles von den Juden übernommen haben.")
(215) Letter from Wagner to H. Levi, October, 1881; cf. F. Kobler, *Juden und Judentum . . .*, pp. 332-3.
(216) Glasenapp, Vol. VI, p. 129.
(217) For information on this episode, I went back to Wagner's letters accompanied by Levi's explanatory notes published in the *Bayreuther Blätter*, with an introduction by H. S. Chamberlain (*Richard Wagners Briefe an Hermann Levi*, XXIV, 1901, pp. 13-41). Cf. also Glasenapp, Vol. VI, pp. 623-4; E. Newman, Vol. IV, pp. 636-8, and T. W. Adorno, *Essai sur Wagner*, Paris, 1966, whose interpretation I have adopted (pp. 17-18).
(218) Letter quoted by M. Gregor-Dellin, *Mein Leben, ed. cit.*, p. 890.
(219) The introduction quoted before, p. 17:
. . . the incomparable way in which Hermann Levi succeeded in reproducing, in his direction of the prelude to the third act, the inconsolable but also witless wandering of Parsifal in search of the Holy Grail. In this significant union of man and artist, essence and talent, a problem that seemed insoluble in real life experienced its first artistic solution.
(220) T. Mann, *Wagner und unsere Zeit*, Frankfurt, 1963, pp. 158 *passim*.
(221) Claude Lévi-Strauss, *Le Cru et le cuit*, Paris, 1964, p. 23.

(222) Henri Lichtenberger, *Wagner,* new ed., Paris, 1948, p. 230.

(223) Marcel Beaufils, *Wagner et le wagnérisme,* Paris, 1946, p. 7.

(224) M. Schneider, *Wagner,* Paris, 1960, p. 52.

(225) Auguste Kubizek, *Adolf Hitler, mon ami d'enfance,* Paris, 1954, p. 91.

(226) From *Hitler's Table Talk 1941-44,* English translation, London, 1953, pp. 241-2:

> At the beginning of this century there were people called Wagnerians. Other people had no special name. What joy each of Wagner's works has given me! And I remember my emotion the first time I entered Wahnfried. To say I was moved is an understatement!

Hitler expressed his Wagnerian enthusiasm on many other occasions, notably in the early pages of *Mein Kampf.* All his biographers bring out this influence, which nonetheless would repay closer study: it emerges, for example, in the arguments he put forward in favor of vegetarianism, in connection with his views on the decadence of mankind.

(227) A. Rosenberg, *Der Mythos des 20, Jahrhunderts,* Munich ed., 1933, p. 433.

(228) Cf. Newman, *op. cit.,* Vol. IV, pp. 638-9.

(229) Cf. F. Kobler, *Juden und Judentum . . . ,* p. 333.

(230) *Wagner's Prose Works (Religion und Kunst).*

(231) *Religion und Kunst,* Vol. VI, p. 229:

> At the first dawning of history we believe we find the aborigines of the present Indian peninsula in the cooler valleys of the Himalayan highlands, supporting themselves as graziers and tillers of the soil . . . a smiling Nature offered them with willing hand its varied products . . . the hunter (to the Brahmin) was an object of horror, and the slayer of man's friends, the domestic animals, unthinkable. . . . But in the self-same valleys of the Indus we think we see at work that cleavage which parted cognate races from those returning southwards to their ancient home, and drove them westwards to the broad expanse of hither-Asia, where in the course of time we find them as conquerors and founders of mighty dynasties, erecting ever more explicit monuments to History. These people had wandered through the wastes that separate the outmost Asiatic confines from the land of Indus; ravenous beasts of prey had taught them here to seek their food no longer from the milk of herds, but from their flesh; till blood alone seemed fitted to sustain the conqueror's courage. . . .
>
> Attack and defense, want and war, victory and defeat, lordship and thralldom, all sealed with the seal of blood: this was henceforth the History of Man. The victory of the stronger is followed close by enervation through a culture supported by their conquered thralls; in turn followed by the uprooting of the degenerate by fresh raw forces, of blood-thirst

still unslaked. Then falling lower and yet lower, the only worthy food for the world-conqueror appears to be human blood and corpses: the Feast of Thyestes would have been impossible among the Indians, but with such ghastly pictures could the human fancy play now that the murder of man and beast had nothing strange for it. And why should the imagination of civilized modern man recoil in horror from such pictures, when it has accustomed itself to the sight of a Parisian slaughterhouse during its early morning traffic, or perhaps of a field of carnage in the evening of some glorious victory? In truth we seem to have merely improved on the spirit of Thyestes' feast. . . .

(232) Glasenapp gives a summary of these views of Wagner's, Vol. VI, p. 307, ff.

(233) See above, pp. 410, 411.

(234) *Wagner's Prose Works*, Vol. V, *Eine Kapitulation*, pp. 3 ff.

(235) Quoted by T. Mann, *Leiden und Grösse der Meister*, Vienna, 1936, p. 149.

(236) *Wagner's Prose Works*, Vol. VI, p. 284.

(237) *Ibid.*, p. 283.

(238) For example, L. von Schroeder, *Das arische Mysterium von Bayreuth*, Munich, 1911. Likewise, A. Rosenberg, in the *Mythos des 20. Jahrhunderts*.

(239) *Lettre ouverte à M. Ernst von Weber, Prose Works*, Vol. VI, pp. 201-2.

(240) Quoted by Glasenapp, *op. cit.*, Vol. VI, p. 262.

(241) June 25, 1872:
> Genau genommen sind Sie, nach meiner Frau, der einzige Gewinn, den mir das Leben zugeführt: nun kommt glücklicherweise noch Fidi dazu; aber zwischen dem und mir bedarf es eines Gliedes, das nur Sie bilden können, etwa wie der Sohn zum Enkel. . . .

(242) "Das Ganze bleibt immer wüst und dumm. Was müsste ich nun mit dem Parzival alles anfangen? Denn mit dem weiss Wolfram nun auch gar nichts: seine Verzweiflung mit Gott ist albern und unmotiviert, noch ungenügender seine Bekehrung," etc. (Letter to Mathilde Wesendonck, May 30, 1859.)

(243) *Ibid.*

(244) *Bayreuther Blätter*, XXIV, 1901, pp. 24 ff, *Richard Wagners Briefe an Hermann Levi* (letter no. 22, p. 29). Thanks are due to Mme Gertrud Strobel, of the Richard Wagner Archiv at Bayreuth, who so kindly sent me the first sentence of this letter, omitted in the above publication.

(245) Glasenapp, VI, pp. 427, 451, and particularly p. 502 (remarks made by Wagner to Levi at Easter, 1881).

(246) Wagner to Levi, October, 1881 (cf. F. Kobler, *Juden und Judentum . . .*, pp. 332-3).

(247) August 30, 1865, note to King Ludwig of Bavaria:

Nicht aber die Schmerzen der Wunde sind es, die Amfortas' Seele umnachten: sein Leiden ist tiefer. Er ist der Erlesene, der das Wundergefäss zu pflegen hat: er und kein anderer hat den heiligen Zauber zu üben, der die ganze Ritterschaft erquickt, stärkt und leitet, während nur *er* einzig zu leiden hat, zu leiden um des schrecklichsten Selbstvorwurfes willen sein Gelübde vorraten zu haben. . . .

(248) "So ward der Opernkomponist vollständig zum Erlöser der Welt, und in dem hilfbegeisterten, von selbstzerfleischendem Schwärmereifer unwiderstehlich hingerissenen Meyerbeer haben wir jedenfalls den modernen Heiland, das weltentsündigende Lamm Gottes zu erkennen" (*Oper und Drama*).

(249) T. Schmid, "Das Kunstwerk der Zukunft und seine Meister," *Stimmen aus Maria-Lach* (*Stimmen der Zeit*), XXV, 1883, pp. 535-6.

(250) *Apocalypse*, XVII, 5 (*ibid.*, XXVI, 1884, p. 159).

(251) Cf. M. André, "Le vrai Parsifal," *Le Correspondant*, Paris, 1914, LXXXVI (254), pp. 68-88. On the eve of the First World War, the Wagnerian enthusiasm of certain Catholics ran high (M. D. Espagnol, *L'Apothéose musicale de la religion catholique, Parsifal de Wagner*, Barcelona, 1902, pp. 1, 3, 245):

Parsifal by Wagner is a new and brilliant argument, added to the old, in favor of religion. . . . It is through the inspiration of the Holy Spirit that Wagner wrote *Parsifal*. . . . Is not *Parsifal* something more than the *musical apotheosis of the Catholic religion?* Is it not a *prophecy?* . . . Is not Parsifal thus the *third man* of History, the third Adam—Adam, Jesus Christ and Parsifal?

(252) Glasenapp, Vol. VI, pp. 231, 435.

(253) " . . . nur durch enhaltendes Vorlesen konnte eine bessere Stimmung hergestellt werden. Webers *Afrika-Reise* ward auf diese Weise zu Ende gebracht, daran schloss sich der Rohlingsche *Talmudjude* unter Staunen über die eigentümlichen Satzungen dieses ausserwählten Volkes an" (Glasenapp, Vol. VI, p. 280).

(254) In 1852, Wagner was enthusiastic about a collection of poems by Daumer, *Hafis*, and recommended his friend Uhlig to read them (*Wagners Briefe an Th. Uhlig*, Leipzig, 1888, pp. 221, 227, 236).

(255) Cf. J. Trachtenberg, *The Devil and the Jews*, Yale University Press, 1943, pp. 124-55.

(256) *Sodome et Gomorrhe*, Proust, La Pléiade ed., Paris, 1963, Vol. II, p. 1105:

. . . A Jew! Moreover, this does not surprise me; this is because of a curious taste for sacrilege specific to that race. . . . When those indecent spectacles that are called the Passion are performed in Holy Week, half the room is filled with Jews, exulting in the thought that they are going to put Christ on the Cross for a second time, at least in effigy. At the

Lamoureux concert one day, my neighbor was a rich Jewish banker. Berlioz's *L'Enfance du Christ* was being performed; he was dismayed. But he soon regained his customary expression of beatitude on hearing the *Good Friday Spell.*

Conclusion

(1) A similar distinction is found at the beginning of this century in Baron de Seillière when he speaks of "two currents in historical Aryanism: . . . the expansive Indo-European current, welcoming, embracing the whole non-Semitic West in its sympathy, and the narrow Indo-Germanic current, suspicious, wanting to reserve the precious heritage of the Veda for Germans alone. . . . " The contrast between the "narrow," "suspicious" current which excludes all non-Germans, and the "expansive," "welcoming" current which only excludes Semites, is symptomatic of the attitude of the period. (Ernest Seillière, *Le Comte de Gobineau et l'aryanisme historique,* Paris, 1903, p. xxv.)

(2) The coincidence in time of the formation of the dogma of trans-substantiation, the development of popular eucharistic piety and the increase in accusations of ritual murder and profanation of hosts, was pointed out to me by Father Gavin Langmuir (Stanford University); cf. his work (in preparation) "From Xenophobia to Prejudice: the Formation of anti-Semitism."

(3) This is the classic theme of the miracle of the profaned host. In this connection, the naïve realism of medieval piety can also be illustrated by a sermon that Berthold de Ratisbonne (thirteenth century) gave, consoling his listeners for their disappointment at not seeing the Child Jesus arise from the consecrated host: "Who would therefore want to tear off the head, arms, or feet of a child with his teeth?" (Cf. H. L. Strack, *Das Blut im Glauben und Aberglauben der Menschheit,* Munich, 1900, p. 14.) The educative role exercised by the Church, faced with the survival of certain outdated anxieties or impulses in the hearts of its worshipers, can be seen from this.

(4) Cf. L. Poliakov, *History of Anti-Semitism,* Vol. I, *From the Time of Christ to the Court Jews,* New York, 1965, pp. 56-64.

(5) Cf. L. Poliakov, *Les Banquiers juifs et le Saint-Siège du XIIIe au XVIIe siècle,* Paris, 1965, notably the conclusion, pp. 291-305.

(6) Historically, the accusation of deicide (preceded by the charge of the denial of Christ) was obviously the first capital charge made by Christians against Jews. As far as its vital relationship

with the eucharistic sacrament is concerned, we think that a serious study (which is beyond our powers) might reveal its existence in various Fathers of the Church (Origen, Tertullian, Gregory of Nyssa). This relationship is obvious in the most anti-Semitic of the Fathers, St John Chrysostom, also called the "Doctor of the Eucharist" (fourteenth century). The following homilies are examples of the association of ardent eucharistic piety with the hatred of Christ's hangmen in his thought (cf. *Eucharistia, encyclopédie populaire sur l'eucharistie,* Paris, 1941, pp. 69, 771):

> When the body of Christ is offered to you, say to yourself: it is thanks to this body that I am no longer earth and ashes, that I am no longer in chains but free. . . . It is this body which, pierced with nails and beaten with rods, has not been destroyed by death. . . . It is from this bloodstained body, pierced by a spear, that the springs of salvation for the whole earth, blood and water, have burst forth. . . . And he has given us this body to hold, to eat: an act of infinite love. For those whom we love passionately, we consume over and over again. . . .
>
> (In 1 Cor. hom., XXIV, 4)

> How many people today say: I would like to see his very expression, his face, his clothes, his shoes. This is how you see him, touch him, eat him. You want to see his clothes; he not only lets you see them, but eat them, touch them, take them inside yourself. . . . Think how your anger rises at the traitors, the wrongdoers who crucified him, and take care not to be responsible yourself for the body and blood of the Lord. They, they have killed his holy body; and you, you would receive it in your defiled soul, after having obtained so many blessings from it. How pure must we be to enjoy such a sacrifice? Should not our hand be more splendid than the rays of the sun to break this flesh? And our mouth which is filled with spiritual fire? Our trembling tongue which is reddened with blood? Think what an honor is being done to you, at which table you are sitting. . . .
>
> (In Matt. hom., XXXIII, 40)

(7) Numbers XXIII, 9.

(8) Freud, who always deserves a hearing, described his feeling of Jewish identity in the following terms in 1926 ("Ansprache an die Mitglieder des Vereins B'nai B'rith," *Gesammelte Werke,* XVII, 51):

> What bound me to Judaism—I have a duty to admit—was not belief, also not national pride, for I was always an unbeliever and was brought up without a religion, though not without respect for the "ethically" termed demands of human civilisation. I have tried to repress a national pride, when I

felt drawn to it, as calamitous and unjust, frightened by the warning example of the peoples amongst whom we Jews live. But there remained enough other things which made the attraction of Judaism and the Jews irresistible, many obscure forces of emotion, the more powerful, the less they allowed themselves to be put into words, as well as the clear awareness of inner identity, the secrecy of the same construction of the psyche.

(9) On this subject, A. Philonenko thinks that the impossibility of giving a contemporary definition of the Jew which is not a "tautology", might spring from the paradox whereby "the Jews' efforts towards assimilating, that is to say of ceasing to be Jews, often arrived . . . at the opposite result." He wrote to me after he had read this Conclusion:

> I would be tempted to say that this paradox removes even the possibility of suggesting a nominal definition, determining a complex by one of its specific qualities . . . for all the terms can be taken in a double meaning. . . . The nominal definition of the Jew will always determine the awareness the stranger acquires of Jewish awareness as much as it determines Jewish awareness itself, for all that the latter tries either to rid itself of its own Jewish-being, or on the contrary affirms it, and that contrary to the will to negate which animates all human definition. This is also why the designation of the Jew—I do not even say its definition—must appear alterable as required, capable of being blended with the refusal of the stranger, which forms the basis for the most misleading assimilation at the same time as the most absurd distinctions.

Here again, on the level of philosophical discussion, are the ambivalent feelings *par excellence* which Jews have at all times aroused in Christianity—and, since their emancipation, in themselves as well.

(10) *From Roman Times to the Court Jews,* pp. vi–vii.

(11) *Les Banquiers juifs . . . , op. cit.,* conclusion *et passim.*

(12) Léon Poliakov, *History of Anti-Semitism,* Vol. II, *From Mohammed to the Marranos,* New York, 1973, pp. 242–3 (Portugal), p. 289 (Balearic Islands) *et passim.*

(13) We are borrowing this expression and idea from the remarkable analyses by N. Cohn, in the conclusion of *Warrant for Genocide, The Myth of the Jewish World-Conspiracy and the Protocols of the Elders of Zion,* London, 1967.

(14) *Ibid.* Particularly significant are certain press comments quoted by Cohn. For example the London *Times* in summer, 1920 asked if the world had only escaped the *pax germanica* to fall under the *pax judaica.* On the other hand, the Protocols were distributed on an international scale by Henry Ford (the pioneer of the automobile industry).

(15) An internationally famous German anthropologist, O. von

Verschuer, noted that the Jew was the very prototype of "urbanized man" (*Stadtmensch*), and exclaimed in 1938: "Urbanized men also exist in other races; but do we not easily resent them as 'Jews'?" (Quoted by K. Saller, *Die Rassenlehre des Nationalsozialismus in Wissenschaft und Propaganda*, Darmstadt, 1961, p. 68.)

(16) Past authors often attributed the historic peregrinations of the Jews to a "nomadism" regarded as a racial characteristic. It will be sufficient to quote the most influential proponent of this view, Werner Sombart. He describes the Jews as a "wandering tribe of Bedouins" and again more expressively as "a desert people, a nomad people, a warm-blooded people lost amongst people of a different essence, humid and cold people with heavy blood, fixed to the land" (*The Jews and Modern Capitalism*).

(17) Cf. above, pp. 345-9.

The violence of the Jews' reaction surprised observers in almost all centers of the diaspora. In the United States, the Jewish thinker, Arthur Hertzberg, wrote ("Israel and American Jewry," *Commentary*, August, 1967):

The main outlines of the effect that the Middle East crisis has had on American Jewry are, then, relatively clear. It has united those with deep Jewish commitments as they have never been united before, and it has evoked such commitment in many Jews who previously seemed untouched by them. . . . The sense of belonging to the worldwide Jewish people, of which Israel is the center, is a religious sentiment, but it seems to persist even among Jews who regard themselves as secularists or atheists. There are no conventional Western theological terms with which to explain this, and most contemporary Jews experience these emotions without knowing how to define them.

(18) G. Friedmann, *Fin du peuple juif?*, Paris, 1964.